2500
CREATIVE
SOLUTIONS TO
THE DAILY
DILEMMA OF
WHAT TO COOK

Fifty Ways to Cook Most Everything

Andrew Schloss with Ken Bookman

Simon & Schuster

NEW YORK • LONDON • TORONTO • SYDNEY • TOKYO • SINGAPORE

SIMON & SCHUSTER
Simon & Schuster Building
Rockefeller Center
1230 Avenue of the Americas
New York, New York 10020

Designed by Irving Perkins Associates
Manufactured in the United States of America

10   9   8   7   6   5   4   3   2   1

Library of Congress Cataloging-in-Publication Data

Schloss, Andrew, date.
    Fifty ways to cook most everything : 2500 creative solutions to
the daily dilemma of what to cook / Andrew Schloss with Ken Bookman.
        p.   cm.
    Includes index.
    1. Quick and easy cookery.   I. Bookman, Ken.   II. Title.
III. Title: 50 ways to cook most everything.
TX833.5.S35   1992
641.5′55—dc20   92-17720
                                                                      CIP

ISBN: 0-671-73451-2

This book is dedicated to our mothers.

To Peggy Schloss. Her dread of the kitchen forced her son to cook,
and her love of words urged him to write.

To Thelma Bookman. She always knew that food and love were connected.

Acknowledgments

There are a lot of fingerprints besides ours on this book. They belong to the people who helped us start this project and then helped us every step of the way.

Anne Farran is at the front of the line. She decided she wanted the experience of recipe testing just as we were going under for the third time from the same experience. We hope she got what she was looking for, because we sure did. Once her cooking talent, energy, and good humor came aboard, we knew for sure that this book would happen.

We're indebted to some youngsters from Cheltenham Elementary School in Cheltenham, Pennsylvania, who gave credibility to our Chapter 12, Fifty Things Kids Will Eat. Our thanks to Meredith Balter, Katelyn Beuttel, Daniel Brennan, Giovanni Brooks, Benjamin Byruch, Rachel Cooper, Jonathan Cooper-Alston, Jessica Daniel, Tremayne Diggs, Mary C. Drach, Maurice Dye, Leah Fauntleroy, Meghan Fitzgerald, Mark Foster, Natasha Garrett, Michael Gettlin, Jennifer Gimbel, Nicholas Goldberg, Eric Grubman, Carly Hall, Sean Heaven, Jason Hinchcliff, Christine Kim, Hopiy Kim, Gabrielle Klaus, Jane Labencki, Paul Lee, Cristin Mann, Julia Martin, Sara Meehan, Erin Moran, Trinity O'Toole, Susan Oswald, Jung Park Min, Bohra Rhee, Brent Rosenthal, Steven Ryan, Amritpal Sandher, Benjamin Schloss, Isaac Schloss, Heather Seo, Melissa Shore, Timothy Sloan, Robert Swift, Don Thomas, Jamil Thompson, Clarence Tong, B. J. Valoris, Eli Vineberg, Denise Widmeier, and Adam Woldow. Thanks also to their teachers, Sandy Katz and Nancy McKernan, and their principal, Helen Fox. The young palate of Brad Farran helped this chapter, too.

Chapter 16, on low-calorie foods, was helped immensely by Mona Sutnick.

Our deep gratitude to Morrie Goldfischer for steering us in the right direction when we had no idea how to start this project; to our literary agent, Judith Weber, the first person in the real world who believed this could be a book; to Bonnie Leblang and her splendid copyediting; and to Toula Polygalaktos, our editor at Simon & Schuster, who did many good things to our manuscript and our spirits. Special thanks to Kerri Conan, a former editor at Simon & Schuster, for her early enthusiasm.

We're especially grateful to the many readers of *The Philadelphia Inquirer*'s food section—and of the food sections of several other newspapers around the country where some of these chapters were later reprinted—for a level of response to the "Fifty Ways" articles that first made us believe that a book was lurking behind all those recipes.

Andrew Schloss
Ken Bookman

March 1992

I wish to acknowledge Tom Hunter, who made the act of cooking clear; Ken Silveri, who let me test my culinary wings with his money; Joanna Smythe, for letting me know that I knew what I was doing when I didn't know what I was doing; Elaine Tait, who thought I might be good at writing food articles; Ken Bookman, whose vision keeps me on track and whose genius for knowing details makes me sound like I'm smart; and Dana, Ben,

Isaac and Karen Shain Schloss, who make everything I do make sense.

A.S.

A few lines are hardly adequate to thank Ruth Adelman, who literally ate, drank, and breathed this book by sharing with me the home in which recipes were tested day and night for nine months. But I'll try: Thank you, Ruth, for enduring the invasions this book imposed on your life and ours, and for the love, support, and good cheer you gave me in return.

Many friends were effusive in their thanks as they sampled one load of food after another. They never seemed to catch on that it was *they* who were doing *me* the favor. I include a lot of folks in this sweeping paragraph, but especially Rick Nichols for the frequent and frank criticism that improved many of these recipes and for unflagging interest in this entire project.

I'd like to thank several of my colleagues from my time as *The Philadelphia Inquirer*'s food editor. Gene Roberts blew my mind by putting me in the job. Andy Schloss was an amazing food teacher, superb work partner, and good friend. Jerry Etter, Marilynn Marter, and Elaine Tait shared an office with me and were patient teachers all. Bob Greenberg was an enthusiastic fan of the "Fifty Ways" articles. And I'm very glad I bumped into Jim Davis one night in 1987, or he might never have shared with me the "Fifty Ways to Love Your Liver" line that amused us both so much and that directly led to this book.

K.B.

Contents

Introduction

We'll be the first to admit that 2500 seems like an absurd number of recipes for any book this side of *Joy of Cooking*. Early on, in fact, we often wondered whether the "50 ways" theme that you'll see woven through these pages was somehow creating a monster, or more literally, creating a cookbook with far more recipes than any rational person could ever need. But once we realized that the number of recipes was merely the vehicle for conveying something more important, we knew we were on precisely the right track.

No, you do not *need* 2500 recipes for your everyday home cooking. But if you are like most home cooks, you are mired in a major cooking rut—one that's defined by an endless rotation of the same ten foods, month after year after decade. And you probably *do* need help getting out of it. That's where this vast collection of recipes comes in, because the more paths you can see out of a dilemma, the more likely you'll be to escape it. Our mission in this book is to extricate you without encroaching on the ever-dwindling number of minutes you can afford to give over to meal preparation. And we are convinced that the way to get out of the rut is to show you how to change your thinking about food and ingredients and cooking.

This book is meant for anyone who has to cook for four people 360 days a year for twenty years (or for two people, or one person). It's for anyone who could use a little help in realizing the enormous variety of dishes that can be extracted from normal, everyday ingredients.

*   *   *

It's all Paul Simon's fault. If he had written a song entitled "Fifteen Ways to Leave Your Lover" instead of "Fifty," this would have been a 15-chapter cookbook containing a more normal 225 recipes, we would have finished writing and testing it many months sooner, and our friends would not have looked at us as though we were slightly crazy for undertaking a project of this scope.

But Simon wrote the song the way he did, which led to the joke that led to this book.

For more than eight years, we worked together on the food section of *The Philadelphia Inquirer*, one of us as the newspaper's food editor, the other as a regular writer for the paper's twice-weekly food section. And one day, a chance conversation in the newspaper's parking lot led a colleague to share an amusing pun he had heard or read somewhere: "Fifty ways to love your liver."

"Fifty ways to love your liver." That struck both of us as a great line that was just crying out to appear as a headline in the *Inquirer*'s food section. There was just one problem—the story that would run under that headline would have to really, truly deliver 50 recipes for making liver, which is arguably the most detested food in America.

Fortunately, we worked for a newspaper that encouraged such bizarre lines of thought. The in-house expression at the *Inquirer* is "zigging while everyone else zags." So in the best tradition of zigging food journalism, we came up with 50 short recipes for cooking liver, we made up some "liver lyrics" to be sung to the tune of "Fifty Ways to Leave Your Lover," and we presented it all under that funny headline.

On May 13, 1987, it was there for the world to

see—the "50 Ways to Love Your Liver" headline, the lyrics, and the 50 recipes. It was a quirky enough story that people read it, spurred on, perhaps, by "Harvey in the Morning," a Philadelphia radio disc jockey who sang our liver lyrics on the air, over the Paul Simon music. (Though you may not believe it now, the liver recipes were really good. Just take a look at Chapter 11.)

It got us to thinking. If 50 easy recipes for a food that everyone *hates* could get so much attention, what would happen if we ran occasional articles featuring 50 easy recipes for foods people *liked*? Chicken breasts, for example, or pizza toppings, or dessert sauces?

Well, we did, and our readers loved them. We think we know why. An array of 50 recipes per article was giving these readers something they were not getting from their usual food sources. Within a minute or two after they came home from work, they could scan the recipes and eliminate those that didn't appeal to them, those they didn't have quite enough time for, and those they couldn't make then and there without going shopping—and there would still be dozens to choose from, all of them different from what they made every single week of their lives.

In other words, it was a way out of their cooking rut.

Many cookbooks and other food sources don't let on how easy it is to change your kitchen habits. It takes only a tiny bit of thought. How tiny? It can be as simple as asking yourself a one-word question: "Why?"

The next time you're in a restaurant, instead of just asking yourself what you want to order ("Roast chicken"), ask yourself why ("Oh, the rosemary seasoning sounded good"). And the next time you're ordering a pizza, instead of just figuring out the topping you want ("Pepperoni"), ask yourself why ("I like the way the pepperoni gets crisped on top of the chewy cheese").

Those answers reveal much more than just your fondness for roast chicken or pepperoni pizza. They also reveal that you appreciate what an imaginative dose of fresh herbs can do to an otherwise neutral meat and that contrasting textures add to your enjoyment of food. Those little morsels of information about what pushes your food buttons can open up hundreds of new cooking possibilities for you.

That's the thinking behind this book. We've chosen 50 chapter topics to accommodate your pantry, your preferences, your mood, or the season of the year, and to help you at breakfast, lunch, dinner, dessert, or snacktime. Within each of those 50 chapters are 50 recipes that combine and flavor everyday foods with everyday ingredients. You'll see combinations that are easy but not obvious. You'll see preparation time minimized with the assertive help of such everyday flavorings as herbs or citrus zests. And you'll see common ingredients in uncommon places, such as popcorn flavored with black pepper. All are intended to spark ideas that you may never have thought of.

There's that word again: *thought*. It doesn't get enough attention. These days, *speed* and *simplicity* are the buzzwords usually associated with everyday cooking. No doubt about it, speed and simplicity are both virtues, and of the 2500 recipes in this book, virtually all are simple and the vast majority are quick. But when speed is hammered home so relentlessly that cooking gets stripped of the thought process, when cooking gets lumped together with laundry and lawn mowing as just another mind-numbing chore on the way to our precious leisure hours, well, that's how boxes of instant mashed potatoes happen. Repeat that sort of atrocity enough times and before you know it, the supermarkets are overtaken by granulated cardboard ingredients, the cooks of the world lose any expectation that cooking can be rewarding, and something that should be a source of daily respite and enjoyment isn't.

No wonder, then, that so many people get trapped in food ruts.

Here's how this book can help. When you're about to cook one of your ten old standards not because that's what you want to eat but out of habit, stop for just a minute. Is it a hamburger? Look at the twenty-two burgers in our ground-meat chapter for one that's appealing and that you don't have to shop for. Then make it. Or is it spaghetti? Go to our chapter on pasta sauces, where you'll find 50 recipes, or to our index, where you'll find other pasta sauces scattered among other chapters, and give one of them a whirl. Got some chicken breasts or fish fillets ready for tonight? Turn to the appropriate chapter, and do the same thing.

Spend a week of dinnertimes doing that with several different foods, including side dishes and desserts, but note the patterns you find as you scan the dozens of recipes and as you try more and more of them. Those patterns show you how all sauces are similar, even as any two of them can be so different, or how different herb and spice and flavoring combinations work together, or which secondary ingredients tend to work well with which main ingredients. Before long, you'll start doing some inventing of your own, creating dishes that might otherwise never have crossed your mind. And one day soon, when you can't decide which of two new recipes to try that night, we hope you'll notice that your food rut is a thing of the past.

Then 2500 recipes will seem to be just about right.

You'll notice the heading "About These Recipes" in each chapter, just before the recipes begin. It's a good idea to read the brief explanation under that heading before proceeding with the recipes from that chapter. That's where you'll find information common to all the recipes in that chapter—on cooking techniques, on ingredients, on seasonings, on yields, and so on.

Recipes are roadmaps that chart a path toward the completion of a particular dish. As on any trip, there are different ways to proceed, and the route you choose depends on your experience. First-time travelers need detailed maps to mark each turn and warn of rocky terrain. More seasoned travelers need to refer to the map only occasionally, such as for unexpected detours or for charting new ground.

We recognize the same diversity of experience among the users of this book. Some will want everything explained, while others will find a recitation of fundamentals unnecessary. To help both groups of cooks, we have included two appendixes in the back of the book—one a compilation of basic recipes, the other of culinary techniques. This has allowed us to streamline the recipes without eliminating information you may need. If you're familiar with the technique or recipe, just ignore the reference to the back of the book. If you want more help, you'll find the advice you need on the designated page.

In regard to ingredients: Although for the most part we avoid the use of prepackaged ingredients, this book is written for the real world. True, the real world sells some abominable commercial food products, but many food manufacturers have cleaned up their act in recent years and now offer some first-rate convenience foods. Pastry made from scratch will always produce a better result than storebought pastry, but there are some fine prepared pie crusts out there and our fillings in those crusts will produce great pies. Your supermarket's freezer case carries a puff pastry so superb that we'd be crazy to suggest you even think of duplicating it at home. And though no one can make a better roasted pepper than you at home, excellent commercial versions are available in jars. You know what the good products are. Don't hesitate to use them.

The way we've managed to present you with 2500 recipes in a book that you can lift is through a recipe format that differs from what you'll find in

Fifty Ways to Cook Most Everything

most cookbooks. Ingredients and procedure are woven together so that each recipe appears as a concise paragraph. Although it may be an unfamiliar format, it's designed to offer a panorama of recipe ideas on every page and to encourage you to read through each recipe and grasp its structure before you start cooking.

Finally, with the possible exception of some baking recipes, remember that the vast majority of our recipes are very forgiving. They allow—and, indeed, we encourage—variation and experimentation. If you don't have spinach, by all means replace it with another green leafy vegetable. Chances are the results will not be that different from ours, and if they are, you'll then have a recipe collection of 2501.

Fifty Marinades, Hundreds of Meals

Good cooks work with food and a thought. Fine ingredients and the right equipment are important, but they do not make a dish great, nor does proper storage or skill alone, though these are all part of the result. Only if the cook thinks does the food come to life, only if he or she breathes life into the food by choosing a flavor direction that brings them to the table newly born.

It is our vision that every cook has the potential to come up with hundreds of culinary creations, and it is our mission in this book to help those visions take form, so we can think of no better chapter to begin with than one that puts the exponential power of marinades at your fingertips.

There is no easier way to infuse a food with flavor than through the use of a marinade. Marinades are as convenient as a bath of barbecue sauce right out of the bottle and as esoteric as a salsa of wild sorrel. They can be rich with oil or sparkling with an acidic bite. There are creamy yogurt marinades and pungent marinades as thin as tea. Marinades can be the vehicle for a blaze of pepper or a gentle perfume of fresh herbs. They are sweet and sour, boozy and piquant, chunky with aromatic vegetables, and silken with purees of fruit. They can be reduced to a glaze or stretched into a sauce, served cold as a dressing or hot as a dip.

All marinades take one of four forms—oily, acidic, salty or sweet. But most are a combination of two or more of these forms. Marinades for fatty or tough meats tend to be salty or acidic because salt and acid help to break down tough fiber and counteract oiliness. Fish marinades are typically acidic and oily. Low-fat foods, such as vegetables, or dehydrating cooking techniques, such as grilling, use oil in their marinades to help moisten the ingredients. Sweet marinades require easily caramelized ingredients. Chicken and beef, or sweet vegetables like carrot, onion and yam, all work well with sweet marinades.

ABOUT THESE RECIPES

These marinades are grouped by the type of ingredient from which they are made and will each be enough for four to six servings. Once marinated, the main ingredient may be roasted, grilled, sautéed, broiled, steamed, fried, or cooked in any other way you wish.

Always marinate under refrigeration to prevent spoilage, and time according to the thickness and density of the ingredient. Most fish, for example, will pick up the flavors of a marinade in an hour or less, while beef or pork steaks may need several hours or overnight. And if you'll be using a marinade as a dipping sauce, be sure to boil the liquid after removing the meat.

Technically, there are only 50 recipes below, but in reality there are hundreds. Following each recipe is a parenthetical list of abbreviations indicating the main ingredients for which that marinade would be well suited. Here is the key to those abbreviations: B = Beef. C = Chicken. D = Duck. F = Fish. FR = Fruit. G = Game Meat. L = Lamb. P = Pork. S = Shellfish. T = Turkey. V = Veal. VG = Vegetable.

 ## Lemon Cilantro Marinade

Mix 1 teaspoon ground coriander seed, salt, and pepper. Work into a thin paste with 4 cloves minced garlic and ⅓ cup olive oil. Beat in the juice and zest of 1 lemon, ¼ cup chopped fresh cilantro, and 1 cup white wine. (C F S T VG)

 ## Lemon Basil Marinade

Mix 1 teaspoon ground fennel seed, salt, and pepper. Work into a thin paste with 4 cloves minced garlic and ⅓ cup olive oil. Beat in the juice and zest of 1 lemon, ¼ cup chopped fresh basil, and 1 cup white wine. (C F S T V VG)

 ## Lemon Garlic Marinade

Mix 2 thinly sliced scallions, salt, and pepper. Work into a thin paste with 4 cloves minced garlic and ⅓ cup olive oil. Beat in the juice and zest of 1 lemon, 2 tablespoons chopped fresh parsley, and 1 cup white wine. (C F P S T V VG)

 ## Lime Jalapeño Marinade

Mix 1 minced jalapeño pepper, salt, and pepper. Work into a thin paste with 4 cloves minced garlic and ⅓ cup olive oil. Beat in the juice and zest of 1 lime, ¼ cup chopped fresh cilantro, and 1 cup white wine. (C D F P S T V VG)

 ## Lime, Olive Oil, and Capers

Mix a pinch crushed red pepper flakes, 1 teaspoon chopped fresh chives, salt, and pepper. Add 4 cloves minced garlic and ⅓ cup olive oil and mix into a thin paste. Beat in the juice and zest of 1 lime, ¼ cup drained capers, and 1 cup white wine. (C D F P S T V)

 ## Orange Walnut Marinade

Mix ½ teaspoon crushed red pepper flakes, 1 teaspoon ground fennel seed, 1 teaspoon dried basil, salt, and pepper. Add 4 cloves minced garlic and ⅓ cup walnut oil and mix into a thin paste. Beat in the juice and zest of 1 orange, ¼ cup ground walnuts, and 1 cup white wine. (B C D F FR L P S T V).

 ## Orange Tarragon Marinade

Mix 2 teaspoons dried tarragon, 1 teaspoon dried chervil, salt, and pepper. Add 2 minced shallots, 1 clove minced garlic, and ⅓ cup peanut oil and mix into a thin paste. Beat in the juice and zest of 1 orange, 2 tablespoons chopped fresh parsley, and 1 cup white wine. (C F FR S T V)

Spicy Citrus Marinade

Mix 1 teaspoon crushed red pepper flakes, 1 teaspoon dried dill, salt, and pepper. Add ¼ cup minced onion, 2 cloves minced garlic, and ⅓ cup olive oil and mix into a thin paste. Beat in the juice and zest of 1 orange, 1 lemon, and 1 lime, and 2 tablespoons chopped fresh parsley. (C D F S T VG)

 Provençale Marinade

Combine 3 cloves minced garlic, 2 mashed anchovies, 1 teaspoon *herbes de Provence*, a pinch of crushed red pepper flakes, salt, and pepper. Work ¼ cup virgin olive oil into the mixture, and stir in ½ cup white wine, ½ cup crushed tomato, and the juice and grated zest of ½ orange. (C F S V VG)

 Jerk Marinade

Toast 1½ teaspoons *each* coriander seed and cumin seed, ½ teaspoon black peppercorns, ¼ teaspoon crushed red pepper flakes, and 1 clove over high heat in a dry skillet until lightly colored and aromatic, about 1 minute. Grind well and strain out hulls. Add 2 teaspoons chopped fresh gingerroot, 1 tablespoon ground allspice, ½ teaspoon salt, 1 tablespoon rum, 3 tablespoons ketchup, 1 teaspoon hot pepper sauce, 2 tablespoons light soy sauce, 1 tablespoon brown sugar, 2 tablespoons vegetable oil, and ¼ cup chopped fresh parsley and mix into a paste. (B C D F G P S T V)

Super-Spicy Jerk Marinade

Follow preceding recipe, adding 2 dried chili peppers to the spices for toasting and using 1 teaspoon black peppercorns. (B C D F G P S T)

 Jerk Citrus Marinade

Follow recipe for Jerk Marinade (above), replacing 2 tablespoons of the ketchup with lime or grapefruit juice. (C D F G P S T V)

 Ginger Soy Marinade

Mix until blended ¼ cup *each* soy sauce, rice vinegar, honey, and water; add ½ teaspoon ground ginger, ¼ teaspoon chili paste, 1 tablespoon peanut oil, 1 teaspoon Oriental sesame oil, 1 tablespoon dry sherry, and 1½ tablespoons grated fresh gingerroot. (C F P S T VG)

 Sweet Sesame Marinade

Follow preceding recipe, replacing the gingerroot with toasted sesame seeds. (C F P S T V VG)

 Tangerine Teriyaki

Mix until blended ¼ cup soy sauce, 1 tablespoon rice vinegar, 3 tablespoons tangerine juice, ¼ cup honey, ¼ cup water, ½ teaspoon ground ginger, ¼ teaspoon chili paste, 1 tablespoon peanut oil, 1 teaspoon Oriental sesame oil, 1 tablespoon dry sherry, 1½ teaspoons grated fresh gingerroot, and 1 tablespoon minced tangerine zest. (C D F P S V)

Apricot Marinade

In a saucepan, brown ¼ cup finely chopped onion in 1 tablespoon vegetable oil. Remove from heat and add 2 cloves minced garlic, 3 tablespoons walnut oil, 1 cup apricot preserves, the juice of 1 lemon, 6 drops hot pepper sauce, 1½ tablespoons Worcestershire sauce, salt, and pepper. (C D L P S T V)

Fifty Ways to Cook Most Everything

 Sweet Tomato Marinade

Follow preceding recipe using olive oil instead of walnut oil and ketchup instead of preserves. Add 1 tablespoon honey. (B C L P T)

 Apple and Spice Marinade

Follow recipe for Apricot Marinade (page 17) using peanut oil instead of walnut oil and apple butter instead of apricot preserves. (B C D G L P)

 All-American Barbecue Marinade

In a saucepan, mix 1 cup ketchup, 2 tablespoons spicy mustard, 2 tablespoons cider vinegar, ¼ cup chopped onion, 1 tablespoon vegetable oil, 2 teaspoons hot pepper sauce, 1 tablespoon brown sugar, 1 tablespoon molasses, and 1 tablespoon Worcestershire sauce. Bring to a boil and season with plenty of salt and pepper. Cool. (B C P V)

 Sweet and Sour Barbecue Marinade

In a saucepan, mix ¼ cup *each* ketchup, cider vinegar, light brown sugar, and chopped onion; add 1 tablespoon vegetable oil, 2 teaspoons hot pepper sauce, ¼ cup orange marmalade, and 1 tablespoon steak sauce. Bring to a boil and season with plenty of salt and pepper. Cool. (B C L P S)

 Fruity Barbecue Marinade

In a saucepan, mix 1 cup apricot preserves, 2 tablespoons cider vinegar, ¼ cup chopped onion, 1 tablespoon vegetable oil, 2 teaspoons hot pepper sauce, and 2 tablespoons soy sauce. Bring to a boil

and season with plenty of salt and pepper. Cool. (B C L P S)

 Smoky Tomato Barbecue Marinade

Crumble 4 strips crisply cooked bacon into a saucepan. Add 1 cup ketchup, 2 tablespoons spicy mustard, 2 tablespoons cider vinegar, ¼ cup chopped onion, 1 clove minced garlic, 2 teaspoons hot pepper sauce, and ¼ cup honey. Bring to a boil and season with plenty of salt and pepper. Cool. (B C L P S V)

 Hot and Sour Barbecue Marinade

In a food processor or blender, process until minced 1 seeded bell pepper with 1 seeded jalapeño pepper, 2 cloves garlic, and ½ cup chopped onion. In a saucepan, simmer with ¼ cup cider vinegar, ⅔ cup water, 2 tablespoons vegetable oil, 1 tablespoon honey, and a pinch of ground allspice for about 10 minutes, until lightly thickened. Season with plenty of salt and pepper. Cool. (B C F P S V)

 Southwest Barbecue Marinade

Follow preceding recipe using 1 teaspoon ground cumin in place of the allspice and adding 2 tablespoons chopped fresh cilantro after cooking. (C F P S V)

 Hot Hot Hot Barbecue Paste

In a food processor or blender, process until minced 1 seeded bell pepper with 2 seeded jalapeño peppers, 3 cloves garlic, and ½ cup chopped onion. In a saucepan, simmer with 2 tablespoons cider vinegar, 1 tablespoon vegetable oil, 1 tablespoon sugar, ½ teaspoon ground cumin, and 2 to 4 tablespoons crushed red pepper flakes for 10 minutes, until lightly thickened. Season with plenty of salt and pepper. Cool. (B C D F P S)

Wine Barbecue Marinade

In a saucepan, mix ¾ cup red wine, ¼ cup red wine vinegar, ½ cup chopped onion, 1 clove minced garlic, 2 tablespoons Worcestershire sauce, 1 tablespoon steak sauce, 1 tablespoon sugar, ¼ cup ketchup, 1 teaspoon Dijon mustard, ½ teaspoon dried thyme, pinch ground allspice, 1 bay leaf, and salt and pepper to taste. Bring to a boil, and simmer for 5 minutes. Cool. (B C D G P)

Easy Red Wine Marinade

Mix 1 cup finely chopped onion, 1 clove minced garlic, 1 cup red wine, 2 tablespoons steak sauce, 3 tablespoons olive oil, 1 teaspoon cracked pepper, and salt and pepper to taste. (B C D G P)

Easy White Wine Marinade

Follow preceding recipe, using white wine instead of red and light soy sauce instead of steak sauce. (C F P S T V)

White Wine Fines Herbes Marinade

Mix 1 cup finely chopped onion with 1 clove minced garlic, 1 cup white wine, 1 tablespoon chopped fresh parsley, 2 teaspoons chopped fresh basil, 2 teaspoons chopped fresh thyme, 1 teaspoon chopped fresh tarragon, 3 tablespoons olive oil, 1 teaspoon cracked pepper, salt, and pepper. (B C F P S T)

Garlic and Wine Marinade

Follow preceding recipe, substituting 2 more cloves minced garlic for the tarragon and thyme. (C F S T V VG)

Hearty Red Wine Marinade

In a saucepan, simmer ½ cup thinly sliced onion, 1 sliced carrot, 12 crushed juniper berries, 1 bay leaf, ¼ teaspoon dried thyme, 2 teaspoons chopped fresh parsley, 10 cracked peppercorns, 6 cloves, 2 tablespoons brown sugar, ¼ cup red wine vinegar, and 3 cups hearty red wine for 10 minutes. Heat ¼ cup cognac, ignite carefully with a match and let the alcohol burn off, and add to marinade. Season with salt. (B D G L P)

Dill Mustard Marinade

Mix 2 cloves minced garlic, ¼ cup chopped dill weed, 3 tablespoons Dijon mustard, 2 tablespoons white wine vinegar, and ¼ cup olive oil. Season with salt and pepper. (C F S T V VG)

Honey Mustard Marinade

Mix 3 tablespoons honey, 6 tablespoons brown mustard, and 1 tablespoon Worcestershire sauce. Season with salt and pepper. (C D L P T V)

Spicy Apple Butter Marinade

Mix ¼ cup apple butter, 2 tablespoons honey, 1 teaspoon brown mustard (such as Gulden's spicy brown), and 2 teaspoons vegetable oil. Season with salt and pepper. (B C D L P)

Orange Cranberry Marinade

Mix ¼ cup orange marmalade, 3 tablespoons whole cranberry sauce, 1 tablespoon honey, 1 tablespoon minced orange zest, a dash of hot pepper sauce, 1 tablespoon soy sauce, and 1 tablespoon cider vinegar. (C D P T V)

Pickling Marinade

In a saucepan, mix 10 cracked peppercorns, 10 cracked coriander seeds, 6 cloves, 3 cloves chopped garlic, 1 tablespoon mustard seed, 2 dried chili peppers, ½ cup thinly sliced onion, 2 tablespoons brown sugar, ¼ cup wine vinegar, 1 tablespoon kosher salt, 3 bay leaves, 1 tablespoon chopped fresh parsley, 1 slice bacon, and 1 cup water. Bring to a boil, then simmer for 10 minutes. Cool, and remove the bacon, bay leaf, and chili peppers. (B C D P T)

Basic Dry Marinade

Mix 2 teaspoons black pepper, 1 teaspoon onion powder, 2 teaspoons garlic salt, ½ teaspoon cayenne pepper, and 1 teaspoon brown sugar. Rub into food, and let rest for 1 hour. (B C L P T V)

Citrus Dry Marinade

Follow preceding recipe adding 1 tablespoon *each* minced orange and lemon zest. (B C L P T V)

Moroccan Dry Marinade

Mix 2 teaspoons black pepper, 1 teaspoon onion powder, 2 teaspoons garlic salt, ½ teaspoon cayenne pepper, 1 teaspoon ground cinnamon, 1 teaspoon ground coriander, ½ teaspoon dried thyme, 1 teaspoon ground ginger, 1 tablespoon minced lemon zest, 1 tablespoon sugar. Rub into food and let rest for 1 hour. (B C L P V)

Charcuterie Dry Marinade

Mix 1 teaspoon salt, 1 teaspoon ground black pepper, 1 teaspoon ground white pepper, and ½ teaspoon *each* ground nutmeg, ginger, and allspice. Rub into food and let rest 1 hour. (C D G P V)

Asian Peanut Marinade

In a small skillet, cook ½ cup chopped onion and 1 clove minced garlic in 1 tablespoon peanut oil until soft. Add ½ teaspoon crushed red pepper flakes, 1 teaspoon ground coriander, and 2 teaspoons grated fresh gingerroot, and cook another minute. Stir in 5 tablespoons peanut butter, 1 tablespoon orange marmalade, 1 tablespoon soy sauce, 2 teaspoons rice wine vinegar, and ¼ cup water. Heat through. Let cool. (C F P S T V)

Chipotle Peanut Marinade

In a food processor or blender, process 2 tablespoons garlic chili paste with ¾ cup tomato puree and 4 dried chili chipotles (smoked jalapeños) until the chilies are well ground and incorporated. Add 2 tablespoons brown sugar, 2 tablespoons cider vinegar, and 1 tablespoon chopped fresh cilantro. Process until smooth. Stir in 2 tablespoons crunchy peanut butter. (B C L P T)

Curry Marinade

In a skillet, cook 1 cup chopped onion in 2 tablespoons vegetable oil until soft. Add 1 teaspoon mustard seed, 1½ teaspoons finely chopped fresh gingerroot, 1 clove minced garlic, 1 teaspoon ground coriander, 1 teaspoon ground cumin, 2 teaspoons curry powder, and a pinch of crushed red pepper flakes. Cook for 2 minutes, stirring frequently. Add salt and pepper to taste, 2 tablespoons lemon juice, and 2 tablespoons chopped fresh cilantro. Heat through, and cool. Mix in ½ cup plain yogurt. (C F L P S V VG)

 Red Curry Marinade

In a saucepan, blend the thick "cream" from the top of 1 can (14 ounces) coconut milk with 3 tablespoons Thai red curry paste and 2 teaspoons garlic chili paste. Simmer 2 minutes. Blend in 1 tablespoon Thai fish sauce (*nam pla*) and juice of 1 lemon. (C F P S T V VG)

 Tandoori Curry Marinade

Combine 1 teaspoon salt, the juice of 1 small lemon, 2 cloves minced garlic, 2 tablespoons minced fresh gingerroot, 1 teaspoon ground cumin seed, 1 teaspoon ground cardamom, 2 teaspoons curry powder, 1 teaspoon paprika, and ½ cup plain yogurt. (C D L P T VG)

 Mint and Anise Marinade

In a small skillet, cook 1 cup chopped onion in 2 tablespoons vegetable oil until soft. Add 1 teaspoon mustard seed, 1½ teaspoons finely chopped fresh gingerroot, 1 clove minced garlic, 1 teaspoon ground coriander, 1 teaspoon curry powder, 1 teaspoon ground aniseed, and ¼ teaspoon crushed red pepper flakes. Cook for 2 minutes, stirring frequently. Add salt, pepper, and 2 tablespoons dried mint leaves. Heat through, and cool. Mix in ½ cup plain yogurt. (C L S P V)

 Sweet Garlic Paste

Bake 2 large heads garlic at 375° F. for 45 minutes, or until soft to the touch. Cool slightly. Cut pointed end off each head and slip cloves from their peels. In a small skillet, heat 2 tablespoons olive oil with 1 dried chili pepper until bubbles form at edges of pepper. Remove pepper. In a blender, purée garlic with the oil, 1 tablespoon honey, and 1 teaspoon wine vinegar. Season with salt and pepper. (B C D F L P S T VG)

 Chili Marinade

In a skillet, cook 1 cup chopped onion, 2 finely chopped canned or fresh chili peppers, and 1 clove minced garlic in 1 tablespoon corn oil. Add 3 to 4 tablespoons chili powder, 1 tablespoon ground cumin, 2 teaspoons dried oregano, and 1 teaspoon ground coriander. Cook 1 minute more. Season with salt and pepper. (C F P S T)

 Yogurt, Garlic and Mint Marinade

Mix 1 cup plain yogurt, ¼ cup virgin olive oil, ½ teaspoon hot pepper sauce, 4 cloves minced garlic, 2 tablespoons lemon juice, and 2½ tablespoons dried mint leaves. Season with salt and pepper. (C F L S T VG)

 All-Coriander Marinade

Follow preceding recipe, adding 2 teaspoons ground coriander seed with the garlic and ⅓ cup chopped fresh cilantro instead of the mint. (C F P S T)

Fifty Sauces to Enhance Any Meal

Why are we so shy about sauces? Is it fear of becoming mired in complicated technique or revulsion at the prospect of unwanted fat and unfamiliar flavors?

For years, our anxiety over sauce-making has held American home cooking hostage. It has helped condemn us to a diet of excess salt as we struggle to eke out flavor without the natural complement of a sauce. It has created a false image of ourselves as a nation of plain eaters, when in fact we're one of the world's most experimental culinary cultures. And it stands in the way of our constant search for quick, healthful, convenient solutions to the nightly quandary of what to make for dinner.

In an effort to change all that, we offer the following 50 sauce recipes. None of them takes more than 10 minutes to prepare, all require little or no salting, and saturated fat is kept to a minimum. Most important, all of them provide fabulous flavor with minimum work.

ABOUT THESE RECIPES

We'll note whether you would do well to serve these sauces with chicken, beef, veal, pork, or fish. But these are only suggestions, and we encourage you to experiment with different combinations, trying the sauces that appeal to you with different main ingredients, or substituting an herb here or a spice there as availability and taste suit you. As with the marinades in the preceding chapter, these 50 sauces lead to hundreds of combinations.

Each recipe is written for two portions of sautéed meat or fish, although they can be doubled or tripled. Before preparing the sauce, sauté the food it will be served with, and remove to a warm platter. In most cases, you'll pour off all but 1 tablespoon fat from the pan, and proceed with the sauce recipe.

If you prefer to steam, poach, or microwave your meat or fish, you can still use these recipes. Follow these procedures instead:

For poaching, remove cooked food to a warm platter, and reduce ½ cup poaching liquid over high heat to 3 tablespoons. Proceed with the sauce recipe of your choice, starting with 1 tablespoon oil in a sauté pan. Add the reduced poaching liquid to the sauce along with the other liquids in the recipe.

For steaming or microwaving, enclose the food in plastic wrap, which will hold in any juices weeping from the ingredients during cooking. When the food is done, remove from the steamer or microwave, carefully snip a hole in the plastic and drain off the juices. Proceed with the sauce recipe of your choice, starting with 1 tablespoon oil in a sauté pan. Add the reserved juices to the sauce along with the other liquids in the recipe.

These recipes make no mention of salt and pepper, which you should add to taste.

Following each recipe is a parenthetical list of abbreviations indicating the main ingredients for which that sauce would be well suited. Here is the key to those abbreviations:

B = Beef. C = Chicken. F = Fish. P = Pork. V = Veal.

Wine and Mushroom Sauce

Add 1 tablespoon minced onion, 8 sliced mushrooms, and 1 tablespoon olive oil to the fat in the pan and sauté until lightly browned. Add 1 cup white wine and boil off the alcohol. Remove from heat. Stir in 2 tablespoons sour cream, plain yogurt, or *crème fraîche*. (C F V)

Lemon Walnut Sauce

Add ½ cup chopped walnuts to the fat in the pan and toast lightly. Remove from heat and stir in 3 tablespoons walnut oil, ½ clove minced garlic, and juice of ½ lemon. (C F V)

Sauce Veronique

Add 1 teaspoon chopped shallot to the fat in the pan and cook until softened. Add ½ cup white wine and boil for 2 minutes. Add ½ cup chicken stock and cook until reduced by half. Finish over low heat by adding 12 halved seedless grapes and 1 tablespoon butter. (C F V)

Yogurt and Herb Sauce

Add 2 tablespoons chopped leek, ¼ clove minced garlic, and 1 tablespoon olive oil to the fat in the pan and sauté until the leek is softened. Add 3 tablespoons chopped fresh herbs and ½ cup chicken, fish, or veal stock. Reduce liquid to ¼ cup. Remove from heat and blend in ½ cup plain yogurt. (C F V)

Watercress and Cream Sauce

Add 2 teaspoons chopped shallot to the fat in the pan and cook until softened. Deglaze pan with ¼ cup dry vermouth and reduce over high heat to a third its volume. Add ½ cup light cream and reduce until thickened, about 1 minute. Stir in ⅓ cup watercress leaves and cook just until leaves wilt. (C F V)

Sorrel and Crème Fraîche Sauce

Follow preceding recipe, using *crème fraîche* instead of cream and sorrel leaves instead of watercress. (C F V)

Beurre Blanc

Add 1 tablespoon minced shallot, ½ cup white wine, and 2 tablespoons white wine vinegar to the fat in the pan and cook until reduced to ⅓ cup. Turn heat to low and swirl in 4 tablespoons butter, 1 tablespoon at a time. (C F V)

 ### Herbed Beurre Blanc

Add 1 tablespoon minced shallot; 2 teaspoons dried tarragon, basil, chervil, or dill; ½ cup white wine, and 2 tablespoons tarragon vinegar to the fat in the pan and cook over high heat until reduced to ⅓ cup. Turn heat to low and swirl in 4 tablespoons butter, 1 tablespoon at a time, and 1 teaspoon minced fresh parsley. (C F V)

 ### Sage Glaze

Add 1 tablespoon chopped onion and 4 fresh sage leaves to the fat in the pan. Sauté until the onion browns lightly. Add ⅔ cup chicken stock and a pinch of dried thyme. Cook until lightly thickened. (C P V)

 ### Spicy Hoisin Sauce

Add ¼ clove minced garlic, 1 teaspoon minced fresh gingerroot, and a pinch of crushed red pepper flakes to the fat in the pan. Sauté for 1 minute. Add 1½ tablespoons hoisin sauce and ⅓ cup chicken stock. Bring to a simmer and serve. (C P V)

 ### Barbecue Pan Sauce

Add 1 tablespoon grated onion and a pinch of sugar to the fat in the pan and brown lightly. Deglaze pan with 1 tablespoon cider vinegar, ¼ cup ketchup, 1 teaspoon brown mustard, and 1 tea-

spoon Worcestershire sauce. Bring to a boil and season to taste with hot pepper sauce. Return the cooked food to the pan and coat with the sauce before serving. (C P V)

 ### Worcestershire and Mustard Sauce

Add 1 tablespoon chopped onion to the fat in the pan and brown lightly. Deglaze pan with 1½ table-spoons Worcestershire sauce. Add ⅓ cup chicken stock and boil for 1 minute. Mix in 1 tablespoon brown mustard. (C P V)

 ### Sauce of Prosciutto, Peas, and Rosemary

Add 1 tablespoon minced onion to the fat in the pan and sauté for 1 minute. Add 2 ounces juli-enned prosciutto, ½ cup defrosted frozen peas, and 2 teaspoons chopped fresh rosemary leaves. Sauté for 1 more minute. Deglaze pan with 2 table-spoons *crème fraîche*, light cream, or mascarpone. Cook and stir until lightly thickened, about 1 minute. (C P V)

 ### Ginger, Soy, and Sesame Sauce

Add ¼ clove minced garlic, 1 teaspoon chopped fresh gingerroot, and 1 tablespoon Oriental sesame oil to the fat in the pan and sauté for 1 minute. Deglaze pan with 1 tablespoon low-sodium soy sauce, ⅓ cup chicken stock, and a pinch of sugar. Simmer for 1 minute. (C P V)

 ### Sweet and Sour Cider Sauce

Add 1 tablespoon chopped onion to the fat in the pan and cook until lightly browned. Add ⅔ cup apple cider, 2 teaspoons apple cider vinegar, and 1 teaspoon brown sugar. Cook until lightly thick-ened, then swirl in 1 tablespoon butter. (C P V)

Sherried Apricot Glaze

Add 1 tablespoon butter, 1 minced shallot, and 1 teaspoon grated fresh gingerroot to the fat in the pan and sauté for 30 seconds. Add 2 tablespoons apricot preserves and stir until melted. Deglaze with 1 tablespoon orange juice and ⅓ cup dry sherry. Ignite carefully with a match and let the alcohol burn off. (C P V)

Crème Fraîche and Mustard Sauce

Add 2 teaspoons chopped shallot to the fat in the pan and cook until soft. Remove from heat and stir in ⅓ cup *crème fraîche* and 1 tablespoon Dijon mustard. (C P V)

Onion, Brandy, and Cream Sauce

Add 1 tablespoon minced onion and ¼ cup brandy to the fat in the pan. Ignite carefully with a match. When flames subside, add 1 cup light cream and reduce until lightly thickened. (C P V)

Beaujolais and Pomegranate Sauce

Add 1 tablespoon chopped shallot to the fat in the pan and sauté for 1 minute. Add ½ cup Beaujolais wine and boil for 2 minutes. Add ½ cup pomegranate juice, squeezed over a strainer to catch the seeds, and boil 1 minute more. Swirl in 1 tablespoon butter. (C P V)

Red Pepper Coulis

In a saucepan, combine 1 large stemmed, seeded, cored, and chopped red pepper, 1 tablespoon chopped onion, ¼ clove minced garlic, ¼ pickled jalapeño, 2 teaspoons Oriental sesame oil, and 1 tablespoon lemon juice. Bring to a boil, cover, and

simmer until the pepper has softened. Purée and strain through a sieve. (C F P V)

Warm Sun-Dried Tomato Vinaigrette

Add 4 finely chopped oil-cured sun-dried tomatoes, ½ clove minced garlic, and 3 tablespoons olive oil to the fat in the pan and sauté for 20 seconds. Add 1½ tablespoons red wine vinegar. (C F P V)

Sauce Provençale

Add 1 clove chopped garlic, 2 tablespoons minced onion, 1 teaspoon *herbes de Provence*, and 2 tablespoons olive oil to the fat in the pan and sauté for 30 seconds. Add 3 finely chopped large plum tomatoes (seeds removed), 12 pitted black olives, and 1 tablespoon chopped fresh basil and heat through. (C F P V)

Tapenade

In a bowl, combine ⅓ cup chopped, pitted, oil-cured black olives, ½ clove finely chopped garlic, and ¼ cup extra-virgin olive oil. (C F P V)

Roasted Pepper Rouille

In a bowl, combine 1 large roasted red pepper that has been stemmed, seeded, cored, and chopped (page 442) with ¼ cup chopped fresh basil, 1 clove minced garlic, and 1 tablespoon extra-virgin olive oil. (C F P V)

Tomato, Chili, and Mascarpone Sauce

Add 1 clove minced garlic, a large pinch of crushed red pepper flakes, and 1 tablespoon olive oil to the fat in the pan and cook to soften the garlic, then add 1½ cups chopped fresh tomatoes. Cook until the tomatoes simmer and stir in 2 tablespoons mascarpone cheese. (C F P V)

Fifty Ways to Cook Most Everything

 Tomato, Olives, and Parmesan Sauce

Add 1 clove minced garlic and 1 tablespoon olive oil to the fat in the pan and cook to soften the garlic, then add 1½ cups chopped fresh tomatoes and 12 pitted black olives. Bring to a simmer and stir in 1 tablespoon grated Parmesan. (C F P V)

 Chilied Peanut Sauce

Add 1 tablespoon chopped onion and ¼ clove minced garlic to the fat in the pan and cook until the onion has softened. Add 1 thinly sliced scallion, ½ teaspoon chili paste, 1 teaspoon soy sauce, 1 teaspoon finely chopped fresh gingerroot, a pinch of ground cumin, and a pinch of coriander. Cook for 1 minute. Stir in 2 tablespoons peanut butter until melted. Remove from the heat and thin with ¼ cup buttermilk, yogurt, or stock to a saucelike consistency. (C F P V)

 Caper and Brown Butter Sauce

Add 1 tablespoon minced onion or shallot and 2 tablespoons butter to the fat in the pan and sauté until browned. Add 2 tablespoons drained capers and 2 more tablespoons butter. Cook 1 minute more and add the juice of ½ lemon. (B C F P V)

 Beurre Rouge

Add 1 tablespoon minced shallot, ½ cup red wine, and 2 tablespoons red wine vinegar to the fat in the pan and cook until reduced to ⅓ cup. Turn heat to low, add ½ teaspoon tomato paste, and swirl in 4 tablespoons butter, 1 tablespoon at a time. (B C F P V)

 Garlic Beurre Blanc

Add 1 clove minced garlic, ½ cup white wine, and 2 tablespoons white wine vinegar to the fat in the pan and cook over high heat until reduced to ⅓ cup. Turn heat to low, and swirl in 4 tablespoons butter, 1 tablespoon at a time. (B C F P V)

 Scotch and Brown Sugar Sauce

Add 2 tablespoons chopped onion and 1 tablespoon butter to the fat in the pan and sauté over moderate heat until the onion is lightly browned. Add 1 teaspoon brown sugar and cook 1 minute more. Deglaze pan with ¼ cup Scotch and ignite carefully with a match. When flames subside, add another tablespoon butter and, after it melts, ½ cup beef broth. Boil until the sauce thickens slightly. (B C F P V)

 Rosemary and Vermouth Sauce

Add 1 tablespoon minced shallot, 2 teaspoons crumbled dried rosemary, ½ cup dry vermouth, and 2 tablespoons tarragon vinegar to the fat in the pan and cook over high heat until reduced to ⅓ cup. Turn heat to low, and swirl in 4 tablespoons butter, 1 tablespoon at a time, and 1 teaspoon minced fresh parsley. (B C F P V)

 Sherry and Balsamic Glaze

Add 1 tablespoon minced shallot, ½ cup sherry, and 2 tablespoons balsamic vinegar to the fat in the pan, and cook over high heat until reduced to ⅓ cup. Turn heat to low and swirl in 4 tablespoons butter, 1 tablespoon at a time. (B C F P V)

 Bordelaise Sauce

Add 1 tablespoon *each* minced shallot and mushroom to the fat in the pan, and sauté until well browned. Add 1 teaspoon tomato paste and a pinch of dried thyme. Sauté 1 minute more. Add ½ cup hearty red wine and reduce by half over high heat. Add ½ cup beef broth and boil 3 minutes. Lower heat and finish sauce by swirling in 1 tablespoon butter or 1 tablespoon chopped beef marrow. (B C F P V)

 Juniper Gin Sauce

Add ¼ clove minced garlic, 1 teaspoon green peppercorns, and 2 crushed juniper berries to the fat in the pan and cook for 2 minutes. Deglaze pan with ¼ cup gin and ignite carefully with a match. Stir in ¼ cup *crème fraîche* or heavy cream after flames subside. (B C F P V)

 Mushroom Ragout

Soak ¼ ounce dried wild mushrooms in ¾ cup warm water for 30 minutes. Remove mushrooms and strain soaking liquid through a coffee filter or cheesecloth. Add the thinly sliced white of 1 leek, the drained dried mushrooms, ¼ pound sliced white mushrooms, and 2 tablespoons butter to the fat in the pan and sauté until softened. Add a pinch of dried thyme, 1 tablespoon chopped fresh parsley, 1 peeled, seeded, and chopped tomato, and the mushroom soaking liquid. Bring to a boil and simmer 3 minutes. (B C F P V)

 Oyster Sauce with Lime and Garlic

In a small bowl, mix ¼ cup Chinese oyster sauce, the juice of 1 large lime, ½ clove minced garlic, 1 teaspoon minced fresh gingerroot, ⅓ cup dry sherry, and ½ cup chicken stock. Add this mixture

to the fat in the pan and boil 3 minutes. Swirl in 1 teaspoon Oriental sesame oil. (B C F P V)

 Curried Onion Sauce

Add ¼ cup chopped onion and 1 tablespoon vegetable oil to the fat in the pan and simmer until softened. Add 2 teaspoons curry powder, ½ teaspoon ground coriander, and a pinch of crushed red pepper flakes and cook for another 2 to 3 minutes. Lower heat and mix in ½ cup plain yogurt. Finish with 1 teaspoon orange marmalade. (B C F P V)

 Marinated Mushroom Sauce

In a small saucepan, combine ¼ pound sliced mushrooms, 1 tablespoon lemon juice, ⅓ cup white wine, 1 bay leaf, 1 minced shallot, ¼ cup olive oil, a pinch of dried thyme, and a pinch of ground coriander. Bring to a boil, remove from heat, and stir in 2 tablespoons chopped fresh parsley. (B C F P V)

 Julienned Pepper and Carrot Sauce

Add 1 minced shallot and 1 tablespoon olive oil to the fat in the pan and sauté for 30 seconds. Add 1 cup *each* julienned carrots and red peppers. Sauté for 2 minutes and add ⅓ cup chicken broth and the juice of ½ lemon. Simmer about 2 minutes, until carrot is barely soft. Finish with 1 tablespoon chopped fresh parsley. (B C F P V)

The following sauces for chicken, fish, and veal are uncooked. They are made separately from the foods they accompany and can be made in advance and held. If you're not sure that your egg supply is free of salmonella, you may want to avoid the first three recipes.

Garlic Vinaigrette

In a small bowl, combine 1 clove minced garlic, 1 egg yolk, 1 tablespoon Dijon mustard, and 2 tablespoons white wine vinegar. In a slow, steady stream, add ⅓ cup olive oil while whisking constantly. (C F V)

 Basil and Garlic Sauce

Follow the preceding recipe, but add 2 tablespoons chopped fresh basil with the garlic. (C F V)

 Lemon Parsley Sauce

Follow the recipe for Garlic Vinaigrette (above), substituting 1 teaspoon finely grated lemon zest for the garlic and using lemon juice instead of vinegar. Add 2 tablespoons chopped fresh parsley at the end. (C F V)

 Anchovy Mayonnaise

Mix 1 ounce finely chopped anchovy fillet with its oil, 2 tablespoons mayonnaise, 1 tablespoon virgin olive oil, 2 teaspoons lemon juice, and ¼ clove minced garlic. (C F V)

Roquefort Buttermilk Sauce

In a small bowl, thin ½ cup Roquefort dressing with ¼ cup buttermilk. (C F V)

 Tarragon Ranch Sauce

In a small bowl, thin ½ cup ranch dressing with 3 tablespoons buttermilk, and 1 tablespoon tarragon vinegar. (C F V)

 Tomato and Artichoke Salsa

Chop contents of a 6-ounce jar marinated artichoke hearts, 1 large tomato, and 1 clove minced garlic. (C F V)

 Garlic Citrus Salsa

Chop 1 cup orange, grapefruit, lemon, lime, or tangerine sections. Mix with ½ clove minced garlic, 1 tablespoon chopped red onion, a dash of hot pepper sauce, and 1 teaspoon white wine vinegar. (C F V)

 Spicy Avocado Sauce

Mash 1 ripe avocado with a fork and mix in 1 clove minced garlic, 1 chopped scallion, a dash of hot pepper sauce, 1½ tablespoons white wine vinegar, and 1 tablespoon olive oil. (C F V)

 Gazpacho Sauce

In a food processor, finely chop 2 stemmed, seeded plum tomatoes, ¼ small cucumber, ¼ pickled jalapeño, 1 tablespoon chopped onion, ½ clove minced garlic, 2 tablespoons olive oil, and 1 tablespoon wine vinegar. (C F V)

Fifty Beautiful Soups

Soup isn't much. A celery stalk, a carrot top, an onion, and a meaty bone are about all you need. Then lots of water, of course. A pinch of salt and a bit of herb to bring the flavor out. Perhaps a potato, chopped in chunks, or sculpted into tiny balls, scattered through the broth, like a string of pearls come unstrung. Maybe a bisque of lobster or crab, finished with a dram of cream, a bit of sweet butter, and a snippet of chive.

No, soup isn't much. Just sustenance for us all.

Most good cooks make good soup. It is a challenge to them, and a delight to extract everything an ingredient has to give, until, from a pile of scraps, a meal emerges. Meat, vegetable, starch, and beverage—neatly packed in one bowl.

Another challenge is to make soups fast. Though perfectly wonderful soups are made with only trimmings and water, it saves time and energy to start with a broth, which is nothing more than a flavorful liquid. It can be the leftover cooking water from vegetables or stews, something concocted from last night's chicken carcass, or a good-quality broth from a can.

A good broth gives you speed. Because it holds most of the flavor of the soup, hours of simmering and long lists of ingredients become unnecessary. Homemade soups can be thrown together in minutes and on the table a half hour later.

To show you how easy it is, we have concocted 50 soups. All but a couple of them can be made in 30 minutes or less if you have your own stock on hand—or if you use one of the good commercial broths.

ABOUT THESE RECIPES

If you'd like to use homemade broth, here are two recipes for basic broths—one for a vegetable broth that can be made in 20 minutes, the other a chicken broth made from a leftover carcass and vegetables that takes somewhat longer. Use these broths as your base, or substitute any good-quality canned or frozen product.

Twenty-Minute Vegetable Broth

In large pot, cook 1 chopped large onion, 3 chopped carrots, 4 ribs chopped celery, and chopped white of 1 large leek in 1 tablespoon oil until softened. Add 4 sprigs dill, 4 sprigs parsley, 1 bay leaf, the juice and zest of ½ lemon, ½ teaspoon salt, 6 peppercorns, 9 cups boiling water, and 2 tablespoons tomato paste. Stir to dissolve the tomato paste and bring to a boil. Simmer for 20 minutes, then strain. Makes 2 quarts.

Chicken Broth

In large pot, combine 2 or 3 chicken carcasses (1 turkey carcass would also be fine), with 1 cup white wine. Boil until aroma of alcohol is gone. Add 2½ quarts water. Bring to a boil and skim away any surface scum. Simmer 20 minutes. Add 2 cups chopped onion, 1 cup chopped carrot, 1 cup chopped celery, 3 tablespoons chopped fresh parsley, 2 tablespoons chopped fresh dill, 1 teaspoon dried thyme, 2 cloves, ¾ teaspoon salt, 6 peppercorns, 1 teaspoon ground turmeric, if desired, and 1 envelope (¼ ounce) unflavored gelatin. Simmer 1 hour more. Strain. Pick off any meat clinging to the carcasses and return to the broth. Makes 2 quarts.

 ## Chicken Soup with Three Rices

In large soup pot, cook 3 chopped carrots, 2 chopped ribs celery and chopped white of 1 large leek in 1 tablespoon hot oil until softened. Add 1 inch fresh gingerroot, 1 dried chili pepper, 1 bay leaf, and 1 cup white wine. Boil for 1 minute. Add 2 quarts chicken broth, and season with salt and pepper. Bring to a boil. Add ¼ cup *each* brown rice and wild rice. Simmer for 45 minutes. Add ¼ cup white rice and simmer 15 minutes more. Remove bay leaf, gingerroot, and chili pepper. (Or use leftover cooked rice to eliminate rice cooking time.) Serves 6.

 ## Curried Chicken Soup

Follow preceding recipe, adding 2 teaspoons curry powder with the gingerroot and chili pepper.

 ## Chicken Noodle Soup

Follow recipe for Chicken Soup with Three Rices, but omit rices, cut initial cooking time to 20 minutes, then add 5 ounces broad egg noodles and cook for 10 minutes more.

 ## Chicken Soup with Tortellini

In large soup pot, cook 3 chopped carrots, 2 chopped ribs celery, and the chopped white of 1 large leek in 1 tablespoon hot oil until softened. Add 1 teaspoon *each* dried thyme, savory, and basil, ½ teaspoon *each* crumbled dried rosemary, oregano, and sage, 1 bay leaf, and 1 cup white wine. Boil for 1 minute. Add 2 quarts chicken broth, 4 chopped canned plum tomatoes, salt, and pepper. Bring to a boil and cook 20 minutes. Add 8 ounces cheese or meat tortellini, and cook for 10 minutes more. Remove bay leaf. Serves 6.

 ## Chicken Matzo Ball Soup

Mix 4 eggs, 2 tablespoons chicken fat or vegetable oil, 1 cup matzo meal, 1 teaspoon salt, 1 tablespoon chopped fresh parsley, and 6 tablespoons of chicken broth until well blended. Cover and refrigerate for 1 hour. Bring a large pot of salted water to a boil. Form matzo balls, each from about 2 teaspoons of the mixture, and simmer in the water for about 30 minutes until they are light and cooked through. Test by cutting one in half. Meanwhile, in a large soup pot, cook 3 chopped carrots, 2 ribs chopped celery, and the chopped white of 1 large leek in 1 tablespoon oil until soft. Add 1 inch fresh gingerroot, 1 dried chili pepper, 1 bay leaf, and 1 cup white wine. Boil for 1 minute. Add 2 quarts chicken broth, salt, and pepper. Bring to a boil, and simmer 5 minutes more. Add matzo balls and simmer until heated through. Remove ginger-root, chili pepper, and bay leaf.

Chicken Barley Soup

Follow recipe for Chicken Soup with Three Rices (opposite), but use 1½ cups pearl barley instead of the rices. Add barley at point in recipe where brown and wild rices are added.

Cream of Mushroom Soup

In heavy soup pot, cook 1 cup chopped onion, 1 clove minced garlic, 1 diced parsnip, and 1 rib diced celery in 2 tablespoons butter over moderate heat until softened. Add ½ pound sliced mushrooms and cook 3 minutes until the mushrooms begin to release their moisture. Add ½ pound minced mushrooms and cook another 3 minutes. Stir in 1 tablespoon flour and cook for 2 minutes more. Add 1 quart chicken broth and season with salt and white pepper. Simmer 20 minutes. Add 2 cups light cream. In separate bowl, beat 2 yolks with 1 cup hot soup, then add this mixture back to soup and stir until lightly thickened. Do not allow soup to boil after yolks have been added. Correct seasonings. Garnish with chopped chive. Serves 6.

Mushroom Chowder

In large heavy soup pot, cook the finely chopped white of 2 large leeks, 2 diced carrots, 2 ribs diced celery, 2 diced peeled boiling potatoes, ½ diced red pepper, and ½ pound diced smoked turkey in 2 tablespoons melted bacon fat over moderate heat until softened. Add 1 pound sliced mushrooms, 1 teaspoon dried thyme, ½ teaspoon *each* ground sage and crumbled dried rosemary, and 1 bay leaf. Stir until mushrooms start to release their liquid. Add 1 quart chicken or vegetable broth, season

with salt and pepper, and simmer for 20 minutes. Dissolve 1 tablespoon cornstarch in 1 cup cold milk, and stir into the soup. Bring to a boil. Remove bay leaf. Serves 6.

Lamb and Mushroom Soup

Generously season 1 pound boneless stewing lamb with salt and pepper. In large heavy soup pot, brown lamb in thin film of oil. Add 1 cup chopped onion and 2 cloves minced garlic. Cook until onion softens. Add 1 pound sliced mushrooms and cook until mushrooms brown lightly. Add 1 teaspoon ground coriander, a pinch of crumbled dried rosemary, and ½ teaspoon dried thyme. Cook for 1 minute more. Add 2 quarts water, 1 cup strong broth (of any type), 2 teaspoons tomato paste, 1 bay leaf, 2 sliced carrots, 1 rib sliced celery, and 1 tablespoon chopped fresh parsley. Adjust seasoning with salt and pepper and simmer for 1 hour until lamb is tender. Add juice of 1 lemon. Remove bay leaf. Serves 8.

Mushroom Barley Soup

Liberally season 1 pound boneless stewing beef with salt and pepper. In large heavy soup pot, brown beef in thin film of oil. Add 1 cup chopped onion, 2 diced carrots, 1 rib diced celery, and 1 diced parsnip. Cook until onion softens. Add 1 pound sliced mushrooms and cook until mushrooms brown lightly. Add a pinch of dried crumbled rosemary and 1 teaspoon dried thyme. Cook for another minute. Add 2 quarts water, 1 cup strong beef broth, 2 teaspoons tomato paste, and 1 bay leaf. Bring to a boil. Add 1 cup pearl barley and 1 tablespoon chopped fresh parsley. Adjust seasoning with salt and pepper and simmer 1 hour until beef and barley are tender. Remove bay leaf. Serves 8.

Wild Mushroom Bisque

Soak ¼ ounce dried wild mushrooms in 1 cup boiling water and ¼ cup Madeira for 15 minutes. Drain mushrooms, trim, and mince. Reserve mushrooms and soaking liquid separately. Meanwhile, in heavy soup pot, cook ¾ cup finely chopped onion in 2 tablespoons butter over moderate heat until softened. Add 1 pound minced mushrooms, the reserved minced wild mushrooms, 1 teaspoon dried thyme, and ½ teaspoon crumbled dried rosemary. Cook until most of the moisture has evaporated, stirring frequently. Add 2 tablespoons flour and stir continuously until flour browns. Add 1 quart chicken broth, salt, and pepper. Simmer for 15 minutes. Add 1 cup light cream and adjust seasoning. Serves 6.

 ## Mushroom Minestrone

In large soup pot, cook 1 cup chopped onion, the chopped white of 1 leek, and 2 cloves minced garlic in 2 tablespoons olive oil until softened. Add 2 sliced carrots, 2 ribs sliced celery, 1 pound whole cleaned button mushrooms, and ½ diced bell pepper. Cook 2 minutes. Add 1 teaspoon *each* dried thyme, savory, and basil and ½ teaspoon *each* dried rosemary, oregano, and sage. Cook 3 minutes more. Add 4 chopped canned tomatoes, 5 cups chicken broth, 1 tablespoon *each* wine vinegar and tomato paste, salt, and pepper. Bring to a boil and simmer for 10 minutes. Serve with grated Parmesan. Serves 8.

 ## Mediterranean Minestrone

Follow preceding recipe, reducing mushroom quantity to ¼ pound and adding 1 cup cooked or canned chick-peas with chicken broth.

 ## Cream of Chestnut Soup

In large heavy pot, cook 2 diced carrots, 2 ribs diced celery, and 1 finely chopped onion in 4 tablespoons butter until tender. Add 1 cup chestnut puree and 1 quart hot chicken broth. Whisk until smooth. Add a pinch of ground cloves, salt, and white pepper. Simmer for 10 minutes, then strain. Add 1 cup light cream and 2 tablespoons brandy. Heat through. Serves 4.

 ## Butternut Squash Soup with Ginger Cream

In a large soup pot, cook the chopped white of 2 leeks, 1 chopped parsnip, ½ pound chopped carrots, and ½ inch grated fresh gingerroot in 2 tablespoons butter until softened. Add 2 pounds peeled, cleaned, and chunked butternut squash, 1 teaspoon dried thyme, a pinch of ground mace, 1½ quarts chicken broth, salt, and pepper. Bring to a boil and simmer for 20 to 30 minutes, until squash is tender. Remove solids and puree in food processor or blender until almost smooth. Return to pot and adjust seasoning. Beat 1 cup heavy cream to a soft peak and fold in 1 tablespoon minced candied ginger. Serve hot soup dolloped with ginger cream. Serves 8.

 ## Potato Cheese Soup

In heavy soup pot, cook the chopped white of 3 leeks and 1 finely chopped onion in 1 tablespoon *each* oil and butter. Add 1½ pounds peeled and diced red-skin potatoes, a pinch of dried thyme, and 1 quart chicken or vegetable broth. Simmer for 15 minutes until potatoes are tender. Add 1 cup *each* light cream and milk, salt, and white pepper. Heat slowly to a simmer. Toss ¼ pound shredded Cheddar with 1 tablespoon cornstarch, then carefully whisk into soup. Cook just long enough to melt the cheese. Serves 6.

 ### Potato Leek Soup

In heavy soup pot, cook 1 chopped onion and the chopped white of 3 large leeks in 3 tablespoons butter over moderate heat until softened. Add 2 pounds peeled and sliced russet potatoes, 6 cups chicken broth, 1 teaspoon salt, ¼ teaspoon white pepper, and a grating of nutmeg. Simmer for 20 minutes, until potatoes are tender. Force solid ingredients with half the liquid through a food mill or coarse strainer. Return to soup pot and add 1 cup *each* light cream and milk. Heat through. Serve hot or chilled, garnished with chopped fresh chives. If soup is served chilled, thin with sour cream or buttermilk before serving. Serves 6.

 ### Potato Fennel Soup

Follow preceding recipe, using just 1 leek and adding 1 chopped fennel bulb and 1 teaspoon ground fennel with leek and onion.

 ### Garlic Potato Soup

Follow recipe for Potato Leek Soup (above), substituting 1 head minced garlic for the onion.

 ### Sweet Potato Vichyssoise

Follow recipe for Potato Leek Soup (above), substituting yams for potatoes. Serve chilled.

 ### Pumpkin Leek Soup

Follow recipe for Potato Leek Soup (above), substituting 2 cups canned or homemade pumpkin puree for the potato. Cut cooking time to 10 minutes.

 ### Caraway Potato Soup

Follow recipe for Potato Leek Soup (above), but use only 1 leek and add 4 ribs chopped celery and 1 teaspoon ground caraway seed with leeks and onions.

 ### Potato Watercress Soup

Follow recipe for Potato Leek Soup (above), adding leaves from 1 bunch watercress with the leeks.

 ### Apple Pumpkin Borscht

In a soup pot, cook ½ cup finely chopped onion in 2 tablespoons butter over moderate heat until softened. Add 2 finely chopped, peeled and cored large apples, 1 tablespoon finely chopped fresh gingerroot, 1 cinnamon stick, and 1 small dried chili pepper. Cook for 1 minute more. Add 2 cups pumpkin puree, 1 quart chicken broth, 2 tablespoons honey, 1 teaspoon apple cider vinegar, a grating of nutmeg, salt, and white pepper. Bring to a boil and adjust seasoning. Serve hot or cold, mixing in ½ cup sour cream just before serving. Remove cinnamon and chili pepper. Serves 6.

 ### Apple Broccoli Borscht

In soup pot, cook ½ cup finely chopped onion in 2 tablespoons butter over moderate heat until softened. Add 2 finely chopped, peeled, and cored large apples, 1 bunch diced broccoli, and 1 quart chicken broth. Cook for 10 minutes until broccoli is soft. Season with salt and white pepper. Puree in a blender or food processor. Reheat, mixing in ¼ cup sour cream. Serve hot or chilled. Thin with some milk if serving chilled. Serves 6.

Roasted Red Pepper Borscht

In heavy saucepan, cook ½ cup finely chopped onion, 1 clove minced garlic, and 1 rib diced celery in 2 tablespoons olive oil over moderate heat until softened. Add 4 diced roasted red bell peppers (page 442), 1 teaspoon curry powder, a pinch of cayenne, 1½ teaspoons paprika, and 1 quart chicken broth. Season with salt and pepper, bring to a boil, and simmer for 10 minutes. Finish with 2 tablespoons lime juice. Serve hot or chilled, garnishing each bowl with 1 tablespoon sour cream and sprinkling of finely chopped canned jalapeño peppers. Serves 4.

 Curried Cucumber Soup

In large soup pot over moderate heat, cook ½ cup chopped onion and 2 minced cloves garlic in 2 tablespoons butter until softened. Add 2 pounds peeled, seeded, and finely chopped cucumber, 2 teaspoons curry powder, salt, and white pepper. Add 1 quart chicken or vegetable broth and simmer for 10 to 15 minutes, until cucumber is soft. Puree in a blender or food processor and stir in ½ cup light cream or sour cream. If serving chilled, thin with bit more cream and adjust seasoning. Serves 6.

 Lime Bisque

In large saucepan, bring 6 cups chicken broth to a full boil. Add ¼ teaspoon salt and ⅓ cup long-grain rice. Reduce heat so soup just simmers and cook 15 minutes, until rice is tender. While soup cooks, mix 3 large egg yolks, ⅓ cup lime juice, and few drops of hot pepper sauce. When rice is tender, slowly whisk 2 cups hot soup into egg mixture. Return this mixture to saucepan and cook gently until soup thickens slightly. Do not boil. Ad-

just seasoning. Serve hot or chilled, garnished with lime slices and chopped fresh cilantro. If serving chilled, thin to desired consistency with extra chilled chicken broth. Serves 4.

 Avgolemono

Season 2 quarts rich chicken broth with salt and pepper and bring to a boil. Add ¾ cup rice and simmer 12 minutes until rice is tender. Meanwhile, mix 3 egg yolks with the juice of 2 lemons. Add a ladleful of boiling soup to egg-yolk mixture, mixing constantly. Reduce heat so soup barely simmers and slowly pour egg mixture into hot soup, stirring constantly. Cook over moderate heat to prevent curdling, stirring until soup thickens slightly. Do not boil. Serve hot or chilled, garnished with chopped fresh chives. If served chilled, thin to desired consistency with bit of chilled broth. Serves 6.

 Lemon Chicken Soup with Orzo

Follow preceding recipe, substituting orzo or another small pastina for rice.

 Lemon Chick-Pea Soup

Follow recipe for Avgolemono (above), substituting 1 cup cooked, drained chick-peas and 1 cup small pasta for rice.

 Tomato Tarragon Consommé

Soften 1 tablespoon gelatin in ½ cup chilled chicken broth. Stir mixture into 5½ cups additional chilled chicken broth in heavy saucepan. Add ¼ cup tomato paste, 1 rib finely chopped celery, 3 tablespoons minced onion, ½ teaspoon dried thyme, 2 teaspoons dried tarragon, 6 peppercorns, 1 crumbled bay leaf, 4 beaten egg whites, and salt. Whisk until well blended and frothy. Cook over moderate heat, stirring frequently, until soup becomes very cloudy. Stop stirring and wait for soup to boil. As soon as it does, a raft of egg whites will form on surface. Immediately reduce heat to a bare simmer and poke a hole in the raft. Simmer 15 minutes. With a large slotted spoon, lift out and discard the raft. Strain soup through several layers of damp cheesecloth. Serve immediately, garnished with fresh tarragon leaves, or chill and serve jellied, garnished with tarragon sprig. Serves 4.

 ### Tomato Basil Consommé

Follow preceding recipe, using 2 tablespoons dried basil instead of the thyme and tarragon and garnishing with ½ cup finely chopped fresh basil instead of fresh tarragon.

 ### New England Clam Chowder

Add 2 dozen scrubbed littleneck clams to 1 quart boiling water, cover, and simmer. As clams open, remove from pot, remove clams from shell, chop, and reserve. Discard any that do not open. Strain cooking liquid through several layers of damp cheesecloth, adding any liquid that seeps from clams. In large heavy soup pot, cook 5 ounces finely diced salt pork until its fat is rendered. Remove cracklings of salt pork from hot fat, and blot on paper towels. Add 1 large diced onion to hot fat and cook until softened. Add 1 tablespoon flour and cook 1 minute, stirring constantly. Add reserved clam cooking liquid and 2 diced red-skin potatoes and cook until potatoes are barely tender. Add chopped clams, reserved cracklings, salt, and pepper. Heat 2 cups *each* light cream and milk in a separate saucepan and add to soup with 2 tablespoons unsalted butter. Serves 4.

 ### Manhattan Clam Chowder

Follow preceding recipe, adding 2 cups chopped canned tomatoes, 1 cup vegetable juice cocktail, 1 diced seeded bell pepper, 1 bay leaf, ¼ teaspoon *each* dried oregano and basil, and a dash of hot pepper sauce when potatoes are cooked. Simmer 5 minutes more. Omit cream, milk, and butter.

 ### Italian Clam Soup

In large heavy saucepan, cook 2 cloves minced garlic in ¼ cup olive oil until softened. Add 1 cup chopped canned tomatoes, 1 tablespoon chopped fresh parsley, and a pinch of crushed red pepper flakes. Simmer for 20 minutes. Add 2 dozen littleneck clams, cover, and simmer for 5 minutes until clams open. Discard any that do not open. Serves 4.

 ### Mussel Marinara Soup

Follow preceding recipe, substituting 2 pounds scrubbed mussels for clams. Cook only 3 minutes to open mussels.

 ### Fish Bisque

In large heavy soup pot, cook 1 finely chopped carrot, 1 rib finely chopped celery, and 1 chopped onion in 2 tablespoons oil over moderate heat until softened. Add 2 cups white wine and 1 tablespoon brandy. Boil for 2 minutes. Add 2 cups chopped boneless lean fish, ⅓ cup rice, 3 cups boiling water, salt, pepper, a dash of cayenne, and 1 teaspoon *each* dill and tarragon. Simmer for 15 minutes until rice is tender. Process in a blender or food processor until smooth, then pass through a fine strainer, forcing as much of the solids as possible into soup pot. Adjust seasoning and add 1 cup light cream. Heat through. Garnish with few sprigs of fresh dill or tarragon, if desired. Serves 4.

Shrimp Bisque

Follow preceding recipe, substituting chopped unshelled shrimp for fish.

Crab Bisque

Follow recipe for Fish Bisque (page 35) using cleaned special crabmeat instead of fish.

Black Bean Soup with Orange and Cilantro

In large soup pot, simmer 4 cups cooked black beans, 2 quarts chicken broth, 2 ounces sliced chorizo, and 1 small chili pepper for 15 minutes. Meanwhile, cook the chopped white of 2 leeks and 2 diced carrots in 2 tablespoons peanut oil over moderate heat until softened. Remove chili pepper, and puree vegetables in a blender or food processor with 2 cups of the bean mixture and stir back into the soup. Adjust seasoning with salt and pepper. Just before serving, heat through and stir in ½ cup chopped fresh cilantro and the finely grated zest of 1 orange. Serves 6.

Garden Split-Pea Soup with Smoked Turkey

In large heavy saucepan, cook 1 medium diced onion, ½ large peeled, seeded, and diced cucumber, 1 head chopped Boston lettuce, and ½ bunch chopped fresh parsley in 2 tablespoons butter over moderate heat for 2 minutes. Add 1 teaspoon sugar and season with salt and pepper. Add 1 quart chicken broth, 1 cup split peas, and ½ cup diced smoked turkey. Simmer until peas are tender,

about 45 minutes. Stir in ½ cup light cream and adjust seasoning. Serves 4.

East African Peanut Soup

In soup pot, cook 2 finely chopped onions and 2 finely chopped carrots in 1 tablespoon peanut oil over moderate heat until soft. Add 1 quart chicken broth and simmer for 20 minutes. In a food processor or blender, puree and return to pot with ¼ cup long-grain rice and 1 small dried chili. Season with salt and simmer 15 minutes. Whisk in ½ cup peanut butter until smooth and add hot pepper sauce to taste. Remove the dried chili and adjust seasoning. Serves 4.

Spicy Red Bean Peanut Soup

In soup pot, cook 2 finely chopped onions, 1 finely chopped carrot, and 1 minced clove garlic in 1 tablespoon peanut oil over moderate heat until soft. Add 1 teaspoon *each* ground coriander and cumin, 2 teaspoons chopped fresh gingerroot, and 1 small dried chili pepper. Add 1 quart chicken broth and simmer 20 minutes. In a food processor or blender, puree and return to pot with ¼ cup long-grain rice. Season with salt and simmer 15 minutes. Add 2 cups canned or homecooked red kidney beans. Dissolve ½ cup peanut butter in 1 cup boiling water, then stir into soup. Remove dried chili and adjust seasoning. Serves 4.

Miso Soup

In a heavy saucepan, sauté ¼ pound sliced mushrooms in 1 teaspoon oil until mushrooms begin to lose their moisture. Add 2 thin slices fresh gingerroot, 2 tablespoons soy miso dissolved in 1 cup boiling water, and 3 cups vegetable broth. Bring to a boil. Add ½ pound cubed firm bean curd and a pinch of cayenne. Simmer for 5 minutes. Remove ginger. Stir in 3 thinly sliced scallions. Serves 4.

 ## Miso Soup with Scallops

Follow preceding recipe, substituting ½ pound bay scallops for bean curd. Cut simmering time to 2 minutes.

 ## Miso Soup with Clams

Prepare Miso Soup (opposite). Place 2 raw shucked littleneck clams in each soup bowl, and ladle simmering soup over the top.

 ## Hot and Sour Soup

In small bowl, dissolve 2 tablespoons cornstarch in ½ cup water. In another bowl, combine ¼ cup rice wine vinegar, ½ teaspoon hot pepper oil, 2 teaspoons Oriental sesame oil, and 1 teaspoon hot pepper sauce. In large heavy saucepan, bring 1 quart vegetable broth to a boil, soften 1 tablespoon soy miso paste with a few spoonfuls of hot broth, then add to pot and stir until miso dissolves completely. Add ¼ cup diced red pepper and ¼ cup julienned carrots to the pot. Simmer 2 minutes. Add dissolved cornstarch and simmer 1 minute more. Add 1 cup drained canned straw mushrooms and 4 ounces cubed firm bean curd. Simmer 1 minute. Add vinegar mixture and 2 thinly sliced scallions. Serve. Serves 4.

 ## Hot and Sour Shrimp Soup

Follow preceding recipe, omitting red pepper and adding 1 cup peeled and cleaned baby shrimp at the end. Immediately after adding shrimp, stir in 1 beaten egg white and simmer 30 seconds before serving.

 ## Hot and Sour Soup with Crab

Follow recipe for Hot and Sour Shrimp Soup (above), using 1 cup cleaned backfin crab for the shrimp.

Fifty Ways to Top a Pizza

All who have sacrificed the roofs of their mouths to a scorching cap of mozzarella know the sadomasochistic ecstasy of pizza fresh from the oven. Reasonable commercial versions abound, but with many arriving tepid and congealed via delivery truck, these discs of dyspepsia can be a far cry from the "real thing."

Many pizzas suffer sensuously. They're frequently packed with so much salt and saturated fat as to undermine the reputation of a wholesome and natural Mediterranean mainstay. You can do better.

Not only are pizzas self-contained balanced meals, but they can be built in just minutes—and with healthful ingredients. The dough is the only part that takes much time, and with the availability of good-quality frozen bread doughs, even this chore can be dispensed with.

Beyond its ease, homemade pizza is just plain fun. Family members can build their own and creative cooks can let their imaginations run wild. We let ours run wild in order to start you off with 50 pizza ideas—beginning with a simple tomato and cheese topping and ending with a trio of sweet, exotic dessert pizzas.

The same simple method of assembly and construction applies to all 50 recipes. It requires no special equipment and guarantees a crisp, high-risen crust. If you have a favorite recipe for making your own dough, or a good storebought dough, go ahead and use it, or use ours (page 432), but the basis for all our recipes is two thirds pound of ready-to-bake bread dough.

ABOUT THESE RECIPES

To build any pizza in this chapter, place a 16-by-18-inch piece of heavy aluminum foil on a work surface. Brush with oil and place ⅔ pound of ready-to-bake bread dough in the center. Flour your hands and spread dough into a rough 15-inch circle, making the circle as thin as you want but leaving a rim at least half an inch high to contain the filling during baking. If the dough tears while you're pushing it into place, pinch to seal it or patch it with a small scrap of dough.

For each of the following pizzas, arrange the desired filling on top, as described in the recipes, and slide the pizza, still on its foil backing, onto the middle rack of a preheated 450° F. oven. All the pizzas should bake for 25 to 30 minutes, until the dough is puffed and crisp. Remove, slice, and serve. All recipes yield 8 small slices, enough for 2 or 3 portions.

Tomato and Cheese Pizza

Brush dough with 1 tablespoon olive oil. Coarsely purée 8 skinned and seeded plum tomatoes and spread over dough. Sprinkle evenly with 4 ounces grated mozzarella, then 2 tablespoons freshly grated Parmesan, salt, pepper, a pinch of oregano, and 1 tablespoon olive oil.

 Tomato and Basil Pizza

Follow preceding recipe, but omit oregano and scatter ¼ cup shredded fresh basil leaves on the oiled dough before adding the tomatoes.

 Tomato, Basil, and Chèvre Pizza

Brush dough with 1 tablespoon olive oil. Scatter ¼ cup shredded fresh basil leaves on the oiled dough. Coarsely puree 8 skinned plum tomatoes and spread over dough. Sprinkle evenly with 6 ounces crumbled fresh chèvre, then 2 tablespoons grated Parmesan, ¼ teaspoon crushed red pepper flakes, salt, pepper, and 1 tablespoon olive oil.

 Tomato, Fennel, and Olive Pizza

Brush dough with 1 tablespoon olive oil. Coarsely puree 8 skinned plum tomatoes and spread over dough. Scatter 1 cup diced fennel over tomato. Sprinkle evenly with 4 ounces grated mozzarella, then 1 cup pitted, coarsely chopped, oil-cured black olives, 2 tablespoons grated Parmesan, salt, pepper, a pinch of oregano, and 1 tablespoon olive oil over top.

 Tomato, Capers, and Anchovy Pizza

Follow recipe for Tomato and Cheese Pizza (above), and top tomato with 2 tablespoons drained capers, 6 julienned anchovy fillets, and 2 teaspoons wine vinegar.

 Tomato and Three-Onions Pizza

Follow recipe for Tomato and Cheese Pizza (above), topping cheese with 1 thinly sliced Spanish onion, 1 thinly sliced red onion, and 2 cloves minced garlic that have all been lightly browned in 2 tablespoons olive oil. Substitute roughly crumbled dried rosemary leaves for oregano.

 Three Tomatoes Pizza

Follow recipe for Tomato and Cheese Pizza (above), topping cheese with 3 sliced fresh plum tomatoes and 3 coarsely chopped sun-dried tomatoes. Substitute dried basil for the oregano.

 Tomato and Wild-Mushroom Pizza

Brush dough with 1 tablespoon olive oil. Coarsely puree 8 skinned plum tomatoes and spread over dough. Sprinkle evenly with 4 ounces grated mozzarella. Top cheese with 6 fresh sliced cepes, oyster, or shiitake mushrooms that have been lightly sautéed in 1 tablespoon butter. Sprinkle with 2 tablespoons grated Parmesan, salt, and a pinch *each* of dried thyme and oregano. Season liberally with freshly ground black pepper and sprinkle with 1 tablespoon olive oil.

 Smoky Tomato and Fontina Pizza

Brush dough with 1 tablespoon olive oil. Skin 8 plum tomatoes by placing them directly over a high stovetop flame and turning so skins char evenly. Rub skins with your fingers to remove. Puree tomatoes and spread over dough, topping with

2 tablespoons capers, 6 julienned anchovies, 4 ounces grated Italian Fontina, 2 tablespoons wine vinegar, 2 tablespoons grated Parmesan, salt, pepper, and a pinch of dried oregano. Sprinkle 1 tablespoon olive oil over top.

 ### Spicy Tomato and Sausage-Meatball Pizza

Combine 1 pound loose Italian sausage meat, 1 beaten egg, 2 teaspoons dried mint, and 2 pieces crumbled bread soaked in ⅓ cup white wine. Form into 24 meatballs and brown in a skillet, greased with thin film of peanut oil. Follow recipe for Tomato and Cheese Pizza (page 39), combining 1 finely chopped pickled jalapeño with the tomatoes. Scatter meatballs over surface of the pizza after adding mozzarella.

 ### Spicy Tomato and Mussel Pizza

Follow recipe for Tomato and Cheese Pizza (page 39), scattering 36 cooked and shelled mussels over the pureed tomatoes. Omit the mozzarella and use 2 tablespoons chopped fresh flat-leaf parsley instead of oregano.

 ### Pepperoni and Meat Sauce Pizza

Brush dough with 1 tablespoon olive oil. Sauté ½ cup chopped onion and 2 cloves minced garlic in 1 tablespoon olive oil until soft, about 2 minutes. Add ¼ pound *each* ground beef and veal and cook until meat loses its raw look. Add 1 cup chopped canned tomatoes and cook until they begin to weep their liquid. Add 2 tablespoons tomato paste. Season with a pinch of crushed red pepper flakes, salt, and black pepper. Stir in 1 teaspoon chopped fresh parsley and heat 1 minute more. Spread sauce over dough. Top with 4 ounces thinly sliced pepperoni. Sprinkle evenly with 4 ounces grated pro-

volone, 2 tablespoons grated Parmesan, salt, pepper, and a pinch of oregano. Sprinkle 1 tablespoon olive oil over top.

 ### Bolognese and Mozzarella Pizza

Brush dough with 1 tablespoon olive oil. Sauté 1 tablespoon *each* chopped onion, diced carrot, and diced celery in 1 teaspoon *each* olive oil and butter until soft, about 2 minutes. Add ¼ pound *each* ground chuck and veal; cook until meat loses its raw look. Add ½ cup milk and cook until mixture is dry. Add 2 cups chopped canned tomatoes and cook until they begin to weep their liquid. Add ¼ cup tomato paste and simmer gently for 1 hour. Season with salt and black pepper. Spread sauce over dough. Sprinkle evenly with 4 ounces grated mozzarella, then 2 tablespoons grated Parmesan, salt, pepper, and ¼ cup chopped fresh flat-leaf parsley. Sprinkle 1 tablespoon olive oil over top.

 ### Lamb and Feta Pizza

Prepare meat sauce as in preceding recipe, but use ½ pound ground lamb instead of the chuck and veal. Brush dough with 1 tablespoon olive oil, spread sauce over dough, sprinkle evenly with 4 ounces crumbled feta cheese, 2 tablespoons grated Parmesan, ½ teaspoon dried oregano, salt, pepper, and ¼ cup chopped fresh parsley. Sprinkle 1 tablespoon olive oil over top.

 ### Basil and Prosciutto Pizza

Sauté 2 cloves minced garlic in ¼ cup olive oil over low heat until soft. Add 1 cup chopped fresh basil leaves and ½ cup julienned prosciutto. Season with a pinch of crushed red pepper flakes, salt, and pepper. Spread over dough and top with ¼ cup grated Parmesan.

Artichoke and Mushroom Pizza

Sauté 1 clove minced garlic in 1 tablespoon olive oil over low heat until soft. Add 8 sliced mushrooms and cook until slightly softened. Coarsely chop 12 ounces marinated artichoke hearts and add with 2 tablespoons chopped fresh parsley, salt, and pepper. Spread over dough and top with 2 tablespoons grated Parmesan.

Crab, Tarragon, and Chèvre Pizza

In a small skillet, gently heat ¼ cup olive oil. Add 2 finely chopped shallots and sauté for 1 minute, until soft. Add 1 pound cleaned lump crabmeat and toss to coat with oil. Add ¼ cup coarsely chopped tarragon leaves and cook for 1 minute. Add juice of 1 lemon, season with salt and pepper, and spread over dough. Top with 4 ounces crumbled chèvre and drizzle with 2 tablespoons walnut oil.

Mixed Roasted Peppers Pizza

Roast 1 each yellow, red, and green pepper (page 442). Stem, seed, peel, and dice the peppers, season with salt and pepper, and toss with ½ teaspoon hot pepper oil. Spread over dough and top with 6 ounces grated mozzarella, 2 tablespoons grated Parmesan, and 2 tablespoons finely chopped fresh parsley. Drizzle with 2 tablespoons olive oil.

Ricotta and Roasted Red Pepper Pizza

Follow preceding recipe, but use only 2 red peppers. Substitute 1 cup ricotta cheese for the mozzarella, arranging it in small spoonfuls atop the pizza.

Roasted Pepper, Caper, and Anchovy Pizza

Roast 1 each yellow, red, and green pepper (page 442). Stem, seed, peel, and dice the peppers and season with salt and pepper. Warm 1 clove minced garlic in 3 tablespoons olive oil and brush the dough with half this mixture. Spread peppers over dough and top with 6 ounces grated mozzarella, 2 tablespoons grated Parmesan, 3 tablespoons drained capers, 6 julienned anchovies, and 2 tablespoons finely chopped fresh parsley. Drizzle on remaining garlic-oil mixture.

Peppers and Walnuts Pizza

Roast 1 each yellow, red, and green pepper (page 442). Stem, seed, peel, and dice the peppers and season with salt and pepper. In a skillet, warm 1 clove minced garlic in 1½ tablespoons each walnut oil and olive oil, then brush dough with half this mixture. Spread peppers over dough and top with 6 ounces grated mozzarella, 2 tablespoons grated Parmesan, ⅓ cup walnut pieces, and 2 tablespoons finely chopped fresh parsley. Drizzle with remaining garlic-oil mixture.

Peppers, Olives, and Olive Oil Pizza

Roast 1 each yellow, red, and green pepper (page 442). Stem, seed, peel, and dice the peppers, season with salt and pepper, and toss with ½ teaspoon hot pepper oil. Warm 1 clove minced garlic in 3 tablespoons olive oil and brush dough with half this mixture. Spread peppers over dough and top with 6 ounces grated mozzarella, 2 tablespoons grated Parmesan, ½ cup chopped pitted oil-cured black olives, and 2 tablespoons finely chopped fresh parsley. Drizzle with remaining garlic-oil mixture.

 Roasted Eggplant and Feta Pizza

Place 1 medium-to-large eggplant over high gas flame or under broiler until its skin is uniformly blackened. Let cool. Slice off stem and peel off skin with your fingers. Dice flesh and sauté in 3 tablespoons olive oil for 1 minute. Add 2 cloves minced garlic, 2 tablespoons lemon juice, 1 tablespoon chopped fresh parsley, salt, and pepper. Brush dough with 1 tablespoon pan liquid and top with eggplant mixture. Crumble 6 ounces feta over top.

Garlic and Parmesan Pizza

In a skillet, warm 2 cloves minced garlic and ½ teaspoon crushed red pepper flakes in ⅓ cup extra-virgin olive oil just until garlic begins to release its aroma, about 45 seconds. Remove from the heat and spread over dough. Cover with ½ to ¾ cup grated Parmesan.

Red, Black, and Green Olive Pizza

In a skillet, heat 1 clove minced garlic in ¼ cup olive oil until garlic begins to release its aroma. Brush dough with half this mixture. Top with ½ cup *each* pitted, chopped salt-cured Niçoise olives, oil-cured Niçoise olives, and green Sicilian olives. Top with 6 chopped anchovies, 8 ounces shredded mozzarella, and remaining oil-garlic mixture.

Tuna, White Bean, and Olive Pizza

Heat 1 clove minced garlic in ¼ cup olive oil just until garlic begins to release its aroma. Brush dough with half this mixture. Top with 1 can (6½ ounces) crumbled drained tuna, 1 cup cooked white beans, and ½ cup pitted, chopped oil-cured Niçoise olives. Season with salt, pepper, and remaining oil-garlic mixture.

 Spinach, Olive, and Feta Pizza

In a skillet, heat 1 clove minced garlic in ¼ cup olive oil just until garlic begins to release its aroma. Brush dough with half this mixture. Top with 10 ounces chopped frozen spinach that has been cooked and thoroughly drained, ½ cup pitted and chopped oil-cured Niçoise olives, 1 julienned pimiento, and 6 ounces crumbled feta cheese. Season with salt, pepper, and remaining oil-garlic mixture.

 Duxelle and Parmesan Pizza

In a skillet, sauté 1 minced onion and 2 cloves minced garlic in 3 tablespoons olive oil until soft. Add 1 pound diced mushrooms and season well with salt and pepper. Cook until mushrooms begin to release their liquid, about 3 minutes. Add ½ cup dry white wine and cook over high heat until liquid is almost completely evaporated. Stir in 1 teaspoon tomato paste and ½ cup chopped fresh parsley. Cook 1 minute more and adjust seasoning. In a skillet, warm 1 clove minced garlic in 2 tablespoons olive oil and brush dough with half this mixture. Top with the mushroom mixture, 3 tablespoons grated Parmesan, and remaining oil-garlic mixture.

 Sweet Sausage, Pine Nuts, and Rosemary Pizza

In a heavy skillet, place 1 pound sweet Italian sausage and enough water to go halfway up the side of the sausage. Cook over moderate heat, turning every 5 minutes, until water has evaporated and sausage has browned lightly. Chop coarsely. Heat 2

tablespoons peanut oil and 1 tablespoon olive oil in the same skillet over low heat. Add ½ cup pine nuts and heat gently until the nuts just begin to color. Add sausage and 1 teaspoon crumbled dried rosemary leaves. Heat 1 minute more. Season with salt and pepper. Add 1 tablespoon grated orange zest, 1 teaspoon minced garlic, and 1 teaspoon fresh rosemary. Spread over dough; top with 4 ounces grated smoked mozzarella.

Pancetta, Hazelnuts, and Garlic Pizza

In a small skillet over low heat, cook 1 cup diced pancetta in 1 tablespoon olive oil for 1 minute. Add ½ cup skinned, chopped hazelnuts and 2 cloves finely julienned garlic. Heat gently until nuts toast lightly. Add 1 clove minced garlic, 1 tablespoon chopped fresh parsley, salt, and pepper. Brush dough with 2 tablespoons fat from the pan, and top with 6 ounces grated mozzarella and the pancetta mixture.

Three-Mushrooms Pizza

In a skillet, sauté ¼ cup minced onion and 1 clove minced garlic in 2 tablespoons butter until soft. Add ¾ cup *each* diced white mushrooms, shiitake mushrooms, and wild mushroom of your choice. Cook until mushrooms are fully softened. Add ¼ cup white wine, bring to a boil, and cook until the mushrooms are soft. Season with salt and pepper. Drain thoroughly. Brush dough with olive oil, top with mushroom mixture, and sprinkle with ½ cup grated Parmesan.

Sausage and Mushroom Pizza

In a large skillet, sauté 1 pound loose Italian sausage until it loses its raw look. Add ¼ cup finely chopped onion and 2 cloves minced garlic and continue to cook until sausage is lightly browned. Add 8 sliced mushrooms and sauté until they soften and lose their white color. Add ½ cup white wine and reduce until pan is almost dry. Spread dough with 2 cups tomato sauce and top with sausage-mushroom mixture. Season with salt and pepper. Top with 3 ounces grated mozzarella, if desired.

Clams and Leeks Pizza

In a heavy saucepan, cook 3 thinly sliced leeks, 1 small finely chopped onion, and 4 cloves minced garlic in ¼ cup olive oil until soft. Add 2 cups canned and drained chopped clams and ¼ cup chopped fresh parsley. Heat through and season with salt and pepper. Arrange on dough and top with 2 tablespoons grated Parmesan.

Peppered Brie and Scallops Pizza

In heavy saucepan, cook 1 small finely chopped onion and 4 cloves minced garlic in ¼ cup olive oil until soft. Add 1 pound sliced sea scallops and cook for 1 minute. Remove scallops and reduce pan liquid until all but 1 tablespoon has evaporated, adding any liquid that collects around the scallops as they sit. Season with salt and pepper, then toss scallops in reduced syrup. Arrange over dough and top with 6 ounces thinly sliced peppered brie.

Scallops and Herbed-Cheese Pizza

Follow preceding recipe, but use 4 ounces herbed cream cheese in small spoonfuls instead of the brie.

Marinated Feta and Artichoke Hearts Pizza

Cut in quarters the drained contents of 12-ounce jar marinated artichoke hearts and mix with ¼ pound crumbled feta. Spread over dough and season with ¼ cup chopped fresh parsley, 2 tablespoons grated Romano, salt, and pepper.

 ### Marinated Sun-Dried Tomato Pizza

Dice 12 oil-cured sun-dried tomatoes, and toss with 1 clove minced garlic, a pinch of crushed red pepper flakes, and about 1 tablespoon olive oil in which the tomatoes were preserved. Spread mixture over dough and top with ¼ cup grated Parmesan cheese and ¼ cup chopped fresh parsley.

 ### Chicken and Olives Pizza

In a skillet, sauté 1 pound diced chicken breast in ¼ cup hot olive oil until it loses its raw look. Add 1 thinly sliced red onion and 1 clove minced garlic and cook 3 minutes more. Add ¼ cup white wine and boil for 1 minute. Add 18 pitted black olives and cook 1 minute more. Season with salt and pepper. Scatter over dough. Drizzle with 1 tablespoon olive oil, 2 tablespoons grated Parmesan, and 2 tablespoons chopped fresh parsley.

 ### Sun-Dried Tomatoes and Tuna Pizza

Mix 6 ounces canned and drained white tuna with 7 chopped oil-cured sun-dried tomatoes, 2 chopped scallions, 2 cloves minced garlic, salt, and pepper. Brush dough with 1 tablespoon virgin olive oil. Top with tuna-tomato mixture, 6 ounces grated provolone, and 1 tablespoon additional olive oil.

 ### Caramelized Onion and Gorgonzola Pizza

In a skillet, sauté 3 large thinly sliced yellow onions in 1 tablespoon *each* butter and olive oil until lightly browned. Spread over dough and top with 4 ounces crumbled Gorgonzola, salt, pepper, 1 tablespoon chopped fresh parsley, and 1 tablespoon additional olive oil.

 ### Onion and Gruyère Pizza

Follow preceding recipe, using 6 ounces shredded Gruyère instead of Gorgonzola, and using peanut oil instead of olive oil.

 ### Smoked Salmon and Onion Pizza

Follow recipe for Caramelized Onion and Gorgonzola Pizza (above), using 8 ounces julienned smoked salmon instead of the cheese and using dill instead of parsley.

 ### Smoked Turkey and Fontina Pizza

In a skillet, sauté 3 large thinly sliced yellow onions in 1 tablespoon *each* butter and walnut oil until lightly browned. Spread over dough and top with ⅓ pound *each* julienned smoked turkey breast and diced Italian Fontina cheese, salt, pepper, 1 tablespoon chopped fresh parsley, and 1 tablespoon additional walnut oil.

 ### Walnuts and Feta Pizza

Follow preceding recipe, but sprinkle 4 ounces chopped walnuts over the onions, and top with 6 ounces crumbled feta instead of Fontina.

 ### Red Onion, Garlic and Herb Pizza

In a skillet, sauté 3 large thinly sliced red onions in 1 tablespoon *each* butter and olive oil with 1 teaspoon *each* dried thyme, tarragon, and chervil until onions are lightly browned. Spread over dough with 2 tablespoons chopped fresh flat-leaf parsley and 1 clove chopped garlic and top with 6 ounces garlic-and-herb cream cheese in small mounds, salt, pepper, 1 tablespoon chopped fresh parsley, and 1 tablespoon additional olive oil.

 ## Marinated Mozzarella Pizza

Marinate 1 pound sliced mozzarella in 4 cloves crushed garlic, 1 teaspoon crushed red pepper flakes, 1 teaspoon salt, pepper, ¼ cup *each* chopped fresh parsley and chopped basil, and enough olive oil to cover. Cover and refrigerate at least 24 hours. Arrange cheese over dough. Moisten with several tablespoons of marinade.

Hot Peppers, Bacon, and Gorgonzola Pizza

In a skillet over moderate heat, cook 4 slices bacon until brown but still soft. Remove and blot excess fat. To the hot bacon fat add 2 julienned hot peppers, 1 thinly sliced onion, and 2 cloves minced garlic and cook for 2 minutes. Season with salt and pepper. Spread on the dough; top with 4 ounces crumbled Gorgonzola and the bacon strips.

 ## Dried Cherry, Tarragon, and Almond Dessert Pizza

Soak 6 ounces dried cherries and 2 teaspoons dried tarragon leaves in enough boiling water to cover. Soak 20 minutes, drain, and blot the cherries of excess moisture. Arrange mixture on dough, drizzle on ¼ cup honey and scatter on ¼ cup toasted sliced almonds.

 ## Banana and Walnut Dessert Pizza

Brush dough with mixture of ¼ cup honey and 1 teaspoon vanilla extract. Top with 3 thinly sliced bananas, ½ cup walnut pieces, and 2 tablespoons brown sugar.

 ## Brown Sugar Curds Dessert Pizza

Mix 8 ounces ricotta cheese, 1 teaspoon vanilla extract, and ¼ cup brown sugar. Beat in 1 egg, then spread over dough.

Fifty Ways to Sauce the Spaghetti

Paesani eat pasta daily, meal after meal—simmered in soup, cut into ribbons and wrapped into rings. From tortes to tortellini, it appears everywhere in every conceivable form, but for the most part, pasta is a simple affair—boiled, drained, and tossed with sauce.

One might expect the great pasta pot of inspiration to soon boil dry, but it never ever does. There is always something new to prepare with pasta, and most of the tried and true methods are so good that a repeat performance is never tiring.

To wake up your palate, here are 50 perfect sauces to make plain boiled pasta extraordinary. They range from a simple coat of parsley and cheese to an exotic melange of caviar, shallots, and smoked salmon.

All are simple to prepare and quick. Most need less than 10 minutes, a few require no cooking at all, and none calls for more than an hour of cooking.

ABOUT THESE RECIPES

All these sauces are presented in sufficient quantity to accompany 12 ounces of pasta, which should be cooked *al dente* in 4 to 6 quarts of rapidly boiling salted water mixed with 1 tablespoon of oil. The cooked pasta should be thoroughly drained, washed briefly in hot running water, and drained again before mixed with the sauce. All recipes yield 4 servings.

 Quick Fresh Tomato Sauce

In a saucepan, sauté 1 cup chopped onion, 2 cloves minced garlic, and 1 dried chili pepper in 2 tablespoons olive oil until onion is just soft, about 2 minutes. Add 12 fresh plum tomatoes that have been skinned, seeded, and coarsely chopped, along with 1 chopped, roasted bell pepper (page

442). Cook until tomatoes begin to weep their liquid, then add 1 tablespoon tomato paste. Season with salt and pepper, stir in ⅓ cup chopped fresh herbs, and heat 1 minute more. Remove chili pepper and serve with hot cooked pasta.

Spicy Tomato Sauce and Red Beans

Follow preceding recipe, doubling chili peppers and adding 1 cup cooked, drained kidney beans. Omit the fresh herbs.

Quick Meat Sauce

In a saucepan, sauté 1 cup chopped onion and 2 cloves minced garlic in 1 tablespoon olive oil until onion is soft, about 2 minutes. Add ½ pound *each* ground beef and veal and cook until meat loses its raw look. Add 3 cups chopped canned tomatoes. Cook until tomatoes begin to weep their liquid and add ¼ cup tomato paste. Season with a pinch of crushed red pepper flakes, salt, and pepper. Stir in 1 tablespoon chopped fresh parsley and heat 1 minute more. Serve over hot cooked pasta.

Bolognese Sauce

In a saucepan, sauté 2 tablespoons *each* chopped onion, diced carrot, and diced celery in 1 tablespoon *each* olive oil and butter until vegetables soften, about 2 minutes. Add ½ pound *each* ground chuck and veal and cook until meat loses its raw look. Add ½ cup milk and cook until mixture is dry. Add 2 cups chopped canned tomatoes. Cook until tomatoes begin to weep their liquid and add ¼ cup tomato paste. Simmer gently for 1 hour. Season with salt and black pepper. Serve over hot cooked pasta.

Ginger Tomato Sauce

In a saucepan, sauté 1 cup chopped onion, 2 cloves minced garlic, and 1 tablespoon finely chopped fresh gingerroot in 2 tablespoons peanut oil until onion is just soft, about 2 minutes. Skin, seed, and coarsely chop 12 fresh plum tomatoes and cook until they begin to weep their liquid. Add 1 tablespoon tomato paste, a pinch of sugar, salt, pepper, and 1 tablespoon finely chopped coriander leaf. Toss with hot cooked pasta.

Parsley Pasta

In a skillet, cook 2 minced shallots and 1 clove minced garlic in ¼ cup olive oil over low heat until soft. Add 1 cup chopped fresh parsley, salt, and pepper. Toss with hot cooked pasta, then again with ¼ cup grated Parmesan.

Basil and Prosciutto Pasta

In a skillet, cook 2 cloves minced garlic in ¼ cup olive oil over low heat until soft. Add 1 cup chopped basil leaves, ½ cup julienned prosciutto, a pinch of crushed red pepper flakes, salt, and pepper. Toss with hot cooked pasta, then again with ¼ cup grated Parmesan.

Artichoke and Mushroom Sauce

In a skillet, cook 1 clove minced garlic in 1 teaspoon olive oil over low heat until soft. Add 8 sliced mushrooms and cook until slightly softened. Coarsely chop contents of 12-ounce jar marinated artichoke hearts and add to skillet with 2 tablespoons chopped fresh parsley, salt, and pepper. Toss with hot cooked pasta.

Fifty Ways to Cook Most Everything

 Warm Tomato Vinaigrette

Place 4 cups crushed plum tomatoes in heavy saucepan and cook over low heat until thick, stirring frequently. Push cooked tomatoes through a fine strainer and whisk in ¼ cup virgin olive oil, 1 tablespoon red wine vinegar, salt, and pepper. Serve over hot cooked pasta.

 Crab, Tarragon, and Shallot Sauce

Gently heat ¼ cup olive oil in small skillet, add 2 finely chopped shallots, and sauté for 1 minute, until softened. Add 1 pound cleaned lump crabmeat and toss to coat with oil. Add ¼ cup coarsely chopped tarragon leaves and cook for 1 minute. Add the juice of 1 lemon, season with salt and pepper, and toss with hot cooked pasta.

 Tomato and Basil Sauce with Chèvre

Slightly heat 1 tablespoon olive oil in a skillet, add 1 split clove garlic, and sauté for 1 minute. Add 8 peeled, seeded, and chopped plum tomatoes and ⅓ cup dry vermouth. Cook over high heat until alcohol evaporates. Season with a pinch of cayenne, salt, and pepper. Toss in 2 tablespoons chopped fresh basil and cook 20 seconds more. Remove garlic and toss with hot cooked pasta and 6 ounces crumbled fresh chèvre.

 Ricotta and Roasted Red Pepper Sauce

Dice 1 *each* roasted green and red pepper (page 442) and sauté in 1 tablespoon olive oil for 2 minutes. Season with salt, pepper, and 1 to 2 teaspoons hot pepper oil. Toss mixture with piping hot cooked pasta, 1 tablespoon butter, ½ cup room-temperature ricotta cheese, 2 teaspoons grated Parmesan, and 2 tablespoons finely chopped fresh parsley. Adjust seasoning.

 Low-Fat Low-Salt Pesto

In a food processor, finely chop 2 cups basil leaves. Blend in 1 clove minced garlic, 3 tablespoons virgin olive oil, 2 tablespoons grated Parmesan, salt, and pepper. Toss with hot cooked pasta.

 Mushroom Persillade

In a large skillet, sauté 1 minced onion and 2 cloves minced garlic in 3 tablespoons olive oil until softened. Add 1 pound diced mushrooms, salt, and pepper. Cook until mushrooms begin to release their liquid, about 3 minutes. Add 1 cup dry white wine and cook over high heat until the liquid is reduced by half. Stir in 1 teaspoon tomato paste and ½ cup chopped fresh parsley. Cook 1 minute more and adjust seasoning. Serve over hot cooked pasta.

 Tomato Sauce with Tequila and Cream

In a large skillet, cook 2 cloves minced garlic over moderate heat in 2 tablespoons olive oil until garlic releases its aroma. Add ½ teaspoon crushed red pepper flakes, and stir briskly. Add 12 large, skinned, seeded, and chopped plum tomatoes and cook until they begin to release their liquid. Add ½ cup light cream and simmer until sauce thickens lightly, about 1 minute. Remove from heat, stir in 2 tablespoons tequila, and season with salt and pepper. Toss with hot cooked pasta.

 Herbs, Tomato, and Cream Sauce

In a large skillet, cook 2 tablespoons minced onion over moderate heat in 2 tablespoons olive oil just until softened. Add ½ cup chopped fresh parsley, 1 tablespoon finely chopped lemon zest, and a pinch *each* dried basil, marjoram, and thyme. Cook another minute, stirring frequently. Add 12 large, skinned, seeded, and chopped plum tomatoes and cook until they begin to release their liquid. Add ½ cup light cream and simmer until sauce thickens lightly, about 1 minute. Season with salt and pepper. Toss with hot cooked pasta.

Smoked Turkey, Pine Nuts, and Rosemary Sauce

In a skillet, heat 2 tablespoons peanut oil and 1 tablespoon olive oil. Add ½ cup pine nuts, 1 cup diced smoked turkey breast, and 1 teaspoon dried, crumbled rosemary leaves and heat gently until pine nuts toast lightly. Add salt, pepper, 1 tablespoon orange zest, 1 clove minced garlic, and 1 teaspoon fresh rosemary leaves. Toss with hot cooked pasta.

Pancetta, Hazelnuts, and Garlic Sauce

In a skillet, brown 1 cup diced pancetta in 1 teaspoon olive oil. Add ½ cup skinned and chopped hazelnuts and 2 cloves finely julienned garlic, heating gently until nuts toast lightly. Add salt, pepper, 1 clove minced garlic, and 1 tablespoon chopped fresh parsley. Toss with hot cooked pasta.

Cheese and Cream Sauce

Bring 2 cups heavy cream to a boil and reduce by a third. Add ⅓ cup grated Parmesan, salt, and pepper. Remove from the heat and toss with hot cooked pasta. Garnish with chopped fresh parsley, if desired.

Hot Pepper and Cream Sauce

Bring 2 cups light cream to a boil and reduce by a third. Add up to ¼ cup hot pepper sauce and reduce until lightly thickened. Add salt and pepper, remove from heat, and toss with hot cooked pasta.

Wild Mushroom, Brandy, and Cream Sauce

Soak ½ ounce dried wild mushrooms in ½ cup boiling water until mushrooms soften, about 30 minutes. Remove mushrooms, chop coarsely, strain soaking liquid through damp cheesecloth, and reserve. In a skillet, sauté 2 minced shallots in 2 tablespoons butter. Add ¼ pound diced cultivated mushrooms and cook until brown. Add 2 tablespoons brandy and carefully ignite with a match. When flames die down, add mushrooms and their soaking liquid and reduce liquid by half. Add 1 cup heavy cream and reduce until lightly thickened. Toss with hot cooked pasta.

Three-Mushroom Sauce

In a skillet, sauté ¼ cup onion and 1 clove minced garlic in 2 tablespoons butter until soft. Add ¾ cup *each* diced white mushrooms, diced shiitake mushrooms, and another diced wild mushroom of your choice and cook until mushrooms are fully softened. Add ¼ cup white wine and bring to a boil. Add 1 cup chopped, peeled, and seeded plum tomatoes and heat through. Season with salt and pepper and toss with hot cooked pasta. Serve with grated Parmesan.

Meatballs

In a bowl, combine with your hands ½ pound *each* ground beef, pork, and veal, 2 crumbled slices firm white bread soaked in milk and squeezed out, 1 beaten egg, ¼ cup minced onion, 1 clove minced garlic, 1 tablespoon chopped fresh parsley, salt, pepper, and 1 teaspoon *each* dried mint and dried basil. Heat 2 tablespoons oil in a large skillet. Form into 24 meatballs and brown on all sides in the hot pan, adding more oil if you do more than one batch. When all have been browned, drain fat from pan, return meatballs, and add 1 inch stock. Simmer until meatballs feel firm. Use with tomato sauce on hot cooked pasta.

 ## Sicilian Turkey Meatballs

In bowl, combine with your hands 1 pound ground turkey, ½ cup fresh bread crumbs, ¼ cup ricotta cheese, 1 tablespoon ketchup, 2 tablespoons Worcestershire sauce, 1 beaten egg, ¼ cup finely chopped onion, 1 tablespoon dried mint, salt, and pepper. Heat 2 tablespoons oil in large nonstick skillet. With wet hands, form into 24 meatballs and brown on all sides in the hot pan, adding more oil if you do more than one batch. When all have been browned, drain fat from pan, return meatballs, and add 1 inch chicken stock. Simmer until meatballs feel firm. Use with tomato pasta sauce on hot cooked pasta.

 ## Sausage Meatballs

Combine 1 pound loose Italian sausage meat, 1 beaten egg, 2 teaspoons dried mint, and 2 pieces crumbled bread soaked in ⅓ cup white wine. Form into 24 meatballs and brown on all sides in a skillet greased with a thin film of peanut oil. When all have been browned, drain fat from pan, return meatballs, and add 1 inch chicken stock. Simmer until meatballs feel firm. Serve with a tomato pasta sauce over hot cooked pasta.

 ## Sausage and Mushroom Sauce

In a large skillet, sauté 1 pound loose Italian sausage until it loses its raw look. Add ¼ cup finely chopped onion and 2 cloves minced garlic and cook until sausage is lightly browned. Add 8 sliced mushrooms and sauté until mushrooms soften and lose their white color. Add ½ cup white wine and reduce until pan is almost dry. Add 2 cups tomato pasta sauce, season with salt and pepper, bring to a boil, and serve over hot cooked pasta.

 ## Fast Clam Sauce

In heavy saucepan, cook 1 finely chopped onion and 4 cloves minced garlic in 2 tablespoons olive oil until soft. Add 1 cup white wine, 2 teaspoons dill leaves, and the juice of 1 lemon. Bring to a boil. Add 2 dozen littleneck clams, cover, and simmer until clams open, about 5 minutes. Remove clams from shells and return to the sauce, discarding the shells and any clams that do not open. Stir in ¼ cup chopped fresh parsley and 2 tablespoons butter. Toss with hot cooked pasta.

 ## Mussels in White Sauce

In a heavy saucepan, cook 1 finely chopped onion and 4 cloves minced garlic in 2 tablespoons olive oil until soft. Add 1 cup white wine, 2 teaspoons dill leaves, and the juice of 1 lemon. Bring to a boil, add 2 dozen cleaned and debearded mussels, cover, and simmer until mussels open, about 2 minutes. Discard any that do not. Stir in ¼ cup chopped fresh parsley and more olive oil, if desired. Toss with hot cooked pasta.

 ## Mussels in Red Sauce

Lightly brown 1 clove minced garlic in 6 tablespoons olive oil. Add 1 tablespoon chopped fresh parsley, 1 cup chopped canned tomatoes with their liquid, and a pinch of crushed red pepper flakes. Simmer for 20 minutes. Add 2 dozen cleaned and debearded mussels, cover, and simmer 2 to 3 minutes until mussels open. Discard any that do not. Serve over hot cooked pasta.

 ### Shrimp, Cucumber, and Dill Sauce

Sprinkle 1 peeled, seeded, and diced cucumber with 1 teaspoon coarse salt, and let sit in a bowl for 20 minutes. Turn into a towel and squeeze out as much water as possible, then rinse thoroughly, drain and set aside. In a skillet, sauté whites of 1 bunch finely chopped scallions and 1 clove minced garlic in 4 tablespoons unsalted butter. When barely softened, add 1 cup white wine and reduce to a third its volume. Add 1 pound shelled, cleaned medium shrimp and 1 tablespoon chopped fresh dill. Stir until shrimp are opaque and firm. Add 1 cup light cream and reduce until lightly thickened. Add reserved cucumbers and season with salt and pepper. Toss with hot cooked pasta.

Smoked Salmon, Cucumber, and Dill Sauce

Follow preceding recipe, omitting the shrimp and adding ¼ pound julienned smoked salmon along with the cucumbers.

Fennel, Shrimp, and Orange Sauce

In a skillet, sauté ¼ cup minced onion and 1 clove minced garlic in 2 tablespoons olive oil until soft. Add 1 cup diced fennel and cook gently until fennel just begins to soften. Add 1 cup white wine, 2 tablespoons finely chopped orange zest, and a pinch of saffron, if desired. Boil until wine is reduced to a third its volume. Add 1 pound shelled, cleaned medium shrimp and 1 tablespoon chopped fennel frond. Stir until shrimp are opaque

and firm. Add 1 cup chopped tomato and season with salt and pepper. Toss with hot cooked pasta.

 ### Smoked Salmon, Caviar, and Cream Sauce

Sauté 2 minced shallots in 4 tablespoons unsalted butter in a skillet until barely soft. Add 1 cup white wine and reduce to a third its volume. Add 1 tablespoon chopped fresh dill and 1 cup light cream. Reduce until lightly thickened. Add 4 ounces julienned smoked salmon and 2 tablespoons salmon caviar. Remove from heat and season with salt and pepper. Toss with hot cooked pasta. Garnish with more caviar and 2 tablespoons chopped fresh parsley.

 ### Roast Pepper and Walnut Sauce

Combine ¼ cup virgin olive oil, 2 large diced roasted peppers (page 442), 1 clove minced garlic, salt, and pepper. Set aside for 10 minutes. Toss mixture with 1 pound hot cooked pasta, ¼ cup walnut pieces, and 2 tablespoons grated Parmesan.

 ### Peppers and Olive Sauce

Combine ¼ cup chopped pitted oil-cured black olives, 2 large diced roasted peppers (page 442), ¼ cup virgin olive oil, 1 clove minced garlic, salt, and pepper. Set aside for 10 minutes. Toss mixture with 1 pound hot cooked pasta and 2 tablespoons grated Parmesan.

 ### Feta and Artichoke Sauce

Mix a 12-ounce jar marinated artichoke hearts and ¼ pound crumbled feta. Set aside for at least 1 hour. Toss with hot cooked pasta, ¼ cup chopped fresh parsley, 2 tablespoons grated Parmesan, salt, and pepper.

Carbonara Sauce

In a deep skillet, gently cook 1 clove crushed garlic in 2 tablespoons olive oil until golden brown. Remove and discard garlic. Add ½ pound diced pancetta, cook until edges brown, and remove from heat. In a large warm bowl, beat 3 eggs with ¾ cup grated Parmesan, then toss with hot cooked pasta. Reheat pancetta mixture and toss with the pasta. (Skip this recipe if you're not comfortable with using uncooked egg yolks.)

 Bacon, Egg, and Cheese Sauce

Follow preceding recipe, substituting bacon for the pancetta.

 Marinated Sun-Dried Tomato Sauce

Dice 12 oil-cured sun-dried tomatoes and toss with about ¼ cup of their oil, and 1 clove minced garlic. Toss with hot cooked pasta, ¼ cup grated Parmesan, and 1 tablespoon chopped fresh parsley.

 Sun-Dried Tomato Rouille

In a food processor, puree 10 sun-dried tomatoes with ⅓ cup of their own oil. Combine with 1 bunch finely chopped basil leaves, 1 small clove minced garlic, 2 tablespoons grated Parmesan, 1 tablespoon virgin olive oil, salt, and pepper. Toss with hot cooked pasta.

 Three-Pepper Sauce

Roast 1 *each* red, yellow and green bell peppers (page 442), then stem, seed, peel, and dice. In a skillet, sauté the peppers in 3 tablespoons olive oil for 2 minutes. Season with salt, pepper, and ½ teaspoon hot pepper oil. Toss with hot cooked pasta, ¼ cup grated Parmesan, and 1 tablespoon chopped fresh parsley.

 Tapenade Sauce

Mix ¼ cup finely chopped pitted oil-cured black olives, 1 clove minced garlic, and 2 minced anchovies. Mix with ¼ to ⅓ cup virgin olive oil until desired consistency is reached. Season with pepper. Toss with hot cooked pasta.

 Spicy Peanut Sauce

In a nonstick skillet, heat 1 tablespoon peanut oil. Add 2 minced shallots and 1 clove minced garlic. Cook over moderate heat until lightly softened. Add 2 thinly sliced scallions, 1 teaspoon chili paste, 1 tablespoon soy sauce, 2 teaspoons grated fresh gingerroot, and ½ teaspoon *each* ground cumin and coriander. Cook for 2 minutes. Stir in ¼ cup peanut butter and heat until melted. Thin with as much buttermilk as necessary to make the mixture saucelike, about 1 cup. Toss with hot cooked pasta.

 Scallop and Herbed-Cheese Sauce

In a skillet, sauté 1 tablespoon finely chopped onion in 1 tablespoon peanut oil until soft. Add 1 cup white wine and 1 tablespoon lemon juice. Reduce by half. Add ¾ pound bay scallops and poach until firm, about 1 minute. Remove from heat and stir in 4 ounces herbed cream cheese until smooth. Add salt, white pepper, and 2 teaspoons chopped fresh parsley, and toss with hot cooked pasta.

Chicken and Olive Sauce

In a skillet, sauté ½ pound diced chicken breast in 1 tablespoon olive oil until it loses its raw look. Add 2 tablespoons minced onion and 1 clove minced garlic and cook another 30 seconds. Add ¾ cup white wine and boil for 1 minute. Add 18 pitted black olives and cook another minute. Season with salt and pepper and swirl in another tablespoon olive oil and 2 teaspoons chopped fresh parsley. Toss with hot cooked pasta.

 Sun-Dried Tomato and Tuna Sauce

Mix 6 ounces flaked white oil-packed tuna with 7 chopped oil-cured sun-dried tomatoes, 2 chopped scallions, 2 cloves minced garlic, 2 tablespoons virgin olive oil, 2 teaspoons lemon juice, salt, and pepper. Toss with hot cooked pasta.

 White Bean, Tuna, and Olive Oil Sauce

In a skillet, sauté 1 teaspoon crumbled rosemary in ¼ cup olive oil for 10 seconds. Add 2 tablespoons minced onion and 1 clove minced garlic. Cook another 30 seconds. Mix in 1 can (6½ ounces) drained oil-packed white tuna and cook another minute. Add 1 cup cooked cannellini beans, salt, pepper, and 1 tablespoon chopped fresh parsley. Heat through and toss with hot cooked pasta.

 Pepper and Anchovy Sauce

Combine 4 roasted bell peppers (page 442) that have been stemmed, seeded, peeled, and cut into strips with 16 slivered anchovy fillets, a pinch of dried oregano, 2 tablespoons drained capers, 1 clove minced garlic, ¼ cup olive oil, salt, and pepper. Allow to rest for at least 1 hour. Toss with hot cooked pasta.

 Roasted Eggplant and Garlic Sauce

Roast 1 medium to large eggplant by placing it over a high gas flame or under a broiler until its skin is uniformly blackened. Remove and cool. Slice off stem, peel skin with your fingers, and dice. In a skillet, sauté in 3 tablespoons olive oil for 1 minute. Add 2 cloves minced garlic, ¼ cup lemon juice, 1 tablespoon chopped fresh parsley, salt, and pepper. Toss with hot cooked pasta.

 Sauce Tonnato

In a saucepan, sauté 1 small clove minced garlic in 3 tablespoons olive oil for 10 seconds. Stir in 2 cups tomato sauce, then add 10 ounces undrained oil-packed tuna. Mix in 3 tablespoons lemon juice, salt, and pepper. Toss with hot cooked pasta.

Fifty Stir-Fries, East and West

Stir-frying has long been imprisoned by the flavors of exotic Asian ingredients. True, it's an Asian technique, and one that has produced many of our most memorable meals. But why does such a versatile cooking method have to be confined to ginger and soy sauce? Why not a stir-fry of steak spiced like a Texas barbecue? How about a bouillabaisse stir-fried in a wok? Why not a shortcake topped with a stir-fry of apples in butter, sugar, and cinnamon?

Stir-frying is nothing more than sautéing or braising in a wok, and it can be applied to any dish in Western cuisine that typically uses these techniques. The biggest difference in stir-frying is the intensity of heat and, as a result, the speed with which food gets cooked.

The unique design and construction of a wok are what permit the cook to control such intense heat without burning the food. A wok is a wide metal pan with sloping sides and a rounded bottom. This design concentrates heat down in the swollen belly of the pan. There, food can be quickly browned and then moved up along the sides, where it can finish cooking more slowly.

If the food requires long cooking with moist heat, liquid can be added to the wok to create a steaming environment that softens tough fibers at the same time that it flavors food and creates a base for a sauce.

Woks can be made from any metal. Traditional Chinese woks are cast iron, are very heavy, and take a long time to heat up, but once hot, they retain heat well. Today, most woks are made of carbon steel, a lighter metal that heats through quickly and cools down in minutes. The biggest drawbacks of carbon steel are that it will discolor with use and will rust if not dried thoroughly and rubbed with oil after each washing.

Because of the wok's rounded base, it will not sit securely on a burner, which is why almost all woks come with a metal ring in which they can rest. The ring is placed narrow-side up on a gas burner to help concentrate the heat near the center of the wok, but it sits wide-side up on an electric burner so the wok can rest closer to the less intense electric heat source. If a gas burner has a wide central opening in its grating the wok will sit securely without any ring at all.

It is often said that a wok is not an essential kitchen tool. Indeed, if you do not have a wok and do not wish to buy one, any stir-fried recipe can be made in a large heavy-gauge skillet instead. But the skillet will not cook food as quickly or as evenly.

Because stir-frying is such a quick method of cooking, all ingredients must be prepared and ready to go before the wok is ever heated. Vegetables must be chopped, sliced, or diced. Meat must be trimmed and sliced. Sauce ingredients should be measured and mixed and spices laid out on a plate.

Place the wok over a high flame until it is red hot and the air above the center of the wok seems to shiver with heat waves, then add a tablespoon or two of oil. If desired flavor the oil with hot pepper, garlic, or ginger by placing the whole spice in the hot oil and pressing it to release its oils. Cook just long enough for the spice to begin to brown—often as little as 10 seconds, then remove and proceed.

Tender, high-moisture vegetables, such as spinach, cabbage, and zucchini need only be wilted in the hot oil. The high heat helps to seal moisture in the vegetables, and, so long as they are stirred continuously, the vegetables will not overcook or burn. By reducing the heat and covering the wok, firmer vegetables, such as broccoli or carrots, can be steamed, which softens their fiber and extracts some of their moisture.

Meat, on the other hand, should sit in the hot oil undisturbed for a moment or two in order to brown properly. When meat and vegetables are cooked together, the meat is added first and, after browning, is either pushed to the sides of the wok or removed to a side plate. Then the vegetables are cooked, the meat is returned, and the whole dish is sauced and seasoned.

Fibrous vegetables and tougher cuts of meat are partially cooked in the oil and then finished in stock, wine, or a sauce mixture. In these cases, the heat is kept high so that the sauce reduces and thickens at the same time that the ingredients finish cooking. Sometimes, however, high-fiber foods require longer, slower cooking. In these cases, the heat is lowered after the liquid is added so that it simmers gently while the ingredients become tender.

These 50 recipes span a wide variety of flavors and techniques applicable to stir-frying. Yet they only skim the surface. Use them and adapt them to your taste, schedule, and imagination.

ABOUT THESE RECIPES

These recipes are written for preparation in a wok. You can use a skillet, but the cooking won't be as quick, so be prepared to adjust cooking times as needed. The water-cornstarch mixture that's added to many of the recipes is known as a slurry. It is used as a thickener late in the recipe and should be thoroughly stirred just before it's added. Salt and pepper should be adjusted to taste before serving. Each of these recipes makes 4 servings.

 ### Stir-Fried Herbed Mushrooms

Stir-fry 2 tablespoons chopped onion in 1 tablespoon olive oil for 30 seconds. Add 1 pound trimmed small white mushrooms and stir-fry until softened. Add 1 clove minced garlic, ¼ cup mixed chopped fresh herbs, and ½ cup chicken stock, cover, and steam for 2 minutes. Stir in 1 teaspoon cornstarch mixed in 2 teaspoons water and simmer until thickened. Finish with 1 teaspoon butter, salt, and pepper.

Stir-Fried Wild Mushrooms with Hazelnuts

Stir-fry 2 tablespoons minced shallots in 2 tablespoons peanut oil for 10 seconds. Add 1 pound trimmed and thickly sliced wild mushrooms, stir-frying until softened. Add 1 tablespoon soy sauce and 1 cup strong beef stock. Cover and steam 2 minutes. Lift mushrooms onto sides of the wok, add 3 finely sliced scallions, ½ clove minced garlic, and 2 teaspoons cornstarch mixed in 4 teaspoons water to the liquid in the wok and simmer until liquid thickens. Toss all with 1 tablespoon walnut oil and ¼ cup coarsely chopped hazelnuts.

 ### Stir-Fried Carrots with Mint and Red Pepper

Stir-fry ½ cup chopped onion, 1 teaspoon minced fresh gingerroot, and 1 pound peeled, trimmed, and thinly sliced carrots in 2 tablespoons olive oil for 1 minute. Add ⅓ cup mint tea and ¼ cup diced red pepper. Cover and steam 4 minutes. Uncover and boil off the excess liquid. Toss with 2 tablespoons finely chopped mint leaves, ½ clove minced garlic, and 1 teaspoon lemon juice.

 ### Italian Stir-Fried Green Beans

Stir-fry 1 pound snapped green beans and 1 clove minced garlic in 1 tablespoon olive oil, until beans turn bright green. Add ⅓ cup water, cover, and steam 3 minutes. Toss with 2 tablespoons toasted pine nuts.

 ### Stir-Fried Garlic Green Beans

Follow preceding recipe, but use 2 cloves minced garlic and omit the pine nuts.

 ### Stir-Fried Pasta Primavera

Stir-fry 1 cup chopped onion in 2 tablespoons virgin olive oil for 30 seconds. Add 1 large clove minced garlic, 2 ounces sliced green beans, ½ cup diced red pepper, 1 cup each small cauliflower and broccoli florets, and ½ cup each diced carrot and celery. Stir-fry 3 minutes. Add 1 teaspoon each dried tarragon, chervil, thyme, and basil, ½ pound asparagus tips, and 1 cup white wine and toss until most of the wine has evaporated. Add 10 ounces hot cooked pasta, salt, and pepper. Stir-fry 1 minute. Add 1 cup light cream and simmer until pasta is coated. Toss with ⅓ cup grated Parmesan.

 ### Spaghetti with Stir-Fried Meat Sauce

Stir-fry 1 cup chopped onion and 2 cloves minced garlic in 1 tablespoon olive oil for 30 seconds. Add 1 pound ground beef and toss until meat loses its raw look. Add 3 cups chopped canned tomatoes, simmer for 3 minutes, and add ¼ cup tomato paste. Season with a pinch of crushed red pepper flakes, salt, and pepper. Add 12 ounces hot cooked spaghetti and 1 tablespoon chopped fresh parsley, tossing until well coated and heated through.

 ### Mussels in Red Clam Sauce

Stir-fry 1 cup chopped onion and 2 cloves minced garlic in 1 tablespoon olive oil for 30 seconds. Add 6½ ounces drained canned clams and 1½ cups crushed canned tomatoes, simmer for 3 minutes, and add ¼ cup tomato paste. Season with a pinch of crushed red pepper flakes, salt, and pepper. Add 4 dozen cleaned and debearded mussels, toss, cover, and steam 3 minutes, until mussels open. Discard any that don't. Toss with 2 tablespoons chopped fresh parsley and 1 tablespoon lemon juice.

Thai Fried Noodles

Soak ¾ pound rice vermicelli in hot water for 15 minutes and drain. Stir-fry 3 cloves finely chopped garlic and ½ teaspoon crushed red pepper flakes in 3 tablespoons oil for 10 seconds. Add 1 tablespoon sugar, 3 tablespoons Thai fish sauce (*nam pla*), and 1½ tablespoons ketchup and stir until sugar dissolves. Add drained noodles and 2 beaten eggs, stir-frying 1 minute. Add ¾ cup bean sprouts and stir-fry another 2 minutes. Turn onto a plate and garnish with ¼ cup raw bean sprouts, 2 tablespoons chopped peanuts, 2 sliced scallions, 2 tablespoons chopped fresh cilantro, and 1 sliced lime.

 ### Shrimp Thai Noodles

Follow preceding recipe, adding 1 tablespoon additional oil and ½ pound small peeled shrimp with the garlic. Stir-fry until shrimp are firm before proceeding.

 ### High-Protein Vegetarian Stir-Fried Noodles

Follow recipe for Thai Fried Noodles (opposite), but stir-fry 1 cake diced tofu and 3 ounces stemmed snow pea pods with the garlic for 1 minute before removing. Return to wok for final minute of cooking.

 ### Stir-Fried Corn with Ham and Sweet Peppers

Stir-fry 1 tablespoon chopped onion and ¼ clove minced garlic in 1 tablespoon corn oil for 30 seconds. Add 4 cups corn kernels, 1 cored, seeded, and diced red bell pepper, a dash of nutmeg, and ¼ pound diced ham, stir-frying another 4 minutes, until corn is tender. Toss with 1 tablespoon chopped fresh parsley, salt, and pepper.

 ### Stir-Fried Broccoli with Hoisin Almonds

Stir-fry 1 whole clove garlic in 2 tablespoons peanut oil until browned, then remove. Add ¼ cup chopped onion and stir-fry until soft. Add ⅛ teaspoon crushed red pepper flakes and 1 bunch broccoli broken into florets, tossing for 1 minute. Add ⅓ cup water and simmer until broccoli is bright green and water evaporates. Remove and reserve. Wipe out wok, add another 1 tablespoon oil, then add ⅓ cup sliced almonds, and cook until lightly colored. Add 1 tablespoon hoisin sauce and 3 tablespoons sugar, cooking until almonds are well glazed. Toss with the broccoli.

 ### Stir-Fried Beans

Heat 3 dried chili peppers in 2 tablespoons corn oil until bubbling. Remove peppers and lightly brown 2 cups chopped onion in the oil. Add 4 cups cooked beans (kidney, white, or black), 1 clove minced garlic, 1 teaspoon ground cumin, 1 teaspoon ground coriander, and ¼ teaspoon dried oregano and stir-fry another 3 minutes. Stir in 2 tablespoons chopped fresh cilantro or parsley.

 ### Stir-Fried Soy-Glazed Potatoes

Blanch 1 pound small red-skin potatoes in 2 quarts salted water until barely tender, about 20 minutes. Drain well and pat dry. Stir-fry potatoes with 1 coarsely chopped onion in 2 tablespoons peanut oil until browned all over. Add ¼ cup low-sodium soy sauce and 1 clove minced garlic and cook until potatoes are glazed with sauce.

 ### Stir-Fried Curried Vegetables

Stir-fry 1 cup finely chopped onion, 2 teaspoons finely chopped fresh gingerroot, ½ clove minced garlic, 1 teaspoon ground coriander, 1 teaspoon ground cumin, 2 teaspoons curry powder, and a pinch of crushed red pepper flakes in 1 tablespoon vegetable oil until onion is soft, about 1 minute.

Remove and mix with 1 tablespoon lemon juice and ¼ cup chopped fresh cilantro. Stir-fry 1 teaspoon mustard seeds in 1 tablespoon vegetable oil until seeds color. Add 1 cup *each* broccoli and cauliflower florets, ½ cup sliced carrots, and 1 cup sliced green beans. Stir-fry until vegetables are brightly colored, about 3 minutes. Add ½ cup water. Cover and steam another 3 minutes. Toss with curried onion mixture.

 ### Curried Lamb with Eggplant

Follow preceding recipe through addition of cilantro, then stir-fry 1 pound thinly sliced leg of lamb and 1 teaspoon mustard seed in 1 tablespoon oil until lightly browned. Add 2 cups cubed eggplant and 1 cup chopped tomato. Stir-fry until eggplant is softened. Add ½ cup chicken stock and toss to moisten. Stir in reserved curried onion mixture.

 ### Stir-Fried Red Curry Chicken

Stir-fry 1 cup finely chopped onion, 2 teaspoons finely chopped fresh gingerroot, ½ clove minced garlic, 1 teaspoon ground coriander, 2 tablespoons Thai red curry paste, and a pinch of crushed red pepper flakes in 1 tablespoon vegetable oil until onion is soft, about 1 minute. Remove and mix with 1 tablespoon lemon juice and ¼ cup chopped fresh cilantro. Stir-fry 1 teaspoon mustard seeds in 1 tablespoon vegetable oil until seeds color. Add 1½ pounds diced boneless and skinless chicken breast, stir-frying until chicken is firm, about 4 minutes. Add ½ cup coconut milk. Cover and steam another 3 minutes. Toss with curried onion mixture.

 ### Sweet and Sour Lemon Pork

Marinate 1½ pounds bite-size cubes boneless pork in 1 tablespoon *each* soy sauce, dry sherry, and lemon juice, 1 teaspoon Oriental sesame oil, and 1 beaten egg white for 30 minutes. Drain, then dredge meat by shaking in plastic bag with equal parts of cornstarch and flour. Stir-fry in batches in ½ cup hot oil until browned and firm. Remove to paper towel and pour off all but thin film of oil. Add 1 tablespoon *each* minced garlic, chopped gingerroot, and grated lemon zest. Stir-fry 10 seconds. Add ¼ cup lemon juice, ¾ cup chicken broth, ¼ cup sugar, and 1 tablespoon soy sauce. Bring to boil and stir in 2 teaspoons cornstarch mixed in 4 teaspoons water. Heat until thickened. Return pork to sauce and finish with 1 tablespoon *each* dry sherry, Oriental sesame oil, and lemon juice.

 ### Sweet and Sour Spicy Shrimp

Marinate, dredge, fry, and set aside 2 pounds cleaned and shelled jumbo shrimp as described in preceding recipe. To a thin film of oil, add 3 cloves minced garlic, 1 tablespoon chopped fresh gingerroot, and 1 teaspoon crushed red pepper flakes and stir-fry 10 seconds. Add 2 tablespoons *each* ketchup and cider vinegar, ¾ cup chicken broth, ¼ cup sugar, and 1 tablespoon soy sauce. Bring to boil, stir in 2 teaspoons cornstarch mixed in 4 teaspoons water, and heat until thickened. Return shrimp to sauce and finish with 1 tablespoon *each* dry sherry, Oriental sesame oil, and lemon juice. Garnish with a sprinkling of sesame seeds.

 ### Sweet and Sour Chicken with Apricots

Marinate, dredge, fry, and set aside 1½ pounds boneless chicken breast as described in recipe for Sweet and Sour Lemon Pork (above). To a thin film of oil, add 1 tablespoon *each* minced garlic, chopped fresh gingerroot, and grated lemon zest. Stir-fry 10 seconds. Add 2 tablespoons *each* lemon juice, orange juice, sugar, ¾ cup chicken broth, 1 tablespoon soy sauce, and ¼ cup diced dried apricots. Bring to boil, stir in 2 teaspoons cornstarch mixed in 4 teaspoons water, and heat until thickened. Return chicken to sauce and finish with 1 tablespoon *each* dry sherry, Oriental sesame oil, and lemon juice.

 ### Stir-Fried Beef and Mushrooms

Soak 12 dried mushrooms in warm water to cover for 30 minutes. Drain and slice. Marinate 1½ pounds thinly sliced flank steak or boneless sirloin in 2 tablespoons soy sauce, 1 tablespoon dry sherry, and 2 teaspoons cornstarch for 15 minutes. Stir-fry 1 thick slice fresh gingerroot, 1 clove garlic, and 1 dried chili pepper in 2 tablespoons oil until garlic browns, then remove. Add marinated beef and stir-fry until lightly browned. Add the mushrooms and ¼ cup beef broth. Simmer until slightly thickened. Finish with 2 thinly sliced scallions and ½ clove minced garlic.

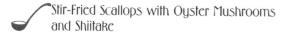 ### Stir-Fried Scallops with Oyster Mushrooms and Shiitake

Soak and slice 8 dried shiitake mushrooms as in preceding recipe. Stir-fry 1 pound trimmed sea scallops in 2 tablespoons oil until firm, then remove. Add 4 ounces cleaned oyster mushrooms, 1 tablespoon minced ginger, and 3 cloves minced garlic, stir-frying for 1 minute. Add 1 tablespoon *each* soy sauce, dry sherry, and lemon juice, and ¼ cup chicken broth. Bring to a boil. Add the shiitake mushrooms, reserved scallops, and 2 teaspoons cornstarch mixed in 4 teaspoons water and simmer until lightly thickened.

 ### Stir-Fried Beef Barbecue

Stir-fry 1½ pounds thinly sliced trimmed flank steak in 1 tablespoon vegetable oil with ¼ to ½

teaspoon crushed red pepper flakes until browned. Remove with slotted spoon and add 1 clove minced garlic, 1 tablespoon grated fresh gingerroot, and ⅓ cup grated onion to oil remaining in the wok. Stir-fry 1 minute. Add ¼ cup ketchup mixed with 2 tablespoons apple cider vinegar, 1 teaspoon brown sugar, and 1 tablespoon Worcestershire sauce and simmer until thickened. Return the steak and toss with sauce. Drizzle with the juice of 1 lime.

 ### Stir-Fried Orange Beef

Follow preceding recipe, but combine 1 cup orange juice with 1 teaspoon cornstarch and use in place of the ketchup and vinegar. Omit the lime juice.

 ### Stir-Fried Pork and Shrimp with Noodles

Stir-fry 1 tablespoon *each* chopped garlic and gingerroot in 1 tablespoon oil for 10 seconds. Add ½ pound thinly sliced strips boneless pork loin and ½ pound peeled and deveined medium shrimp. Cook until they lose their raw look. Add ½ cup *each* thinly sliced strips carrot and bamboo shoots and toss briefly. Add ½ cup chicken stock and simmer for 3 minutes. Add ½ pound cooked egg noodles, 3 tablespoons soy sauce, and 1 tablespoon *each* sugar and Chinese oyster sauce. Simmer until sauce clings to the noodles. Finish with 1 teaspoon Oriental sesame oil.

 ### Stir-Fried Garlic Chicken with Noodles

Follow preceding recipe, using 1 pound bite-size pieces boneless, skinless chicken instead of the pork and shrimp. Add 1 clove minced garlic with the sesame oil.

Fifty Ways to Cook Most Everything

 Stir-Fried Spicy Peanut Pork

Stir-fry ½ cup peanuts in 1 teaspoon peanut oil until toasted, remove, toss with 2 thinly sliced scallions and 1 clove minced garlic, and reserve. Add an additional 1 teaspoon oil to wok and stir-fry 1 pound thinly sliced strips trimmed boneless pork loin until lightly browned. Add ¼ cup finely chopped onion, ½ cup diced red pepper, 2 teaspoons grated fresh gingerroot, ½ teaspoon ground cumin, and ½ teaspoon ground coriander and toss until onion softens. Add 1 teaspoon chili paste, 2 teaspoons low-sodium soy sauce, and ½ cup chicken stock. Cover and simmer for several minutes until pork is tender. Stir in 2 teaspoons cornstarch mixed in 4 teaspoons water, bring to a boil, and add ¼ cup peanut butter mixed with 1 tablespoon dry sherry, along with the peanut garnish.

 Stir-Fried Peanut Chicken

Follow preceding recipe substituting 1 pound boneless, skinless chicken for the pork.

 Stir-Fried Spicy Peanut Shrimp

Follow recipe for Stir-Fried Spicy Peanut Pork (above), substituting 1½ pounds peeled and deveined large shrimp for the pork. Do not cover after the chicken stock is added. Simmer for only 1 minute and add the juice of ½ lemon in place of the sherry.

 Stir-Fried Veal with Olives

Toss 1½ pounds boneless leg of veal, cut in strips, with 1 clove chopped garlic, salt, and pepper. Stir-fry in 2 tablespoons olive oil for 2 minutes and remove. Add 1 teaspoon dried basil, ¼ cup finely chopped onion, 3 tablespoons pitted oil-cured black olives, and 2 cloves minced garlic to oil in pan and stir-fry for 1 minute. Add 4 chopped, seeded, and skinned plum tomatoes and bring to a simmer. Return veal to sauce and heat through. Finish with 2 teaspoons chopped fresh parsley.

 Stir-Fried Veal with Hot and Sweet Peppers

Follow preceding recipe, using 1 tablespoon finely diced and seeded fresh hot pepper and 1 diced roasted red bell pepper (page 442) instead of the olives.

 Stir-Fried Chicken with Glazed Red Pepper

Toss 1 pound boneless, skinless chicken breast, cut in bite-size pieces, in 1 tablespoon cornstarch. Stir-fry in 3 tablespoons oil until firm, then remove. Add a pinch of crushed red pepper flakes, ¼ cup finely chopped onion, and 1 clove minced garlic to remaining oil and stir-fry for 1 minute. Add 2 roasted red peppers (page 442), cut in strips, and stir-fry 1 minute more. Deglaze pan with 1 teaspoon Worcestershire sauce, 3 tablespoons apple cider vinegar, and 2 tablespoons sugar. Return chicken to pan and toss.

 Creamy Chicken and Corn Stir-Fry

Follow preceding recipe, but use only 1 roasted pepper and add 1 can (17-ounce) cream-style corn with the red pepper. Omit the vinegar and sugar.

 Stir-Fried Caramel Chicken

Stir-fry and set aside chicken as in recipe for Stir-Fried Chicken with Glazed Red Pepper (above).

Add ½ cup finely chopped onion and 1 clove minced garlic to remaining oil and stir-fry for 1 minute. Add 2 roasted red peppers (page 442), cut in strips, and stir-fry 1 minute more. Deglaze pan with 1 teaspoon Worcestershire sauce, 3 tablespoons apple cider vinegar, and 2 tablespoons sugar and cook until sugar begins to color, about 1 minute. Return chicken to pan and toss.

Sweet Anise Chicken

Soak 8 dried mushrooms in warm water for 30 minutes. Slice. Stir-fry 1½ pounds boneless, skinless chicken, cut into bite-size pieces, in 2 tablespoons oil until lightly browned. Add 1 tablespoon *each* minced fresh gingerroot and garlic, ½ teaspoon crushed red pepper flakes, 1 teaspoon ground aniseed, and 1 cup sliced fennel, cooking 1 minute more. Add 3 tablespoons low-sodium soy sauce, ¼ cup dry sherry, 1 cup chicken stock, 2 tablespoons sugar, and the sliced mushrooms. Simmer 4 to 5 minutes. Add 2 teaspoons cornstarch mixed in 4 teaspoons water. Finish with 1 teaspoon Oriental sesame oil.

Spicy Anise Lamb

Follow preceding recipe substituting leg of lamb for the chicken and finishing dish with hot pepper oil rather than sesame oil.

Stir-Fried Turkey with Garlic Black Beans

Dredge 1 pound boneless, skinless turkey breast, cut in bite-size pieces, in 1 tablespoon cornstarch. Stir-fry in 3 tablespoons oil until firm, then remove. Add a pinch of crushed red pepper flakes, ¼ cup finely chopped onion, ½ cup *each* sliced celery and carrots, and 1 clove minced garlic to remaining oil, and stir-fry for 1 minute. Return turkey to pan. Add

1 tablespoon garlic black bean sauce dissolved in 1 cup chicken stock, bring to a boil, and thicken with 2 teaspoons cornstarch mixed in 4 teaspoons water. Finish with 2 sliced scallions and 1 tablespoon dry sherry.

Stir-Fried Chicken with Rosemary and Sage

Dredge 1 pound boneless, skinless chicken breast, cut in bite-size pieces, in 1 tablespoon cornstarch. Stir-fry in 3 tablespoons oil until firm, then remove. Add a pinch of crushed red pepper flakes, ¼ cup finely chopped onion, ½ cup *each* sliced celery and carrots, 1 clove minced garlic, and 1 tablespoon *each* chopped fresh rosemary and sage leaves to remaining oil and stir-fry for 1 minute. Return chicken to pan. Add 1 cup chicken stock. Bring to a boil and thicken with 2 teaspoons cornstarch mixed in 4 teaspoons water. Finish with 1 tablespoon dry sherry.

Herbed Shrimp

Stir-fry 1 cup chopped onion and 3 cloves minced garlic in 2 tablespoons olive oil for 10 seconds. Add 2 tablespoons dry vermouth and cook for 15 seconds. Add 1½ pounds shelled, cleaned jumbo shrimp. Stir-fry 1 minute more. Add ¼ cup clam juice, 1 tablespoon chopped fresh parsley, 1 tablespoon chopped fresh dill, and 1 teaspoon fresh tarragon leaves. Cook another minute. Season with salt, pepper, and 1 teaspoon lemon juice.

Stir-Fried Scallops with Garlic

Stir-fry 1 cup chopped onion and 3 large cloves minced garlic in 2 tablespoons olive oil for 10 seconds. Add 2 tablespoons dry vermouth and cook for 15 seconds. Add 1½ pounds sea scallops and stir-fry 1 minute more. Add ¼ cup clam juice and

1 tablespoon chopped fresh parsley. Cook 1 minute. Season with salt, pepper, and 1 teaspoon lemon juice.

Ginger Sesame Salmon

Dredge 1½ pounds boneless, skinless salmon fillet, cut in 1-inch-wide strips, in a mixture of ¼ cup ground sesame seeds, ¼ cup cornstarch, and ½ teaspoon ground ginger. Fry in ½ cup hot oil until golden brown. Remove and discard all but a thin film of oil. Add 1 tablespoon finely chopped fresh gingerroot and 3 cloves minced garlic. Stir-fry 10 seconds. Add ½ cup bean sprouts and 16 stemmed snow peas. Stir-fry 30 seconds. Add 2 tablespoons each low-sodium soy sauce, lemon juice, and sherry and 2 teaspoons sugar. Stir in 1 teaspoon cornstarch mixed in 2 teaspoons water and simmer until thickened. Pour over fish and garnish with ¼ cup toasted sesame seeds.

Stir-Fried Fish and Vegetables

Dredge 1½ pounds skinless flounder fillet, cut in 1-inch-wide strips, in seasoned flour. Fry in ½ cup hot oil until golden brown. Remove and discard all but a thin film of oil. Add ¼ cup each thinly sliced carrots, cucumbers, and water chestnuts, and 1 clove minced garlic. Stir-fry 30 seconds. Add 2 tablespoons rice wine vinegar, 1 teaspoon sugar, and 1 tablespoon sherry. Heat through and pour over fish.

Stir-Fried Crab with Salsa

Stir-fry 1 pound cleaned lump crabmeat with 3 cloves minced garlic in 2 tablespoons olive oil until lightly browned. Remove from heat and toss with 1 tablespoon lemon juice, 1 cup spicy salsa, and 1 diced, peeled, and seeded avocado. Serve with corn chips.

Stir-Fried Apple Shortcake

Stir-fry 4 large peeled, cored, and sliced tart apples in 6 tablespoons butter, ⅓ cup sugar, and 1 tablespoon lemon juice until pan liquid is boiling. Boil for 3 minutes. Add 2 teaspoons cornstarch dissolved in 2 teaspoons water and 1 teaspoon vanilla extract and cook until thickened. Pour over 8 split Shortcake Biscuits (page 435).

Stir-Fried Poached Pears

Stir-fry 4 cored and sliced pears in 4 tablespoons butter for 1 minute. Add ¼ cup honey dissolved in the juice of ½ lemon, the juice of ½ orange, ¼ cup white wine, and ¼ cup water. Add julienned zest from the orange and lemon, bring to a boil, reduce to a simmer, and toss gently until pears are soft, about 3 minutes. Remove pears with slotted spoon. Add 2 teaspoons cornstarch dissolved in 2 tablespoons orange liqueur and 1 teaspoon vanilla extract and simmer until lightly thickened. Pour over pears and serve warm.

Peaches Stir-Fried with Framboise

Stir-fry 4 large peeled, pitted, and sliced freestone peaches in 6 tablespoons butter, ¼ cup sugar, and 1 teaspoon raspberry vinegar until pan liquid is boiling. Boil for 2 minutes. Add 2 teaspoons cornstarch dissolved in 2 teaspoons raspberry liqueur. Serve over ice cream or pound cake.

Stir-Fried Banana Split

Stir-fry 4 peeled and sliced bananas in 2 tablespoons butter over moderate heat. Add 3 tablespoons brown sugar and 2 tablespoons dark rum and stir-fry until sugar melts. Serve over 4 scoops vanilla ice cream and top with Wet Bourbon Pecans (page 403), which can be made in the wok.

Rum Raisin Bananas

Follow preceding recipe. After cooking, add ¼ cup raisins plumped in ¼ cup dark rum. Serve over ice cream or slices of plain cake.

Sweet Fried Rice

Soak 1 cup mixed dried fruit in 1¼ cups water and 1 teaspoon vanilla extract for 40 minutes. Stir-fry ½ cup whole almonds in 1 tablespoon peanut oil until toasted, about 1 minute. Remove with slotted spoon. Reduce heat to moderate and add 2 tablespoons butter. Add ⅓ cup thinly sliced onions and stir-fry until lightly browned. Add ¼ cup sugar and stir-fry until sugar melts and is lightly caramelized. Add ½ teaspoon ground cinnamon and the fruit mixture. Stir for 3 minutes and remove. Stir-fry 3 cups cooked rice in 2 tablespoons butter, 1 teaspoon vanilla extract, 1 tablespoon sugar, and a pinch of salt for 1 minute. Push rice up sides of wok, pour fruit in the center, and mix together. Turn out onto a platter and sprinkle with the toasted almonds, ½ teaspoon ground cinnamon, and ⅛ teaspoon ground cloves.

7

Fifty Ways to Build a Sandwich

There are few foods more soulful than an honest sandwich. It's easy to prepare, effortless to serve, and so common to our way of eating that we are apt to take it for granted. But there is more to building a great sandwich than just slapping a couple of things between two slices of bread.

The bread must never dominate. It certainly can give a sandwich textural interest, such as when it's toasted for a BLT or when it's bread-dough soft for a PBJ. But really, the bread serves as little more than a casing for the filling, making the sandwich easier to hold and eat.

Meat sandwiches need chewier breads—rye for roast beef and pastrami, hard rolls for submarines and steak sandwiches. More intricate and delicate club and tea sandwiches, with three bread slices, should get thinner bread that's toasted to prevent sogginess. If a sandwich is served hot with a sauce, the bread must be sturdy and flexible, such as rye bread or rolls.

Rolls demand more filling because of their thickness, and a buttery roll, like a croissant, should be served only warm with a warm filling. Sometimes large rolls, such as torpedo rolls, must be trimmed of some of their interior bread in order to make room for the filling.

Fillings should be moist, yet not overly wet. For years, almost all sandwich bread was buttered, but now diners are seeking more flavor with less fat, so mustard, horseradish, creamy vinaigrettes, herbed and spiced mayonnaises, and yogurt-based sauces have become the lower-calorie, most preferred sandwich spreads.

More and more, vegetables are providing savory flavors and moisture for sandwiches. There are, of course, the ubiquitous tomato, the mandatory iceberg leaf, and the sloppy crunch of cole slaw, but think, too, about the peppery bite of watercress and arugula, the exotic touch of marinated artichokes, or a garlic-laced eggplant puree. Cucumbers marinated in a vinaigrette, peppers preserved in oil, or an onion salad can add spark to almost any meat sandwich, and a relish of pickled vegetables is great with grilled cheese or broiled meat.

There's an old construction trick, of which veteran sandwich makers are very fond, that adds flavor to a sandwich while reducing its cost. It takes advantage of the physical phenomenon that no matter how delicious the ingredients are in a sandwich, their flavors will be lost if there is no space around them. Space is air and air carries food's aroma to the nose. Without aroma, our perception of flavor falls to a fraction of what it could be.

Space is created in a sandwich by loosely folding flat ingredients, such as meat and cheese slices; by overlapping vegetables, such as tomato slices and lettuce leaves, and by fluffing shredded or finely chopped condiments.

ABOUT THESE RECIPES

All 50 of these recipes are written to make 4 sandwiches unless otherwise noted and assume that you will season to taste with salt and pepper.

 ### Ham, Apple, and Mustard on Rye

Mix 1 tablespoon apple butter with 3 tablespoons brown mustard and spread on 8 slices rye bread. Arrange 3 thin slices folded baked ham on each of 4 slices of the bread, top each with 3 thin wedges cored apple, and top with the remaining bread.

 ### Egg Salad with Olives

Mix 8 chopped hard-cooked eggs, 1 tablespoon *each* mayonnaise, extra-virgin olive oil and finely chopped fresh parsley, ½ teaspoon mustard, 1 teaspoon lemon juice, and ¼ cup diced ripe olives. Sandwich between 8 slices toasted bread, garnished with 4 leaves Romaine.

 ### Spicy Anchovy Egg Salad

Mix 8 chopped hard-cooked eggs, 2 tablespoons minced anchovy fillets, 1 tablespoon oil from the anchovy can, 1 tablespoon mayonnaise, ½ teaspoon mustard, 1 teaspoon lemon juice, 1 tablespoon finely chopped fresh parsley, and ¼ teaspoon crushed red pepper flakes. Sandwich between 8 slices toasted bread, garnished with 4 leaves Romaine.

 ### Peanut Butter, Honey, and Raisins

Spread 4 slices raisin bread with ¾ cup peanut butter and sprinkle each with 2 tablespoons raisins. Top with 4 more slices raisin bread, spread with ¼ cup honey.

 ### Walnut Butter and Figs

In a food processor or blender, process ⅓ pound walnut pieces, ¼ teaspoon brown sugar, and a pinch of salt, until smooth and thick. Spread on 4 slices whole wheat bread and top each with 2 sliced dried figs. Top with 4 more slices whole wheat bread, each spread with a thin layer of raspberry preserves, using 3 tablespoons total.

 ### Rolled-Up Pop-Up Health Sandwich

Soak 1 cup bulgur in 1½ cups cold water and ¼ cup olive oil for 30 minutes, and drain off excess liquid. Mix in juice of 1 lemon, 2 tablespoons finely chopped mint leaves, 3 finely chopped scallions, 1 clove minced garlic, 1 shredded carrot, 1 chopped tomato, salt, and pepper. Toast 6 8-inch flour tortillas in a hot dry skillet for 30 seconds per side, spread with ¾ cup tahini, and top each with a line of ¼ cup bulgur salad and ⅔ cup alfalfa sprouts. Roll tortillas around their fillings. They will be shaped like fat cigars. Wrap in wax paper or parchment, leaving one end open. Eat like a banana, peeling back paper as you go. Serves 6.

Rolled-Up Pop-Up Corned Beef Special

Toast 6 (8-inch) flour tortillas in a hot dry skillet for 30 seconds per side, spread with a mixture of ½ cup mayonnaise and 2 tablespoons ketchup, and fill with ½ pound thinly sliced deli corned beef and 1 cup cole slaw. Wrap and eat as described in preceding recipe. Serves 6.

 ### Rolled-Up Pop-Up Ham and Cheese

Toast 6 (8-inch) flour tortillas in a hot dry skillet for 30 seconds per side, spread with a total of 6 table-spoons mustard, and fill with ½ pound sliced baked ham and ⅓ pound sliced Swiss cheese. Wrap and eat as described in Rolled-Up Pop-Up Health Sandwich (page 65). Serves 6.

 ### Roast Beef on Rye with Horseradish Sauce

Mix 2 tablespoons *each* white horseradish and may-onnaise, and 1 tablespoon sour cream. Spread on one side of 8 slices rye bread. Loosely mound ½ pound thinly sliced rare roast beef on 4 of the bread slices and top each with one of the remain-ing bread slices.

 ### Salami, Provolone, and Olives

Slice tops off 4 kaiser rolls and hollow out the in-teriors. Mix ½ pound diced Genoa salami, ¼ cup chopped pitted oil-cured black olives, 5 ounces diced provolone, ½ clove minced garlic, ¼ cup chopped tomato, 2 tablespoons chopped red on-ion, 1 tablespoon chopped fresh parsley, 2 table-spoons olive oil, and 1 tablespoon wine vinegar and fill the rolls.

 ### Fennel Salmon Salad Sandwich

Toss 2 ribs diced fennel, 2 drained (6½-ounces) cans salmon, and 1 tablespoon chopped fennel leaf. Mix 2 tablespoons lemon juice, 1 tablespoon sour cream, and 3 tablespoons mayonnaise, spread 1 teaspoon on each of 8 slices black bread, and mix remaining sauce with salmon. Build sandwiches using the salmon salad and 1 leaf Romaine per sandwich.

 ### Smoked Salmon Salad Sandwich

Toss 1 rib diced celery, 1 drained (6½-ounce) can salmon, ¼ pound chopped smoked salmon, and 1 tablespoon chopped fresh dill. Mix 2 tablespoons lemon juice, 1 tablespoon sour cream, and 3 table-spoons mayonnaise, spread 1 teaspoon on each of 8 slices black bread, and mix remaining sauce with the salmon. Build sandwiches using the salmon salad and 3 slices cucumber per sandwich.

 ### Smoked Salmon, Feta, and Tapenade

Sandwich 6 ounces thinly sliced smoked salmon, 4 spinach leaves, and 2 ounces feta cheese between 8 slices black bread or 4 split bagels, spread with ¼ cup Tapenade (page 25).

 ### Waldorf Salad on Rye

Mix ¾ pound diced baked ham or smoked turkey breast, 1 large grated Granny Smith apple, ⅔ cup coarsely chopped walnuts, 3 tablespoons mayon-naise, and 1 teaspoon cider vinegar. Brush 8 slices rye bread with 1 tablespoon mayonnaise. Top each slice with 1 lettuce leaf, mound 4 of the slices with the salad, and top with the remaining slices.

French Shrimp Salad Sandwich

Mix 12 ounces small, peeled, cleaned and boiled shrimp, 2 tablespoons mayonnaise, 1 teaspoon lemon juice, 1 teaspoon Dijon mustard, ½ teaspoon fresh or ¼ teaspoon dried tarragon leaves, 1 rib diced celery, and ¼ cup chopped walnuts. Sandwich between 8 slices brioche-type bread (challah will do), garnishing each with a few sprigs watercress.

Dilled Tuna Sandwich

Seed and thinly slice 1 cucumber, toss with ½ teaspoon salt, set aside for 20 minutes, then squeeze out as much moisture as possible. Toss with 2 drained (6-ounce) cans tuna, 2 tablespoons chopped fresh dill, 1 tablespoon lemon juice, and 5 tablespoons any ranch dressing. Spread each of 8 slices black bread with 1 teaspoon Ranch Dressing and build sandwiches using the tuna salad and 2 thin slices tomato per sandwich.

Dill Tuna Melt

Prepare cucumber and tuna salad as in preceding recipe. Spread each of 4 slices black bread with 1 teaspoon any ranch dressing and top each with tuna salad and 2 thin slices tomato. Lay ½ ounce sliced dill havarti on top of each sandwich and brown under a broiler or in a toaster oven until cheese melts, about 2 minutes.

Smoked Turkey with Grilled Smoked Mozzarella

Spread 4 slices rye bread with 2 tablespoons brown mustard and top each with 1 ounce sliced smoked turkey breast. In a skillet, sauté 1 thinly sliced small onion in 1 teaspoon corn oil until lightly browned, then place over the turkey. Top each with 1 ounce sliced smoked mozzarella and brown under a broiler or in a toaster oven until cheese is bubbly, about 2 to 3 minutes.

Meatloaf with Sauerkraut and Mustard on Rye

Spread 8 slices rye bread with 3 tablespoons brown mustard. Sandwich with 4 slices leftover meatloaf and ½ cup drained and rinsed sauerkraut. Wrap each sandwich in foil and warm in preheated 375° F. oven for 20 minutes.

Meatloaf with Barbecue Sauce

Brush 4 slices leftover meatloaf with ¼ cup barbecue sauce and warm in preheated 400° F. oven for 15 minutes, or microwave at full power for 2½ minutes. Warm 4 kaiser rolls in an oven or toaster. Brush each with 1 tablespoon barbecue sauce, top with warm slices of meatloaf and ½ cup cole slaw.

Hot Dog and Chilied Mustard

In a skillet, cook 2 tablespoons chopped onion in 1 teaspoon corn oil until soft. Add 2 tablespoons chili powder and 1 teaspoon *each* ground cumin and coriander. Cook for 1 minute, remove from heat, and stir in 2 tablespoons brown mustard. Broil, grill, or boil 4 hot dogs or knockwurst until plump and steaming. Serve on toasted hot dog rolls or small torpedo rolls, spread with the chili mustard.

Chicken Franks with Avocado Salsa

Rub interior of 8 split hot dog rolls with 2 tablespoons olive oil and toast lightly. Grill, broil, or boil 8 chicken franks until puffed and steaming and sandwich each in a roll. Spoon ½ cup Avocado Salsa (page 164) on top.

 ## Bratwurst with Mustard Applesauce

In a small skillet, brown ¼ cup minced onion in 2 teaspoons butter. Add 1 teaspoon brown sugar and melt. Mix into ½ cup applesauce mixed with 2 tablespoons brown mustard. Boil, grill, or broil 4 bratwurst until plump and steamy. Serve in 4 split hot dog rolls, *each* brushed with 2 teaspoons brown mustard. Top with mustard applesauce.

 ## Hot Dogs Grilled with Bacon and Honey Mustard

Split 8 hot dogs lengthwise and spread 3 tablespoons honey mustard on them. Wrap 1 slice bacon around each, securing ends with toothpicks. Grill or broil hot dogs 4 inches from a high fire, turning once, until bacon is crisp and hot dogs browned. Serve in warm hot dog rolls and additional honey mustard on the side.

 ## Grilled Chèvre and Sun-Dried Tomatoes

Place 16 slices French bread on a sheet pan. Moisten surface of each slice with oil from 1 cup oil-cured sun-dried tomatoes. Place 1 basil leaf on each bread and top with ½ sun-dried tomato. Place 1 thin slice chèvre over each tomato and bake in 400° F. oven until cheese melts and is lightly browned, about 4 to 5 minutes.

 ## Grilled Bacon, Tomato, and Cheese

In large skillet, cook 8 slices bacon until crisp and brown, drain on paper towels, and reserve a thin film of fat in the pan. Place a total of 6 ounces sliced muenster on 4 slices crusty white bread. Top each with 2 slices tomato and 2 slices bacon. Place 4 more slices bread on top. Brown sandwiches on both sides over moderate heat in the reserved fat until golden.

 ## Grilled Farmer Cheese and Smoked Salmon on a Bagel

Spread 3 ounces farmer cheese among each half of 4 split bagels. On each bagel half, place 1 paper-thin slice red onion and 1 thin slice smoked salmon, using about 5 ounces total. Top each with about 1 ounce farmer cheese. Broil 4 inches from a high flame for 3 to 4 minutes, until the cheese melts and very lightly browns.

 ## Baked Brie Sandwich

Split 1 large baguette down the middle, fill with 6 ounces sliced brie, wrap in foil, and bake in a preheated 400° F. oven for 15 minutes. Serve in slices.

 ## Crabcake Sandwich with Creole Tartar Sauce

Mix ½ pound backfin crabmeat, ½ cup fresh bread crumbs, 2 tablespoons mayonnaise, 1 small egg, 2 teaspoons chopped fresh parsley, 1 teaspoon Worcestershire sauce, ½ teaspoon hot pepper sauce, 2 teaspoons lemon juice, and ½ teaspoon dry mustard. Form into 4 patties and coat with ½ cup seasoned bread crumbs. Refrigerate for 30 minutes. In a skillet, fry for 3 minutes per side in ¼ inch hot oil. Serve on 4 split buns spread with ½ cup Creole Tartar Sauce (page 166) and top with ½ cup shredded lettuce.

Shrimp Cake Sandwich with Lemon Yogurt Sauce

Follow preceding recipe but use ½ pound chopped cooked shrimp instead of the crab. Serve on 4 split buns, replacing the tartar sauce with a mixture of ¼ clove minced garlic, ½ cup plain yogurt, and 1 tablespoon lemon juice. Top with ½ cup bean sprouts.

Fillet Panier with Wine Butter Sauce

In a hot iron skillet, sauté four 4-ounce fillet steaks, seasoned with salt and pepper, to desired doneness. Add 1 tablespoon butter and ¼ cup chopped shallot and cook until shallots soften. Add ½ cup red wine and reduce by half. Swirl in 2 tablespoons butter and simmer until sauce thickens lightly. Slice steaks and arrange on 4 small French breads, split open lengthwise. Pour sauce over meat and close rolls.

Italian Sausage with Prosciutto and Capers

Split 1 pound mild Italian sausage into 4 sections. Place in a skillet with ½ inch water, cover, bring to a boil, and cook for 4 minutes. Turn over sausage and continue cooking until the water evaporates. Continue cooking until the sausage browns. Flip and brown on the other side. Meanwhile, sauté ⅓ cup drained capers in 1 tablespoon olive oil for 1 minute. Add 1 tablespoon chopped fresh parsley, then spread on the interiors of 4 split torpedo rolls. Wrap each sausage in 1 thin slice prosciutto and place 1 in each roll.

Fried Salmon Sandwich with Dill Tartar Sauce

Dip four 5-ounce pieces salmon fillet in 1 egg beaten with ¼ cup milk, then coat with a mixture of ½ cup cornmeal, ¼ cup flour, ¼ teaspoon salt, and ⅛ teaspoon cayenne pepper. Refrigerate for 20 minutes. Mix 6 tablespoons mayonnaise, 1½ tablespoons lemon juice, 1 minced shallot, 2 teaspoons finely chopped fresh dill, and 1 finely chopped hard-cooked egg. Pan-fry breaded salmon for 2 minutes per side and drain on paper towel. Spread 4 split kaiser rolls with the sauce, place 1 salmon fillet on each, and top each with ½ cup shredded lettuce, 1 slice tomato, and a bit more of the sauce.

Barbecued Pork Sandwich

Rub 2 pounds boneless pork shoulder with salt, pepper, and 2 cloves minced garlic. Roast on a rack in a small roasting pan in a preheated 400° F. oven for 30 minutes. Mix ½ cup finely chopped onion, ¾ cup ketchup, 1 tablespoon mustard, ¼ cup dark brown sugar, 2 tablespoons apple cider vinegar, 1 tablespoon Worcestershire sauce, 1 tablespoon hot pepper sauce, 2 cups chicken stock, and 1 cup water. Remove rack from roasting pan, pour off fat and pour mixture over pork. Roast at 350° F. for 1½ hours, until pork is quite tender. Slice thinly and break pork into small pieces. Toss with liquid remaining in pan and heap onto 8 hamburger buns. Serves 8.

Barbecued Pork Sandwich with Sauerkraut

Follow preceding recipe, topping each sandwich with the following mixture: Render fat from 4 strips bacon, reserve bacon, and add ½ cup finely chopped onion to the fat. Add 1 pound drained sauerkraut and ¾ cup apple juice and cook until all liquid evaporates. Crumble in the bacon.

Barbecued Pork Sandwich with Cole Slaw

Follow recipe for Barbecued Pork Sandwich (above), topping each sandwich with ¼ cup cole slaw, using the Red Cabbage, White Cabbage, Sweet and Sour, or Creole Cole Slaw (pages 293, 288).

 ### Marinated Mozzarella, Olives, and Sun-Dried Tomatoes

Whisk together 1 tablespoon red wine vinegar, ½ large clove minced garlic, 3 tablespoons olive oil, ⅛ teaspoon salt, pepper, 1 teaspoon minced fresh parsley, and ½ teaspoon dried basil. Toss with ½ pound diced mozzarella, ¼ cup chopped oil-cured black olives, and 8 chopped oil-cured sun-dried tomatoes. Serve with 2 sliced baguette French breads.

 ### Marinated Mozzarella Grinder

Follow preceding recipe, packing cheese mixture into 4 long torpedo rolls. Wrap each sandwich in foil and bake in a preheated 400° F. oven for 20 minutes.

 ### Gorgonzola Grinder

Mix ½ cup olive oil, ⅓ cup wine vinegar, 2 cloves minced garlic, 2 tablespoons *each* chopped fresh basil, chives, and parsley, ½ teaspoon crushed red pepper flakes, and lots of freshly ground black pepper. Brush 4 split torpedo rolls with a thin film of this dressing, pack rolls with 1 pound cubed Gorgonzola cheese, and pour remaining dressing over the cheese. Close rolls, wrap each in foil, and bake 10 minutes in preheated 400° F. oven.

 ### Three-Meat Deli Hoagie

Brush 4 split torpedo rolls with ⅓ cup hot pepper oil. Layer 1 ounce *each* sliced baked ham, Genoa salami, roast turkey breast, and aged provolone on each roll and top each with ¼ cup shredded lettuce, ½ sliced tomato, and 2 ounces sliced onion. Drizzle each with 1 tablespoon olive oil and 1½ teaspoons wine vinegar.

 ### Grilled Eggplant and Smoked Mozzarella Grinder

Slice 1 medium eggplant into thin rounds, brush slices lightly with olive oil, and grill over a high fire for 1 to 2 minutes per side. In a skillet, cook ¼ cup chopped onion and 1 clove minced garlic in 1 tablespoon olive oil until soft. Add ¾ pound sliced mushrooms and brown lightly. Brush 4 split torpedo rolls with 1 tablespoon olive oil. Arrange eggplant down the length of each roll and drizzle each with 1 teaspoon lemon juice. Spoon onions and mushrooms, 1½ ounces sliced smoked mozzarella, and 1 chopped plum tomato over each. Wrap individually in foil and bake 15 minutes in a 400° F oven.

 ### Chèvre and Roasted Pepper Mini-Sandwiches

Brush 8 split torpedo-shaped dinner rolls with 3 tablespoons Garlic Herb Dressing (page 296). Pack each roll with ½ ounce crumbled chèvre and 1 tablespoon diced roasted pepper (page 442), wrap each roll in foil and bake in a 400° F. oven for 10 minutes.

 ### Caesar Salad Sandwich

In a food processor, combine 1 clove garlic, 6 anchovies, 2 egg yolks, 2 teaspoons Dijon mustard, 5 tablespoons wine vinegar, 2 tablespoons lemon juice, and a dash of Worcestershire sauce. Add ½ cup olive oil and ½ cup vegetable oil in slow, steady stream with processor running until mixture is smooth and thick. Slice an end off each of 8 warm pita breads to make a pocket and spread interiors with this dressing. Toss together 1 head Romaine leaves and 1 head curly endive leaves broken into bite-size pieces, 3 ounces sliced mushrooms, ½ thinly sliced medium-size sweet onion, ¼ cup grated Parmesan, and the remaining dressing. Heap into the pitas and garnish each with 2 thin tomato slices. (Skip this recipe if you're uncomfortable using uncooked egg yolks.) Serves 8.

 ### Spinach Salad with Warm Bacon Dressing in a Baguette

Cook 10 slices bacon until crisp, crumble, and reserve. In the same skillet, cook 1 cup chopped onion and 2 cloves minced garlic in 2 tablespoons of the bacon fat. Add ½ cup wine vinegar, ¼ cup olive oil, 1 tablespoon sugar, and plenty of salt and pepper and heat through. Brush 2 split (1-pound) French baguettes with ¼ cup of this dressing. Toss remaining dressing with 12 ounces cleaned spinach and the reserved bacon, mound into the breads, close, and cut each in half.

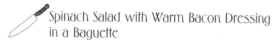 ### Grilled Lamb and Artichoke in a Pita

Season 2 pounds sliced boneless leg of lamb with 2 cloves minced garlic, salt, and pepper and let rest for 15 minutes. Meanwhile, quarter 6 ounces marinated artichoke hearts and toss with 2 diced roasted red bell peppers (page 442), ½ peeled, seeded, and finely diced cucumber, ¼ cup chopped fresh mint, and 6 tablespoons plain yogurt. Slice an end off each of 4 pitas to make a pocket, brush with 2 teaspoons olive oil, and warm in a 375° F. oven for 5 minutes. Grill lamb over high heat to desired degree of doneness, slice into strips, and divide among pitas. Top each with some of the artichoke mixture.

 ### Tuna and Guacamole Pita

Slice an end off each of 4 pitas and brush insides with 1 tablespoon olive oil. Fill with Tuna Salsa Salad (page 353) and top with a mixture of California avocado, ¼ clove minced garlic, ¼ teaspoon hot pepper sauce, and 1 teaspoon lemon juice pureed in a food processor or blender. Top each with 1 tablespoon finely chopped tomato.

 ### Middle Eastern Turkey Pita

Slice an end off each of 4 pitas to make a pocket and brush with ½ recipe Sesame Chick-Pea Spread (page 165), top with ½ pound shredded roast turkey breast and spoon over Minted Yogurt Dressing (page 300).

 ### Chicken Chick-Pea Salad in a Pita

In a bowl, toss 1 cup diced cooked chicken, 1 cup cooked or canned chick-peas, 1 teaspoon ground coriander, ½ teaspoon ground cumin, 2 tablespoons olive oil, 1 tablespoon lemon juice, 1 clove minced garlic, ½ teaspoon hot pepper sauce, and 1 cup plain yogurt. Slice an end off each of 4 small pitas to make a pocket, and brush interiors with 1 tablespoon sauce from the chicken. Fill with chicken salad and top each with ¼ cup shredded lettuce.

 ### Cold Crab and Avocado Taco

Toss 1 pound lump crabmeat, 2 thinly sliced scallions, 1 tablespoon lemon juice, and ¼ teaspoon hot pepper sauce. In a food processor or blender, puree 1 California avocado, ¼ teaspoon minced garlic, ¼ teaspoon hot pepper sauce, and 1 teaspoon lemon juice. Layer the 2 mixtures in 8 warm taco shells and top with Mild Red Salsa (page 268).

Crab and Smoked Salmon Tea Sandwiches

Butter 1 side of each of 8 thin slices of sandwich bread and both sides of 4 toasted slices. On the buttered side of 4 of the untoasted slices, spread a mixture of 6 ounces cleaned backfin crabmeat, 3 finely chopped scallions, and 3 tablespoons mayonnaise, then top with toasted slices. Spread each with mixture of 1 ounce chopped smoked salmon, 2 ounces softened cream cheese, and 1 tablespoon chopped dill leaves and top with remaining bread, buttered sides down. Cut off crusts and slice each sandwich into 3 fingers.

Fifty Foods for Romance

Anthropologists tell us that early on in human evolution, men and women were brought together primarily for two physical necessities—eating and procreation. Food and love have remained intimately entwined ever since.

We are seduced by food and we hunger for love. Our loved ones are "sweet" and "look good enough to eat," just as we "desire" our favorite flavors and find the most delicious dishes "lip-smacking." Whether it's a notorious aphrodisiac or a homebaked bread, beautiful sensual food, thoughtfully prepared, is not just the fastest way to soften a lover's heart, it opens all the senses for pleasure.

But food does not seduce alone. Timing, setting, lighting, and mood must all play their part if the full effect is to be irresistible. Candlelight, crisp linen, and champagne flutes on a table set for two are always a good bet, provided they're unexpected, for the one element of romantic dining that can't be overestimated is the subtle surprise that is the essence of romance.

For example, winter can be the perfect time for a picnic—in bed. Set the bed with a cloth and dishes or serve on large trays while you snuggle under a quilt. Then select foods that can be eaten without utensils—room-temperature hens that can

be ripped apart by hand and dipped into a warm cranberry glaze; raw oysters studded with pearls of cavier to slide from their half shells between awaiting lips; or strawberries in a pool of warm chocolate that rise from their bath delicately dangling a droplet of sauce.

Or start off an entire day of romance with wedges of ripe peach dipped in sweetened framboise or heart-shaped biscuits slathered with spiced brown-sugar butter. Fill a melon with champagne the night before and serve it with fresh raspberries to create a morning that will never be forgotten, or stuff croissants with anything from chocolate-butter to smoked-salmon mousse.

Try an herb-infused savory rendition of a classic French *coeur à la crème* for midday. Or greet your lover with a steak sandwich like no other, crowning a grilled filet with sautéed mushrooms and a cloak of bearnaise. Keep dinner light and passions keen with a simple poached fish, a seafood stew, or a rare roast beef. Serve asparagus, artichokes, or a fanciful salad. Dessert can be nothing more than a few pieces of perfectly ripened fruit or it can be one of our more spectacular creations, such as Sinful Chocolate Tartlets or Grand Marnier White Chocolate Truffles. If they don't do the trick, nothing will. For beautiful food taken with the one you

Fifty Ways to Cook Most Everything

love is all the more memorable when you rise from the table with your hungers soothed and your appetite yearning for more.

ABOUT THESE RECIPES

The following 50 recipes are grouped according to the time of day or the nature of the occasion when they might be presented, but feel free to use them any way you like. Note that several recipes call for a *coeur à la crème* mold. This is a ceramic, heart-shaped mold with holes in the bottom to permit drainage, available at gourmet stores. If you don't want to buy one, you can mold the cheese in a small strainer lined with a damp cheesecloth, although the resulting "*coeur*" will not be heart-shaped.

All recipes are written for 2 generous portions, unless otherwise noted.

THE MORNING AFTER OR BEFORE

Ultra-Rich Spiked French Toast

Beat 1 egg, 2 yolks, 2 tablespoons sugar, 2 tablespoons orange liqueur, a pinch of grated nutmeg, a pinch of salt, ¼ cup light cream, and ½ cup milk. Dip 4 thick slices challah into the batter until all of it has been absorbed, then in a skillet, brown over moderate heat in 4 tablespoons unsalted butter.

Souffléd French Toast

Beat 2 egg yolks, 2 tablespoons *each* sugar, brandy and milk, a pinch of grated nutmeg, and ¼ cup light cream. With an electric mixer, beat 2 egg whites to a soft peak with a pinch salt, then gently fold into batter. Dip 4 thick slices challah into the batter until all of it has been absorbed, then brown in a skillet over moderate heat in 4 tablespoons unsalted butter.

Buttermilk Biscuits with a Heart

Sift 1½ cups flour, 1 teaspoon baking soda, 1½ teaspoons baking powder, 2 tablespoons sugar, and a pinch of salt. Using a pastry cutter or two knives, cut in 6 tablespoons butter until the mixture resembles a coarse meal. Beat 1 extra-large egg, 1 teaspoon vanilla, and ⅓ cup buttermilk. Reserve 3 tablespoons and mix the rest into the dry ingredients to moisten. Knead lightly on a floured board for 30 seconds, pat ¼ inch thick, and cut into 8 biscuits using a 3-inch heart-shaped cutter. Brush with some of reserved liquid, place a hulled strawberry on 4 of the biscuits, and cover with the remaining biscuits, easing the dough over the berries to enclose them. Press lightly on edges to seal. Brush with remaining liquid. Bake on sheet pan in 400° F oven for 20 minutes.

Herbed Biscuits with a Secret

Follow preceding recipe, but add 2 tablespoons chopped fresh herbs with the flour. Replace strawberries with 1 frozen teaspoon-size nugget of herbed cream cheese.

Croissants with Scallops in Beurre Blanc

Remove a thin slice from the top of 2 large croissants and hollow out interiors. Warm in a 350° F. oven for 10 minutes. Poach ¾ pound trimmed sea scallops in ⅓ cup white wine for 2 minutes. Remove scallops and keep warm. Add ¼ cup white wine vinegar and 1 tablespoon finely chopped shallot to the wine and reduce to ¼ cup volume. Add 1 tablespoon heavy cream and bring to a simmer over low heat, then swirl in 6 tablespoons butter, a bit at a time. Toss with the scallops and 1 tablespoon chopped fresh parsley. Fill croissants with the scallops, pour sauce over all, and lean the croissant lids to the side.

Shrimp in Croissants

Follow preceding recipe, replacing scallops with 12 peeled, cleaned, and butterflied jumbo shrimp.

FOREPLAY

Cajun Oysters

Simmer 12 large shucked oysters in a thin film of their liquor until they plump, remove oysters, and reduce liquid to 3 tablespoons. Add 1 cup heavy cream and 2 to 3 teaspoons hot pepper sauce and reduce until lightly thickened. Return oysters and heat through. Serve in 2 large hollowed-out croissants with their tops sliced off. Top each croissant with 1 teaspoon caviar, if desired.

Caviar Coeur à la Crème

Blend 1 ounce cream cheese, ¼ pound ricotta cheese, and ⅛ teaspoon salt. Add 1 teaspoon lemon juice, a pinch of cayenne pepper, a grating of nutmeg, 2 minced scallions, 1 ounce golden caviar, and 1 ounce salmon caviar. Spoon into two ½-cup *coeur à la crème* molds lined with damp cheesecloth. Cover with plastic, weight lightly and refrigerate in a pan to drain overnight. Invert onto plates and serve with 4 slices black bread, cut into small hearts with a cookie cutter and toasted.

Smoked Salmon Coeur à la Crème

Follow preceding recipe, but add 1 teaspoon lemon juice, a pinch of cayenne pepper, a grating

of nutmeg, 1½ teaspoons chopped fresh chive, and 2 ounces finely chopped smoked salmon to the cheeses and salt. Serve with 4 slices toasted black bread, cut into small hearts with a cookie cutter.

Spicy Shiitake Mushrooms

Mix ¼ clove minced garlic, 1 teaspoon minced ginger, a pinch of crushed red pepper flakes, 1½ tablespoons hoisin sauce, 1 teaspoon dry sherry, and 1½ teaspoons Oriental sesame oil. Toss 12 large trimmed fresh shiitake mushrooms in this marinade and refrigerate for 1 hour. Spear mushrooms on long-handled skewers and grill over an open fire or under a broiler until firm, 1 to 2 minutes per side. Serve with 2 lemon wedges.

French Fries with Tapenade

Prepare ½ recipe Perfect Fries (page 259) and serve with ½ recipe Tapenade (page 25).

Garlic and Walnut Baguette

In a food processor or blender, process 1 clove garlic, ½ cup walnut pieces, 2 tablespoons olive oil, and a pinch of salt. Slice 1 small French baguette into diagonal slices leaving them attached on one side. Spread the garlic-nut paste on 1 side of each slice. Tightly wrap loaf in foil and bake in preheated 375° F. oven for 15 minutes.

Spinach Artichoke Bread

In a skillet, cook the finely chopped white of 1 leek and 1 clove minced garlic in 1 tablespoon olive oil until soft. Add half a 10-ounce package frozen chopped spinach, cooked until almost dry. Season to taste with salt, pepper, and a pinch of mace, remove from heat, and add ¼ cup chopped marinated artichoke hearts. Spoon over ½ pound white-bread dough, storebought or homemade, patted into a 6-by-8-inch rectangle and roll up, jelly roll–style, starting with the 8-inch side. Pinch ends closed, place seam-side down on greased sheet pan, cover with damp towel, and let rise until doubled in bulk. Slash top of loaf with knife, brush with ice water, and bake in a 400° F. preheated oven with a pan of water on the oven floor for 35 to 40 minutes until the bread is crisp and golden on top and bottom. Cool on a rack for 15 minutes, then serve at once.

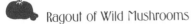

Shrimp on a Stick with Spicy Avocado Sauce

Toss 12 peeled, cleaned jumbo shrimp in 2 tablespoons olive oil mixed with 1 tablespoon lemon juice. Spear 2 shrimp at a time on long-handled skewers and grill over an open fire or broil until shrimp are firm, 1 to 2 minutes per side. Serve with Spicy Avocado Sauce (page 28) as a dip.

Roasted Anchovy Potatoes

Rub oil from 2 ounces anchovy fillets all over 2 large russet potatoes, pierce with a fork, and bake 50 to 60 minutes in 400° F. oven. Meanwhile, mash the anchovies with 2 tablespoons each mayonnaise and olive oil, ½ clove minced garlic, and pepper to taste. When potatoes are ready, split and dollop with the sauce.

Ragout of Wild Mushrooms

Soak ¼ ounce dried morels and ¼ ounce dried chanterelles (or other dried wild mushrooms) in ¾ cup warm water for 30 minutes. Squeeze mushrooms, rinse well, set aside, and strain soaking liq-

uid through cheesecloth or a coffee filter. In a skillet, reduce liquid to a third its volume and set aside. In the same skillet, cook the sliced white of 1 leek in 2 tablespoons butter until soft. Add 2 ounces each stemmed fresh shiitake mushrooms, oyster mushrooms, and sliced white mushrooms along with the soaked mushrooms and cook for 1 minute. Add ½ teaspoon chopped fresh rosemary leaves, 1½ teaspoons chopped fresh parsley, 1 chopped, peeled, and seeded plum tomato, 1 teaspoon lemon juice, and the reduced soaking liquid. Season liberally with salt and pepper. Simmer 2 minutes.

Warm Orange Walnut Spinach Salad

Toss 8 ounces cleaned spinach leaves, ¼ cup thinly sliced red onion, ¼ cup walnut pieces, 1 peeled and sectioned orange, and ½ rib thinly sliced celery. In a saucepan, heat ¼ cup walnut oil, 1½ teaspoons orange juice concentrate, 1½ tablespoons wine vinegar, salt, and a pinch of cayenne until simmering, remove from heat, and stir in 2 tablespoons sour cream. Toss with the salad and serve immediately.

THE MAIN COURSE

Salmon en Papillote with Shrimp and Asparagus

Wrap a 10-ounce salmon fillet, sliced into 6 thin pieces, on one side of a large heart of parchment paper with 1 teaspoon butter, 8 peeled and cleaned baby shrimp, 1 tarragon leaf, 6 asparagus tips, and 2 tablespoons dry white wine. Cover, secure parchment, and bake on a sheet pan in a preheated 350° F. oven for 12 minutes. Serve in the parchment, slitting it open at the table and sliding contents onto a platter. Garnish with 2 lemon wedges.

Grilled Lobster with Red Pepper Coulis

Kill a 2- to 3-pound lobster (page 440) and split in half lengthwise. Sprinkle meat with 2 tablespoons lemon juice, 1 tablespoon olive oil, salt, and pepper. Wrap lobsters in foil and place on a hot grill for 12 minutes for the first pound and 6 minutes for every additional pound, turning halfway through the cooking time. Serve with Red Pepper Coulis (page 25).

 Lobster Bouillabaisse

Boil a 1-pound live lobster in 2 quarts water until bright red, about 12 minutes. Remove and cut into 8 pieces. Add 4 cleaned clams to the water and simmer until they open, remove, and reserve. Peel and clean 8 large shrimp, adding the shells to the water. Boil the water until reduced to 2 cups, strain, and reserve. In a heavy soup pot, cook 1 cup chopped onion, ¼ teaspoon *each* dried thyme, basil, and fennel seed, and 1 clove chopped garlic in 2 tablespoons olive oil until the onion is soft. Add ½ cup white wine, ½ teaspoon saffron threads, 1 bay leaf, and 2 cups crushed tomatoes along with reserved cooking liquid. Bring to a boil, add ¾ pound fish fillets cut into 2-inch strips, and simmer 3 minutes. Add lobster, clams, and shrimp and simmer 2 minutes more. Stir in 2 tablespoons chopped fresh parsley.

 Lobster with Avocado Lobster Salsa

Drop 2 female lobsters, 1½ pounds each, in boiling salted water, bring back to boil, and simmer for 5 minutes. Remove and cool under cold water. Split in half lengthwise with a large butcher knife, and scoop out any red coral from the central cavity. Remove gills and green tomalley and discard. Crumble the coral into Avocado Salsa (page 164)

and reserve. To serve, brush interior of each lobster with 1 teaspoon hot pepper oil and grill or broil for 3 minutes on each side. Fill central cavity with the salsa and serve with a mixture of 4 tablespoons warm melted butter, 1 teaspoon minced fresh hot pepper, and 1 tablespoon lemon juice for dipping.

 Squab Roasted with Garlic and Molasses

In a skillet, cook 2 strips bacon until fat is rendered. Remove and reserve bacon for another use. In the bacon fat, sauté 20 whole cloves garlic until lightly browned. Remove with slotted spoon and drain on paper towel. Mix ¼ cup molasses, 1 tablespoon cider vinegar, salt, and pepper with the remaining bacon fat and brush over the surface of 2 cleaned squabs. Place squabs in nonmetallic roasting pan surrounded by the garlic cloves and roast in preheated 400° F. oven for 25 minutes, basting 3 more times during roasting. Serve birds surrounded by roasted garlic cloves.

EATING IN BED

 Oysters and Caviar

Open 1 dozen large oysters. Serve each with 2 to 3 drops hot pepper sauce, 1 thin lemon wedge, and ⅛ teaspoon caviar. Place on a bed of cracked ice.

 Cold Roasted Cranberry Game Hens

Marinate in refrigerator 2 game hens in ½ cup cranberry juice, 1 tablespoon raspberry vinegar, ¼ cup frozen orange juice concentrate, 1 tablespoon honey, salt, and cayenne pepper for several hours. Remove hens from marinade and roast on a rack in a preheated 400° F. oven for 50 minutes. In a saucepan, reduce marinade by half and baste the hens with it twice in the last 20 minutes. Serve at room temperature, using the remaining marinade as a dip.

Cold Roast Szechuan Chicken

Follow preceding recipe, substituting double recipe of Spicy Hoisin Sauce (page 24) for the cranberry marinade and a 3½ pound chicken for the game hens. Increase roasting time to 1 hour.

Chicken Fingers with Roasted Pepper Dip

Cut ¾ pound boneless and skinless chicken breast into fingers, dust with flour seasoned heavily with salt and cayenne pepper, and deep-fry at 375 ° F. until golden brown. Serve with a dip of 1 large stemmed and seeded roasted red pepper (page 442), ¼ cup basil leaves, 1 clove minced garlic, and 1 tablespoon olive oil chopped together in a food processor.

Baked Brie with Croissants

In an ovenproof dish, bake a 4½-ounce round of brie in preheated 425° F. oven for 10 minutes. Place 4 croissants in the oven and bake 5 minutes more. Remove brie and croissants. Slice off the top of the brie, scraping back any cheese clinging to the skin. Serve the warm, lightly melted cheese surrounded by the croissants. Scoop up spoonfuls of cheese and spread on the croissants.

Shrimp Marinated in Wine and Lemon

In a saucepan, bring to a simmer 12 cleaned jumbo shrimp, 2 cloves thinly sliced garlic, sliced whites of ½ bunch scallions, 2 tablespoons white wine, and 1 tablespoon extra-virgin olive oil. As soon as the liquid begins to bubble, toss the shrimp for 1 minute. Remove from heat and add 1 tablespoon olive oil, 2 tablespoons lemon juice, a pinch of cayenne pepper, salt, and pepper. Transfer to a serving bowl and refrigerate. Serve with toothpicks.

Fillet Steak Sandwich with Bearnaise

In a skillet, cook 6 thinly sliced large mushrooms in 2 tablespoons unsalted butter until soft, remove from heat, and keep warm. Season two 4-ounce fillet steaks with salt and pepper and grill or broil to desired doneness. While steaks are cooking, reduce 2 minced shallots, ½ teaspoon dried tarragon, 2½ tablespoons white wine vinegar, and ¼ cup white wine in a small saucepan to 2 tablespoons liquid. In top of small double boiler set over simmering water, whisk the reduced liquid into 2 small egg yolks until fluffy and thick. Remove from heat and beat in 4 to 6 tablespoons melted butter. Spoon mushrooms over bottoms of 2 split French bread dinner rolls. Place 1 steak on each, top with sauce, and garnish each with 1 sprig tarragon.

SWEET SEDUCTION AND LOVE TOKENS

Melon Filled with Port

Cut a plug from the stem end of 1 small cantaloupe, large enough for a soup spoon to fit through. Remove the plug and scrape away any seeds clinging to its underside. Scoop out and discard seeds from interior. Fill cavity with ¾ cup red seedless grapes and ½ cup ruby port, then replace plug. Set melon in a bowl with plug facing up and refrigerate for several hours. To serve, cut melon in half and serve each half filled with the grapes and a few tablespoons of the port.

Honeydew Filled with Champagne

Follow preceding recipe, using 1 honeydew instead of the cantaloupe, 1 cup raspberries instead of grapes, and ½ cup champagne instead of port.

 Chocolate Butter

Cream 4 tablespoons butter and beat in 1 ounce cooled melted semisweet chocolate. Pour into a small ramekin and chill until firm. Serve with 2 warm brioches or croissants.

 Spicy Brown-Sugar Butter

Cream together 4 tablespoons butter, 1 tablespoon brown sugar, ¼ teaspoon ground cinnamon, and a pinch *each* of ground allspice and ginger. Spread on warm cinnamon rolls.

 Orange Saffron Honey

Combine 10 threads saffron and 2 tablespoons warm orange liqueur, then blend in ½ cup honey. Drizzle over fruit or spread on bread or biscuits.

 Hot Pepper Honey

Blend ¼ cup honey with 2½ teaspoons hot pepper sauce. Serve with corn muffins, corn cakes, or warm biscuits.

 Lemon Ginger Honey

Blend 2 tablespoons minced candied ginger, 2 tablespoons honey, and 1 teaspoon lemon juice. Serve on muffins, biscuits, or buns.

 Berries with Framboise Honey

Blend 1 tablespoon framboise with 2 tablespoons honey. Use as a dip for 1 pint cleaned berries.

 Champagne Granita

In a saucepan, bring 1 cup sugar, 1¼ cups water, and 2 tablespoons raspberry vinegar to a boil without stirring. Remove from heat and cool. Add a pinch of salt and ½ cup champagne. Pour into a shallow pan and set in the freezer. After 1 hour, stir the ice crystals forming at the edge of the pan into the more liquid portions. Continue to freeze, stirring every 30 minutes until the whole mixture is a firm slush, about 3 hours. Pour into champagne flutes and eat with a spoon.

 Margarita Water Ice

Follow preceding recipe, substituting lime juice for the vinegar. Replace champagne with 3 tablespoons tequila, 1 tablespoon Triple Sec, and ¼ cup water. Serve in glasses with rims moistened and dipped in salt.

 Mimosa Sorbet

Blend 1 cup chilled Simple Syrup (page 436), 1 cup orange juice, the juice of 1 lemon, 1 tablespoon wine vinegar, ½ cup champagne, ½ cup water, 1 tablespoon brandy, and 1 beaten egg white. Cool and freeze in an ice-cream freezer according to the manufacturer's directions. Makes 1½ pints.

 Soft Irish Ice Cream

Scald 1 cup milk, ½ cup sugar, ½ teaspoon salt, and ½ vanilla bean. With an electric mixer, beat 3

egg yolks and ½ cup sugar, add scalded milk in a slow, steady stream, return to low heat, and cook until mixture coats a spoon; don't overcook. Remove from heat and cool. Add 3 tablespoons Irish whiskey and 1 cup heavy cream and chill in a tightly closed container in the freezer for 2 hours. Freeze in an ice-cream freezer according to manufacturer's directions until consistency of soft ice cream. Serve sprinkled with a bit of ground cinnamon.

Raspberry Chocolate Bombe

Press 1 quart softened raspberry sherbet into a frozen 8-cup metal bowl so it forms a ½-inch-thick shell. Line with plastic wrap to hold in place and freeze until firm, at least 1 hour. Remove plastic. Sprinkle 2 ounces shaved semisweet chocolate over the sherbet, fill center with 2 cups softened chocolate ice cream, cover with plastic, and freeze overnight. To unmold, dip in warm water for 10 seconds and invert onto a platter. Serve with any chocolate sauce (some of ours are in Chapter 47). Serves 8.

Espresso Anise Bombe

Dissolve 1 tablespoon instant espresso in 1½ teaspoons warm milk. Add 1½ tablespoons coffee-flavored liqueur and beat into 2 cups softened coffee ice cream. Freeze in small covered container. Blend 1 tablespoon anise-flavored liqueur and ¼ teaspoon anise extract in 1½ cups softened vanilla ice cream. Freeze in small covered container. Follow preceding recipe, using the frozen coffee mixture for the outer shell and the frozen anise mixture for the center filling. Omit the raspberries.

Coeur à la Crème

Blend 1 ounce cream cheese, ¼ pound ricotta cheese, ⅛ teaspoon salt, and 1 tablespoon confec-

tioners' sugar, fold in ½ cup whipped cream, and spoon into two ½-cup *coeur à la crème* molds lined with damp cheesecloth. Cover with plastic, weight lightly and refrigerate in a pan to drain overnight. Invert onto plates. Toss 6 halved strawberries with 1 teaspoon honey and 1½ teaspoons orange liqueur, pour excess honey mixture over all, and top with the berries.

Warm Pink Pear Purée

In a heavy saucepan combine 1½ pounds coarsely chopped pears, ¼ cup sugar, 1 tablespoon lemon juice, 1 cup red wine, 1 split vanilla bean, and a pinch of salt, and bring to a boil. Simmer 8 to 10 minutes, until pears are tender. Remove the pears and purée in a food processor or blender. Reduce pan liquid until lightly thickened, remove the vanilla bean, and add the reduced liquid to the purée along with 2 tablespoons butter. Serve warm.

Sinful Chocolate Tartlets

Melt 2 ounces semisweet chocolate and 2 tablespoons sugar in double boiler over simmering water. Gradually whisk in ⅓ cup scalded heavy cream and cook for 15 minutes, scraping sides occasionally with rubber spatula. Remove from heat and chill the chocolate over ice until cool to the touch. Pour into 4 prebaked (3-inch) tartlet shells made from Sweet Pastry (page 434) and chill until set.

Peaches in Chianti

Blanch 2 large perfectly ripe peaches, peel, and slice into thin wedges. Pour ¾ cup Chianti Classico over top and chill for 30 minutes.

Warm Peaches with Sesame Praline

In a small heavy saucepan, melt ¼ cup sugar until it turns amber, stirring frequently. Stir in ½ cup toasted sesame seeds and turn out onto a cookie sheet. Spread as thin as possible with the back of a spoon and allow to cool to room temperature. Break into pieces and grind to a fine powder in a food processor. Heat 2 blanched, peeled, and sliced ripe peaches over moderate heat for 30 seconds, add 1 tablespoon sugar, and toss. Add 2 tablespoons white wine and simmer for 1 minute. Flavor with a dash of vanilla extract and serve warm topped with a generous sprinkling of the sesame praline powder.

Grand Marnier White Chocolate Truffles

In a saucepan set over low heat, melt 1 tablespoon butter with ½ cup heavy cream. Remove from heat, add 8 ounces finely chopped white chocolate, stirring until melted, then transfer to a bowl and whisk in ¼ cup Grand Marnier. Refrigerate several hours to firm. Shape into rough tablespoon-size balls, place on a sheet pan, and freeze until solid. Dip into 4 ounces melted bittersweet chocolate, place on wax paper, and refrigerate until chocolate sets. Makes 1 dozen.

Praline Lace Hearts

Mix ¾ cup sugar, ½ cup quick-cooking oats, ½ cup finely chopped pecans, and ¾ cup flour sifted with ½ teaspoon baking powder. Combine 10 tablespoons melted butter, ¼ cup milk, ¼ cup dark corn syrup, and ¼ teaspoon almond extract and mix into dry mixture. Using 2 teaspoons batter, form a V shape on a greased sheet pan; each line of the V should be about 1½ inches long. Make a total of five Vs about 3 inches apart. Bake in a preheated 350° F. oven until well browned around the edges, 10 to 12 minutes, rotating the pan once during baking. Let cool about 2 minutes, remove from pan with a wide spatula, and cool completely on a rack.

Fifty Main Courses on a Real Tight Budget

Good food doesn't have to cost a lot. You could bust a gut on pasta without breaking a buck, drown in chowder without jumping tax brackets, or eat your fill of chili and have enough cash left over to retain your own private gastroenterologist.

Too often we elevate a food's status to match its price, as if the cost of caviar defines its sensual charm or the rarity of a truffle elevates the prestige of the cook who slices it.

To the contrary, frequently the best food is also the cheapest. Budget-priced chuck has more beefy flavor than top-of-the-line fillet. A main-course soup fills the belly with heartwarming goodness as it fills your larder with a week's worth of meals. Sausages or meatballs paired with braised vegetables make low-cost stews, and curry or chili powder provides a wealth of flavor with little more than a pot of rice or beans and a handful of other spices.

To prove our point, we have come up with 50 recipes that cost us about 50 cents a serving to prepare—with the help of the right sales at the right time. Please grant us some literary license

here; obviously, inflation will eventually overtake all these calculations, and we admit that the 50-cent limit is arbitrary and has more to do with extending our "50 ways" theme than with strict kitchen economics. The main point is that all the recipes below are guaranteed to be delicious, to be inventive, and to fit well within a modest budget.

ABOUT THESE RECIPES

All recipes make 4 servings unless otherwise noted.

 Chili-Baked Chicken Drumsticks

In a large bowl, mix 1 tablespoon chili powder, 1 teaspoon ground cumin, 1 tablespoon hot paprika, ½ teaspoon oregano, ½ teaspoon salt, and ¼ teaspoon freshly ground pepper in ¼ cup boiling water and cool. Mix in 1 beaten egg, 1 tablespoon ketchup, and 1 teaspoon hot pepper sauce. Add 2 pounds chicken drumsticks, toss, and marinate in refrigerator at least 1 hour. Remove from marinade and coat with 1 cup bread crumbs. Bake at 350° F. for 50 minutes.

 ### Pungent Orange Turkey Meatballs

Mix 1 pound ground turkey, 2 tablespoons minced onion, 2 cloves minced garlic, 1 tablespoon ketchup, 1 teaspoon mustard, 1 egg, 2 tablespoons seasoned bread crumbs, salt, and pepper. Form into 24 meatballs and simmer in 2 cups chicken stock until the meatballs are firm. In a skillet, cook 2 slices bacon until crisp. Remove from pan and crumble. Brown meatballs on all sides in the hot fat. Add a pinch *each* of ground ginger and cayenne pepper, ⅓ cup orange juice, 1 tablespoon honey, 2 teaspoons soy sauce, and 1 tablespoon rice wine vinegar. Simmer 2 minutes. Dissolve 1 teaspoon cornstarch in 1 tablespoon water. Stir into sauce until thickened. Add crumbled bacon.

 ### Cranberry Turkey Burgers

Mix 1 pound ground turkey, 2 tablespoons minced onion, 2 cloves minced garlic, 1 tablespoon ketchup, 1 teaspoon mustard, 1 egg, 2 tablespoons seasoned bread crumbs, salt, and pepper. Form into 4 burgers and brown on both sides in 1 tablespoon hot oil in a skillet. Add a pinch *each* of ground ginger and cayenne pepper and 1 cup chicken stock. Boil until stock has reduced to 1 tablespoon. Flip burgers and add 2 tablespoons orange juice, ⅓ cup whole-berry cranberry sauce, 2 teaspoons soy sauce, and 1 tablespoon cider vinegar. Simmer for 2 minutes, until sauce thickens lightly.

 ### Garlicky Pasta Primavera

In a skillet, cook the whites of 6 scallions in 1 tablespoon olive oil over low heat until soft. Add 3 cloves minced garlic and 8 sliced mushrooms. Cook until slightly softened. Add ½ cup defrosted baby peas, 1 cup defrosted baby carrots, 1 cup defrosted broccoli florets and1 diced roasted red bell pepper (page 442). Heat through. Add 2 tablespoons chopped fresh parsley, salt, and pepper. Toss with 12 ounces hot cooked pasta and 2 tablespoons grated Parmesan.

 ### Fettuccine with Ricotta and Spinach

In a skillet, cook 10 ounces defrosted chopped spinach, 1 clove minced garlic, ¼ cup minced onion, and a pinch of crushed red pepper in 3 tablespoons olive oil until dry. Season with salt and pepper to taste. Set aside in a bowl. Mix 1 cup ricotta cheese with 1 egg white and add to bowl. Toss 1 pound hot cooked fettuccine with spinach-cheese mixture.

 ### Corn, Black Beans, and Roasted Tomato Salad

Place 2 large tomatoes over an open flame and turn until their skins char and blister all over. Run under cold water to remove skin. Core, seed, and cut into bite-size pieces. Toss with 2 cups cooked corn kernels and 1 cup cooked black beans. In a saucepan, heat with 1 cup Lime Vinaigrette (page 296) until simmering, and toss with rinsed and dried leaves from 1 head *each* escarole and curly endive.

 ### Corn and Lentil Salad

Toss 2 cups *each* cooked lentils and corn kernels and the sliced whites of 4 scallions, ½ cucumber cut in dice, 1 diced roasted bell pepper (page 442), 1 cup chunky salsa, 2 tablespoons olive oil, 2 tablespoons lime juice, salt, and pepper.

Fifty Ways to Cook Most Everything

 Pasta with Garlic and Pea Beans

Sauté 2 tablespoons minced onion, 1 teaspoon dried basil, and 1 clove minced garlic in ¼ cup olive oil for 30 seconds. Add 2 cups cooked pea beans, ¼ teaspoon crushed red pepper flakes, salt, pepper, and 1 tablespoon chopped fresh parsley. Heat through. Toss with 12 ounces hot cooked small macaroni of any shape.

 Tortellini with Roasted Vegetables

Slice 1 small zucchini and 1 small yellow squash lengthwise and slice ½ small eggplant and 1 tomato in rounds, brush with olive oil, and season with salt and pepper to taste. Grill 2 to 4 minutes on each side until lightly browned and tender, then dice all the vegetables. Toss 12 ounces hot cooked cheese tortellini with 3 tablespoons olive oil, ¼ cup finely chopped fresh basil, ½ teaspoon crushed red pepper, 2 tablespoons grated Parmesan, the roasted vegetables, salt, and pepper.

 Roasted Shallot Frittata

Break 2 ounces shallots and 1 large head garlic into cloves and toss with ½ teaspoon olive oil and salt. Place in a microwave-safe pan and microwave at full power for 4 minutes, until tender. Slice ends from each clove, peel and reserve. Beat 10 eggs until frothy with a dash of cayenne pepper, salt, and pepper. Heat 1 teaspoon olive oil for 30 seconds in a 10-inch iron skillet. Add eggs and cook until set across the bottom. Scatter shallots and garlic over top and broil until puffed and brown, about 2 minutes.

 Fried Potato Frittata

Cut 2 russet potatoes into thin slices and sauté in ¼ cup peanut oil with ½ sliced onion in a 10-inch skillet. Season liberally with salt and pepper. Beat 10 eggs until frothy with a dash of cayenne pepper, salt, and pepper. Add to skillet and cook until eggs set across bottom. Broil until puffed and brown, about 2 minutes.

 Potatoes with Anchovies and Tomatoes

Boil 2 pounds peeled russet potatoes for 12 to 15 minutes, until barely tender. Meanwhile, in a skillet, cook 4 skinned and chopped large tomatoes in 2 tablespoons olive oil with 1 clove minced garlic for 5 minutes. Add 2 tablespoons chopped anchovy fillets. Slice potatoes and layer with the tomato mixture in a 2-quart casserole, top with ¼ cup grated Parmesan, and bake in a preheated 400° F. oven for 40 minutes.

 Sautéed Potatoes with Garden Vegetables

In a skillet, sauté 2 pounds scrubbed and thinly sliced russet potatoes, blotted to absorb surface moisture, in 3 tablespoons hot olive oil, tossing occasionally until brown and tender, about 20 minutes. Add ¼ cup *each* diced zucchini, yellow squash, mushrooms, red bell pepper, and carrots and sauté 5 minutes more, until vegetables are tender. Season with salt, pepper, and a dash of nutmeg. Toss with 1 clove minced garlic and 1 tablespoon chopped fresh parsley at the end of cooking.

 Orzo with Peas and Rosemary

Cook ¾ cup chopped onion, 1 clove minced garlic, and 2 teaspoons fresh rosemary leaves in 2 tablespoons butter in a large saucepan until soft. Add 1½ cups orzo and toss to coat. Stir in 3 cups hot chicken stock, salt and pepper. Simmer for 8 minutes. Mix in 10 ounces defrosted peas. Simmer 4 to

5 minutes more until all the stock has been absorbed. Finish with 1 tablespoon finely chopped fresh parsley.

Brown Rice with Red Beans

In a saucepan, cook ½ cup finely chopped onion and ⅓ cup finely diced bell pepper in 2 tablespoons butter until soft. Add 1 cup long-grain brown rice and coat with butter. Add 3 cups water or stock and bring to a boil, reduce the heat, cover, and simmer 45 minutes. Add 1 cup cooked or canned kidney beans, 1 cup hot salsa, and 1 to 2 tablespoons chopped fresh cilantro. Toss lightly.

Mixed Grilled Vegetables with Hummus

Toss 1 *each* large red and yellow pepper cut into 6 spears, 1 zucchini and 1 yellow squash cut in large chunks, 1 large sweet onion cut in wedges, 1 large tomato, sliced, and 12 large stemmed mushrooms in 1 cup Oil and Vinegar Dressing (page 296). Marinate for 1 hour. Meanwhile, process until smooth 1 drained (10-ounce) can chick-peas, 1 clove garlic, the juice of ½ lemon, 3 tablespoons olive oil, 1 tablespoon tahini, salt, and hot pepper sauce. Grill or broil vegetables until browned and tender. (Onion needs about 12 minutes; peppers, squash, and mushrooms, 6 to 8 minutes; tomatoes, 4 minutes). Garnish marinade with 1 tablespoon toasted sesame seeds, and serve with vegetables.

Turkey Mushroom Sloppy Joes

In a skillet, cook ½ cup *each* chopped onion, diced celery, and diced green pepper, and 1 cup diced mushrooms in 3 tablespoons corn oil until soft. Add 1 pound ground turkey and brown lightly. Add ¼ cup beef broth, 3 tablespoons ketchup, and

1 teaspoon hot pepper sauce, simmer 1 minute, and serve on 4 toasted hamburger buns.

Braised Turkey Legs

In a skillet, brown 2 small turkey legs, cut into thighs and drumsticks, in 1 tablespoon butter melted with 1 tablespoon olive oil. Add 1 chopped onion, 2 cloves minced garlic, 1 rib chopped celery, 1 diced carrot, ½ teaspoon dried thyme leaves, ½ teaspoon dried marjoram, 1 bay leaf, ¼ teaspoon oregano leaves, a pinch of nutmeg, a pinch of cloves, and ½ teaspoon dry mustard and cook until vegetables soften. Stir in 2 tablespoons flour and cook 1 minute more. Add 2 cups hot chicken stock, stir to mix, and simmer, covered, for 35 minutes. Add 2 tablespoons chopped fresh parsley and cook 10 minutes more. Remove bay leaf.

Turkey and Brown Rice

Follow preceding recipe, but omit flour, add 1 cup brown rice, and increase stock to 3 cups.

Tuscan Chicken Legs

Cut 1 onion, 1 rib celery, and 2 carrots in large chunks and cook in a skillet in 3 tablespoons oil with 2 ounces ham, cut in chunks, and 2 cloves minced garlic until vegetables soften. Remove and reserve. Add 2 pounds thighs and drumsticks to the pan and brown. Add ½ cup red wine, ¼ teaspoon freshly grated nutmeg, salt, and pepper. Simmer until chicken is tender and most of the wine has reduced, about 45 minutes. Return vegetables to pan, heat through, and adjust seasoning.

Teriyaki Burgers

Mix ½ pound *each* ground turkey and beef, ¼ teaspoon ground ginger, salt, pepper, and 2 tablespoons light soy sauce. Form into burgers and grill or pan-fry to desired doneness. As each side is browned, brush with mixture of ¼ cup soy sauce, 3 tablespoons honey, and 1 teaspoon hot pepper sauce, cooking each side for another minute after glazing it. Serve on 4 buns each topped with 1 tablespoon bean sprouts and 1 slice tomato.

 ## Mushroom Strudel

In a skillet, cook 1 chopped onion and 2 cloves minced garlic in 2 tablespoons butter until soft. Add 1½ pounds cleaned and chopped mushrooms, 1 teaspoon dried thyme leaves, a pinch of rubbed sage, salt, and pepper and cook for 5 minutes more. Add ½ cup white wine and simmer until most evaporates. Let cool. Brush 4 sheets defrosted phyllo dough with 1 tablespoon melted butter and lay one on top of the other. Place half the mushroom mixture in a line parallel to a short edge and roll dough around filling. It should look like a large cigar. Roll another with 4 more phyllo sheets, more melted butter, and the remaining filling. Brush both with melted butter and bake on a sheet pan at 400 ° F. for 35 minutes. Cut each strudel in half and serve with a tomato pasta sauce.

 ## Tuna Strudel

Follow preceding recipe, using only ½ pound mushrooms, dried dill weed instead of thyme, and dried tarragon instead of sage. After wine has evaporated, add 1 (6-ounce) can drained and crumbled water-packed tuna. Sauce is optional.

 ## Potatoes au Gratin with Three Cheeses

Butter an 8-inch square baking pan. Peel and slice 1¼ pounds russet potatoes and 1 small onion. Mix 2 ounces each shredded mozzarella and Swiss cheese and 1 ounce grated Parmesan. Place a third of the potato slices in the pan, season with salt and pepper, and top with half the onion and a third of the cheeses. Make another layer of potatoes, salt, and pepper, the remaining onion, and another portion of cheese. Finish with remaining potatoes and cheese. Pour 1 cup milk over top, dot with 2 teaspoons butter, cover, and bake at 400° F. for 40 minutes. Remove cover and bake another 15 minutes.

 ## Brown Rice with Three Cheeses

Follow preceding recipe, substituting Brown Rice Pilaf (page 241) for the potatoes and onion.

 ## Sweet and Sour Stuffed Red Cabbage

In a skillet, cook ¼ cup finely chopped onion, 2 cloves minced garlic, 1 peeled, cored, and diced Granny Smith apple, and 1 rib diced celery in 1 tablespoon butter until soft. Add ½ teaspoon dried thyme, 1 tablespoon chopped fresh parsley, salt, and pepper. Stir in 2 cups cooked long-grain rice. Place 2 tablespoons of this filling in each of 12 large blanched red cabbage leaves. Fold loosely around filling and secure ends with a toothpick. Place close together in a casserole. Bring ¼ cup ketchup, ¼ cup honey, 3 tablespoons apple cider vinegar, 1 tablespoon Worcestershire sauce, 1 cup chicken stock, ½ cup apple juice, salt, and pepper to a boil. Pour over cabbage, cover, and bake 1 hour at 350° F.

 ## Sausage Stuffed Cabbage

Follow preceding recipe, but use green cabbage leaves instead of red and add ½ pound cooked crumbled sausage with the onion.

Cabbage Stuffed with Orzo and Cheese

In a skillet, cook 3 tablespoons finely chopped onion and 2 cloves minced garlic in 2 tablespoons olive oil until soft. Add 1 tablespoon chopped fresh dill weed, 1 tablespoon chopped fresh parsley, a pinch of cayenne pepper, salt, pepper, and 1½ cups hot cooked orzo. Mix in 3 tablespoons ricotta cheese and 3 tablespoons grated Parmesan. Divide filling among 8 large blanched cabbage leaves, wrap like packages, and secure ends with toothpicks. Place snugly in a baking pan, pour ½ cup white wine, the juice of ½ lemon, and ½ cup water over top, cover, and bake 1 hour at 350° F.

 ### Bell Peppers Stuffed with Macaroni and Cheese

Prepare filling from Cabbage Stuffed with Orzo and Cheese (above), using 3 cups hot cooked small elbow macaroni instead of orzo. Cut ¼ pound Cheddar cheese in small dice. Cut around the stems of 4 large bell peppers, remove stems with the attached cores, and wipe out any stray seeds. Place a few cheese cubes in each pepper, fill halfway with the macaroni mixture, add a few more cheese cubes, more pasta, another cheese cube, and top with pasta. Pack a casserole small enough to hold the peppers upright, pour ½ cup chicken broth over top, and cover. Bake for 45 minutes at 350° F., uncover, and bake another 15 minutes.

 ### No-Fuss No-Crust Macaroni and Cheese

Cook ½ pound macaroni until *al dente*. Toss in a 2-quart casserole with 2 tablespoons butter and a dash of cayenne pepper. Mix ⅓ cup milk, 1 egg, and 1 teaspoon brown mustard and stir in ¼ pound shredded Cheddar cheese, salt, and pepper. Bake at 350° F. for 10 minutes. Add ¼ pound more shredded Cheddar and mix well. Bake 10 minutes more.

 ### Crusty Macaroni and Cheese

In a 2-quart casserole, mix ½ pound cooked and cooled macaroni, 1 cup Béchamel Sauce (page 429), 1 teaspoon prepared mustard, a dash of cayenne pepper, ½ pound shredded sharp Cheddar cheese, and salt and pepper to taste. Top with ¼ cup grated Parmesan mixed with 2 tablespoons bread crumbs, dot with 1 tablespoon butter, and bake at 375° F. for 30 minutes.

 ### Rolled-Up Lasagna

Mix 2 cups drained ricotta cheese, 1 egg, ¼ cup grated Parmesan, salt, and pepper. Spread cheese mixture over each of 8 cooked lasagna noodles and roll, as you would a sleeping bag. Place on end, side side by side, in an oiled baking dish, cover with 2 cups meat-flavored pasta sauce, cover, and bake at 350° F. for 50 minutes.

 ### Stuffed Shells

Follow preceding recipe, substituting 12 cooked jumbo shells for the lasagna noodles and filling shells with the cheese mixture.

Eggplant Rollatini

Peel and slice 1 large eggplant, lengthwise, into thin slices, brush with 2 tablespoons olive oil, and grill until tender. Prepare cheese filling from Rolled-Up Lasagna (above). Place ¼ cup filling in the center of a slice and roll eggplant around it. Place rolls side by side in an oiled baking dish and cover with 2 cups tomato pasta sauce. Cover and bake at 350° F. for 40 minutes.

Grilled Smoked Sausage with Hot Apple Chutney

In a skillet, cook ⅓ cup finely chopped onion, ¼ teaspoon *each* crushed red pepper flakes and dried thyme, ½ teaspoon *each* curry powder and ground cinnamon, and a pinch of ground clove in 2 tablespoons peanut oil until the onion is soft. Add 2 peeled, seeded, and diced Granny Smith apples, ¼ cup apple cider vinegar, 2 tablespoons brown sugar, salt, pepper, and ⅓ cup raisins. Cover and simmer for 15 minutes. Grill or broil 8 smoked sausage links until brown and crisp and serve on 8 hot dog rolls with the warm chutney.

 ### Knockwurst Simmered in Beer with Sauerkraut

In a saucepan, cook 2 chopped slices bacon until almost crisp. Add 1 sliced onion, 2 pounds rinsed and drained sauerkraut, 2 teaspoons brown sugar, and 1 pint dark beer, bring to a boil, and add 8 knockwurst. Cover and simmer until knockwurst is plump and most of the beer has been absorbed, about 15 minutes.

 ### Hot Dog Nuggets

Mix together 1 cup flour, 1 teaspoon baking powder, ½ teaspoon baking soda. ¼ teaspoon salt, 1 tablespoon yellow mustard, 1 egg and 1 cup buttermilk until smooth and thick. Cut 6 hot dogs into 4 sections each and toss into batter. Deep-fry in small batches in several inches of 375° F. oil until golden brown. Dip into barbecue sauce or honey mustard.

 ### Sweet and Sour Hot Sausage Potato Salad

In a skillet, brown ½ pound sliced hot sausage. Add 5 tablespoons cider vinegar and 3 tablespoons sugar and heat until the sugar dissolves. Transfer to a salad bowl and add 1 finely chopped small onion, 1 teaspoon salt, pepper, 1 tablespoon ketchup, and 3 tablespoons mayonnaise. Boil 1½ pounds peeled red-skin potatoes in salt water, drain, quarter and add to the salad bowl, along with 2 ribs diced celery and 2 tablespoons chopped fresh parsley. Toss well.

 ### Potato and Tuna Vinaigrette

Boil 1½ pounds peeled red-skin potatoes in salt water, drain, quarter, and keep warm. In a saucepan, bring 2 cloves minced garlic, ½ cup white wine, and ¼ teaspoon crushed red pepper flakes to a boil and reduce to 2 tablespoons. Add ¼ cup olive oil, 2 tablespoons wine vinegar, 2 tablespoons chopped fresh dill weed, 2 tablespoons chopped olives, and 1 can (6-ounce) drained water-packed tuna. Toss with the potatoes and 1 tablespoon chopped fresh parsley.

 ### Bacon and Potato Soufflé

Bake 1¼ pounds Idaho potatoes until tender, then skin and mash. In a skillet, brown 6 slices bacon, remove, and crumble. Cook 1 cup chopped onion in the hot fat until soft. Add the potatoes and mix in 1½ cups heated milk, ½ cup at a time. Season with 1 teaspoon salt, ¼ teaspoon pepper, and a pinch *each* cayenne pepper and grated nutmeg. Add 6 egg yolks, 1 at a time, and ¼ cup shredded Cheddar cheese along with reserved bacon. Cool to room temperature. Beat 6 egg whites with a pinch of cream of tartar to a soft peak and gently fold into potatoes in 2 additions. Turn into a greased and floured 2-quart soufflé dish and bake at 450° F. for 20 minutes, reduce oven temperature to 350° F., and bake another 20 minutes. Serve immediately. Serves 6.

Cheddar Corn Soufflé

In a skillet, cook 1 cup onion, 1 clove minced garlic, 1 rib diced celery, and ½ cup diced bell pepper in 1 tablespoon butter until soft. Add 1 cup cornmeal, ½ cup boiling water, and 1 cup milk. Cook until mixture is smooth and thick. Season with ⅛ teaspoon cayenne pepper, a pinch of nutmeg, salt, pepper, and ⅔ cup shredded sharp Cheddar cheese. Add 6 egg yolks, 1 at a time, and cool to room temperature. Beat 6 egg whites with a pinch of cream of tartar to a soft peak and gently fold into mixture in 3 additions. Turn into a greased and floured 2-quart soufflé dish, bake at 450° F. for 20 minutes, reduce oven temperature to 350° F., and bake another 20 minutes. Serve immediately. Serves 6.

Bacon Breakfast Cookie

With an electric mixer, beat ¼ pound softened butter, 1½ cups chunky peanut butter, and 1⅓ cups brown sugar until creamy. Beat in 3 eggs. Add 1 tablespoon baking soda dissolved in 2 teaspoons strong coffee, then pour over 4½ cups quick-cooking oats, 4 crumbled slices crisp bacon, 1 cup unsalted dry-roasted peanuts, and 1 cup raisins. Mix to moisten. Drop in ¼-cup mounds 2½ inches apart on greased cookie sheets. Bake at 350° F. for 21 minutes per batch, cool on the pan for 2 minutes and transfer to cooling racks. Makes 2 dozen or 12 servings.

Whole-Grain Breakfast Cookie

Follow preceding recipe, replacing 2½ cups of the oats with 1 cup rye flakes, 1 cup bran cereal, and ½ cup toasted wheat germ. Eliminate the bacon.

Peanut Butter Raisin Bran Breakfast Cookie

Follow the recipe for Bacon Breakfast Cookie (above), substituting vanilla extract for the coffee and raisin bran for the oats. Eliminate the bacon.

Smoky Vegetable Chowder

Cook ½ cup chopped onion, 1 peeled and diced potato, 1 peeled and diced carrot, 1 diced rib celery, ¼ diced red pepper, and 4 ounces diced smoked turkey breast in 1 tablespoon oil until vegetables are soft. Add ½ pound sliced mushrooms, ½ teaspoon dried thyme, ¼ teaspoon *each* dried marjoram and crumbled rosemary, and 1 bay leaf. Cook for 2 minutes. Add 1 quart chicken stock, salt, and pepper and simmer for 20 minutes. Remove bay leaf. Dissolve 1½ teaspoons cornstarch in ½ cup milk. Stir into the soup and simmer for 2 minutes more. Adjust seasoning.

Lemon Lamb Soup with Oatmeal

In a saucepan, brown ½ pound cubed lamb shoulder in 2 tablespoons oil along with 2 *each* peeled and sliced carrots and celery ribs, and 1 diced onion. Mix in 1 tablespoon minced lemon zest, 3 cloves minced garlic, 1 teaspoon ground coriander, and a pinch *each* of ground ginger and crushed red pepper flakes. Add 2 cups water, 2 cups beef broth, and the juice of 1 lemon. Season with salt and pepper and simmer for 45 minutes. Add ⅓ cup old-fashioned oats to the broth in a slow stream, stir, and simmer 15 minutes more, until the oatmeal is tender but not mushy. Stir in ¼ cup chopped fresh parsley.

 ### Lamb and Mushroom Barley Soup

In a saucepan, brown ½ pound cubed lamb shoulder in 2 tablespoons oil along with ½ pound sliced mushrooms, 2 each peeled and sliced carrots and ribs celery, and 1 diced onion. Add 3 cloves minced garlic, 1 teaspoon ground coriander, ½ teaspoon crumbled rosemary, and a pinch of crushed red pepper flakes. Mix. Add 2 cups water, 2 cups beef broth, 1 bay leaf, ½ cup pearl barley, 1 tablespoon tomato paste, salt, and pepper and simmer for 1 hour. Remove bay leaf. Stir in ¼ cup chopped fresh parsley.

 ### Spicy Black Bean Soup

Soak 2 cups black beans. Drain. In a saucepan, cook 4 minced slices bacon until crisp. Add 2 cloves minced garlic and 2 stemmed, seeded, and chopped fresh chili peppers and cook until soft. Add 6 cups chicken stock and the beans. Simmer for 1½ hours. Meanwhile in a skillet, cook 1 cup chopped onion, 2 diced carrots, and 2 diced celery ribs in 2 tablespoons butter until soft. Add ½ finely diced red pepper and 2 tablespoons grated orange zest, cook another 2 minutes, and add to the soup. Serves 6 to 8.

 ### Potato Fennel Vichyssoise

In a saucepan, cook 1 finely chopped onion, the chopped white of 1 large leek, ½ diced fennel bulb, and 1½ teaspoons ground fennel seed in 3 tablespoons butter until soft. Add 1½ pounds peeled and diced russet potatoes and toss to coat. Add 3 cups chicken stock, ½ to 1 teaspoon salt, ½ teaspoon white pepper, and a grating of nutmeg. Cook until potatoes are soft. In a food processor or blender, process until almost smooth, then chill. Thin with 1 cup milk, ½ cup buttermilk, and ½ cup half-and-half before serving. Garnish with ¼ cup chopped fresh chives.

 ### Yam, Leek, and Bacon Soup

In a skillet, brown ¼ pound diced rindless slab bacon, remove, and blot off fat with paper towels. In the same skillet, cook 1 finely chopped onion and chopped white of 3 leeks in the hot fat until soft. Add 2 pounds peeled and diced sweet potatoes and toss to coat. Add 4 cups chicken stock, 1 to 2 teaspoons salt, ½ teaspoon white pepper, and a grating of nutmeg. Cook until potatoes are soft. Puree in a food processor. Return bacon to the soup and thin with 1 cup milk. Heat through.

Fifty Wonderful Muffins

Muffins. The word alone stirs an immediate response, bringing back a flood of memories. Phantoms of fragrances swirl in the mind as we remember the flavors—apple, walnut, buttermilk, blueberry, cornmeal, bran—that made the prospect of a warm muffin in the morning reason enough to wake.

It's not surprising that homemade muffins are so much a part of our collective past, for American cookbooks are full of muffin recipes, both savory and sweet. But they've changed over the years. Originally leavened with yeast and baked on griddles, like English muffins, today's muffins are more likely to be leavened with baking soda and baking powder and to have a high proportion of liquid to dry ingredients. The result is something closer to a miniature cake than to a bread. Load them up with fruit and nuts, and they're almost confections.

How a muffin's ingredients go together determines the type of muffin you'll end up with. Fats in the batter (such as butter or oil) produce a flaky, crumbly texture, while eggs make a muffin chewier. Although most muffin recipes call for both, one usually dominates. Muffins that start by beating sugar into butter and then adding egg will turn out cakier. Those in which sugar is beaten with egg, then melted butter added, will be more elastic. So if you're baking muffins with a chewy ingredient, such as dried fruit, a cakelike batter works best. But bran, which tends to make baked goods crumble, is better with an egg-based batter.

The only substantial differences between a muffin and a cake are that muffins aren't as sweet and aren't as big, resulting in a drier interior, a crisper crust, and a faster baking time. Most muffins bake in 15 to 30 minutes, making them one of the most convenient home-baked breakfast foods.

To facilitate early-morning preparation, measure ingredients the night before, sift the dry ingredients together, and prepare the muffin tins. Come morning, just mix in the liquids, pop the tin in the oven, and pull out another muffin memory.

ABOUT THESE RECIPES

The following 50 recipes are written to yield 1 dozen medium-size muffins—some sweet, some savory. All of them use a 12-cup tin where each muffin cup has a capacity of 4 fluid ounces and a top diameter of 3 inches. Prepare the pan by greasing the interior of each cup and the top surface of the tin (spray shortening works well), or place a paper or foil cupcake liner in each cup. It's best to use a nonstick tin if you are not using cupcake liners.

Muffins are done when fully risen, browned, and slightly pulling away from the sides of the tin. A tester inserted into the middle of the largest muffin should come out with a moist crumb clinging to it. Let all muffins cool in the pan for 5 minutes, unless otherwise noted.

All recipes should use extra-large eggs, unless otherwise noted.

Two of the corn-muffin recipes call for cornstick pans. These heavy iron pans are traditional for making cornbreads and are available at most cookware stores. If you don't have one, bake them in mini-muffin pans.

 ## Orange Currant Muffins

Sift 2 cups flour, 2 teaspoons baking powder, and ½ teaspoon ground cardamom (optional). Mix 1 cup currants into the dry ingredients and set aside. With an electric mixer, beat ¼ pound softened butter with ¾ cup sugar until pale and fluffy. Add 1 teaspoon vanilla extract and 1 tablespoon finely grated orange zest. Beat in 2 eggs, 1 at a time. Mix in the dry ingredients in 2 additions alternating with ½ cup milk. Spoon batter into prepared muffin tin and bake at 375° F. for 25 minutes.

 ## Blueberry Muffins

Follow preceding recipe, omitting the orange zest and currants. Add 2 cups blueberries before spooning batter into tins. Bake for 30 minutes.

 ## Toasted Walnut Muffins

Follow recipe for Orange Currant Muffins (above), but use ground cinnamon instead of cardamom and chopped toasted walnuts instead of currants. Increase milk to ⅔ cup.

 ## Apple Walnut Muffins

Follow recipe for Orange Currant Muffins (above), but use ground cinnamon instead of cardamom and ½ cup chopped walnuts instead of currants. Add 1 peeled, seeded, and diced Granny Smith apple before spooning batter into tins. Before baking, sprinkle tops of the muffins with mixture of 1 tablespoon sugar and ¼ teaspoon ground cinnamon. Bake for 30 minutes.

 ## Jam-Filled Muffins

Follow recipe for Orange Currant Muffins (above). When filling the muffin tins, place 2 tablespoons batter in each prepared cup. Make an indentation in the batter with the back of a spoon and place 1 teaspoon jam, marmalade, or preserves on top. Top with the remaining batter.

 ## Ginger Peachy Muffins

Sift 2 cups flour with 2 teaspoons baking powder and 1 teaspoon ground ginger. With an electric mixer, beat ¼ pound softened butter with ¾ cup sugar until pale and fluffy. Add 1 teaspoon vanilla extract and 1 tablespoon finely grated lemon zest. Beat in 2 eggs, 1 at a time. Mix in the dry ingredients in 2 additions alternating with ½ cup milk. Add 2 peeled, pitted, and diced peaches, and spoon batter into prepared muffin tin. Bake at 375° F. for 30 minutes.

 ## Cinnamon Swirl Muffins

Mix ¼ cup brown sugar, ½ teaspoon ground cinnamon, and ¼ cup chopped pecans or walnuts.

Set aside. Sift 2 cups flour, 2 teaspoons baking powder, and ½ teaspoon ground cinnamon. Mix 1 cup chopped raisins into the flour mixture, and set aside. With an electric mixer, beat ¼ pound softened butter with ¾ cup sugar until pale and fluffy. Add 1 teaspoon vanilla extract and 1 tablespoon finely grated orange zest. Beat in 2 eggs, 1 at a time. Mix in the dry ingredients in 2 additions alternating with ½ cup milk. Spoon 2 tablespoons batter into each prepared muffin cup, top each with 2 teaspoons of the brown-sugar mixture, then the remaining batter. Bake at 375° F. for 25 minutes.

Raspberry Chocolate-Chip Muffins

Sift 2 cups flour with 2 teaspoons baking powder. Mix in 1 cup semisweet chocolate mini-morsels. Set aside. With an electric mixer, beat ¼ pound softened butter with ¾ cup sugar until pale and fluffy. Add 1 teaspoon vanilla extract and 1 tablespoon finely grated orange zest. Mix in dry ingredients in 2 additions, alternating with ½ cup milk. Fold in 2 cups raspberries. Spoon into prepared muffin tin and bake at 375°F. for 30 minutes. Cool for 10 minutes before unmolding.

Date Nut Muffins

Sift 2 cups flour, 2 teaspoons baking powder, and ¼ teaspoon ground allspice. Mix in 1 cup chopped pitted dates and 1 cup chopped walnut pieces. Set aside. With an electric mixer, beat ¼ pound softened butter with ⅓ cup granulated sugar and ⅓ cup brown sugar until pale and fluffy. Add 1 teaspoon vanilla extract and 1 tablespoon finely grated orange zest. Beat in 2 eggs, 1 at a time. Add the dry ingredients in 2 additions alternating with ½ cup milk. Spoon into prepared muffin tin and bake at 375°F. for 25 minutes. Cool for 10 minutes before unmolding.

Brown Sugar Pecan Muffins

Follow preceding recipe substituting cardamom for the allspice and 2 cups pecan pieces for the dates and walnuts. Substitute lemon zest for orange.

Sour Cream Banana Muffins

Sift 2 cups flour, ½ teaspoon baking powder, and ¾ teaspoon baking soda. Set aside. In a food processor or blender, process 3 ripe bananas with ¼ cup sour cream until smooth. With an electric mixer, beat ¼ pound softened butter with 1 cup sugar and 1 teaspoon vanilla extract until light and fluffy. Beat in 2 eggs, 1 at a time. Add dry ingredients in 3 additions, alternating with banana mixture in 2 additions, beating only until blended. Fold in ½ cup chopped walnuts. Spoon into prepared muffin tin and bake at 350°F. for 20 minutes.

Banana Bran Muffins

Follow preceding recipe, substituting mixture of ¾ cup all-purpose flour and ¾ cup whole-wheat flour for the 2 cups flour. After sifting dry ingredients, add ½ cup bran cereal.

Banana Oat Bran Raisin Muffins

Follow recipe for Sour Cream Banana Muffins (above), substituting mixture of ¾ cup all-purpose flour and ¾ cup whole-wheat flour for the 2 cups flour. After sifting dry ingredients, add ½ cup oat bran. Replace walnuts with ½ cup chopped raisins.

Tropical Banana Muffins

Follow recipe for Sour Cream Banana Muffins (page 93), but replace walnuts with ½ cup chopped pitted dates and ½ cup coconut.

 Bran Muffins

Beat 2 extra-large eggs, 1 teaspoon vanilla extract, 2 tablespoons dark brown sugar, and 2 tablespoons granulated sugar until well mixed. Add ¼ cup vegetable oil and beat until smooth. Add 2 cups bran cereal, 1 cup at a time, alternating with 1 cup milk. Allow to rest for 5 minutes. Add 1 cup flour sifted with 2 teaspoons baking powder. Spoon into prepared muffin tin and bake in preheated 375°F. oven for 25 minutes.

 Raisin Bran Muffins

Follow preceding recipe, substituting raisin bran for bran cereal. Add ½ cup raisins along with the cereal.

 Blueberry Bran Muffins

Follow recipe for Bran Muffins (above), adding 1½ cups blueberries and 1 tablespoon finely grated lemon zest to the batter before spooning batter into prepared muffin tin.

 Nutty Bran Muffins

Follow recipe for Bran Muffins (above), adding 1 cup chopped walnuts before spooning batter into prepared muffin tin.

 Honey Bran Muffins

Follow recipe for Bran Muffins (above), using ¼ cup honey instead of the sugars, melted butter instead of oil, and raisin bran in place of bran cereal.

 Oat Bran and Fig Muffins

Follow recipe for Bran Muffins (above) substituting oat bran cereal for the bran cereal and adding 12 diced and stemmed dried figs with the cereal.

 All-Bran Muffins

Mix 2½ cups bran (any type), 1 tablespoon baking powder, ¼ teaspoon salt, ⅓ cup raisins, 2 extra-large egg yolks, ½ cup honey, 2 tablespoons peanut oil, and ¾ cup milk. Beat the 2 egg whites to a soft peak and fold into the batter. Spoon into the prepared muffin tin and bake at 400°F. for 20 minutes.

 Blueberry Corn Muffins

Mix ⅔ cup flour, 1⅓ cups yellow cornmeal, ½ teaspoon salt, and 2 teaspoons baking powder. Toss in 2 cups blueberries. Separately, beat 1 extra-large egg with ¼ cup sugar until blended. Beat in 1 cup milk and 3 tablespoons corn oil. Mix with dry ingredients until all is moist. Spoon into prepared muffin tins and bake at 400°F. for 20 to 25 minutes. Cool for 3 minutes before unmolding.

 Cranberry Orange Corn Muffins

Follow preceding recipe, replacing blueberries with mixture of 1 cup chopped cranberries, 2 teaspoons grated orange zest, and ¼ cup sugar.

Pecan Peach Corn Muffins

Follow recipe for Blueberry Corn Muffins (opposite), replacing blueberries with 1 large peeled, diced peach and 1 cup chopped pecans. Add ¼ teaspoon ground ginger with the dry ingredients.

 ### Garden Corn Muffins

Dice ¼ cup *each* red bell pepper, carrot, onion, and celery and cook in a skillet with ½ cup corn niblets in ¼ cup corn oil until soft. Follow recipe for Blueberry Corn Muffins (opposite), but use this mixture for the corn oil and add after beating in the milk. Omit the blueberries and reduce sugar to 2 tablespoons.

 ### Cheddar Corn Muffins

Follow recipe for Blueberry Corn Muffins (opposite). Reduce sugar to 1 tablespoon, replace blueberries with 1 cup shredded sharp Cheddar cheese, and add a pinch of cayenne pepper to the dry ingredients.

 ### Bacon and Apple Corn Muffins

Cook 4 strips bacon until crisp, blot with paper towels, and crumble. In a skillet, cook ⅓ cup chopped onion and 1 peeled, seeded, and diced Granny Smith apple in ¼ cup corn oil until soft. Mix ⅔ cup flour, 1⅓ cups yellow cornmeal, ½ teaspoon salt, and 2 teaspoons baking powder. Mix in bacon. Separately, beat 1 extra-large egg with 2 tablespoons sugar until blended. Beat in 1 cup milk and the apple-onion mixture. Mix with dry ingredients until all is moist. Spoon into prepared muffin tins and bake at 400°F. for 20 to 25 minutes. Cool for 3 minutes before unmolding.

 ### Spicy White Cornsticks

Place a 7-stick iron cornstick pan in a preheated 400°F. oven. Meanwhile in a skillet, cook 2 tablespoons minced onion in 3 tablespoons butter until soft and let cool. Mix ¾ cup white cornmeal, ¼ cup flour, ½ teaspoon salt, ¼ teaspoon cayenne, 3 tablespoons sugar and 1½ teaspoons baking powder. Stir in onion and butter, followed by 1 extra-large egg and 1 cup heavy cream. Carefully grease the hot cornstick pan by brushing with 1 tablespoon corn oil and spoon batter into pan. Bake for 15 minutes. They're delicate, so unmold carefully. Makes 7 cornsticks.

 ### Blue Corns

Follow preceding recipe, using blue cornmeal instead of white cornmeal. Omit the cayenne.

 ### Bacon Cornsticks

Cook 2 strips bacon until crisp, blot with paper towels, and crumble. Follow recipe for Spicy White Cornsticks (above), but use the bacon fat in place of the oil and use yellow cornmeal instead of white. Add crumbled bacon to the dry ingredients.

 ### Pepperoni Pepper Corn Muffins

Mix 1 cup yellow cornmeal, 1 cup flour, ¼ cup sugar, 4 teaspoons baking powder, and ½ teaspoon salt. In a skillet, cook ¼ cup finely chopped onion and 1 diced red pepper in ¼ cup corn oil until soft. Add ⅓ cup chopped pepperoni and ¼ cup chopped scallion. Remove from heat and mix into dry ingredients with 1 beaten extra-large egg and 1 cup milk. Spoon into prepared muffin tin and bake at 400°F. for 20 minutes.

Pecan Corn Muffins

Sauté 3 tablespoons minced onion and 1 cup finely chopped pecans in 4 tablespoons butter until lightly browned. Follow preceding recipe, but use this mixture in place of the onion, pepper, oil, pepperoni, and scallions.

 Corn and Green Chili Muffins

Follow recipe for Pepperoni Pepper Corn Muffins (page 95), replacing the red bell pepper with 1 cup corn niblets and 2 tablespoons finely chopped pickled jalapeño pepper. Eliminate the pepperoni.

 Carrot Muffins

Beat 2 eggs, 1 teaspoon vanilla extract, and ¾ cup sugar until very light and thick. In a slow stream, add ¾ cup vegetable oil. Sift 1 cup flour, 1 teaspoon baking soda, ½ teaspoon salt, and 1 teaspoon ground cinnamon. Mix into wet ingredients and fold in 1½ cups shredded carrots and ½ cup chopped walnuts. Spoon into prepared pan and bake at 375°F. for 20 to 25 minutes. Cool for 10 minutes, unmold, and dust with confectioners' sugar, if desired.

 Orange Carrot Muffins

Follow preceding recipe, adding 1 tablespoon finely grated orange zest with the carrots. Use pecans instead of walnuts.

 Currant Carrot Muffins

Follow recipe for Carrot Muffins (above), adding 1 cup dried currants in place of ½ cup of the carrots.

 Zucchini Walnut Muffins

Beat 2 medium eggs, 1 teaspoon vanilla extract, and 1 cup sugar until light and fluffy. Add ½ cup vegetable oil in a slow stream. Sift 1½ cups flour with ½ teaspoon *each* salt, ground cinnamon, and baking soda, and ¼ teaspoon baking powder. Mix dry ingredients into the wet ingredients. Fold in 1 cup shredded zucchini and ¾ cup chopped walnuts. Spoon into prepared pan and bake at 350°F. for 27 minutes.

 Lemon-Lime Zucchini Muffins

Follow preceding recipe, adding 1 tablespoon *each* finely grated lime zest and lemon zest and 1 tablespoon lemon juice to the batter after the oil.

 Candied Ginger Zucchini Muffins

Follow recipe for Zucchini Walnut Muffins (above), adding 2 tablespoons finely chopped candied ginger with the walnuts. Replace cinnamon with ground ginger.

 Zucchini Apple Muffins

Follow recipe for Zucchini Walnut Muffins (above), replacing ½ cup of the zucchini with ½ cup coarsely shredded tart apple.

 Applesauce Walnut Muffins

Sift 1½ cups flour with 1 teaspoon baking powder, 1 teaspoon baking soda, 2 teaspoons ground cinnamon, and ½ teaspoon salt. Stir in ¾ cup quick or old-fashioned oats and set aside. Beat 1 tablespoon softened butter with ⅔ cup brown sugar and 1 egg until smooth. Add ⅔ cup chunky applesauce. Mix in half the dry ingredients, ⅔ cup buttermilk, remaining dry ingredients, and ⅔ cup chopped walnuts just until incorporated. Spoon into prepared muffin tin and bake at 350°F. for 25 to 30 minutes.

Apple Oatmeal Spice Muffins

Follow preceding recipe, but use ½ cup granulated sugar in place of the brown sugar and apple butter in place of the applesauce.

Banana Oatmeal Muffins

Follow recipe for Applesauce Walnut Muffins (opposite), replacing brown sugar with ½ cup granulated sugar and using 2 mashed ripe bananas instead of the applesauce.

Yogurt Muffins

Sift 1½ cups flour with 1 teaspoon baking powder, ½ teaspoon baking soda, and a pinch of salt and set aside. With an electric mixer, beat ¼ pound softened butter with 1 cup sugar until light and fluffy. Beat in 2 extra-large eggs, 1 at a time, followed by half the dry ingredients. Add 1 cup vanilla yogurt and remaining dry ingredients, beating just until smooth. Spoon into prepared pan and bake at 375°F. for 30 minutes. Cool in pan for 10 minutes before unmolding. Dust tops with confectioners' sugar, if desired.

Lemon Yogurt Muffins

Follow preceding recipe, substituting 1 cup lemon yogurt mixed with 1 tablespoon finely grated lemon zest and 2 tablespoons lemon juice for the vanilla yogurt.

Apricot Cardamom Muffins

Follow recipe for Yogurt Muffins (above), sifting 1 teaspoon ground cardamom with the dry ingredients and adding 1 cup chopped dried apricots with the yogurt.

Walnut Fig Sinkers

Combine 3 cups quartered stemmed dried figs with 3 cups walnut pieces and set aside. Sift ½ cup flour, ½ teaspoon baking powder, and ¼ teaspoon salt. Toss 2 tablespoons of the dry ingredients with the figs and walnuts. With an electric mixer, beat 2 extra-large egg yolks with ½ cup sugar until light and thick. Add 2 tablespoons lemon juice and the sifted dry ingredients, beating until smooth. Beat 2 egg whites to firm peaks and gently fold in, then mix with the figs and nuts. There will be just enough batter to coat the fruit and nuts. Pack into muffin tin lined with foil cupcake papers, mounding each muffin slightly. They will not rise. Bake at 350°F. for 45 minutes.

Ricotta Rosemary Muffins

In a skillet, cook ½ cup chopped onion, ¼ cup diced celery, ¼ teaspoon crumbled dry rosemary, and ¼ teaspoon rubbed sage in 4 tablespoons butter until vegetables soften. Season with salt and pepper. Sift 2 cups flour with 1 tablespoon baking powder. Mix vegetables and butter into dry ingredients, followed by 1 extra-large egg, 1 cup ricotta cheese, and ½ cup milk. Spoon into prepared muffin tin and bake at 400°F. for 20 minutes.

Herb Cheese Muffins

In a skillet, cook ½ cup chopped onion, ½ clove minced garlic, 1 tablespoon *each* chopped fresh chive and parsley in 4 tablespoons butter until vegetables soften. Season with salt and pepper. Sift 2 cups flour with 1 tablespoon baking powder. Mix vegetables and butter into dry ingredients followed by 1 extra-large egg, ½ cup herbed cream cheese, and ¾ cup milk. Spoon into prepared muffin tin and bake at 400°F. for 20 minutes.

Ham and Cheese Muffins

Sift 2 cups flour, 1 tablespoon baking powder, ½ teaspoon salt, ¼ teaspoon pepper, and a pinch of cayenne pepper. Mix in 1 extra-large egg, 2 tablespoons brown mustard, 1 cup milk, and 4 tablespoons melted butter. Beat in ¾ cup shredded sharp Cheddar cheese and ¾ cup finely chopped smoked ham. Spoon into prepared pan and bake at 400°F. for 20 minutes.

Fifty Ways to Love Your Liver

I flipped through the pages of my cookbooks yesterday,
Thinking to myself that liver could be cooked in just one way,
And there I found to my surprise and my dismay
There must be 50 ways to love your liver.

You can cook it up real nice with bacon or with ham.
Don't forget the onions, peppercorns, or currant jam.
Bake it, broil it, stew it, or flambé it in a pan.
There must be 50 ways to love your liver.

Just make a purée, Ray.
Or give it a grill, Lil.
Try a sauté, Mae.
Whatever you will.
Slice it quite thin, Lynn.
Then watch while it's cookin'.
Don't let it get too done.
Making liver is fun.

In the name of liver, I will offer this critique.
Knowing all too well its reputation's worse than bleak.
Take a taste; I am quite sure you'll find you're rather chic
Once you know 50 ways to love your liver.

Fifty ways to love your liver? You probably have trouble believing there could be even one. If so, we'd like to share a morsel of wisdom from a friend of ours: Every five years give another try to a food you hate.

It's sound advice, especially because the odds are that many a food dislike stems not from the food itself but from flawed cooking. So here's hoping that you'll find liver happiness somewhere in the 50 short recipes below. If not, the other 49 chapters should keep you busy for five years. By that time, we hope you'll be ready to come back to this one and try again.

Fifty Ways to Cook Most Everything

ABOUT THESE RECIPES

These recipes all make 4 servings, which should be served immediately unless noted otherwise. Season each one to taste with salt and pepper at some point during preparation.

The first group of recipes calls for sautéing calf's liver. Use a large skillet, unless otherwise noted. For these recipes, cut liver into slices ¼ inch thick or less, season on both sides with salt and pepper after slicing, sauté in hot fat for 1 to 2 minutes per side, and adjust the seasoning before serving.

 Liver, Bacon, and Capers

Cook 4 strips bacon until crispy, drain on paper towels, and sauté ¼ cup minced onion in the fat until lightly browned. Add ¾ pound calf's liver and sauté. Deglaze pan with 2 tablespoons capers and their liquid and use as a sauce on the liver. Garnish with the bacon.

 Liver and Lemon

Sauté 1 tablespoon minced shallot and 1 clove minced garlic in 4 tablespoons butter for 30 seconds. Add ¾ pound calf's liver and sauté. Deglaze pan with juice of 1 lemon and use as a sauce on the liver.

 Liver and Green Peppercorns

Sauté 1 tablespoon minced shallot in 4 tablespoons butter for 30 seconds. Add ¾ pound calf's liver and sauté. Deglaze pan with ½ cup white wine, 1 tablespoon green peppercorns, and a dash of cayenne. Pour sauce on the liver.

 Liver Glazed with Raspberry Vinegar

Sauté 1 tablespoon minced shallot and ½ clove minced garlic in 4 tablespoons butter for 30 seconds. Add ¾ pound calf's liver and sauté. Deglaze pan with ¼ cup white wine and ¼ cup raspberry vinegar. Add ½ cup fresh raspberries and reduce until liquid thickens. Pour sauce on the liver.

 Liver, Onions, and Sherry Vinegar

Cook 4 strips bacon until crisp, drain on paper towels, and reserve for another use. Sauté ½ cup thinly sliced onion in the fat until soft. Sauté ¾ pound calf's liver. Deglaze pan with ¼ cup sherry vinegar and pour sauce on liver.

 Liver and Mushrooms

Sauté 1 tablespoon minced shallot and 8 sliced mushrooms in 6 tablespoons butter until lightly browned. Add ¾ pound calf's liver and sauté. Deglaze pan with 3 tablespoons balsamic vinegar. Pour liquid over liver.

 Liver in Brown Butter

Sauté 1 small minced onion in 4 tablespoons butter for 30 seconds. Add ¾ pound calf's liver and sauté. Remove liver, add 4 more tablespoons butter and cook until lightly browned. Add juice of 1 lemon and pour mixture on the liver.

 Liver Flamed in Brandy

In a small skillet, sauté 2 tablespoons minced onion in 2 tablespoons butter until soft. Add ¾ pound calf's liver and sauté. Deglaze pan with ¼ cup brandy and flame. When flames subside, finish with 2 tablespoons heavy cream and pour sauce on liver.

Liver Sautéed with Avocado

Sauté 1 sliced avocado with ¾ pound calf's liver in 3 tablespoons avocado oil and 2 tablespoons butter. Deglaze pan with juice of ½ lemon. Pour liquid on liver.

Liver with Rosemary and Marsala

Sauté 1 tablespoon minced shallot and 2 teaspoons fresh rosemary leaves in 4 tablespoons butter. Add ½ pound calf's liver and sauté. Deglaze pan with ½ cup marsala wine and cook until alcohol evaporates. Pour sauce on liver.

Liver Sautéed with Sweet Pickles

Sauté 4 slices bacon until crisp, drain on paper towels, and reserve for another use. Cook ¼ cup chopped onion and 1 clove minced garlic in the fat in the pan until soft. Add ½ pound calf's liver and sauté. Deglaze pan with ¼ teaspoon ground coriander, ⅓ cup chopped gherkins, and ¼ cup pickle liquid. Pour liquid on liver.

Liver with Currant Glaze

Sauté 1 tablespoon minced shallot in 2 tablespoons butter for 30 seconds. Add ¾ pound calf's liver and sauté. Deglaze pan with juice of 1 lime, 2 tablespoons rich beef stock, and 3 tablespoons currant jelly. Pour sauce on liver.

Liver in Mustard Crumbs

Cut ¾ pound liver into thin strips. Dip in mixture of ½ cup Dijon mustard and 1 egg yolk, then roll liver in seasoned bread crumbs. Sauté liver in ¼ cup peanut oil until browned and crisp.

Soy and Anise Liver

Sauté 1 tablespoon minced scallion with ½ teaspoon ground aniseed in 4 tablespoons butter for 30 seconds. Add ¾ pound calf's liver and sauté. Deglaze pan with 2 tablespoons soy sauce, 1 clove minced garlic, 1 teaspoon sugar, and the juice of 1 orange. Pour sauce on liver.

Liver Braised with Duxelles

Sauté 1 tablespoon minced shallot in 4 tablespoons butter for 30 seconds. Add ¼ pound minced mushrooms and cook until all the liquid evaporates. Add 1 teaspoon tomato paste and ¼ cup dry vermouth. Cook until alcohol evaporates. Add ½ pound calf's liver and sauté. Serve liver with sauce.

Liver Sautéed with Roasted Peppers and Cilantro

Sauté 1 tablespoon minced shallot in 4 tablespoons butter for 30 seconds. Add ¾ pound calf's liver and sauté. Deglaze pan with the juice of 1 lime and 1 cup minced roasted pepper (page 442). Toss with ¼ cup chopped fresh cilantro. Pour sauce on liver.

Liver and Leeks

Sauté thinly sliced white of 2 leeks in 4 tablespoons butter for 1 minute. Add ¾ pound calf's liver and sauté. Deglaze pan with ¼ cup white wine and 2 tablespoons white wine vinegar. Pour sauce on liver.

 Liver and Cranberries

Sauté 2 cloves minced garlic with ½ pound calf's liver in 4 tablespoons butter. Deglaze pan with the juice of 1 orange and ¼ cup whole-berry cranberry sauce. Pour sauce on liver.

 Liver Stir-Fried with Ginger

In a wok, sauté ¾ pound calf's liver strips in 2 tablespoons hot pepper oil. Add 1 clove minced garlic, 1 tablespoon minced fresh gingerroot, 1 tablespoon soy sauce, and ⅓ cup Chinese oyster sauce.

 Liver with Pickled Onions

Sauté 4 slices bacon until crisp, drain on paper towels and reserve for another use. Cook ¼ cup chopped onion and 1 clove minced garlic in the fat in the pan until soft. Add ½ pound calf's liver and sauté. Deglaze pan with ⅓ cup pickled pearl onions, ¼ cup white wine, and ¼ cup pickle liquid. Pour sauce on liver.

 Bacon, Liver, and Chinese Apples

Sauté 4 slices bacon until crisp, drain on paper towels, and cook ¼ cup chopped onion and 1 clove minced garlic in the fat in the pan until soft. Add 1 sliced Chinese apple and ¾ pound calf's liver and sauté. Deglaze pan with ¼ cup apple brandy.

 Sweet and Sour Liver

Sauté 4 slices bacon until crispy, drain on paper towels, and cook ½ thinly sliced red onion and 1 clove minced garlic in the fat in the pan until soft. Add ½ pound calf's liver and sauté. Deglaze pan with ¼ cup currant jelly and ¼ cup cider vinegar. Pour sauce on liver, and garnish with bacon.

 Liver Paprikash

Sauté ½ cup chopped onion in 4 tablespoons butter for 30 seconds. Add ¾ pound calf's liver and sauté. Deglaze pan with ½ cup Beef Broth (page 430), 1 tablespoon sweet paprika, and 1 teaspoon tomato paste. Remove from heat and swirl in 2 tablespoons sour cream. Pour sauce on liver.

 Liver with Poblanos and Cream

Sauté ½ minced onion in ¼ cup corn oil. Add ¾ pound calf's liver and sauté. Remove and keep warm. Add 2 chopped roasted poblano peppers, ½ cup chicken stock, and 1 cup heavy cream. Reduce by a third. Add 1 bunch chopped fresh cilantro and purée in food processor. Add 1 teaspoon lime juice and pour sauce over liver.

 Jalapeño Liver

Sauté 2 tablespoons minced onion in 4 tablespoons butter for 30 seconds. Add 1 minced jalapeño and ½ pound calf's liver and sauté. Deglaze pan with juice of 1 lime and ¼ cup jalapeño jelly. Pour sauce over liver.

 Liver with Pears and Parsley

Sauté 1 tablespoon minced shallot in 4 tablespoons butter for 30 seconds. Add ¾ pound calf's liver and sauté. Remove to a warm plate. Deglaze pan with the juice of 1 lime, ½ cup white wine, and 1 sliced, peeled, and cored pear. Reduce until lightly thickened. Add 1 tablespoon chopped fresh parsley and pour over the liver.

Liver and Kidneys

Sauté 4 slices bacon until crisp, drain on paper towels, and cook ¼ cup chopped onion and 1 clove minced garlic in the fat in the pan until soft. Add ½ pound calf's liver and 1 trimmed and sliced veal kidney and sauté. Deglaze pan with ¼ cup cider vinegar. Pour sauce over liver, and garnish with bacon.

Liver, Apples, and Cream

Sauté 1 tablespoon minced shallot in 4 tablespoons butter for 30 seconds. Add ¾ pound calf's liver and 1 peeled, cored, and sliced apple and sauté. Deglaze pan with ¼ cup apple brandy and reduce by half. Add ⅓ cup heavy cream and reduce until lightly thickened. Serve liver with sauce.

Deep-Fried Honey-Mustard Liver

Cut ¾ pound calf's liver into 1-by-1-by-¼-inch squares, season with salt and pepper, dip in mixture of ½ cup honey mustard and 1 egg yolk, then roll in seasoned bread crumbs. Heat several inches of oil in a saucepan to 325° F. Deep-fry a few pieces at a time in the hot oil until golden brown and drain before serving.

Baked Liver with Garlic

Rub a 1-pound piece calf's liver with olive oil and season with salt and pepper. Cut slits in the liver and insert thin slices of garlic. Roast in a shallow roasting pan at 450° F. for 5 minutes. Reduce oven temper-

ature to 350° F. and roast for 15 minutes more. Turn off oven and baste liver with pan juices. After 10 minutes, remove liver, and slice for serving.

Liver Roasted with Shallots

Rub a 1-pound piece calf's liver with olive oil and season with salt and pepper. Cover with ½ cup chopped shallots and roast in a shallow roasting pan at 450° F. for 5 minutes. Reduce oven temperature to 350° F. and roast for 15 minutes more. Turn off oven and baste liver with pan juices. Remove liver after 10 minutes and slice for serving.

Roasted Liver in a Mustard-Seed Crust

Rub a 1-pound piece calf's liver with olive oil and season with salt and pepper. Roll in mustard seeds to cover and roast in a shallow roasting pan at 450° F. for 5 minutes. Reduce oven temperature to 350° F. and roast for 15 minutes more. Turn off oven, remove liver 10 minutes later, and slice for serving.

Grilled Liver with Caramelized Onions

Slowly simmer 1 large chopped onion in 6 tablespoons butter until golden brown. Stir in 1 tablespoon sugar until melted. Add salt, pepper, and 1 tablespoon brandy. Brush ¾ pound sliced calf's liver with oil. Grill over high flame or broil for 2 to 3 minutes per side. Serve with the caramelized onions.

Grilled Liver with Mustard

Brush ¾ pound sliced calf's liver with brown mustard and season well with salt and pepper. Grill over high flame or broil for 2 to 3 minutes per side.

Fifty Ways to Cook Most Everything

 Grilled Liver in Chili Paste

Brush ¾ pound sliced calf's liver with a thin film of chili paste. Grill over high flame or broil for 2 to 3 minutes per side.

 Grilled Liver in Worcestershire Marinade

In a low, flat dish, combine ¼ cup Worcestershire sauce, 1 tablespoon molasses, and 1 tablespoon dark mustard. Add ¾ pound sliced calf's liver and marinate for 30 minutes. Grill over high flame or broil for 2 to 3 minutes per side.

 Barbecued Liver

Brush ¾ pound sliced calf's liver liberally with any barbecue sauce. Grill over high flame or broil for 2 to 3 minutes per side.

 Broiled Peppered Liver

Liberally brush ¾ pound sliced calf's liver with olive oil. Sprinkle with salt and generously with freshly cracked black pepper. Grill over high flame or broil for 2 to 3 minutes per side.

The following 9 recipes call for chicken livers. Trim by splitting the livers in half and removing the tendon between the two halves.

 Chicken Livers with Hazelnuts and Garlic

In a large skillet, sauté 1 tablespoon minced shallot in ¼ cup walnut oil for 30 seconds. Add ¼ cup coarsely chopped hazelnuts and 1 pound chicken livers. Sauté for 2 minutes per side. Add 1 clove minced garlic and deglaze pan with 3 tablespoons heavy cream. Pour sauce on liver.

 Chicken Livers on Pasta

Sauté thinly sliced white of 1 leek in ¼ cup olive oil. When soft, add ½ clove minced garlic and 1 pound chicken livers and sauté until firm. Add ⅓ cup julienned prosciutto and ¼ cup white wine, reduce for 1 minute, remove from heat, and stir in ½ cup sour cream. Serve over 1 pound freshly cooked fettuccine.

 Chicken Liver Omelet

In a small skillet, sauté 2 tablespoons minced onion in 2 tablespoons butter until soft. Add 3 split, trimmed chicken livers to the pan and brown on all sides. Deglaze pan with 2 tablespoons brandy and reduce by half. Add 2 tablespoons cream, bring to a boil, and use as a filling in a 3-egg omelet.

 Chicken Livers Sautéed with Cucumber and Grapes

Sauté ¾ pound chicken livers and 2 minced shallots in 2 tablespoons butter until firm. Add ¼ cup brandy, ignite carefully with a match and transfer to a plate after flames subside. Add 2 more tablespoons butter, 2 cups peeled and blanched cucumber slices, 1 cup halved seedless grapes, and 1 tablespoon chopped fresh parsley. Cook for 1 minute, add reserved livers, and serve.

 Chicken Livers and Cabbage

In a large skillet, sauté 4 strips bacon until crisp, remove bacon, and drain on paper towels. Sauté ¾ pound chicken livers in the fat and remove to a warm plate. Add 1 small chopped onion, a pinch of dried thyme, and 1 clove minced garlic to the pan and brown lightly. Add ½ head shredded red cabbage, cook until wilted, and add ¼ cup cider vinegar and 1 tablespoon sugar. Toss in the livers and serve garnished with bacon.

 Warm Chicken Liver Salad

Mix 1 cup heavy cream, ½ cup oil, ½ cup wine vinegar, 3 cloves minced garlic, 1 chopped red onion, 2 tablespoons sugar, 1 teaspoon salt, and ½ teaspoon pepper. Sauté 1 pound chicken livers in the rendered fat from 4 bacon slices. Add the liquid and cook for 1 minute. Pour over a pile of greens in a large bowl. Toss and garnish with bacon.

 Chopped Liver Overcome with Onions

In a covered dry skillet, cook 2 large minced onions over low heat until soft. Remove and reserve. Add ⅓ cup rendered chicken fat and 2 more chopped onions to pan and sauté until brown. Add ¾ pound chicken livers and a pinch of thyme and sauté until livers are firm. Combine everything in food processor and finely chop. Mix in 2 chopped hard-boiled eggs and adjust seasoning. Chill.

 Warm Chicken Liver Flan

Purée 3 tablespoons rendered chicken fat, ¾ pound chicken livers, 1 egg yolk, ½ clove garlic, ½ teaspoon salt, a pinch *each* of pepper and grated nutmeg, 2 eggs, ⅓ cup heavy cream, and 1½ cups milk. Strain and pour into four greased 8-ounce ramekins. Place ramekins in a pan, fill with enough water to come halfway up the side of the ramekin, cover with foil, and bake in a preheated 250° F. oven for 50 minutes. Unmold and serve with drained capers for garnish.

 Chicken Liver Mousse

Sauté 1 pound chicken livers in 2 tablespoons butter until lightly browned. Add ¼ cup cognac, ignite carefully with a match, and season with a pinch of dried thyme after flames subside. Purée in food processor while adding 4 tablespoons softened butter through the feed tube a tablespoon at a time. Chill in ramekins.

For the following recipes use prepared or fresh foie gras. Slice it ¼ inch thick and sauté for 30 seconds per side.

 Foie Gras Flamed with Cognac and Morels

In a large skillet, sauté ½ pound sliced fresh morels and 1 minced shallot in 2 tablespoons butter. Sauté 8 thin slices foie gras and remove to a warm plate. Deglaze pan with ¼ cup cognac and ignite carefully with a match. When the flames subside, finish with 2 tablespoons rich brown stock. Pour over foie gras.

 Foie Gras on Toast

Sauté 2 minced shallots in 3 tablespoons butter until soft. Sauté 4 slices foie gras in the same pan and place each on a slice toast. Keep warm. Deglaze pan with ¼ cup red wine and ¼ cup rich brown stock, cook until lightly thickened, and swirl in 1 teaspoon Dijon mustard. Pour over liver.

 Foie Gras with Capers in Brown Butter

Sauté 8 slices foie gras in 4 tablespoons butter. Remove to a warm plate and add 2 tablespoons drained capers and juice of ½ lime to the pan. Bring to a boil and pour over the liver.

Fifty Things Kids Will Eat

Born with the ability to spot a speck of spinach from across a room, children constitute the most reactionary audience a cook is apt to face. They are naturally cautious and unnaturally conservative, and their lists of suspect foods can be encyclopedic. Eventually, even the most gastronomically committed parents acknowledge that preparing meals for grade-schoolers means simply deciding which side of the bread gets the peanut butter.

One mother we know was so determined to get her 7-year-old to eat vegetables that she decreed a special dinner routine. She would start at the beginning of the alphabet and each dinnertime would present a vegetable beginning with that day's letter. After a week of serving asparagus through eggplant, all cooked in the tradition of the 1950s (for about 24 hours), she ended the experiment with the kid making dinnertime quite unpleasant and with him further than ever from making his peace with vegetables.

There are better tactics. She might have tried expanding the child's palate slowly. There are three methods that, though not foolproof, work most of the time.

The first is to sneak a new or unpopular food in with an old favorite. Celery filled with peanut butter is a classic example of this technique, but con-temporary ones also abound. Salsa and chips fill up a kid's belly with vegetables that otherwise might never get there. Banana sandwiches mask the low-fat protein of farmer cheese with slices of potassium-rich bananas. Bean sprouts add nutrition to a hoagie, and whole-wheat flour is incognito when baked into chocolate-chip cookies.

The second method is to make the food so much fun that no child could resist it. Make tiny finger sandwiches and challenge children to see how many they can eat. Accompany vegetables with a tub of peanut butter or sweetened cream cheese for dipping. Give kids a pencil with their glass of milk and show them how, by tapping on the glass, they'll hear a different musical tone after every sip. The problem of unfinished milk vanishes with a song.

The third method is to slightly sweeten a new food when you introduce it. No one wants to load a child's diet with sugar, but the fact remains that most children are attracted to sweetness beyond all other flavors. So a cheese dip sweetened with a bit of chutney is much more likely to convince a child that a cheese dip is good stuff than one that's pungent with fresh herbs and Parmesan. Whole grains go down much easier in muffins or cookies than they do as side dishes, and yogurt becomes a treat when puréed with fruit and served as a shake.

To help you further, we've put together 50 kid-proof recipes—for breakfast, lunch, dinner, and anything in between.

All of the recipes that we considered even slightly iffy from a kid's perspective have been tested on real children with real appetites and real food prejudices. The most suspect of the bunch underwent even more rigorous kid testing: the votes of 50 third-graders whose teachers allowed us to cater their lunchtime using a dozen of these recipes.

Some of their critiques might surprise you. A minted cucumber salad sweetened enough that we were sure it would win over the kids was nearly run out of town. (It wasn't run out of town, but it *was* run out of this chapter.) But lots of other vegetable combinations won their approval, as did a couple of unusual dishes, such as turkey meatballs and an Asian-style noodle dish.

Although no single recipe got universal applause from our young testers, nothing made it into this chapter without widespread support.

Don't stop here when serving kids. There are many recipes throughout the other chapters that kids will enjoy. By the same token, you might find yourself sneaking a bite of one or two of the following. They're not for kids *only*.

ABOUT THESE RECIPES

All recipes are written for 4 portions unless otherwise noted.

Grilled Cheddar and Apple

Spread 8 slices of bread with butter on one side, turn the slices over, and top each with 1 slice mild Cheddar cheese. Divide 16 thin apple slices among 4 pieces of the bread and top each with 1 of the remaining bread slices so the buttered sides face outward. Grill on a dry griddle or skillet over mod-erate heat until bread is toasted and cheese has melted.

Grilled Muenster with Pickles

Follow preceding recipe using sweet muenster cheese in place of the Cheddar and pickle slices in place of the apple.

Healthy Hoagie

Spread 2 split Italian rolls with 4 teaspoons olive oil. Scatter ¼ cup bean sprouts down the interiors followed by ⅔ cup tuna fish salad (your own or Traditional Tuna Salad on page 351), 4 split tomato slices, and ¼ cup additional sprouts. Drizzle each sandwich with another 1 teaspoon olive oil and 1 teaspoon lemon juice. Halve and serve.

Banana Sandwiches

Blend 1 tablespoon honey with 4 ounces farmer cheese. Spread mixture on one side of 4 slices raisin bread. Slice 1 banana and arrange in a layer on 2 of the slices. Place the other 2 slices on top. Halve and serve. Makes 2 servings.

Peanut Butter and Banana Sandwiches

Follow preceding recipe substituting peanut butter for the farmer cheese.

Peanut Butter and Apple Raisin Sandwiches

Spread 2 tablespoons peanut butter on one side of each of 4 slices raisin bread. Sprinkle each slice with 1 tablespoon raisins, lightly pressing them into the peanut butter. Core and thinly slice 1 apple and arrange in a layer on 2 of the bread slices. Place the other slices on top. Halve and serve. Makes 2 servings.

 Roast Beef Pita Pocket

Mix 2 tablespoons mayonnaise with 2 teaspoons ketchup. Spread over interiors of 4 small pitas with one end removed, to form a pocket. Fill each pita with 2 deli slices of roast beef. Add 1 tablespoon cole slaw, 2 more roast beef slices, and 2 teaspoons additional cole slaw.

 Vegetable "Dogs"

Spread 4 hot-dog rolls with 2 tablespoons mayonnaise mixed with 1 teaspoon ketchup. Mix ½ cup alfalfa sprouts, ½ cup shredded carrot, ½ cup shredded mozzarella, and 1 tablespoon *each* finely chopped tomato, lettuce, and cucumber and divide among rolls.

 Vegetable Spread for Sandwiches

In a small saucepan, bring 1 small peeled and diced carrot, ½ rib diced celery, 1 diced scallion, 1 clove minced garlic, and 2 tablespoons milk to a boil. Cool and beat into 4 ounces cream cheese. Season with salt and pepper. Use as a spread for 4 sandwiches.

 Turkey Tacos

In a skillet, sauté 1 pound ground turkey, 3 tablespoons finely chopped onion, and 1 tablespoon chili powder in 2 teaspoons oil. Serve with 2 cups shredded lettuce, 1 cup shredded Monterey Jack cheese, and mild salsa. To make the salsa, blend the whites of 2 scallions, 3 chopped tomatoes, ¼

clove minced garlic, 2 tablespoons olive oil, 2 tablespoons chopped fresh parsley, salt, and pepper in a food processor or blender until finely chopped. Serve with 8 taco shells warmed for 1 minute in a microwave or for 5 minutes in a 350° F. oven.

 Chicken Fajitas

Toss 1 pound chicken tenders in 1 tablespoon Worcestershire sauce and 1 tablespoon ketchup. Marinate in the refrigerator for 1 hour. In a skillet, sauté 1 *each* julienned red and green bell pepper and 1 cup diced onion in 2 teaspoons corn oil until softened. Remove vegetables, add chicken to pan, and cook until firm and brown. Return vegetables to pan, toss to mix, and serve with 8 tortillas warmed in a 350° F. oven, 2 cups chopped tomatoes, 1 cup shredded mild Cheddar cheese, ¼ cup sour cream, and ¼ cup sliced black olives.

 Make Your Own Pizza

Cut 1 pound defrosted frozen bread dough into 4 pieces. Roll each into a 6-inch circle, rub with 1 teaspoon olive oil, and place on sheet of heavy foil. Place any 3 or 4 of the following on the dough: 1 cup tomato pasta sauce, 1½ cups shredded mozzarella, ¼ cup grated Parmesan, 4 slices sautéed mushrooms, ½ diced bell pepper, ½ cup blanched broccoli florets, ½ cup browned ground meat, ¼ pound cooked and chopped sausage or salami, and ¼ pound small cleaned shrimp. Place on lower rack of preheated 425° F. oven, still on the foil. Bake for 20 to 25 minutes until puffed and brown. Cool for 5 minutes.

 Tuna Lettuce Pockets

Drain and crumble contents of one (6-ounce) can white tuna and mix with 1 finely shredded carrot,

2 tablespoons mayonnaise, and 1½ tablespoons Italian dressing. Remove 4 large or 8 small perfect whole leaves from 1 head iceberg lettuce. Cut out center rib. Place 2 to 3 tablespoons tuna in center of each leaf. Fold leaf around filling to form an edible cup. Make 1 or 2 per serving, depending on size.

 Chicken and Grapes Lettuce Pocket

Follow preceding recipe using the following mixture in place of the tuna salad: Mix 1 cup diced cooked chicken, ½ cup halved seedless grapes, 1 sliced rib celery, ¼ cup chopped walnuts, 2 tablespoons mayonnaise, 1 teaspoon mustard, and 1 teaspoon lemon juice.

 Inside-Out Taco

Sauté 1 pound ground turkey, 3 tablespoons finely chopped onion, and 1 tablespoon chili powder in 2 teaspoons oil. Divide among the 6 large or 12 small lettuce cups, formed as described in Tuna Lettuce Pockets (opposite). Top each with 2 teaspoons shredded Monterey Jack cheese, 1 tablespoon crumbled taco chips and 1 teaspoon mild salsa, made as described in Turkey Tacos (opposite). Serves 6.

 Inside-Out Lasagna

In a skillet, cook ½ cup chopped onion and 1 clove minced garlic in 1 tablespoon vegetable oil until soft. Add 1 jar (26 ounces) tomato pasta sauce, 2 tablespoons tomato paste, salt, and pepper. Simmer 5 minutes. Meanwhile, mix together 4 cups hot cooked macaroni, ¼ pound shredded mozzarella, 2 beaten eggs, 1 cup ricotta cheese, salt, and pepper. Spread in bottom of rectangular pan. Top with sauce. Bake at 350° F. for 40 minutes.

 Mild Macaroni and Cheese

In a casserole, toss ½ pound hot cooked macaroni with a mixture of ⅓ cup milk, 1 egg, ¼ pound shredded sharp Cheddar cheese, ½ pound shredded mozzarella, ½ teaspoon mustard, salt, and pepper. Bake at 350° F. for 20 minutes.

 Noodles and Cheese

Toss ¾ pound cooked hot noodles (any type) with 1 tablespoon butter, 1 cup small-curd cottage cheese, 2 tablespoons grated Parmesan, salt, and pepper.

 Spaghetti with Fresh Tomato Sauce

In a skillet, cook ¼ cup chopped onion, 1 clove minced garlic, a dash of crushed red pepper, and 1 teaspoon dried basil in 1 tablespoon olive oil until vegetables soften. Add 1½ cups tomato purée and 3 cups chopped skinned tomatoes. Season with salt and pepper and simmer for 15 to 20 minutes. Toss with 1 pound hot cooked spaghetti and serve with grated Parmesan.

 Cheesy Bread Pudding

Trim crusts from 10 slices stale bread. Spread each slice with 1 teaspoon butter and layer in a greased casserole with ¼ pound shredded Monterey Jack cheese. Beat 3 eggs with 2 cups milk, pour over bread and cheese, and refrigerate for several hours. Bake for 45 minutes at 350° F.

 Cottage Cheese Pancakes

Beat 2 cups drained cottage cheese, 6 egg yolks, ¼ cup sugar, 6 tablespoons flour, and ½ teaspoon vanilla extract. With an electric mixer, beat 6 egg whites to a soft peak with pinch of salt, then fold into batter. Make 2- to 3-inch pancakes on a hot greased griddle and brown on both sides over moderate to high heat, flipping after 2 to 3 minutes. Serve immediately with fruit.

Chicken and Noodle Salad with Peanut Butter Sauce

Toss ½ pound boneless, skinless chicken breast, cut in strips, with 1 teaspoon cornstarch, ¼ teaspoon Oriental sesame oil, salt, and pepper. Stir-fry in 1 tablespoon vegetable oil and toss with 5 ounces cooked Asian-style noodles, 1 teaspoon Oriental sesame oil, 1 tablespoon peanut oil, 1 julienned seeded cucumber, 1 cup shredded carrot, and this sauce: Mix ¼ cup creamy peanut butter with 5 tablespoons water, then add 1½ tablespoons rice vinegar, 1 tablespoon soy sauce, ⅛ teaspoon hot pepper oil, and salt.

Sweet and Sour Apricot Chicken

Mix ¾ cup orange juice, ½ cup apricot preserves, 1½ teaspoons lemon juice, 1 tablespoon brown mustard, a pinch of ground cloves, and ¼ teaspoon ground ginger and brush on 4 pounds chicken pieces. Place in 1 layer on a baking pan and bake at 350° F. for 1 hour, basting a few times with the remaining sauce.

Teriyaki London Broil

Marinate in the refrigerator 2 pounds London broil cut from the top round in 2 tablespoons Oriental sesame oil, 3 tablespoons brown sugar, ¼ teaspoon ground ginger, ⅓ cup light soy sauce, 1 tablespoon dry sherry, and 1 clove minced garlic for at least 2 hours. Broil to desired degree of doneness.

Japanese Grilled Shrimp

Toss 1 pound cleaned large shrimp in 1 teaspoon Oriental sesame oil, 1 tablespoon honey, ¼ teaspoon ground ginger, 2 tablespoons light soy sauce, 1 tablespoon lemon juice, 1 tablespoon dry sherry, and 1 clove minced garlic. Marinate in the refrigerator for 30 minutes. Grill or broil for 2 minutes per side.

Barbecued Shrimp

Sauté 1 pound large butterflied shrimp in 1 tablespoon corn oil until firm. Remove with slotted spoon. Add 1 tablespoon grated onion and a pinch of sugar to the pan and brown lightly. Deglaze pan with 1 tablespoon cider vinegar, ¼ cup ketchup, and 1 teaspoon *each* brown mustard and Worcestershire sauce. Bring to a boil and season to taste with hot pepper sauce. Return shrimp to pan and coat with the sauce before serving.

Turkey Meatball Chili

Mix 1 pound ground turkey, 1 tablespoon ketchup, 1 teaspoon mustard, 1 slice crumbled bread soaked in 2 tablespoons milk, 1 small beaten egg, salt, and pepper. Form into 2 dozen small meatballs and brown on all sides in 2 tablespoons vegetable oil in a deep skillet. When almost done, add 1 chopped onion and 1 clove minced garlic. Cook until onion softens. Add 2 tablespoons flour, 2 tablespoons chili powder, 1 tablespoon ground cumin seed, and 1 teaspoon dried oregano and simmer 1 minute more. Add 2 cups chicken broth, 1 cup crushed tomatoes, and 2 tablespoons tomato paste and simmer for 10 minutes. Add 2 cups drained cooked or canned kidney beans and heat through. Serve with crusty bread.

Surprise Cheeseburgers

Mix 1 pound ground beef, 3 tablespoons ice water, salt, and pepper. Form into 8 thin patties, top 4 of the patties with ¼ cup shredded Cheddar cheese, top each with 1 of remaining patties, and mold into burgers. Brown in a lightly oiled skillet until burgers reach desired degree of doneness—about 3 to 5 minutes per side for rare, 5 to 8 for medium, 10 for well done. Serve on 4 split hamburger buns.

Initial Burgers

Mix 1 pound ground beef, 2 tablespoons ketchup, 1 tablespoon water, 1 small beaten egg, salt, and pepper. Divide into 4 portions and shape each into the first letter of one child's name. Brown in a lightly oiled skillet until burgers reach desired degree of doneness, referring to preceding recipe for a timing guide. Some letters, such as W, can be quite fragile, so turn carefully. Serve without buns.

Hamburger Hot Dogs

Mix ¾ pound ground beef, 2 tablespoons ketchup, 1 small beaten egg, salt, and pepper. Mold into 4 sausage shapes and brown on all sides in thin film of oil in a nonstick skillet—about 2 minutes per side if you turn them 3 times. Place each in a split hot dog roll and serve with mustard, ketchup, and relish.

All-American Turkey Cheeseburgers

Mix 1 pound ground turkey, 2 tablespoons ketchup, 2 tablespoons grated onion, 2 teaspoons steak sauce, 3 tablespoons seasoned bread crumbs, and ¼ pound sliced muenster cheese. Form into 4 patties. Grill over white-hot charcoal or under a broiler until browned and cooked through, about 4 minutes per side.

Kiddie Nachos

For each portion, place a large handful of tortilla chips on a microwave-safe plate in a single layer. Top with 1 ounce grated Cheddar or Monterey Jack cheese. Microwave at full power for 1 minute until cheese melts. Serve warm with the mild salsa in the Turkey Tacos recipe (page 108).

Ham and Honey Mustard "Cigars"

Mix 1 tablespoon honey with 1 tablespoon brown mustard. Spread over 12 deli slices of baked ham along with ¼ cup applesauce and roll each slice into a cigar shape.

Banana French Toast

Combine 4 eggs, ¾ cup milk, 2 tablespoons sugar, 1 teaspoon vanilla extract, 2 very ripe puréed bananas, and a pinch of salt. Soak 8 thick slices slightly stale bread in the egg mixture until bread has absorbed all the liquid. Lightly grease a nonstick skillet with butter. Add as many slices of bread as will fit in a single layer, and brown on both sides over moderate heat, about 3 minutes on the first side, 1 to 2 on the second. Remove to a warm platter. Brown remaining slices in the same way. Serve with 2 cups fruit yogurt.

Chocolate Chip Pancakes

Sift 1 cup sifted unbleached all-purpose flour, 1 cup whole-wheat flour, 1 teaspoon baking soda, 2 teaspoons baking powder, 2 tablespoons sugar, and ½ teaspoon salt. Mix in 2 beaten eggs and 2 cups buttermilk until blended. Mix in 2 table-spoons melted butter, 1 cup raisins, and 1 cup semisweet chocolate morsels. Heat 2 teaspoons butter in a skillet or on a griddle until butter foams. For each pancake, pour ¼ cup batter on the hot surface, cook over moderately high heat until pan-cakes are covered with bubbles, then flip and cook another minute or two, until pancakes feel springy. Keep warm while preparing remaining pancakes, greasing pan for every batch. Serve alone, with syrup if you must, or with fruit. Or top with ice cream and chocolate sauce for a decadent dessert. Makes 18 pancakes.

Applesauce Sweetened with Apples

In a 3-quart microwave-safe bowl, combine 6 cored McIntosh apples cut into 1-inch chunks, the juice of ½ lemon, ½ cup chopped dried apples, and 2 tablespoons sugar. Cover tightly with plastic wrap vented at one corner and microwave at full power for 6 minutes. Pierce plastic, lift, stir, re-cover, and cook 3 minutes more at full power. Pierce again and uncover. Process mixture through a food mill. Adjust sugar depending on sweetness of the apples. Yields approximately 3 cups.

Peanut Butter Apple "Canapes"

Core 1 large apple. Cut into 16 slices. Pipe ½ tea-spoon creamy peanut butter through a star-tipped pastry bag onto each apple slice. Top each rosette of peanut butter with 1 raisin.

Sweet Potato Chips

Slice 1 pound peeled sweet potatoes in ⅛-inch slices. Deep-fry potatoes in batches in several inches of oil heated to 350° F. until chips are lightly browned. Drain and salt to taste. Serve with the following dip.

Sweet Chutney Mustard Dip

Combine 3 tablespoons mayonnaise, 1½ table-spoons yellow mustard, and 2 tablespoons chopped mango chutney.

Apple Kugel

Sauté 2 sliced peeled apples in 4 tablespoons but-ter with ¼ cup sugar until softened. Mix 1 pound hot cooked egg noodles, ½ pound farmer cheese, 3 tablespoons sour cream, ¾ cup milk, ¼ cup cot-tage cheese, 6 eggs, 4 tablespoons melted butter, ¼ cup sugar, and a pinch of salt. In a 9-by-13-inch buttered glass baking dish, layer noodles in 3 layers alternating with apples in 2 layers, and bake for 1 hour at 350° F.

Julienned Vegetables with Lemon Honey Dip

Cut enough vegetables (carrots, bell peppers, cu-cumbers, broccoli stems, celery) into thin sticks to equal 2 cups. Serve with 1 cup plain yogurt mixed with 1½ tablespoons lemon juice, ¾ tablespoon honey and a pinch of salt.

High-Protein Chocolate Peanut Butter Shake

Blend ¼ cup smooth peanut butter with ½ cup chocolate syrup. Mix in 1½ cups vanilla yogurt and ¼ cup powdered milk and thin with 2 cups low-fat milk. Chill.

Watermelon Slush

Bring ¾ cup sugar and ¾ cup water to a boil with-out stirring. Cool and freeze in a low-sided pan until solid. With a small knife, slice into cubes and chop coarsely in a food processor or blender. Add 4 cups seeded watermelon chunks and process to a slush. Serve in chilled glasses.

 Xylophone Milk

For each serving, place 1 generous tablespoon chocolate syrup in a 6-ounce drinking glass and freeze for 30 minutes. Remove from freezer and with a small, thin, clean watercolor brush, paint a 2-inch horizontal line of chocolate at a point one-quarter of the way up from the bottom of the glass on the inside of the glass. Paint another line halfway up and a third line three-quarters of the way up. Store in freezer until needed. To serve, fill glass with milk and serve with a pencil. Have the child lightly tap the glass with the pencil and listen to the tone. Then drink down to the first line and tap again, noticing how the tone changes.

 Yogurt Shake

For each serving, in a food processor or blender, combine 1 cup fruit-flavored yogurt, ½ cup milk, and ½ teaspoon vanilla extract.

 Fig Bars

Gently simmer 3 cups finely chopped stemmed dried figs, ¼ cup brown sugar, 2 tablespoons honey, ¼ cup water, 3 tablespoons orange juice, and 1 tablespoon lemon juice for 10 minutes, stirring constantly. Pour into a pie plate to cool. Follow recipe for Peanut Butter Sandwich Bars (page 118), but use this fig mixture in place of the peanut butter.

 Fruit and Nut Bricks

Melt 6 tablespoons peanut butter in a large heavy saucepan, add 40 regular-size marshmallows, and stir until melted. Stir in 4 cups crisp cereal, such as Kix, Rice Krispies, or Chex, and 1 cup *each* roasted peanuts and raisins. Press into a greased 8-inch square pan with the back of an oiled spoon. Cool for 20 minutes. Run a knife around the edge of the pan and unmold on a clean surface. Cut into 4 two-inch strips with a serrated knife and cut each strip in 6 bricks. Makes 24 bricks.

 Ice Cream Sandwich

For each serving, place a 3-ounce scoop of ice cream on a chocolate chip cookie and top with another cookie. Gently press together and serve immediately.

 Chocolate Ice Cream Cupcakes

With a sharp serrated knife, remove tops from 6 large bakery or homemade chocolate cupcakes. Hollow out the interiors, leaving a ½-inch-thick wall of cake all the way around. Fill each with 2 to 3 tablespoons softened chocolate-chip ice cream. Replace tops and freeze until ice cream is firm, at least 3 hours. If not iced, sprinkle with ⅓ cup confectioners' sugar. Serves 6.

 Girl Scout Thin Mint Cookie Ice Cream Log

Using ½ gallon mint chocolate ice cream and 10 ounces (1 box) Thin Mint Girl Scout Cookies, place 1 tablespoon ice cream in center of 1 cookie. Top with another cookie and another 1 tablespoon ice cream. Continue until you have 5 cookies and 4 layers of ice cream in a stack. Place in the freezer.

Make 5 more stacks. Coarsely chop 10 remaining cookies. Place the cookie stacks side by side across an oblong tray to form a tight rectangle. Cover rectangle with remaining ice cream to form a large "log." Freeze until firm. Lightly press chopped cookies into top of log. Cover with plastic wrap and freeze several hours more. Remove 10 minutes before serving in slices.

Fifty Pots of Chili

Although chili is easy to prepare and is as unpretentious as any slop you can ladle into a bowl, the flavors in a great chili are overwhelmingly complex. They start with a slow burn of jalapeño, scorched with a crackle of cayenne, and cooled by a balm of ancho. There's also a scent of black pepper and the floral perfume of cumin and coriander, followed by a bittersweet hint of oregano. The effect is greater than the sum of its parts, and once tasted, the raucous harmony that is chili forever demolishes any old preconceptions about American food being bland.

There are countless "best" chili recipes—from county-fair prize winners to treasured family formulas. Although most chilis still use ground beef and kidney beans, there are no rules. The possibility of making chili from any meat-and-bean variation gives this dish spectacular versatility.

That's why this chapter exists. A handful of these 50 combinations are probably pretty close to some of the concoctions you've enjoyed over the years, but many of them may surprise you at first glance. If so, give them a moment's thought and you'll realize that turkey chili is perfect with chick-peas and lamb chili is complemented well by lentils. To broaden your chili horizons, there are seafood chilis, pork chilis, sausage chilis, and chili sauces to serve over grilled meats.

Some chili aficionados have gone so far as to market their particular secret chili ingredients in premixed spice blends, thus creating such well-known products as 2-Alarm Chili, Chili Man Chili, and Texas Chili. We'll join their ranks with our own chili mix, which is more than a chili powder. Our Basic Chili Mix (below) precooks the spices with onions, peppers, and garlic. Once that's made, it's quick work to finish many of these recipes by just browning the meat, adding the liquid, and simmering.

A common problem when making chili is finding the right pot. Those who fix chili regularly usually own what they affectionately call a "chili pot." Often a standard saucepan is not wide enough for browning the meat and a skillet is not deep enough for simmering the chili once the liquid has been added, so most of us have to improvise. Therefore, if you don't have a "chili pot" at your disposal, choose the deepest skillet or widest saucepot available. A heavy soup pot or Dutch oven works well for large amounts of chili.

Fifty Ways to Cook Most Everything

ABOUT THESE RECIPES

The recipes in this chapter use our Basic Chili Mix, which we will call BCM, combined with a variety of meats and accompaniments. All recipes make 6 servings plus some leftovers, unless otherwise noted. Since chili is such a popular party dish, you may want to make some of these in large batches. Because all chilis are stews, and therefore forgiving by nature, you can easily double or triple any chili recipe without worrying about adjusting the proportion of seasonings or liquid separately. However, as in any cooking, it is advisable to spice lightly at first and then heighten the seasoning near the end to fit your taste.

Basic Chili Mix (BCM)

Cook 1 cup chopped onion, 2 finely chopped canned or fresh chili peppers, and 1 clove minced garlic in 1 tablespoon corn oil until the onion has softened. Add 3 to 4 tablespoons chili powder to taste, 1 tablespoon ground cumin, and 2 teaspoons dried oregano, and cook 1 minute more. Add 2 tablespoons flour and cook until flour is completely absorbed.

 Ground Beef Chili

Brown 3 pounds ground beef in 2 tablespoons vegetable oil. Add BCM, 1 chopped green bell pepper, 2 cups tomato sauce, 1 cup beef broth, and 1 teaspoon black pepper. Simmer, partially covered, for 1 hour, and adjust seasoning by adding hot pepper sauce. Stir in 4 cups drained cooked or canned kidney beans. Heat through.

 Ground Turkey Chili

Follow preceding recipe, substituting turkey for beef and adding 1 tablespoon ground coriander to

the BCM and ¼ cup chopped fresh cilantro with the beans.

 Stew Beef Chili

Brown 3 pounds beef stew meat, cut into large bite-size pieces and dredged in flour, in 2 tablespoons corn oil. Add BCM, 1 chopped green bell pepper, 1 clove minced garlic, and 2 tablespoons tomato paste and cook 1 minute more. Add 3 cups beef broth, 1 teaspoon black pepper, and 1 teaspoon cider vinegar. Simmer, covered, for 2 hours, until meat is very tender. Season to taste with 1 teaspoon to 1 tablespoon hot pepper sauce. Add 1 (19 ounce) can or 2 cups homecooked drained kidney beans and heat through.

 All-Pork Chili

Brown 2 pounds boneless pork shoulder, cut into large bite-size pieces and dredged in flour, in 2 tablespoons corn oil. Add 1 pound sliced sausage and cook until it loses its raw look. Add BCM along with 1 teaspoon rubbed sage, 1 chopped green bell pepper, 1 clove minced garlic, and 2 tablespoons tomato paste and cook another minute. Add 3 cups chicken broth, 1 teaspoon black pepper, and 1 teaspoon cider vinegar. Simmer, covered, for 2 hours, until meat is very tender. Season to taste with 1 teaspoon to 1 tablespoon hot pepper sauce. Add 1 (19 ounce) can or 2 cups homecooked drained kidney beans and heat through.

 Three-Sausage Chili

Follow preceding recipe, substituting 1 pound garlic sausage and 1 pound Italian sausage for the pork shoulder. Reduce simmering time to 1 hour.

Char-Broiled Sirloin Chili

Brown 3 pounds beef sirloin over a high charcoal fire. Cut into 1-inch cubes. Combine in a large pot with BCM, 1 chopped green bell pepper, 1 clove minced garlic, and 2 tablespoons tomato paste and cook another minute. Add 3 cups beef broth, 1 teaspoon black pepper, and 1 teaspoon cider vinegar. Simmer, covered, for 40 minutes, until meat is very tender. Season to taste with 1 teaspoon to 1 tablespoon hot pepper sauce. Add 19 ounces canned or 2 cups homecooked drained kidney beans and heat through.

 ### Venison Chili

Brown 3 pounds boneless leg of venison, cut into large bite-size pieces and dredged in flour, in rendered fat of 3 bacon slices. Add BCM, 1 chopped green bell pepper, 1 clove minced garlic, and 2 tablespoons tomato paste and cook another minute. Add 1 cup red wine, 2 cups beef broth, and 1 teaspoon black pepper. Simmer, covered, for 1 hour, until the meat is tender. Add 19 ounces canned or 2 cups homecooked drained kidney beans and heat through.

 ### Chili Inferno

Follow recipe for Stew Beef Chili (opposite), but double quantities of green chilies, black pepper, and hot pepper sauce.

 ### Chili with Beer

Follow recipe for Stew Beef Chili (opposite), but substitute 12 ounces beer for half the beef broth.

 ### Smoked Sausage Chili with Porter

Brown 3 pounds smoked sausage in 2 tablespoons corn oil. Add BCM, 1 chopped green bell pepper, 1 clove minced garlic, and 2 tablespoons tomato paste and cook another minute. Add 1½ cups beef broth, 1 (12-ounce) bottle of porter or dark beer, 1 teaspoon black pepper, 1 teaspoon dry mustard, and 1 teaspoon cider vinegar. Simmer, covered, for 40 minutes, then season to taste with 1 teaspoon to 1 tablespoon hot pepper sauce. Add 1 (19 ounce) can or 2 cups homecooked drained kidney beans and heat through.

 ### Roasted Pepper Chili

Brown 3 pounds sliced flank steak, dredged in flour, in 2 tablespoons corn oil. Add BCM, 1 clove minced garlic, and 2 tablespoons tomato paste and cook another minute. Add 3 cups beef broth. 1 teaspoon black pepper, and 1 teaspoon cider vinegar. Simmer, covered, for 1½ hours, until meat is very tender, adding 1 *each* red, yellow, and green roasted bell pepper cut into strips (page 442) for the last half hour. Season to taste with 1 teaspoon to 1 tablespoon hot pepper sauce. Add 1 (19 ounce) can or 2 cups homecooked drained kidney beans and heat through.

 ### Herbed Chili

Follow recipe for Stew Beef Chili (opposite), adding 1 teaspoon *each* dried thyme, crumbled rosemary, and basil to the BCM and ¼ cup chopped fresh parsley with the beans.

 ### Baked Chili

Follow recipe for Stew Beef Chili (opposite), baking it in a covered casserole for 3 hours in a 350° F. oven rather than simmering it.

Chili Baked with Cheese

Follow recipe for Stew Beef Chili (page 116), baking it in a covered casserole for 3 hours in a 350° F. oven rather than simmering it and sprinkling 2 cups shredded Cheddar or Monterey Jack cheese over the chili for last 15 minutes of baking. Do not re-cover after adding cheese.

Corn Bread Chili

Follow recipe for Ground Beef or Stew Beef Chili (page 116). After it is finished, pour it into a large casserole, top with Corn Bread (page 433), and bake in a 400° F. oven for 40 minutes.

All-Bean Chili

Combine 2 tablespoons tomato paste and 2 cups beef broth, add to BCM, and bring to a boil. Stir in 4 cups cooked drained beans, 1 teaspoon black pepper, salt, and hot pepper sauce and simmer for 10 minutes.

Ancho Chili

Follow preceding recipe, substituting the following mixture for half the beef broth: Brown 3 dried ancho chili peppers in a skillet in a thin film of oil. Stem, seed, and break the peppers into small pieces, then grind in a blender or spice grinder. Add to 1 cup simmering beef broth and steep for 15 minutes.

Chili with Cornmeal Dumplings

Use any chili recipe. While chili is simmering, sift ¾ cup cornmeal, ¾ cup flour, 2 tablespoons sugar, 1 tablespoon baking powder, and a pinch of salt. Beat in 2 tablespoons corn oil, ¼ cup chopped scallions, and ½ cup milk. Let rest for 5 minutes. When chili is almost done cooking, drop teaspoon-size pieces of cornmeal batter on top of the chili, leaving an inch or more between dumplings. Cover and simmer for 15 minutes more.

Black-Eyed Pea Chili

Follow recipe for Stew Beef or All-Pork Chili (above), substituting cooked drained black-eyed peas for kidney beans.

Shrimp Chili with Black Beans

In a saucepan, cook 1 diced red bell pepper, ½ cup finely chopped onion, and 1 clove finely chopped garlic in 2 tablespoons peanut oil until vegetables soften. Add BCM and 1½ teaspoons ground coriander and cook for 1 minute. Add 1 pound peeled and cleaned medium shrimp, cooking until they lose their raw look, about 4 minutes. Add 1½ cups bottled clam juice or Quick Fish Stock (page 430) and ½ cup pureed cooked black beans. Bring to a boil, add 4 more cups cooked black beans and 1 teaspoon black pepper, and simmer 5 minutes. Finish with salt to taste, the juice and freshly grated zest of 1 lemon, and 2 tablespoons chopped fresh dill.

Shrimp Chili with Garbanzos

Follow preceding recipe, substituting chick-peas for black beans.

Chilied Scampi with Cannellini

Follow recipe for Shrimp Chili with Black Beans (above), substituting 1½ pounds jumbo shrimp for the medium and cannellini beans for black. Increase simmering time from 5 minutes to 10.

Crabmeat Chili

In a saucepan, cook 1 diced red bell pepper, ½ cup finely chopped onion, and 1 clove finely chopped garlic in 2 tablespoons peanut oil until vegetables soften. Add BCM and 1½ teaspoons ground coriander and cook for 1 minute. Add 1½ pounds lump crabmeat and cook about 4 minutes. Add 1½ cups bottled clam juice or Quick Fish Stock (page 430) and ½ cup pureed cooked kidney beans. Bring to a boil, add 4 more cups cooked kidney beans and 1 teaspoon black pepper and simmer 5 minutes. Finish with salt to taste, the juice and freshly grated zest of 1 lemon, and 2 tablespoons chopped fresh parsley.

Smoked Turkey Chili

Follow preceding recipe, substituting 2 pounds diced smoked turkey for the crabmeat and chicken broth for the clam juice.

Chili Gumbo

In a saucepan, cook 1 diced red bell pepper, 1 rib diced celery, 1 cup finely chopped onion, and 1 clove finely chopped garlic in 2 tablespoons peanut oil until vegetables soften. Add ½ recipe BCM and 2 tablespoons ground coriander and cook for 1 minute. Add 1 pound peeled and cleaned medium shrimp and 1 pound lump crabmeat and cook 3 to 4 minutes. Add 2 cups chicken broth, bring to a boil, add 2 cups cooked black-eyed peas, ½ teaspoon filé powder, and 1 teaspoon black pepper, and simmer 5 minutes. Finish with salt to taste, the juice and freshly grated zest of 1 lemon, and 2 tablespoons chopped fresh parsley.

Chinese Shrimp Chili

Combine 2 tablespoons soy sauce, 1 tablespoon Thai fish sauce, 2 teaspoons chili paste, 2 teaspoons tomato paste, 1 cup beef broth, 2 teaspoons cornstarch, a pinch of sugar, and the juice of ½ lemon. Set aside. Toss 1 pound peeled and cleaned large shrimp in 2 tablespoons cornstarch mixed with 2 tablespoons chili powder and stir-fry in ¼ cup peanut oil until shrimp are firm. Add 2 chopped scallions, 2 cloves minced garlic, and 1 tablespoon minced fresh gingerroot and stir-fry 1 more minute. Add the reserved liquid and simmer until lightly thickened. Serve over 4 cups cooked rice or noodles.

Chilied Clams

Combine 2 tablespoons soy sauce, 1 tablespoon Thai fish sauce, 2 teaspoons chili paste, 2 teaspoons tomato paste, 1 cup beef broth, a pinch of sugar, 1 tablespoon cornstarch, 1 tablespoon chili powder, and the juice of ½ lemon. Set aside. Place 2 dozen littleneck clams in a hot wok with 1 tablespoon Oriental sesame oil and cook, covered, until clams open, about 4 minutes. Add reserved liquid and cook until lightly thickened. Remove from heat and toss with 2 chopped scallions, 2 cloves minced garlic, and 1 tablespoon minced fresh gingerroot, discarding any clams that do not open.

Chocolate Chicken Chili

Brown 3 dried ancho or mulato chilies in a skillet in a thin film of oil. Stem, seed and break peppers into small pieces, then grind them in blender or spice grinder. Add to 2 cups simmering chicken stock and let steep 15 minutes. Set aside while you cook 2 cups finely chopped onion and 4 cloves minced garlic in the oil remaining in skillet until they soften. Add 2 teaspoons ground cumin seed (ground in a spice grinder), 1 teaspoon dried oregano, 1 teaspoon dried thyme, ½ teaspoon ground cinnamon, and 2 pounds boneless chicken meat cut into bite-size chunks and cook until the chicken loses its raw look. Stir in 2 tablespoons flour and cook 1 minute more. Add 2 chopped tomatoes, 1 tablespoon tomato paste, and the stock mixture. Simmer, partially covered, until chicken is firm, about 15 minutes. Stir in ¼ cup chopped fresh cilantro and 1 ounce bittersweet or unsweetened chocolate until the chocolate melts. Serve over rice or beans.

Turkey Chili Mole

Follow preceding recipe, substituting turkey breast for chicken.

Lamb Chili Mole

Brown 3 pounds boneless lamb stew meat, cut in large bite-size pieces and dredged in flour, in 2 tablespoons olive oil. Add BCM, 2 teaspoons ground anise, and 1 tablespoon ground coriander and cook another minute. Add 2 chopped tomatoes, 1 clove minced garlic, ¼ cup chopped mint leaves, and 1 tablespoon tomato paste and cook 1 minute more. Add 3 cups beef broth and 1 teaspoon black pepper. Simmer, covered, for 1 hour, until the meat is very tender. Stir in 1 ounce bittersweet chocolate until it melts. Serve over rice or beans.

Duck Chili

Follow preceding recipe, substituting 4 pounds skinned duck pieces for the lamb. Skim off any fat

that collects on the surface of the chili. If desired, garnish with thin strips of duck skin rendered until crisp.

Lamb and Lentil Chili

In a large skillet over high heat, brown 4 pounds lamb shoulder pieces on the bone and dredged in flour, in 3 tablespoons olive oil. Add BCM, 1 tablespoon ground coriander, 1 whole dried chili or cayenne pepper, 2 tablespoons dried mint leaves, and 1 clove minced garlic and cook for 30 seconds, stirring constantly. Add 3 cups chicken broth, 1 tablespoon orange juice, and at least ½ teaspoon freshly ground black pepper. Cover and simmer for 1 hour, stirring occasionally. Remove whole chili pepper and serve lamb with its sauce on a bed of 4 cups warm cooked lentils.

Curried Lamb Chili

Follow preceding recipe, adding 2 tablespoons garam masala (available at many specialty food shops) with the coriander.

Chilied Chicken Stew

Brown 4 pounds chicken parts dredged in flour in 2 tablespoons oil. Add BCM, 2 cloves minced garlic, 2 tablespoons ground coriander, 1 teaspoon ground ginger, and 1 teaspoon thyme leaves and cook for 1 minute. Add enough chicken stock, 3 to 4 cups, to come two thirds of the way up the chicken and the juice of 1 lemon. Simmer, partially covered, for 30 minutes. Add 2 sliced carrots, 2 diced potatoes, 2 tablespoons chopped fresh parsley, and 1 cup sliced mushrooms. Simmer, partially covered, 30 minutes more.

Chorizo Chicken Chili

Brown 4 pounds chicken parts dredged in flour in 2 tablespoons oil. Add 1 pound sliced chorizo sausage, BCM, 2 cloves minced garlic, 2 tablespoons ground coriander, 1 teaspoon ground ginger, and 1 teaspoon thyme leaves and cook for 1 minute. Add 3 to 4 cups chicken stock and the juice of 1 lemon. Simmer, partially covered, for 30 minutes. Add 1 pound cooked chick-peas and 2 tablespoons chopped fresh cilantro, and simmer, partially covered, another 30 minutes.

Sausage and Quail Chili

Follow preceding recipe, substituting 8 quail for the chicken and garlic sausage for the chorizo. Simmer, partially covered, for 15 minutes, not 30, after adding chick-peas.

Rabbit Chili

Cut each of 2 large rabbits, each 2 or 3 pounds, into 6 pieces. Dredge in flour and brown in 2 tablespoons vegetable oil. Add BCM, 2 cloves minced garlic, 2 tablespoons ground coriander, 1 teaspoon ground ginger, and 1 teaspoon thyme leaves and cook for 1 minute. Add 3 cups chicken stock, ½ cup white wine, and the juice of 1 lemon. Simmer, partially covered, for 30 minutes. Add 1 pound cooked black-eyed peas and simmer, partially covered, another 30 minutes.

Curried Chicken Chili

Brown 4 pounds chicken parts dredged in flour in 2 tablespoons oil. Add ½ recipe BCM, 2 tablespoons curry powder, 2 cloves minced garlic, 2 tablespoons ground coriander, 1 teaspoon ground ginger, and 1 teaspoon dry mustard and cook for 1 minute. Add 3 cups chicken stock and the juice of 1 lemon. Simmer, partially covered, for 30 minutes. Add 2 sliced carrots, 2 diced potatoes, 1 cup dried lentils, and 1 cup sliced mushrooms. Simmer, partially covered, 30 minutes more.

Turkey and Avocado Chili

Brown 2 pounds bite-size chunks of boneless turkey breast, dredged in flour, in 2 tablespoons oil. Add BCM, 2 cloves minced garlic, 2 tablespoons ground coriander, 1 teaspoon ground ginger, and 1 teaspoon thyme leaves and cook for 1 minute. Add 3 cups chicken stock and the juice of 1 lemon. Simmer, partially covered, for 40 minutes. Add 1 pound cooked drained chick-peas and 2 tablespoons chopped fresh cilantro and simmer, partially covered, 10 minutes more. Serve garnished with 1 diced avocado.

Vegetarian Chili

Sauté 2 cloves chopped garlic, 2 bell peppers cut in strips, 2 sliced carrots, 2 peeled and sliced ribs celery, and 1 cup sliced mushrooms in 2 tablespoons vegetable oil for 3 to 4 minutes. Add BCM, 1 tablespoon ground coriander, and 1 teaspoon *each* ground ginger, dried thyme, and dried tarragon and cook for 1 minute more. Add 1 cup crushed tomatoes, 2 tablespoons tomato paste, and 2 cups vegetable broth. Simmer 10 minutes more. Stir in 1 sliced zucchini, 2 cups cooked drained kidney or white beans, 1 teaspoon black pepper, salt, and hot pepper sauce and simmer for 10 minutes. Garnish with ¼ cup chopped fresh cilantro and 1 diced avocado. Serve with corn bread.

Corn Chili

Sauté 2 cloves garlic, 2 diced bell peppers, 3 cups cooked corn kernels, and 2 peeled and sliced ribs celery in 2 tablespoons vegetable oil for 3 to 4 minutes. Add BCM, 1 tablespoon ground coriander, and 1 teaspoon *each* ground ginger, dried thyme and dried tarragon and cook for 1 minute more. Add 1 cup crushed tomatoes, 2 tablespoons tomato paste, and 2 cups vegetable broth. Simmer 10 more minutes. Stir in 2 cups cooked kidney beans, 1 teaspoon black pepper, salt, and hot pepper sauce and simmer for 10 minutes. Garnish with ¼ cup chopped fresh cilantro and 1 diced pimiento.

Garden Chili

Sauté 1 large diced eggplant, 2 cloves chopped garlic, 1 diced bell pepper, 2 peeled and sliced ribs celery, and 1 cup sliced mushrooms in 3 tablespoons olive oil for 3 to 4 minutes. Add BCM, 1 tablespoon ground coriander, and 1 teaspoon *each* ground ginger, dried thyme, and dried tarragon and cook for 1 minute more. Add 1 cup crushed tomatoes, 2 tablespoons tomato paste, and 2 cups vegetable broth. Simmer 10 minutes more. Stir in 2 cups cooked drained black beans, 1 teaspoon black pepper, salt, and hot pepper sauce and simmer for 10 minutes. Garnish with 2 tablespoons chopped fresh parsley.

Wild Mushroom Chili

Sauté 2 cloves garlic, 1 pound sliced wild mushrooms, 2 peeled and sliced ribs celery, and 1 cup sliced white mushrooms in 2 tablespoons vegetable oil for 3 to 4 minutes. Add BCM, 1 tablespoon ground coriander, and 1 teaspoon *each* ground ginger, dried thyme, and dried tarragon and cook for 1 minute more. Add 1 cup crushed tomatoes, 2 tablespoons tomato paste, and 2 cups beef broth. Simmer 10 minutes more. Stir in 2 cups cooked lentils, 1 teaspoon black pepper, salt, and hot pepper sauce and simmer for 10 minutes. Garnish with

¼ cup chopped fresh cilantro and 1 diced avocado. Serve with corn bread.

Veal Chili with Artichoke

Brown 3 pounds veal stew meat, dredged in seasoned flour, in 2 tablespoons olive oil. Add BCM, 2 cloves minced garlic, 1 bay leaf, 1 teaspoon dried basil, and 1 teaspoon dried thyme, and cook 1 minute more. Add ½ cup white wine and cook until alcohol boils off. Add 3 cups chicken broth and 5 peeled and chopped plum tomatoes. Simmer, partially covered, for 1 hour until veal is tender. Add 1 pound cooked chick-peas and 1 drained 8-ounce can quartered artichoke hearts. Heat 10 minutes and finish with 1 tablespoon lemon juice.

Bourbon Chili

Brown 3 pounds pork stew meat, dredged in seasoned flour, in 2 tablespoons corn oil. Add BCM, 2 cloves minced garlic, 1 bay leaf, and 1 teaspoon *each* dried sage, crumbled rosemary, and thyme, cooking another minute. Add ¼ cup bourbon and cook until the alcohol boils off. Add 3 cups chicken broth and 5 peeled and chopped plum tomatoes. Simmer, partially covered, for 1 hour until pork is tender. Add 1 pound cooked chick-peas and heat 10 minutes more.

Honeyed Pork Chop Chili

Brown 3 pounds pork shoulder chops, dredged in seasoned flour in 2 tablespoons corn oil. Add BCM, 2 cloves minced garlic, 1 bay leaf, and 1 teaspoon *each* ground coriander and dried thyme, cooking another minute. Add ½ cup bourbon and cook until the alcohol boils off. Add 2 cups chicken broth and 2 tablespoons honey. Simmer, partially covered, for 1 hour until pork is tender. Add 1 pound cooked black-eyed peas and 1 teaspoon cider vinegar. Heat 10 minutes more.

Chilied Chicken Salad

Toss 2 pounds barbecued chicken meat, 2 cups cooked corn, 1 pound cooked kidney beans, 1 thinly sliced bunch scallions, 1 diced roasted red pepper (page 442), 1 diced avocado, 2 tablespoons chopped fresh cilantro, and a dressing made from 3 tablespoons mayonnaise, 2 tablespoons chili powder, 1 tablespoon ground cumin, ⅓ cup corn or peanut oil, 2 tablespoons hot pepper sauce, and 1 tablespoon cider vinegar.

Grilled Salmon Chili

Heat BCM with 1 tablespoon virgin olive oil, 1 tablespoon ground coriander, the juice of 1 lemon, and 1 teaspoon hot pepper sauce and brush a thin film on 2 pounds salmon steak. Refrigerate for 1 hour. Add 1 cup bottled clam juice to mixture remaining in pan and simmer 3 minutes. Add 2 cups cooked or canned cannellini beans and 1 tablespoon chopped fresh cilantro or parsley. Grill salmon steaks 4 inches from a hot fire for 8 minutes per inch of thickness, about 5 to 6 minutes per side. Serve each salmon steak on a bed of beans. Makes 4 servings.

Chilied Scallop Kebabs

Follow preceding recipe, substituting 1 pound sea scallops for the salmon steaks. Thread scallops onto 4 skewers after marinating, and grill 8 to 10 minutes total.

Grilled Tuna Chili on Black Beans

Follow recipe for Grilled Salmon Chili, substituting tuna steaks for salmon and black beans for cannellini. Add the grated zest from the lemon, along with its juice, to the marinade.

Fifty Foods Hot Off the Grill

We Americans are fanatical about grilling, leaving the technology of our kitchens for the primitive facilities of cooking outdoors at the first sign of fair weather. Without ovens to preheat or burners to adjust, we return to our pioneer roots, facing flare-ups and dying embers for the glory of meal preparation over an open fire.

One of the oddest facets of our national ardor for grilling is that it's the only form of home cooking considered macho. Not only are most men eager to cook outdoors, they often consider themselves experts in the field, jealously harboring recipes for sauces and techniques to make their grilled foods better than the next guy's. Such culinary one-upsmanship has given birth to countless barbecue sauces and grilling tricks, but very few recipes.

We have 50, including some innovative ideas for grilling fish, shellfish, chicken, steaks, chops, and sausages. We even have a few for grilled salads, breakfast breads, and desserts. (See Chapter 23, on ground meat, for some novel burger ideas.)

All the recipes are fast, requiring less than 20 minutes of actual cooking time. Although some ask for several hours of marination, this can be done the day before or overnight.

ABOUT THESE RECIPES

Unfortunately, timing directions for grilled foods can be only approximate. Because most grills do not have a thermostat, exact temperatures are impossible to control. Fires can flare up or die away without warning, so it is imperative to keep a close watch and check the food regularly. It is more important that food be cooked through and properly browned than that it sit over the heat for some prescribed time.

Do not allow the fire to flame uncontrolled. Although some scorching is unavoidable when cooking over an open fire, it's never desirable (unless you're executing a blackening technique). To ensure an even brownness, turn food frequently and move it away from flare-ups when they occur. It helps to keep a spray bottle of water by the grill to douse any flames immediately.

These recipes are all written for 4 portions. Unless otherwise stated, all items are grilled 4 to 6 inches from a hot fire. Be careful not to overcook fish. When you grill it, you can tell the fish is done when it flakes with gentle pressure.

Grilling and broiling are two names for the same technique, so go ahead and adapt any of these grilling recipes for your broiler.

Grilled Salmon Steak with Lemon and Olive Oil

Marinate 4 salmon steaks, each 1 inch thick, in ¼ cup virgin olive oil, the juice of ½ lemon, salt, and pepper for 1 hour, turning halfway through. Grill for 4 minutes per side, basting with a bit of marinade every minute.

 Grilled Trout with Bacon and Dill

Season 4 boneless brook trout inside and out with salt and pepper. Place 1 sprig dill in the cavity of each fish and wrap 1 slice bacon around the outside. Grill over a moderately hot fire for 5 to 6 minutes per side.

Mesquite-Grilled Swordfish

In a small saucepan, combine 4 cloves minced garlic, 1 crumbled bay leaf, a pinch of dried oregano, and ⅓ cup olive oil and heat gently until warm. Pour into a dish large enough to hold four 6-ounce swordfish steaks in one layer and add the juice of 1 large lemon, salt, and pepper. Place swordfish in this marinade and turn to coat the fish. Prepare grill by heating a bed of charcoal briquettes until they are white with ash. Place 4 or 5 pieces mesquite on the hot coals and heat until the wood starts to burn. Shake steaks to remove excess marinade, and grill 3 to 4 minutes per side, basting with the marinade every minute.

 Whole Fish Grilled in Foil with Vegetables

On large sheet of oiled foil, place a row of sliced tomatoes, 1 thinly sliced red onion half, 1 peeled and sliced navel orange, and 1 small minced fresh chili pepper. Place 1 whole, lean gutted and scaled fish (1½ to 2 pounds) on top of the vegetables. Season the fish with salt and pepper inside and out and squeeze lemon juice over all. Wrap foil around the fish and grill for 12 to 15 minutes.

 Grilled Tuna Salad

Rub four 1-inch-thick tuna steaks with a thin film of oil and season with salt and pepper. Grill 3 to 4 minutes per side. Trim off skin and bone and break meat into small pieces. Mix with 2 thinly sliced scallions, 2 chopped ribs celery, 1 tablespoon chopped fresh parsley, the juice of ½ lemon, and 6 tablespoons mayonnaise. Serve on a bed of lettuce or as a sandwich filling.

 Grilled-Salmon Potato Salad

Combine 2 tablespoons chopped fresh herbs, 6 tablespoons mayonnaise, 1 tablespoon wine vinegar, salt, and pepper. Set aside. Cut 2 russet potatoes into 1-inch-thick slices, brush with 2 tablespoons vegetable oil, and grill 4 to 5 minutes per side. When potatoes have grilled for 2 minutes, rub four 1-inch-thick salmon steaks with oil and grill for 3 to 4 minutes per side. Trim away skin and bones and break meat into small pieces. Cut potato slices in quarters. Toss fish and potatoes with the sauce. Serve on a bed of lettuce or as a sandwich filling.

 Grilled Salmon with Avocado Salsa

Make salsa by mixing the diced flesh of 1 large avocado with 2 finely chopped scallions, 3 peeled and seeded chopped plum tomatoes, the juice of 1 lemon, 1 clove minced garlic, 2 teaspoons chopped fresh parsley, salt, and crushed red pepper flakes. Cover and refrigerate. Rub four 1-inch-thick salmon steaks with 2 tablespoons lemon juice, salt and pepper and grill for 4 minutes per side. Serve with dollops of salsa.

Fifty Ways to Cook Most Everything

 Grilled Chilied Shrimp

Marinate 1 pound peeled, cleaned jumbo shrimp in ⅓ cup olive oil, 1 tablespoon chili paste with garlic, and 1 teaspoon light soy sauce. Allow to marinate, refrigerated, at least 1 hour. Grill shrimp until firm and opaque.

 Grilled Rosemary Shrimp

Marinate 1 pound peeled, cleaned jumbo shrimp in ⅓ cup olive oil, 1 tablespoon crushed rosemary leaves, 2 cloves minced garlic, salt, and pepper. Marinate, refrigerated, for at least 1 hour. Throw 6 branches fresh rosemary on the hot coals of a charcoal fire. Remove shrimp from marinade and grill, covered, for 1 to 2 minutes per side, until shrimp are firm and opaque.

 Grilled Orange-Spice Clams and Mussels

Steep ½ cup loose orange-spice tea leaves in 1 cup boiling water for 10 minutes, then drain. Throw tea leaves on a hot charcoal fire and grill 2 dozen cleaned clams, covered, for 1 minute. Uncover and add 2 dozen mussels. Cover again, and cook 3 minutes more until all shells have opened. Discard any clams or mussels that do not open.

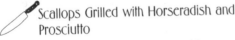 Scallops Grilled with Horseradish and Prosciutto

In a nonmetallic bowl, combine 3 tablespoons peanut oil, the juice of ½ lemon, 1 clove minced garlic, 2 tablespoons white horseradish, salt, and pepper. Toss 1 pound sea scallops, trimmed of their hard side muscles, in this marinade, and re-frigerate 1 to 2 hours. Cut ¼ pound thinly sliced prosciutto into ½-inch-wide strips. Wrap each scallop with 1 strip prosciutto and secure with a toothpick or place 3 on a skewer. Grill for 2 minutes per side, basting with a bit of marinade every minute until scallops are opaque and firm.

 Grilled Scallop Kebabs in Hazelnut Garlic Glaze

Follow preceding recipe, but substitute the following marinade: 3 tablespoons mayonnaise, 1 tablespoon lemon juice, 1 clove minced garlic, 1 tablespoon finely ground toasted hazelnuts, salt, and pepper. Garnish with 1 tablespoon finely chopped toasted hazelnuts.

 Grilled Curried Scallops

In a small saucepan, combine 3 tablespoons peanut oil, 2 tablespoons minced onion, 1 tablespoon curry powder, and 1 teaspoon ground coriander. Cook gently until onion is softened, about 2 minutes. Add a dash of cayenne, salt, and 2 teaspoons orange marmalade, mix well, and toss with 1 pound sea scallops, trimmed of their hard side muscles. Refrigerate for 1 hour. Grill for 2 minutes per side, basting with a bit of marinade each minute until scallops are opaque and firm.

 Grilled Cilantro Softshell Crabs

In a large bowl, combine 2 minced scallions, 2 cloves minced garlic, 3 tablespoons chopped cilantro leaves, 1 tablespoon chopped fresh parsley, 1 cup plain yogurt, and the juice of 1 lime. Kill and clean 8 live softshell crabs (page 439). Dry crabs thoroughly, and place in the yogurt sauce so they are completely covered. Refrigerate for 30 minutes. Remove from the marinade, and grill 3 to 4 minutes per side.

 ## Barbecued Softshell Crabs

Prepare crabs as described in preceding recipe, substituting this marinade: Sauté 1 small chopped onion and 1 clove minced garlic in 1 tablespoon corn oil until softened. Add 2 tablespoons apple cider vinegar, ½ cup ketchup, 1 teaspoon Dijon mustard, 1 teaspoon Worcestershire, 1 teaspoon hot pepper sauce, and the juice of ½ lemon.

 ## Chili Grilled Lobster

Kill 4 small lobsters by splitting them in half lengthwise with a large sharp knife. Remove the light green tomalley and rub the exposed meat with oil. Grill 4 minutes per side, starting with the shell side. When the lobster is done, brush the exposed tail meat with mixture of ¼ cup chili paste, 2 tablespoons Thai fish sauce, 1 tablespoon light soy sauce, 1 tablespoon finely grated fresh gingerroot, and 1 tablespoon peanut oil. Bring extra sauce to a simmer and serve on the side for dipping.

 ## Chilled Grilled Creamy Garlic Chicken Breast

Combine 2 tablespoons mayonnaise, salt, and pepper and rub over 4 split chicken breasts with bone and skin. Grill 4 to 5 minutes per side, turning frequently. While still warm, toss with ⅔ cup Garlic Ranch Dressing (page 299). Cover and chill.

 ## Paillard of Chicken Oriental

Rub 4 split boneless, skinless chicken breasts with Soy Ginger Dressing (page 298). Pound between sheets of plastic wrap to ⅛-inch thickness, then marinate 1 hour in another ½ cup dressing. Cook each breast 2 inches from a white-hot charcoal fire for 30 to 60 seconds per side. Boil extra marinade, and brush on chicken before serving.

 ## Marinated Paillard of Veal

Follow preceding recipe, but substitute four 8-ounce veal scallops for the chicken, and use Caesar Dressing (page 298) instead of Soy Ginger Dressing.

 ## Grilled Chicken Breast with Pesto

In a food processor, puree 2 cups cleaned basil leaves, 4 cloves garlic, and ½ cup pine nuts. Add enough virgin olive oil to make a smooth paste and about ½ cup grated Parmesan. Make a pocket in the center of each of 4 split chicken breasts still on the bone. Place 2 teaspoons pesto inside each breast and rub the outside of each breast with ½ teaspoon olive oil. Grill 5 minutes per side, turning frequently. Serve dolloped with more sauce.

 ## Grilled Turkey Genovese

In a blender or food processor, purée 2 ounces anchovy fillets with their oil, ¼ cup mayonnaise, 2 tablespoons olive oil, ½ clove minced garlic, and pepper to taste and rub 1 tablespoon on each of 4 trimmed turkey cutlets. Grill 2 to 3 minutes per side. Serve dolloped with remaining sauce.

 ## Grilled Veal Saté

In a nonstick skillet, sauté ¼ cup chopped onion and 1 clove minced garlic in 1 teaspoon peanut oil until softened. Add 2 sliced scallions, 1 teaspoon chili paste, 2 teaspoons soy sauce, 2 teaspoons grated fresh gingerroot, ½ teaspoon ground cumin, and ½ teaspoon ground coriander. Cook for 2 minutes. Stir in ¼ cup peanut butter and heat until peanut butter melts. Remove from heat and stir in 1 cup yogurt. Pound eight 3-ounce veal scallops until ¼ inch thick. Brush with 1 tablespoon Oriental sesame oil and grill 2 to 3 minutes per side. Serve topped with sauce.

 ### Grilled Chicken Breast with Roquefort Dressing

Pound 4 split, boneless, skinless chicken breasts to ⅜-inch thickness. Grill 2 to 3 minutes per side. Serve with a sauce made from 1 cup blue cheese dressing thinned with ¼ cup buttermilk.

 ### Barbecued Chicken

Bring ¾ cup ketchup, ¼ cup grated onion, 2 tablespoons cider vinegar, 1 tablespoon mustard, 1 tablespoon Worcestershire sauce, 1 tablespoon molasses, and 1 tablespoon hot pepper sauce to a simmer. Remove from heat and marinate a 3- to 4-pound chicken, cut into serving pieces, in the sauce for 1 hour. Remove chicken from sauce and grill over medium heat until firm—about 20 minutes for legs and thighs, 15 minutes for wings, 10 minutes for breasts. Turn chicken frequently to keep it from burning, basting with sauce after each turn.

 ### Barbecued Chicken Sandwich

Follow preceding recipe but use two 12-ounce boneless and skinless chicken breasts, split and trimmed. Grill breasts for 4 to 5 minutes per side and serve hot on 4 kaiser rolls.

Leftover Barbecued Chicken Salad

In a large skillet, sauté until softened 1 clove chopped garlic and ½ minced small onion in hot rendered fat from 4 slices bacon. Add 3 tablespoons cider vinegar, 2 teaspoons Worcestershire sauce, ¼ teaspoon hot pepper sauce, 1 tablespoon sugar, salt, and pepper and keep warm. Just before serving, toss with 1 to 1½ pounds leftover barbecued chicken meat in bite-size pieces, 1 diced roasted red pepper (page 442), 2 large sliced mushrooms, ½ head cleaned Romaine lettuce broken into bite-size pieces, and 1 chopped scallion.

 ### Grilled Ranch-Style Chicken Legs

Marinate 8 chicken legs in 1 cup ranch dressing for 1 hour. Lift from marinade and grill over moderate heat for 20 minutes, turning frequently and basting after each turn.

 ### Grilled Chicken Breast with Tomato-Dill Salsa

Combine 2 chopped large seeded and stemmed tomatoes, ½ finely chopped red onion, ¼ cup chopped dill leaves, 1 clove minced garlic, ¼ cup olive oil, 3 tablespoons vinegar, salt, and pepper. Pound 2 large split skinless, boneless chicken breasts to ⅜-inch thickness. Grill 3 to 4 minutes per side. Dollop with sauce.

 ### Grilled Chicken Basted with Sage Butter

Simmer 2 tablespoons rubbed sage in ¼ cup chicken stock until almost all the liquid has evaporated, remove from heat, swirl in ¼ pound butter and season with pepper. Brush on pieces of a cut-up 3- to 4-pound chicken and cook over medium heat until firm—about 20 minutes for legs and thighs, 15 minutes for wings, 10 minutes for breasts. Turn chicken frequently to keep it from burning, basting with the butter after each turn.

Grilled Chicken Salad

Rub 2 large split skinless, boneless chicken breasts with olive oil, salt, and pepper. Grill 4 to 5 minutes per side. Cut chicken into chunks and toss with ¼ cup olive oil, 2 tablespoons red wine vinegar, ¼ cup chopped red onion, 2 tablespoons drained capers, salt, and pepper. Serve over lettuce.

Grilled Oriental Chicken Salad

Rub 2 large split skinless, boneless chicken breasts with olive oil, salt, and pepper. Grill 4 to 5 minutes per side, cut chicken into chunks and toss with 1 tablespoon finely grated fresh gingerroot, 1 clove minced garlic, 2 tablespoons low-sodium soy sauce, 2 tablespoons Oriental sesame oil, 2 tablespoons peanut oil, 2 tablespoons rice vinegar, a pinch of cayenne pepper, 2 chopped scallions, 1 cup tangerine sections, 1 tablespoon toasted sesame seeds, salt, and pepper. Serve over lettuce.

Grilled Chicken Livers with Worcestershire Marinade

In a bowl, combine ¼ cup Worcestershire sauce, 1 tablespoon molasses, 1 tablespoon brown mustard, and 1 pound trimmed chicken livers and marinate for 20 minutes. Place 3 to 4 livers on a skewer and grill for 2 minutes per side, basting frequently with marinade, until the livers are firm.

Mustard-Grilled Veal Chops

Coat four 1-inch-thick veal chops with a mixture of 3 tablespoons mustard, ½ clove minced garlic, 1

tablespoon olive oil, salt, and pepper. Grill for 4 to 5 minutes per side.

Veal Chops Stuffed with Fontina and Sun-Dried Tomato

Cut a small pocket in each of four 1-inch-thick veal chops. Stuff each veal chop with 1 oil-cured sun-dried tomato and ½-ounce slice Italian Fontina cheese. Rub exterior of chops with some oil from the tomatoes and grill 4 to 5 minutes per side.

Grilled Liver with Onions

Sauté 1 large thinly sliced onion in 2 tablespoons *each* butter and olive oil over low heat until onion is golden brown. Brush ¾ pound calf's liver sliced into ⅜-inch-thick slices with some fat from the pan and season with salt and pepper. Grill liver for 2 to 3 minutes per side. Serve with onions.

Grilled Steak with Caramelized Garlic

Break 2 heads garlic into cloves, peel, and cook gently in 4 tablespoons butter until golden brown. Stir in 1 tablespoon sugar and cook until mixture darkens slightly. Add 1 tablespoon brandy, season with salt, and set aside. Season four 8-ounce boneless sirloin strip steaks with salt, pepper, and a pinch of minced fresh garlic. Grill to desired doneness. Serve with the caramelized garlic over top.

Grilled Honey-Mustard Pork Chops

Brush 8 thin pork chops with a mixture of 3 tablespoons brown mustard and 3 tablespoons honey. Grill 2 to 3 minutes per side.

Grilled Corn

Grill, covered, 8 ears unhusked corn for 15 minutes, turning every 3 to 4 minutes. Allow to cool for 2 minutes, remove husks and silks, and serve with butter, salt, and pepper.

Grilled Lamb Chops with Cucumber Yogurt Sauce

Peel, halve, and seed 1 large cucumber and cut into thin slices. Toss with 1 teaspoon kosher salt and set aside for 15 minutes. Rinse well and drain. Mix with 1 cup yogurt, the juice of ½ lemon, 1 tablespoon olive oil, 1 tablespoon chopped mint leaves, salt, and pepper. Season 8 rib or loin lamb chops with salt, pepper, and a pinch of ground coriander. Grill 3 to 4 minutes per side. Serve dolloped with the sauce.

Mushroom Kebabs

Marinate 16 cleaned, large mushrooms for at least 2 hours in ¼ cup olive oil, the juice of 1 lemon, 2 cloves minced garlic, 2 tablespoons chopped fresh chive, 1 teaspoon dried thyme leaves, a pinch of crushed red pepper flakes, and salt. Place 3 or 4 mushrooms on a metal skewer, leaving at least ¼ inch between each mushroom. Grill over moderate heat for 9 minutes, turning every 3 minutes, and basting with some of the marinade at each turn.

Grilled Lamb Steak Provençale

In a shallow nonmetallic pan, combine 2 cloves chopped garlic, 1 minced onion, 1 tablespoon *herbes de Provence*, ⅓ cup olive oil, and 2 finely chopped canned plum tomatoes. Season eight 5-ounce shoulder lamb chops or slices of lamb leg with salt and pepper. Place lamb in marinade, coat well, and marinate 1 to 2 hours. Grill about 5 minutes per side, basting with marinade every minute.

Charcoal-Grilled Potato Chips

Slice 1½ pounds russet potatoes in slices ¹⁄₁₆ inch thick. Dip slices in oil and grill 3 to 4 minutes per side, until brown and crispy. Dust with salt before serving.

Lamb and Leek Kebabs

Mix 2 tablespoons virgin olive oil, 2 tablespoons red wine vinegar, 2 cloves minced garlic, ¼ cup chopped fresh basil, 1 chopped tomato, 1 crumbled bay leaf, salt, and pepper. Add 1½ pounds trimmed and cubed boneless leg of lamb and whites of 4 cleaned leeks, cut in 2-inch lengths. Marinate several hours. Alternately skewer 3 pieces lamb and 2 pieces leek on each of 4 metal skewers. Grill over moderate fire for 20 to 30 minutes, turning every 5 minutes and basting with some remaining marinade before each turn.

Grilled Ratatouille

In a large bowl, toss the whites of 2 leeks cut into 2-inch segments, 1 large zucchini cut in 1-inch-thick slices, 12 large mushroom caps, 1 peeled medium eggplant cut into 3-inch-long batons, 2 large thickly sliced beefsteak tomatoes, and 1 red onion cut in thick slices in ½ cup olive oil until well coated. Grill vegetables in the following order, turning each several times while it cooks: leeks for 8 to 10 minutes; mushrooms, onion, and eggplant for 5 to 7 minutes; zucchini and tomatoes for 3 to 4 minutes. Arrange grilled vegetables on a large platter and serve with Garlic Vinaigrette (page 28).

Grilled Maple-Glazed Breakfast Sausage

Grill 12 breakfast sausages for 8 minutes, turning every 2 minutes. Brush each sausage with 1 teaspoon maple syrup, cover the grill, and cook 1 minute more.

Grilled Honey Corn Cakes

Cream 4 tablespoons softened butter with 2 teaspoons honey and brush ½ teaspoon on each side of 8 corn toaster cakes or 8 slices corn bread. Grill for 1 minute per side. Serve warm with extra honey butter on the side.

Grilled Pound Cake with Honey Butter

Cream ¼ pound softened butter with ¼ cup honey. Set aside. Brush 8 slices pound cake with 6 tablespoons melted butter and grill 6 inches from a moderate fire until slices brown lightly, about 90 seconds per side. Serve with the honey butter and fresh fruit.

Bananas Grilled with Vanilla and Candied Ginger

Place each of 4 peeled bananas on an 8-inch piece of foil. Place ¼ vanilla bean and 1 teaspoon chopped candied ginger next to each banana. Top each with 1 teaspoon butter, 1 teaspoon honey, and 1 tablespoon orange liqueur. Wrap in the foil, sealing tightly. Grill 5 minutes. Serve with ice cream.

Grilled Brandied Peaches

Follow preceding recipe, but substitute 1 quartered, peeled, and pitted peach for each banana, and brandy for the liqueur.

Chocolate Fondue on a Grill

Over a low charcoal fire, place a small saucepan containing ½ cup light cream and 1 tablespoon instant coffee powder and bring to a simmer. Move the pot to the edge of the fire, whisk in 8 ounces finely chopped sweet chocolate, then stir in ¼ cup rum, brandy, or fruit liqueur. Keep chocolate warm by the side of the fire while guests dip in pieces of fruit, pound-cake fingers, or plain butter cookies.

Fifty Do-Ahead Recipes That Let You Go to Your Own Party

Just about everyone who loves to cook eventually gets pressured, either from external or inner forces, into showing off with a party. Although this can begin innocently enough as a way of sharing one's talents and good feelings with friends, it can easily become overwhelming. No one can pinpoint the exact moment at which an evening of gracious entertaining becomes a sentence of dinner with no parole, but it has happened to all of us. So we offer the following advice to help you avoid the pitfalls.

Start with a menu containing many types of foods and a detailed cooking plan. Serve some items chilled and others heated. Think about what can be cooked ahead and what ingredients will be hard to purchase or store well. Decide mostly on tried-and-true dishes that are quick and easy, and if you want to make a good impression, go for it once and once only in the meal, rather than trying for fireworks at every course.

Don't try to do everything yourself. Unless you live with a staff of four in your kitchen, you will probably need some outside help even for a dinner party with as few as, say, a dozen people. Help can be as simple as having guests cook and bring a dish or deciding that you will buy the dessert rather than prepare it yourself.

But if you insist on cooking everything from scratch with your own two hands and you want to be able to attend the party as well, it is essential that you prepare as much of the food ahead of time as possible. Freeze whatever you can and plan dishes that do not require last-minute fussing.

Hors d'oeuvre or appetizers wrapped in commercially prepared frozen puff pastry are infinitely elegant and keep for weeks in the freezer. You can make chilled soufflés and soups a day ahead and serve them without so much as reheating. Pâtés keep for weeks, each providing a score or more of servings, while marinated salads provide brilliant colors and piquant flavors that only get better after a day in the refrigerator.

ABOUT THESE RECIPES

The following 50 recipes for hors d'oeuvre, appetizers, and desserts are virtually ready to go long before the party begins, requiring no more than last-minute cooking or reheating.

Many are written for a large number of servings and can be multiplied or divided to fit your guest count.

All of these foods can be refrigerated and most can be frozen without ill effect. To ensure good results, wrap them tightly in plastic wrap and then in foil. To freeze, do not pack too many pieces together so that freezing occurs rapidly. For soft foods, first place on a sheet pan and freeze solid before wrapping to keep the food from becoming crushed.

You'll find these recipes a notch more elegant than most others in this book, making them suitable for parties or company dinners, but they are just as easy and no more time-consuming.

Creole Crab Mini-Turnovers

In a saucepan, cook 1 minced scallion in 1 tablespoon butter until soft. Toss in ½ pound cleaned lump crabmeat, add ¼ cup heavy cream mixed with 1 teaspoon cornstarch and 2 teaspoons hot pepper sauce, and simmer until lightly thickened. Season with salt and pepper and let cool. Using ½ pound defrosted frozen puff pastry sheets, assemble mini-turnovers (page 445) and refrigerate for several hours or freeze for several weeks. Before baking, defrost if frozen and brush with 1 egg yolk mixed with 1 tablespoon water. Bake at 400° F. for 10 minutes until puffed and brown. Makes 16.

Liver and Bacon Mini-Turnovers

In a skillet, brown and crumble 2 slices bacon. Add 2 tablespoons minced onion and cook in the hot fat until softened. Add 3 split, trimmed chicken livers and brown on all sides. Deglaze pan with 2 tablespoons bourbon. Finely chop livers, add the bacon and cool. Using ½ pound defrosted frozen puff pastry sheets, assemble mini-turnovers (page 445) and refrigerate for several hours or freeze for several weeks. Before baking, defrost if frozen and brush with 1 egg yolk mixed with 1 tablespoon water. Bake at 400° F. for 10 minutes until puffed and brown. Makes 16.

Apple Mincemeat Turnovers

Cook 1 large peeled, cored, and diced apple with ½ cup sugar until tender. Stir in ¾ cup mincemeat and 2 teaspoons cornstarch dissolved in 1 tablespoon lemon juice, stirring until lightly thickened. Add 1 teaspoon vanilla extract and let cool. Using ½ pound defrosted frozen puff pastry sheets, assemble turnovers (page 445) and refrigerate for several hours or freeze for several weeks. Before baking, defrost if frozen and brush with 1 egg yolk mixed with 1 tablespoon water. Bake at 400° F. for 20 to 25 minutes, until fully puffed and brown. Cool for 10 minutes before serving. Makes 4.

Lemon Pear Turnovers

Toss 2 peeled, cored, and diced pears in the juice of ½ lemon. In a saucepan, cook in 2 tablespoons butter and 2 tablespoons sugar until pears are soft. Add 1½ teaspoons cornstarch dissolved in 1 tablespoon water and 1½ teaspoons vanilla extract, along with the finely grated zest of ½ lemon. Cook until thickened, then let cool completely. Using ½ pound defrosted frozen puff pastry sheets, assemble turnovers (page 445) and refrigerate for several hours or freeze for several weeks. Before baking, defrost if frozen and brush with 1 egg yolk mixed with 1 tablespoon water. Bake at 400° F. for 20 to 25 minutes before serving. Makes 4.

Chicken Wellington

Season 2 split boneless, skinless chicken breasts with salt and pepper and brown in a hot skillet in 2 tablespoons olive oil. Let cool. Cut a pocket in each breast half. Insert ¼ roasted red bell pepper (page 442) and 2 basil leaves in each pocket and wrap 1 slice prosciutto around each piece. Roll ¾ pound defrosted frozen puff pastry 3/16 inch thick, cut in quarters, and wrap each breast half in 1 section of pastry. Refrigerate for a day or freeze for several weeks. If frozen, defrost, place seam-side down on a dry sheet pan, and brush with 1 egg yolk mixed with 1 tablespoon water. Bake for 10 minutes at 400° F., reduce heat to 375° F and bake 10 minutes more. Makes 4.

Puff Pastry Mini-Pizzas

Roll 1 pound defrosted frozen puff pastry to 3/16-inch thickness. Sprinkle with ⅓ cup grated Parmesan, top with 1½ cups tomato pasta sauce, ¼ pound sliced and sautéed mushrooms, 1 finely diced red or yellow bell pepper, and ½ pound shredded mozzarella and drizzle with 1 tablespoon olive oil. Punch out 16 mini-pizzas with a 3-inch cutter, freeze on a sheet pan until solid before cooking, then wrap well and freeze for up to several weeks. Bake frozen at 400° F. for 15 to 20 minutes until bubbly and crisp. Makes 16.

Cheese Straws

Roll 1 pound defrosted frozen puff pastry to 3/16-inch thickness. Brush both sides with 1 egg yolk mixed with 1 tablespoon water, then coat with a mixture of 1 cup grated Parmesan, 1 teaspoon cayenne pepper, ½ cup finely shredded Cheddar cheese, and 1 teaspoon paprika. Cut into ½-inch-wide, 6-inch-long strips, twist each strip 4 times, and place on a dry sheet pan, pressing ends down to hold the twist in place. Refrigerate for up to several hours or freeze for several weeks. If frozen, defrost, then bake for 15 minutes at 400° F. Makes 3 dozen.

Fried Herbed Shrimp

Mix 6 tablespoons softened butter with 1 teaspoon lemon juice, 1 tablespoon chopped fresh parsley, ½ teaspoon dried tarragon, 1½ teaspoons chopped shallot, salt, and pepper. Butterfly 20 shelled jumbo shrimp. Spread interior of each shrimp with about ½ teaspoon of the butter, close shrimps, dip in 1 beaten egg, and dredge in 2 cups bread crumbs. Refrigerate for at least 1 hour or freeze up to 1 month. Bring to refrigerator temperature before cooking. Deep-fry at 375° F. until golden brown, about 2 minutes. Makes 20.

Pepper Peanut Shrimp

Follow preceding recipe substituting this mixture for the butter: Mix 1 clove minced garlic, 1 teaspoon chili paste, 2 teaspoons finely chopped fresh gingerroot, ¼ teaspoon ground cumin, ¼ teaspoon ground coriander, and ¼ cup peanut butter. Freeze. Makes 20.

Chilled Salmon Soufflé

In a food processor, mix 2 teaspoons mustard, the juice of ½ lemon, 1½ cups mayonnaise, salt, and pepper. Add 2 pounds cooked, boned, and skinned salmon and process with the sauce. Soften 1 envelope gelatin in the juice of ½ lemon, add to ⅓ cup boiling white wine, and stir to dissolve. Blend into salmon mixture. Beat 1 cup heavy cream to a soft peak and fold into salmon. Attach a paper collar to a 1-quart soufflé dish, turn salmon mixture into dish, smooth top, cover loosely with plastic, and chill for at least several hours, until firm. Remove collar before serving. Serves 6 to 8.

 Chilled Crab and Chive Soufflé

Follow preceding recipe substituting 1 pound cooked white-fleshed fish fillet and 1 pound cleaned crabmeat for the salmon. Stir in ¼ cup chopped chive along with the gelatin.

 Balsamic Shrimp

In a saucepan, bring 4 cloves sliced garlic, the sliced whites of 1 bunch scallions, and ¼ cup dry white wine to a boil. Add 1 pound peeled medium shrimp and toss until firm; do not overcook. Remove from heat and stir in ¼ cup extra-virgin olive oil, 1 tablespoon balsamic vinegar, a pinch of cayenne pepper, salt, and pepper. Refrigerate for up to 3 days. Serves 6 as an appetizer.

 Eggplant Rillettes

Bake 2 medium eggplants at 400° F. for 45 minutes, let cool 10 minutes, then halve lengthwise, and scoop out flesh. Mash the flesh. Mix in 1 clove minced garlic, 2 tablespoons mayonnaise, the juice of 1 lemon, 6 minced anchovy fillets, and 1 tablespoon drained small capers. Chill up to several days. Serve as a dip or cracker spread. Makes 2 to 3 cups.

 Baba Ghanoush

Bake 2 medium eggplants in a 400° F. oven for 45 minutes, let cool 10 minutes, then halve lengthwise and scoop out the flesh. Mash with 1 clove minced garlic, 2 tablespoons olive oil, and the juice of ½ lemon. Makes 2 to 3 cups.

 Niçoise Pizzas

In a food processor, blend 1 cup black olives, 2 cloves garlic, 1 tablespoon anchovy fillet, black pepper, and 2 teaspoons drained capers. Add enough olive oil to make a smooth paste. Refrigerate for several days. Cut 1 French baguette into 24 slices, brush with thin film of olive oil, and toast. Store at room temperature in airtight container for a few days. To serve, spread paste on the toast, top each with 1 slice plum tomato and 2 teaspoons shredded mozzarella and broil until cheese melts. Serves 12.

 Roasted Garlic Puree

Cut tips off 6 heads garlic, place in baking dish with ¼ cup water, drizzle with 2 tablespoons olive oil, and sprinkle with salt and pepper. Bake at 400° F. for 40 minutes and let cool. Squeeze flesh from garlic skins and puree in a food processor with the pan juices, adding more olive oil to make it a dip consistency. Season with salt and pepper. Use as a dip for vegetables, poached shellfish, or as a bread spread. Serves 12.

 Roasted Pepper Dip

Roast 3 large red peppers (page 442), chop the flesh, and puree in a food processor with 2 tablespoons mayonnaise, 1 tablespoon olive oil, salt, and pepper. Refrigerate for several days. Use as dip with vegetables or poached shellfish. Serves 12.

 Marinated Roasted Peppers and Olives

Marinate 6 sliced roasted bell peppers (page 442) and 1 cup black olives in ⅓ cup olive oil, 2 cloves minced garlic, ½ teaspoon crushed red pepper flakes, 2 tablespoons wine vinegar, salt, and pepper. Refrigerate up to several days. Serves 12.

 Sausage-Stuffed Mushrooms

Brown caps from 24 large mushrooms in 2 tablespoons olive oil, then set aside. Chop mushroom stems and brown with 2 cloves minced garlic, 2 tablespoons chopped scallion, and 6 ounces sausage meat. Mix in ¾ cup bread crumbs and 3 tablespoons grated Parmesan. Mound mixture into mushroom caps and refrigerate up to 3 days. Bake at 400° F. for 15 to 20 minutes. Serves 12.

Spinach-Stuffed Mushroom Caps

Follow preceding recipe, omitting the sausage. Add 10 ounces frozen chopped spinach, defrosted and squeezed dry, and ½ teaspoon Dijon mustard to the sautéed vegetables. After assembly, freeze for several weeks, but defrost before cooking. Serves 12.

 Spanakopita

In a skillet, cook ½ cup chopped onion and 3 cloves minced garlic in 3 tablespoons olive oil until softened. Add 10 ounces defrosted frozen chopped spinach and cook until dry. Blend in ¼ pound *each* crumbled feta cheese and cream cheese

and season with salt and pepper. Cut 8 sheets phyllo dough into 4 strips each. Using 1 strip at a time, brush with a thin film of melted clarified butter (page 430). Place 1 tablespoon of the cheese mixture at the end of the strip and fold into a triangle, continuing as you would fold a flag. Brush with more clarified butter. Repeat until all ingredients have been used. Refrigerate several days or freeze for several weeks. Bake at 400° F. until golden brown, about 20 minutes. Serves 12.

 Cheese Pockets

Mix 1 cup crumbled feta cheese, 8 ounces farmer cheese, 2 eggs, 2 tablespoons chopped fresh dill, ½ clove minced garlic, salt, and pepper. Follow preceding recipe, using this cheese mixture in place of the spinach mixture. Serves 12.

 Blue Cheese Grapes

Toast ½ pound walnuts and chop well. Mix 6 ounces *each* blue cheese and softened cream cheese and a dash of hot pepper sauce. Mold cheese mixture around 24 seedless grapes and roll in the toasted nuts. Refrigerate for 2 to 3 days before dredging in the nuts. Roll in the nuts no more than 4 hours before serving. Arrange like a bunch of grapes on serving tray. Serves 12.

 Vegetable Pâté Niçoise

In a skillet, cook ½ cup onion in 3 tablespoons olive oil until softened. Add 2 cloves minced garlic and 15 ounces defrosted frozen chopped spinach and cook until dry. Blend in 2 tablespoons flour, then add 1 cup milk, and cook until thick. Remove from heat and beat in ½ cup ricotta cheese, ½ cup grated Parmesan, 10 egg yolks, ½ teaspoon brandy, salt, and pepper. Line a greased 5-by-7-inch loaf pan with parchment or wax paper, then grease the paper. Alternate 5 layers of spinach mixture with a layer each of 1 cup cooked chick-peas, 1 cup diced roasted red pepper (page 442), 1½ cups chopped black olives, and 5 canned artichoke bottoms. Top with greased parchment and foil, place in a pan of water and bake at 375° F. for 1½ hours. Let cool, unmold, and chill for up to 1 week. Serve in slices with Warm Tomato Vinaigrette (page 298). Serves 8.

 ## Fennel Pâté

Follow preceding recipe substituting 1 finely chopped fennel bulb (including leaves) for half the spinach. Add 1 tablespoon *herbes de Provence* with the flour and replace the brandy with Pernod.

 ## Tricolor Fish Terrine

In a food processor, blend until smooth 1½ pounds trimmed and skinned flounder fillet, 3 egg whites, and 3¼ cups cold heavy cream. Mix in 2 teaspoons salt, 1 teaspoon white pepper, and 1 teaspoon finely chopped shallot. Line a buttered 5-by-7-inch loaf pan with parchment paper. Layer half the fish mixture in the pan. Cut 6 ounces salmon fillet in 2 strips, season with salt and pepper, and brush with 1 beaten egg white. Blanch 6 ounces trimmed spinach leaves until wilted, pat dry, and wrap salmon in leaves. Lay wrapped salmon down the center of the mousse and pack remaining mousse on top. Cover with buttered parchment paper and 2 layers of foil. Bake in a pan of water in a preheated 350° F. oven for 1¼ hours until firm. Cool, chill, and unmold. Serve with Creamy Orange Fennel Dressing (page 297), if desired. Serves 8.

 ## Anise Tea Eggs

Cook 6 eggs in 2 quarts simmering water for 10 minutes. Let cool completely. Crack the shells without removing them by tapping all over the surface of the eggs with the back of a spoon or rolling them gently on a countertop or table. Cover with cold water, add 2 tablespoons aniseed, ¼ cup soy sauce, and 2 hibiscus-blend tea bags, cover saucepan, and simmer 1 hour. Let cool and store in the liquid in the refrigerator at least 2 days. Shortly before serving, peel and cut in quarters. Serve with Dipping Sauce for Potstickers (page 205). Serves 6.

 ## Lemon-Soy Smoked Shrimp

Marinate 2 pounds large shrimp in the juice and finely grated zest of 2 lemons, 1 dried chili pepper, 2 tablespoons soy sauce, and 2 tablespoons cider vinegar in the refrigerator for 2 to 3 hours or overnight. Line a heavy wok, iron skillet, or Dutch oven with heavy foil, mix ½ cup loose hibiscus-tea with ½ cup sugar, place in bottom of pan and place a rack over top. Heat over high flame until tea smokes. Drain shrimp, place on rack, cover, and smoke for about 10 minutes. Remove and refrigerate for up to several days. Serve with Dipping Sauce for Potstickers (page 205). Serves 12.

 ## Marinated Mozzarella

Marinate 1 pound sliced mozzarella in ½ cup virgin olive oil, 3 cloves minced garlic, 2 tablespoons chopped basil leaves, ¼ cup wine vinegar, salt, and pepper. Refrigerate up to 1 week. Serve with lots of fresh French bread. Serves 6.

 ## Quick Chopped Chicken Liver

In a nonstick skillet, cook 2 large chopped onions in a covered pan over low heat until very soft and lightly browned. Add ⅓ cup rendered chicken fat and sauté until well brown. Add 1 pound trimmed chicken livers and a pinch of thyme and sauté until firm. Finely chop in a food processor and mix in 2 chopped hard-cooked eggs, salt, and pepper. Chill and serve with toast. Serves 6 to 8.

 ### Escabeche of Softshell Crab

In a large skillet, sauté 8 cleaned softshell crabs (page 439) in ½ cup olive oil. Add ¾ pound thinly sliced onion, 2 cloves minced garlic, 2 tablespoons wine vinegar, and the juice of 1 lemon, 1 orange, and 1 lime. Bring to a boil and season with cayenne pepper, salt, and pepper. Let cool. Stir in 2 tablespoons chopped fresh parsley. Refrigerate for up to 4 days. Serves 4.

 ### Mahogany Chicken Wings

Section 2 pounds chicken wings between the first and second joints and discard the small third joint. Cook 2 cloves minced garlic, 1 dried hot chili pepper, and 1 tablespoon grated fresh gingerroot in 2 tablespoons peanut oil. Mix in ⅓ cup soy sauce, ¼ cup water, ¼ cup dry sherry, 1 tablespoon rice vinegar, 2 tablespoon molasses, and ¼ cup honey and bring to a boil. Add the wings, cover, and simmer for 5 minutes. Uncover and cook until the liquid reduces enough to glaze wings. Toss gently near the end of cooking, then stir in 1 tablespoon Oriental sesame oil. Refrigerate up to 2 days. Reheat or serve chilled. Serves 6.

 ### Ginger Black Bean Chicken Wings

Follow preceding recipe, replacing soy sauce with ¼ cup black bean sauce, 1 tablespoon garlic chili paste, 1 tablespoon hoisin sauce, and ½ cup water.

 ### Charred Raw Beef with Jalapeño Salsa

Heat a large iron skillet over high flame for 10 to 12 minutes. Rub 3 pounds trimmed beef tenderloin with salt and pepper on all sides and char on all sides in the hot pan. Do not lower heat and do not overcook. Remove and let cool. Refrigerate up to 3 days. Slice thin and serve on sliced French bread, topping each slice with 1 teaspoon Jalapeño Salsa (page 64). Serves 10.

 ### Raw Charred Lamb with Roasted Garlic

Follow preceding recipe using boneless loin of lamb instead of beef. Use Roasted Garlic Puree (page 135) in place of the salsa.

Shrimp With Smoked Salmon

In mixture of 2 cups white wine, 2 cups water, 1 strip lemon zest, the juice of ½ lemon, 6 peppercorns, ½ teaspoon salt, and 1 bay leaf, poach 24 peeled and cleaned jumbo shrimp until firm and opaque, about 2 minutes. Marinate in Mustard Vinaigrette (page 297) mixed with 2 tablespoons chopped dill weed. Refrigerate up to 2 days. Up to 24 hours before serving, cut 6 ounces smoked salmon into 24 strips. Wrap each shrimp with 1 strip smoked salmon and secure with toothpick. Wrap tightly to store. Serves 6.

Turkey Kebabs Glazed with Jalapeño Jelly

Slice 2 pounds boneless, skinless turkey breast into fingers and toss in a mixture of ¼ cup olive oil, 2 tablespoons cider vinegar, 1 clove minced garlic, and 1 teaspoon crushed red pepper flakes. Refrigerate overnight. Spear each piece of meat with a bamboo skewer and refrigerate up to 1 day or, if turkey was fresh, freeze for several weeks. If frozen, defrost before cooking. Brush with ½ cup melted jalapeño jelly and broil or grill for 2 to 3 minutes per side. Serves 8.

 ### Chicken Tandoori Brochettes

Slice 2 pounds skinless, boneless chicken breast in 1-inch-wide strips and marinate overnight in Tandoori Curry Marinade (page 21). Thread each piece of meat on a bamboo skewer and refrigerate up to 1 day or, if chicken was not frozen, freeze for several weeks. If frozen, defrost, then broil or grill for 2 to 3 minutes per side and serve with Asian Peanut Marinade (page 20). Serves 8.

 ### Gingered Carrots with Hot Pepper Vinaigrette

Blanch 2 pounds peeled spiral-cut carrots, drain, and while still hot, toss with a mixture of ¼ cup peanut oil, 2 tablespoons Oriental sesame oil, 2 tablespoons white wine vinegar, the juice of 1 lemon, 1 clove minced garlic, 1 teaspoon crushed red pepper flakes, 2 teaspoons minced fresh gingerroot, salt, and pepper. Refrigerate up to 1 week. Before serving, toss with 2 tablespoons chopped fresh chives. Serves 12.

 ### Marinated Roasted Peppers with Black Olives and Tortellini

Mix 4 julienned roasted red bell peppers (page 442) with 24 pitted oil-cured black olives, 2 cups cooked cheese tortellini, ½ chopped red onion, 1 clove minced garlic, ¼ cup olive oil, 3 tablespoons wine vinegar, salt, and pepper. Refrigerate up to 1 week. Before serving, toss with 2 tablespoons chopped fresh basil. Serves 12.

 ### Marinated Garlic Mushrooms

Sauté 1 pound small mushrooms and 2 cloves minced garlic in ¼ cup olive oil until softened. Toss with 1 tablespoon olive oil, the juice and zest of 1 lemon, ⅛ teaspoon cayenne pepper, salt, and pepper. Refrigerate up to 1 week. Before serving, toss with 2 tablespoons chopped fresh flat-leaf parsley. Serves 12.

 ### Lemon Cheese

Mix 8 ounces farmer cheese with 1 tablespoon lemon juice. Mash 1 tablespoon minced lemon zest with 1 teaspoon sugar and mix into cheese. Shape into a dome on a small plate. Serve with crackers or fresh bread. Refrigerate up to 3 days. Serves 4 to 6.

 ### Garlic Cheese

Follow preceding recipe replacing lemon juice with 1 teaspoon wine vinegar. Add 3 cloves minced garlic and 1 teaspoon coarsely ground pepper with the vinegar.

 ### Angel-of-Death Cheese

Follow recipe for Lemon Cheese (above) using 1 teaspoon wine vinegar instead of the lemon. Add 2 teaspoons rubbed sage and 6 cloves minced garlic. Sprinkle surface of cheese with 2 tablespoons cracked pepper.

 ### Smoked Salmon and Gruyère Cheesecake

In a skillet, cook 1 chopped onion, 1 clove minced garlic, and ⅓ cup chopped fresh dill in 3 tablespoons olive oil until the onion softens. Remove from heat and stir in ½ pound coarsely chopped smoked salmon. With an electric mixer, cream 2 pounds room-temperature cream cheese. Add 3 tablespoons wine vinegar, ¼ cup whiskey, ¼ pound shredded Gruyère cheese, ¼ cup grated Parmesan, 6 eggs, salt, and pepper and beat until smooth. Fold in salmon mixture. Pour into a 2-quart soufflé dish, greased and dusted with Parmesan, and bake in a pan of water in a preheated 200° F. oven for 8 hours. Allow to cool in the pan, then unpan (page 444) and chill. Serve with sliced black bread. Serves 16 to 20.

Blue Cheese Apple Cheesecake

Cook ½ pound bacon until crisp, remove from skillet and blot off excess fat with paper towels. Crumble bacon and set aside. Discard all but 3 tablespoons bacon fat, add 1 chopped onion, 1 clove minced garlic, and 1 cup diced peeled apple and cook in the fat until softened. Add the reserved bacon and set aside. Follow preceding recipe using this mixture in place of the smoked salmon mixture. Substitute ½ pound crumbled blue cheese for the Gruyère.

Eight-Hour Brandy Cheesecake

With an electric mixer, beat 2 pounds room-temperature cream cheese, 1 cup sugar, 2 tablespoons vanilla extract and ¼ cup brandy until very smooth. Add 5 eggs and beat just long enough to incorporate. Pour into a greased 2-quart soufflé dish, dusted with cookie crumbs, and bake in pan of water in a preheated 200° F. oven for 8 hours. Allow to cool in pan. Invert to unpan (page 444). Chill before serving. Serves 12 to 16.

Avocado Ice Cream

In a food processor, mix 3 ripe California avocados with the juice of 1 lime until smooth. Scald 2 cups milk with 1 cup sugar and mix into avocado mixture along with 1 cup sour cream, 1 cup light cream, 1 teaspoon lemon extract, a pinch of cayenne pepper, and ¼ teaspoon salt. Cool completely and freeze in an ice-cream freezer according to manufacturer's directions. Freeze tightly covered for up to 3 days. Serve as a summer appetizer, palate cleanser, or dessert. Makes 1½ quarts.

Chocolate Coronary

Scald 1 cup milk with 1 tablespoon instant coffee. Stir in 1 pound finely chopped semisweet chocolate until melted. Add 1 tablespoon vanilla extract and 2 tablespoons orange liqueur. With an electric mixer, beat in ½ pound softened butter and 8 egg yolks. Pour into a 9-inch greased springform pan, lined with wax or parchment paper and bake at 350° F. for 23 minutes. It will not look done. Cool and refrigerate until completely firm. Cut around sides and remove springform. Refrigerate up to 1 week. Serve with whipped cream. Serves 16.

Crème Caramel

Caramelize ¾ cup sugar and pour into a low flat ovenproof baking dish of at least 1½-quart capacity. Tilt the dish so the caramel covers the bottom in a sheet. Set aside. Scald 1 quart milk with ½ cup sugar. Add slowly to 4 eggs beaten with ¼ cup sugar. Mix in 2 teaspoons vanilla extract. Pour into baking dish on top of caramel. Bake in pan of water in preheated 350° F. oven for 1 hour 15 minutes. Cool on a rack to room temperature, then refrigerate 24 hours. Run a knife around the edge and invert onto large platter, letting caramel fall around the custard. Serve in wedges. Serves 8.

Fifty Ways to Trade Calories for Flavor

From a culinary tradition steeped in calories, fat, cholesterol, salt, and sugar, nothing short of a food revolution has occurred in recent years. All those things have become our kitchen enemies, and we want less of them.

Calories and complexity in particular have become the standards by which recipes are judged by today's home cooks. Those that call for pints of heavy cream and hours in the kitchen are the ones inevitably left unused by busy, calorie-conscious cooks. Like unsung songs and unseen art, such untried recipes might just as well not exist.

The following 50 recipes were built with those constraints in mind. They are as simple and streamlined as everything else in these pages, but in this chapter we pay special attention to calories. In most cases, we've done so by drastically cutting fat. Anyone can make food flavorful by using lots of butter and oil. The trick to these recipes lies in our reliance on highly flavored ingredients—herbs, broths, and purées—that have the added benefit of reducing the need for salt. And to help you keep tabs on everything going into your meals, we've

minimized the use of processed food and packaged ingredients.

These recipes explore a wide variety of ingredients, including shellfish, fish, poultry, game meats, veal, pork, and vegetables. Look through them, find one that fits your palate, and try it. If you're pleased, try another. Soon you'll have a whole new repertoire of easily prepared, low-calorie dishes that give you and your diners much more with much less. By the way, calories, while important, tell only part of the nutrition story. Be sure to look at the low-fat recipes in Chapter 17, which pay close attention to fat without the severe calorie restrictions that we've worked with here.

ABOUT THESE RECIPES

Each of these recipes contains fewer than 300 calories per serving, allowing you ample room for side dishes and a reasonable dessert while remaining well within the calorie boundaries of most diets.

The number in parentheses at the end of the

recipe is the calorie count per serving. But to get those counts, you must follow ingredient quantities carefully. One tablespoon of oil means exactly that; another tablespoon would add 30 calories to one portion of a 4-serving dish. "Trimmed" means all excess fat and skin are removed. Recipes are written for 4 portions unless otherwise noted and all should be seasoned to taste with salt and pepper.

All chicken breasts in the following recipes are skinless, boneless, and trimmed. When pounding breasts, do so between 2 sheets of wax paper or kitchen parchment to ¼-inch thickness. Remove the paper before cooking.

 Chicken Steamed with Roasted Pepper and Cilantro

Cook 2 cloves minced garlic, ½ teaspoon ground coriander, ½ teaspoon ground cumin, and ⅛ teaspoon cayenne pepper in 1 tablespoon walnut oil for 30 seconds. Mix with 2 tablespoons lemon juice and spread on four 8-ounce chicken breasts. Refrigerate 1 hour. Pound, remove paper, and roll each piece around ¼ roasted red pepper (page 442) cut in julienne strips and 1 tablespoon chopped fresh cilantro. Roll each in a large piece tightly sealed plastic wrap and steam for 20 to 25 minutes, until chicken feels firm. Snip one end of the plastic, pour any juices into a small saucepan, and reduce until lightly thickened. Slice chicken and pour reduced juices on top. (228)

 Middle Eastern Chicken Salad

Steam 1½ pounds chicken breast for 14 minutes, until firm. Cut in small pieces and toss with 2 ounces thinly sliced white part of scallion, 6 ounces peeled, seeded, and diced cucumber, 1 clove minced garlic, 2 teaspoons virgin olive oil, 1 tablespoon lemon juice, 2 tablespoons chopped fresh parsley, 2 tablespoons chopped mint leaves, and 8 ounces plain nonfat yogurt. Season with a pinch of cayenne pepper, salt, and black pepper. (208)

 Curried Tandoori-Style Chicken

Poke four 6-ounce pieces chicken breast all over with a fork. Rub with ½ teaspoon salt, toss with the juice of 1 large lemon, and refrigerate 30 minutes. Mix 2 large cloves minced garlic, 2 tablespoons finely chopped fresh gingerroot, 1 teaspoon ground cumin seed, 1 teaspoon ground cardamom seed, 2 teaspoons curry powder, and 2 teaspoons tandori masala (available at many specialty food stores) and thoroughly rub into the chicken. Pour ½ cup plain nonfat yogurt over top and rub into the meat. Cover and refrigerate at least 4 hours. Broil 4 inches from heat for 4 to 5 minutes per side. (243)

 Stir-Fried Chicken Chicory Salad

Cut 1 pound chicken breast into chunks and soak in 2 tablespoons cornstarch dissolved in ¼ cup cold water. Stir-fry 1 coarsely chopped red onion, 2 cloves minced garlic, 1 dried chili pepper, and ¼ pound diced smoked turkey breast in 2 teaspoons corn oil for 1 minute and remove. Remove chicken from cornstarch, add 2 teaspoons corn oil to the wok, and stir-fry chicken for 3 minutes. Add ¼ cup dry sherry, ½ cup chicken stock, and ¼ cup water. Cover and simmer for 3 minutes until chicken is firm. Add 1 tablespoon cider vinegar, 1 tablespoon honey mustard, 1 teaspoon soy sauce, and the reserved vegetables. Heat through. Remove chili pepper and pour mixture over 3 cups shredded chicory or curly endive. (268)

 Grilled Chicken with Artichoke Mole

In a food processor finely chop 6 ounces drained canned artichoke hearts, 2 cloves garlic, 2 tablespoons lemon juice, 1 tablespoon fresh cilantro, 1 tablespoon fresh parsley, 1 seeded jalapeño pepper, 2 tablespoons toasted pumpkin seeds, and 1 tablespoon olive oil. Brush four 6-ounce pieces chicken breast with 1 tablespoon additional olive oil. Pound chicken and grill 4 inches from fire for 4 minutes per side. Serve dolloped with the relish. (258)

 ### Stir-Fried Chicken in Orange Black Bean Sauce

Cut 1 pound chicken breast in bite-size pieces and soak in 1 tablespoon cornstarch dissolved in ¼ cup water. Mix 1 tablespoon Chinese black bean sauce, ½ cup orange juice, 1 tablespoon finely grated orange zest, and 1 clove minced garlic. Lift chicken from cornstarch mixture and stir-fry in a large wok in 1 tablespoon peanut oil until chicken loses its raw look. Add 1 tablespoon grated fresh gingerroot and ¼ teaspoon crushed chili pepper and cook another 30 seconds. Add orange juice mixture, bring to a boil, add cornstarch mixture, and cook until sauce thickens. Remove to a platter and drizzle with 1 teaspoon Oriental sesame oil and 2 finely shredded scallions. Serve over ¼ pound cooked *somen* or other Oriental noodles. (276)

Grilled Chicken with Roasted Pepper and Smoked Eggplant

Rub four 6-ounce pieces chicken breast with a mixture of 1 teaspoon hot paprika, 1 clove minced garlic, 2 teaspoons olive oil, salt, and pepper. Pound and set aside. In a food processor, puree the flesh of ½ pound roasted eggplant, 1 clove garlic, 1½ tablespoons lemon juice, and 1 tablespoon olive oil. Keep warm. In a nonstick skillet, cook 1 diced red pepper in 1 teaspoon olive oil until softened. Season with salt, pepper, 2 table-

spoons minced fresh parsley, and 1 tablespoon finely chopped fresh chive. Grill chicken over hot fire for 3 minutes per side until firm. Spoon warm eggplant sauce over top and scatter pepper mixture over all. (210)

 ### Grilled Turkey Breast with Tomato Basil Salsa

In a food processor, chop ½ pound cored ripe tomatoes, 1 ounce chopped onion, ½ ounce fresh basil leaves, ½ clove garlic, 2 teaspoons olive oil, and 2 teaspoons wine vinegar. Rub eight 3-ounce turkey cutlets with a total of 1 teaspoon olive oil, pound, and grill or broil 4 inches from a hot fire for 1½ minutes per side, until firm. Serve with salsa. (225)

 ### Spaghetti with Turkey Bolognese

In a skillet, cook 2 tablespoons finely chopped onion in 1 tablespoon olive oil until softened. Add 1 finely diced small carrot and 1 finely diced small rib celery and cook 2 more minutes. Add ½ pound lean ground turkey breast, cooking until it loses its raw look. Add ½ cup nonfat milk and a pinch of grated nutmeg and cook until milk has been absorbed. Add 12 peeled, seeded, and chopped plum tomatoes, 1 teaspoon tomato paste, and 1 teaspoon dried basil. Cover partially, and simmer slowly for 2 hours, until lightly thickened. Serve tossed with 12 ounces cooked hot spaghetti. (295)

 ### Lemon Cilantro Turkey Breast

Rub a 6-pound (bone in) skinned turkey breast with 3 cloves minced garlic, 1 tablespoon ground coriander, and 3 tablespoons virgin olive oil. Squeeze the juice of 1 lemon over top. Coarsely chop the lemon shell, toss with 1 bunch cilantro, and spread mixture over floor of a roasting pan. Place turkey on top, and roast at 375° F. until internal temperature reaches 165° F., about 1 hour 45 minutes. Baste frequently with any pan drippings. Serves 12. (274)

 Roasted Turkey Breast with Mint

Rub a 6-pound (bone-in) skinned turkey breast with 4 cloves minced garlic, ¼ cup dried mint, 1 teaspoon virgin olive oil, 1 tablespoon lemon juice, and ¼ cup plain nonfat yogurt. Place in a shallow roasting pan and stuff 12 to 14 mint sprigs in the cavity. Roast for 45 minutes at 425° F. Reduce heat to 350° and roast for another 1½ hours, or until the internal temperature reaches 165° F. Slice and serve with pan juices and 1 pound blanched asparagus. Serves 12. (276)

 Fillets of Sole Steamed with Lemon and Cilantro

Arrange 4 skinned sole fillets, dark-side down, on a plate. Pour the juice of 1 lemon and 1 teaspoon Oriental sesame oil over top and season with salt, pepper, and a grating of nutmeg. Sprinkle 2 tablespoons chopped fresh cilantro over top and cover with another plate. Place over a pot of simmering water and steam for 8 minutes, until fish is opaque. Garnish with lime wedges. (93)

 Steamed Flounder with Yogurt Dill Sauce

Season each of eight 2-ounce flounder fillets with salt, pepper, and ½ teaspoon lemon juice. Roll each fillet lengthwise into a tight roll, seal each roll tightly in a large sheet of plastic wrap, and steam for 8 minutes. Snip one end from each plastic package, pour any juices into a small saucepan, add 1

minced shallot, and reduce for 1 minute. Blend in 2 tablespoons chopped fresh dill and ½ cup plain nonfat yogurt. Remove fish from plastic and pour sauce over top. (109)

 Dilled Salmon Salad

Poach 1 pound salmon fillet in 3 cups Court Bouillon (page 430) for 6 to 8 minutes, turning once after 4 minutes, until salmon flakes when gently prodded. Remove skin and excess fat from salmon, and flake fish. Add to 2 tablespoons extra-virgin olive oil, 2 tablespoons herb vinegar, 1 tablespoon lemon juice, and 2 tablespoons finely chopped fresh dill. (200; on lettuce leaves, 202; with toast, 245)

 Flounder and Salmon Steamed in Romaine

Blanch 4 large Romaine leaves for 10 seconds and halve each one lengthwise. Split four 3-ounce flounder fillets lengthwise and cut an 8-ounce salmon fillet in 8 slices. On each piece of Romaine, place 1 piece flounder and 1 slice salmon. Roll the 3 layers tightly and steam rolls for about 10 minutes. While the fish steams, prepare Beurre Rouge (page 26) and serve with the steamed rolls. (270)

 Snapper Steamed with Green Peppercorns

Make 4 slits in each side of a cleaned 2-pound red snapper. Rub well with 1 tablespoon walnut oil, 2 tablespoons crushed green peppercorns, 1 clove minced garlic, and ½ teaspoon soy sauce. Steam for 15 minutes. Transfer to a platter, pour 2 tablespoons lime juice over top, halve the top and bottom fillets, and serve one piece to each diner. (194)

Salmon Stewed with Fennel and Mushrooms

Lightly dredge in flour four 4-ounce pieces skinned salmon fillet. In a nonstick skillet, brown the salmon in 1 teaspoon olive oil, remove fish, add 1 teaspoon olive oil to the pan, and cook ¼ cup finely chopped onion until softened. Add ½ pound thinly sliced mushrooms and ½ teaspoon tomato paste and brown lightly. Deglaze pan with 2 tablespoons lemon juice. Add 1 cup diced fennel, ½ cup beef stock, and ½ cup fish stock. When simmering, add salmon fillets, cover, and poach for 3 minutes. With a slotted spoon, remove all solids to a platter, reduce liquid until lightly thickened, and pour over fish. (220)

Mexican Stewed Monkfish

Rub 1 pound monkfish fillets, cut in 8 chunks, with ¼ cup lemon juice, salt, and pepper and set aside. In nonstick skillet, cook ⅓ cup minced onion, 2 cloves minced garlic, 2 minced jalapeño peppers, and 1 finely chopped red bell pepper in 1 teaspoon olive oil until softened. Add 4 peeled, chopped plum tomatoes and ½ cup Fish Stock (page 430) and bring to a simmer. Add fish and simmer, covered, for 10 minutes. While fish cooks, chop 6 skinned, quartered tomatillos with ¼ cup fresh cilantro in a food processor. When fish is done, remove it to a platter and reduce the sauce until lightly thickened. Cover half the fish with the pan sauce, the other half with the tomatillo mixture. (240)

Codfish and Cabbage

Sprinkle 1 pound cod fillet with 2 tablespoons lemon juice, salt, pepper, and a grating of nutmeg and refrigerate. Grease the interior of a 3-quart casserole with a thin film of butter. Build up alternating layers of ½ pound peeled and thinly sliced celery root, ¾ pound washed and thinly sliced red potatoes, and 1 pound thinly sliced Napa cabbage, seasoning each layer with salt and pepper and dabbing each with butter, using a total of 2 tablespoons butter. Pour 1½ cups Fish Stock (page 430) over top and bake in preheated 375° F. oven for 40 minutes. Uncover, place cod on top, and bake for another 20 minutes. Sprinkle with 1 tablespoon chopped fresh parsley. (260)

Gingered Black-Bean Bluefish

Mix 1 tablespoon Chinese black bean sauce with 2 teaspoons chili paste, 1 tablespoon hoisin sauce, and 2 tablespoons finely chopped fresh gingerroot, rub over a 1½-pound bluefish fillet, and place in roasting pan in a 350° F. oven for 25 minutes. Garnish with 1 sliced scallion and lime or lemon wedges. (189)

Flounder with Arugula

Split 4 skinless flounder fillets down their center line. Roll each piece, starting at thicker end, and secure with a toothpick. In a skillet, combine 1 cup white wine, 2 cups water, the juice of ½ lemon, and 4 finely chopped shallots and bring to a boil. Place the flounder rolls on end in the liquid, cover, and poach at a slow simmer for 8 minutes. Remove with a slotted spoon and keep warm. Reduce the poaching liquid to ⅔ cup, then add 1 diced roasted red bell pepper (page 442) and any liquid that has accumulated on the fish plate and boil 2 minutes more. Over low heat, mix in ½ cup chopped fresh arugula and 4 tablespoons butter, and pour over fish. (227)

Stir-Fry of Crab and Asparagus

Stir-fry ½ pound trimmed asparagus tips in 1 tablespoon peanut oil until bright green and remove. Add 1 halved clove garlic and 1 dried chili pepper, stir-fry 30 seconds and remove with slotted spoon. Add 1 pound cleaned lump crabmeat, 1 tablespoon finely chopped fresh gingerroot, ¼ cup diced red bell pepper, the reserved asparagus, and ¼ cup water, cover, and steam 3 minutes. Finish with 1 teaspoon soy sauce, 1 teaspoon Oriental sesame oil, 1 tablespoon lemon juice, 1 clove minced garlic, and 2 finely sliced scallions. (160)

 Crab and Shrimp Stir-Fried with Lime and Grapes

Stir-fry ½ pound large shelled and deveined shrimp with 2 tablespoons finely chopped shallot in 1 tablespoon olive oil just until the shrimp lose their raw look, about 30 seconds. Add 1 pound lump crabmeat, ½ teaspoon fresh tarragon leaves, and 2 dozen halved green seedless grapes. Stir-fry 1 minute more. Finish with 1 tablespoon sweet sherry, a pinch of sugar, a pinch of cayenne pepper, salt, and the juice of 1 lime. (228)

 Middle Eastern Barbecued Softshell Crabs

Combine 2 minced shallots, 2 cloves minced garlic, 2 dozen finely chopped mint leaves, 1 tablespoon chopped fresh parsley, 1 cup plain nonfat yogurt, and the juice of ½ lemon. Add 8 cleaned softshell crabs, and marinate for 30 minutes. Remove crabs from marinade and grill 4 inches from a hot fire for 3 to 4 minutes per side. (247)

 Hardshell Crabs Cooked in Beer

In a large pot, bring 12 ounces beer, 1 cup water, 1 cup bottled clam juice, ¼ cup white vinegar, 2 teaspoons hot pepper sauce, 1 teaspoon salt, and ¼ cup Old Bay Seasoning to a boil, add 8 to 12 large blue crabs, totaling 3 pounds, cover, and shake pot once. Steam crabs for 10 to 12 minutes, turn off heat, uncover, and allow crabs to cool in the liquid. Serve some of the liquid on the side as a dip. (124)

 Tea-Smoked Mussels and Clams

Place ½ cup black tea leaves in 1 cup boiling water and let steep for 5 minutes. Drain and toss leaves on a hot charcoal fire. Place 2 dozen large cleaned clams on a rack over the fire, cover tightly, and smoke for 2 minutes. Add 2 dozen large cleaned mussels, cover, and smoke for 3 to 4 minutes more. Serve with lemon and lime wedges, discarding any clams or mussels that do not open. (78)

 Mussels in Tomato over Orzo

Cook ½ cup orzo in boiling water until al dente, drain, rinse, and keep warm in each of 4 wide soup bowls. In large saucepan, cook 2 cloves minced garlic in 2 tablespoons virgin olive oil for 1 minute. Add 1 cup drained, chopped canned plum tomatoes, a pinch of crushed red pepper flakes, and 2 pounds cleaned, debearded mussels. Cover and simmer until mussels open, about 5 minutes. Ladle mussels and broth over the orzo, discarding any mussels that do not open. (181)

 Orange and Fennel Mussels

Bring to a boil 2 tablespoons grated orange zest, 2 cloves minced garlic, 1 tablespoon basil leaves, 2 teaspoons crushed fennel seed, ⅓ cup chopped fresh fennel, ½ cup chopped onion, ½ cup white wine, ½ cup orange juice, and ¼ cup water. Add 4 dozen cleaned, soaked and debearded mussels, cover, and simmer until mussels open, about 5 minute. Discard any mussels that do not open. (210)

 Clams Steamed in Tomato Broth

In a deep skillet, lightly brown 3 cloves coarsely chopped garlic in 1 tablespoon olive oil. Add the grated zest of 1 lemon, 1 dried chili pepper, and ½ cup white wine and bring to a boil. Add 1 cup vegetable juice cocktail, return to a boil, and remove the pepper. Add 4 dozen cleaned littleneck clams, cover, and cook until clams open, about 5 minutes. Stir in ¼ cup finely chopped fresh parsley and serve over ¾ pound hot cooked fettuccine, discarding any clams that do not open. (193)

 Curried Tandoori-Style Shrimp

Rub 1½ pounds large peeled, cleaned shrimp with ½ teaspoon salt, toss with the juice of 1 large lemon and refrigerate 15 minutes. Mix 2 large cloves minced garlic, 2 tablespoons finely chopped fresh gingerroot, 1 teaspoon ground cumin seed, 1 teaspoon ground cardamom seed, 2 teaspoons curry powder, and 2 teaspoons tandori masala (available at many specialty food stores) and thoroughly rub into the shrimp. Pour ½ cup plain nonfat yogurt over top and rub into shrimp. Cover and refrigerate at least 2 hours. Broil 4 inches from a high broiler for 2 minutes per side. Serve with lemon wedges. (247)

 Shrimp Stew with Mint Pesto

In a food processor, purée 2 cups cleaned mint leaves, 1 clove garlic, 1 tablespoon olive oil, and 2 tablespoons plain nonfat yogurt and set aside. In a deep skillet, cook the thinly sliced whites of 2 leeks and 2 cloves minced garlic in 1 teaspoon additional olive oil until softened. Add 1 cup white wine, 2 tablespoons lemon juice, and 2 large seeded and chopped tomatoes and boil for 2 minutes. Add 1 pound large shelled and deveined shrimp, and simmer 3 to 4 more minutes. Stir in mint pesto, and serve. (238)

 Stir-Fried Sesame Oysters

Stir-fry 1 clove minced garlic, ½ minced jalapeño pepper, and 1 rib diced celery in 1 teaspoon Oriental sesame oil for 30 seconds. Add 1 pint shucked oysters and their liquid and cook until oysters plump, about 1 minute. Remove oysters with a slotted spoon. Mix 1 tablespoon Chinese oyster sauce, 1 teaspoon cornstarch, and 1 tablespoon water, add, and cook until the liquid thickens. Return oysters, sprinkle with 1 tablespoon sesame seeds, and serve over 3 cups cooked rice. (281)

 Shrimp and Oysters with Basil

In a saucepan, cook thinly sliced white sections of 2 leeks and 2 cloves minced garlic in 1 tablespoon olive oil until softened. Add 1 cup white wine, 2 tablespoons lemon juice, and 2 chopped tomatoes and bring to a boil. Add 1 cup chopped basil leaves and ½ pound large peeled, cleaned shrimp and simmer for 2 minutes. Add 1 cup shucked oysters and simmer 1 minute more. (200)

 Asparagus, Shrimp, and Grapefruit Salad

Crush ½ cup raspberries with 1 tablespoon raspberry vinegar and 2 tablespoons walnut oil and pour over ½ pound blanched asparagus spears arranged on 4 plates with 1 peeled pink grapefruit, broken into sections, and 6 ounces cleaned shrimp, simmered for 1 minute in salted water and cooled. (150)

Fifty Ways to Cook Most Everything

Sautéed Shrimp on Cucumber "Noodles"

With a vegetable peeler, cut long, thin ribbons from 3 large peeled cucumbers that have been split lengthwise and seeded. Toss with 1 teaspoon kosher salt, set aside for 10 minutes, then rinse well and wring dry in a kitchen towel. In a skillet, cook 2 cloves minced garlic in 2 tablespoons olive oil until softened. Add 1 pound large peeled and deveined shrimp and sauté until they lose their raw look. Add ½ cup white wine, salt, pepper, and ½ teaspoon ground Szechuan peppercorns and simmer until shrimp are firm, about 1 minute. Remove shrimp, reduce pan juices to ¼ cup, add 2 tablespoons chopped dill, and remove from heat. Whisk in ⅓ cup plain nonfat yogurt until smooth. Toss shrimp in sauce and serve on the bed of cucumber "noodles." (240)

Seafood Pot au Feu

In a saucepan, cook the thinly sliced white of 1 large leek and 3 cloves chopped garlic in 1 tablespoon olive oil until softened. Add 3 cups white wine, 1 cup water, the juice of 1 lemon, ½ teaspoon dried thyme leaves, and 1 teaspoon dried dill leaves and bring to a boil. Add 4 skinned, chopped tomatoes and 12 cleaned littleneck clams, cover, and simmer 3 minutes. Add 24 scrubbed and debearded mussels, cover, and simmer 1 to 2 minutes, or until mussels open. Add 12 peeled and deveined large shrimp, ½ pound lean fish fillet cut in 4 pieces, and 2 tablespoons finely chopped fresh parsley. Bring to a boil. Serve, discarding any mussels that do not open. (252)

Artichoke Ratatouille

In a saucepan, cook 1 finely chopped onion and 2 cloves minced garlic in 2 tablespoons olive oil until softened. Add the grated zest of 1 lemon, 1 teaspoon dried basil leaves, ½ teaspoon dried oregano leaves, and 1 bay leaf and cook for 2 minutes. Stir in 1 diced red bell pepper and 12 sliced mushrooms and cook until softened. Add 6 boiled and sliced artichoke bottoms, 8 chopped plum tomatoes, 1 cubed zucchini, the juice of 1 lemon, and 1 tablespoon wine vinegar and simmer for 5 minutes. Add ½ cup pitted black olives. Serve hot or cold. (117)

Tofu Braised with Wild Mushrooms

In a saucepan, cook 1 tablespoon minced shallots in 2 tablespoons olive oil. Add ½ pound trimmed and thickly sliced wild mushrooms and ½ pound trimmed and sliced button mushrooms and sauté 1 minute more. Add 1 tablespoon soy sauce, 1 cup strong beef stock, and ¾ pound tofu cut in 1-inch cubes and simmer for 2 minutes. With a slotted spoon, remove mushrooms and tofu to a warm platter. Add 3 finely sliced scallions and 1 teaspoon cornstarch dissolved in 1 tablespoon water to the pan. Simmer until liquid thickens and pour over mushrooms. (162)

Asparagus Salad

Cook 1 pound trimmed asparagus in simmering water until bright green. Keep warm. Bring 3 tablespoons walnut oil, 1½ tablespoons wine vinegar, ¼ cup orange juice, 1 clove minced garlic, ½ teaspoon salt, and ½ teaspoon pepper to a boil. Toss ⅓ of this dressing with ¼ pound julienned Belgian endive, ¼ pound bite-size arugula pieces, and ¼ pound bite-size radicchio pieces. Mound on a platter, top with hot asparagus, and pour remaining dressing on top. Scatter 2 ounces finely chopped walnuts over all. Serve warm or chilled. (143)

Stir-Fried Sesame Vegetables

Stir-fry 1 small chopped onion and 1 clove minced garlic in 1 teaspoon safflower oil for 10 seconds. Add ½ pound peeled and diagonally cut carrots, ¼ pound sliced fennel stalks, ½ pound cleaned and halved medium mushrooms, 2 teaspoons finely chopped fresh gingerroot, and a pinch of crushed red pepper flakes. Stir-fry 30 seconds more. Add ⅔ cup water and 2 tablespoons light soy sauce, bring to a boil, and add ¾ pound asparagus, cut in 2-inch lengths, and ½ pound snapped green beans. Cover for 3 to 4 minutes. Add ⅓ pound sliced summer squash and 2 thinly sliced scallions and stir-fry another minute. Remove from heat and toss in 2 teaspoons lime juice, 1 teaspoon Oriental sesame oil, and 1 ounce toasted sesame seeds. (145)

 Grilled Rabbit

Marinate overnight in the refrigerator 1½ pounds rabbit pieces in ½ cup red wine, 1 tablespoon walnut oil, 2 tablespoons orange juice, 1 clove minced garlic, ¼ cup minced onion, 5 peppercorns, 1 chili pepper, 1 whole clove, 2 crushed juniper berries, ½ teaspoon thyme leaves, ¼ teaspoon crushed rosemary leaves, 2 teaspoons minced fresh gingerroot, and ¼ teaspoon salt. Remove meat, strain liquid into small saucepan, add ½ cup chicken broth, and reduce to ⅓ cup. Grill rabbit 4 inches from a high flame for 8 to 10 minutes per side. Brush with liquid and grill 2 minutes more per side. (275)

 Venison in Mustard Crust

Brush 1 pound trimmed venison loin, cut in 12 slices, with a mixture of 1 teaspoon whole-grain mustard, 1 clove minced garlic, and 1 teaspoon dry sherry. Pat ¼ cup black mustard seeds over the slices and brown in a nonstick skillet in 4 teaspoons olive oil to desired doneness. Serve with 3 ounces baked potato per serving. (290)

 Veal Scallops with Asparagus and Capers

Brush four 3-ounce veal scallops with a total of 1 teaspoon olive oil and pound between 2 sheets of wax paper until ⅛ inch thick. Heat 2 teaspoons olive oil in a heavy skillet until smoking, sauté meat for 1 minute per side, and remove. Deglaze pan with ½ cup chicken stock, add 2 dozen blanched asparagus tips, heat through, and transfer with a slotted spoon on and around the veal. Add 2 tablespoons drained capers and 2 tablespoons lemon juice to the pan, reduce until liquid thickens lightly and pour over veal. (237)

 Grilled Mustard-Glazed Veal Chops

In a dry skillet, toast 1 tablespoon whole mustard seeds and 12 whole peppercorns for 45 seconds. Grind and mix with ⅓ cup Dijon mustard, 2 tablespoons bourbon, and 2 teaspoons walnut oil. Brush four 6-ounce rib veal chops with this mixture and grill for 4 to 5 minutes per side. (279)

 Veal au Poivre

Rub four 6-ounce pieces trimmed lean veal loin with 2 tablespoons cracked peppercorns and salt to taste. Broil 4 to 5 minutes per side. (253)

 Pork Medallions with Mustard and Capers

In a large nonstick skillet coated with a thin film of spray shortening, brown ¾ pound trimmed center-cut pork loin, cut in ¼-inch slices and seasoned with salt and pepper. Turn the pork and add

1 halved clove garlic. When fully browned, add 2 tablespoons Dijon mustard, 2 tablespoons capers with their liquid, and 1 cup apple juice. Simmer for 2 minutes. Remove pork to a warm platter and reduce until liquid thickens lightly. Remove garlic and pour liquid over pork. (255)

 Grilled Pork Medallions with Mustard and Rosemary

Cut 1 pound boneless pork loin into 12 slices. Rub slices on both sides with 1 split clove garlic, salt, and pepper. Mix 1 tablespoon crumbled rosemary with ¼ cup Dijon mustard and brush on the pork. Broil 3 minutes per side. Serve sprinkled with 1 tablespoon chopped fresh parsley. (296)

 Pork Braised in Apple Cider

Brown 12 ounces trimmed lean pork loin in a non-stick skillet greased with a thin film of spray shortening. Add ½ cup chopped onion, 1 clove chopped garlic, and 2 teaspoons thyme leaves and cook until softened. Add 1 cup apple cider and ½ cup white wine, cover, and simmer for 35 minutes.

Remove pork and reduce pan liquid until lightly thickened. Slice pork and reheat in the sauce. (300)

 Lamb Chops Braised with Belgian Endive

Dredge four 6-ounce shoulder lamb chops lightly in seasoned flour. Brown in 1 tablespoon olive oil in a nonstick skillet, remove, and add 1 more teaspoon olive oil. Add 2 cloves minced garlic, 3 minced shallots, and 4 trimmed and halved Belgian endive, searing the endive on both sides. Return chops to pan and add ¼ cup white wine, ½ teaspoon dried thyme, and ½ cup beef stock. Cover and simmer for 40 minutes. Remove chops and endive to a platter and reduce pan liquid until lightly thickened. Pour over meat and garnish with 2 tablespoons chopped fresh parsley. (300)

 Lamb with Lemon and Mint

Rub 2 pounds trimmed lean leg of lamb with 2 cloves minced garlic, 2 teaspoons olive oil, ¼ cup lemon juice, and 1 tablespoon dried mint. Roast on a rack in a roasting pan for 1 hour at 375° F. Makes 7 servings. (250)

Fifty Ways to Fight Fat

From childhood, we are conditioned to think that gravy goes on mashed potatoes and butter on bread. And for such conditioning we have paid a heavy toll in heart disease, obesity, and circulatory problems. Perhaps it's time to recondition ourselves—not just by finding substitutes for saturated fat and cholesterol, but by getting away from the very notion of substitution.

There is no perfect substitute for butter or ice cream or eggs. Most margarines taste no more like butter than carob tastes like chocolate. Ice milk and frozen yogurt can't approach the charm of ice cream, no matter how delusional one becomes on a diet, and egg substitutes whip up into "scrambled eggs" that resemble the real thing only in advertising photographs.

There may not be substitutes for your favorite forbidden foods, but there are alternatives. Unlike substitutes, alternatives do not attempt to imitate. Instead, they stand on their own merits. Rather than margarine on a baked potato, try a low-fat ranch dressing or serve a pepper purée, instead of gravy, to spark the flavor of roast chicken. As an alternative to ice cream, try peaches pungent with ginger and flamed in bourbon.

Not all alternatives to fat need be completely fat-free. Though all fats give rich flavors and creamy textures to food, different fats have different nutritional properties. Cutting out fat completely frequently results in bland-tasting or unsatisfying dishes. But by switching to fats that have no cholesterol or are lower in saturated fatty acids, and by cutting the amount of fat used in a recipe, we can reduce a recipe's liabilities without sacrificing its sensory properties.

This premise guides the 50 recipes that follow. Unlike the recipes in Chapter 16, which put an upper limit on calories, not all of these foods are geared to weight loss. Rather, they attack what most nutritionists consider America's number-one dietary villain: too much fat.

ABOUT THESE RECIPES

None of these recipes is fat-free, but by relying on small amounts of highly flavorful fats—like sesame, walnut, and olive oils—and by adding richness with low-fat cheese, yogurt, or a reduced portion of meat, we have been able to offer 50 dishes that deliver wonderful flavor with a fraction of the fat of traditional American fare.

Each of these recipes uses less than 1 tablespoon of fat per serving. Unless otherwise noted, all yield 4 portions.

Tomato, Tarragon, and Chèvre "Tartlets"

Skin 1 large ripe tomato by charring its skin over a high flame and then peeling. Cut into 8 slices. Toast 4 split English muffins until lightly browned, then sprinkle each with 1½ teaspoons grated Parmesan. On each muffin half, place 3 tarragon leaves, 1 tomato slice, and 1 ounce sliced chèvre. Broil until cheese has melted, about 1 minute.

 Eggplant and Feta au Gratin

Slice 1 large eggplant into 18 slices, sprinkle with salt and pepper, and broil for 3 minutes on one side and 2 minutes on the other. Sprinkle 2 tablespoons grated Parmesan over the bottom of a 9-inch pie pan. Top with 3 ounces crumbled feta and 4 chopped basil leaves, half the eggplant, ½ cup chopped tomato, 2 tablespoons additional Parmesan and 4 more chopped basil leaves. Cover with the remaining eggplant, another ½ cup chopped tomato, and sprinkle 2 more ounces crumbled feta over top. Bake in preheated 375° F. oven for 35 minutes. Serves 6.

 Tea-Smoked Grilled Softshell Crabs

Place ½ cup black tea leaves in 1 cup boiling water and let steep for 5 minutes. Drain and toss on a hot charcoal fire. Place 8 cleaned softshell crabs rubbed with 2 teaspoons Oriental sesame oil on an oiled rack over the fire, cover tightly, and smoke for 5 minutes. Turn, cover, and smoke for 3 to 4 minutes more. Serve with lemon and lime wedges.

 Fennel, Shrimp, and Walnut Salad

Whisk together 2 tablespoons nonfat buttermilk, 2 tablespoons walnut oil, the finely grated zest and juice of 1 lemon, salt, and pepper. Toss with 8 cups washed greens (spinach, chard, sorrel or escarole), ¾ pound peeled and deveined medium shrimp poached for 45 seconds, ½ diced red onion, 3 ribs thinly sliced fennel, 1 peeled and diced Granny Smith apple, ⅓ cup walnut pieces, and ¼ cup chopped fresh flat-leaf parsley. Chill.

 Chick-pea, Tomato, and Onion Salad

Toss 2 cups cooked chick-peas, ⅓ cup chopped onion, 1 clove minced garlic, 1 ripe chopped tomato, 2 tablespoons lemon juice, 1 tablespoon virgin olive oil, 3 tablespoons nonfat plain yogurt, ⅛ teaspoon crushed red pepper flakes, 2 tablespoons finely chopped fresh parsley, salt, and pepper. Serve chilled.

 Chicken Chili Bean Salad

Toss 3 cups cooked kidney beans, 1 bunch thinly sliced trimmed scallions, 1 diced roasted red pepper (page 442), and 1 pound grilled, boneless, skinless diced chicken breast. Mix 2 tablespoons light mayonnaise, 2 tablespoons chili powder, 1 tablespoon ground cumin, ⅓ cup low-fat buttermilk, 2 tablespoons hot pepper sauce, salt, and pepper and toss with the bean salad and 2 tablespoons chopped fresh flat-leaf parsley.

 Lime-Laced Gazpacho

In a food processor, blend 4 slices crustless diced black bread, 1 teaspoon extra-virgin olive oil, and ¼ cup lime juice until finely chopped. Add and finely chop 1 large sweet onion, 2 cloves garlic, 1 rib celery, 1 peeled and seeded cucumber, 1 large red bell pepper, 1 chili pepper, ¼ cup fresh parsley, and the zest of 2 limes and mix with 4 seeded large ripe tomatoes, 4 cups vegetable cocktail juice, salt, pepper, and the bread mixture. Chill and serve with 6 lime wedges. Serves 6 as an entree.

Raspberry Borscht

Boil 1 cup dry white wine for 1 minute. Add 1 pint raspberries, ¼ cup sugar, and a pinch of salt, return to a boil, and cool slightly. Add the juice of ½ lemon, 1 cup orange juice, and 3 ice cubes and stir until ice melts. Chill completely and finish with ½ cup nonfat yogurt.

Chilled Red Corn Chowder

Skin 2 large ripe tomatoes by charring their skins over a high flame and then peeling. Chop coarsely with 1 large roasted red pepper (page 442), ¼ onion, 1 clove garlic, 1 teaspoon hot pepper sauce, 2 teaspoons virgin olive oil, salt, and pepper. In a food processor, blend with 6 ice cubes until finely chopped. Stir in 2 cups cooked corn niblets and 2 tablespoons chopped fresh cilantro.

Risotto with Lentils

Boil 1 cup lentils in 3 cups water for 20 minutes, drain, and set aside. Meanwhile, cook 1 chopped onion and 2 cloves chopped garlic in 2 teaspoons virgin olive oil in a saucepan until softened. Add 1 teaspoon dried thyme, ½ teaspoon crumbled rosemary, a pinch of ground allspice, and 1½ cups Arborio rice, stir, and cook for 1 minute. Add ½ cup white wine and simmer until absorbed, stirring frequently. Add 1 cup defatted chicken broth and stir until absorbed. Add the lentils and 5 cups additional broth, 1 cup at a time, stirring. Wait for each cup to be absorbed before adding the next. Stir in

2 tablespoons finely chopped fresh parsley, 1 tablespoon grated Parmesan, salt, and pepper.

Brown Rice Risotto with Sage and Potatoes

In a saucepan, cook 1 chopped onion and 2 cloves chopped garlic in 2 teaspoons virgin olive oil until softened. Add 1 teaspoon rubbed sage, ½ teaspoon crumbled rosemary, a pinch of ground allspice, and 1½ cups short-grain brown rice, stir, and cook for 1 minute. Add ½ cup white wine and simmer until absorbed, stirring frequently. Add 1 cup defatted chicken broth and stir until absorbed, stirring. Add 5½ cups additional broth, 1 cup at a time. Wait for each cup to be absorbed before adding the next. After the first 3 cups have been absorbed, add ¾ pound peeled new potatoes. Stir in 2 tablespoons fresh sage leaves, 1 tablespoon grated Parmesan, salt, and pepper.

Wild Rice Risotto

Boil ⅔ cup wild rice in 3 cups water for 20 minutes, then drain. Meanwhile, cook 1 chopped onion, ¼ cup diced mushrooms and 2 cloves chopped garlic in 2 teaspoons virgin olive oil until softened. Add 1 cup Arborio rice and the wild rice. Stir and cook for 1 minute. Add ½ cup white wine and simmer until absorbed, stirring frequently. Add 5 cups defatted chicken broth, 1 cup at a time, stirring until each cup is absorbed before adding the next. Cook until rice is soft and moist. Stir in 2 tablespoons finely chopped parsley, 1 tablespoon grated Parmesan, salt, and pepper.

Warm Buckwheat Pasta and Sesame Salad

Boil 1 pound Japanese buckwheat noodles (soba) in a large pot of salted water with 1 teaspoon Oriental sesame oil until tender, about 10 minutes. Drain, rinse, and toss with a mixture of 1 tablespoon Oriental sesame oil, 6 tablespoons nonfat yogurt, 3 tablespoons rice wine vinegar, ¾ teaspoon sugar, 4½ tablespoons light soy sauce, a pinch of crushed red pepper flakes, 4 teaspoons finely chopped fresh gingerroot, and 1½ cloves minced garlic. Mix in ¼ thinly sliced red onion, 3 thinly sliced scallions, 1 peeled and diced seeded cucumber, and ¼ cup toasted sesame seeds. Serve warm.

 ## Whole-Wheat Pasta with Roasted Peppers

Toss 1 pound hot cooked whole-wheat fettuccine with 4 large roasted bell peppers cut in strips (page 442), ½ finely chopped red onion, 2 cloves minced garlic, 1 tablespoon virgin olive oil, 2 tablespoons grated Parmesan, 1 tablespoon red wine vinegar, salt, and pepper.

 ## Feta and Basil Macaroni and Cheese

Toss 1 pound hot cooked macaroni with 6 ounces crumbled feta cheese, ½ cup skim milk, 2 cloves minced garlic, 3 tablespoons finely chopped fresh basil, ¼ teaspoon hot pepper sauce, 1 lightly beaten egg white, salt, and pepper in a casserole. Bake uncovered at 350° F. for 30 minutes.

 ## Yogurt and Garlic Grilled Chicken Breast

In the refrigerator, marinate 2 split, skinless, boneless, and pounded chicken breasts in 1 cup nonfat plain yogurt, 1 teaspoon virgin olive oil, 10 cloves crushed garlic, ⅓ cup chopped mint leaves, salt, and pepper for at least 2 hours. Grill for about 5 minutes per side, basting with the marinade every minute.

 ## Stir-Fried Chicken with Chicory

Dissolve 3 tablespoons cornstarch in ¼ cup cold water and toss 1 pound boneless, skinless chicken breast chunks in the mixture. Stir-fry 1 chopped onion in 2 teaspoons virgin olive oil and 1 teaspoon safflower oil for 30 seconds. Add chicken and stir-fry until meat loses its raw look. Add 2 cloves minced garlic, 1 dried chili pepper, ¼ pound finely chopped skinless smoked turkey breast, ½ cup dry sherry, 1 teaspoon sugar, and ½ cup defatted chicken stock, cover, and simmer 4 minutes. Add 2 tablespoons cider vinegar, 1 tablespoon honey mustard, salt, and pepper. Bring to a boil and pour over 1 head cleaned and stemmed chicory leaves.

 ## Stir-Fried Shrimp with Watercress

Follow preceding recipe, using 1½ pounds cleaned large shrimp instead of chicken, rice wine vinegar instead of cider vinegar and 2 bunches watercress leaves instead of chicory.

 ## Stir-Fried Velvet Chicken and Shiitakes

Toss 1 pound boneless, skinless chicken breast chunks in 1 teaspoon cornstarch and 1 lightly beaten egg white. Dissolve 2 tablespoons cornstarch and 1 teaspoon sugar in 1 tablespoon rice wine vinegar and 2 tablespoon light soy sauce. Stir-fry ½ pound sliced shiitake mushrooms in 1 teaspoon Oriental sesame oil until softened. Add 2 tablespoons lemon juice and remove mushrooms. Add 1 tablespoon peanut oil to the wok, then add the chicken and stir-fry until it loses its raw look. Add a pinch of crushed red pepper flakes, 1 tablespoon dry sherry, and ¾ cup defatted chicken stock, cover, and simmer for 3 minutes.

Add the mushrooms and cornstarch mixture and cook until lightly thickened. Stir in 2 thinly sliced scallions.

Grilled Chinese Chicken Breast

Rub 4 lightly pounded boneless skinless chicken breast halves with 1 teaspoon Oriental sesame oil and season with salt, pepper, and a pinch of ground ginger. Grill or broil until firm, about 4 minutes per side. Meanwhile, in a small skillet, bring 1 teaspoon minced garlic, 2 tablespoons light soy sauce, 1 sliced scallion, a pinch of sugar, and 2 tablespoons dry sherry to a boil. Add ½ teaspoon cornstarch dissolved in 1 tablespoon water and boil 10 seconds. Brush over cooked chicken and sprinkle with 2 tablespoons toasted sesame seeds.

Grilled Marinated Game Hen

Split 2 game hens in half lengthwise, removing backbone and skin. Marinate overnight in the refrigerator in ½ cup red wine, 1 teaspoon walnut oil, ¼ cup orange juice, 2 cloves minced garlic, ¼ cup minced onion, 12 peppercorns, 2 chili peppers, 2 whole cloves, 4 crushed juniper berries, 1 teaspoon thyme leaves, ½ teaspoon crushed rosemary leaves, 2 tablespoons minced fresh gingerroot, and ¼ teaspoon salt. Lift hens from marinade, strain liquid into small saucepan, and reduce to ⅓ cup. Grill for 6 to 8 minutes, brush with reduced liquid, and grill 2 minutes longer. Flip, brush with liquid, and grill another 5 minutes.

Marinated Grilled Rabbit

Follow preceding recipe, substituting 1½ pounds small farm-raised rabbit pieces for the split hens.

Grilled Chicken Breast with Buttermilk and Herbs

Marinate 2 pounded, split, skinned, and boned chicken breasts in 1 cup low-fat buttermilk, 1 teaspoon crushed red pepper flakes, ¼ cup chopped celery, the thinly sliced whites of 2 scallions, 1 tablespoon chopped fresh parsley, 1 tablespoon chopped fresh herb of your choice and 1 tablespoon finely grated orange zest. Refrigerate at least 2 hours. Grill chicken for 5 to 6 minutes per side on an oiled rack until firm and browned, basting with marinade every 2 minutes.

Grilled Scallops on Cucumber "Noodles"

With a vegetable peeler, pare length-long strips from 2 large peeled and seeded cucumbers, toss with ½ teaspoon salt and set aside for 10 minutes. Squeeze out excess moisture and pile on each of 4 plates. Toss 1 pound cleaned sea scallops in ½ cup nonfat plain yogurt, 1 clove minced garlic, the juice of ½ lemon, 1 tablespoon chopped dill leaves, salt, and pepper and set aside for 10 minutes. Grill on an oiled mesh or broil for 2 to 3 minutes per side, basting with marinade every minute. Serve scallops over the cucumber noodles.

Broiled Coriander Salmon

Follow preceding recipe, using four 1-inch-thick salmon steaks in place of scallops. Add 1 teaspoon ground coriander to the marinade and use cilantro instead of dill.

Salmon Poached in Basil Tea with Pine Nuts

Bring 1½ cups white wine, 1½ cups water, the juice of 1 large lemon, salt and pepper to a boil. Cut 1½ pounds skinned, trimmed salmon fillet on an angle into ½-inch-thick slices. Add ¼ cup chopped fresh basil leaves to the liquid and return to a boil. Add salmon in a single layer, cover, and remove from heat. Let rest for 2 minutes, remove salmon with slotted spatula, and garnish with 3 tablespoons chopped toasted pine nuts and 8 thin lemon wedges.

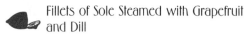

Steamed Fish with Yogurt Herb Sauce

Season 4 fillets of lean fish with salt and pepper. Mix ¼ cup chopped fresh herbs (basil, tarragon, thyme, dill, mint) with 2 tablespoons chopped fresh parsley, sprinkle each fillet with 1 tablespoon of the herbs, and wrap in plastic. Cook ¼ cup finely chopped onion and 1 clove minced garlic in 1 teaspoon olive oil until softened. Add ½ cup clam juice, and reduce to 3 tablespoons liquid. Steam plastic-wrapped fish for 6 to 8 minutes. Snip plastic, add the juices to the reduction along with remaining herbs, reduce back to 3 tablespoons, remove from heat, and whisk in ¾ cup nonfat plain yogurt. Pour sauce over fish.

Fillets of Sole Steamed with Grapefruit and Dill

Arrange 4 skinned sole fillets, dark-side down, on a plate. Pour ½ teaspoon Oriental sesame oil and the juice of ½ grapefruit over top and season with salt, pepper, and a grating of nutmeg. Sprinkle 3 tablespoons finely chopped dill leaves on top and cover with another plate. Place over a pot of simmering water, and steam for 4 to 5 minutes, until fish is opaque. Let rest for 1 minute. Garnish with 4 lemon wedges.

Flounder with Starfruit in Parchment

Place each of 4 skinned flounder fillets on a large parchment heart. Season each fillet with ¼ tea-

spoon hot pepper oil, ¼ teaspoon Oriental sesame oil, 1 teaspoon lemon juice, a grating of nutmeg, salt, and pepper. Top each with 2 slices starfruit, close and seal the parchment, and bake at 350° F. for 12 minutes. Open parchment and serve.

 ### Steamed Salmon with Orange, Basil, and Tomato.

In a saucepan, cook ¼ cup chopped onion, 2 cloves minced garlic, 1 tablespoon finely grated orange zest, ½ cup orange juice, and ½ cup white wine until reduced to ¼ cup. Add 4 chopped canned plum tomatoes, salt, and pepper. Season four 4-ounce pieces skinless salmon fillet with salt and pepper and drizzle with 1 teaspoon virgin olive oil. Top each piece of fish with 1 basil leaf and place on the simmering sauce. Cover and steam for 8 to 10 minutes, until fish is opaque.

Monkfish and Mussel Stew with Pasta

Cook the whites of 2 thinly sliced leeks, ¼ teaspoon crushed red pepper flakes, and 2 cloves minced garlic in 2 teaspoons virgin olive oil until softened. Add ½ cup white wine and 1 cup clam juice and boil 2 minutes. Add the juice of ½ lemon, 2 large seeded chopped tomatoes, 1 cup chopped fresh basil leaves, and ¾ pound monkfish fillet, cut in 1½-inch pieces, and simmer 5 minutes. Add 1 dozen scrubbed and debearded mussels, cover, and simmer another 3 minutes. Stir in 3 cups hot cooked shell-shaped pasta.

 ### Broiled Catfish with Vinegar Glaze

Cook 1 cup defatted beef broth, 1 cup red wine, 2 cloves crushed garlic, ¼ teaspoon crumbled dried rosemary, and pepper until reduced to ½ cup. Strain, return to saucepan, and set aside. Meanwhile, rub four 5-ounce trimmed catfish fillets with 1 teaspoon olive oil and a mixture of ½ teaspoon *each* salt, pepper, and paprika and ¼ teaspoon *each* ground ginger and rubbed sage. Broil on a lightly oiled pan for about 3 minutes per side, until firm, then transfer to a platter. Deglaze the broiling pan with ¼ cup balsamic vinegar, add to the strained liquid, and reduce back to ½ cup, adding any drippings from the catfish plate. Pour glaze over fish.

Steamed Flounder and Cilantro Rolls with Red Pepper Puree

Split 4 flounder fillets in half lengthwise, season with salt, pepper, and the juice of ½ lime and top with leaves from 6 large sprigs cilantro. Roll fillets, secure each with a toothpick, place spiral-side up in a lightly oiled steamer, and steam over boiling water for 4 to 6 minutes. Serve with 1½ cups Red Pepper Coulis (page 25).

Baked Trout Stuffed with Fennel and Apple

Cook the whites of 2 thinly sliced leeks, 3 ribs diced fennel, and 2 cloves minced garlic in 2 teaspoons safflower oil until vegetables soften. Add 6 chopped basil leaves, ½ teaspoon dried thyme, and 2 cups peeled and diced Granny Smith apple and simmer 3 minutes. Season with 2 teaspoons lemon juice, salt, and pepper. Fill interior cavities of 4 gutted rainbow trout, place in a roasting pan, and bake at 400° F. for 12 to 15 minutes.

Fish Poached in Tomato Sauce over Pasta

Prepare Quick Fresh Tomato Sauce (page 46) using 2 teaspoons extra-virgin olive oil instead of 2 tablespoons olive oil and bring to a simmer in a large skillet. Place four 4-ounce pieces skinned salmon fillet in sauce, cover, and poach for 5 minutes.

Meanwhile, cook ¾ pound fettuccine to *al dente* in plenty of salted water, drain, toss with some of the sauce, and divide among 4 plates. Place 1 fillet on each pile of pasta and top with remaining sauce.

Sesame Scallops Steamed over Tea

Boil ½ pound thin Chinese noodles in plenty of salted water until tender, about 5 minutes, then drain. Bring 2 cups water to a boil, add ¼ cup loose black tea, let steep 5 minutes, then strain out the leaves. Toss 1½ pounds cleaned and trimmed sea scallops, 1 teaspoon Oriental sesame oil, and 1 teaspoon soy sauce. Steam over the simmering tea for 6 to 8 minutes, until barely firm. Remove and toss with 1 teaspoon Oriental sesame oil, 2 tablespoons toasted sesame seeds, 2 tablespoons lemon juice, salt, pepper, and 2 thinly sliced scallions. Reheat noodles in the hot tea, drain, and serve scallops on the noodles.

Paupiettes of Flounder Steamed in Romaine

Blanch 8 large Romaine leaves until wilted, then cool. Sauté thinly sliced whites of 2 leeks in 1 teaspoon olive oil. Add 1 diced roasted red pepper (page 442), a pinch of crushed red pepper flakes, and 1 tablespoon minced lemon zest and cook another 2 minutes. Add ½ cup white wine and reduce until almost dry. Season with salt, pepper, and 1 tablespoon chopped fresh basil. Place 2 Romaine leaves end to end, slightly overlapping. Top with a 3-ounce flounder fillet, then with a quarter of vegetables. Roll up completely in the Romaine, securing with a toothpick. Repeat with 3 more fillets. Steam for about 6 minutes.

Peppered Roast Venison Loin

Rub 3 pounds well-trimmed boneless venison loin with 1 tablespoon Charcuterie Dried Marinade

Fifty Ways to Cook Most Everything

(page 20) and roast at 350° F. for 1 hour, or to an internal temperature of 135° F. to 140° F. for medium-rare. Rest for 10 minutes before carving. Serves 8.

 ## Loin of Pork Baked in a Crust of Salt

Rub 2 pounds well-trimmed rolled boneless pork loin with 2 tablespoons crushed peppercorns. Combine 6 cups kosher salt and 1¼ cups cold water into a mixture as cohesive as damp snow and make a thin layer of it in the bottom of a glass roasting pan. Place 6 sage leaves on the salt, the pork on top, 6 more sage leaves, and mound the remaining salt paste all around the meat to enclose it. Roast at 350° F. for 1 hour. Rest 10 minutes. Crack away the salt crust, remove the meat, and wipe off excess salt. Slice.

Herbed Turkey Breast Baked in Salt Crust

Follow preceding recipe, but use a 4-pound boneless, skinless turkey breast in place of the pork, and roast for 2 hours to an internal temperature of 165° F.

Chicken Livers with Mustard Yogurt Sauce

Trim 1 pound chicken livers and separate each into 2 lobes. Sauté in a nonstick pan in 1 tablespoon virgin olive oil until firm, about 3 minutes per side. Add salt, pepper, and 1 clove minced garlic. Turn heat to low and stir in 2 tablespoons Dijon mustard and ½ cup nonfat plain yogurt.

Chicken Livers in Balsamic Green Peppercorn Sauce

Trim 1 pound chicken livers and separate each into 2 lobes. In a nonstick skillet, sauté 1 tablespoon

minced shallot in 1 tablespoon virgin olive oil for 30 seconds. Add livers and brown lightly on both sides. Deglaze pan with ½ cup white wine, 1 tablespoon balsamic vinegar, 1 tablespoon green peppercorns, and a dash of cayenne pepper. Simmer until livers are firm. Serve on 4 slices toast.

 ## Grapefruit Cloud

Bring 1⅓ cups each sugar and water to a boil without stirring, cook 1 minute, then let cool. Combine with 2 cups unsweetened grapefruit juice and ¼ cup lemon juice and chill. Beat 4 egg whites with ¼ teaspoon salt until frothy, stir into the juice, and freeze in an ice-cream freezer according to the manufacturer's directions. Store in a tightly closed container.

 ## Spicy Tomato Water Ice

Bring ⅓ cup each sugar and water to a boil without stirring, cook 30 seconds, then let cool. Combine with 3 cups tomato juice, 2 tablespoons hot pepper sauce, and the juice of 1 lime. Freeze in an ice-cream freezer according to the manufacturer's directions. Store in a tightly closed container.

 ## Chili Mango Sorbet

Bring 1 cup each sugar and water and 1 dried chili pepper to a boil. Cool to room temperature and remove pepper. In a food processor, purée 2 peeled and pitted large ripe mangoes and strain out skin. Add to sugar syrup with the juice of 1 lime, 1 teaspoon hot pepper sauce, and 1 egg white beaten lightly with pinch salt. Freeze in an ice-cream freezer according to manufacturer's directions. Store in a tightly covered container.

Frozen Irish Coffee Yogurt

Combine ¾ cup sugar with ¼ cup water and bring to a boil. Add 3 tablespoons instant coffee powder. Remove from heat, stir in 1 tablespoon Irish or other whiskey and ¼ teaspoon ground cinnamon, and chill. Add 4 cups coffee yogurt and a pinch of salt and freeze in an ice-cream freezer according to manufacturer's directions. Store in a tightly covered container.

 Berries and "Cream" Mousse

Line a strainer with 4 layers of cheesecloth and set over a deep bowl. Mix 3 cups nonfat vanilla yogurt with 1 cup nonfat lemon yogurt and pour into the cheesecloth. Wrap the extra cheesecloth up around the yogurt and place a plate on top. Refrigerate and allow to drain for up to 12 hours. Mix the drained yogurt with 1 cup skim-milk ricotta cheese. Beat 2 egg whites until frothy, add 2 teaspoons honey, and beat until peaked. Fold into the yogurt mixture. Serve in 6 small dishes, topped with 1 pint cleaned berries. Serves 6.

 Cantaloupe, Apricot, and Mango
Mint Compote

Scoop 1 small seeded cantaloupe into balls and toss with 6 diced fresh apricots, 1 diced large peeled mango, ¼ cup chopped fresh mint leaves, ¼ cup orange liqueur, and 1 teaspoon to 1 tablespoon honey, depending on sweetness of the fruit. Chill. Serves 6.

 Warm Spiced Bourboned Peaches

Warm 2 large, peeled, and sliced peaches in 1 tablespoon walnut oil over moderate heat with 2 tablespoons finely chopped candied ginger. Add 1 tablespoon sugar and cook a bit more until the sugar melts. Finish with 3 to 4 tablespoons bourbon. Ignite carefully with a match. Serve warm or use as a dessert topping.

 Honey and Orange Summer Fruit

Two hours before serving, toss 1 sliced peach with 3 quartered apricots, ½ cup halved cherries, 1 peeled and sliced kiwi, 3 stemmed and quartered fresh figs, 8 large stemmed strawberries, and 1 cup blueberries with 3 tablespoons orange liqueur, 1 tablespoon honey, and 1 teaspoon raspberry vinegar. Chill.

Fifty Ways to Beat the Heat

The survival of many a cook has rested as much in knowing when to turn off a stove as when to turn it on.

Take summer, for example. The only trick to cooking during summer's swelter is figuring out how not to do it. For most of us, this is no mean feat. After using up our quota of dinner reservations and tuna-stuffed tomatoes, we tend to yearn for inspiration. So how about 50 inspirations? Here are 50 ways to beat the heat of summer, even when getting out of the kitchen is out of the question.

They include appetizers, entrées, desserts, salads, soups, and sauces and you don't have to use a range, oven, or grill to make any of them. Many are stand-alone dishes, while a number of sauces accompany leftovers that were originally cooked and can now be eaten without reheating, such as meats, rice or hard-cooked eggs. You can, of course, elect to reheat the meat or fish they'll accompany, but whether served with hot or cold foods, they're great for dressing up a steak or recycling a cold roast without ever being accused of serving up leftovers.

Though pestos are traditionally tossed with hot pasta, you can use them without boiling a huge pot of water, because they are equally good mixed with cold salads made from tuna, potatoes, or rice. Mix them into egg salad or with hard-cooked egg yolks for Genovese-style deviled eggs. Use pesto to flavor a simple vinaigrette or mayonnaise, serve it as a dip for shrimp or crab claws, or dollop it over vine-ripened tomatoes for the ultimate summer treasure.

Most often we think of marination as a way to flavor ingredients that are being cooked conventionally, but in this chapter we offer several dishes that are cooked without ever being exposed to heat. The cooking is done by soaking the ingredient, usually fish or shellfish, in a salty or acidic liquid until its flesh becomes firm and its color changes from translucent to opaque. When you consider that these are the same changes that happen when a fish is heated, you can see that the fish prepared in the seviche or gravlax recipes below are as cooked by exposure to acid and salt as they would be if they came out of the oven.

Many of these recipes are exciting and all yield beautiful results that will delight any cook who can't stand the heat but can't get out of the kitchen.

ABOUT THESE RECIPES

Many of the ingredients in this chapter are served raw. This will cause no one concern with fruits and vegetables, but you may balk at the prospect of serving raw meat or fish, both for esthetic and sanitary reasons.

Though food preference is individual, concern over parasites and the problems they cause is widespread. All published cases of parasite infection related to consumption of raw fish have involved fresh-water and anadromous fish, such as salmon. The only sea fish associated with parasites are those in the herring and cod families, such as scrod, whiting, rockfish, haddock, and mackerel.

If the threat of parasites is even remotely possible, follow the U.S. Food and Drug Administration's September 28, 1990, advisory on purchasing fish that will be served raw, marinated, or partially cooked—that it be blast-frozen to at least −31° F. for 15 hours, or frozen by conventional means to at least −10° F. for seven days.

However, this process will alter the texture of the fish, making it less appealing when served raw. If you cannot verify the safety of your fish source, we suggest you avoid any recipe that calls for fish to be served less than fully cooked.

The following recipes can all be prepared without turning on the stove. Some are complete dishes unto themselves, while others complement cold leftovers.

All are written for 4 portions unless otherwise noted.

 ### Four-Color Fish Seviche

In the refrigerator, marinate ¾ pound skinned, boned, and thinly sliced flounder fillet in 1 cup fresh lemon juice for 1½ hours. Drain, add ¼ pound chopped smoked salmon, 2 thinly sliced scallions, and 1 tablespoon finely chopped red onion, and serve on lettuce leaves.

 ### Mexican Seviche

In the refrigerator, marinate 1 pound cleaned, thinly sliced scallops in ½ cup lemon juice, ½ cup lime juice, and 2 tablespoons cider vinegar for 2 hours. Drain and add 1 diced avocado, 1 minced pickled chipotle or jalapeño pepper, 2 thinly sliced scallions, 2 tablespoons chopped fresh cilantro, and 1 diced tomato. Remove from marinade and serve on a bed of lettuce.

 ### Green Seviche

In the refrigerator, marinate 1 pound cleaned thinly sliced scallops in ½ cup lemon juice, ½ cup lime juice, and ¼ cup orange juice for 2 hours. Drain and add ⅓ cup chopped fresh herbs and 1 tablespoon olive oil. Serve on a bed of lettuce.

 ### Honey-Cured Gravlax

In the refrigerator, marinate 2 pounds boneless skin-on salmon fillet in ⅓ cup honey and the juice of ½ lemon for 2 hours. Mix 1 cup kosher salt, ¼ cup sugar, and ½ teaspoon white pepper and spread a third of the mixture over bottom of a glass dish large enough to hold salmon. Lift salmon from marinade and place on the salt. Pour remaining salt mixture over salmon, mounding it at the thickest part of the fish. Cover with plastic wrap, weight with a dish, and refrigerate 48 to 72 hours, depending on thickness. Lift fish from the salt and rinse thoroughly. Thinly slice at an angle, and serve as you would lox or smoked salmon. Makes 10 servings.

Fifty Ways to Cook Most Everything

 Fennel-Cured Bluefish

Lay 3 fronds fennel on each side of a 2-pound piece skin-on bluefish fillet. Mix 1 cup kosher salt, ¼ cup sugar, 1 tablespoon ground fennel seed, and ½ teaspoon ground black pepper and spread a third of the mixture over bottom of a glass dish large enough to hold the fish. Place fish on the salt, cover with remaining salt mixture, cover with plastic wrap, weight with a dish, and refrigerate 36 hours. Lift fish from salt and rinse thoroughly. Slice thinly on an angle and serve on rye bread with sour cream, sliced red onion, and horseradish. Makes 8 servings.

 Brandied Summer Fruit

At least 2 hours before serving, toss ½ pound stemmed, pitted, and halved cherries, 1 sliced and pitted peach, 3 pitted and quartered apricots, 1 peeled and thinly sliced kiwi, 3 stemmed and quartered figs, 8 stemmed and halved large strawberries, and 1 cup blueberries in ¼ cup brandy, 1 tablespoon honey, and 1 teaspoon Berry Vinegar (page 397).

This group of recipes is made entirely with raw ingredients:

 Three-Endive Slaw

Toss 1 head stemmed curly endive broken in small pieces, 1 head shredded radicchio, 1 head julienned Belgian endive, and 3 tablespoons sesame seeds with a dressing made from 1 tablespoon Oriental sesame oil, 3 tablespoons peanut oil, 2 tablespoons white wine vinegar, 4 teaspoons honey, and 1 tablespoon light soy sauce whisked together.

 Chilled Tomato and Roasted Pepper Soup

In a food processor or blender, process 2 large skinned tomatoes, 2 jarred roasted red peppers, ¼ chopped onion, 1 clove minced garlic, 3 tablespoons olive oil, and 3 ice cubes until finely chopped. Stir in 3 more ice cubes and serve garnished with chopped fresh parsley when the ice has melted.

 White Gazpacho

In a food processor or blender, puree 2 peeled, seeded, and chopped cucumbers, 2 ribs peeled and chopped celery, the chopped whites of 3 scallions, and 1 clove minced garlic. Blend with 2 cups chilled and defatted chicken stock, 2 tablespoons white wine vinegar, 1 cup yogurt or sour cream, and a dash of hot pepper sauce. Chill well and serve in chilled bowls garnished with 1 tablespoon chopped fresh dill and 2 teaspoons finely grated lemon zest.

 Honeydew Mint Soup

In a food processor or blender purée the seeded meat of 2 medium honeydews, the juice of 1½ lemons, ¼ teaspoon grated nutmeg, a pinch of salt, 8 mint leaves, and 1 tablespoon superfine sugar. Chill for several hours.

Gingered Mango Soup

Cut 2 large mangoes lengthwise on either sides of their pits. Scoop out the flesh and puree in a food processor with 1 cup orange juice, 2 teaspoons minced fresh gingerroot, ½ cup white wine, and 4 teaspoons honey. Serve chilled as a dessert, garnished with 4 teaspoons chopped candied ginger.

Mango Orange Soup with Plums and Blueberries

Cut 2 large mangoes lengthwise on either sides of their pits. Scoop out the flesh and puree in a food processor with 1 cup orange juice, ½ cup white wine, and 4 teaspoons honey. Serve chilled, garnished with 1 cup blueberries frozen for several hours until solid and 2 pitted, diced red plums.

 Sesame Tuna Sashimi

Cut ½ pound trimmed, 1-inch-thick best-quality fresh tuna fillet into thin slices. Brush with ½ teaspoon wasabi softened in 4 teaspoons light soy sauce. Roll in ½ cup toasted sesame seeds and arrange on a platter garnished with thin slices of lemon. Cut 2 sheets toasted nori into julienne strips and sprinkle over top.

 Carpaccio

In a food processor, finely chop 6 cornichons, 3 tablespoons chopped fresh parsley, 1 large clove garlic, 3 anchovies, 1 tablespoon drained capers, and 1 tablespoon chopped shallot. Whisk in 1 tablespoon Dijon mustard, 1 tablespoon wine vinegar, and 5 tablespoons virgin olive oil until thick. Pour this sauce over ½ pound raw tenderloin fillet, trimmed of fat and gristle, cut in paper-thin slices, arranged on a platter, and seasoned with kosher salt and freshly ground black pepper.

 Carpaccio Jalapeño

Mix ¼ cup minced onion, 1 clove minced garlic, 2 to 3 minced jalapeño peppers, ¼ cup minced cilantro leaves, and 3 tablespoons corn oil. Serve over ½ pound tenderloin fillet as described in the preceding recipe.

 Carpaccio Tonnato

Whisk together 1 minced shallot, 1 clove minced garlic, 1 tablespoon finely grated fresh gingerroot, ¼ teaspoon crushed red pepper flakes, ¼ teaspoon ground coriander, 1 tablespoon lemon juice, 1 tablespoon virgin olive oil, and 1 tablespoon peanut oil. Cut ⅓ pound best-quality fresh tuna across its narrow side into ½-inch-thick slices. Dip slices into the sauce and pound gently between sheets of wax paper to an even thickness of 1⁄16 inch. Arrange tuna slices on a platter, slightly overlapping, and top with any remaining sauce.

SAUCES

 Cold Sage Sauce

Whisk 2 egg yolks with 2 teaspoons mustard until lightly thickened. Whisk in the juice of ½ orange and 1 teaspoon balsamic vinegar. In a slow stream, whisk in 1½ cups vegetable oil. (To avoid uncooked eggs, substitute 1½ cups mayonnaise mixed with the orange juice, vinegar, and mustard.) Add 1 tablespoon minced sage leaves. Season with salt, white pepper, and a dash of cayenne pepper dissolved in 1 tablespoon water. Serve with leftover roasts, especially pork, veal, and poultry.

 Fennel Grapefruit Sauce

Whisk 2 egg yolks with 2 teaspoons mustard until lightly thickened. Whisk in 3 tablespoons grapefruit juice and 1 teaspoon lemon juice. In a slow stream, whisk in 1½ cups vegetable oil. (To avoid uncooked eggs, substitute 1½ cups mayonnaise mixed with the mustard and grapefruit and lemon juices.) Add 1 teaspoon ground fennel seed. Season with salt, white pepper, and a dash of cayenne pepper dissolved in a tablespoon of water. Try it with poached fish or in tuna salad.

Tarragon Raspberry Sauce

Follow recipe for Raspberry Vinaigrette (page 297), adding 1 teaspoon dried or 1 tablespoon fresh tarragon leaves. Use with grilled meats or sautéed liver.

Spicy Red Tomato Salsa

In a blender or food processor, chop 1 small onion, 3 large tomatoes, 2 seeded and stemmed fresh jalapeño peppers, 2 tablespoons olive oil, 2 tablespoons chopped fresh parsley, ¼ cup chopped fresh cilantro, salt, and pepper. Serve with chips, french fries and grilled meats.

Spicy Green Tomato Salsa

Follow preceding recipe, but substitute green tomatoes for red.

Confetti Salsa

Follow recipe for Spicy Red Tomato Salsa (above), substituting 4 or 5 chopped scallions for the onion and adding ½ cup diced yellow pepper. Use as a dip or a sauce for plain meats.

Jalapeño Salsa

In a blender or food processor, finely chop 1 large clove garlic, 6 or 7 stemmed and seeded pickled jalapeño peppers, 2 stemmed tomatoes, and ⅓ cup water. Use as a dip or a sauce for chicken, fish, or pork.

Gazpacho Salsa

In a blender or food processor, finely chop 2 stemmed tomatoes, ¼ small cucumber, ¼ stemmed and seeded jalapeño pepper, 1 tablespoon chopped onion, ½ clove minced garlic, 2 tablespoons olive oil, and 1 tablespoon wine vinegar. Try with grilled or poached fish and shellfish.

Artichoke Salsa

In a food processor or blender, finely chop the contents of a 6½-ounce jar marinated artichoke hearts, 1 small clove minced garlic, the juice of ½ large lemon, and ⅓ cup pine nuts. Serve with grilled steaks, lamb, fish, or chicken.

Tomato Dill Salsa

Mix 2 large stemmed, seeded, and finely chopped tomatoes, ½ finely chopped red onion, ¼ cup finely chopped fresh dill, 1 clove minced garlic, ¼ cup olive oil, and 3 tablespoons vinegar. Serve with fish, chicken, veal, pork, or shellfish.

Roasted Pepper Salsa

Finely chop 2 large jarred roasted red bell peppers, ½ teaspoon minced garlic, the juice of ½ lemon, and ¼ teaspoon crushed red pepper flakes. Blend in 1 tablespoon olive oil. Serve with roasted or grilled meats, poultry, or seafood.

Avocado Salsa

Mix 1 peeled, pitted, and diced large avocado, 2 finely chopped scallions, 1 stemmed and chopped large tomato, 3 tablespoons lemon juice, 1 tablespoon virgin olive oil, 1 clove minced garlic, 2 teaspoons chopped fresh parsley, and crushed red pepper flakes to taste. Serve with grilled meats, fish, or seafood.

Cucumber Mint Salsa

In a food processor or blender, finely chop 2 peeled, seeded, and chopped large cucumbers, 1 clove garlic, chopped whites of 2 scallions, ¼ cup fresh mint leaves, 2 tablespoons olive oil, 1 teaspoon wine vinegar, ¼ cup water, and 3 tablespoons plain yogurt. Serve with fish, chicken, or veal.

Ginger Lychee Salsa

In a food processor or blender, finely chop 24 peeled and pitted lychees (canned or fresh), ½ teaspoon light soy sauce, 1 clove minced garlic, 1 teaspoon grated fresh gingerroot, 2 teaspoons Oriental sesame oil, 1 teaspoon lemon juice, 1 tablespoon fresh cilantro, and 2 to 3 tablespoons water. Serve with grilled or poached fish or chicken.

Fresh Basil Pesto

In a food processor or blender, finely chop 1 large garlic clove and 2 tablespoons pine nuts. Add ⅔ cup firmly packed basil leaves and chop finely. Blend in ⅓ cup virgin olive oil in a slow, steady stream, 3 tablespoons grated Parmesan, salt, and pepper. Serve on pastas, grilled meats, and fish.

Spicy Basil Pesto

Follow preceding recipe and add ¼ teaspoon crushed red pepper flakes and freshly ground black pepper with the pine nuts.

Spinach Pesto

In a food processor or blender, finely chop 1 clove garlic and 2 tablespoons pine nuts. Add 10 ounces defrosted frozen spinach with about half the liquid squeezed out and 1 tablespoon dried basil, and chop finely. Blend in ⅓ cup extra-virgin olive oil in a slow, steady stream, 3 tablespoons grated Parmesan, salt, and pepper. Serve on pastas, grilled meats, and fish.

Mint Pesto

In a food processor or blender, finely chop 1 clove garlic with 2 tablespoons sliced unblanched almonds and 2 cups fresh mint leaves. Add ½ cup olive oil, 1 tablespoon lemon juice, salt, and pepper and puree. Serve on pastas, grilled meats, and fish.

Oregano Walnut Pesto

In a food processor or blender, finely chop ½ cup oregano leaves, ½ cup basil leaves, 2 cloves garlic, and ¼ cup walnuts. Add ¼ cup olive oil and ¼ cup walnut oil in a slow, steady stream, processing continually. Blend in ¼ cup freshly grated Parmesan. Serve on pastas, grilled meats, and fish.

Anchovy Olive Pesto

Add 8 anchovy fillets to a double recipe of Tapenade (page 25). Serve on pastas, grilled meats, and fish.

Sesame Chick-Pea Spread

In a food processor or blender, puree 1 cup canned chick-peas, 1 clove garlic, 1 tablespoon tahini, 2 tablespoons Oriental sesame oil, 2 tablespoons olive oil, 1 teaspoon soy sauce, and ½ teaspoon hot sauce. Serve with crudités, crackers, or bread.

 ### Avocado Coulis

In a food processor or blender, puree 2 medium peeled, pitted, and chopped avocados, the juice of ½ lime, 1 teaspoon hot pepper sauce, and 1 clove minced garlic. Use with chicken, veal, fish, or shellfish. Serve with crudités or grilled chicken or fish.

 ### Green Herb Oil

Mince 2 tablespoons *each* fresh rosemary leaves, thyme leaves, chives, flat-leaf parsley, tarragon leaves, and 1 small clove garlic and blend with ¼ cup olive oil and ¼ cup peanut oil. Use for vegetables, fish, or shellfish. It is especially good with corn on the cob.

 ### Creole Tartar Sauce

Mix 2 tablespoons finely chopped onion, ½ clove minced garlic, ½ cup grated apple, 1 teaspoon cider vinegar, 1 tablespoon lemon juice, 1 cup mayonnaise, 3 tablespoons pickle relish, and 1 to 2 teaspoons hot pepper sauce. Serve with seafood, fried fish, or chicken breasts.

This group includes recipes served frozen or chilled:

 ### Three-Can Salad

Cut into quarters the drained contents of 1 can (16-ounce) small boiled potatoes. 1 can (16-ounce) boiled beets, and 1 jar (12-ounce) pickled herring and toss with ½ cup *each* mayonnaise and sour cream, 3 chopped dill pickles, and 2 cups walnut pieces. Serve chilled.

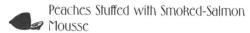 ### Prosciutto and Summer Fruit Relish

Cut up ½ skinned and seeded honeydew, 3 fresh figs, 4 pitted apricots or 2 pitted peaches, and ½ cup halved grapes. Toss with ½ pint raspberries and 2 tablespoons chopped fresh mint. Serve with ½ pound thinly sliced imported prosciutto.

 ### Peaches Stuffed with Smoked-Salmon Mousse

Blend ½ pound softened cream cheese, 6 ounces finely chopped smoked salmon, the grated zest and juice of ½ lemon, 1 tablespoon minced fresh dill, a dash of grated nutmeg, 3 tablespoons sour cream, and ¼ clove minced garlic. Slice off tops of 4 large freestone peaches and reserve for "lids." Hollow out peaches with a melon baller, discard pits, and cut a thin slice from the bottoms so they sit upright. Rub cut surfaces with lemon juice. Fill hollowed-out peaches with the mousse, place "lids" on top, and garnish each with a dill sprig.

 ### Peaches Stuffed with Ham Mousse

Follow preceding recipe, but substitute 6 ounces boneless baked ham for the salmon and use parsley instead of dill.

 ### Vegetable-Stuffed Deviled Eggs

Halve lengthwise 4 peeled and chilled hard-cooked eggs. Mash the yolks with 1 teaspoon mustard, 2 tablespoons mayonnaise, and ½ clove minced garlic. Mix in 1 cup finely diced garden vegetables (carrots, scallions, onions, celery, cucumber, zucchini, radishes) and mound into the hollow of each egg-white half.

 ### Smoked Trout and Horseradish Deviled Eggs

Follow preceding recipe, substituting boneless, skinless, crumbled smoked trout for the vegetables and adding 1 tablespoon horseradish.

 ### Cherries in Orange Honey Over Melon

Whisk together 1 tablespoon honey, ½ cup orange juice, and 1 teaspoon brandy. Toss with 1 pint pitted and stemmed cherries and serve over 1 honeydew or cantaloupe, seeded, peeled, and sliced in wedges.

 ### Kiwi and Honeydew in Margarita Glaze

Toss 4 peeled, quartered, and sliced kiwis, ¼ cup tequila, 2 tablespoons orange liqueur, ½ teaspoon salt, 3 tablespoons confectioners' sugar, and 3 tablespoons lime juice. Serve over 1 thinly sliced peeled and seeded honeydew.

 ### Espresso Granita

Mix 3 cups brewed or instant espresso or strong coffee with ½ cup light corn syrup. Freeze in a shallow pan until ice crystals begin to form, then remove from freezer and stir. Continue freezing and stirring every half hour for about 3 hours, until the whole mixture is a firm slush. (If it should freeze solid, break into small pieces, and crush in a food processor or blender.) Serve in 4 chilled espresso cups garnished with curls of lemon rind.

 ### Bourbon-Spiked Peach and Praline Bombe

Remove the center of ½ gallon peach ice cream to a bowl, leaving 1 inch of ice cream across bottom and sides of the carton. Return carton to freezer. Work ¼ cup bourbon, 1 tablespoon molasses, and 1 cup chopped pecans into the ice cream from the center and fold in ½ cup heavy cream, whipped firm. Pour this mixture into the hollowed-out ice cream. Cover tightly and freeze for several hours or overnight, until the center is firm. To serve, rip the carton away from the ice cream and invert onto a serving plate. Slice and serve with Brandied Peaches (page 401).

19
Fifty Ways to Clean Out the Refrigerator

It's a jungle in there. Rummaging through the underbrush in the inner reaches of a refrigerator, one can capture a miniature menagerie of lemon bits and onion fragments, a dab of tomato paste, a lonely anchovy or a solitary sardine. Perhaps a half-eaten yogurt is lurking or a deserted celery stalk.

Beneath veils of plastic wrap and shields of foil hide the remnants of bygone recipes, destined for either disposal or resurrection. The choice is yours.

The quandary is not so much what to do as how to do it. We can all agree on the shamefulness of wasting food, but when we're confronted with a plateful of odds and ends and not a clue of how to turn them into anything edible, the disposal seems like an attractive alternative.

Fortunately, there are a slew of options for combining the specks and spots of sundry ingredients into all-purpose preparations that are more likely to serve a useful role in day-to-day meal planning. A homemade salad dressing can use up half a yogurt or a wedge of lemon. A quick pasta sauce will finish off the last of the tomato paste, onion, or celery. Making vegetable soup clears out the refrigerator in a clean sweep when vegetable ends pile up, and chicken soup is practically free of charge with a leftover carcass or two and a few cups of vegetable tops.

Leftovers are not only the mother of many distinguished culinary inventions, they are the original convenience food. What could be better than a perfect roast ready to be wrapped in frozen puff pastry for an elegant return engagement? Or flavorful meat simmered with vegetables for a stew that takes 20 minutes to prepare instead of 2 hours? What cook would complain about a pasta salad providing complete protein and savory flavors yet requiring little more work than mixing vinaigrette with a can of tuna, a can of beans, and last night's spaghetti?

Leftover egg whites can be the base for meringue cookies, macaroons, or a quick cheese soufflé. The soufflé carries the added advantage of using the block of Cheddar that has been quietly moldering in the refrigerator door.

Make sandwich spreads by combining vegetable trimmings with tidbits of cheese, or with sour cream and cottage cheese blended with scallion and cucumber, or by puréeing the liver from last night's roast chicken with some browned onions and butter. Use the giblets from that chicken to make a quick stock that can be reduced into a flavorful glaze for effortless professional-quality sauces. Embellished with mushrooms, capers, mustard, or cream, glaze-based sauces turn ordinary grilled, roasted, and poached meats into elegant entrées in seconds.

Create your own frozen dinners by arranging portions of leftover meats and vegetables on plastic plates, ready to be wrapped and frozen for another night, when they can be popped into the microwave to deliver a finished dinner in 5 minutes.

Once you get into the right frame of mind and begin transforming unused remainders into useful convenience foods, you won't be able to stop. What else can single-handedly clean out the refrigerator, cut back the food bill, and dress up the table while wiping away the guilt of wasting good food?

ABOUT THESE RECIPES

Because the contents of refrigerators differ from house to house and from day to day, the yield on each recipe is intended to be approximate. Unless otherwise noted, each recipe is written for 4 portions, but if you find yourself a tablespoon shy of tomato paste or wanting to get rid of a cup more chicken broth than a recipe calls for, make the appropriate adjustments. All of these recipes are very forgiving.

Likewise, we encourage you to adjust the ideas in this chapter to your own needs. Chicken soup can mean turkey soup if a turkey carcass is what you have on hand. Steak sauce can be used on any roasted meat. A lemon half can be replaced with a lime half. The point here is not to follow recipes

exactly but to use the ever growing pile of leftovers and recipe refuse in your refrigerator to your culinary advantage.

 Lemon Yogurt Dressing

Mix ½ cup plain yogurt, the finely chopped zest and juice of ½ lemon, 1 clove minced garlic, ½ teaspoon chopped fresh parsley, salt, and pepper.

 Garlic Yogurt Dressing

Mix ½ cup yogurt, ¼ cup olive oil, 1 clove minced garlic, salt, and pepper.

 Yogurt Dessert Sauce

Mix ½ cup fruit yogurt (any flavor), 2 tablespoons milk, 1 tablespoon honey, ¼ teaspoon vanilla, ¼ teaspoon lemon juice, and 1 tablespoon orange liqueur.

 Eggless Caesar Dressing

Mix 1 clove crushed garlic, 2 minced anchovies, and 1 tablespoon Dijon mustard, then blend in 1 tablespoon wine vinegar, 1½ teaspoons lemon juice, and 2 teaspoons Worcestershire. In a slow, steady stream, whisk in a blend of ½ cup olive oil and ½ cup vegetable oil. Season with salt and pepper.

 Red Caesar Dressing

Follow preceding recipe, replacing 2 teaspoons of the mustard with 1 tablespoon tomato paste.

Fifty Ways to Cook Most Everything

 Spicy Tuna Sauce

Follow recipe for Eggless Caesar Dressing (page 169), adding 1 cup leftover tuna salad to the garlic-mustard mixture. Replace half the Worcestershire sauce with hot pepper sauce.

 Hot Pepper Peanut Vinaigrette

Mix ¼ clove minced garlic, 2 finely chopped scallions, ½ teaspoon hot pepper sauce, 1 teaspoon soy sauce, 3 tablespoons rice wine vinegar, 1 teaspoon finely chopped fresh gingerroot, a pinch of ground cumin, a pinch of ground coriander, 2 tablespoons peanut butter, and 2 tablespoons peanut oil.

 Tomato Vinaigrette

Whisk together 1 tablespoon tomato paste, 2 tablespoons red wine vinegar, ¼ cup olive oil, 1 teaspoon chopped fresh parsley, salt, and pepper.

 Homemade Steak Sauce

Melt 4 tablespoons butter, then whisk in 2 tablespoons Worcestershire sauce, 1 tablespoon tomato paste, and 1 tablespoon brown mustard.

 Anchovy Steak Sauce

Follow preceding recipe, substituting a minced anchovy fillet for the tomato paste.

Spicy Steak Sauce

Follow recipe for Homemade Steak Sauce (above), adding 1 teaspoon hot pepper sauce.

 Scraping-the-Jar Russian Dressing

Whisk together ¼ cup mayonnaise, ¼ cup sour cream, 1 tablespoon tomato paste, 3 tablespoons lemon juice, and a pinch of sugar. Makes 6 portions.

 Easy Tomato Sauce

In a saucepan, cook ½ chopped onion, 1 clove minced garlic, a pinch of crushed red pepper flakes, and ½ diced bell pepper in 2 tablespoons olive oil until vegetables soften. Add one (14-ounce) can crushed tomatoes and 2 tablespoons tomato paste and simmer 5 minutes. Season with salt and pepper, add 1 tablespoon chopped fresh parsley, and heat another minute.

 Mediterranean Tomato Sauce

Follow preceding recipe, but double the garlic and add ¼ cup chopped black olives and 2 teaspoons chopped anchovies with the bell pepper. If desired, replace the parsley with basil.

 Capered Tomato Sauce

Follow recipe for Easy Tomato Sauce (above), but add 2 tablespoons drained capers with the bell pepper.

 Chicken Glaze

Bring ½ chopped onion with skin, 1 small chopped carrot, 1 chopped rib celery or 3 celery tops, the chopped giblets from 1 chicken (excluding the liver), 1 cup white wine, the juice of ½ lemon, 3 cups water, ½ teaspoon thyme leaves, 1

clove garlic, 1 parsley sprig, 1 bay leaf, and ¼ teaspoon cracked black pepper to a boil. Skim away the scum and simmer 1 hour. Strain, return the liquid to a small pot, and reduce the liquid to a third its volume. Strain and use as a flavor base for soups, stews, sauces, and gravies.

Meat Glaze

Follow preceding recipe, using 1 to 2 pounds leftover roasted meat bones instead of the giblets and 2 teaspoons tomato paste instead of lemon juice. Simmer for 1½ hours before straining.

Saltless Seasoning From Leftover Lemon

Peel and finely chop the zest from ½ lemon and mix with its juice, 1 teaspoon olive oil, ¼ teaspoon coarsely ground black pepper, 2 tablespoons chopped fresh parsley, and 1 clove minced garlic. Rub over chicken, beef, veal, or pork before roasting, scatter on baked fish, add to the poaching liquid for a fish or chicken breast, stir into stews, soups, and stir-fries, or mix into eggs. Makes about 2 tablespoons, enough for 6 to 8 portions of food.

Celery-Top Seasoning Mix

Follow preceding recipe, but use chopped celery leaves instead of parsley and add ½ teaspoon ground celery seed.

Vegetable Top and Chicken Carcass Soup

In a stock pot, combine 3 chicken carcasses with 1 cup white wine and boil for 3 minutes. Add 2½ quarts water, bring to boil, skim the surface, and simmer 20 minutes. Dice 1 quart vegetable tops and trimmings, discarding soiled or unsightly sections, and add to the soup along with 3 tablespoons chopped fresh parsley, 2 tablespoons chopped fresh dill, 1 teaspoon dried thyme, 1 clove, ½ cup pearl barley, salt, pepper, and 1 envelope (¼ ounce) unflavored gelatin softened in 2 tablespoons water. Simmer for 1 hour. Remove the bones, let cool, then pick off and return any meat to the soup. Reheat.

 ## Turkey Carcass Split Pea Soup

Follow preceding recipe, using 1 turkey carcass instead of the chicken carcasses. Add ⅓ cup diced smoked turkey along with the vegetables, and use 1 cup split peas instead of the barley.

 ## Leftover Chicken Noodle Soup

Follow recipe for Vegetable Top and Chicken Carcass Soup (above), omitting the barley. Add 3 cups cooked leftover pasta along with the meat from the carcasses.

 ## Leftover Chicken Rice Soup

Follow recipe for Vegetable Top and Chicken Carcass Soup (above), omitting the barley. Add 2 cups cooked leftover rice along with the meat from the carcasses.

Lemon Chicken Soup

Follow the recipe for Vegetable Top and Chicken Carcass Soup (above), replacing the dill with 1 tablespoon ground coriander, 1 teaspoon ground cumin, ½ teaspoon crushed red pepper flakes, and 1 tablespoon finely chopped lemon zest. Add the juice of 1½ lemons and ⅓ cup chopped fresh cilantro with the meat from the carcasses.

Fifty Ways to Cook Most Everything

Pasta, Bean, and Tuna Salad

Toss 3 cups leftover cooked pasta with drained and crumbled tuna from a 6-ounce can, 1 drained (19-ounce) can white kidney beans, 4 sliced scallions, and 2 tablespoons chopped fresh parsley. Toss with dressing made from 2 tablespoons olive oil whisked with 2 tablespoons lemon juice, 2 tablespoons wine vinegar, ½ teaspoon crushed red pepper flakes, salt, and pepper.

Chili Pasta Salad

Chop 3 cups leftover pasta (plain or with tomato sauce) into bite-size pieces. Toss with 1 cup chopped cooked meat, 1 drained (19-ounce) can red kidney beans, 3 sliced scallions, and a mixture of 3 tablespoons mayonnaise, 2 tablespoons chili powder, 1 tablespoon ground cumin, ⅓ cup corn or peanut oil, 2 tablespoons hot pepper sauce, salt, and pepper.

Pepper Pasta Salad

Chop 3 cups leftover plain pasta into bite-size pieces. Toss with 4 large roasted bell peppers (page 442), cut into strips, and ½ recipe Garlic Herb Dressing (page 296).

Chicken and Bean Salad

Toss 1 drained (19-ounce) can chick-peas (garbanzo beans), ⅓ cup thinly sliced scallion, 1 sliced roasted red pepper (page 442), 4 crumbled slices browned bacon, and ½ pound diced leftover skinned chicken meat with a mixture of 3 tablespoons mayonnaise, 2 tablespoons chili powder, 1 tablespoon ground cumin, ⅓ cup corn or peanut oil, 2 tablespoons hot pepper sauce, salt, and pep-

per. Just before serving, toss in 2 tablespoons chopped fresh parsley.

Leftovers Tabouleh

Soak 2 cups bulgur in 2½ cups hot tap water for 30 minutes until most of the water has been absorbed and the bulgur is tender, then drain. Mix ⅓ cup olive oil, the juice of 1 lemon, 1 clove minced garlic, 1 teaspoon hot pepper sauce, 3 tablespoons chopped fresh parsley, 1 tablespoon dried mint, salt, and pepper and toss with the soaked bulgur along with 2 cups diced leftover vegetables and/or meat, such as tomatoes, bell peppers, celery, cucumbers, fennel, mushrooms, cooked chicken. Chill.

Leftover Fish Salad for Sandwiches

Toss 2 cups flaked cooked boneless and skinless fish with 3 tablespoons mayonnaise, 2 chopped ribs celery, salt, pepper, and 2 teaspoons lemon juice.

Rice and Bean Salad

Toss 2 cups leftover rice, 2 cups cooked black beans, 2 diced roasted red bell peppers (page 442), ½ clove minced garlic, ⅓ cup olive oil, ¼ cup red wine vinegar, the juice of 1 lime, ¼ cup chopped fresh parsley, salt, and pepper.

Leftover Chicken Chili

In a saucepan, cook 1 finely chopped onion in 2 tablespoons corn oil until softened. Add 1 clove minced garlic, 1 chopped fresh chili pepper, 1 tablespoon chili powder, 1 teaspoon ground cumin and 1 tablespoon flour and cook 30 seconds. Add

¾ cup chicken stock, ¼ cup crushed tomatoes in puree, salt, and pepper. Bring to a boil, add 3 cups chopped cooked and skinless chicken, and simmer until the sauce is lightly thickened.

 ## Leftover Steak Chili

Follow preceding recipe, using ½ cup beef broth and 1 tablespoon Worcestershire sauce in place of the chicken stock, and using chopped leftover steak or roasted beef for the chicken.

 ## Stir-Fried Chicken with Apples and Walnuts

Stir-fry ½ cup walnuts in 2 teaspoons peanut oil until lightly toasted. Remove. Add ¼ cup chopped onion and stir-fry 10 seconds. Add 2 ribs sliced celery and 1 diced Granny Smith apple and stir-fry until the apple softens slightly. Add 3 cups diced cooked skinless chicken, a pinch of crushed red pepper flakes, 2 tablespoons lemon juice, and 1 clove minced garlic and toss for 30 seconds. Add the walnuts, 1 teaspoon walnut oil, salt, and pepper.

Leftover Fried Chicken Cole Slaw

Remove 1 pound fried chicken meat and its skin from the bones and toss with 2 cups shredded cabbage, 1 shredded carrot, 3 sliced scallions, and 2 teaspoons orange marmalade mixed with 1 teaspoon honey. Whisk in 1 tablespoon mayonnaise, 1½ tablespoons sour cream, 1 tablespoon red wine vinegar, 2 teaspoons ketchup, 1 tablespoon hot pepper sauce, salt, and pepper.

Leftover Grilled Meat with Escabeche Sauce

In a skillet, cook 1 sliced onion and 2 cloves chopped garlic in ¼ cup olive oil until softened. Add 1 to 2 pounds leftover grilled meat and toss in hot oil. Add the juice of 2 oranges, 2 lemons, and 2 limes, ¼ cup red wine vinegar, 1 teaspoon hot pepper sauce, salt, and 1 tablespoon chopped fresh parsley. Chill.

 ## Meat and Potato Salad with Blue Cheese Dressing

Finely chop 1 pound leftover roasted, grilled, or sautéed meat with a dressing made of 1 clove minced garlic, 2 tablespoons olive oil, 1½ tablespoons red wine vinegar, ¼ cup sour cream, 3 tablespoons milk, and 2 ounces crumbled blue cheese. Toss with 1½ pounds warm boiled, peeled, and large-diced red-skin potatoes and 2 ribs sliced celery.

 ## Cold Sliced Meats with Red and Green Sauces

Mix ¼ cup finely chopped fresh parsley, 6 finely chopped anchovy fillets, 1 clove minced garlic, 1 teaspoon spicy mustard, 4 teaspoons red wine vinegar, 5 tablespoons olive oil, salt, and pepper and chill. Combine 2 chopped red bell peppers, 1 chopped chili pepper, ¼ cup chopped onion, 1 clove garlic, 2 tablespoons wine vinegar, the juice of ½ lemon, and 2 tablespoons olive oil and simmer until the peppers are soft. Season with salt and pepper and keep warm. Serve the two sauces with 4 to 6 portions cold sliced roast meat or poultry.

 ## Barbecued Pork Salad

In a skillet, brown ¼ pound bacon, remove, blot on paper towels, and crumble. Cook ½ minced onion in the bacon fat until soft. Add 2 cloves minced garlic, ¼ cup cider vinegar, 1 tablespoon Worcestershire sauce, ½ teaspoon hot pepper sauce, 2 tablespoons sugar, salt, and pepper. Bring to a boil and toss with 1 to 2 pounds diced leftover boned barbecued pork spareribs, 1 diced roasted red pepper (page 442), ¼ pound sliced mushrooms, 2 sliced scallions, and the reserved bacon.

Wilted Salad Gazpacho

In a food processor, chop 2 cups wilted dressed salad, 1 chopped small onion, 1 clove minced garlic, 3 cups vegetable cocktail juice, 1 to 2 teaspoons hot pepper sauce, salt and pepper. Chill and serve garnished with 1 cup seasoned croutons.

Asian Fried Noodles

Stir-fry 3 cloves finely chopped garlic and ½ teaspoon crushed red pepper flakes in 3 tablespoons oil for 10 seconds. Add 1 tablespoon sugar, 3 tablespoons soy sauce, and 1½ tablespoons ketchup and stir until sugar dissolves. Add ½ pound cooked spaghetti and 2 beaten eggs, stir-frying for 1 minute. Add ¾ cup bean sprouts and ½ cup chopped cooked meat, poultry, or seafood and stir-fry another 2 minutes. Turn onto a plate and garnish with ¼ cup raw bean sprouts, 2 tablespoons chopped peanuts, 2 sliced scallions, 2 tablespoons chopped fresh cilantro and 1 sliced lime.

Fried Rice from Leftovers

Follow preceding recipe, using 4 cups cooked rice instead of the spaghetti and toasted sesame seeds instead of the peanuts. Omit the sugar and lime.

Leftover Minestrone

In a large soup pot, cook 1 cup chopped onion and 2 cloves minced garlic in 2 tablespoons olive oil until soft. Add 2 to 3 cups sliced vegetables and cook 2 minutes. Add 1 teaspoon *each* dried thyme, savory, and basil and ½ teaspoon *each* dried rosemary (crumbled), oregano, and sage and cook 3 minutes more. Add 4 chopped canned tomatoes, 5 cups chicken broth, 1 tablespoon *each* wine vinegar and tomato paste, salt, and pepper. Bring to a boil and simmer for 10 minutes. Add 2 cups cooked pasta in tomato sauce and heat through. Serve with grated Parmesan. Serves 8.

Baked Potato Skins with Garlic Yogurt Dressing

Cut shells from 4 baked potatoes in 6 pieces each, deep-fry at 375° F. until crisp and serve with Garlic Yogurt Dressing (page 169).

A Little Chopped Liver

Cook 1 cup minced onion in a nonstick skillet until soft. Add 2 tablespoons butter and cook until onion is brown. Add 3 chicken livers and a pinch of thyme, cooking until the livers are firm. Season with salt and pepper and chop finely. Mix in 1 teaspoon chopped fresh parsley, chill, and serve with crackers. Serves 1.

Onion Dip

Brown 1 cup finely chopped onion in 2 teaspoons oil until crisp. Beat into ⅓ cup mayonnaise and ⅓ cup yogurt or sour cream. Season with salt, pepper, and a dash of hot pepper sauce.

Chicken and Gravy Frozen Dinner

Arrange 3 ounces sliced roast chicken on part of a microwave-safe plastic dinner plate and cover with

¼ cup chicken gravy. Place 1 portion leftover vegetable beside it and 1 portion leftover rice or noodles tossed with 2 teaspoons melted butter in the remaining space. Cover tightly with plastic wrap vented at one corner, then with foil. Freeze until solid. To serve, remove foil and microwave at full power for 4 to 6 minutes until plastic swells. Serves 1.

Stale-Cookie Pie Crust

Process ½ pound old plain cookies into fine crumbs. Blend with 1 teaspoon ground cinnamon, 3 tablespoons brown sugar, and 3 tablespoons melted butter until uniform. Press into a 10-inch pie pan to form an even crust. Bake at 350° F. for 10 minutes. Refrigerate until firm.

Chocolate Bread Pudding

In a food processor, process ½ pound diced stale bread with 1 teaspoon ground cinnamon and 1 cup strong coffee. Add 2 eggs and 6 tablespoons butter, and process well. Process in 1 cup sugar, 5 ounces sweetened condensed milk, ¾ cup evaporated milk, 2 tablespoons milk, 1 teaspoon vanilla extract, and 2 ounces melted unsweetened chocolate. Pour into greased 9-inch square baking dish set in a larger pan of water and bake at 350° F. for 1 hour 15 minutes, until set. Cool before serving. Serves 6.

White Chocolate Rice Pudding

Heat ¼ cup honey until melted, mix in 2 tablespoons brandy, ¼ cup dried currants, and 1 cup cooked rice and heat through. Stir in 5 ounces finely chopped white chocolate until it melts. Cool and fold in 2 cups unsweetened whipped cream. Chill.

Fifty Herbs and Spices and How to Use Them

Most home cooks are chicken when it comes to herbs. They confine themselves to two or three favorites and rely on salt and pepper to fill in the gaps. Set in their ways, they think of herbs and spices as exotic gourmet ingredients, meant for the fancy restaurant kitchen rather than for everyday home cooking.

Nothing could be further from the truth, for herbs are natural flavor enhancers, just waiting to take a plain roasted chicken and transform it—with white wine and tarragon, or curry and orange, or ginger and soy, with little more than a pinch of this and a dash of that.

Herbs are the soft parts of aromatic plants, such as leaves and blossoms, which can be bought fresh or dried. Spices are the harder parts, like the root, seed, or pod, and they are always dried.

When using whole dried herbs and spices, grind them as close to when you plan to use them as possible, for once a seasoning is ground, its aroma and flavor begin to dissipate. So given a choice between ground thyme and leaf thyme, for example, choose the leaf. It will have a shelf life of nearly

six months, while the ground thyme will have begun losing its oomph before you even lift the lid on the bottle. Whole seeds and other hard spices will keep for up to a year.

Dried leafy herbs can simply be crushed between your fingers, but seeds must be ground. Though you can use a mortar and pestle, it takes considerable time and elbow grease. A better solution is a coffee mill or an electric spice grinder. These mini–food processors will pulverize the hardest dried seeds in no time. But they will have no effect on dried barks and hard roots, such as turmeric, cinnamon stick, or dried gingerroot. These must be bought in ground form if that's what the recipe calls for.

Store dried seasonings in cool, dark places, packed in small containers with tight-fitting lids. Because all the flavor in an herb or spice comes from its volatile oils, degeneration of these oils from exposure to light, heat, or air will cause the seasoning to lose power and, in time, turn rancid. So never keep dried seasonings over a stove or near a sunny window.

When using fresh herbs in place of dried herbs in a recipe, triple the quantity called for in the recipe and expect a slightly sweeter and more subtle product. Because dried herbs are dehydrated, their flavors are concentrated, but so is the natural bitterness of the leaf. Fresh herbs are less bitter but do not have the same intensity as dried herbs, especially when they are cooked too long.

In cooking, think of fresh herbs as you would other leafy vegetables. Cook them quickly. When the leaf is wilted, the herb is cooked. Any additional heat will only dissipate the herb's flavor and destroy its color.

ABOUT THESE RECIPES

The following 50 recipes each highlight an herb or spice. All recipes serve 4 unless otherwise noted.

 Lemon Anise Spinach

In a skillet, cook ½ cup chopped onion until softened in 2 tablespoons butter with 1 teaspoon ground aniseed and 1 teaspoon finely chopped lemon zest. Add 20 ounces defrosted frozen chopped spinach and cook until fairly dry. Season with salt and pepper.

 Star-Anise Duck

In a deep skillet, brown 1 sectioned duck, about 4 pounds, in 1 inch peanut oil. Remove browned duck pieces and discard oil. Add 1 tablespoon additional oil, 1 tablespoon minced fresh gingerroot, 3 cloves minced garlic, ½ teaspoon crushed red pepper flakes, and 6 star anise, cooking another minute. Add the browned duck, 3 tablespoons soy sauce, ¼ cup dry sherry, 1 cup chicken stock, 1 cup water, and 2 tablespoons sugar, cover, and simmer for 25 minutes. Degrease and add 8 sliced scallions and 8 soaked dried black mushrooms. Add 2 tea-

spoons cornstarch dissolved in 1 tablespoon water, and stir until thickened. Finish with 1 teaspoon Oriental sesame oil.

 Chicken Breast Steamed in Basil Leaves

Pound 2 split boneless, skinless chicken breasts between sheets of wax paper until very thin. Season one side of each breast with salt and pepper and cover with fresh basil leaves. Roll up and wrap in several layers of plastic wrap. Steam over boiling water for 10 minutes until the rolled breasts are firm. Unwrap, draining juices from each roll into a saucepan. Reduce juices until lightly thickened and swirl in 1 tablespoon butter, if desired. Slice each roll and nap with some sauce.

 Out-of-Fresh-Basil Pesto

Place 2 tablespoons dried basil in ⅔ cup warm olive oil and let steep for 10 minutes. In a food processor, finely chop 4 cloves garlic, ⅓ cup pine nuts, and ½ pound cleaned and stemmed spinach leaves. Add oil mixture and process to a smooth sauce. Stir in ¾ cup grated Parmesan, salt, and pepper. Use as a sauce for pasta, grilled meats, roasts, or poached fish.

 Veal Shanks with Tomato and Bay

Using string, tie 2 bay leaves around the perimeters of each of 4 veal shanks, cut into 2-inch segments. Dredge flat sides of the shanks in flour and brown on both sides in 2 tablespoons butter melted with 2 tablespoons olive oil. Add ⅔ cup finely chopped onion, ⅓ cup finely chopped celery, and 1 clove minced garlic halfway through browning. When meat is browned, add ½ cup white wine, 2 cups chopped and skinned plum tomatoes, ½ teaspoon dried thyme, 1 teaspoon dried basil leaves, ¼ teaspoon dried oregano, salt, and pepper. Bring to a boil, cover, and place in a 350° F. oven for 2 hours, until tender. Skim off fat and stir in ½ clove minced garlic and 1 tablespoon finely chopped fresh parsley. Remove string and discard bay leaves.

Black Mustard

Soak ¼ cup black mustard seed in 1 tablespoon balsamic vinegar and 1 tablespoon wine vinegar for 1 hour. Mix in 2 tablespoon molasses and 1 cup brown mustard. Serve with grilled meats.

Caraway Raisin Soda Bread

Sift 2 cups unbleached all-purpose flour, 2 teaspoons baking soda, 2 teaspoons baking powder, ¼ teaspoon salt, and ½ cup sugar. Cut in 4 tablespoons butter to the size of small peas. Mix in 1 tablespoon caraway seeds. Add 1 cup buttermilk and ½ cup raisins, mixing just until moistened. Form into a ball on a lightly floured board and place on a dry sheet pan. Slit a cross in the top of dough and sprinkle with 1 tablespoon sugar. Bake in preheated 375° F. oven for 30 to 35 minutes, until brown. Serves 6.

Cardamom Tea Cake

Sift 1½ cups sifted all-purpose flour, 1 teaspoon baking powder, and 1 tablespoon ground cardamom. Set aside. With an electric mixer, beat 5 egg whites with a pinch of salt until they hold a shape. Add ¾ cup confectioners' sugar and beat until very thick. Set aside. Beat 5 egg yolks with ¾ cup sugar until thick. Set aside. Cream ½ pound unsalted butter until soft. Beat in 1 teaspoon vanilla extract and the finely grated zest of 1 large orange. Mix in half the dry ingredients, followed by the yolk mixture and remaining dry ingredients. Fold in the egg whites in 2 additions. Bake in greased and floured

standard loaf pan at 350° F. for 1 hour 10 minutes or until a tester comes out with a crumb clinging to it. Cool for 10 minutes and unpan. Serves 10 to 12.

Cayenne Pepper Gingerbread

Sift 2½ cups sifted all-purpose flour, 2 teaspoons baking soda, ½ teaspoon salt, 1 teaspoon ground cinnamon, ½ teaspoon ground cloves, ½ teaspoon dried mustard, ⅛ teaspoon cayenne pepper, and ½ teaspoon ground black pepper. Beat ¼ pound unsalted butter, 2 tablespoons grated fresh gingerroot, and ½ cup firmly packed brown sugar until fluffy. Beat in 2 eggs, one at a time, with 1 cup dark molasses. Dissolve 2 tablespoons instant coffee powder in 1 cup boiling water. Alternately add sifted dry ingredients in three additions and the coffee in two additions. Bake in 9-inch square pan at 375° F. for 40 to 45 minutes, until tester comes out with crumbs clinging to it.

Chilled Garden Soup with Celery Seed

In a food processor, finely chop 2 skinned and chopped tomatoes, 1 chopped roasted red pepper (page 442), ¼ onion, 1 clove minced garlic, ¼ cup celery leaves, 3 tablespoons olive oil, salt, pepper, and 3 ice cubes. The ingredients should not be completely smooth. Stir in another 3 ice cubes, 1 tablespoon crushed celery seed, and 1 tablespoon chopped fresh parsley. Chill.

Grilled Chicken Breast with Buttermilk and Chervil

Marinate 2 split, lightly pounded, boneless, skinless chicken breasts in 1 cup buttermilk mixed with the chopped whites of 2 scallions, 2 tablespoons chopped fresh chervil, 1 tablespoon finely grated orange zest, a pinch of cayenne pepper, salt, pepper and 1 tablespoon virgin olive oil. Refrigerate at least 2 hours. Remove from marinade and grill until firm, about 4 minutes per side, basting frequently with the extra marinade.

 ### Chili Pepper Chutney

In a skillet, cook 1 finely chopped onion, 2 cloves minced garlic, and 1 minced and seeded fresh serrano chili in 2 tablespoons peanut oil until softened. Add 1 toasted and ground dried chili pepper, 1 teaspoon ground coriander, ¼ teaspoon ground cloves and 1 tablespoon grated fresh gingerroot and cook for 1 minute. Add 1 *each* roasted and diced poblano, red bell, yellow bell, and green bell pepper (page 442), along with ¼ cup cider vinegar, ¼ cup sugar, and ¼ cup water. Stir, cover, and simmer for 20 minutes, until peppers are soft. Cook off excess liquid, and stir in ¼ cup chopped fresh cilantro leaves. Store in refrigerator. Makes 2 cups. Serve with poultry, pork, eggs, or fish.

 ### Chicken with Ginger, Soy, and Chive

Season with salt and pepper 2 pounded, split, skinless, boneless chicken breasts and brown in 2 tablespoons peanut oil. Add ¼ clove minced garlic and 1 teaspoon chopped fresh gingerroot, and cook another minute. Deglaze pan with 1 tablespoon lowsodium soy sauce, ⅓ cup chicken stock, and a pinch of sugar, simmer for 3 minutes, then add 1 tablespoon sliced fresh chives, 1 teaspoon Oriental sesame oil, and 1 teaspoon dry sherry.

 ### Poached Salmon with Lemon and Chive Blossoms

Bring 1 cup white wine, ½ cup water, the juice of 1 large lemon, salt, and pepper to a boil, add 4 pieces skinned salmon fillet, each 3 to 4 ounces, and poach for 8 to 10 minutes. Remove to a warm plate. Reduce pan liquid to a third its volume, add ⅓ cup

finely chopped fresh chives and, if available, 12 chive blossoms, and boil 1 minute more. Swirl in 4 to 6 tablespoons butter. Pour over fish and serve.

 ### Lime and Coriander Roast Chicken

Rub a 5-pound roasting chicken inside and out with a mixture of 1 tablespoon ground coriander, 1 teaspoon salt, ½ teaspoon pepper, 3 cloves minced garlic, and 3 tablespoons extra-virgin olive oil. Refrigerate overnight. Place in a roasting pan, squeeze the juice of 3 limes over top. Place lime shells in chicken cavity and roast at 375° F. for 2 hours, basting occasionally.

 ### Cilantro Catfish Soup

Toss 3 pounds trimmed catfish fillets, cut in bite-size chunks, in ¼ cup lemon juice. Season with salt and pepper. In a food processor, finely chop 1 onion, 2 cloves garlic, 1 stemmed and seeded jalapeño pepper, and 1 stemmed and seeded red bell pepper, then cook until softened in 2 tablespoons olive oil in a saucepan. Add 1 cup crushed canned tomato and 1 quart Fish Stock (page 430) and bring to a boil. Add fish to broth and simmer for 6 minutes. Just before serving, stir in 6 tablespoons chopped fresh cilantro and 1 diced avocado.

 ### Grilled Shrimp in Cumin Paste

In a skillet, cook 1 cup chopped onion, 1 minced seeded jalapeño pepper, and 1 clove minced garlic in 1 tablespoon olive oil until softened. Add 1 tablespoon ground cumin, ½ teaspoon dried oregano, and 1 teaspoon ground coriander and cook 1 minute more. Add 2 tablespoons lemon juice, salt, and pepper. Butterfly 1 pound cleaned jumbo shrimp, spread with the spice paste, and marinate in the refrigerator for 1 hour. Grill until firm and opaque, about 2 minutes per side.

Fifty Ways to Cook Most Everything

 Curried Cabbage Flowers

Toast 1 tablespoon black mustard seed in 1 table-spoon hot clarified butter (page 430) for 10 seconds. Add 1 cup chopped onion, 1 tablespoon curry powder, 1 teaspoon ground cardamom, 1 teaspoon ground coriander, and 1½ teaspoons ground cumin and cook until onion softens. Add 2 cups small cauliflower florets and 2 cups small broccoli florets, mix well and add 1 cup water. Simmer until vegetables are tender, about 15 minutes, and most of the liquid has evaporated. Add ½ cup yogurt and season with salt and pepper.

 Dill Popovers

Place a 12-well nonstick muffin tin or a 6-deep-well popover pan in a preheated 450° F. oven. Beat 1 cup milk with 1 tablespoon melted butter. Sift 1 cup all-purpose flour with a pinch of salt, then beat in the liquid ingredients just until blended. Beat in 2 eggs, one at a time, and ¼ cup minced fresh dill. Grease the hot tin with melted butter and sprinkle the wells with flour. Divide batter evenly among the wells. Bake for 15 minutes, then reduce oven temperature to 375° F. and bake 10 to 15 minutes more, until fully puffed, brown, and crisp all over the surface.

 Dilly Cabbage

In a saucepan, cook 1 sliced onion until soft in 2 tablespoons vegetable oil with 2 teaspoons dill seed. Add 1 pound sliced cabbage and cook until softened. Season with salt and pepper.

 Fines Herbes Vinaigrette

Whisk together 1 clove minced garlic, ¼ cup red wine vinegar, ¾ cup olive oil, ½ teaspoon salt, freshly ground pepper, 1 tablespoon minced fresh parsley, 2 teaspoons chopped fresh chervil, 2 teaspoons fresh dill, and 1 teaspoon chopped fresh tarragon. Makes enough for 8 portions of salad.

 Five-Spice Eggs

Simmer 6 eggs in 2 quarts simmering water for 10 minutes. Let cool completely. Crack shells all over without removing them by tapping them all around with the back of a spoon or by rolling them gently over a countertop. Cover with cold water and add 2 teaspoons five-spice powder, ¼ cup soy sauce, and 2 tea bags. Cover and simmer gently for 1 hour. Cool in refrigerator and store in liquid for at least 2 days. Shortly before serving, peel and cut in quarters. Serve with Dipping Sauce for Potstickers (page 205).

Blackened Beef Steaks with Fennel

Mix 2 tablespoons *each* ground black pepper, dried minced garlic, salt, and ground fennel seed, 1 tablespoon onion powder, ½ teaspoon dried mustard, and ½ teaspoon cayenne pepper. Rub into surface of 4 loin steaks (T-bone or porterhouse) and refrigerate for several hours. Heat a large iron skillet over a high flame for 15 minutes, brush with oil (be careful, it will flame up) and cook the steaks for 2 to 3 minutes per side.

Fennel and Orange Salad

Break 1 fennel bulb into ribs and slice thinly. Toss with the split sections of 2 navel oranges, ½ cup walnut pieces, and a pinch of grated nutmeg. Whisk together ⅓ cup olive oil, 1 teaspoon ground fennel seed, ⅓ cup orange juice, 1 tablespoon lemon juice, a pinch of cayenne pepper, salt, and pepper. Toss with the vegetables.

 ### Indian Steamed Clams with Garam Masala

In a skillet, cook 1 finely chopped onion, 2 teaspoons finely chopped fresh gingerroot, ½ clove minced garlic, 1 teaspoon ground coriander, 1 teaspoon ground cumin, 1 tablespoon garam masala (available at many specialty stores), and a pinch of crushed red pepper flakes in 1 tablespoon vegetable oil until the onion softens. Add 4 dozen cleaned littleneck clams, cover, and steam 5 to 8 minutes, until clams open. Remove clams, discarding any that do not open, add 1 tablespoon lemon juice and ¼ cup chopped fresh cilantro to the pan juices, and spoon over clams.

 ### Ginger Apple Cobbler

Toss 3 pounds peeled and sliced tart apples with the juice of 1 lemon and cook in 2 tablespoons butter, ¾ cup sugar, and 2 teaspoons ground ginger until the apples begin to release their moisture. Mix 1 tablespoon cornstarch in 1 tablespoon water, add 2 tablespoons brandy, mix thoroughly, add to the apples, and simmer until thickened. Remove from heat and stir in 2 tablespoons chopped candied ginger, 1 cup raisins, and 1 teaspoon vanilla extract. Grease a 9-inch casserole, line the bottom with whole gingersnaps, pack in the apple mixture, and top with 12 crumbled gingersnaps mixed with 1 tablespoon softened butter and ¼ cup sugar. Bake at 450°F. for 25 minutes.

Garlic and Ginger Lamb Chops

Mix 2 cloves minced garlic, ¼ cup finely chopped fresh gingerroot, and 2 tablespoons olive oil. Rub 8 rib or loin lamb chops with salt and pepper and coat with this marinade. Refrigerate at least 1 hour. Grill or broil 3 to 4 minutes per side.

 ### Trout Stuffed with Pickled Ginger and Scallion

Mix the thinly sliced whites of 1 bunch scallions, 3 tablespoons chopped Japanese pickled ginger (*gari*), and the finely chopped zest of 1 lemon. Open 4 cleaned and boned rainbow trout, divide the mixture among the fish, and close the fish over the stuffing. Douse with the juice of 1 lemon, rub each with 1 teaspoon olive oil, and broil for 4 minutes per side.

 ### Veal Scallops Sautéed with Herbes de Provence

Dredge 8 pounded veal scallops, 2 to 3 ounces each, in flour seasoned with salt and pepper, sauté in 2 tablespoons olive oil, remove and keep warm. Add 2 teaspoons *herbes de Provence*, 1 minced shallot, and 2 cloves minced garlic and cook for 30 seconds. Add 1 cup white wine and 2 tablespoons white wine vinegar and reduce to ¼ cup. Add the juices from the veal, bring to a boil, remove from heat and swirl in 4 tablespoons softened butter. Pour over veal.

 ### Roasted Garlic Horseradish Paste

Bake 2 large heads garlic at 375° F. for 45 minutes, or until soft to the touch. Let cool slightly. Cut the pointed end off each garlic head and slip cloves from their peels. In a food processor, puree the roasted garlic, 5 tablespoons white prepared horseradish, and 1 teaspoon Dijon mustard. Season with salt. Serve with plain roasted meats or steaks.

Fifty Ways to Cook Most Everything

 Jalapeño Bloody Marys

Whisk or shake together ½ cup tequila, 2 cups vegetable cocktail juice, 1 tablespoon Worcestershire sauce, 1 minced stemmed and seeded jalapeño pepper, and 4 teaspoons lime juice. Make 2 slits in either side of 4 whole pickled jalapeño peppers and insert 1 thin slice garlic in each slit. Drop 1 pepper into each drink.

 Frittata with Ham, Walnuts, and Marjoram

Heat 2 tablespoons peanut oil and 1 tablespoon olive oil in a skillet. Add ½ cup walnuts, 1 cup diced baked ham, and 1 teaspoon crumbled dried marjoram leaves. Heat gently until the walnuts toast lightly. Season with salt and pepper, and add 1 tablespoon orange zest, 1 clove minced garlic, 1 teaspoon fresh marjoram leaves, and 8 eggs beaten with 2 tablespoons water and ¼ teaspoon hot pepper sauce. Cook until the eggs set up completely across the bottom, about 2 minutes. Place under a broiler until frittata is puffed and brown, 2 to 3 minutes.

 Green Pea Soup with Mint

In a saucepan, cook 1 cup chopped onion in 1 tablespoon butter until soft. Add 1 tablespoon dried mint, 20 ounces frozen peas, 1½ quarts chicken stock, 1 tablespoon sugar, salt, and pepper and simmer for 20 minutes. In a food processor or blender, process until smooth, adjust seasoning, reheat, and add 1 cup light cream. Garnish with chopped fresh mint leaves. Serve hot or chilled. Serves 6.

 Watermelon Spearmint Water Ice

Boil 3 tablespoons dry mint, ½ cup sugar, and ⅓ cup water for 3 minutes, strain, and let cool. In a food processor or blender, process 8 cups seeded watermelon pulp with the cooled syrup. Add a pinch of salt, 3 tablespoons lemon juice, and ¼ cup chopped spearmint leaves. Pour into a flat pan and freeze for 1½ hours. Stir well, and return to freezer, stirring every 30 minutes until completely frozen. If mixture should freeze solid, cut into cubes and process until finely chopped.

 Salmon With Molasses and Mustard

Mix 2 tablespoons brown mustard, 1 teaspoon lemon juice, and 1 teaspoon molasses. Brush over the surfaces of 4 salmon steaks, each ¾ inch thick, and dredge in seasoned bread crumbs. Set on a rack for 10 minutes. Cook over moderate heat in ⅛ inch olive oil for 5 to 6 minutes per side, until salmon has browned and flakes to gentle pressure.

 Salad of Garden Lettuces and Nasturtium

Toss cleaned leaves of 1 small head red leaf lettuce, 1 bunch arugula, 1 head Boston lettuce, and 4 dozen small nasturtium leaves. Pluck petals from 16 rinsed and dried nasturtium blossoms and toss with the greens. In a small bowl, combine 1 minced shallot, 2 tablespoons raspberry vinegar, 2 tablespoons walnut oil, ¼ cup peanut oil, salt, and pepper and toss with salad. Top with 2 dozen sliced unblanched almonds.

 Mussels Oreganato

In a large heavy saucepan, cook 2 cloves minced garlic in ¼ cup olive oil until soft. Add 1 cup chopped canned tomatoes, 1 tablespoon chopped fresh parsley, 1 teaspoon dried oregano, and a pinch of crushed red pepper flakes and simmer for 20 minutes. Add 2 pounds scrubbed and debearded mussels, cover, and simmer for 3 minutes until mussels open, discarding any that don't. Serve with crusty bread.

 Reddened Blackfish with Paprika.

In a skillet, cook 2 cloves minced garlic and 1 finely chopped small onion in 2 tablespoons peanut oil until soft. Add 1 tablespoon chili powder, 1 tablespoon Hungarian paprika, and ½ teaspoon salt and cook 1 minute more. Rub all but 1 tablespoon of this paste over 4 thick black bass fillets. To the remaining spice paste, add 2 diced red bell peppers, 1 tablespoon wine vinegar, 1 tablespoon lime juice, 1 teaspoon sugar and ¾ cup water. Reduce to a third its volume, and puree in a food processor. Season with salt and pepper, reheat, and swirl in 1 tablespoon butter. Grill fish for 2 minutes per side and serve covered with the sauce.

 Parsley Green Pasta

Pour 1 quart boiling water over 1 bunch parsley leaves. Drain, cool, and squeeze dry. In a food processor, blend to a paste with 1 clove garlic and add 1 large egg and ⅛ teaspoon salt. Add 1 cup unbleached all-purpose flour and process until a smooth dough forms. Add up to ¼ cup more flour, 1 tablespoon at a time, until dough forms a ball in the center of the workbowl. Rest the dough for 10 minutes. Roll and cut into any shape pasta. Boil and serve tossed with grated Parmesan, garlic, olive oil, salt, and pepper.

 Szechuan Pepper Popcorn

Mix ¼ teaspoon freshly ground black pepper, ¼ teaspoon freshly ground Szechuan peppercorns, ½ teaspoon ground coriander seed, ¼ teaspoon ground ginger, and 1 teaspoon finely grated lemon zest and set aside. Heat 3 tablespoons peanut oil

over high heat in a large heavy pot until oil smokes. Add 1 kernel popping corn and heat until kernel pops. Add ¾ cup popping corn. Cover and shake gently until corn starts to pop. Shake vigorously until popping subsides. Remove from heat. Toss with reserved spice mixture and 1 clove minced garlic. Serves 6.

 Veal Chops with Rosemary, Sage, and Aïoli

Dust 4 (8-ounce) veal chops in ½ cup flour seasoned with 2 teaspoons crumbled dried rosemary, 2 teaspoons rubbed sage, salt, and pepper. Brown in 2 tablespoons butter mixed with 1 split clove minced garlic, and 2 tablespoons olive oil. Turn down heat, cover, and cook chops through, turning two more times, about 10 minutes. Serve with ½ cup mayonnaise blended with 2 teaspoons lemon juice and 1 clove minced garlic.

 Sage Roast Pork with Sage Mayonnaise

Rub surface of 2 pounds boneless pork loin with salt, pepper, and 1 tablespoon olive oil. Lay 12 fresh sage leaves over surface of the pork and roast at 375° F. for 1 hour, or until internal temperature reads 155° on a meat thermometer. Let rest 10 minutes. Slice and serve with 1 cup mayonnaise mixed with 1 teaspoon wine vinegar, 2 tablespoons orange juice, 1 teaspoon rubbed sage, and 1 tablespoon of the pan drippings.

Sicilian Mushrooms with Savory

In a skillet, cook 1 cup chopped onion, the chopped white of 1 leek, and 2 cloves minced garlic in 2 tablespoons olive oil until softened. Add 2 ribs sliced celery, 1 pound cleaned whole button mushrooms, and ½ diced bell pepper and cook 2 minutes. Add 1 teaspoon *each* dried thyme and basil, ½ teaspoon *each* dried crumbled rosemary and sage, and 2 teaspoons dried savory and cook 3 minutes more. Add 4 chopped canned tomatoes, ½ cup chicken broth, and 1 tablespoon *each* wine vinegar and tomato paste. Simmer 15 minutes. Season with salt and pepper.

Sorrel Beurre Blanc

Combine 1 tablespoon minced shallot, ¼ teaspoon dried tarragon, ½ cup white wine, and 2 tablespoons tarragon vinegar and reduce over high heat to ⅓ cup. Add 1 cup sorrel leaves and cook 30 seconds. Reduce heat to low and swirl in 6 tablespoons butter. Serve over fish, shellfish, chicken, or veal.

Tamarind Eggplant with Peanuts

Cook 1 cup chopped onion and 2 cloves minced garlic in 1 tablespoon olive oil until softened. Add 1 tablespoon curry powder, 1 teaspoon ground cumin, and 1 teaspoon chili powder and cook 2 minutes more. Add 1 large peeled and diced eggplant, ¼ cup split yellow peas, ¼ cup ketchup, 2 teaspoons hot pepper sauce, and ¼ teaspoon ground saffron soaked in 1 cup boiling water. Simmer for 20 minutes until peas are tender, adding more water if necessary. Stir in 1 tablespoon tamarind paste dissolved in ¼ cup water and simmer 3 more minutes. Add ½ cup roasted peanuts.

Cherry Tarragon Compote

Simmer 1 pound stemmed cherries with ¼ cup sugar, a pinch of salt, the juice of 2 limes, 1 small cinnamon stick, 1 whole clove, and ¼ cup kirsch for 5 minutes. Remove from heat and toss in 1 tablespoon fresh tarragon leaves and the finely

chopped zest of ½ lime. Cool and serve as is, with cookies or over ice cream.

Lime and Thyme Vinaigrette

Whisk together ⅓ cup virgin olive oil, the juice of 2 limes, 2 teaspoons dried thyme, 1 clove minced garlic, salt, and pepper.

Golden Turmeric Tomato Relish

Toss together 2 chopped and seeded tomatoes, ¼ thinly sliced red onion, the juice of ½ lemon, ¼ cup chopped mint leaves, 1 teaspoon sugar, 1 teaspoon chili powder, 2 teaspoons ground turmeric, and 1 tablespoon plain yogurt. Serve with grilled meats or poached seafood.

Watercress and Grapefruit Salad

Toss 4 cups watercress leaves trimmed of all stems, the sections of 2 peeled grapefruit trimmed of their membrane, the thinly sliced whites of 4 scallions, and ⅓ cup chopped pistachio nuts. Separately, whisk together 3 tablespoons peanut oil, 1 tablespoon Oriental sesame oil, 3 tablespoons lemon juice, a pinch of cayenne pepper, salt, and pepper. Toss with salad.

Zesty Salt Substitute

Mix 1 teaspoon freshly ground black pepper, 1 teaspoon freshly ground Szechuan peppercorns, 1 teaspoon ground coriander seed, ¼ teaspoon ground ginger, 1 tablespoon finely grated lemon zest, and 2 teaspoons *each* finely grated orange and lime zests.

Fifty Chicken Breast Recipes for Every Pot

The chicken is an odd bird. Its legs are those of a sumo wrestler, its Mae West breast seems better suited to take to a sauce than to the skies, and its puny wings haven't the remotest chance of lifting its girth aloft.

Bred far from its ornithological roots, the chicken is now primarily a culinary animal, and anyone who cooks should be eternally grateful for it. We would be hard-pressed to find another ingredient as versatile, as convenient, or as easy to prepare—especially the breast, which can be quickly grilled, poached, baked, or broiled in hundreds of ways without risk of repetition.

In this chapter, we offer 50 chicken breast recipes. Be sure, also, to look at Chapter 22 for some ideas on preparing chicken legs.

ABOUT THESE RECIPES

All the recipes in this chapter call for whole, skinless, boneless chicken breasts that have been trimmed of excess fat. When a recipe calls for pounded breasts, pound them between oiled sheets of wax paper. Each recipe makes 4 servings, unless otherwise noted. Many use clarified butter, described on page 430.

Sautéed Chicken Breast with Tarragon

Brown 2 large split chicken breasts in 1 tablespoon clarified butter. Add 2 tablespoons minced onion, 1 cup dry vermouth, 2 tablespoons wine vinegar, and 1 tablespoon dried tarragon. Cook until chicken is firm and liquid is lightly thickened. Remove from heat and swirl in 4 tablespoons butter.

Chicken Lemon Veronique

Brown 2 large split chicken breasts in 1 tablespoon clarified butter. Add 1½ cups chicken stock and reduce until chicken is firm and liquid is lightly thickened. Add the juice of 1 lemon and simmer for 30 seconds more. Add 2 dozen split seedless grapes, remove from heat, and swirl in 1 tablespoon butter.

Fifty Ways to Cook Most Everything

 Lemon Mushroom Chicken

Brown 2 large split chicken breasts in 1 tablespoon clarified butter. Add 2 cups sliced mushrooms and cook over low heat until mushrooms are tender and chicken is firm. Add the juice of 1 lemon and simmer for 30 seconds more. Season with salt and pepper.

 Pecan Chicken Breast with Mustard Sauce

Dip 2 chicken breasts, split and lightly pounded, in 4 tablespoons melted butter mixed with 2 tablespoons mustard. Press 6 tablespoons ground pecans into the breasts, and sauté in mixture of 2 tablespoons butter and 2 tablespoons peanut oil. When browned and firm, remove to warm platter. Deglaze pan with ⅔ cup sour cream and 1 tablespoon mustard, season with salt and pepper, and pour sauce over the chicken.

 Chicken Breast with Vodka, Tomatoes, and Cream

Brown 4 split chicken breasts in 2 tablespoons olive oil. Add 2 cloves minced garlic and cook just until garlic is soft. Add ½ teaspoon crushed red pepper flakes, 12 peeled, seeded, and chopped plum tomatoes, salt, and pepper and simmer until breasts are firm. Remove chicken to a warm platter. Add ¼ cup vodka and ½ cup heavy cream. Simmer just until cream thickens. Pour over chicken. Serves 6 to 8.

 Sautéed Chicken Breast in Capers and Brown Butter

Brown 2 pounded large split chicken breasts in 1 tablespoon clarified butter until firm. Remove to warm platter. Add 4 tablespoons butter, cook until bubbly, add ¼ cup capers with their liquid, and cook until sauce is brown and lightly thickened. Pour over breasts.

 Sage and Rosemary Chicken Breasts Meunière

Dredge 2 lightly pounded large chicken breasts in ½ cup bread crumbs seasoned with salt, pepper, and 1 teaspoon *each* ground sage and crumbled dried rosemary. Cook in 2 tablespoons clarified butter until firm. Add ⅛ clove minced garlic, 1 tablespoon fresh rosemary, and 1 tablespoon shredded sage leaves. Cook 1 minute more.

 Sautéed Chicken Breast with Brandy Cream

Brown 2 large split chicken breasts in 1 tablespoon clarified butter. Add 2 tablespoons minced onion and ½ cup brandy and ignite carefully with a match. Add 1½ cups light cream and reduce until lightly thickened. Season with salt and white pepper.

 Deviled Chicken Breast

Brush 2 lightly pounded large split chicken breasts with 2 tablespoons mustard and dredge in 1 cup bread crumbs seasoned with salt, pepper, and ½ teaspoon cayenne pepper. Cook in 3 tablespoons clarified butter until firm and brown. Deglaze with 1 tablespoon hot pepper sauce and 1 tablespoon lemon juice.

 Sesame Chicken Breast

Brush 2 lightly pounded large split chicken breasts with Oriental sesame oil and dredge in 1 cup sesame seeds seasoned with salt, pepper, and ½ teaspoon cayenne pepper. Cook in ¼ cup Oriental sesame oil over moderate heat until firm. Add 1

teaspoon minced garlic and deglaze pan with 2 tablespoons light soy sauce.

 Sautéed Chicken Breast with Apple Glaze

Brown 2 large split chicken breasts in 1 tablespoon clarified butter. Add 2 tablespoons minced onion, 1 cup apple juice, 2 tablespoons cider vinegar, and 1 teaspoon brown sugar. Reduce until chicken is firm and liquid is lightly thickened. Remove from heat and swirl in 2 tablespoons butter.

 Chicken Baked in Foil with Clams

Place each of 4 small chicken breasts rubbed with olive oil and lemon juice in the center of a piece of foil, each 18 inches square. Season *each* with 1 teaspoon dill leaves, salt, and pepper and surround with 8 littleneck clams in their shells. Wrap foil around the chicken and clams and seal edges. Bake at 400° F. for 30 minutes. Discard any clams that do not open.

 Chicken Breast Baked with Smoked Turkey and Fontina

Rub 2 whole chicken breasts with olive oil and season with salt and pepper. Pound to ¼-inch thickness. Place 1 slice smoked turkey breast and 1 slice Fontina cheese atop each half of each chicken breast. Fold one side over the other, sandwiching turkey and cheese in the middle. Wrap each in foil and bake in 400° F. oven for 15 minutes.

 Poached Chicken Breast with Warm Tomato Vinaigrette

In a saucepan, mix together 1 cup tomato puree, ¼ cup olive oil, 2 tablespoons wine vinegar, 2 tablespoons chopped fresh parsley, salt, and pepper,

bring to a simmer, and keep warm. Split 2 large chicken breasts and poach in simmering chicken stock to cover until firm. Remove to a platter and pour sauce over top.

 Quick Chicken Chili

Cut 3 whole chicken breasts into bite-size chunks, dredge in flour, and brown in 2 tablespoons corn oil in a large skillet. Add 1 minced onion, 1 clove minced garlic, 1 tablespoon chili powder, and 1 teaspoon ground cumin and cook 30 seconds. Add ¾ cup chicken stock, ¼ cup crushed tomatoes in puree, salt, and pepper. Simmer 3 minutes more until chicken is firm and sauce is lightly thickened.

 Poached Chicken Breast in Beurre Blanc

Poach 4 split breasts in 2 cups white wine, 2 tablespoons minced shallot, and ¼ cup wine vinegar until firm. Remove chicken and keep warm while reducing pan liquid to a glaze. Swirl in ¼ pound butter, a bit at a time, over very low heat and season with salt and pepper. Pour sauce over chicken. Serves 8.

 Chicken Salad with Tarragon and Grapes

Poach 3 whole chicken breasts until firm. While still warm, cut into chunks and mix with 1 cup mayonnaise, 1½ teaspoons dried tarragon, 1 teaspoon sugar, 1 cup halved seedless grapes, and 2 ribs diced celery. Season with salt and pepper. Serves 6.

Spicy Tahini Chicken Salad

Sauté ¼ cup chopped onion and 1 clove minced garlic in 1 teaspoon Oriental sesame oil until softened. Add 2 tablespoons lemongrass, 1 teaspoon chili paste, 2 teaspoons soy sauce, 2 teaspoons grated fresh gingerroot, ½ teaspoon ground cumin, and ½ teaspoon ground coriander and cook for 2 minutes. Stir in ¼ cup tahini and heat until melted. Remove from heat and stir in 1 cup yogurt. Grill or broil 2 lightly pounded large split chicken breasts 4 inches from high flame until firm. Thinly slice chicken and toss with the tahini sauce. Serve over chilled, cooked cellophane noodles.

 Old-Fashioned Chicken Salad

Poach 3 split chicken breasts until firm. Cut into chunks while still warm and toss with ⅔ cup mayonnaise, 1 tablespoon cider vinegar, 2 ribs finely diced celery, ½ seeded and diced cucumber, 1 shredded carrot, 1 tablespoon minced fresh parsley, salt, and pepper. Chill. Serves 6.

 Yogurt-Dill Chicken Salad

Poach 3 split chicken breasts until firm. Cut into chunks while still warm and toss with 8 ounces plain yogurt, 2½ tablespoons chopped fresh dill, 1 tablespoon lemon juice, and 1 peeled, seeded, and diced cucumber. Season with salt and pepper. Chill. Serves 6.

 Waldorf Chicken Salad

Poach 3 split chicken breasts until firm. Cut into chunks while still warm and toss with 1 cored and diced Granny Smith apple, 1 large rib diced celery, ½ cup coarsely chopped walnuts, ⅓ cup mayonnaise, ⅓ cup sour cream, salt, and pepper. Chill. Serves 6.

 Warm Chicken Salad on Wilted Lettuce

In a saucepan, bring 1 clove minced garlic, 2 tablespoons wine vinegar, 1 tablespoon peanut oil, 3 tablespoons walnut oil, 1 teaspoon salt, and 2 teaspoons sugar to a simmer. Meanwhile, grill 3 whole chicken breasts until firm. Slice thinly. Toss chicken and hot dressing with 1 head cleaned escarole torn into bite-size pieces, ¼ cup chopped onion, and ⅓ cup chopped pecans. Serves 6.

 Fried Chicken Salad

Trim and cut 3 whole chicken breasts into bite-size chunks. Toss with ¾ cup flour heavily seasoned with salt and cayenne pepper. Fry in several inches of hot oil until golden brown. Drain well and toss with ½ cup chopped fresh chives and a dressing made of 2 teaspoons mustard, 1 tablespoon balsamic vinegar, salt, and pepper. Serves 6.

 Cold Chicken with Guacamole Vinaigrette

Rub 2 large split chicken breasts with olive oil and grill 4 inches from a high flame until firm. Chill. In a blender, purée 2 avocados, 2 cloves minced garlic, 3 tablespoons white wine vinegar, a dash of cayenne, salt, and pepper. Serve chilled breasts with the avocado sauce.

 Capered Chicken Salad

Poach 3 split chicken breasts until firm. Cut into chunks while still warm and toss with ⅓ cup mayonnaise, 1 tablespoon lemon juice, 2 tablespoons drained capers, salt, and pepper. Chill and serve with sliced cucumbers. Serves 6.

 Grilled Chicken Salad with Pine Nuts

Rub 3 whole chicken breasts with Oriental sesame oil and grill until firm. Cut into chunks and toss with 2 tablespoons mayonnaise, 2 tablespoons Oriental sesame oil, ¼ cup wine vinegar, 1 teaspoon tomato paste, ¼ cup toasted pine nuts, 1 bunch sliced scallions, salt, and pepper. Serves 6.

Chicken Breast and Orange Salad

Poach 3 split chicken breasts until firm. Cut into chunks while still warm and toss with ⅓ cup mayonnaise, 2 ribs diced celery, 2 navel oranges separated into sections and cut into bite-size chunks, a dash of nutmeg, salt, and pepper. Chill. Serves 6.

Escabeche of Chicken Breast

Dredge 4 split chicken breasts in flour and sauté in ½ inch olive oil until firm, add 1 sliced onion and 2 cloves chopped garlic, remove from heat, and transfer to a wide, nonmetallic bowl. Combine the juice of 2 oranges, 2 lemons, and 2 limes with ¼ cup red wine vinegar, 1 teaspoon hot pepper sauce, salt, and 1 teaspoon dried tarragon and pour over the chicken. Marinate in the refrigerator for 12 hours. Serve chilled. Serves 8.

Chilled Grilled Marinated Chicken Breast

Split 4 chicken breasts and rub with olive oil, salt, and pepper. Grill 4 inches from a high flame until almost firm, 3 to 5 minutes per side. While still warm, toss with ⅔ cup Italian dressing, cover, and chill. Serve on a bed of chilled greens. Serves 8.

Marinated Paillard of Chicken

Rub 2 split chicken breasts with Italian dressing. Pound between sheets of plastic wrap to ⅛-inch thickness. Remove from plastic and marinate in refrigerator for 1 hour in ½ cup additional dress-

ing. Cook each breast in a white-hot, lightly oiled, ridged skillet for 30 to 60 seconds per side. Bring marinade to a boil, and serve chicken brushed with a little marinade.

Grilled Chicken Breast with Artichoke Relish

Thoroughly chop contents of 6-ounce jar of marinated artichoke hearts. Blend in juice of ½ large lemon and ⅓ cup toasted pine nuts. Set aside. Pound 2 large chicken breasts to ¼-inch thickness. Grill or broil until brown and firm, 3 to 5 minutes per side. Serve with a dollop of sauce.

Grilled Saltimbocca Chicken Breast

In a food processor, puree 2 cups cleaned basil leaves, 4 cloves garlic, and ½ cup pine nuts. Add enough virgin olive oil to make a smooth paste and about ½ cup grated Parmesan. Pound 2 large split chicken breasts to ¼-inch thickness. Brush one side with the basil paste and place 1 thin slice prosciutto on top. Fold each breast in half, enclosing the prosciutto, and secure with a toothpick. Brush outside of each breast with ½ teaspoon olive oil. Grill or broil until browned and firm, 3 to 5 minutes per side. Remove toothpick and serve with a dollop of the sauce.

Grilled Chicken Anchoïade

In a food processor, purée 2 ounces anchovy fillets and their oil, and mix with ¼ cup mayonnaise, 2 tablespoons olive oil, ½ clove garlic, and pepper. Set aside. Pound 2 large split chicken breasts to ¼-inch thickness. Grill or broil until browned and firm, about 3 to 5 minutes per side. Serve with a dollop of the sauce.

Grilled Chicken Breast with Tapenade

Combine ⅓ cup pitted and finely chopped oil-cured black olives, 1 clove minced garlic, 5 tablespoons extra-virgin olive oil, and plenty of salt and pepper. Pound 2 large split chicken breasts to ¼-inch thickness. Grill or broil until browned and firm, about 3 to 5 minutes per side. Serve with a dollop of the sauce.

 Grilled Chicken Breast with Roasted Pepper Salsa

Finely chop 2 large roasted bell peppers (page 442), and mix with ½ clove minced garlic, ¼ teaspoon crushed red pepper flakes, and salt. Pound 2 large split chicken breasts to ¼-inch thickness. Grill or broil until browned and firm, about 3 to 5 minutes per side. Serve with a dollop of the sauce.

 Lime-Thyme Broiled Chicken

In nonmetallic baking pan, combine the juice of 1 lime, 2 tablespoons olive oil, 1 teaspoon dried thyme, 1 minced shallot, salt, and pepper. Rub 2 large split chicken breasts with this mixture and marinate in baking pan in the refrigerator for 1 hour. Remove from marinade and broil until firm.

 Chicken Saté

In nonstick skillet, sauté ¼ cup chopped onion and 1 clove minced garlic in 1 teaspoon peanut oil until softened. Add 2 sliced scallions, 1 teaspoon chili paste, 2 teaspoons soy sauce, 2 teaspoons grated fresh gingerroot, ½ teaspoon ground cumin, and ½ teaspoon ground coriander. Cook for 2 minutes. Stir in ¼ cup peanut butter until it melts. Remove from heat and stir in 1 cup yogurt. Flatten 2 large split chicken breasts and grill until

firm, 5 to 6 minutes per side. Top grilled chicken with sauce.

 Grilled Chicken Breast with Herbed Blue Cheese Dressing

Mix 1 cup blue cheese dressing with ¼ cup Italian dressing. Divide into two equal amounts. Pound 2 large split chicken breasts to ¼-inch thickness, and brush with one container of the dressing. Set aside for 30 minutes. Grill or broil the chicken 4 inches from a high flame until browned and firm, about 3 to 5 minutes per side. Serve with the other container of dressing as a sauce.

 Honey Barbecued Chicken Breast

In a saucepan, bring ¾ cup ketchup, ¼ cup grated onion, 2 tablespoons cider vinegar, 1 tablespoon honey mustard, 1 tablespoon Worcestershire sauce, 2 tablespoons honey, and 1 tablespoon hot pepper sauce to a simmer. Split 4 chicken breasts and marinate in the sauce in the refrigerator for 1 hour. Remove breasts from sauce and grill 5 to 6 minutes per side, basting frequently with the extra sauce, until the breasts are firm. Serves 6 to 8.

 Forget-Fast-Food Chicken Sandwich

Mix 2 tablespoons of the preceding barbecue sauce with 2 tablespoons mayonnaise before marinating chicken. Set aside. Continue to follow preceding recipe, serving the barbecued chicken breasts on 8 split kaiser rolls, each spread with the reserved mayonnaise and with ¼ cup coleslaw. Serves 8.

 Grilled Chicken Breast with Cucumber Yogurt Sauce

Thinly slice 1 large peeled, halved, and seeded cucumber, toss with 1 teaspoon kosher salt, and set aside for 15 minutes. Rinse well and drain. Mix with 1 cup yogurt, the juice of ½ lemon, 1 tablespoon olive oil, 1 tablespoon chopped mint leaves, salt, and pepper. Pound 2 large split chicken breasts to ¼-inch thickness. Grill or broil 4 inches from high flame until browned and firm, about 3 to 5 minutes per side. Serve with a dollop of the sauce.

 Grilled Chicken Breast with Sun-Dried Tomato and Basil Rouïlle

In a food processor, puree 10 oil-cured sun-dried tomatoes in ⅓ cup of their own oil. Combine with 1 bunch finely chopped basil leaves, 1 clove minced garlic, 2 tablespoons grated Parmesan, 1 tablespoon virgin olive oil, salt, and pepper. Pound 2 large split chicken breasts to ¼-inch thickness. Grill or broil until browned and firm, about 3 to 5 minutes per side. Serve with a dollop of the sauce.

 Broiled Honey Mustard Chicken

Pound 2 large split chicken breasts to ¼-inch thickness. Brush one side of each breast with 1 teaspoon honey mustard. Broil until browned and firm, about 3 to 5 minutes. Flip, brush with 1 teaspoon additional mustard, and broil another 3 to 5 minutes until browned and firm.

 Broiled Ranch-Style Chicken Breast

Pound 2 large split chicken breasts to ¼-inch thickness. Marinate in ¾ cup ranch dressing for 1 hour. Lift from marinade and broil until browned and firm, about 3 to 5 minutes per side.

 Broiled Chicken Breast with Tomato Dill Salsa

Combine 2 large seeded, stemmed, and chopped tomatoes, ½ finely chopped red onion, ¼ cup chopped dill leaves, 1 clove minced garlic, ¼ cup olive oil, 3 tablespoons vinegar, salt, and pepper. Pound 2 large split chicken breasts to ¼-inch thickness. Broil until browned and firm, about 3 to 5 minutes per side. Top with sauce.

 Broiled Chicken Breast Basted with Sage Butter

Simmer 2 teaspoons rubbed sage in ¼ cup chicken stock until almost all the liquid has evaporated. Remove from heat and swirl in 2 tablespoons butter. Season with pepper and strain. Pound 2 large split chicken breasts to ¼-inch thickness. Brush with all the sage butter and broil until browned and firm, about 3 to 5 minutes per side, basting frequently with more sage butter. Top with any sauce in the broiler pan.

 Chicken Breast Stuffed with Herbed Cheese

Pound 2 split chicken breasts to ⅛-inch thickness, thinner near the edges. Place 2 tablespoons of a soft herb cheese in the center of each portion and wrap the pounded breast around it, as if wrapping a package. Dip into a beaten egg, dredge in bread crumbs, dip in the egg again, and coat with bread crumbs again. Deep-fry in 325° F. oil until golden brown and firm.

 Tangy Fried Chicken Breast

Dip 4 split small chicken breasts in a mixture of 1 cup plain yogurt, 1 clove minced garlic, 1 tablespoon hot sauce, and 1 beaten egg. Dredge in flour and fry in 1 to 1½ inches oil heated enough to make the chicken sizzle vigorously. Cook about 10 minutes, until chicken breast is browned and firm.

Stir-Fried Orange Chicken

Dissolve 2 tablespoons cornstarch in ¼ cup water. Cut 3 chicken breasts into bite-size chunks and soak in cornstarch mixture. In another bowl, mix 2 tablespoons hoisin sauce, 1 clove minced garlic, and 2 teaspoons orange marmalade. Stir-fry chicken in 2 tablespoons peanut oil until meat loses its raw look. Add ½ cup chicken stock and ½ cup orange juice. Simmer until chicken is firm. Add hoisin mixture and any remaining cornstarch mixture. Simmer until thickened, about 30 seconds. Toss in 2 finely chopped scallions. Serves 6.

Stir-Fried Chicken Breast with Cashews

Dissolve 2 tablespoons cornstarch in ¼ cup water. Cut 3 split chicken breasts into bite-size chunks, and soak in the cornstarch mixture. Reserve. In another bowl, mix 2 tablespoons light soy sauce, ⅓ cup Chinese oyster sauce, and the juice of 1 lemon. Set aside. Stir-fry chicken in 2 tablespoons peanut oil. Add 1 dried hot pepper and 1 cup chicken stock, cover, and simmer until chicken is firm. Add oyster-sauce mixture and any remaining cornstarch mixture. Simmer 1 minute. Remove from heat and toss in 1 clove minced garlic, 2 thinly sliced scallions, and 1 cup cashews. Serves 6.

Fifty Chicken Leg Recipes for Every Pot

Where the white meat of chicken lends itself to the broiler, grill, and sauté pan, the leg sections shine when moisture comes into play, as in soups, stews, and broths. They spring to life when fried or fricasseed. They become the very essence of home cooking in braising, and they take on a natural elegance when stuffed and baked.

People can be divided into two groups—those who prefer light meat and those who prefer dark. We've organized our chicken recipes to please both groups of chicken eaters. While Chapter 21 takes care of the light meat, this one is for the leg.

ABOUT THESE RECIPES

The legs called for in the following recipes should include both drumstick and thigh with their skin still on, unless otherwise noted.

As is the case with all stews, those in this chapter need to be skimmed of fat before serving.

Three pounds of chicken legs will be about six full legs. All recipes will feed 4 to 6 people, unless otherwise noted.

Chicken Braised with Apples and Cabbage

Brown 3 pounds sectioned chicken legs in 3 tablespoons rendered bacon fat and remove to a large baking dish. Add ½ cup chopped onion and 4 cups shredded cabbage to remaining fat and cook until soft. Add ½ teaspoon crumbled rosemary, ½ teaspoon dried thyme, ½ teaspoon rubbed sage, salt, pepper, and 2 large diced Granny Smith apples. Pour over the chicken, cover, and bake at 350°F. for 1 hour.

Chicken Braised with Sauerkraut and Sausage

Brown 1 pound Italian sausage, cut in disks, and reserve. Follow preceding recipe, using the fat from the sausage in place of bacon fat, 1 pound rinsed sauerkraut instead of cabbage, and only 1 apple.

Garlic and Ginger Chicken Legs

Rub surface of 3 pounds sectioned chicken legs with 2 large cloves minced garlic, 1 inch grated fresh gingerroot, salt, pepper, and 2 teaspoons Oriental sesame oil. Place on a foil-lined sheet pan and bake for 45 minutes in a 375°F. oven.

 Chicken Legs in Pumpkin Seed Mole

Lightly brown ½ cup bread cubes, ⅓ cup pumpkin seeds, and 3 whole cloves garlic in 1 tablespoon olive oil. Add 1 finely diced jalapeño pepper, ¼ finely chopped onion, and ⅛ teaspoon ground cumin and cook another 30 seconds. Deglaze pan with 1 tablespoon wine vinegar. In a food processor, process into a paste with 2 tablespoons cilantro leaves and add to 1½ cups hot chicken stock. Brown 3 pounds sectioned chicken legs in 2 tablespoons olive oil, add the prepared sauce, cover, and cook for 35 minutes. Remove chicken, whisk 1 tablespoon lime juice and 1 tablespoon mayonnaise into sauce, and pour over chicken.

 Chicken Cacciatore

Dredge 3 pounds sectioned chicken legs in seasoned flour and brown in olive oil. Remove chicken and set aside. Add 1 cup sliced onion and 2 cups sliced mushrooms to the hot oil and brown. Add 2 cloves minced garlic, ¼ teaspoon dried oregano, ½ teaspoon crushed red pepper flakes, and 1 cup white wine and reduce liquid by half. Add 6 skinned and chopped plum tomatoes, salt, pepper, and 1 cup chicken stock. Return chicken to pan and simmer, covered, for 35 minutes. If liquid is too thin, reduce, and stir in 1 tablespoon minced anchovy fillets and 1 tablespoon minced parsley.

 Cacciatore with Olives

Follow preceding recipe, adding 1 tablespoon lemon juice and ⅓ cup slivered black olives with the anchovy.

 Chicken Legs Braised with Garlic

Dredge 3 pounds sectioned chicken legs in seasoned flour and brown in 3 tablespoons olive oil. Add 1 chopped onion and all but 6 cloves of 1 peeled head of garlic and brown along with the chicken after turning. Mince the 6 cloves of garlic and add half of it along with 2 cups white wine, 2 cups chicken stock, 2 tablespoons tomato paste, 1 tablespoon *herbes de Provence*, 2 bay leaves, salt, and pepper and simmer 40 minutes. Meanwhile, roast 3 finger eggplants, peel, and puree. Stir into the braising liquid, along with the remaining garlic, and heat through.

 Chicken with Coriander, Lemon, and Rice

Combine 1 tablespoon ground coriander, 1 teaspoon salt, and ½ teaspoon pepper, rub into 3 pounds chicken legs, and set aside for 10 minutes. Brown in a thin film of olive oil. Add 1 coarsely chopped onion, 2 cloves minced garlic, and pinch of crushed red pepper flakes, and 2 tablespoons ground coriander and cook until the onion is brown. Add 2 cups white wine, 2 cups chicken broth, and the finely grated zest of 1 lemon and simmer 20 minutes. Stir in 1 cup rice and add ¼ cup chopped fresh cilantro, 2 tablespoons chopped fresh parsley, salt, and pepper. Cover and simmer for 15 minutes more. Add the juice of 1 lemon and serve.

 Lemon and Thyme Chicken Stew

Combine 1 teaspoon dried thyme, 1 teaspoon salt, and ½ teaspoon pepper, rub into 3 pounds chicken legs, and set aside for 10 minutes. Brown in a thin film of olive oil. Add 1 coarsely chopped onion, 1 sliced carrot, 1 rib sliced celery, 2 cloves minced garlic, a pinch of crushed red pepper flakes, and 2 teaspoons dried thyme and cook until the onion is brown. Add 2 cups white wine, 2 cups chicken broth, and the finely grated zest of 1 lemon and simmer 20 minutes. Stir in 4 quartered small red-skin potatoes and add ¼ cup chopped fresh cilantro, 2 tablespoons chopped fresh parsley, salt, and pepper. Cover and simmer for 15 minutes more. Add the juice of 1 lemon and serve.

 Chicken Marseille

Brown 3 pounds sectioned chicken legs in 2 tablespoons olive oil. Remove chicken and set aside. Add ½ cup chopped onion, 2 cloves minced garlic, 1 chopped bell pepper, 1 teaspoon dried basil, and 1 teaspoon *herbes de Provence* and cook until softened. Deglaze pan with 1 cup white wine and let boil 2 minutes. Add 2 strips lemon zest, 1 bay leaf, and 1 cup chopped plum tomatoes. Return chicken to pan, cover, and simmer for 40 minutes. Garnish with 2 tablespoons chopped fresh parsley and season with salt and pepper.

 Orange, Tomato, and Anise Chicken Stew

Follow preceding recipe, replacing *herbes de Provence* with ground aniseed and lemon zest with 1 tablespoon finely grated orange zest.

 Chicken and Mussels

Brown 3 pounds sectioned chicken legs on one side in 3 tablespoons olive oil. Add 1 cup chopped onion, ½ cup diced carrot, and ½ cup diced celery, turn and brown the chicken's other side. Add 1¼ cups white wine, 1 bay leaf, 1 strip lemon zest, 1 teaspoon dried thyme leaves, 2 sprigs parsley, salt, and pepper and simmer, covered, for 30 minutes. Add 2 pounds debearded and cleaned mussels and simmer 10 minutes more until mussels open; discard any that do not. Remove parsley and bay leaf and sprinkle with 2 tablespoons chopped fresh parsley.

 Chicken with Sausage and Clams

Slowly brown ¾ pound sliced chorizo or other spicy sausage in 1 tablespoon olive oil. Remove and proceed with previous recipe. Substitute 2 dozen cleaned clams for the mussels, and return the sausage to pan with the clams.

 Chicken Stewed with Parsleyed Dumplings

Dredge 5 pounds sectioned chicken legs in seasoned flour and brown in thin film of peanut oil in a heavy soup pot. Remove chicken and set aside. Add 1 chopped onion, 2 cloves minced garlic, 4 ribs sliced celery, 4 sliced carrots, 1 teaspoon dried thyme, 1 bay leaf, ½ teaspoon crumbled dried rosemary, and ½ teaspoon poultry seasoning to oil remaining in pot and cook until vegetables soften. Return chicken to pot with 5 cups chicken stock and 1 tablespoon lemon juice and simmer for 30 minutes. Meanwhile, sift together 1 cup flour, 2 teaspoons baking powder, and a pinch of salt. Blend in ¼ cup chopped fresh parsley, 2 tablespoons butter, and ½ cup milk. Drop teaspoons of dough across surface of stew, cover, and simmer for 10 minutes without disturbing. Serves 6.

 Chicken with Dirty Rice

Brown 3 pounds sectioned chicken legs in 2 tablespoons olive oil. Remove chicken and set aside.

Fifty Ways to Cook Most Everything

Add ½ pound *each* finely chopped chicken giblets and livers, 1 cup chopped onion, 1 finely diced bell pepper, and ½ cup chopped celery to fat in pan and brown well. Add salt, pepper, and 1 cup long-grain rice. Toss to coat and add 2½ cups hot chicken stock. Return chicken to liquid, cover, and simmer for 30 minutes until liquid has been absorbed. Toss to fluff rice.

 Chicken and Sausage Gumbo

Rub 5 pounds sectioned chicken legs with plenty of salt, garlic powder, and cayenne pepper. Set aside. In a large iron skillet, cook ½ cup flour in ½ cup lard over low heat, stirring frequently, for about 20 minutes, until chocolate brown. Add 2 cups chopped onion, 1 chopped bell pepper, and 1 cup chopped celery and stir for 1 minute. Add 2 cloves minced garlic, cook briefly, slowly stir in 3 quarts hot chicken broth, and bring to a boil. Add 1 pound sliced smoked sausage and 2 cups sliced okra (fresh or frozen). Simmer 15 minutes. Meanwhile, brown chicken in a thin film of oil, add to gumbo, and simmer 40 minutes more. Serve over rice. Serves 6.

 Chicken Braised with Caramelized Onions

Dredge 3 pounds sectioned chicken legs in flour and brown in 2 tablespoons vegetable oil. Remove chicken and set aside. Add 3 large thinly sliced onions, 4 cloves minced garlic, and 6 tablespoons butter. Cook gently until the onion is golden brown, about 15 minutes. Add 1 teaspoon dried thyme leaves, the chicken, 3 cups chicken stock, and 1 teaspoon lemon juice. Cover and simmer 30 minutes. Remove chicken to a platter, reduce liquid until lightly thickened, and pour over chicken.

 Chicken Braised with Cider

Brown 5 pounds sectioned chicken legs in ¼ cup clarified butter. Add 1 coarsely chopped onion, 1 rib chopped celery, 1 sliced carrot, 1 teaspoon *each* dried rosemary (crumbled), sage, and thyme, and 2 large sliced tart apples. Cook for several minutes more to soften vegetables, add 1 quart apple cider, cover, and simmer for 40 minutes. Remove chicken, reduce liquid until lightly thickened, and pour over chicken. Season with salt. Serves 6.

 Moroccan Chicken Stew

In a large pot, place 3 pounds sectioned chicken legs, 4 tablespoons butter, 2 cups chopped onion, 2 cloves minced garlic, 2 sliced carrots, 2 ribs sliced celery, 1 dried chili pepper, 1 tablespoon ground coriander, 1½ teaspoons ground cumin, 1 teaspoon *each* ground ginger, dried thyme, and ground turmeric, 2 cinnamon sticks, ¼ cup *each* chopped fresh cilantro and chopped fresh parsley, and 1 bay leaf. Cover with water, bring to a boil, and simmer for 1 hour. Meanwhile, toast ½ cup almonds in 1 tablespoon oil. In a food processor, finely chop with 1 teaspoon cinnamon and 1 tablespoon confectioners' sugar. Set aside. Remove chicken and vegetables from liquid and reduce liquid by half. Remove cinnamon stick, bay leaf, and chili pepper and return chicken and vegetables to reduced broth. Heat through and serve over rice. Garnish with the almond mixture.

 Chicken Couscous

In a large heavy pot, brown 3 pounds sectioned chicken legs in 2 tablespoons olive oil. Add 2 coarsely chopped onions, 3 cloves minced garlic, 1 teaspoon ground turmeric, 1 tablespoon ground coriander, 2 teaspoons ground cumin, 1 ground dried chili pepper, 2 sliced carrots, 3 ribs thickly sliced celery, 1 peeled, seeded, and chunked acorn squash, 1 large peeled and chunked sweet potato, 3 peeled and chunked turnips, and 2 quarts chicken stock, bring to a boil, and simmer for 30 minutes. Add 2 sliced zucchini and simmer another 10 minutes. Stir in 2 cups quick-cooking couscous, remove from heat, cover, and let sit for 10 minutes.

Chicken and Leek Pot Pie with Herb Biscuit Crust

Remove meat from 3 pounds skinless chicken thighs and dredge in seasoned flour. Brown in the fat rendered from 4 strips bacon. Add 1 sliced onion, 1 rib sliced celery, ¼ pound sliced mushrooms, 1 clove minced garlic, and the sliced white part of 3 leeks and cook 3 minutes. Add ½ cup *each* white wine and chicken stock, 1 teaspoon crumbled rosemary, 1 tablespoon soy sauce, 1 tablespoon lemon juice, and 1 tablespoon lemon zest, and simmer 15 minutes. Crumble and add bacon. Place in a large ovenproof casserole. Shape the dough from ½ recipe Herbed Biscuits with a Secret (page 74) to match the shape of the casserole, and place dough on top of chicken mixture. Brush with the buttermilk mixture left from the biscuit dough and bake in a preheated 400°F. oven for 20 minutes.

Chicken and Fennel Pot Pie

Follow preceding recipe, replacing mushrooms and leek with 4 ribs sliced fennel and using 1 teaspoon *each* ground fennel seed and dried thyme in place of the rosemary.

Anise Chicken Braised in a Wok

In a hot work, sear 3 pounds sectioned chicken legs in ¼ cup peanut oil in 2 batches. Add 3 slices fresh gingerroot, 2 dried chili peppers, and 2 star anise near the end of each batch. Add ¼ cup dry sherry, ⅓ cup soy sauce, 1½ cups water, and 2 tablespoons light brown sugar. Return chicken to pan, cover, and simmer 20 minutes. Add 4 chopped scallions and 1 teaspoon cornstarch mixed in 2 teaspoons water and simmer 30 seconds more. Remove ginger, star anise, and chili. Finish with ½ teaspoon Oriental sesame oil. Serve over rice.

Chicken Legs Braised with Sauerkraut and Beer

In a large deep skillet, cook 4 strips bacon until crisp, then remove and set aside. Brown 3 pounds sectioned chicken legs in the fat, remove, and brown 1 large sliced onion in remaining fat. Add 2 pounds drained and rinsed sauerkraut, 2 bay leaves, 8 juniper berries, ⅛ teaspoon ground cloves, 1 teaspoon ground coriander, 3 cloves chopped garlic, 8 ounces diced ham, and 12 ounces beer. Cover and simmer 1 hour. Add chicken and 12 halved small red-skin potatoes. Cover and simmer 1 hour more.

Chicken Braised with Mint and Yogurt

Dredge 3 pounds sectioned chicken legs in flour and brown in 2 tablespoons olive oil. Add 2 coarsely chopped onions, 6 cloves minced garlic, 1 tablespoon ground coriander seed, 2 teaspoons ground cumin seed, and 1 ground dried chili pepper and cook until onion is soft. Add 3 cups chicken stock and simmer for 30 minutes. Stir in 2 tablespoons dried mint leaves and simmer 15 minutes more. Remove chicken to a platter, reduce liquid until slightly thickened, remove from heat, and stir in ½ cup plain yogurt. Pour over chicken.

Braised Chicken with Red Wine and Mushrooms

Dredge 3 pounds sectioned chicken legs in seasoned flour and brown in 2 tablespoons each butter and peanut oil. Remove chicken and set aside. Add ½ pound sliced mushrooms and 2 minced shallots and brown lightly. Deglaze pan with 1 cup red wine and ½ cup brandy and reduce by half. Add ½ cup tomato sauce and 1½ cups beef stock, bring to a boil, add chicken, cover, and simmer for 45 minutes.

Chicken Curry with Lentils

Dredge 3 pounds sectioned chicken legs in flour and brown in ¼ cup vegetable oil. Remove chicken and set aside. Add 2 teaspoons black mustard seed to remaining fat and cook until seeds turn gray. Add 1½ cups finely chopped onion, 1 clove minced garlic, and 1 tablespoon finely diced fresh gingerroot and cook until vegetables soften. Add ½ cup lentils, 2 teaspoons ground coriander, 2 teaspoons curry powder, 1 teaspoon ground aniseed, and ½ teaspoon crushed red pepper flakes and cook 1 minute. Return chicken to pan, add 3 cups chicken stock, cover, and simmer for 45 minutes, until lentils are tender. Stir in ½ cup plain yogurt.

Stewed Chicken with Black Beans and Lime

Soak 2 cups black beans and simmer in 1 quart each chicken stock and water with 2 ounces diced smoked turkey, salt, and pepper for 1¾ hours. Meanwhile, brown 2 pounds sectioned chicken legs in 2 tablespoons olive oil. Remove chicken and set aside. Add 2 sliced leeks, 2 diced carrots, 1 clove chopped garlic, and 1 chopped onion to the pan and sauté 2 minutes. Return chicken to pan, add 2 cups chicken stock and the juice of 2 limes, cover, and simmer for 40 minutes. Remove chicken, add ½ cup chopped fresh cilantro and 1 tablespoon finely chopped lime zest, and reduce pan liquid by half. Serve chicken with the sauce on a bed of beans.

Chicken Legs and Sausage in Red Gravy

Brown 1 pound Italian sausage cut in 2-inch pieces. Remove. Add 1 tablespoon olive oil and brown 2 pounds sectioned chicken legs in the fat, adding 1 cup chopped onion and 2 cloves minced garlic at the end and cook until softened. Return sausage to pan along with 4 cups chopped canned tomatoes, 1 cup chicken stock, and ¼ cup tomato paste. Season with a pinch of crushed red pepper flakes, salt, and black pepper. Simmer for 1 hour. Stir in 1 tablespoon chopped fresh parsley and heat 1 minute more. Serve over hot pasta.

Chicken Braised with Spicy Peanut Sauce

Brown 3 pounds sectioned chicken legs in 3 tablespoons peanut oil. Add 1 tablespoon chopped onion and ¼ clove minced garlic and cook until softened. Add 1 sliced scallion, ½ teaspoon chili paste, 1 teaspoon soy sauce, 1 teaspoon finely chopped fresh gingerroot, and a pinch each of ground cumin and coriander. Cook for 1 minute, add 2 cups chicken broth, cover, and simmer 40 minutes. Remove chicken and reduce pan liquid to ¼ cup. Stir in ¼ cup peanut butter until melted, remove from heat, and add ¼ cup plain yogurt, stirring until smooth. Coat chicken with sauce.

Meaty Chicken Noodle Soup

Sauté 2 pounds bite-size pieces boneless, skinless chicken thigh meat with 3 chopped carrots, 2 ribs chopped celery, and the chopped white of 1 large leek in 3 tablespoons oil until the meat loses its raw look. Add 1 inch fresh gingerroot, 1 dried chili pepper, 1 bay leaf, and 1 cup white wine. Boil for 1 minute. Add 2 quarts chicken broth and salt and pepper to taste, bring to a boil, and simmer for 45 minutes. Add ⅓ pound broad egg noodles and simmer 12 minutes more. Remove bay leaf, gingerroot, and chili pepper. Serves 6.

 ### Chicken Soup with Lemon and Mint

Sauté 2 pounds bite-size pieces boneless, skinless chicken thigh meat in 1 tablespoon olive oil until meat loses its raw look. Add 2 quarts chicken broth and bring to a boil. Add ¾ cup rice and 3 tablespoons dried mint. Simmer 12 minutes until rice is tender. Meanwhile, mix 3 egg yolks with the juice of 2 lemons. Add a ladleful of boiling soup to the egg yolk mixture, mixing constantly. Over low heat, slowly pour egg mixture into the hot soup, stirring constantly. Cook over moderate heat, stirring constantly, until soup thickens lightly. Serves 6.

 ### Chunky Chicken Minestrone

Sauté 1 pound bite-size pieces boneless, skinless chicken thigh meat in 2 tablespoons olive oil until meat loses its raw look. Add 1 cup chopped onion, the chopped white of 1 leek, and 2 cloves minced garlic and cook until softened. Add 2 sliced carrots, 2 ribs sliced celery, 12 sliced mushrooms, and ½ diced bell pepper and cook 2 minutes. Add 1 teaspoon *each* dried thyme, savory, and basil and ½ teaspoon *each* dried rosemary (crumbled), oregano, and sage. Cook 3 minutes more. Add 4 chopped canned tomatoes, 5 cups chicken broth, 1 tablespoon *each* wine vinegar and tomato paste, salt, and pepper. Bring to a boil and simmer 30 minutes. Serve with grated Parmesan. Serves 8.

 ### Chicken Split Pea Soup

Gently cook 1 pound bite-size pieces boneless, skinless chicken thigh meat in 4 tablespoons butter

until meat loses its raw look. Add 1 minced onion, ½ peeled, seeded, and minced cucumber, 1 head finely chopped stemmed Bibb lettuce, and ½ cup minced fresh parsley and cook 2 minutes more. Add 1 teaspoon sugar, salt, pepper, 1 cup green split peas, and 4 cups chicken stock. Simmer 45 minutes until peas are tender. Puree 1 cup of the soup in a processor or blender and return to pot. Finish with ½ cup light cream.

 ### Boiled Chicken with Mushrooms and Noodles

Tie 2 whole cloves, 1 teaspoon dried thyme leaves, 12 black peppercorns, 6 parsley stems, 1 dried chili pepper, and 1 bay leaf in a piece of cheesecloth. Place in pot with 2 halved carrots, 2 halved celery ribs, and 1 peeled and halved onion. Add 4 pounds chicken legs, 1½ quarts *each* chicken broth and water, salt, and the juice of 1 lemon and simmer for 1¼ hours. Add 1½ pounds trimmed small mushrooms and ¾ pound broad egg noodles. Simmer for 15 minutes more. Serve chicken with the mushrooms and horseradish. Serve broth as soup with the noodles. Serves 6.

 ### Chicken Pot au Feu with Sausage

Prepare cheesecloth bag and vegetables as in preceding recipe. Add 4 pounds chicken legs, 1½ quarts *each* chicken broth and water, salt, and the juice of 1 lemon and simmer for 1 hour. Add 2 pounds halved red-skin potatoes and simmer 15 minutes more. Add 2 cups rice and simmer another 15 minutes. Serve chicken, sausage, and potatoes with small pickles and brown mustard. Serve broth with the rice.

 ### Chicken and Corn Chowder

Cook 4 slices bacon until crisp, remove, and crumble bacon. Brown 1 pound bite-size pieces boneless, skinless chicken thigh meat in the hot fat. Add 1 cup diced onion, 2 ribs diced celery, 1 clove minced garlic, 1 diced red bell pepper, and ⅛ teaspoon crushed red pepper flakes and cook until vegetables soften. Add 2 cups corn kernels, 6 cups chicken broth, 2 tablespoons chopped fresh dill, and 1 tablespoon chopped fresh parsley and simmer for 40 minutes. Add 2 cups milk and heat through.

Stir-Fried Chicken with Clams

Dredge 1 pound bite-size pieces boneless, skinless chicken in cornstarch and fry in a wok until crisp in 3 tablespoons peanut oil. Remove chicken and discard all but 1 tablespoon of the oil. Add a pinch of crushed red pepper flakes, ¼ cup finely chopped onion, ½ cup sliced celery, and 1 clove minced garlic and stir-fry for 30 seconds. Add 2 dozen cleaned littleneck clams, the chicken, and 1 tablespoon garlic black bean sauce dissolved in 1 cup chicken stock. Cover and simmer until clams open, discarding any that don't. Thicken sauce with ½ teaspoon cornstarch dissolved in 1 teaspoon water. Finish with 2 sliced scallions and 1 tablespoon dry sherry.

Southern-Fried Chicken

Shake 3 pounds sectioned chicken legs in a bag with 1 cup seasoned flour. Shake off excess flour, place in equal parts hot lard and shortening totaling ½ inch, cover, and fry over moderate heat, about 325° F., until dark brown on one side, checking to make sure chicken does not burn. Turn, cover, and fry the other side. Hold in a warm oven until all pieces are fried.

Sweet and Sour Fried Chicken

Follow preceding recipe. After frying, dip chicken in a sauce made by browning 1 tablespoon

chopped onion in 4 tablespoons butter, adding ⅔ cup apple juice, 2 teaspoons apple cider vinegar, and 1 teaspoon brown sugar and boiling for 3 minutes.

Parmesan-Coated Chicken Legs

Shake 3 pounds sectioned chicken legs in a bag with ½ cup finely grated Parmesan, 2 tablespoons flour, and pepper, Shake off excess and dip pieces in 2 beaten eggs. Add remaining cheese mixture to 1 cup seasoned Italian bread crumbs and dredge chicken well in this mixture. Set aside to dry for 15 minutes. Place in ½ inch hot olive oil, cover, and fry pieces over moderate heat, about 325°F., until richly browned on one side, about 6 to 7 minutes, checking to make sure they do not burn. Turn, cover, and fry the other side. Hold in a warm oven until all the chicken has been fried.

Italian Fried Chicken

Follow preceding recipe, but replace beaten egg with ¼ cup Italian salad dressing beaten with 1 egg yolk.

Buffalo Drumsticks

Fry 3 pounds small chicken drumsticks in several inches of 350°F. oil until crisp and brown, about 15 minutes. Remove, drain on paper towels, and dip into a mixture made from 4 tablespoons melted butter and ¼ cup Durkee Red Hot Sauce.

Chicken Chicharrones

In a small saucepan, boil the alcohol off ¼ cup dark rum. Add ¼ cup each low-sodium soy sauce and lime juice. Pour over 3 pounds small chicken drumsticks and toss well. Marinate under refrigeration for 1 hour. Pat dry and dredge in seasoned flour. Place in ½ inch hot olive oil, cover, and fry until dark brown on one side, checking to make sure they do not burn. Turn, cover, and fry the other side. Hold in a warm oven until all the chicken has been fried. Serve with lime wedges and hot pepper sauce.

Chicken Leg Saté

Follow preceding recipe, serving the chicken legs with this sauce: In a skillet, cook 1 tablespoon chopped onion and ¼ teaspoon minced garlic in 1 tablespoon peanut oil until softened. Add 1 sliced scallion, ½ teaspoon chili paste, 1 teaspoon soy sauce, 1 teaspoon finely chopped fresh gingerroot, and a pinch *each* of ground cumin and coriander. Cook 1 minute. Stir in 2 tablespoons peanut butter until melted. Remove from heat and thin with ¼ cup buttermilk, yogurt, or stock to a saucelike consistency.

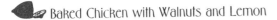

 Baked Chicken with Walnuts and Lemon

Liberally season 3 pounds sectioned chicken legs with salt and pepper. Brush with ½ cup sour cream mixed with 1 tablespoon mustard and 2 tablespoons lemon juice. Coat well with 2 cups finely ground walnuts. Place on a lightly oiled sheet pan and bake at 375°F., for 1 hour, turning legs after 30 minutes. Serve with lemon wedges.

Cornflake Baked Chicken

Liberally season 3 pounds sectioned chicken legs with salt and pepper. Brush with ½ cup mayonnaise and coat well with 2 cups crushed cornflakes. Place on a lightly oiled sheet pan and bake at 375°F. for 1 hour, turning legs after 30 minutes.

 Baked Chicken Legs with Balsamic Glaze

Brown 3 pounds chicken legs in rendered fat from 4 bacon slices. (Reserve bacon for another use.) Place in a baking dish and cook for 10 minutes at 375°F. Meanwhile, pour all but 2 tablespoons fat from the pan. Add 4 cloves chopped garlic and cook for 30 seconds. Add 2 cups beef broth, ⅓ cup balsamic vinegar, and 6 peppercorns and reduce to ¾ cup. Brush legs with the glaze and bake for 50 minutes more, basting with additional glaze every 10 minutes.

 Garlic and Molasses Chicken Legs

Brown and bake chicken as in preceding recipe, but brush it with this glaze: Pour all but 2 tablespoons fat from the pan, add 4 cloves chopped garlic, and cook for 30 seconds. Add 1½ cups beef broth, ½ cup dark molasses, ⅓ cup cider vinegar and 6 peppercorns and reduce to ¾ cup.

 Baked Chicken with Grapefruit Glaze

Rub surface of 3 pounds chicken legs with 1 tablespoon Oriental sesame oil and bake in 375°F. oven for 15 minutes. Meanwhile, mix ½ cup grapefruit juice, ¼ cup honey, 2 tablespoons soy sauce, and 1 tablespoon wine vinegar, brush on chicken, and roast another 30 minutes, basting with more glaze every 10 minutes.

Fifty Ways Out of the Ground-Meat Grind

Centuries before Hamburger Helper helped to reset the parameters of quick cooking in America, the ancient Romans, Greeks, and Phoenicians knew just how easy it was to cook ground meat. Not only was it faster than a whole mutton on a spit, but it could be preserved and flavored effortlessly just by mixing it with spices.

Today, we often forget the versatility of ground meat, resorting to it for easy, unimaginative meals—foods that everyone will eat but that no one will relish. In an effort to change that approach, we've put together 50 easy, tasty ground-meat meals. You'll find lots of burgers, along with dumplings, salads, meatballs, sausages, pâtés, casseroles, sandwiches, and a tartare. (There are no meatloafs, but that's because we've got 50 of those in Chapter 40.)

If your local butchers give you an odd look when you ask for ground meat other than beef, it's probably because they don't get much call for them. Just ask the butcher to run the desired variety of stew meat through a grinder twice. (Chicken and pork may have to be ordered ahead.) (Of course, if you have a meat grinder at home, you can grind the meat yourself, which can save money and ensure freshness. Ground meat is quite perishable.)

Although a food processor can chop meat, the machine will not grind it. Instead, you'll end up with pulverized meat, which can result in a flaccid, unpleasantly textured puree if you're not careful. Quick pulsing of the processor throughout the chopping will give best results.

ABOUT THESE RECIPES

None of the ideas or techniques we employ for working with ground meat are difficult, but some of them might be new to you, such as the caramelizing of sugar in the Sweet Sesame Meatballs and the technique for forming potstickers.

Two simple techniques contribute to the exceptional flavor of the burgers in this chapter. One is that many of the additions get mixed in with the meat, instead of sitting on top of the burger. The other is that a small quantity of liquid is added to the meat to make the finished burger juicier.

We tested all the beef recipes with an all-purpose ground beef, although ground round, chuck, sirloin, or any combination of them could be used to suit your own taste.

The following recipes are written for 4 portions unless otherwise noted. It is assumed that you will season all recipes to taste with salt and pepper.

Great Burgers

Using your hands, blend ¼ cup ice water into 1½ pounds ground chuck or ground round, and form into 4 patties, each 1 to 1½ inches thick. Do not pack too tightly. Grill or broil 3 inches from a high fire until browned and cooked to desired degree of doneness—about 3 to 5 minutes per side for rare, 6 to 8 minutes for medium, 10 minutes for well done. If desired, during the last 45 seconds of grilling, place 4 split hamburger buns next to the burgers to lightly toast the interior surfaces.

Deli-Style Burger

Follow preceding recipe using kaiser rolls instead of hamburger buns. After toasting rolls, brush their interiors with a mixture of 3 tablespoons mayonnaise, 2 teaspoons ketchup, and 1 teaspoon pickle relish. Place 1 lettuce leaf on one side of each roll and 1 tomato slice on the other. Place burgers on the lettuce leaves and top each with 2 tablespoons cole slaw.

Peppercorn Burger

Follow recipe for Great Burgers (above), rubbing tops and bottoms of burgers with mixture of

1 teaspoon *each* crushed black, dried green, and Szechuan peppercorns.

Mustard Burger

Follow recipe for Great Burgers (above), adding 1 clove minced garlic and 1 tablespoon Dijon mustard to the ground meat, and rubbing surface of burgers with ⅓ cup mustard seed before cooking.

Steak and Onion Burger

Follow recipe for Great Burgers (above), adding ¼ cup finely chopped onion cooked in 1 teaspoon oil until soft, 2 tablespoons steak sauce, and 1 teaspoon brown mustard to the ground meat.

Apple and Sage Burger

In a skillet, cook ¼ cup finely chopped onion, ½ cup finely diced, peeled and cored apple, 1 clove minced garlic, ¼ teaspoon dried thyme, and ½ teaspoon rubbed sage in 2 teaspoons oil until softened. Follow recipe for Great Burgers (above), adding onion mixture to the ground meat.

Mexican Burgers

Follow recipe for Great Burgers (above), substituting ¼ cup spicy salsa for the ice water and adding 1 tablespoon chili powder, 1 teaspoon ground cumin, and 1 tablespoon chopped fresh cilantro to the ground meat. Serve with ½ cup more salsa and ¾ cup shredded lettuce on top.

Smoked Bacon Burger

Prepare patties as described in Great Burgers recipe (above). Wrap each with 1 bacon strip and grill 4

Fifty Ways to Cook Most Everything

inches from a charcoal fire strewn with ½ cup hardwood chips that have been soaked in water for 30 minutes.

 ## Three-Cheese Burger

Follow recipe for Great Burgers (page 203), substituting ⅓ cup ricotta cheese for the water and adding ¼ cup grated Parmesan to the meat. Two minutes before burgers are done, top with ¼ pound thinly sliced Provolone and cook until cheese melts.

 ## Ham and Swiss Cheese Burger

Follow recipe for Great Burgers (page 203), adding ½ pound finely diced ham sautéed with 2 tablespoons finely chopped onion and a pinch of nutmeg in 1 tablespoon oil until onion browns lightly. Two minutes before burgers are done, top with ¼ pound thinly sliced Swiss cheese, and cook until cheese melts.

 ## Blue Cheese Burger

Follow recipe for Great Burgers (page 203), substituting 3 tablespoons blue cheese dressing and 2 ounces crumbled blue cheese for the water.

 ## Blackened Cajun Burger

Make meat patties as described in recipe for Great Burgers (page 203) and pat each one with a portion of the following mixture: 1 tablespoon *each* salt, white pepper, ground fennel, ground black pepper, and garlic powder, plus 1½ teaspoons *each* dry mustard and cayenne pepper. Cook burgers in a white-hot iron skillet for 4 minutes per side. Turn off heat and transfer burgers to buns. Deglaze pan

with ¼ cup water and 3 tablespoons Worcestershire sauce, and pour over burgers.

 ## Meatloaf Burger

With your hands, mix ¾ pound *each* ground veal and ground beef, 1 beaten egg, 1 tablespoon ketchup, 2 teaspoons Worcestershire sauce, 1 teaspoon mustard, and 1 tablespoon finely chopped onion. Soak 1 slice crustless bread cubes in ¼ cup milk and mix in with the meat. Form into 4 patties and cook as described in the Great Burger recipe (page 203).

 ## Turkey Burger

With your hands, mix together 1 pound ground turkey, 2 tablespoons ketchup, 2 tablespoons grated onion, 2 teaspoons steak sauce, and 3 tablespoons Italian bread crumbs. Form into 4 patties. Grill or broil until browned and cooked through, about 5 minutes per side.

 ## Teriyaki Turkey Burger

With your hands, mix together 1 pound ground turkey, 1 tablespoon hoisin sauce, 1 tablespoon honey, 2 tablespoons grated onion, 1 tablespoon grated fresh gingerroot, 2 teaspoons light soy sauce, and 3 tablespoons unseasoned bread crumbs. Form into 4 patties. Grill or broil until browned and cooked through, about 5 minutes per side.

 ## Chicken Burger with Mustard and Green Peppercorns

With your hands, combine 1½ pounds ground chicken, 1 tablespoon Dijon mustard, 2 tablespoons grated onion, 2 teaspoons green pepper-corns, 1 beaten egg, and 1 slice crumbled bread soaked in ¼ cup milk. Form into 4 patties. Grill or broil until browned and cooked through, about 5 minutes per side.

 ### Chicken Burger Laced with Brandy

With your hands, combine 1½ pounds ground chicken, 1 tablespoon chopped tarragon leaves, 2 teaspoons brandy, 2 tablespoons chopped shallots, a pinch of nutmeg, 1 teaspoon Dijon mustard, 2 tablespoons fresh bread crumbs, and 1 beaten egg. Form into 4 patties. Grill or broil until browned and cooked through, about 5 minutes per side.

 ### Herb-Cheese Veal Burger

Freeze 4 tablespoon-size nuggets of herb cream cheese until solid. With your hands, combine 1½ pounds ground veal, ⅓ cup chopped basil leaves, ¼ cup grated Parmesan, ½ clove minced garlic, 3 finely chopped anchovy fillets, and 2 tablespoons ice water. Form into 4 patties with 1 frozen cheese nugget encased in the middle of each. Grill or broil 4 inches from a high fire, following cooking times in Great Burgers recipe (page 203).

 ### Roasted Pepper Veal Burger

Follow preceding recipe, adding ⅓ cup chopped roasted red pepper (page 442) with the ground meat and eliminating the herb cream cheese.

 ### Veal Oscar Burger

Follow recipe for Great Burgers (page 203), substituting ground veal for ground beef and mixing in ⅓ cup chopped cooked asparagus. Top with ¼ pound lump crabmeat and ¼ cup mayonnaise mixed with 1 teaspoon lemon juice.

 ### Garlic Spinach Lamb Burger

With your hands, combine 1½ pounds ground lamb, 10 ounces cooked frozen chopped spinach that has been squeezed dry, 1 clove minced garlic, 2 tablespoons plain yogurt, 1 beaten egg, and 2 teaspoons chopped fresh parsley. Form into 4 patties and grill or broil 4 inches from a high fire, following cooking times in Great Burgers recipe (page 203).

 ### Minted Lamb Burgers

With your hands, combine 1½ pounds ground lamb, 1 clove minced garlic, 2 tablespoons plain yogurt, 2 teaspoons chopped fresh parsley, and 2 tablespoons finely chopped mint leaves. Form into 4 patties and grill or broil 4 inches from a high fire, following cooking times in Great Burgers recipe (page 203).

Serve this sauce on the side with each of the next four recipes:

Dipping Sauce for Potstickers. Boil ¼ cup soy sauce, ½ cup chicken stock, ½ cup water, 1 teaspoon ground Szechuan or black peppercorns, 1 whole star anise, 1 teaspoon Oriental sesame oil, a pinch of sugar, and 1 crushed clove garlic for 3 minutes. Add 1 teaspoon cornstarch dissolved in 2 teaspoons water and boil 1 minute more.

 ### Potstickers

Mix ½ pound ground pork, 2 tablespoons finely chopped white part of scallion, 2 tablespoons chopped fresh parsley, 1 tablespoon finely chopped fresh gingerroot, 1½ teaspoons Oriental sesame oil, 1 clove minced garlic, and 1½ tablespoons soy sauce. Using meat mixture, 40 Chinese wonton wrappers, and 1 egg beaten with 2 tablespoons water to seal edges, form into 40 potstickers (page 442). Brown the bottoms in a skillet in 3 tablespoons hot peanut oil, then finish cooking by adding 1 cup chicken stock and covering pan. Serve with Dipping Sauce for Potstickers (above).

 ## Veal and Pork Potstickers

Form and cook potstickers as in preceding recipe using this filling: Mix ¼ pound each ground pork and veal, 2 tablespoons finely chopped white part of scallion, 2 tablespoons *each* chopped fresh cilantro and mint, 1 tablespoon finely chopped fresh gingerroot, 1½ teaspoons Oriental sesame oil, 1 clove minced garlic, and 1½ tablespoons soy sauce. Serve with Dipping Sauce for Potstickers (page 205).

 ## Chicken Spinach Potstickers

Follow recipe for Potstickers (above), but use this filling: Mix ¼ pound *each* ground veal and chicken, ¼ cup cooked and drained chopped spinach, 2 tablespoons finely chopped white part of scallion, 2 tablespoons chopped fresh cilantro, 1 tablespoon finely chopped fresh gingerroot, 1½ teaspoons Oriental sesame oil, 1 clove minced garlic, and 1½ tablespoons soy sauce. Serve with Dipping Sauce for Potstickers (page 205).

 ## Asian Fish Balls

In a food processor, finely chop ½ pound *each* chunked white fish fillets and cleaned shrimp, ½ cup chopped onion, ¼ jalapeño pepper, ¼ teaspoon ground turmeric, 1 tablespoon chopped fresh cilantro, 1 teaspoon chopped fresh gingerroot, and ½ clove chopped garlic. Add ¼ cup

beaten egg and process until smooth. Spoon heaping teaspoon-size balls of this mixture into ¼ cup sesame seeds ground to a powder with 2 tablespoons cornstarch. Roll the balls until well coated and deep fry until golden brown, then drain. Serve with Dipping Sauce for Potstickers (page 205).

 ## Sweet Sesame Meatballs

Combine 3 tablespoons cornstarch, 2 teaspoons ground ginger, and 1 clove minced garlic and mix with 1 pound ground pork. Form into 1-inch meatballs and brown in a film of oil in a nonstick skillet until firm. Reserve meatballs, discard oil. Add ¼ cup sugar to pan and cook until melted and caramelized, about 1 minute. Return meatballs to pan and coat with the syrup. Working quickly, place meatballs on a platter and sprinkle with ¼ cup toasted sesame seeds.

 ## Meatball Chili

Mix 2 pounds ground beef, 3 tablespoons minced onion, 2 cloves minced garlic, 1 tablespoon ketchup, 1 teaspoon mustard, 1 egg, and 3 tablespoons seasoned bread crumbs. Form into 1-inch meatballs and brown in a nonstick skillet in 2 tablespoons vegetable oil. Remove meatballs, add ½ recipe Basic Chili Mix (page 116), 1 chopped bell pepper, 2 cups tomato sauce, 1 cup beef broth, and 1 teaspoon black pepper, and bring to a boil. Return meatballs to the pan and simmer for 1 hour. Adjust seasoning with hot sauce. Stir in 2 cups cooked or canned drained kidney beans and heat through. Serves 6.

 ## Spicy Cocktail Meatballs

Mix 1 pound ground beef, 2 tablespoons minced onion, 2 cloves minced garlic, 1 tablespoon ketchup, 1 teaspoon Dijon mustard, 1 teaspoon hot pepper sauce, 1 tablespoon chili powder, 1 teaspoon minced jalapeño pepper, ¼ teaspoon cayenne pepper, 1 beaten egg, and 2 tablespoons seasoned bread crumbs and form into 1-inch meatballs. Roll in ½ cup cornmeal seasoned to taste with cayenne pepper and salt and fry in ½ inch hot fat until browned and crisp. Serve with warm dipping sauce made from 4 tablespoons melted butter mixed with 1 to 2 tablespoons hot pepper sauce.

 Bacon Meatballs

With your hands, mix 1 pound ground beef, 1 beaten egg, 3 tablespoons minced onion, 1 clove minced garlic, 2 tablespoons water, 1 tablespoon chopped fresh parsley, and 3 tablespoons seasoned bread crumbs and form into 24 meatballs. Wrap each with ½ slice bacon and secure with a toothpick. Bake at 375°F. until bacon and meatballs are firm, about 25 minutes.

 Sicilian Mint and Ricotta Meatballs

With your hands, mix 1 pound ground beef, 1 beaten egg, 3 tablespoons minced onion, 1 clove minced garlic, ¼ cup ricotta cheese, 2 tablespoons minced mint leaves, and 3 tablespoons seasoned bread crumbs and form into 24 meatballs. Brown in a thin film of fat in a nonstick skillet, then simmer in 2 quarts tomato pasta sauce until firm, about 15 minutes. Serve with 1 pound cooked pasta.

 Meatball Sandwich

Follow preceding recipe, substituting 2 tablespoons grated Parmesan and 2 tablespoons milk for the ricotta and 1 tablespoon chopped fresh parsley for the mint. Serve spooned into torpedo rolls.

 Cheesy Chicken Meatballs

With your hands, mix 1 pound ground chicken, 2 tablespoons minced onion, 2 cloves minced garlic, 2 tablespoons ricotta cheese, 2 tablespoons grated Parmesan, 1 ounce grated Fontina cheese, 1 tablespoon ketchup, 1 teaspoon chopped fresh basil, 1 tablespoon chopped fresh parsley, 1 beaten egg, and 2 tablespoons seasoned bread crumbs and form into 24 meatballs. Roll in a mixture of ½ cup grated Parmesan, 1 teaspoon ground fennel, and ½ cup seasoned bread crumbs. Pan-fry until browned and firm.

 Sweet and Sour Turkey Meatballs

With your hands, mix 1 pound ground turkey, 2 tablespoons minced onion, 2 cloves minced garlic, 1 tablespoon ketchup, 1 teaspoon Dijon mustard, 1 beaten egg, and 2 tablespoons seasoned bread crumbs. Form into 24 meatballs. In a nonstick skillet, brown in 2 tablespoons vegetable oil, adding ¼ cup chopped onion, 1 clove minced garlic, and 2 teaspoons finely chopped fresh gingerroot during last minute of cooking. Sprinkle with 3 tablespoons *each* brown sugar and cider vinegar, 1 tablespoon soy sauce, ⅛ teaspoon cayenne pepper, and 2 cups chicken stock. Simmer until liquid is reduced by half. Stir in 2 teaspoons cornstarch dissolved in 1 tablespoon water and cook until lightly thickened.

 Sweet and Sour Sesame Meatballs

With your hands, mix 1 pound ground pork, 1 tablespoon chopped fresh gingerroot, 1 clove minced garlic, ¼ cup Oriental Sesame oil, 1 teaspoon soy sauce, 1 beaten egg, and 5 tablespoons bread crumbs. Form in 24 meatballs and cook in the same way with the same sauce as in preceding recipe.

Cranberry Turkey Meatballs

With your hands, mix 1 pound ground turkey, 2 tablespoons minced onion, 2 cloves minced garlic, 2 tablespoons whole-berry cranberry sauce, 1 teaspoon Dijon mustard, 1 beaten egg, and 2 tablespoons seasoned bread crumbs and form into 24 meatballs. In a nonstick skillet, brown meatballs in 2 tablespoons vegetable oil, adding ¼ cup chopped onion, 1 clove minced garlic, and 2 teaspoons finely chopped fresh gingerroot during last minute of cooking. Sprinkle with 3 tablespoons *each* brown sugar, and cider vinegar, ¼ cup whole-berry cranberry sauce, and 2 cups cranberry juice. Simmer until liquid is reduced by half. Stir in 2 teaspoons cornstarch dissolved in 1 tablespoon water and cook until lightly thickened.

 ### Kibbeh with Yogurt Sauce

Soak 1 cup bulgur in 2 cups water for 5 minutes. Squeeze out as much moisture as possible and process with 1 pound ground leg of lamb and 1 cup chopped onion in a food processor until smooth. Form into 24 olive-shaped meatballs and brown on all sides in a thin film of oil in a nonstick skillet. Drain off excess oil. Add 1 cup water, 4 cloves minced garlic, and 2 tablespoons crushed dried mint until all water evaporates. Add 2 cups plain yogurt and heat through. Do not boil.

 ### Königsberg Klos

In a food processor, briefly process 1 pound ground pork, 4 slices chopped bacon, 1½ cups chopped onion, 2 slices crustless bread, 2 eggs, 2 teaspoons chopped anchovy, salt, pepper, and ½ teaspoon dried thyme. Form into 24 meatballs and simmer in 4 cups chicken broth until firm, about 20 to 25 minutes. In a separate pot, cook 2 table-spoons butter and 2 tablespoons flour until lightly browned. Add cooking liquid from meatballs and simmer for 10 minutes. In a slow stream, add 2 egg yolks beaten with 2 teaspoons white wine vinegar, 2 teaspoons drained capers, and 1 teaspoon dried thyme. Add meatballs and warm through.

 ### Garlic Sausage

In a nonstick skillet, sauté 2 tablespoons minced onion, ½ head peeled and minced garlic, ½ teaspoon *each* dried thyme, sage, and ginger, and a pinch *each* of ground nutmeg and cloves. Season liberally with salt and pepper. Mix with 1 pound sausage meat and form into 12 patties. Brown and cook though over medium heat in an iron skillet.

 ### Apple Gorgonzola Sausage

Follow preceding recipe, adding 1 peeled, cored, and grated tart apple in place of all but ½ clove minced garlic. Mix 3 ounces crumbled Gorgonzola with the sausage meat.

 ### Wild Mushroom Sausage

Soak ¼ cup dried wild mushrooms in ⅓ cup boiling water for 10 minutes. In a nonstick skillet, sauté 2 tablespoons minced onion and ½ clove minced garlic with ½ teaspoon *each* dried thyme, sage, crumbled rosemary, and ginger, and a pinch *each* ground nutmeg and cloves. Add soaking liquid from mushrooms and reduce to 1 tablespoon. Chop mushrooms and add. Mix with 1 pound sausage meat and form into 12 patties. Brown and cook through over medium heat in an iron skillet.

 ### Country Pâté

In a food processor, chop 1 pound ground veal, 1 pound chopped fatback, 1 pound chicken livers, and ½ pound chopped pork butt. Mix with ½ pound diced smoked ham, 2 tablespoons chopped onion, ¼ cup light cream, 2 teaspoons ground white pepper, ¼ teaspoon *each* ground cloves, ginger, nutmeg, and crumbled rosemary, 1 tablespoon salt, and ¼ cup brandy. Pack into loaf pan lined on bottom and sides with ¼ pound sliced bacon. Cover top with another 2 ounces bacon, cover with foil, and bake in a water bath at 375°F. for 1½ hours. Cool with a weight on top. Remove from pan and chill. This will keep for 1 to 2 weeks before slicing. Serve with mustard. Makes 10 servings.

 Herbed Chicken Pâté

In a food processor, chop 2 pounds boneless chicken meat with 1 pound fatback. Mix with 2 chopped shallots, 1 beaten egg, ½ cup Madeira, ¼ cup cream, 1 tablespoon salt, 1 teaspoon ground white pepper, ¼ teaspoon ground ginger, ¼ cup chopped fresh parsley, ¼ cup chopped fresh tarragon, 1 tablespoon fresh rosemary leaves, and ½ pound diced smoked turkey breast. Bake in a loaf pan lined with chicken skin or thin slices of fatback and cover top with more skin or fatback. Cover with foil and bake at 375°F. for 1½ hours. Cool with a weight on top. Remove from pan and chill. Slice and serve with herb mayonnaise. Makes 10 servings.

 Brandied Liver Mousse

In a food processor, finely chop ½ pound fatback, 1 pound chicken liver, 6 anchovies, 5 eggs, ¼ cup brandy, 2 teaspoons salt, ½ teaspoon ground white pepper, a pinch of ground allspice, and 1 cup heavy cream. Line bottom and sides of a loaf pan with strips of bacon, pour mousse in center, and wrap bacon over top. Cover with foil and bake in a water bath in a 300°F. oven for 2½ hours. Chill overnight

and remove from pan. Slice and serve with toast, mustards, and pickles. Makes 10 servings.

 Spicy Sausage Potato Salad

Boil 2 pounds small red-skin potatoes until tender, 25 to 30 minutes. While potatoes are cooking, simmer ½ pound sweet and ½ pound spicy Italian sausages until firm, then slice thinly. Drain, quarter, and toss potatoes with the sausage, 1 diced red bell pepper, 3 ribs diced celery, 4 sliced scallions, and the following dressing while still hot. Cook 1 cup finely chopped onion, 1 clove minced garlic, and 1 dried hot pepper in 2 tablespoons olive oil until softened. Add ¼ cup red wine vinegar, 2 tablespoons sugar, and 1 tablespoon salt. Remove from heat and stir in ¼ cup sour cream.

 Thai Turkey Salad

Stir-fry 1½ cloves finely chopped garlic and ¼ cup finely chopped onion in 2 tablespoons peanut oil for 30 seconds. Add 1 pound ground turkey, 2 teaspoons ground coriander, ½ teaspoon salt, ½ teaspoon black pepper, 3 tablespoons sugar, and ½ teaspoon crushed red pepper flakes and stir-fry for 3 minutes. Add ½ cup coarsely chopped roasted peanuts, 2 tablespoons lemon juice, 1 tablespoon Thai fish sauce, and 1 teaspoon Oriental sesame oil. Heap on a plate surrounded by 1 cup bean sprouts, 2 peeled and sectioned tangerines, and ½ thinly sliced cucumber.

Shepherd's Pie

Cook 1 cup chopped onion and 1 clove minced garlic in 1 tablespoon olive oil until softened. Add 1 pound ground lamb and cook until it loses its raw look. Add 2 tablespoons chopped pitted oil-cured black olives, 1 cup canned crushed tomatoes, and ½ teaspoon dried oregano and simmer 10 minutes. Place in bottom of a 2-quart casserole and top with Classic Mashed Potatoes (page 258) mixed with 1 clove minced garlic. Bake in a pre-heated 375°F. oven for 40 minutes.

 Spicy Pork Tacos

Cook 1 cup chopped onion, 1 minced jalapeño, and 1 clove minced garlic in 1 tablespoon olive oil. Add 1 pound ground pork and cook until it loses its raw look. Add 2 tablespoons chopped fresh cilantro and 1 tablespoon chili powder and cook for 10 minutes. Warm 8 taco shells in a 350° F. oven for 8 minutes. Divide meat mixture among the taco shells. Top with 1 julienned roasted bell pepper (page 442), 1 cup crumbled farmer cheese, and 1 cup Mild Green Salsa (page 268). Serve with Re-fried Beans (page 429).

 Ground Chicken Fajitas

Cook 1 cup chopped onion, 1 minced jalapeño pepper, 1 diced bell pepper, and 1 clove minced garlic in 2 teaspoons vegetable oil until vegetables soften. Add 1 pound ground chicken and 1 table-spoon Worcestershire sauce and cook until chicken is firm. Cook 8 flour tortillas in a lightly oiled nonstick skillet for 10 seconds per side. Serve with the chicken accompanied by 2 cups salsa of your choice, 1 diced avocado, 2 cups chopped to-mato, and 2 cups grated Monterey Jack cheese. Let diners roll their own fajitas.

 Veal Tartare

Coarsely chop ½ pound well-trimmed milk-fed veal. Add 1 clove minced garlic, 1 tablespoon extra-virgin olive oil, salt, and freshly ground pepper and chop finely. Serve with 8 thin lemon wedges and 12 triangles of toasted black bread.

24

Fifty Recipes for Twenty-five Fish

In this age of dietary doomsaying, everything from three square meals a day to the goodness of milk is being re-evaluated. Even fish, yesterday's messiah, is suffering its share of food bashing. But think twice before you jump on this bandwagon, because the fault lies within ourselves, not the fish. Water pollution and handling are the problem. The fish is loaded with virtues. Even its fat content—the bane of all other animal proteins—seems blessed with health benefits.

Fish has little cholesterol and is naturally low in calories. It cooks quickly and radiates flavor even in the simplest presentations. It lends itself to every known cooking technique, pairs with hundreds of seasonings, and comes in more varieties than flavored potato chips.

The only problem is that most of us don't know the first thing about cooking fish. Even good cooks, reared on frozen flounder and tinned tuna, frequently find themselves at a loss when confronting a swordfish steak or a red snapper shining crimson beneath its scales. Add to this the phenomenal number of new fish varieties appearing at the mar-

ket and it's easy to see why fish cookery in most homes amounts to preheating the broiler and juicing a lemon.

To help broaden your horizons, we have assembled 50 recipes—for 25 of the most commonly available fish. Virtually all the recipes are quite quick. Though each recipe is unique and complete, none is definitive. Feel free to alter a seasoning here or a sauce there. If a recipe appeals to you but the fish listed is unavailable, just substitute a fish of similar fat content: replace a flat fish with a flat fish, a fresh-water fish with another fresh-water fish, and so on.

Use this guide for making substitutions:

Lean round fish: Black bass, catfish, cod, grouper, haddock, ocean perch, pike, pompano, porgy, orange roughy, scrod, sea trout, snapper, tilefish, whiting.

Fatty round fish: Bluefish, salmon, shad, smelt, freshwater trout, tuna.

Dense-muscled fish: Mahimahi, monkfish, shark, sturgeon, swordfish.

Flat fish: Flounder, fluke, halibut, sole, turbot.

Fifty Ways to Cook Most Everything

ABOUT THESE RECIPES

Pollution and handling are real problems. Your job is to be vigilant in picking a market—and in being careful to keep the fish thoroughly chilled until you're ready to cook.

Although all of the following recipes have been tested as written, cooking times will vary with the thickness of a particular piece of fish. Judge 8 minutes of cooking for every inch of thickness when grilling, sautéing, boiling, broiling, or frying; 10 minutes per inch of thickness when steaming, baking, or using dense-muscled fish.

It is assumed that you will season all recipes to taste with salt and pepper, including the salt for seasoned flour and for finishing sauces. For that reason we have specifically mentioned salt and pepper only where the amounts differ. All recipes yield 4 servings, unless otherwise noted.

Black Bass on Cucumber "Noodles"

Pare long strips from 2 large peeled and seeded cucumbers, toss with 1 teaspoon kosher salt, and let sit 10 minutes. Rinse well, shake dry, and arrange in a ring on a platter. Brush four 6-ounce black bass fillets with ¼ cup yogurt and dredge in ½ cup seasoned flour and 1 tablespoon dried dill. Sauté 2 to 3 minutes per side in 2 tablespoons olive oil. Place in the center of the cucumber "noodles." Deglaze pan with 1 tablespoon olive oil, 1 clove minced garlic, the juice of 1 lemon, and 1 tablespoon chopped fresh dill. Pour sauce over fish and cucumbers.

Tea-Steamed Black Bass

Make four slashes in the sides of a 2-pound black bass. Rub with 1 teaspoon soy sauce and 1 tablespoon Oriental sesame oil, place in a large bamboo

steamer, and set over a pot of boiling water infused with a cup of loose black tea leaves. Steam 10 to 12 minutes, until fish flakes easily to gently prodding. Transfer to a platter and serve garnished with wedges of lemon or pomegranate.

Bluefish Baked with Easy Mustard Sauce

In a flame-resistant baking dish, cook 2 tablespoons minced onion and 1 clove minced garlic in 3 tablespoons butter until softened. Add ½ cup white wine and reduce by half. Place 1½ pounds bluefish fillet in the liquid in one layer. Bake at 375°F. for 12 to 15 minutes, until fish flakes to a gentle push. Mix 3 tablespoons Dijon mustard with ⅔ cup sour cream or yogurt. When the fish is done, transfer to a warm platter, bring pan juices to a boil, add mustard mixture, and heat through. Do not allow to boil. Cover fish with sauce.

Ranch-Style Bluefish Fillets

Sauté 1½ pounds bluefish fillet in a thin film of peanut oil for 3 to 4 minutes per side. Remove to a warm platter and brown 2 tablespoons chopped onion and 1 clove minced garlic in fat remaining in the pan. Remove from heat and deglaze pan with ⅔ cup any variety Ranch Dressing (page 299) and 2 tablespoons lemon juice. Pour sauce over fish.

Barbecued Catfish

Lightly brown ½ cup chopped onion and 1 clove minced garlic in 1 tablespoon corn oil. Add 2 tablespoons apple cider vinegar, ½ cup ketchup, 1 teaspoon mustard, 1 teaspoon Worcestershire sauce, 1 teaspoon hot pepper sauce, 1 tablespoon sugar, and the juice of ½ lemon. Marinate 1½ pounds catfish fillet in this sauce for 1 hour in the refrigerator. Grill over moderate heat for 6 to 8 minutes per side, basting frequently with sauce.

 ### Pecan Catfish Fingers and Sweet Potato Chips

Cut 1½ pounds catfish fillet into ½-by-2-inch fingers. Brush with 2 tablespoons brown mustard mixed with 2 teaspoons honey. Dredge in a mixture of ⅔ cup pecans ground with ⅓ cup seasoned bread crumbs and set aside. Sauté ¾ pound thinly sliced sweet potato in peanut oil until crisp and brown and drain on paper towels. Add oil to pan and sauté fish until it flakes to the touch, 4 to 5 minutes per side. Serve fish with the chips and orange wedges.

 ### Cod and Avocado Salad

Steam 1 pound cod fillet for 10 minutes until fish flakes easily, then let cool. Peel, pit, and dice 1 large avocado. Toss fish with avocado, 1 clove minced garlic, 2 sliced scallions, the juice of 1 lemon, 3 tablespoons chopped fresh cilantro, and cayenne pepper. Serve on bed of lettuce, endive, or radicchio.

 ### Microwaved Mediterranean Cod

Rub 1½ pounds cod fillet and the interior of a 10-inch glass baking dish with 1 tablespoon virgin olive oil. Rub fish with the finely grated zest of 1 orange, ¼ cup finely chopped basil leaves, and 1 clove minced garlic and pour ¼ cup orange juice and 2 tablespoons lemon juice over all. Cover with plastic wrap and microwave at full power for 2½ minutes in a high-wattage oven. Poke plastic wrap to release steam. Serve immediately.

 ### Flounder Poached in Fresh Tomato Sauce

Cook ½ cup chopped onion and 1 clove minced garlic in 2 tablespoons olive oil until soft. Add ½ cup white wine, 2 teaspoons dried basil, and a pinch of marjoram. Simmer until most of the liquid evaporates. Add 3 cups chopped, skinned, and seeded ripe tomatoes and simmer 3 minutes. Place 4 skinned flounder fillets into the simmering sauce, cover, and cook gently for 2 minutes—just until fish is firm. Remove fish, add the juice of ½ lemon to the sauce and pour over fish.

 ### Fried Flounder in Buttermilk Batter

Sift together ½ cup seasoned flour, ¼ teaspoon baking soda, and 1 teaspoon dried dill leaves. Beat in 1 large egg yolk and ¾ cup buttermilk. Beat egg white until firm and fold in. Cut 1½ pounds flounder fillets into 2-inch sections and dust with cornstarch and 1 to 2 teaspoons chopped fresh dill. Dip flounder into batter and fry in several inches of 375°F. vegetable oil until golden—2 to 3 minutes. Do not crowd pan. Drain on paper towels and serve with lemon wedges.

 ### Fluke Paupiettes Stuffed with Smoked Salmon Mousse

In a food processor, puree ¼ pound *each* lean white-meat fish fillet and smoked salmon cut in chunks. Add 1 egg white, salt, white pepper, cayenne pepper, and ½ cup cold heavy cream. Roll four 4-ounce skinless fluke fillets around portions of this mixture and place in greased baking dish. Top with the juice of 1 lemon, ½ cup white wine, and 2 finely chopped shallots. Cover and bake at 350°F. for 30 minutes, until mousse is set. Remove fish and keep warm. Add 1 tablespoon fresh tarragon leaves to pan juices and reduce over high heat to about one third their volume. Remove from heat, swirl in 3 tablespoons butter, and pour over top.

 Fluke Fillets Andalouse

Cook ½ cup chopped onion, 1 cup diced red and green bell pepper, ⅓ cup diced carrot, 1 clove minced garlic, and ½ teaspoon saffron in 2 tablespoons olive oil until vegetables soften. Add ½ cup white wine and simmer until most of the liquid evaporates. Add 3 cups chopped, skinned, and seeded ripe tomatoes and simmer 5 minutes. Place 4 pieces skinned fluke fillet, 5 to 6 ounces each, in the simmering sauce, cover, and cook gently for 4 minutes, just until fish flakes. Remove fish, add the juice of ½ lemon and 2 tablespoons chopped fresh parsley to the sauce. Pour sauce over fish.

 Curried Grouper Chowder

Cook 1 cup chopped onion, ½ cup diced carrot, ½ cup diced celery, 1 clove minced garlic, and 1 tablespoon curry powder in 2 tablespoons clarified butter until softened in a heavy-bottomed pot. Add 1 pound peeled, diced potato and 1 cored, peeled, diced green apple, mix well, add 4 cups chicken broth, and simmer 15 minutes until potatoes are tender. Add 1½ pounds skinless grouper fillet cut into ½-inch cubes, simmer 5 minutes, remove from heat, and stir in 1 cup plain yogurt or milk. Adjust seasoning. Garnish with ¼ cup toasted nuts.

 Sautéed Grouper Fillets
with Corn-Pepper Relish

Brown ⅓ cup chopped onion in 1 teaspoon corn oil. Add 1 teaspoon pickling spice, ¼ teaspoon crushed red pepper flakes, ½ cup water, ⅓ cup apple cider vinegar, 1 bay leaf, 2 tablespoons sugar,

and 1 peeled, diced carrot. Bring to a boil and simmer 5 minutes. Remove from heat, add 4 cups cooked corn and 2 stemmed, seeded, diced roasted red peppers (page 442). Dredge eight 4-ounce grouper fillets in seasoned flour and sauté in a thin film of corn oil for 2 to 4 minutes per side, depending on thickness. Serve fillets with the relish.

 Baked Mahimahi with Grapefruit
Butter Sauce

Place 1 skinned 1½-pound mahimahi fillet in a greased baking pan. Add ½ cup grapefruit juice, the julienned whites of 4 scallions, and the julienned zest of 1 grapefruit. Bake at 350° F. for 30 minutes. Remove fish to a warm platter. Over high heat, reduce pan juices by half, remove from the heat, and swirl in 3 tablespoons unsalted butter. Pour sauce over the fish.

 Mahimahi Meunière with Asian Peanut
Sauce

Cut 1½ pounds mahimahi fillet into 1-inch cubes and dredge in seasoned flour. Sauté in a thin film of peanut oil over moderately high heat until firm, about 4 minutes per side. Remove fish to a warm platter. Add ¼ cup chopped onion to pan and brown lightly. Add 1 clove minced garlic, 2 thinly sliced scallions, 1 teaspoon chili paste, 2 teaspoons light soy sauce, 2 teaspoons grated fresh gingerroot, ½ teaspoon ground cumin, and ½ teaspoon ground coriander and cook 2 minutes. Stir in ¼ cup smooth peanut butter until it melts. Add 2 tablespoons plain yogurt, the fish cubes, and their juices and heat through.

 Mexican Baked Monkfish

Cook ½ cup chopped onion, 1 clove minced garlic, 1 minced jalapeño pepper, and 1 chopped red bell pepper in 2 tablespoons olive oil until vegetables soften. Add ½ cup crushed tomatoes and simmer for 3 minutes. Pour over 1½ pounds monkfish fillet in a baking dish; add the juice of ½ lemon and bake at 350°F. for 25 minutes or until fish is firm. Garnish with 1 thinly sliced avocado.

 ### Provençale Monkfish Soup

Soak 1 teaspoon saffron threads in 1 cup white wine with the zest and juice of 1 large orange. In a soup pot, sauté 1 large chopped onion and 2 cloves minced garlic in 2 tablespoons olive oil until soft. Add 2 ribs chopped celery, 1 teaspoon ground fennel seed, 1 teaspoon dried basil, ½ teaspoon thyme, and 1 bay leaf. Cook 1 minute more, add wine mixture, and bring to a boil. Add 12 skinned, seeded, and chopped tomatoes, 1 teaspoon crushed red pepper flakes, and 3 cups fish stock or clam juice, bring to a boil, and add 1½ pounds monkfish fillet cut in 1-inch chunks. Simmer for 10 minutes and stir in ¼ cup chopped fresh parsley.

 ### Perch Seviche

Cut 1 pound skinless perch fillet into thin slices, and marinate in a glass or ceramic bowl with the juice of 4 lemons, 2 limes, and 1 orange, cover, and refrigerate 3 hours. Drain and toss with a pinch cayenne pepper and 1 teaspoon olive oil.

 ### Pan-Fried Perch with Homemade Tartar Sauce

Sauté ½ cup chopped onion, 2 cloves minced garlic, and 1 cup peeled, diced, and seeded apple in 2 tablespoons vegetable oil until tender. Deglaze pan with 1 teaspoon cider vinegar and 1 tablespoon lemon juice. Cool and blend with 1 cup mayonnaise, 3 tablespoons pickle relish, and 2 teaspoons hot pepper sauce. Dredge 2 whole perch, about 1½ pounds each, first in milk, then in ¾ cup seasoned bread crumbs. Pan-fry in ½ inch hot oil about 5 minutes per side. Serve with the prepared tartar sauce.

 ### Pike Mousse with Beurre Blanc

In a food processor, puree 1 pound boneless pike with 2 egg whites and a grating of nutmeg. Set in a bowl placed over ice until very cold. Beat in 2 cups heavy cream a bit at a time until the mixture has consistency of softly beaten cream, then turn into 6 well-greased 5-ounce ramekins. Cover with buttered parchment and bake in a water bath in a preheated 350°F. oven until set, about 25 minutes. Invert onto plates. Blot up liquid and serve with Beurre Blanc (page 24). Serves 6.

 ### Grilled Pompano with Lime and Dill

Plan 1 gutted and scaled pompano (or butterfish) per person. Cut 3 slits on each side of each fish and rub with lime juice and olive oil. Place 2 or 3 dill sprigs in each fish cavity and grill on a well-oiled rack 4 inches from a high fire for 4 minutes per side.

 ### Pompano en Papillote with Baby Shrimp and Chervil

Wrap each of 4 cleaned pompano in a large piece of heart-shape parchment paper with 1 teaspoon butter, 8 peeled and cleaned baby shrimp (about 60 count), 1 teaspoon minced chervil or tarragon leaves, and 2 tablespoons dry white wine. Bake on sheet pan in preheated 350°F. oven for 20 to 25 minutes until parchment is puffed and browned. Slit the parchment sacks and slide contents onto dinner plates. Garnish each with 2 lemon wedges.

Whole Smoked Porgy

Cut 3 slits in the sides of two 2-pound porgies. Marinate in ¼ cup olive oil, the juice and finely grated zest of 1 lemon, and 1 teaspoon dried basil or tarragon for 1 hour under refrigeration. Scatter 1 cup soaked hardwood chips over a charcoal fire and place marinated fish on an oiled rack about 6 inches from the fire. Cover grill and cook 8 minutes per side. Bring extra marinade to a boil, transfer fish to plates and spoon several tablespoons marinade over each fish.

 ### Sesame Porgy Fillets

Brush eight 4-ounce porgy fillets with 1 egg white beaten with 1 tablespoon soy sauce. Dredge in 1 cup sesame seeds tossed with ¼ cup cornstarch and a pinch of cayenne pepper. Sauté in 2 tablespoons peanut oil and 1 tablespoon Oriental sesame oil until browned on each side and flaky to the touch. Squeeze the juice of 1 lemon over top and garnish with 1 minced scallion.

 ### Bourride of Orange Roughy

Cook 1 large chopped onion, 1 clove minced garlic, and 1 chopped carrot in 2 tablespoons olive oil in a large soup pot until vegetables soften. Add 1½ cups *each* white wine and fish broth, 2 tablespoons grated orange zest, ½ teaspoon *each* ground fennel seed and thyme, and 1 bay leaf and simmer 10 minutes. Add 2 pounds orange roughy fillet cut into 1-inch-wide strips and simmer for 5 minutes. Place 1 slice of garlic bread in each of 6 soup bowls. Divide fish among the bowls. Whisk 3 minced garlic cloves and ⅓ cup mayonnaise into the broth and ladle over the fish.

 ### Sautéed Roughy in Anise-Parmesan Crust

Dredge four 6-ounce orange roughy fillets in a mixture of 1 cup grated Parmesan, 2 teaspoons ground anise, and 1 tablespoon finely chopped fresh parsley and shake off excess. Gently dip fish in 1 egg beaten with 3 tablespoons water, and dredge in 1½ cups bread crumbs until well coated. Allow to rest at least 10 minutes (or several hours under refrigeration). In a large skillet, sauté fish in thin film of olive oil until browned, about 3 minutes per side. Remove fish and drain on paper towels. Garnish with lemon wedges.

 ### Cold Poached Salmon with Middle Eastern Cucumbers

In a large skillet, bring 2 cups water, 1 cup white wine, 1 thick onion slice, 1 clove, and 1 bay leaf to a boil and reduce to a simmer. Add four 6-ounce pieces salmon fillet and simmer 8 minutes. Remove fish and cool, moistening occasionally with a bit of the poaching liquid. Toss together 2 peeled, seeded, thinly sliced cucumbers, 2 tablespoons olive oil, 1 tablespoon lemon juice, 1 clove minced garlic, and 1 tablespoon plain yogurt. Serve cooled salmon with cucumber salad on the side.

 ### Dill-Cured Salmon (Gravlax)

Mix 1 cup kosher salt, ½ cup sugar, and 1 teaspoon white pepper. Spread a third of this mixture in a thin layer in a large, deep-sided dish. Place 6 dill branches and a 2- to 3-pound salmon fillet, skin-side down, on top. Arrange 6 dill sprigs across surface of salmon, and mound remaining salt mixture on top, using more salt on the thicker parts. Cover with several layers of plastic wrap or wax paper and weight with a full tin can atop a dish. Refrigerate 36 to 48 hours, depending on thickness of fish. Remove fish, rinse well, pat dry, and slice thinly on an angle against the grain. Serve as you would lox. Makes 10 to 12 servings.

 Charcoal-Grilled Salmon with Spicy Black Beans

Marinate four 6-ounce salmon steaks in the juice of 1 lemon, ⅓ cup olive oil, and 2 tablespoons chopped basil leaves in the refrigerator for 1 hour. Grill salmon over moderately high flame for 4 to 5 minutes per side, basting with marinade every minute. Serve with 1 recipe Spicy Black Beans (page 319).

Shad in Mustard Crumbs

Brush 1½ pounds boneless shad fillet with 3 tablespoons brown mustard. Dredge in 1 cup seasoned bread crumbs and dab another 3 tablespoons mustard over the breading. Dredge again in the bread crumbs (surface may look crumbly). Sauté in 2 tablespoons olive oil until fish flakes, about 4 minutes per side. Serve with lemon wedges.

Steamed Paupiettes of Shad Stuffed with Roe

Poach a split set of shad roe until firm and lay end to end down center of 1 boneless fillet of shad. Place another boneless fillet on top. Tie in several places with string to secure. Place in top section of a steamer and sprinkle with 2 tablespoons *each* lemon juice and chopped fresh dill. Steam over boiling water for 10 to 15 minutes until fish is cooked through. Carefully remove to a service platter with 2 wide spatulas, remove string, and cover with 1 recipe Herbed Beurre Blanc (page 24) made with dill.

Brochettes of Shark, Sturgeon, and Salmon

Cut ½ pound *each* skinless salmon fillet, skinless shark, and sturgeon into 8 chunks each. Marinate in ¼ cup olive oil, the juice of 1 lemon, 2 tablespoons chopped basil leaves, and 1 clove minced garlic for 1 hour in the refrigerator. Skewer 1 piece of each fish variety with a 1-inch section of red pepper and 1 mushroom on each of 8 skewers. Grill 4 inches from a hot charcoal fire for 10 to 12 minutes, basting with marinade.

Chilied Grilled Shark Steak

Rub 1½ pounds shark steak with salt and pepper and marinate in juice of 2 lemons for 1 hour in the refrigerator. In small skillet, warm 2 cloves minced garlic, 2 tablespoons chili powder, 1 tablespoon ground cumin, and a pinch of oregano in ⅓ cup olive oil until aroma of chili is strong. Pour warm mixture over shark, refrigerate and marinate another hour. Grill 6 minutes per side over a hot fire, basting frequently with marinade. Serve with lemon wedges.

Pan-Fried Breaded Smelts with Pickled Peppers

Dip 2 pounds pan-dressed 3- to 4-inch smelts in 1 cup milk, then dredge in 1½ cups seasoned bread crumbs. Pan-fry in ¼ inch olive oil until skin is crisp and fish flakes to the touch, about 3 minutes per side. Drain on paper towels and serve with jarred pickled peppers.

Smelt Tempura

Mix 1 jumbo egg, 2 cups ice water, and 2 cups sifted flour until barely blended. Dredge 2 pounds

Fifty Ways to Cook Most Everything

pan-dressed 3- to 4-inch smelts in 1 cup cornstarch and dip into prepared batter. Deep-fry in 375° F. oil until pale brown, about 2 minutes. Drain on paper towels and serve with soy sauce for dipping.

Broiled Red Snapper with Green Chili Cream Sauce

In a saucepan, combine 4 roasted, skinned, seeded, and stemmed poblano peppers, 1 clove chopped garlic, the chopped whites of 4 scallions, and 1 cup chicken broth, bring to a boil, and reduce by half. Add 2 cups light cream and boil until lightly thickened. Rub four 6-ounce red snapper fillets with 2 tablespoons olive oil, salt, and pepper. Grill or broil 4 inches from a moderately high flame for 3 to 4 minutes per side, depending on thickness. While fish is cooking, puree sauce in a blender or food processor and finish with ¼ cup chopped cilantro leaves, salt, pepper, and 1 teaspoon lime juice. Nap the fish with this sauce.

Whole Steamed Red Snapper

Cut 4 slits in each side of a 2- to 3-pound red snapper and rub with 2 teaspoons Oriental sesame oil. Place on a platter and scatter 1 inch julienned fresh gingerroot, 2 cloves julienned garlic, and 2 julienned scallions over the top. Cover with foil and steam for 20 minutes over simmering water, uncover, and pour the juice of 1 lime over the top.

Escabeche of Sole

Lightly flour 1½ pounds sole fillet and brown in ¼ cup olive oil. Remove fish and add 1 sliced onion, 2 smashed cloves garlic, and 2 more tablespoons olive oil to the pan. Sauté until soft. Add the juice of 2 oranges, 2 lemons, and 2 limes, ¼ cup wine vinegar, 1 dried hot pepper, and 1 bay leaf. Bring to

boil and stir in 2 tablespoons chopped fresh parsley and 2 tablespoons dill leaves. Pour hot marinade over fish and marinate in the refrigerator for 3 to 4 hours. Serve chilled, using marinade as a sauce.

 Sole Steamed with Tangerine and Chive

Arrange 4 skinned 5- to 6-ounce fillets of sole, dark sides down, on a heat-safe platter. Sprinkle with 1 tablespoon walnut oil, ¼ cup tangerine juice, 1 teaspoon lemon juice, a grating of nutmeg, and ⅓ cup chopped fresh chive. Cover with foil, and steam over large skillet of simmering water for 8 to 10 minutes until fish is opaque. Uncover and garnish each fillet with a blade of chive and a wedge of lime.

Broiled Swordfish Steak with Mignonette Sauce

Mix together 2 minced shallots, 1 teaspoon crushed red pepper flakes, ⅓ cup red wine vinegar, and 1 tablespoon water. Rub 4 swordfish steaks, each 1 inch thick, with oil, and broil 4 inches from a high flame for 4 minutes per side. Serve splashed with the sauce.

Lemon Rosemary Swordfish Steak

Heat 2 cloves minced garlic, 1 dried chili pepper, 1 tablespoon rosemary leaves, and ⅓ cup virgin olive oil until warm. Add the juice of 2 lemons and pour over four 8-ounce, 1-inch-thick swordfish steaks in a glass bowl. Marinate for at least 1 hour in refrigerator. Place oiled rack 4 inches from a white-hot charcoal fire, remove fish from marinade, and place on rack. Grill 4 to 5 minutes per side. Bring extra marinade to a boil, and serve with a splash of marinade.

Mediterranean Tilefish Stew

In a soup pot, sauté 1 large chopped onion, ½ cup quartered mushrooms, and 2 cloves minced garlic in 3 tablespoons olive oil until onions are soft. Add 2 ribs chopped celery, 1 cup peeled and diced eggplant, 1 teaspoon ground fennel seed, 1 teaspoon dried basil, ½ teaspoon dried oregano, and 1 bay leaf. Cook 1 minute more, add ½ cup white wine, bring to a boil and add 4 skinned, seeded, and chopped tomatoes, 1 teaspoon crushed red pepper flakes, and 3 cups fish stock or clam juice. Bring to a boil and add 1½ pounds tilefish fillet in 2-inch chunks. Simmer 8 minutes, and stir in ¼ cup chopped fresh parsley.

 Tortellini, Tilefish, and Pesto

In a food processor, finely chop 2 cups fresh basil leaves and blend in 1 clove minced garlic and ¼ cup virgin olive oil to make pesto. Steam 1 pound skinless tilefish fillets until flaky, about 6 minutes. Flake and toss with 1 pound hot cooked tortellini, ¼ cup grated Parmesan, and the pesto.

 Grilled Trout with Bacon and Tarragon

Rub 4 cleaned (8-ounce) brook trout inside and out with the juice of 1 lemon. Place 1 sprig tarragon in the cavity of each fish and wrap 1 strip bacon around each one. Grill 4 inches from a hot fire on a covered grill until bacon is crisp and fish flakes to the touch, about 4 minutes per side. Garnish with lemon wedges.

 Pan-Fried Trout with Tapenade Relish

Toss together 1 cup finely chopped pitted oil-cured black olives, 1 clove minced garlic, and ¼ cup extra-virgin olive oil. Dip 4 cleaned (8-ounce) brook trout into ½ cup milk and dredge in ½ cup seasoned bread crumbs. Pan-fry in ¼ inch olive oil until skin is crisp and flesh flakes to the touch, about 3 minutes per side. Drain on paper towels and serve with the sauce.

 Smoky Tuna Salad

Rub three 4-ounce tuna steaks with oil. Grill over moderate fire or under broiler for 1 to 2 minutes per side, until tuna is opaque. Remove skin and bone and set aside to cool. Whisk together ⅓ cup mayonnaise, ¼ teaspoon ground celery seed, and 1 tablespoon lemon juice, add flaked cooked tuna, and toss with ½ cup peeled, seeded, and diced cucumber and ½ diced roasted pepper (page 442).

 Grilled Tuna Steak with Warm Tomato Vinaigrette

In heavy saucepan, bring 2 cups chopped skinless plum tomatoes to a boil and cook vigorously for 5 minutes. Remove from the heat and stir in 3 tablespoons extra-virgin olive oil, 1 tablespoon wine vinegar, a pinch of crushed red pepper flakes, and 2 chopped scallions. Keep warm. Rub four 4-ounce tuna steaks with olive oil and grill over a hot fire or under a broiler for 1 to 2 minutes per side, until firm. Serve with the vinaigrette poured over top.

 Whiting Baked with Apples and Thyme

Sauté 1 small chopped onion and 1 clove minced garlic in 1 tablespoon butter. Add 1 peeled, cored, and diced Granny Smith apple, 2 ribs chopped celery, 2 teaspoons thyme leaves, and ½ teaspoon minced sage leaves. Cook 2 minutes more, add juice of ½ lemon, and pour over 1½ pounds whiting fillet set in a greased baking pan. Cover and bake 20 minutes at 375°F. until the fish flakes.

Whiting, Asparagus, and Pine Nut Salad

Simmer 1 pound whiting fillet in lightly salted water for 8 minutes, until flaked. Cool and drain. Toss with ½ pound cooked asparagus cut into 1½-inch lengths, 2 sliced scallions, the juice of 1 lemon, ¼ cup virgin olive oil, ¼ cup toasted pine nuts, 1 tablespoon chopped fresh parsley, and cayenne pepper. Serve on a bed of Bibb lettuce.

Fifty Recipes for Any Fish

Now that the preceding chapter has given you a couple of recipes for every fish variety you are likely to find at the market, let's multiply your repertoire in one fell swoop by dividing the fish of the world into two broad categories—lean and oily.

After all, the main culinary differences among fish are reflected in their fat content, and for that reason fish are classified for cooking purposes as lean or oily. A lean fish is any one with a fat content of less than 5 percent. This would include all flatfish, codfish, snappers, perch, whiting, catfish, and drum. Oily fish can have fat percentages up to 45 percent. Salmon, shark, bluefish, tuna, and mackerel are examples.

Typically, as the fish fat content increases so does the flesh color, aroma, and flavor. For that reason, high-fat fish tend to work best with dry cooking techniques, such as grilling and baking, where their natural oils keep the meat moist. High-fat fish are usually served with stronger-flavored sauces.

Lean fish are better suited for moist cooking methods, such as poaching and steaming, where the meat keeps moist in a bath of warm liquid. Lean fish are usually served with buttery and creamy sauces to lend needed richness.

There are exceptions, of course, among cooking techniques and among fish. For example, both lean and oily fish fry and sauté well, provided the fillet is thin enough, and salmon (the most popular of all oily fish) is equally good whether grilled or poached.

The following 50 recipes appear in two groups—30 for lean fish, 20 for oily fish. The recipes do not specify one variety, but use the following partial list as a guide. Because new varieties of fish are always coming to market and because the same fish can be known by different names in different seasons or parts of the country, it is possible that the fish you have in hand may not be listed. In that case, use the guidelines given before each list.

Lean fish have snow-white flesh and no perceptible aroma. They can have a round or flat body, but all flatfish are lean. This group includes black bass, sea bass, catfish, cod, drum, flounder, fluke, grouper, halibut, John Dory or St. Peter's fish, perch, pompano, porgy, redfish, rockfish, orange roughy, sheepshead, snapper, sunfish, tilefish, whiting, and yellow perch.

Oily fish all have a round body and tinted flesh that can be beige, gray, or pink-to-salmon color, depending on the variety. Although no fish should ever smell fishy, oily fish will have an aroma characteristic of their type. The group includes anchovy, bluefish, butterfish, carp, chub, dolphinfish (or mahimahi), eel, herring, mackerel, sable, salmon, sardine, sea robin, shad, shark, smelt, sturgeon, swordfish, and tuna.

ABOUT THESE RECIPES

Unless otherwise noted, the following recipes are written for boneless, skinless fish fillets, serve 4 portions, and should be seasoned to taste with salt and pepper.

Some of the recipes in this chapter call for a *court bouillon* as an added liquid. Use this recipe.

Court Bouillon

Bring 2 cups water, 2 cups white wine, ½ cup chopped onion, ¼ cup *each* chopped carrot and celery, 1 bay leaf, a pinch thyme, 1 tablespoon chopped fresh parsley, 4 peppercorns, 1 clove, and 1 tablespoon lemon juice to a boil. Simmer 15 minutes and strain.

The first 30 recipes use lean fish, such as flounder, sole, fluke, or any other flat fish, and white-meat round fish, such as red snapper, black bass, ocean perch, or cod-family fish.

 Poached Fish with Beurre Blanc

Poach 1½ pounds fillet in Court Bouillion (above) for 8 minutes per inch of thickness. Remove with slotted spatula to warm platter. Combine ½ cup poaching liquid, 2 tablespoons white wine vinegar, any liquid that has collected on the fish platter, and 2 tablespoons finely chopped shallot, and reduce to ⅓ cup over high heat. Reduce heat to low and swirl in 4 tablespoons butter. Pour over the fish.

 Fish Poached in Vegetable Juice

Poach 1½ pounds fillet in 1½ cups vegetable cocktail juice for 8 minutes per inch of thickness. Re-move with slotted spatula to a warm platter. Add 2 tablespoons chopped basil leaves and reduce pan liquid by half. Whisk in 2 tablespoons virgin olive oil and 2 teaspoons lemon juice. Pour over the fish.

 Poached Fish with Tomato Mint Salsa

Combine 2 finely chopped large ripe tomatoes, 2 thinly sliced scallions, 5 tablespoons finely chopped mint leaves, the juice of ½ lemon, a pinch of sugar, and ¼ teaspoon chili powder. Refrigerate at least 30 minutes. Poach 1½ pounds fillet in Court Bouillon (above) for 8 minutes per inch of thickness. Remove with slotted spatula to a warm platter. Top with the salsa.

 Poached Fish with Wine Hollandaise

Poach 1½ pounds fillet in Court Bouillon (above) for 8 minutes per inch of thickness. Remove with slotted spatula to a warm platter. Strain poaching liquid and reduce 2 cups of it to ½ cup. Beat in 2 egg yolks and the juice of ½ lemon in top of a double boiler over simmering water, and continue whisking until thick and fluffy. Remove from heat and whisk in 5 tablespoons melted butter.

 Bourride

Place 1 slice toast rubbed with a cut garlic clove in each of 4 large soup bowls. Set aside. Cook 1 large chopped onion, 1 clove minced garlic, and 1 chopped carrot in 2 tablespoons olive oil until vegetables soften. Add 2½ cups Court Bouillon (above), 2 tablespoons julienned orange zest, ½ teaspoon ground fennel seed, ½ teaspoon dried thyme, and 1 bay leaf and simmer for 10 minutes. Strain broth back into saucepan. Cut 2 pounds fish fillets in 2-inch-wide strips and poach in the hot broth for 6 to 8 minutes. With a slotted spoon, distribute fish over the toasts. Whisk 1 cup Aïoli (page 432) with 1 egg yolk and mix into the hot broth and simmer very gently, stirring constantly, until lightly thickened. Do not allow to boil. Ladle sauce over fish.

Chilled Poached Fish with Citrus Vinaigrette

Poach 1½ pounds fillet in Court Bouillon (opposite) for 8 minutes per inch of thickness. Let cool, then chill fish in poaching liquid. Carefully remove fish from the liquid onto a serving platter. Sauce with ⅓ cup virgin olive oil whisked with 1 clove minced garlic and juices of 1 lemon and ½ orange.

Chilled Poached Fish with Creamy Cucumbers

Follow preceding recipe, but substitute this sauce for the vinaigrette: Toss 1 thinly sliced, peeled, and seeded cucumber with 1 teaspoon salt and set aside for 15 minutes. Rinse well and toss with 1 clove minced garlic, 1 tablespoon lemon juice, 1 tablespoon chopped fresh dill, and ¼ cup *crème fraîche*, yogurt, or sour cream.

Fried Fish in Ranch Buttermilk Batter

Sift together ½ cup flour, half a 1-ounce packet ranch dressing mix, and ¼ teaspoon baking soda. Beat in 1 large egg yolk and ¾ cup buttermilk. Beat egg white until firm and fold in. Dust 1½ pounds fish fillets, cut into 2-inch-long sections, with ½ cup cornstarch mixed with the remaining half of the dressing mix. Dip into the batter and fry in several inches of 375°F. fat until golden brown, 2 to 3 minutes. Do not crowd pan. Drain on paper towels and serve with lemon wedges.

Tempura

Mix 1 extra-large egg, 2 cups ice water, and 2 cups sifted flour until barely blended. Dredge 1½ pounds fish fillets, cut in 2-inch-long sections in 1 cup cornstarch and dip into prepared batter. Deep-fry in 375°F. oil until pale brown, about 2 minutes. Drain on paper towels and serve with soy sauce for dipping.

Old Bay Fried Fish

Dust 1½ pounds fish fillets with ½ cup flour seasoned with 2 teaspoons Old Bay Seasoning. Dip in 1 beaten egg mixed with 1 tablespoon water and dredge well in 1 cup bread crumbs seasoned with 1 tablespoon Old Bay Seasoning. Dry on a rack for 10 minutes and pan-fry in 1 inch hot oil until golden brown, 2 to 3 minutes. Drain on paper towels and serve with lemon wedges.

Buffalo "Fins"

Dust 1½ pounds fish fillets, cut into 2-by-3-inch fingers, with ½ cup seasoned flour. Deep-fry in several inches of 375°F. fat until golden brown, about 3 minutes. Do not crowd pan. Drain on paper towels and dip into a warm mixture of 4 tablespoons melted butter and 1 to 2 tablespoons Durkee Red Hot sauce. Serve with ranch or blue cheese dressing for dipping.

Whole Fried Sesame Fish

Score each side of a 1½- to 2-pound cleaned lean fish right down to the bone at 1½-inch intervals. Liberally dust fish surface with cornstarch. Carefully lower fish, head first, into a large wok filled with several inches of vegetable oil that bubbles when a small bread cube touches it. (Most of the head and tail will probably extend out of the oil.) Fry for 8 minutes, ladling hot oil over the exposed parts of the fish to ensure even browning. Lift fish with a large flat strainer to a platter. Douse with mixture of 1 tablespoon Oriental sesame oil, 1 tablespoon lemon juice, 2 teaspoons light soy sauce, and 1 teaspoon honey. Sprinkle with 2 tablespoons toasted sesame seeds. Makes 2 servings.

 ### Orange Fennel Fillets

Dredge 1½ pounds fish fillets in a mixture of 1 cup grated Parmesan, 2 teaspoons ground fennel seed, and 1 tablespoon minced orange zest. Shake off excess and dip in 1 egg beaten with 3 tablespoons water. Dredge in 1½ cups bread crumbs until well coated. Sauté fish in thin film of olive oil until browned, about 3 minutes per side. Remove with slotted spatula and drain on paper towels. Serve garnished with orange wedges.

 ### Fish in Balsamic Brown Butter with Capers

Dust 1½ pounds fish fillets with seasoned flour. Sauté in 6 to 8 tablespoons butter, remove to warm plate, and add 2 tablespoons drained capers and 1 tablespoon balsamic vinegar to pan. Bring to a boil and pour over the fish.

 ### Sautéed Fish in Lemon Butter

Follow preceding recipe, substituting 2 tablespoons lemon juice for the capers and vinegar.

 ### Sautéed Fish with Lime and Olives

Dust 1½ pounds fish fillets with seasoned flour. Sauté in 4 to 6 tablespoons butter, remove to warm plate, and add ¼ cup chopped pitted oil-cured black olives, 2 tablespoons chopped fresh parsley, and the juice of 1 lime to the pan. Bring to a boil and pour over the fish.

 ### Fish Sautéed in Hazelnut-Garlic Crust

Dip 1½ pounds fish fillets in 4 tablespoons melted butter mixed with 2 tablespoons Aïoli (page 432). Press 6 tablespoons ground hazelnuts into the fish and sauté in 2 tablespoons Garlic Butter (page 431) mixed with 2 tablespoons olive oil until browned. Serve with lemon wedges.

 ### Rosemary, Sage, and Garlic Fillets

Dust 1½ pounds fish fillets in a mixture of ½ cup flour, 2 teaspoons crumbled dried rosemary, 2 teaspoons dried sage, salt, and pepper. Sauté in 2 tablespoons Garlic Butter (page 431) mixed with 2 tablespoons olive oil until browned. Serve with lemon wedges.

 ### Fish Fillets Steamed with Lime and Chive.

Arrange 4 fish fillets in single layer on a platter. Squeeze the juice of 1 large lime over fish and scatter 3 tablespoons chopped chive over top. Dot with 2 teaspoons butter. Steam over boiling water, covered, for 4 to 5 minutes. Garnish with lime wedges.

 ### Fish Steamed with Baby Shrimp in Tarragon Vinaigrette

Arrange 4 fish fillets in a single layer on a platter. Drizzle with olive oil and scatter ¼ pound peeled and cleaned baby shrimp and 1 teaspoon tarragon leaves over the top. Steam over boiling water, covered, for 4 to 5 minutes. Serve topped with ½ recipe Tarragon Mustard Vinaigrette (page 297), made with fresh tarragon.

 ### Fish Steamed with Vegetables

Place a cleaned 1½- to 2-pound whole fish on a dinner plate. Dot with 1 teaspoon butter and sprinkle with 2 teaspoons lemon juice. Surround fish with 2 cups julienned vegetables (any combination of carrots, bell pepper, green beans, leeks, celery, fennel, tomato). Dot vegetables with butter and season with salt and pepper. Steam, covered, in the top of a flat-bottomed steamer over boiling water for 8 minutes. Remove from the steamer. Makes 2 servings.

 ### Steamed Paupiettes Rolled with Fresh Herbs

Split 4 fish fillets in half lengthwise. Season with salt and pepper and top with a layer of fresh herb leaves. Roll up fillets and secure each with a toothpick. Place spiral-side up in a steamer and steam over boiling water for 4 minutes. Serve with lemon wedges.

 ### Fish en Papillote with Leeks

Wrap each of 4 fish fillets in a large parchment paper heart with 1 teaspoon butter, 3 tablespoons julienned leeks, ½ clove minced garlic, 1 teaspoon chopped fresh parsley, salt, and pepper. Bake on a sheet pan in a preheated 350°F. oven for 12 to 15 minutes, until parchment is puffed and browned. Slit parchment sacks and slide contents on each of 4 dinner plates. Garnish each with 2 lemon wedges.

Fish en Papillote with Julienne of Garden Vegetables

Follow preceding recipe, substituting 1 tablespoon *each* julienned carrot and celery for 2 tablespoons of leeks.

 ### Fish en Papillote with Olives and Tomatoes

Wrap each of 4 fish fillets in a large heart of parchment paper with 1 teaspoon olive oil, 1 tablespoon minced onion, 2 tablespoons chopped black olives, ¼ cup chopped tomato, ½ clove minced garlic, 1 teaspoon chopped fresh parsley, salt, and pepper. Bake and serve as described in recipe for Fish en Papillote With Leeks (above).

 ### Fish en Papillote with Melon and Capers

Wrap each of 4 fish fillets in a large heart parchment paper with ½ cup diced honeydew melon, ½ teaspoon drained capers, 1 teaspoon lemon juice, and a dot of butter. Bake on a sheet pan in a preheated 350°F. oven for 10 to 15 minutes, until parchment is puffed and browned. Slit parchment sacks and slide contents on each of 4 dinner plates. Garnish with lime wedges.

 ### Fish en Papillote, Bouillabaisse-Style

Wrap each of 4 fish fillets in a large heart parchment paper with an equal portion of sauce, made as follows: Cook 2 tablespoons finely chopped onion, 1 clove minced garlic, ¼ cup diced fennel, and 2 teaspoons finely grated orange zest in 1 tablespoon olive oil until vegetables soften. Add 2 chopped tomatoes, 1 tablespoon chopped basil leaves, a pinch of saffron, and the juice of ½ orange and simmer 1 minute. Bake on sheet pan in preheated 350°F. oven for 10 to 15 minutes, until parchment is puffed and browned. Slit parchment sacks, and slide contents on each of 4 dinner plates. Serve with crusty bread.

 ### Fish en Papillote with Pickled Ginger

Rub each of 4 fish fillets with ½ teaspoon Oriental sesame oil. Wrap each in a large heart parchment paper with 1 tablespoon julienned pickled ginger, a few slivers garlic, 1 teaspoon low-sodium soy sauce, 1 tablespoon lemon juice, and 3 fresh chives. Bake on sheet pan in preheated 350°F. oven for 10 to 15 minutes, until parchment is puffed and browned. Slit parchment sacks and slide contents on each of 4 dinner plates.

 ### Fish Sautéed with Bacon and Scallions

Rub 4 fish fillets with the juice of 1 lemon. Place 1 julienned scallion on each fillet and fold fillets in half lengthwise. Wrap 1 strip bacon around each fillet so the bacon is spiraled. Sauté in a dry skillet until bacon is crisp and fish flakes to the touch, about 3 to 4 minutes per side. Garnish with lemon wedges.

 ### Broiled Fish with Walnut Butter

Brush 1½ pounds fish fillets with 2 tablespoons walnut oil. Broil 4 inches from the flame for 4 to 5 minutes. While fish is cooking, brown ½ cup walnut pieces in a skillet with 1 tablespoon walnut oil. When toasted, stir in 1 tablespoon butter and 1 tablespoon lime juice. Pour over fish.

The following 20 recipes use oily fish, such as bluefish, tuna, salmon, swordfish, or mackerel.

 ### Baked Fish in Mustard Glaze

Bake 1½ pounds fish fillet in a preheated 375°F. oven for 15 to 20 minutes. Meanwhile, mix 3 tablespoons Dijon mustard with ⅔ cup sour cream or yogurt. When fish is done, transfer to warm platter with a slotted spatula. Add the mustard mixture to juices in the pan, blend, and pour over the fish. Garnish with 1 tablespoon chopped fresh parsley.

 ### Fish Baked with Horseradish and Sour Cream

Follow preceding recipe, substituting 2 tablespoons prepared horseradish for the mustard.

 ### Sweet and Sour Cranberry Fish

Bake fish as described in following recipe or fry as described in Whole Fried Sesame Fish (page 223) and serve with the following sauce: Bring 1 tablespoon dry sherry, 3 cloves minced garlic, 1 tablespoon minced fresh gingerroot, 1 teaspoon Worcestershire sauce, 2 tablespoons minced orange zest, ¼ cup cider vinegar, ⅓ cup sugar, and ½ cup orange juice to a boil. Add 1½ cups cranberries and simmer about 5 minutes.

 ### Whole Fish Baked with Sauce

Rub exterior of a 4-pound cleaned fish with salt, pepper, 1 tablespoon vegetable oil, and the juice of 1 lemon. Place in oiled baking dish and bake in preheated 375°F. oven for 10 minutes per inch of thickness, about 30 minutes. Serve with one of the following sauces: Red Pepper Coulis (page 25), Warm Sun-Dried Tomato Vinaigrette (page 25), Sauce Provençale (page 25), Chilied Peanut Sauce (page 26), Mushroom Ragout (page 27), Oyster Sauce with Lime and Garlic (page 27), Marinated Mushroom Sauce (page 27), or Julienned Pepper and Carrot (page 27).

 ### Fish Baked in a Glaze of Herb Oil

Bake a whole fish as described in preceding recipe, omitting the vegetable oil and basting every 5 minutes during baking with ¼ cup finely chopped fresh herbs steeped in ⅓ cup olive oil.

Smoky Grilled Fish

Slash 3 slits in sides of two 2-pound whole, cleaned fish. Marinate 1 hour under refrigeration in ¼ cup olive oil, the juice and finely grated zest of 1 lemon, and 1 teaspoon dried basil. Soak 1 cup hardwood chips in water to cover for 10 minutes, drain, and scatter over a hot charcoal fire. Place marinated fish on an oiled rack about 6 inches from fire, cover grill, and cook 8 to 10 minutes per side. Transfer to plates and moisten fish with a generous amount of boiled marinade over each fish.

 ## Grilled Fish in Chili Paste

Rub 1½ pounds fish steak with salt and pepper and marinate in the juice of 2 lemons in the refrigerator for 30 minutes. In a small skillet, warm 2 cloves minced garlic, 2 tablespoons chili powder, 1 tablespoon ground cumin, and a pinch of dried oregano in ⅓ cup olive oil until the aroma of chili is strong. Pour mixture over fish and marinate in the refrigerator for 1 hour more. Grill 6 minutes per side over hot fire, basting frequently with marinade. Serve with lemon wedges.

Grilled Fish in Garlic Herb Marinade

Marinate 1½ pounds fish steak in ½ recipe Garlic Herb Dressing (page 296) in the refrigerator for 1 hour. Grill 5 to 6 minutes per side over hot fire, basting frequently with marinade.

Barbecued Fish

Prepare and grill fish as described in the previous recipe, but substitute this marinade: Sauté 1 small chopped onion and 1 clove minced garlic in 1 tablespoon corn oil until softened. Add 2 table-spoons apple cider vinegar, ½ cup ketchup, 1 teaspoon mustard, 1 teaspoon Worcestershire sauce, 1 teaspoon hot pepper sauce, and the juice of ½ lemon.

 ## Teriyaki Grilled Fish

Follow recipe for Grilled Fish in Garlic Herb Marinade (above), substituting this marinade: Mix 1 teaspoon Oriental sesame oil, 1 tablespoon lemon juice, 2 tablespoons light soy sauce, 1 tablespoon dry sherry, and 1 tablespoon honey.

 ## Broiled Fish in Garlic Sage Marinade

Marinate in the refrigerator for 1 hour 1½ pounds fish steak or fillets in ½ recipe Garlic Herb Dressing (page 296) using sage for the herb. Broil for 8 minutes per inch of thickness, turning once and basting several times with marinade.

 ## Broiled Fish Glazed with Vinaigrette

Follow preceding recipe, but using Basic Wine Vinaigrette (page 296) as marinade.

 ## Broiled Fish Steaks with Olive Oil and Balsamic Vinegar

Marinate in the refrigerator for 1 hour 1½ pounds fish steak or fillets in ½ recipe Balsamic Olive Oil Vinaigrette (page 297). Broil for 8 minutes per inch of thickness, turning once and basting several times with marinade.

 ## Marinated Fish Kebabs

Marinate in the refrigerator 1½ pounds fish fillets cut in 1½-inch cubes in ¼ cup olive oil, the juice of

1 lemon, 2 tablespoons chopped basil leaves, and 1 clove minced garlic for 1 hour. Skewer 3 pieces fish with a 1-inch section of red pepper and 1 mushroom on each of 8 skewers. Grill 4 inches from hot charcoal fire for about 10 minutes, basting with marinade.

Broiled Fish with Lemon Ranch Dressing

Marinate in the refrigerator for 1 hour 1½ pounds fish steak or fillets in ⅔ cup ranch dressing mixed with 2 tablespoons lemon juice. Broil 4 inches from a high broiler flame for 3 to 4 minutes per side, basting with marinade throughout.

Fish Chili

In a large pan, cook 1½ cups finely chopped onion and 2 cloves minced garlic in 2 tablespoons vegetable oil until softened. Add 1 diced roasted pepper (page 442), 2 tablespoons chili powder, ½ teaspoon ground coriander, ½ teaspoon crushed red pepper flakes, and 1½ tablespoons ground cumin and cook for 1 minute, stirring constantly. Add 2 cups Quick Fish Stock (page 430) or clam juice and bring to a boil. Add 4 cups cooked, drained kidney beans and 1½ pounds fish fillet cut into large chunks and simmer 5 minutes. Add the juice and finely grated zest of 1 lemon and 2 tablespoons chopped fresh dill and simmer 1 minute more.

Fish, Black Beans, and Cilantro

In a large pan, cook 1½ cups finely chopped onion, 1 minced chili pepper, and 2 cloves minced garlic in 2 tablespoons vegetable oil until vegetables soften. Add 1 diced roasted pepper (page 442), 2 tablespoons chili powder, 2 teaspoons ground coriander, ½ teaspoon crushed red pepper flakes,

and 1½ teaspoons ground cumin and cook for 1 minute, stirring constantly. Add 2 cups Quick Fish Stock (page 430) or clam juice and bring to a boil. Add 4 cups cooked, drained black beans and 1½ pounds fish fillet cut into large chunks and simmer 5 minutes. Add the juice and finely grated zest of 1 lime and ¼ cup chopped fresh cilantro. Simmer 1 minute more.

 All-Fish Bouillabaisse

Soak 1 teaspoon crumbled saffron threads in 1 cup white wine with the finely grated zest and juice of 1 large orange. Set aside. In a large pot, cook 1 large chopped onion and 2 cloves minced garlic in 2 tablespoons olive oil until softened. Add 2 ribs chopped celery, 1 teaspoon ground fennel seed, 1 teaspoon dried basil, ½ teaspoon dried thyme, and 1 bay leaf along with the reserved wine mixture and bring to a boil. Add 2 cups skinned, seeded, and chopped tomatoes and 3 cups Quick Fish Stock (page 430) or Court Bouillon (page 222). Simmer for 10 minutes. Add a total of 2 pounds of three kinds of fish fillet cut into large chunks, and simmer for 5 minutes. Add ¼ cup chopped fresh parsley and simmer 1 minute more. Serve with crusty bread.

Clam and Fish Stew with Lots of Basil

Cook 2 cloves minced garlic and the white part of 2 thinly sliced leeks in 3 tablespoons virgin olive oil until softened. Add 1 cup white wine and boil for 2 minutes. Add the juice of ½ lemon and 2 large seeded and chopped tomatoes. Add 1 cup chopped basil leaves and 16 littleneck clams, and simmer for 5 minutes. Add 1 pound fish fillet, cut in large pieces, and simmer another 5 minutes. Discard any clams that do not open.

Fish Braised with Mussels and Orange

Follow preceding recipe, but substitute the juice and finely grated zest of 1 orange for the lemon juice, and use cleaned, debearded, and soaked mussels instead of clams.

Fifty Ways to Bring Shellfish Out of Their Shells

It is miraculous that anyone ever thought to eat a shellfish, since they are armored like medieval warriors and possess all the innate appeal of a sea-washed rock. Yet every time we feast on a lobster or imbibe the brackish essence of a newly opened oyster, we are grateful to that long-gone Neanderthal gourmet who had the vision and courage to taste the unknown.

Though increasingly difficult to procure and consequently ever more expensive, shellfish are easy and fast to prepare and so naturally flavorful that they call for the barest embellishment on their way to the table. In fact, the surest way to ruin good shellfish is by fussing too much.

Fresh shellfish are best with just a dash of spice, a splash of something acidic, and, most important, a minimum of heat. Bivalves, which include any shellfish with one hinge and two shells, such as mussels, clams, oysters, and scallops, are made tough and rubbery when heated too long. And crustaceans, those shellfish with multiple hinges—such as shrimp, prawns, crayfish, lobsters, and crabs—will get tough and dry from overcooking.

Steam bivalves just until their shells open, crustaceans until the flesh is firm and opaque. Anything more is overkill. Only single-shelled mollusks, such as abalone, conch, and snails, and cephalopods, such as squid and octopus, will tenderize during extended cooking.

Buy shellfish from a reputable and busy fish purveyor to ensure reasonable prices and fresh products. All shellfish should smell of fresh sea water. If they smell like fish, then something fishy is going on. Except for scallops, squid, octopus, and single-shelled mollusks, all fresh shellfish should be alive or frozen at the time of purchase.

Live shellfish must be cooked while still alive. Live bivalves will be tightly closed or will close their shells quickly after a firm tap, except for steaming clams. They have a veil-like membrane across the opening between the shells. Live crustaceans will show considerable movement. Because these animals harbor large amounts of bacteria that will spread rapidly after they die, it is quite risky to eat any of them if their time of death is uncertain. If a bivalve remains closed after cooking, it's probably spoiled and should be discarded.

Simply plopping a shellfish in boiling liquid is the easiest method of killing and cooking it. But for some preparations, it's important to open a bivalve's shell with a knife or to section a lobster before cooking it. These procedures require special techniques, which are described in Appendix B. If you do not wish to go through the mess of doing it yourself, many fish markets will open or section shellfish to your specifications.

ABOUT THESE RECIPES

The most opulent of shellfish, the lobster, will not be found in this chapter. Its role as a special-occasion food convinced us to present it among our romantic foods (Chapter 8) and our grilled foods (Chapter 14).

The following recipes serve 4 unless otherwise noted.

 Scallop Seviche Skewered with Avocado

Marinate ½ pound cleaned bay scallops in ½ cup lime juice, 1 minced jalapeño pepper, and 1 clove minced garlic, cover, and refrigerate 6 hours. Drain and toss with 1 teaspoon extra-virgin olive oil, salt, and pepper. Just before serving, toss 2 large diced avocados in 2 tablespoons lime juice. Skewer 2 scallops followed by 1 piece avocado and repeat twice more on each of 10 bamboo skewers. Serve as hors d'oeuvres.

 Scallops Vinaigrette

Bring 1 quart Court Bouillon (page 430) to a boil. Add 1 pound trimmed sea scallops, remove from heat, cover, and let rest for 8 minutes. Remove scallops. Whisk together 1 clove minced garlic, 2 tablespoons red wine vinegar, ¼ cup olive oil, salt, pepper, and 1 tablespoon minced fresh parsley.

Toss with scallops and 1 peeled, seeded, and diced cucumber.

 Grilled Marinated Scallops

Prepare dressing from preceding recipe. Toss 1 pound trimmed sea scallops in the dressing and set aside for 10 minutes. Grill on oiled mesh or broil, for 2 to 3 minutes per side, basting with a bit of marinade every minute.

 Scallops in Wine and Lemon Sauce

Cook 4 cloves chopped garlic and the sliced whites of 1 bunch scallions in 2 tablespoons virgin olive oil until soft. Add ¼ cup dry white wine and bring to a boil. Add 1 pound trimmed sea scallops and cook, tossing frequently, until scallops are barely firm, about 3 to 4 minutes. Do not overcook. Remove scallops. Add the juice of 1 lemon, a pinch of cayenne pepper, salt, and pepper and reduce pan liquid to about 3 tablespoons. Remove from heat and swirl in 4 tablespoons softened butter. Pour over scallops.

 Scallop Escabeche

Cook ¾ pound thinly sliced onion and 2 cloves minced garlic in ⅓ cup olive oil until soft. Add ½ teaspoon ground ginger, ¼ teaspoon dried thyme, and 1 pound trimmed sea scallops. Cook until scallops are barely firm, about 3 minutes. Remove scallops, add 2 tablespoons wine vinegar and the juice of 1 lemon, 1 orange, and 1 lime. Bring to a boil, and season with cayenne pepper, salt, and pepper. Return scallops and cool. Stir in 2 tablespoons chopped fresh parsley. Store in refrigerator up to 4 days.

Scallops Poached with Cider and Cream

Poach 1 pound trimmed sea scallops in ½ cup apple cider, 1 cup white wine, and 2 tablespoons finely chopped onion until scallops are barely firm, about 3 minutes. Remove scallops and reduce liquid to ¼ cup. Brown ⅓ pound sliced mushrooms in 2 tablespoons butter. Add 1 peeled and thinly sliced Granny Smith apple, and cook until browned. Add 2 tablespoons brandy and ignite carefully with a match. Add scallops, reduced poaching liquid, and 1 cup heavy cream and simmer until lightly thickened, about 1 minute

 ### Dill and Fennel Scallops

Mix together 1 cup flour, 1 tablespoon dill weed, 2 teaspoons ground fennel seed, salt, and pepper. Dredge 1 pound trimmed sea scallops in the flour and shake off excess. Brown 1 split clove garlic in ¼ cup olive oil, remove, and cook the scallops in the hot oil until firm and browned on all sides. Serve with a mixture of 1 cup mayonnaise, 1 tablespoon lemon juice, and 3 cloves minced garlic.

 ### Tempura Scallops and Shrimp

Toss ½ pound *each* trimmed and halved sea scallops and shelled and deveined medium shrimp, 1 tablespoon minced fresh gingerroot, 1 clove minced garlic, 2 teaspoons soy sauce, and 1 teaspoon Oriental sesame oil. Refrigerate for at least 1 hour. Beat 2 cups ice water into 2 egg yolks. Stir in 2 cups sifted flour, but not too thoroughly, leaving some clumps of flour. Blot excess moisture from the seafood and toss with ½ cup cornstarch, shaking off excess. Dip in batter and deep-fry in batches in 375°F. oil until lightly browned and crisp.

 ### Shrimp Étouffée

In an iron skillet, cook ¼ cup flour in ¼ cup vegetable oil over low heat until dark chocolate brown, stirring frequently, about 15 to 20 minutes. Add 2 cups chopped onion, 1 chopped rib celery, and 1 diced red bell pepper and cook until wilted, about 1 minute. Toss in 1 pound shelled and deveined large shrimp and 1 tablespoon minced garlic. Add ½ cup hot chicken stock, ½ cup hot beef broth, a large pinch of cayenne pepper, salt and pepper. Simmer for 10 minutes, garnish with 1 tablespoon chopped fresh parsley and 1 tablespoon minced scallion. Serve over 3 cups cooked rice.

 ### Mustard Tarragon Shrimp Cocktail

Bring 4 cups Court Bouillon (page 430) to a boil. Add 1 pound shelled and deveined jumbo shrimp, remove from heat, cover, and let rest for 8 minutes. Remove shrimp. Whisk together 1 clove minced garlic, 2 tablespoons Dijon mustard, 1 teaspoon dried tarragon, and 3 tablespoons wine vinegar. In a slow, steady stream, whisk in ⅓ cup *each* peanut and olive oils. Season to taste with salt and pepper and toss ⅓ of this sauce with the shrimp. Chill and serve with remaining sauce as a dip.

 ### Jalapeño Shrimp Cocktail

Bring 1 quart Court Bouillon (page 430) to a boil. Add 1 pound shelled and deveined jumbo shrimp, remove from heat, cover, and let rest for 8 minutes. Remove shrimp and let cool. In a food processor, finely chop 1 large clove garlic, 3 to 4 stemmed, seeded pickled jalapeño peppers, and 2 stemmed tomatoes. Mix with ¼ cup ketchup and 1 tablespoon lemon juice. Serve with shrimp as a dip.

Deep-Fried Shrimp Cocktail

Butterfly 1 pound shelled and deveined jumbo shrimp, and marinate in the refrigerator in 3 tablespoons dry sherry, 1 tablespoon soy sauce, 1 teaspoon minced fresh gingerroot, 1 minced scallion, and a pinch *each* salt, pepper, and cayenne pepper for 1 hour. Mix ½ cup flour, ½ cup cornstarch, and 1 teaspoon baking powder. Add ½ cup water to make a thick batter. Drain shrimp and dust lightly with cornstarch. Dip in the batter and deep-fry in 375°F. oil until browned and crisp. Serve with dipping sauce made of 2 tablespoons *each* ketchup, honey, and cider vinegar, and 1 tablespoon soy sauce.

 ## Shrimp and Guacamole Salad

Bring 4 cups Court Bouillon (page 430) to a boil. Add 1 pound shelled and deveined medium shrimp, remove from heat, cover, and rest for 4 minutes. Remove shrimp and toss with 3 sliced scallions and 1 teaspoon lemon juice. With a fork, mash together 1 large ripe avocado, 1 clove minced garlic, 1 tablespoon grated onion, ¼ teaspoon hot pepper sauce, 1 tablespoon lemon juice, and 1 tablespoon olive oil. Season lightly with salt and toss with the shrimp. Serve on Romaine leaves.

 ## Grilled Shrimp with Pesto

Marinate 1 pound large unpeeled shrimp overnight in 2 tablespoons virgin olive oil, ½ teaspoon salt, ¼ teaspoon crushed red pepper flakes, and 1 tablespoon lemon juice. Remove shrimp from marinade and grill, still unpeeled, 2 minutes per side, until firm and opaque. Let cool for 5 minutes. Serve with Fresh Basil Pesto (page 165) as a dip. Diners will peel their own shrimp.

 ## Grilled Barbecued Shrimp

Brown 1 tablespoon minced onion in 1 tablespoon vegetable oil. Add 3 cloves minced garlic, 1 tablespoon cider vinegar, 1 teaspoon brown sugar, ¼ cup ketchup, 1 teaspoon brown mustard, and 1 teaspoon Worcestershire sauce, bring to a boil, and season with hot pepper sauce. Let cool and toss 1 pound shelled, deveined and butterflied jumbo shrimp with a third of the sauce. Grill until firm, basting frequently with sauce. Serve with extra sauce for dip.

 ## Shrimp Poached in Tomato Vinaigrette

Peel and devein 1 pound large shrimp. Prepare Warm Tomato Vinaigrette (page 298) without the parsley, add the shrimp, and simmer for 2 to 3 minutes. Add 1 tablespoon chopped fresh dill and serve with crusty bread.

 ## Shrimp with Herbs and Pasta

Dredge 1 pound shelled and deveined large shrimp in flour, seasoned with salt and pepper. Cook until lightly brown and firm in ¼ cup olive oil. Remove shrimp. Add 1 cup onion and cook until softened. Add 2 cloves minced garlic and ¾ cup white wine and reduce by half. Add 1 cup crushed tomatoes, reduce by half, and stir in the shrimp, 2 tablespoons butter, and 1 tablespoon *each* chopped fresh parsley and fresh basil. Toss with ¾ pound hot cooked shell-shaped pasta.

 ## Fried Shrimp in Beer Batter

Mix ¾ cup flour, 2 egg yolks, 2 tablespoons oil, and ¾ cup beer. Beat 2 egg whites to a peak and fold into batter. Dredge 1 pound large shelled and deveined shrimp in cornstarch, shake off excess, coat with batter, and deep-fry at 375°F. until golden brown. Serve with a mixture of ½ cup ketchup, ¼ cup prepared horseradish, and 2 tablespoons mayonnaise.

Clams in Tomato Vinaigrette

Scrub 3 dozen littleneck clams. Heat 1 cup Warm Tomato Vinaigrette (page 298) in a large deep skillet. Add the clams, cover, and simmer 5 to 7 minutes until clams open. Serve with pasta, rice, or crusty bread.

Clams Casino

Blend ¼ cup *each* chopped green bell pepper, red bell pepper, and scallion, 1 clove minced garlic, 1 tablespoon chopped fresh parsley, 2 tablespoons chopped green olives, 6 tablespoons butter, salt, and pepper. Open 16 cherrystone clams and place clams on half shells. Pack each with a portion of the pepper mixture and top each with 2 teaspoons bread crumbs. Bake at 400°F. for 12 minutes, then brown briefly under a broiler.

Niçoise Clams

Blend ¼ cup *each* chopped green pepper, seeded tomato, and minced scallion, 1 clove minced garlic, 1 tablespoon chopped fresh basil, 1 tablespoon chopped oil-cured black olives, 5 tablespoons butter, 1 tablespoon virgin olive oil, salt, and pepper. Open 16 cherrystone clams and place clams on half shells. Pack each with a portion of the vegetable mixture and top each with 2 teaspoons bread crumbs. Bake at 400°F. for 12 minutes, then brown briefly under a broiler.

Clams with Capers and Lemons

Cook 1 tablespoon minced onion in 1 tablespoon butter until soft. Add 2 tablespoons drained capers and 1 more tablespoon butter and cook another minute. Add 2 dozen scrubbed littleneck clams, cover, and cook until clams open, 5 to 8 minutes. Remove clams. Add 2 tablespoons lemon juice and 1 finely sliced scallion and pour over clams.

Curried Clams

Slowly cook ¼ cup chopped onion in 1 tablespoon vegetable oil until softened. Add 2 teaspoons curry powder, ½ teaspoon ground coriander, and a pinch of crushed red pepper flakes and cook 2 to 3 minutes more. Add 1 cup coconut milk and simmer 1 minute. Add 2 dozen scrubbed littleneck clams, cover, and cook until clams open, 5 to 8 minutes. Remove clams. Lower heat, mix in ½ cup plain yogurt, and pour over clams.

Ginger Soy Clams

Sauté ¼ clove minced garlic, 1 teaspoon chopped fresh gingerroot and a pinch of crushed red pepper flakes in 1 tablespoon Oriental sesame oil for 1 minute. Add 1 tablespoon soy sauce, ¼ cup dry sherry, ¼ cup water, and a pinch of sugar. Add 2 dozen scrubbed littleneck clams. Cover, and cook until clams open, 5 to 8 minutes. Remove clams. Boil pan liquid for 1 minute, and pour over clams.

Hoisin Clams

Sauté ¼ clove minced garlic, 1 teaspoon minced fresh gingerroot, and a pinch of crushed red pepper flakes in 1 tablespoon peanut oil for 1 minute. Add 1½ tablespoons hoisin sauce and ¼ cup chicken stock and bring to a simmer. Add 2 dozen scrubbed littleneck clams, cover, and cook until clams open, 5 to 8 minutes. Remove clams. Boil pan liquid for 1 minute and pour over clams.

Spicy Black Bean Clams

Follow preceding recipe, substituting ¼ cup garlic black bean sauce and 1 teaspoon chili paste for the hoisin sauce. Omit the crushed red pepper flakes.

Barbecue Steamed Clams

Brown 1 tablespoon minced onion and a pinch of sugar in 1 tablespoon vegetable oil. Add 1 table-spoon cider vinegar, ¼ cup ketchup, 1 teaspoon brown mustard, and 1 teaspoon Worcestershire sauce, bring to a boil, and season with hot pepper sauce. Add 2 dozen scrubbed littleneck clams, cover, and cook until clams open, 5 to 8 minutes. Remove clams. Boil pan liquid for 1 minute and pour over clams.

Tex-Mex Clams

Cook 1 cup chopped onion, 2 finely chopped chili peppers, and 1 clove minced garlic in 1 tablespoon corn oil until softened. Add 2 tablespoons chili powder, 2 teaspoons ground cumin, and 1 tea-spoon ground coriander and cook 1 minute more. Add 1 tablespoon tomato paste and ¼ cup beer and bring to a boil. Add 2 dozen scrubbed little-neck clams, cover, and cook until clams open, 5 to 8 minutes. Remove clams. Boil pan liquid for 1 minute and pour over clams.

Puerto Rican Clams

In a food processor, finely chop 1½ cups chopped onion, 2 diced bell peppers, 3 cloves finely chopped garlic, and 2 tablespoons cilantro. Cook in 3 tablespoons olive oil for 10 minutes. Add 1 cup finely diced ham, 2 cups chopped tomato, salt, and pepper and simmer 20 to 30 minutes. Add 2 dozen scrubbed littleneck clams, cover, and cook until clams open, 5 to 8 minutes. Remove clams. Boil pan liquid for 1 minute and pour over clams.

Mussels Niçoise

Cook 3 cloves chopped garlic, 2 tablespoons minced onion, and 1 teaspoon *herbes de Provence* in 2 tablespoons olive oil until vegetables soften. Add ½ cup dry vermouth and cook until reduced to 3 tablespoons. Add 4 skinned and finely chopped large plum tomatoes and 12 pitted black olives and bring to a boil. Add 36 scrubbed and debearded mussels, cover, and cook for 3 to 5 minutes, until the mussels open. Stir in 1 tablespoon chopped fresh basil.

Portuguese Mussel Stew

Cook the thinly sliced whites of 2 leeks and 2 cloves minced garlic in 3 tablespoons olive oil until soft. Add 1 cup white wine, and boil for 4 minutes. Add the juice of ½ lemon and 1½ cups chopped tomato and cook until the tomato starts to release its liquid. Add 4 dozen large scrubbed and de-bearded mussels, cover, and cook until mussels open, 3 to 5 minutes. Stir in ½ cup chopped basil leaves and 2 tablespoons grated Parmesan.

Mussels Marseille

Cook 1 finely chopped onion, 2 cloves minced garlic, 1 diced bell pepper, 1 teaspoon dried basil, 1 teaspoon finely chopped orange zest, and ¼ tea-spoon ground fennel seed in 2 tablespoons olive oil until vegetables soften. Season with salt and pepper, add 4 chopped canned plum tomatoes, ¼ cup orange juice, and 1 bay leaf, and simmer for 5 minutes. Add 3 dozen scrubbed and debearded large mussels, cover, and cook until the mussels open, 3 to 5 minutes. Stir in 1 tablespoon chopped fresh flat-leaf parsley.

Oysters on the Half Shell with Jalapeño Cocktail Sauce

In a food processor, finely chop 1 large clove garlic, 3 to 4 stemmed, seeded pickled jalapeño peppers, and 2 stemmed tomatoes. Mix with ⅓ cup ketchup and 1 tablespoon lemon juice. Open 2 dozen oysters and place oysters on half shells on a bed of thinly sliced lettuce or other greens. Top each oyster with a portion of sauce and garnish with lemon wedges.

Oysters Florentine

Open 2 dozen oysters and place oysters on half shells on a broiling pan lined with a layer of rock salt. Cook the minced white of 1 leek in 2 tablespoons butter until soft. Add 20 ounces defrosted frozen chopped spinach and cook until dry. Add ½ cup heavy cream and simmer 3 minutes. Add 2 tablespoons grated Parmesan, salt, pepper, and a pinch of grated nutmeg. Top each oyster with a portion of spinach and 1 tablespoon shredded Gruyère cheese. Bake at 450°F. for 10 minutes, then brown under a broiler.

Oyster-Stuffed Mushroom Caps

Brown caps from 24 large mushrooms in 2 tablespoons olive oil and set aside. Chop stems and brown in the oil with 2 cloves minced garlic and 2 tablespoons chopped scallion. Mix in ¾ cup bread crumbs and 3 tablespoons grated Parmesan and let

cool. Place 1 shucked oyster in each mushroom cap and pack some of the bread-crumb mixture on top. Bake at 400°F. for 10 minutes, then brown under a broiler.

Oyster Stew

Combine 1 quart milk and 2 dozen oysters with their liquor and heat very slowly, stirring occasionally, until oysters plump and curl at their edges. Do not boil. Add salt, a pinch of cayenne pepper, 1 tablespoon ground paprika, and 2 to 4 tablespoons butter and heat until butter melts. Serve with oyster crackers.

Poached Oysters in Butter Sauce

Brush 8 slices French bread with ⅓ cup olive oil and rub with 1 split clove garlic. Toast and place 2 slices on each of 4 plates. Combine ¼ cup white wine, 2 tablespoons clam juice, 2 tablespoons white wine vinegar, and 1 minced shallot and bring to a simmer. Add 2 dozen shucked oysters and simmer until oysters plump and their edges start to curl. Remove oysters with slotted spoon, place on the toasts, and keep warm. Reduce pan liquid to 3 tablespoons. Add 1 tablespoon lemon juice and swirl in 6 tablespoons butter over very low heat. Pour over oysters.

Baked Creole Crabmeat

Cook 1½ cups chopped onion and 4 cloves minced garlic in 4 tablespoons butter until soft. Add ½ teaspoon dried thyme, ¼ teaspoon dried oregano, ¼ teaspoon dried chervil, 2 tablespoons chopped fresh parsley, ¼ teaspoon cayenne pepper, ¼ teaspoon black pepper, and ½ teaspoon salt and simmer 1 minute. Add 1 pound cleaned lump crabmeat and heat through. Fold in 5 tablespoons grated Parmesan and turn into a small casserole. Top with ¼ cup seasoned bread crumbs mixed with 2 tablespoons grated Parmesan. Bake at 375°F. for 20 to 25 minutes, until browned and bubbly.

Fried Oysters with Tartar Sauce

Dust 2 dozen chilled shucked oysters in flour, dip in 2 beaten eggs, and dredge in 2 cups seasoned bread crumbs. Dry on a rack for 5 minutes. Deep-fry at 375°F. until browned, about 2 to 3 minutes and serve with a mixture of 1 cup mayonnaise, 1 teaspoon hot pepper sauce, 1 tablespoon lemon juice, and ¼ cup chopped pickle.

Fried Clam Sandwich

Follow preceding recipe using topneck clams instead of oysters. Serve 6 clams on each of 4 large soft rolls spread with the tartar sauce and topped with chopped lettuce and tomato.

Sautéed Softshell Crabs with Lime Mayonnaise

Mix 2 cups mayonnaise, the finely grated zest of 1 lime, the juice of 2 limes, 3 tablespoons minced onion, 1 clove minced garlic, and ½ teaspoon hot pepper sauce. Dredge 8 trimmed softshell crabs in flour seasoned with salt and pepper and brush with ¾ cup of the mayonnaise. Dredge well in 2 cups bread crumbs. Let rest on a rack for 10 minutes. Brown in 2 batches in a mixture of ¼ cup *each* hot peanut oil and clarified butter for 3 to 4 minutes per side. Serve with remaining mayonnaise.

Grilled Softshells

Marinate in the refrigerator 8 trimmed softshell crabs in 1 cup Italian dressing for 1 hour. Remove and grill 4 minutes per side, basting frequently with marinade.

Softshell Crab Sandwich

Prepare crabs according to either of the two preceding recipes. Serve each on 1 split kaiser roll spread with the lime mayonnaise or Italian dressing, 1 Romaine leaf, 3 slices cucumber, and 1 large slice ripe tomato. Omit tomato if ripe ones are unavailable.

Marinated Softshell Crab

Dredge 8 trimmed softshell crabs in flour seasoned with salt and pepper. Brown on both sides in ¼ cup olive oil. Add 4 cloves sliced garlic, the sliced white parts of 1 bunch scallions, and ¼ cup dry white wine and bring to a boil. Remove from heat and stir in juice of 1 large lemon, a pinch of cayenne pepper, salt, and pepper. Store in refrigerator for up to 3 days. Serve chilled.

Crab and Caviar Custard

Scald 1 cup light cream with 1½ cups milk. Mix into 4 eggs beaten with 2 yolks, salt, white pepper, and a pinch *each* of cayenne pepper and grated nutmeg. Scatter ½ pound cleaned backfin crabmeat on the bottom of a well-greased 10-inch ovenproof glass pie plate and pour the liquid over top. Place in a larger pan of water and bake at 350°F. for 1 hour, until a tester comes out almost clean. Let cool for 20 minutes. Run a knife around the edge and invert on large tray. Garnish top with 2 ounces salmon caviar. Serve in wedges.

Crab and Avocado Salad

Whisk together ¼ cup chili sauce, 1 tablespoon minced onion, ½ teaspoon hot pepper sauce, ½ cup mayonnaise, 2 tablespoons sour cream, salt, and pepper. Toss in 1 pound cleaned lump crabmeat. Mound into 4 avocado halves and serve with 4 lemon wedges.

Quick Crab Chowder

Cook 4 chopped slices bacon until crisp. Remove bacon and reserve for another use. Add 1 finely chopped onion to the hot fat and cook until soft. Add 1 clove minced garlic, 2 ribs sliced celery, ½ diced red bell pepper, and ½ pound peeled and diced red-skin potatoes and toss together. Add 2 cups clam juice, salt, pepper, and a pinch *each* of grated nutmeg and cayenne pepper and cook until potatoes are tender, about 15 minutes. Add 1 pound cleaned lump crabmeat and 3 cups milk. Adjust seasoning and heat through.

Italian Seafood Sandwich

Bring to a boil 6 tablespoons *each* olive oil and red wine vinegar, ½ teaspoon *each* dried oregano, dill, thyme, and basil, 1 dried chili pepper, salt, and pepper. Add ½ pound cleaned medium shrimp and return to a boil. Add ½ pound bay scallops and remove from heat. Cover for 5 minutes. Add ½ pound cleaned lump crabmeat, ¼ cup chopped fresh parsley, and ½ thinly sliced red onion. Heat 4 split torpedo rolls at 400°F. for 10 minutes. Place ½ cup shredded Romaine in each roll. Top with a

quarter of the seafood mixture, and moisten with some of the liquid.

Squid Salad

Slice tentacles and sacs of 1 pound cleaned squid in ¼-inch slices. Simmer in salted water until opaque, about 30 to 60 seconds, drain, and let cool. Toss with 2 large diced tomatoes, 24 pitted black olives, and ¼ cup finely chopped red onion. Dress with a sauce made by whisking together 1 clove minced garlic, 1 chopped scallion, ¼ teaspoon dried oregano, ¼ cup lemon juice, ¼ teaspoon crushed red pepper flakes, salt, pepper, 1 tablespoon chopped fresh parsley, and ½ cup olive oil. Chill. Serve on bed of Romaine leaves accompanied by pita triangles.

Calamari with Potatoes and Tomatoes

Slice sacs of 2 pounds cleaned squid into 1-inch rings. Cut tentacles in 1-inch pieces. Cook 1 cup chopped onion, ½ cup diced green pepper, ½ cup diced red pepper, and 1 clove minced garlic in 2 tablespoons olive oil until vegetables soften. Add squid and cook until opaque, about 30 to 60 seconds. Add ¼ teaspoon *each* dried marjoram and oregano. Add 1 pound sliced red-skin potatoes and toss. Add 2 cups chopped canned plum tomatoes, salt, pepper, and a large pinch of crushed red pepper flakes, cover and simmer until potatoes are tender, about 45 minutes. Add ¼ cup chopped fresh basil.

Fifty Recipes for Rice and Other Grains

Grain is basic to every cuisine on earth: rice in Asia, millet in Africa, bulgur in the Middle East, semolina in Italy, masa in Mexico, barley in Scotland, and a humble slice of wheat bread practically anywhere. Grain is also basic to nutrition, providing necessary fiber, protein, and B vitamins with hardly a trace of fat, and is basic to world agriculture, forming the great bulk of all edible crops.

Yet in America, whole grains are blatantly missing from our diets, and grain cookery remains a mystery. Though doctors and nutritionists chide us to eat more whole grains, few have much advice about how to do it.

The way to proceed is one step at a time—especially if your repertoire begins and ends with instant rice.

If that's the case, longer-cooking rices, which give better nutrition and more flavor, would make a good second step. Long-grain rice takes only 15 to 20 untended minutes to prepare and, so long as you don't stir it, there is little danger that it will get sticky. Use chicken broth in place of water or add soy sauce, onion, or garlic to the liquid for more flavor with no more work.

After that, try an aromatic rice, such as Basmati or Jasmine, which have a redolent floral perfume that makes them flavorful even when cooked in water alone. They still need only 15 minutes to cook. The difference is that if imported, these rices need rinsing to remove surface debris. Rinse rice in a strainer and run it under cold water until the water coming through the strainer runs clear.

The technique for making pilaf is another way to ensure grains that aren't stuck together. With pilafs, the raw rice is tossed with oil or melted butter to coat each grain. The coating keeps the grains of rice from clinging to one another as they soften, resulting in exceptionally fluffy, and separate, rice grains.

Once you have mastered white rice pilaf, try the same technique with brown or wild rices. These take longer to cook, but they provide added nutrition and a rich nutty flavor that white rice can't match.

Next, try risotto, the exquisitely creamy rice concoction from Venice and Milan, and then try less conventional grains, such as millet, bulgur, barley, cornmeal, buckwheat, or sorghum.

One of the newest grains to hit the American market is an ancient South American species called qui-noa (pronounced *keen-WAH*), a small round seed that resembles a pale lentil. Quinoa cooks in less than 15 minutes, during which time it doubles in size and sprouts a tiny curled thread. This unique appearance, along with its high protein content and delicate flavor, makes it one of the most interesting new ingredients at market. Though more and more supermarkets have begun to enlarge their selection of whole grains, you still might have trouble finding it there. Health-food stores, though, are a good source—they tend to have a quick turnover, thus usually providing a fresh product.

Grains can be kept in bulk up to a year under refrigeration or for several months tightly covered in a cool dark cupboard. Avoid exposing grains to light, which can destroy some of their B vitamins, and keep them away from heat and humidity, which cause grains to ferment.

ABOUT THESE RECIPES

The following recipes serve 4 to 6 portions unless otherwise noted.

 ### Simple Rice Pilaf

Cook ¼ cup finely chopped onion in 1 tablespoon butter until soft. Add 1 cup long-grain white rice and stir until the grains are well coated with butter. Add 2 cups chicken broth, salt, and pepper. Bring to a boil, reduce heat, cover, and simmer 15 to 20 minutes, until all the liquid has been absorbed. Do not stir rice when checking for doneness. Remove from heat and let rest 10 minutes. Fluff with fork and adjust seasoning.

 ### Curried Rice Pilaf

Follow preceding recipe, adding 1-inch piece cin-namon, ½ teaspoon curry powder, ¼ teaspoon

ground cumin, a pinch of ground cloves, and ¼ teaspoon ground pepper to the onions.

 ### Black Pepper Pilaf

Follow recipe for Simple Rice Pilaf (above), adding 2 teaspoons coarsely ground black pepper and 1 bay leaf with the onion. Toss 1 tablespoon lemon juice with the rice while fluffing. Remove bay leaf.

 ### Rice Pilaf with Walnuts

Follow recipe for Simple Rice Pilaf (above). While rice is cooking, toast ⅓ cup chopped walnuts in 1 tablespoon walnut oil. Toss with the cooked rice.

 ### Sweet Curried Rice with Pistachio

Cook ¼ cup finely chopped onion, 1-inch piece cinnamon, ½ teaspoon curry powder, a pinch of ground cloves, and ¼ teaspoon ground cardamom in 1 tablespoon butter until onion softens. Add 1 cup long-grain white rice and stir until grains are well coated with butter. Add 2 cups water, salt, and pepper. Bring to a boil, reduce heat, cover, and simmer 15 to 20 minutes, until all the liquid has been absorbed. Do not stir when checking for doneness. Remove from heat and let rest 10 minutes. While rice is cooking, sauté ¼ cup chopped raisins and ¼ cup chopped pistachios in 2 table-spoons peanut oil until raisins are plump and nuts are toasted. Add 2 tablespoons sugar. Toss with the cooked rice. Remove cinnamon.

 ### Low-Sodium Rice Pilaf

Cook ⅓ cup chopped onion, 1 rib chopped celery, 1 clove minced garlic, and 1 teaspoon finely chopped hot fresh pepper in 2 teaspoons Oriental sesame oil until onion softens. Add 1 cup long-grain white rice and toss to coat with oil. Add 1 bay leaf, ¼ cup toasted sliced almonds, and 2 cups low-sodium chicken stock. Bring to a boil, reduce heat, cover, and simmer 15 to 20 minutes, until all the liquid has been absorbed. Do not stir rice when checking for doneness. Remove from heat and let rest 10 minutes. Add 1 teaspoon additional Oriental sesame oil, fluff rice with fork, and adjust seasoning. Remove bay leaf.

 Rice and Split-Pea Pilaf

Simmer ½ cup soaked split peas in 3 cups boiling salted water for 20 minutes and drain. Cook ¼ cup finely chopped onion, 1 teaspoon curry powder, ½ teaspoon ground cumin, and ½ teaspoon coarsely ground pepper in 1 tablespoon butter until onion softens. Add 1 cup long-grain white rice and stir until grains are well coated with butter. Add the parcooked peas, 4 cups water, salt, and pepper. Bring to a boil, reduce heat, cover, and simmer 20 minutes, until all the liquid has been absorbed. Do not stir rice when checking for doneness. Remove from heat and let rest 10 minutes. Fluff with fork and adjust seasoning.

 Wild Rice Pilaf

Rinse 1 cup wild rice in several changes of cold water and drain well. Cook ½ cup finely chopped onion and ⅓ cup finely diced mushroom in 2 tablespoons butter until soft. Add rice and coat with the butter. Add 4 cups beef stock and salt. Bring to a boil, reduce heat, and simmer, covered, 45 to 60 minutes, until rice grains burst. Remove from heat and let rest 10 minutes. Fluff with a fork and stir in 1 to 2 tablespoons chopped fresh parsley.

 Brown Rice Pilaf

Rinse 1 cup long-grain brown rice in several changes of cold water and drain well. Cook ½ cup finely chopped onion and ⅓ cup finely diced mushroom in 2 tablespoons butter until soft. Add rice and coat with the butter. Add 3 cups water or chicken stock and salt to taste. Bring to a boil, reduce heat, and simmer, covered, 45 minutes. Remove from heat and let rest 10 minutes. Fluff with a fork and stir in 1 to 2 tablespoons chopped fresh parsley.

 Brown Rice with Wheat Berries

Follow preceding recipe, substituting ¼ cup whole-wheat berries for ¼ cup of the rice.

 Brown Rice with Toasted Coconut

Follow recipe for Brown Rice Pilaf (above), replacing mushrooms with 1 cup shredded coconut and cooking until onions and coconut are both browned, watching coconut carefully to avoid burning. Add 1 cup shredded carrots and 1 tablespoon orange juice with the rice.

 Brown Rice and Vegetable Pilaf

Follow recipe for Brown Rice Pilaf (above). Sauté 1 cup vegetables (peas, corn, or diced zucchini, celery, eggplant, carrot, red pepper, or green beans) in 2 tablespoons butter until soft. Add to the rice during the last 15 minutes of cooking, but do not mix together until rice is fluffed.

 Confetti Brown Rice

Rinse 1 cup long-grain brown rice in several changes of cold water. Bring 3 cups water, ¼ cup minced onion, 1 tablespoon currants, ½ teaspoon curry powder, 1½ teaspoons soy sauce, ½ teaspoon salt, and the rice to a boil. Reduce heat, cover, and simmer about 40 minutes. Set aside to rest 5 minutes while you sauté 2 tablespoons *each* finely chopped scallions, green peppers, and tomatoes in 1 tablespoon oil for 1 minute. Toss with rice along with 2 tablespoons sliced toasted almonds and 1 tablespoon chopped fresh parsley.

 Dirty Rice

Brown ½ pound *each* finely chopped chicken giblets and livers, 1 cup chopped onion, 1 finely diced bell pepper, and ½ cup chopped celery in 3 tablespoons oil. Season with salt and pepper, add 1 cup long-grain rice, and toss. Add 2½ cups hot chicken stock, bring to a boil, cover, reduce heat, and simmer 30 minutes until all the liquid has been absorbed. Fluff the rice.

 Basmati Rice

Rinse 1 cup Basmati rice in several changes of cold water until water is clear. Bring 1¾ cups salted water to a boil. Stir in the washed rice, cover tightly, reduce heat, and simmer over low heat 15 minutes, until all the water has been absorbed. Remove from heat and let rest 5 minutes. Fluff with a fork, mixing in 2 tablespoons butter.

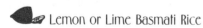 Lemon or Lime Basmati Rice

Follow preceding recipe. While cooked rice is resting, toast ½ cup pine nuts in 1 tablespoon butter with ½ teaspoon curry powder. Toss with the cooked rice along with 2 tablespoons fresh lemon or lime juice.

 Fragrant Basmati Rice

Rinse 1 cup Basmati rice in several changes of cold water until water is clear. Cook ¼ cup finely chopped onion in 1 tablespoon butter until soft with 1-inch piece cinnamon, ½ teaspoon curry powder, ¼ teaspoon ground cumin, a pinch of ground clove, and ¼ teaspoon pepper. Add rice and stir until grains are coated with butter. Add 1¾ cups chicken broth, 1 teaspoon lemon juice, salt, and pepper. Bring to a boil, reduce heat, cover, and simmer 15 minutes, until all the liquid has been absorbed. Remove from heat and let rest 5 minutes. Fluff with fork as you add 2 tablespoons chopped fresh cilantro. Remove cinnamon.

 Risotto

Cook ¼ cup finely chopped onion in 2 tablespoons olive oil until soft. Add 1 cup Arborio rice and toss with oil. Add ½ cup white wine and, stirring with a wooden spoon, cook over moderate heat until wine has been absorbed. Add 4½ cups chicken broth to the rice, ½ cup at a time, stirring and waiting for each addition to be absorbed before adding the next. Simmer until rice is *al dente* and a creamy sauce has developed throughout the rice. Stir in ¼ cup grated imported Parmesan and 1 tablespoon butter.

 Risotto Milanese

Follow preceding recipe, but soften 1 teaspoon saffron threads in wine for 10 minutes before adding it.

 Spinach Risotto

Cook 10 ounces frozen chopped spinach in 3 tablespoons olive oil with ¼ cup chopped onion until spinach is completely defrosted. Add 1 clove minced garlic and cook until almost dry. Set aside. Follow recipe for Risotto (opposite), adding spinach mixture with last addition of stock.

Risotto with Mushrooms and Chicken Livers

Follow recipe for Risotto (opposite), browning 1 cup finely chopped onion and 2 cloves minced garlic in the olive oil. While rice is cooking, sauté ¼ pound sliced mushrooms with 1 pound trimmed and quartered chicken livers in 2 tablespoons olive oil. Toss with the rice when you add the Parmesan.

Risotto with Rosemary

Follow recipe for Risotto (opposite), adding 2 teaspoons crumbled dried rosemary, 1 teaspoon dried thyme, and 1 bay leaf with the onion. Add ½ clove minced garlic with the Parmesan. Remove bay leaf.

Apple Raisin Risotto Pudding

Cook 1 large peeled and diced apple in 4 tablespoons butter until soft. Add 1 cup Arborio rice and toss to coat. Add ½ cup brandy and simmer until absorbed. Add ½ cup apple cider, stirring constantly until absorbed. Repeat with another ½ cup cider. Add 1-inch piece cinnamon, 1 tablespoon finely grated orange zest, and 2 tablespoons sugar. Add 2½ cups milk, ½ cup at a time, in the same way as the cider. Mix 2 egg yolks, ½ cup light cream, and 1 teaspoon vanilla extract. Stir in ½ cup raisins after the last ½ cup of milk is almost absorbed. Remove from heat and stir until mixture is incorporated. Serve warm. Remove bay leaf.

Rice Pudding

Parboil ½ cup long-grain rice in 1 quart salted water for 10 minutes. Drain well. In an ovenproof pan, scald 1 quart milk, add rice, and bring to a gentle boil. Add ½ cup granulated sugar, 1 teaspoon butter, 2 teaspoons finely grated orange rind, ½ cup raisins, and 1 vanilla bean. Cover and bake at 350°F. 1 hour, stirring occasionally. Combine 2 eggs with ½ cup light cream and mix into pudding. Bake another 15 minutes, covered. Remove vanilla bean. Pour in individual dishes and chill.

Brown Rice Pudding

Follow preceding recipe using brown rice in place of long-grain rice and light brown sugar instead of granulated. Parboil rice for 25 minutes.

Stir-Fried Rice

Stir-fry ¼ cup finely chopped onion, 1 rib diced celery, and ½ diced red bell pepper in 1 tablespoon peanut oil. Push up the sides of the wok, add another 1 tablespoon oil in the center, and stir-fry 4 ounces chopped shrimp and 4 ounces diced ham for 1 minute. Add 3 cups cooked white rice and stir-fry with the vegetables and meat until rice browns lightly. Add 1 beaten egg, 1 cup bean sprouts, ½ cup shredded fresh spinach, and 2 chopped scallions. Heat through.

Stir-Fried Rice with Spring Vegetables

Follow preceding recipe substituting ½ pound asparagus tips and 1 cup cooked peas for the shrimp and ham. Instead of spinach, use ½ cup finely chopped tomato.

Fifty Recipes for Rice and Other Grains   243

Polenta

Bring 5 cups water and 1½ teaspoons salt to a rapid boil in a large heavy saucepan. Using a sifter, add 1 cup cornmeal very, very slowly to avoid lumping, while stirring constantly. Simmer 20 minutes, stirring occasionally, until mixture is very thick and smooth, and pulls away from the sides of the pan. Mix in 3 tablespoons butter, ¼ cup grated Parmesan, and plenty of freshly ground pepper.

 Fried Polenta with Tomato Sauce

Follow preceding recipe. When polenta is finished, pour into a ½-inch-thick layer on a sheet pan and chill until set. Cut into 2-inch squares or diamonds. Dredge in flour, dip into 1 beaten egg, and coat well with 1 cup bread crumbs. Refrigerate at least 15 minutes. Brown polenta squares in thin film of olive oil over moderately high heat. Blot with paper towels and serve with Quick Fresh Tomato Sauce (page 46).

 Fontina Polenta

Follow recipe for Polenta (above), substituting ⅓ pound shredded Fontina cheese for the Parmesan.

 Polenta with Green Salsa

Follow recipe for Polenta (above), substituting 6 ounces crumbled farmer cheese for the Parmesan. Serve with Spicy Green Tomato Salsa (page 164).

 Buttermilk Spoonbread with Garlic

Place a 6-cup soufflé dish in a preheated 350°F. oven. Mix 1 cup white cornmeal, 3 cloves minced garlic, 1½ cups boiling water, and 1 tablespoon butter until smooth. Mix 1 extra-large egg, 1 cup buttermilk, ½ teaspoon salt, and 1 teaspoon baking soda and beat into the cornmeal. Remove soufflé dish from oven and carefully grease with 1½ teaspoons butter. Pour in batter and bake 1 hour, spooning 2 tablespoons light cream over top every 15 minutes. Serve immediately.

 Mascarpone Spoonbread

Follow preceding recipe, substituting mascarpone cheese for the buttermilk.

 Hominy Grits with Cheese

Add ¾ cup quick-cooking grits in a thin stream to 3 cups simmering salted water, stirring constantly. Simmer 10 minutes until thick and creamy. Season with pepper and stir in ¾ cup shredded Cheddar cheese and 1 tablespoon butter.

 Hominy with Peppers

Cook 1 cup diced green bell pepper, ½ cup diced red bell pepper, and ¼ chopped onion in 4 tablespoons butter until vegetables soften. Season with salt, pepper, and a dash of hot pepper sauce. Follow preceding recipe, adding pepper mixture instead of the cheese and butter.

 Hominy Soufflé

Add ¾ cup quick-cooking grits in a thin stream to 3 cups simmering salted water, stirring constantly. Simmer 10 minutes until thick and creamy. Meanwhile, cook 1 cup diced green bell pepper and 3 sliced scallions in 4 tablespoons butter until softened. Add 1 cup diced baked ham and ½ cup diced pimiento. Beat into the cooked grits along with 3 egg yolks, a dash of hot pepper sauce, ¾ cup shredded Cheddar cheese, salt, and pepper. Whip 5 egg whites to soft peaks. Fold into grits in 3 additions. Pour into a 6-cup greased and crumbed soufflé dish and bake at 400°F. for 20 minutes. Reduce oven to 350° and bake 20 minutes more. Serve immediately.

Kasha with Onion and Dill

Cook ½ cup chopped onion in 2 tablespoons chicken fat or butter and set aside. Beat 1 cup whole or coarsely cracked buckwheat groats with 1 large egg in a heavy skillet until combined. Cook over low heat until egg cooks and kasha grains separate from each other. Add the onions, 2 cups chicken stock, salt, and pepper and simmer, covered, for 15 minutes. Mix in 1 tablespoon minced fresh dill.

Kasha with Tortellini

Follow preceding recipe, substituting fresh parsley for dill and tossing the cooked kasha with 2 cups cooked cheese or spinach tortellini. Serves 6.

Kasha with Wild Mushrooms

Soak 1 ounce dried wild mushrooms in ½ cup boiling water for 30 minutes. Remove mushrooms and squeeze out excess water. Trim stems and slice the larger mushrooms. Strain soaking liquid through a coffee filter. Follow recipe for Kasha with Onion and Dill (above), adding the mushrooms with the onions. Use strained soaking liquid in place of a like amount of chicken stock.

Kasha with Walnuts and Garlic

Follow recipe for Kasha with Onion and Dill (above), adding 1 clove minced garlic with the onion and ½ cup toasted walnut pieces with the dill.

Tabouleh with Lentils

Parboil 1 cup lentils in 1 quart water for 40 minutes, and place in a large bowl. Rinse and drain ¾ cup medium-grain bulgur wheat in several changes of cold water, drain, and combine with the lentils. Bring 1 cup water to a boil with a pinch of ground allspice and ½ teaspoon salt and pour over the bulgur and lentils. Let soak until all the liquid is absorbed. Toss with 1 peeled, seeded, and diced cucumber, 2 cloves minced garlic, 1 cup seeded, diced tomato, and ¼ cup *each* chopped mint leaves, fresh parsley, scallions, lemon juice, and olive oil. Serve on lettuce leaves garnished with lemon wedges.

Quinoa Tabouleh

Rinse 1 cup quinoa in several changes of cold water. Combine in a saucepan with 2 cups water and ¼ teaspoon salt. Bring to a boil, reduce heat and simmer, covered, 12 to 14 minutes until all the water has been absorbed and quinoa is tender. Spread out on a sheet pan to cool. Toss quinoa with ⅓ cup extra-virgin olive oil and 3 tablespoons lemon juice, separating clumps with your fingers. Toss with 6 thinly sliced scallions, 2 tablespoons chopped fresh mint, 1 clove minced garlic, 2 seeded and chopped tomatoes, and 1 peeled, seeded, and diced cucumber.

Quinoa Pilaf

In a heavy saucepan, sauté 2 tablespoons *each* minced onion, diced celery, and diced carrots in 1½ tablespoons peanut oil. Add 1 cup quinoa that has been rinsed in several changes of water and stir until quinoa grains separate. Add 2 cups hot stock, salt, and pepper, bring to a boil, reduce heat, and simmer, covered, about 20 minutes until all the liquid has been absorbed. Fluff with a fork.

Fifty Ways to Cook Most Everything

 Quinoa with Pecans

Follow preceding recipe, adding ¼ cup chopped pecans toasted in 2 tablespoons butter when you fluff the quinoa. Omit the carrots.

 Millet Pilaf with Pistachios and Apricots

In heavy saucepan, sauté ¼ cup *each* minced onion and diced dried apricot in 3 tablespoons peanut oil. Add 1 cup millet and stir until millet is lightly toasted. Add 3 cups hot chicken stock, salt, and pepper, bring to a boil, reduce heat, cover, and simmer 15 minutes until all the liquid has been absorbed. Add ¼ cup toasted and chopped pistachios and fluff with a fork.

 Black Bean and Bulgur Salad with Orange and Pepperoni

Soak 1 cup bulgur wheat in 1¼ cups hot tap water until tender, about 30 minutes. Drain and combine in a large bowl with 2 cups cooked, drained black beans, ½ finely chopped onion, 1 small minced chili pepper, 1 peeled, seeded, and diced cucumber, ¼ pound finely diced pepperoni, and the finely grated zest of 1 large orange. Combine the juice from the orange, ¼ cup cider vinegar, ⅓ cup vegetable oil, salt, and pepper, pour over salad, and let marinate for several hours in the refrigerator.

 Corn Chili Salad

Toss 4 cups cooked corn kernels, 1 pound cooked and drained kidney beans, 1 bunch trimmed and sliced scallion, and 1 diced roasted red pepper (page 442). Mix 3 tablespoons mayonnaise, 2 table-spoons chili powder, 1 tablespoon ground cumin, ⅓ cup corn or peanut oil, and 2 tablespoons hot pepper sauce. Toss with salad along with 1 diced avocado and 2 tablespoons chopped fresh cilantro. Serves 6.

 Succotash Salad

Toss 2 cups *each* cooked corn kernels, lima beans, and diced ham, and ¼ cup minced sweet pickles. Whisk together 6 tablespoons corn oil, ¼ cup cider vinegar, 3 tablespoons light corn syrup, 2 tea-spoons brown mustard, salt, and pepper. Toss with salad.

 Barley Chicken Salad

Simmer 1 cup pearl barley in 6 cups boiling water with ½ teaspoon salt in a covered pot for 40 minutes. Drain. Meanwhile, grill 2 pounds skinless, boneless chicken breast until firm. Dice and toss with the barley, 3 ribs diced celery, and 1 cup chopped walnuts. Whisk together 1 cup mayonnaise, 1 teaspoon mustard, 2 teaspoons dried tarragon, 2 tablespoons tarragon vinegar, salt, and pepper and toss with the salad. Serves 6 to 8.

 Barley and Sausage Soup

Brown 2 cups chopped onion in 4 tablespoons butter. Add ½ cup pearl barley and toss to coat. Add ¼ cup sliced mushrooms, 2 cloves minced garlic, 1 cup chopped tomato, 2 tablespoons *each* fresh dill and chopped parsley, and ¼ pound *each* sliced smoked sausage and diced smoked ham. Add 6 cups water, bring to a boil, cover, reduce heat, and simmer until barley is tender, about 40 minutes. Whisk in ½ cup sour cream and serve.

Fifty Ways to Eat Your Vegetables

There is nothing so gracious as a vegetable. Happy to move aside when meat or fish take center stage, many vegetables never get their due. This is unfortunate, for vegetables comprise the most varied food source available and nothing matches their innate versatility. Especially as side dishes, vegetables round out a meal nutritionally, reinforce or modify the entrée style, and provide the principal source of color on a plate.

Because of their natural good looks and basic sweet flavor, most vegetables practically prepare themselves, as long as you choose the right way to cook them. That choice depends on just two things—the vegetable's fiber content and its color. Hard, tough, high-fiber vegetables, such as beets, carrots, and turnips, are cooked in liquid. Softer, moister vegetables, such as summer squashes, mushrooms, and eggplant, are sautéed, baked, or grilled. If you want to sauté or grill a tough vegetable, first finely chop it to break down its fibers or blanch it in boiling water to soften them.

Maintaining a vegetable's color requires a differ-
ent technique for each pigment. Chlorophyll, the pigment in green vegetables, is destroyed by excessive heat or by exposure to acid, which means green vegetables cannot be marinated, cooked for long periods, or cooked in an acidic liquid, such as wine or lemon. Cooking them in a covered pot will trap the vegetable's natural acids and cause the same problem.

To the contrary, the color of red-pigmented vegetables is enhanced by exposure to acid and destroyed in an alkaline or low-acid environment. So when cooking red cabbage or red peppers, always add a bit of wine or lemon to the mixture or keep the lid on the pot.

White vegetables discolor with long storage or overcooking, both of which allow oxygen to mix with the pigment and turn it gray or brown. That's why mushrooms and cauliflower are best cooked quickly and why potatoes must be cooked as soon as they are peeled.

Orange-colored vegetables, however, are almost impervious to culinary abuse. Nothing short of incineration will destroy their pigment.

Fifty Ways to Cook Most Everything

ABOUT THESE RECIPES

The following 50 vegetable side dishes offer ideas for hot and cold vegetables, stews, sautés, poached and boiled vegetables, and casseroles.

Zucchini, potatoes, tomatoes, and greens make relatively few appearances in this chapter because each gets a chapter on its own. Be sure to look at the four chapters following this one for more vegetable ideas.

The recipes in this chapter are all written for 4 portions. It is assumed that you will add salt and pepper to taste to each recipe.

 Artichokes with Tofu Dressing

Trim 4 artichokes of their stems and thorns and immediately rub cut surfaces with lemon juice or rice wine vinegar. Boil, stem-end down, in several quarts boiling water, acidulated with ¼ cup rice wine vinegar until the stem end can be pierced easily, 30 to 40 minutes. Drain well, stem ends up, in a colander, and serve with Sesame Tofu Vinaigrette (page 298) for dipping.

 Sicilian Artichokes

Trim top and stems from 8 baby artichokes or 8 globe artichokes that have been peeled down to their inner tender leaves; rub cut surfaces with lemon juice. Cook in several quarts boiling water, acidulated with ¼ cup wine vinegar and seasoned with 6 peppercorns, 1 bay leaf, and 2 cloves garlic, until the stem end can be pierced easily, about 30 minutes. Drain and quarter. While artichokes are cooking, cook ½ cup chopped onion and 4 cloves minced garlic in ¼ cup olive oil until soft. Add quartered artichokes and sauté 3 minutes, turning carefully. Add 1 cup chopped tomato, 1 cup chicken broth, the juice of 1 lemon, and a pinch of red pepper flakes and simmer 20 minutes, until artichokes are tender.

 Asparagus with Lemon Oil

Snap tough white ends from the stalks of 1 pound thin to medium asparagus. Simmer the trimmed asparagus in a skillet filled with water seasoned with salt and 3 or 4 peppercorns until bright green. Drain well and serve bathed with ¼ cup extra-virgin olive oil whisked with the juice of 1 lemon and 1 clove minced garlic.

 Asparagus with Tomato Vinaigrette

Follow preceding recipe, but sauce asparagus with Warm Tomato Vinaigrette (page 298) instead of lemon oil.

 Stir-Fried Asparagus with Cashews

Dissolve 2 teaspoons cornstarch in 2 tablespoons light soy sauce, ⅓ cup Chinese oyster sauce, and the juice of ½ lemon. Set aside. Stir-fry 1 pound trimmed asparagus, cut into 2-inch sections, in 2 tablespoons hot peanut oil until bright green. Add a pinch of crushed red pepper flakes and 1 cup chicken stock. Cover wok and steam for 3 minutes. Add cornstarch mixture and toss until sauce thickens. Remove from heat and toss in 1 clove minced garlic, 2 thinly sliced scallions, and 1 cup cashews.

 Honey Baked Beets

Scrub four 8-ounce beets and trim stem to within 2 inches. Wrap each beet in plastic wrap, place on a dish, and microwave at full power for 15 to 18 minutes. Cook for several minutes, remove plastic, cut off ends of beets, and peel off skins. Quarter each beet and toss in ¼ cup honey and 1 teaspoon lemon juice. Microwave at full power for 1 minute.

Orange Saffron Beets

Peel, trim, and cook beets as in preceding recipe. Cut beets in thin wedges and sauté for 1 minute in 2 tablespoons butter. Add ½ cup orange juice and ¼ teaspoon crumbled saffron threads and cook until liquid reduces to a glaze.

 Braised Fennel

Brown 1 large head fennel, trimmed of leaves and quartered lengthwise, in 2 tablespoons olive oil. Add ¼ cup finely chopped onion, 1 clove minced garlic, and ½ teaspoon crumbled dried rosemary and sauté 1 minute more. Add 2 skinned, seeded, and finely chopped plum tomatoes and ⅔ cup white wine. Bring to a boil, then reduce heat, cover, and simmer for 20 to 25 minutes until fennel is tender.

 Mediterranean Braised Leeks

Follow preceding recipe, using 4 leeks split in half instead of the fennel.

 Braised Lemon Celery

Follow recipe for Braised Fennel (above), using 2 celery hearts split in half instead of the fennel. Substitute ½ cup chicken stock mixed with the juice of ½ lemon for the wine.

 Pearl Onions Stewed with Olives

Brown 1 pint peeled pearl onions in 2 tablespoons olive oil. Add 1 clove minced garlic, ¼ cup chopped and pitted oil-cured black olives, and ¼ cup finely diced red bell pepper. Sauté 1 minute more. Add ½ cup chicken stock and simmer until onions are tender, about 25 minutes. Finish with 2 tablespoons chopped fresh parsley.

 Broccoli with Apples and Bacon

Blanch 1 bunch broccoli florets until bright green. Cook ¼ cup chopped onion in rendered fat of 2 slices bacon until soft along with 1 peeled, cored, and diced green apple. Add broccoli and toss until heated through. Finish with 1 teaspoon lemon juice and 2 crumbled slices bacon.

 Broccoli with Cider and Rosemary

Reduce ½ cup apple cider to 2 tablespoons and set aside. Blanch 1 bunch broccoli florets until bright green. Cook ¼ cup chopped onion in 1 tablespoon vegetable oil until soft along with 1 teaspoon crumbled fresh rosemary. Add broccoli and toss until heated through. Finish with 1 teaspoon lemon juice and reduced cider.

 Broccoli with Walnuts

Cook 1 clove minced garlic in 1 tablespoon walnut oil until soft. Blanch 1 bunch broccoli florets until bright green, and toss with oil, garlic, and ⅓ cup toasted chopped walnuts.

 Carrots with Green Peppercorns

Poach 1 pound peeled and diagonally cut carrots until *al dente* in 2 cups boiling water, 3 tablespoons honey, and 1 tablespoon lemon juice for about 8 minutes. Drain and rewarm carrots in 1 tablespoon butter heated with 2 teaspoons drained green peppercorns. Finish with 1 teaspoon chopped fresh parsley.

Fifty Ways to Cook Most Everything

 Carrots and Red Peppers

Sauté 1 minced shallot in 1 tablespoon olive oil for 30 seconds. Add 1 cup *each* finely julienned carrots and red pepper, sauté 2 minutes, add the juice of ½ lemon and 2 tablespoons chicken broth, and simmer 2 minutes, until carrots are barely soft. Finish with 1 tablespoon chopped fresh parsley.

 Carrots, Parsnips, and Chives

Sauté 1 minced shallot in 1 tablespoon olive oil for 30 seconds. Add 1 cup *each* finely julienned carrots and parsnips. Sauté 2 minutes. Add the juice of ½ lemon, and 2 tablespoons chicken broth. Simmer for 4 to 5 minutes, until carrot is barely soft. Finish with 1 tablespoon chopped fresh chives.

 Cauliflower in Mustard Cream

Blanch ½ head cauliflower florets and refresh under cold water. Cook 1 tablespoon chopped onion in 1 tablespoon butter until soft. Add 1 cup light cream and 1 tablespoon mustard and reduce to half its volume. Add cauliflower and warm through. Season with salt and white pepper.

 Curried Cauliflower

Blanch ½ head cauliflower florets and refresh under cold water. Toast 1 tablespoon black mustard seeds in 1 tablespoon clarified butter for 10 seconds. Add 1 cup chopped onion, 1 tablespoon curry powder, 1 teaspoon ground cardamom, 1 teaspoon ground coriander, and 1½ teaspoons ground cumin and cook until onion has softened. Add 1 cup light cream and reduce to half its volume. Add cauliflower and warm through. Season with salt and white pepper.

 Cauliflower with Capers

Blanch ½ head cauliflower florets and refresh under cold water. Combine ¼ cup mayonnaise, 1 teaspoon heavy cream, 2 teaspoons lemon juice, a dash hot pepper sauce, and 1 teaspoon drained nonpareil capers. Toss with cauliflower.

 Indian Braised Vegetables

Cook 1 finely chopped onion in 1 tablespoon vegetable oil until soft with 2 teaspoons finely chopped fresh gingerroot, ½ clove minced garlic, 1 teaspoon ground coriander, 1 teaspoon ground cumin, 2 teaspoons curry powder, and a pinch of crushed red pepper flakes. Season with 1 tablespoon lemon juice and ¼ cup chopped fresh cilantro. Set aside. (This paste can be stored indefinitely in the refrigerator.) Before serving, toast 1 teaspoon black mustard seeds in 1 tablespoon vegetable oil until seeds turn gray. Add 1 cup *each* broccoli and cauliflower florets, ½ cup sliced carrots, and 1 cup sliced green beans. Stirring frequently, cook vegetables over moderately high heat in a covered pot until they are just tender, about 5 minutes. Add ¼ cup water, cover, and cook another 3 minutes. Uncover, add reserved onion-spice mixture, and stir to blend.

 Broiled Corn with Roasted Garlic Butter

Roast 2 large heads garlic at 350°F. for 40 minutes, until soft. Slice off points of garlic cloves and squeeze the soft flesh from skins into ¼ pound softened butter. Rub 8 ears shucked corn with thin film olive oil and broil 2 inches per side for a total of 8 minutes. Serve with the garlic butter.

 Corn with Red Pepper Coulis

Boil 8 ears shucked corn for 3 minutes, and serve with Red Pepper Coulis (page 25).

Corn on the Cob with Paprika Butter

Grill 8 ears unshucked corn over hot charcoal fire for about 15 minutes, turning regularly, until husks are uniformly browned and corn is steamed inside (peek under husk of 1 ear). Husk the corn and serve with ¼ pound softened butter beaten with ¼ cup paprika, ½ teaspoon lemon juice, and ¼ teaspoon freshly ground pepper.

 Chilied Corn and Peanuts

Cook 1 tablespoon chopped onion and ¼ clove minced garlic in 1 tablespoon corn oil until soft. Add 4 cups corn kernels removed from the cobs, 1 tablespoon chili powder, 1 sliced scallion, ½ teaspoon chili paste, 1 teaspoon soy sauce, 1 teaspoon finely chopped fresh gingerroot, a pinch of ground cumin, and a pinch of ground coriander. Cook 4 to 5 minutes until corn is tender. Stir in 2 tablespoons peanut butter and 3 to 4 tablespoons chicken stock, stirring until peanut butter melts and liquid thickens to a light saucelike consistency.

 Corn and Smoked Salmon

Sauté 1 tablespoon chopped shallot and 2 teaspoons chopped fresh dill in 1 tablespoon olive oil. Add 4 cups cooked corn kernels and heat through. Finish with 2 ounces finely chopped smoked salmon.

Grilled Mediterranean Finger Eggplant

Cut each of 10 finger eggplants into 4 lengthwise slices. Brush slices with a thin film of olive oil taken from ⅓ cup and grill until softened. Brush 2 sliced tomatoes with more of the oil and grill for 2 minutes per side. Toss with remaining oil, 2 cloves minced garlic, 2 tablespoons wine vinegar, the juice of 1 lemon, a pinch of crushed red pepper flakes, 2 tablespoons finely chopped basil leaves, 1 tablespoon chopped fresh chives, and 2 tablespoons drained capers.

 Eggplant with Garlic Jam

Simmer 4 cloves peeled garlic, ¾ cup white wine, and 2 teaspoons sugar until liquid turns amber. Puree until smooth and reserve. Lightly brown ¼ cup finely chopped onion in 1 tablespoon olive oil. Add 1 peeled and diced eggplant and sauté for 1 minute. Add 2 cups chicken stock, ¼ cup finely chopped fresh parsley, and pepper, simmering until most of the liquid evaporates. Stir in garlic mixture and adjust seasoning.

 Fennel with Tomatoes and Garlic

Cook ½ cup chopped onion, 1 clove minced garlic, and 2 bulbs trimmed and julienned fennel in 2 tablespoons olive oil until soft. Add 4 chopped, skinned, and seeded plum tomatoes and place in a baking dish. Top with ¼ cup bread crumbs seasoned with ¼ cup grated Parmesan, 1 teaspoon grated lemon zest, and ½ clove minced garlic. Bake in a 375°F. oven for 20 minutes.

 Garlic Green Beans

Blanch 1 pound snapped green beans until bright green and *al dente*. Cook 1 clove minced garlic in 2 teaspoons olive oil until soft and toss garlic with the beans.

 Green Beans with Pine Nuts

Follow preceding recipe, adding 2 tablespoons toasted pine nuts with the garlic.

Fifty Ways to Cook Most Everything

Green Beans in Thyme

Blanch 1 pound snapped green beans until bright green and *al dente*. Cook 1 clove minced garlic and 1 teaspoon dried thyme in 2 teaspoons olive oil until soft. Toss with the beans.

Green Beans Sautéed with Pimiento

Blanch 1 pound snapped green beans until bright green and *al dente*. Cook 1 tablespoon chopped onion, 1 clove minced garlic, and ¼ cup diced pimiento in 2 teaspoons olive oil until soft. Toss with the beans.

Mushrooms Boiled with Lots of Garlic

Break 1 head garlic into cloves and peel. If cloves are very large, cut into ½-inch pieces. Warm garlic with 1 pound cleaned small mushrooms in 2 tablespoons olive oil with a pinch of crushed red pepper flakes, ½ teaspoon dried thyme, and 2 tablespoons chopped fresh parsley until mushrooms have lost their raw look and garlic is aromatic. Add 1½ cups chicken stock and simmer for 12 minutes. Strain out mushrooms and garlic and reduce pan liquid to ¼ cup. Return mushrooms and garlic to pan, and warm through.

Marsala Mushrooms with Pancetta

Render fat from 2 ounces pancetta. Add 1 clove minced garlic, 2 tablespoons chopped onion, and ¼ teaspoon crumbled rosemary leaves and cook for 1 minute, adding up to 2 teaspoons olive oil if there is not enough fat in the pan. Add 1 pound quartered mushrooms and sauté until lightly browned. Deglaze with 2 tablespoons marsala wine and 1 teaspoon lemon juice. Sprinkle crumbled pancetta over mushrooms.

Parslied Mushrooms

Cook 2 tablespoons chopped onion and 1 clove minced garlic in 2 tablespoons olive oil until soft. Add 1 pound sliced mushrooms, and brown lightly. Add ¼ cup chopped fresh parsley.

Mushrooms in Balsamic Glaze

Follow preceding recipe. After removing mushrooms, deglaze pan with 1 tablespoon balsamic vinegar and pour over mushrooms.

Mushrooms in Tomato Broth

Cook ¼ cup chopped onion and 1 rib chopped celery in 2 tablespoons olive oil until soft. Add 1 pound small whole mushrooms to the pan along with ¼ teaspoon dried thyme, ½ teaspoon dried basil, and 1 bay leaf and cook until mushrooms lose their raw look. Add 3 chopped tomatoes and ½ cup chicken stock. Simmer for 10 minutes. Lift solids from broth to a warm platter, reduce pan liquid to a glaze, and pour over mushrooms. Remove bay leaf.

Creamed Parsnips

Cook 1 tablespoon onion in 1 tablespoon butter until soft. Add 1 pound chopped parsnips and ½ cup water, simmering until parsnips are tender. Add more water if needed. Drain well, and puree until smooth with dash each nutmeg and cayenne. Enrich with 1 tablespoon *crème fraîche*, sour cream, or yogurt.

Minted Peas

In a saucepan, toss 1 pound shelled peas with 2 tablespoons chopped onion in 2 tablespoons melted butter until well coated. Add ⅓ cup boiling water, 2 teaspoons sugar, and 2 tablespoons dried mint, cover, and simmer over moderate heat until the peas are tender, 10 to 15 minutes. Uncover and boil off any remaining liquid. Toss with 1 tablespoon butter.

Peas with Brown Shallots

Boil 1 pound shelled peas in plenty of water, seasoned with a pinch of sugar, for 10 to 15 minutes, until tender. Drain well and set aside. Sauté 2 tablespoons chopped shallots in 2 tablespoons butter with a pinch of dried thyme until lightly brown. Deglaze pan with 3 tablespoons white wine, boil off alcohol, and toss with the peas.

Stir-Fried Snow Peas with Minced Shrimp

In a wok or skillet, heat 1 slice fresh gingerroot in 1 tablespoon peanut oil for 1 minute. Remove ginger and add 2 sliced scallions, ⅔ pound stemmed snow peas, and ¼ pound finely chopped cleaned shrimp. Stir-fry 1 minute, or long enough for snow peas to turn bright green and for shrimp to lose their raw look. Remove from heat and season with salt, pepper, 1 clove minced garlic, and 1 teaspoon dry sherry.

Pickled Peppers

Cook ½ cup chopped onion and 2 cloves minced garlic in 1 tablespoon olive oil until soft. Add 4 stemmed and seeded red and/or yellow bell peppers, cut into strips, and sauté until barely softened, about 4 minutes. Add ½ cup Italian dressing or Garlic Herb Dressing (page 296) and simmer for 2 minutes more.

Mélange of Roasted Peppers

Roast 2 red, 2 yellow, and 2 green bell peppers and slice into strips (page 442). Toss with 1 thinly sliced onion and 2 cloves minced garlic and cook in 2 tablespoons olive oil until vegetables soften. Add the juice of 1 lemon, a pinch of crushed red pepper flakes, and ¼ cup freshly chopped parsley.

Hash of Ham, Peppers, and Peppercorns

Lightly brown 1 chopped onion in 1 tablespoon vegetable oil. Add ½ pound finely diced ham, 2 stemmed and seeded finely diced bell peppers, and 1 tablespoon drained green peppercorns. Cook until peppers soften, about 5 minutes.

Broiled Peppers with Anchovies

Roast 4 bell peppers and slice into strips (page 442). Toss with 1 clove minced garlic, 6 julienned anchovies, 1 tablespoon of the anchovy oil, a pinch of crushed red pepper flakes, and 1 teaspoon wine vinegar.

Acorn Squash with Gingered Applesauce

Halve 2 acorn squash at their equators, remove seeds and fibers, and rub interiors with 1 tablespoon minced fresh gingerroot. Brush with mixture of ¼ cup applesauce, 2 tablespoons honey, 1 teaspoon lemon juice, and a dash of salt and pepper. Dot each half with ½ teaspoon butter and bake, covered, in 1 inch water in a 350°F. preheated oven for about 1 hour, until squash can be pierced easily with a fork.

Acorn Squash with Orange Molasses

Cut and clean 2 acorn squash as described in previous recipe and rub interiors with 1 clove minced garlic. Brush with a mixture of 2 tablespoons light molasses, 2 tablespoons honey, 1 teaspoon balsamic vinegar, 1 tablespoon orange juice, and a dash of salt and pepper. Dot each half with ½ teaspoon butter and bake, covered, in 1 inch water in a 350°F. preheated oven for 1 hour, until squash can be pierced easily with a fork.

Acorn Squash with Spiced Honey

Cut and clean 2 acorn squash as described in recipe for Acorn Squash with Gingered Applesauce (page 253), and brush with mixture of ⅛ teaspoon cayenne pepper, ½ teaspoon ground cinnamon, ½ teaspoon ground ginger, ⅛ teaspoon ground allspice, 1 tablespoon lemon juice, and ⅓ cup honey. Dot each half with ½ teaspoon butter and bake, covered, in 1 inch water in a 350°F. preheated oven for 1 hour, until squash can be pierced easily with a fork.

Crookneck Squash Parmesan

Cook 1 thinly sliced small red onion and 1 clove minced garlic in 2 tablespoons olive oil until soft. Add 4 cups sliced yellow crookneck squash and sauté until tender, about 4 minutes. Remove from heat and toss with ¼ cup grated Parmesan and 1 tablespoon chopped fresh parsley.

Fifty Ways to Rediscover Potatoes

Potatoes tend to go without notice—barely visible through a smokescreen of country ham, the sidekick to a steak, the filler in corned-beef hash. The fact that they're such an afterthought is a deficiency with us, not with the spud, for there is no other food that moves with such flawless grace from dish to dish and meal to meal.

Potatoes are cheap, plentiful, and effortless to prepare, yet most of us never take advantage of their potential. Ignoring an international arsenal of potato recipes, we dig the rut of our cooking routines deeper by mindlessly repeating the same baked- and boiled-potato dishes year after year.

The following 50 recipes are designed to help you out of the spud rut with style, rewarding flavor combinations, and ease. They include baked, fried, sautéed, roasted, and casseroled potatoes. Although a few recipes for sweet and red-skin potatoes are included, most call for russet potatoes.

Russet potatoes are known by several different names, including baking potatoes and Idaho potatoes. Look for russets with thick rough skins and a well-formed oblong shape. Avoid potatoes with soft spots, deep pits, and bruises. Sprouting indicates age and is often accompanied by a softening of the potato. A green tinge to the skin of a potato comes from the alkaloid solanine, produced when a potato is exposed to light for extended periods. Some sensitive people have allergic reactions to solanine, but to all of us it results in a bitter, unpleasant taste. So always store potatoes away from light.

Never refrigerate potatoes or store them below 40°F. Store them at room temperature if you must, but they store longest when kept cool and dry. The best storage choice is a paper or burlap sack or a wooden box kept on a shelf in a cool cellar. At room temperature, some potatoes will sprout and shrivel in as little as a week and in the refrigerator, their starch breaks down into sugar, which destroys the texture and taste of the potato. Although it is possible to reverse this process by leaving the potato at cellar temperature for a week or more, the vegetable will never regain its original firmness.

Fifty Ways to Cook Most Everything

ABOUT THESE RECIPES

The following recipes are written for 4 portions unless otherwise noted. They assume that you will season to taste with salt and pepper, so those ingredients are mentioned only in recipes where unusual amounts are necessary or where their absence would be disastrous. Potatoes are bland. They need salt and pepper to be palatable and they often require liberal seasoning.

Potato Pancakes

Grate 1 pound scrubbed russet potatoes, then rinse well in cold water, drain, and wring dry in a towel. Add 3 beaten eggs, 2 tablespoons flour, 1 teaspoon salt, pepper, and 3 tablespoons finely chopped onion. Fry heaping soupspoonfuls of this batter in ¼ inch hot oil in a deep skillet, flattening the mounds into pancakes about 3 inches in diameter. Brown well, 4 to 5 minutes per side. Drain on paper towels and serve hot with sour cream.

Potato Fennel Pancakes

Follow preceding recipe, adding 1 cup finely chopped fennel with the onion.

Potato Leek Pancakes

Follow recipe for Potato Pancakes (above), replacing onion with 2 finely chopped leeks and ½ clove minced garlic.

Sweet Potato Pancakes with Ham

Grate 1 pound scrubbed sweet potatoes and mix with 3 beaten eggs, 2 tablespoons flour, 1 teaspoon salt, pepper, ⅓ cup finely chopped ham, and 3 tablespoons finely chopped onion. Fry heaping soupspoonfuls of this batter in ¼ inch hot oil in a deep skillet, flattening the mounds into pancakes about 3 inches in diameter. Brown well, 4 to 5 minutes per side. Drain on paper towels.

Sweet Potato Apple Pancakes

Follow preceding recipe, but increase flour by 2 teaspoons and add 1 cup grated tart apple to the batter.

Potato Garlic Galette

Grate 1 pound scrubbed russet potatoes, then rinse well in cold water, drain, and wring dry in a towel. Melt 2 tablespoons butter in a large nonstick skillet until foamy, add half the potatoes, and press into an even layer. Sprinkle with 1 clove minced garlic, salt, and pepper. Place remaining potatoes on top and pack into an even layer. Season with more salt and pepper. Cover pan and brown potatoes on the bottom, about 15 minutes over medium high heat. Flip onto a plate. Melt 2 more tablespoons butter in the pan and slide the galette, brown side up, back into the pan. Cook another 10 minutes, until the other side is brown.

Potato Cheese Galette

Follow preceding recipe, adding ¼ cup grated Parmesan with the garlic, and topping with ⅓ cup grated Gruyère or Fontina cheese after galette has been flipped. Cover for last 5 minutes of cooking.

Galette Provençale

Grate 1 pound scrubbed russet potatoes, then wash well in cold water, drain, wring dry in a towel, and mix with 1 teaspoon *herbes de Provence*. Melt 1 tablespoon butter and 1 tablespoon olive oil in a large nonstick skillet until foamy, add half the potatoes, and press into an even layer. Sprinkle with 1 clove minced garlic, 2 tablespoons chopped ripe black olives, 1 tablespoon minced anchovy, salt, and pepper. Place remaining potatoes on top and pack into an even layer. Season with more salt and pepper, cover pan, and brown potatoes on the bottom, about 15 minutes over medium high heat. Flip onto a plate. Melt 2 more tablespoons butter in the pan and slide the galette, brown side up, back into the pan. Cook another 10 minutes, until the other side is brown.

Potatoes au Gratin

Make an even layer of ½ pound sliced russet potatoes mixed with ½ sliced small onion in shallow 8-inch baking dish. Season liberally with salt and pepper and top with 1 ounce grated Swiss cheese, 1 tablespoon grated Parmesan, and ½ cup milk mixed with half-and-half in any proportion. Make another layer of the same ingredients in the same proportion and same order and bake in preheated 375°F. oven for 1 hour, until potatoes are tender and top is bubbly and brown.

Raclette Gratin

Follow preceding recipe, substituting 2 ounces grated raclette cheese for every 1 ounce Swiss cheese. Omit the Parmesan. Substitute light cream for the milk and half-and-half for a richer version.

Gorgonzola Gratin

Follow recipe for Potatoes au Gratin (above), substituting 2 ounces crumbled Gorgonzola for the Swiss cheese, eliminating the Parmesan, and adding ¼ clove minced garlic with the onion.

Ham and Swiss Gratin

Follow recipe for Potatoes au Gratin (above), adding ¼ pound diced baked ham with the potato and onion.

Potato and Celeriac Gratin

Blanch ½ pound peeled, sliced celery root in acidulated water for 10 minutes. Make an even layer of the celery root, 6 ounces sliced russet potatoes, and ½ sliced small onion in shallow 8-inch baking dish. Season liberally with salt and pepper and top with 1 ounce grated Swiss cheese and ½ cup plain yogurt. Make another layer of the same ingredients in the same proportion and same order and bake in preheated 375°F. oven for 1 hour, until potatoes are tender and top is bubbly and brown.

New Potatoes with Bacon

Boil 1½ pounds new potatoes for about 10 minutes, until they are no longer hard but not fully tender. Cool, skin, and slice thickly. Make an even layer of half the potatoes mixed with ½ sliced small onion in a shallow 8-inch baking dish. Season liberally with salt and pepper and top with 1 ounce grated Cheddar cheese, 1 tablespoon grated Parmesan, 2 crumbled slices crisply cooked bacon, and ½ cup milk mixed with half-and-half in any proportion. Make another layer of the same ingredients in the same proportion and same order and bake in preheated 375°F. oven for 1 hour, until potatoes are tender and top is bubbly and brown.

Caramelized Potatoes au Gratin

Caramelize 2 cups thinly sliced onion in 2 table-spoons melted butter over low heat until deeply browned. Follow recipe for Potatoes au Gratin (page 257), using these onions instead of the on-ions in that recipe.

 Scalloped Potatoes with Feta

Follow recipe for Potatoes au Gratin (page 257), substituting crumbled feta for the Swiss, eliminat-ing the Parmesan and drizzling 1 teaspoon olive oil over each layer.

 Scalloped Potatoes with Onions and Anchovies

Follow recipe for Potatoes au Gratin (page 257), doubling the amount of onion and adding 4 chopped anchovies to each layer.

 Potatoes Parmesan

Follow recipe for Potatoes au Gratin (page 257), substituting Parmesan for the Swiss cheese and adding 1 clove minced garlic with the onion.

 Tomato and Basil Potatoes

Boil 2 pounds peeled russet potatoes for 12 to 15 minutes, until barely tender. Meanwhile, cook 4 large, skinned, chopped tomatoes and 1 clove minced garlic in 2 tablespoons olive oil for 5 min-utes. Add 3 tablespoons chopped fresh basil. Slice potatoes and layer in 2-quart casserole with the tomatoes. Top with ¼ cup grated Parmesan and bake in preheated 400°F. oven for 40 minutes.

 Classic Mashed Potatoes

Bake 3 pounds russet potatoes in preheated 400°F. oven for 1 hour until tender. Split, scoop out the flesh into a large heavy saucepan, and beat in 1 cup sour cream, half-and-half, or plain yogurt until light and fluffy. Beat in 2 to 4 tablespoons butter and season liberally with salt and pepper. Reheat in pan or microwave.

 Mashed Potatoes with Roasted Garlic

Follow preceding recipe. Bake 1 large head garlic along with potatoes. Remove garlic from oven af-ter 40 minutes. Cut off pointed end of garlic head and squeeze roasted flesh from the skin. Beat garlic into potatoes along with the butter.

 Potato Celeriac Puree

Follow recipe for Classic Mashed Potatoes (above), but use only 2 pounds potatoes. While potatoes bake, simmer 1 pound peeled, diced celery root in water for 10 minutes, until softened. Puree in a blender with ¼ cup milk and beat into potatoes.

 Potato Fennel Purée

Follow recipe for Classic Mashed Potatoes (above), but use only 2 pounds potatoes. While potatoes bake, cook 1 pound peeled, diced fennel and 1 clove minced garlic in 2 tablespoons butter until soft. Puree in a blender with ¼ cup milk and beat into potatoes, reducing butter to 2 tablespoons or less.

 Sweet Potato and Apple Purée

Follow recipe for Classic Mashed Potatoes (above), but use sweet potatoes instead of russets. While potatoes bake, cook 1 pound peeled, diced tart apple and 1 clove minced garlic in 2 tablespoons butter until soft. Puree in a blender with ¼ cup milk and 1 tablespoon sugar. Beat into potatoes, reducing butter to 2 tablespoons or less.

Mashed Potatoes with Yogurt and Herbs

Follow recipe for Classic Mashed Potatoes (opposite), using plain yogurt for the liquid. Cook any combination of minced fresh parsley, thyme, tarragon, chervil, and basil totaling 3 tablespoons in the butter until soft before adding to potatoes.

Mashed Potatoes with Ham and Cheese

Follow recipe for Classic Mashed Potatoes (opposite). Beat in 2 ounces shredded sharp Cheddar cheese and 2 ounces finely diced baked ham after reheating.

Blue Cheese Mashed Potatoes

Follow recipe for Classic Mashed Potatoes (opposite), using 1 cup blue cheese dressing (yours, or ours on page 299) instead of cream, yogurt, or half-and-half.

Potato Chips

Soak 2 pounds scrubbed russet potatoes, sliced paper-thin, in 1 quart ice water mixed with 1 tablespoon salt. Pat dry and fry in 375°F. oil until golden and crisp. Drain on paper towels and salt lightly.

Spicy Potato Chips

Soak 2 pounds scrubbed russet potatoes, sliced paper-thin, in 1 quart ice water mixed with 1 tablespoon salt. Pat dry, and fry in 375°F. oil until golden and crisp. Drain on paper towels and season with mixture of 1 teaspoon *each* salt, cayenne pepper, and black pepper.

Perfect Fries

Soak 2 pounds russet potatoes, cut into ¾-inch-thick rods, in 1 quart ice water mixed with 1 tablespoon salt. Drain and dry completely. Deep-fry in several inches of 300°F. oil until softened. Lift from oil with slotted spoon and drain on paper towels. Heat oil to 375°F. and fry potatoes in several batches until crisp and golden brown. Drain on paper towels and salt lightly.

Buffalo Fries

Follow preceding recipe, tossing finished fries with 2 tablespoons *each* melted butter and hot pepper sauce.

Parmesan Fries

Follow recipe for Perfect Fries (above), tossing finished fries with ¼ cup grated Parmesan along with the salt.

Sautéed Potatoes with Walnuts

In a large nonstick skillet, sauté ½ cup chopped walnuts in 1 teaspoon walnut oil. Remove nuts and set aside. Add 3 tablespoons walnut oil to pan, heat, and cook 2 tablespoons minced shallot in it. Add 2 pounds scrubbed, thinly sliced russet potatoes, blotted to absorb surface moisture, and sauté, tossing occasionally until browned and tender. Season with salt, pepper, and a dash of ground ginger as you sauté. Return walnuts to mixture for last few minutes of cooking.

Sautéed Potatoes with Garlic and Olives

Sauté 2 pounds scrubbed and thinly sliced russet potatoes, blotted to absorb surface moisture, in 3 tablespoons hot olive oil, tossing occasionally until browned and tender, about 20 minutes. Season with salt, pepper, and a dash of nutmeg as you sauté. Toss with 2 cloves minced garlic, 1 tablespoon chopped fresh parsley, and ¼ cup chopped oil-cured black olives at the end of cooking.

 Sautéed Potatoes with Capers

Follow preceding recipe, substituting ¼ cup drained capers for the olives.

 Sautéed Potatoes, Onions, and Smoked Salmon

Prepare and sauté potatoes as in recipe for Sautéed Potatoes with Garlic and Olives (above), adding ½ cup thinly sliced onions with the potatoes. When done, toss with 2 cloves minced garlic, 1 tablespoon chopped fresh parsley, and 2 ounces chopped smoked salmon.

 Bacon, Peppers, and Potatoes

Cook 4 slices bacon in large nonstick skillet until crisp. Reserve bacon. Sauté 2 pounds scrubbed and thinly sliced russet potatoes, blotted to absorb surface moisture, in the hot bacon fat with ½ cup thinly sliced onion, tossing occasionally until browned and tender, about 20 minutes. Season with salt, pepper, and a dash of grated nutmeg as you sauté. Toss with 2 cloves minced garlic, 1 tablespoon chopped fresh parsley and 1 diced roasted red pepper (page 442). Crumble reserved bacon over top.

 Roasted Potatoes with Turnips

Cut 1¼ pounds scrubbed russet potatoes and 1 pound peeled turnips into wedges. Boil in salted water for 10 minutes, drain, and pat dry. Toss with 1 tablespoon melted butter, sprinkle liberally with salt and pepper, and roast at 375°F. for 50 minutes, turning 3 or 4 times, until tender and brown.

 Roasted Potatoes with Pearl Onions

Follow preceding recipe, substituting 1 pound peeled pearl onions for the turnips.

 Perfect Hash-Brown Potatoes

Soak 2 pounds grated scrubbed russet potatoes in ice water until water is cloudy. Drain and wring out in a kitchen towel until dry. In heavy skillet, melt 1 tablespoon rendered bacon or chicken fat, or 1 tablespoon *each* butter and oil, until smoking. Add 1 cup finely sliced onion and the potatoes and cook until they begin to brown on the bottom, about 5 minutes. Chop coarsely with spatula and turn pieces over, continuing to chop and turn potatoes every 3 to 5 minutes until they are uniformly tender and brown. Season liberally with salt and pepper.

 Peppered Hash Browns

Follow preceding recipe, adding 1 cup diced bell pepper and ¼ teaspoon crushed red pepper flakes with the onions.

 Hash Browns and Cabbage

Follow recipe for Perfect Hash Brown Potatoes (above), adding 3 cups shredded cabbage in place of half the onions.

Chilied Hash Browns

Follow recipe for Perfect Hash Brown Potatoes (opposite). Halfway through cooking, sprinkle potatoes with 1 tablespoon chili powder, 1 tablespoon paprika, 1 teaspoon ground cumin, and 1 teaspoon ground coriander.

 Baked Potatoes with Sour Cream Vinaigrette

Rub 4 scrubbed ½-pound russet potatoes with 2 teaspoons vegetable oil. Poke each in several places with a fork. Place on rack in a roasting pan and bake 20 minutes in preheated 425°F. oven. Reduce heat to 375°F. and bake 40 minutes more. While potatoes are baking, whisk 5 tablespoons sour cream with 3 tablespoons Italian dressing. Cut a cross through the skin of each potato and squeeze gently to lightly fluff the interior. Spoon 2 tablespoons of the sauce over each potato.

 Baked Potatoes with Minted Yogurt

Prepare and bake potatoes as in preceding recipe. Top with ½ cup plain yogurt mixed with ½ clove minced garlic, 1 tablespoon chopped mint leaves, 1 tablespoon lemon juice, and 1 tablespoon olive oil.

 Baked Potatoes with Mustard Sauce

Prepare and bake potatoes as in recipe for Baked Potatoes with Sour Cream Vinaigrette (above), but top with a mixture of 2 tablespoons Dijon mustard, 1 clove minced garlic, and 5 tablespoons sour cream.

 Twice-Baked Cheddar Jalapeño Potatoes

Rub 4 scrubbed ½-pound russet potatoes with 2 teaspoons vegetable oil. Poke each in several places with a fork. Place on a rack in a roasting pan and roast 20 minutes in a preheated 425°F. oven. Reduce heat to 375°F. and bake 30 minutes more. Cut a 2-inch slit in the length of each potato, squeeze sides to force the slit open, and scoop out all but a thin shell of potato from the interior. Mix potato flesh with 1 minced pickled jalapeño pepper, ¼ cup sour cream, and 6 ounces shredded Cheddar cheese. Refill potato shells with this mixture and return to oven for 20 minutes more.

 Twice-Baked Roasted Garlic Potatoes

Prepare and bake potatoes as in preceding recipe. Bake 1 head garlic for the last 40 minutes that the potatoes bake. Cut off the pointed end of the garlic head and squeeze the roasted flesh from the skins. Before refilling potato shells, beat together garlic, potato flesh, ¼ cup sour cream, and 2 tablespoons butter, and return potatoes to oven for final 20 minutes.

 Twice-Baked Blue Cheese Potatoes

Prepare and bake potatoes as in recipe for Twice-Baked Cheddar Jalapeño Potatoes (above). Refill potato shells with mixture of potato flesh, 1 clove minced garlic, ¼ cup sour cream, and 4 ounces crumbled blue cheese. Return potatoes to oven for final 20 minutes.

 Corned Beef and Potato Salad

Whisk 2 tablespoons whole-grain mustard with ¼ cup cider vinegar. Slowly whisk in ½ cup peanut oil until thick. Season with salt and pepper. Boil 1½ pounds red-skin potatoes in a large pot of salted water until tender, about 20 minutes. Peel and cut in bite-size pieces. Toss with the dressing, ¼ pound cooked shredded corned beef, 3 tablespoons finely chopped onion, and 2 tablespoons finely chopped fresh parsley.

30

Fifty Garden-Fresh Ways to Use Tomatoes

What cook could hope to compete with a tomato newly picked? Who could improve on its color or its fragrance of sunshine and freshly tilled land? Who could contrive another flavor as intricately sweet and tart, or boast a new ingredient better able to turn a bowl of plain pasta or a stale crust of bread into a meal?

Smart cooks don't try, for they know that the best thing to do with tomatoes in summer is to do as little as possible—and to do it whenever they can.

If you're lucky enough to be able to buy top-quality vine-ripened tomatoes, we have a reward for you: 50 quick and easy ways for serving them. From salads and soups to throw-together pasta sauces, each recipe is designed to require minimal cooking and less than 20 minutes' preparation.

ABOUT THESE RECIPES

Unless otherwise stated, all of these recipes were tested with large, vine-ripened, locally grown tomatoes that have been washed and stemmed, and each recipe yields 4 servings.

 Quick Tomato Salad

In a salad bowl, mix ½ minced onion, 1 clove minced garlic, ⅓ cup olive oil, ¼ cup wine vinegar, 1 tablespoon balsamic vinegar, 2 tablespoons minced fresh parsley, a pinch of crushed red pepper flakes, salt, and pepper. Toss in 3 tomatoes cut into wedges.

 Tomato with Pesto

In a food processor, finely chop 1 clove garlic and 2 tablespoons pine nuts. Add ⅔ cup firmly packed basil leaves and chop finely. Add ⅓ cup virgin olive oil in a slow, steady stream. Mix in 2 to 3 tablespoons grated Parmesan and season with salt and pepper. Slice 3 tomatoes into ½-inch-thick slices and drizzle with 1 tablespoon olive oil, salt, and pepper. Dollop each slice with 2 teaspoons pesto and serve the rest on the side.

Tomato Pesto Pasta Salad

Prepare pesto as in preceding recipe. Toss with 2 diced tomatoes, 4 thinly sliced scallions, 20 sliced pitted black olives, and 12 ounces hot cooked pasta.

 Chilled Tomato and Pesto Soup

In a food processor, finely chop 2 tomatoes and 1 stemmed and seeded roasted red pepper (page 442), ¼ onion, 1 clove garlic, 3 tablespoons olive oil, salt, pepper, and 3 ice cubes. Do not make mixture completely smooth. Stir in another 3 ice cubes and 1 tablespoon chopped fresh parsley. Chill and serve garnished with ¼ cup pesto, made as in Tomato with Pesto (page 263).

 Tomato Salad with Mozzarella and Herbs

In a salad bowl, mix 1 diced red onion, 2 cloves coarsely chopped garlic, ½ cup olive oil, ⅓ cup wine vinegar, ½ cup minced fresh herbs, ¼ teaspoon crushed red pepper flakes, salt, and pepper. Toss 3 tomatoes cut into wedges and 8 ounces sliced mozzarella in this dressing and refrigerate. Serve with crusty bread.

 Tomato with Caper Vinaigrette

In a salad bowl, mix together 1 minced shallot, ½ clove minced garlic, ⅓ cup olive oil, ¼ cup wine vinegar, 2 tablespoons drained capers, and pepper. Toss in 3 tomatoes cut into wedges and chill.

 Roasted Tomato and Pepper Salad

In a salad bowl, mix 2 cloves minced garlic, ⅓ cup olive oil, 2 tablespoons lemon juice, 2 tablespoons white wine vinegar, 1 finely chopped and seeded chili pepper, and salt. Set aside. Place 2 large tomatoes and 2 yellow bell peppers over a high gas flame or beneath a high broiler until their skins char and blister—about 20 seconds a side for the tomatoes, 2 minutes for the peppers. Rub under cold running water to remove skins. Remove stems and seeds from the peppers. Slice tomatoes and peppers and toss in the dressing. Chill.

 Marinated Tomato with Chèvre and Onion

In a salad bowl, mix 1 thinly sliced sweet onion, 2 halved cloves garlic, ½ cup olive oil, 2 tablespoons white wine vinegar, ½ cup coarsely chopped basil leaves, ¼ teaspoon crushed red pepper flakes, salt, and pepper. Toss in 3 stemmed, sliced tomatoes and 6 ounces sliced fresh chèvre and refrigerate. Serve with crusty bread.

Tomato with Black Pepper and Lime

Slice 2 beefsteak tomatoes. Arrange on a plate and drizzle with 2 tablespoons extra-virgin olive oil, the juice of 1 lime, coarse salt, and a liberal grinding of black pepper.

 Tomato and Crab Salad

In a large bowl, toss 2 chopped tomatoes, 1 peeled, seeded, and diced cucumber, kernels from 2 ears cooked corn, 2 sliced scallions, 1 pound cleaned lump crabmeat, and 1 diced small avocado. In a separate bowl, mix ½ cup mayonnaise, 2 tablespoons wine vinegar, the juice of 1 lemon, 1 teaspoon hot pepper sauce, salt, and pepper. Toss with salad mixture.

Tomato Niçoise

In a salad bowl, mix 1 sliced onion, 1 clove minced garlic, ⅓ cup olive oil, ⅓ cup red wine vinegar, ¼ cup chopped fresh basil, ¼ cup finely chopped fennel, 2 minced anchovies, salt, and pepper. Toss in 3 tomatoes cut into wedges, 6 ounces drained canned tuna, and 12 pitted Niçoise olives, and chill.

 Tomato and Prosciutto in Garlic Vinaigrette

In a salad bowl, mix 3 sliced scallions, 2 cloves minced garlic, ⅓ cup olive oil, ¼ cup wine vinegar, 1 tablespoon sherry vinegar, 2 tablespoons minced fresh parsley, 1 teaspoon dried oregano, a pinch of crushed red pepper flakes, salt, and pepper. Toss in 3 tomatoes cut into wedges and 2 ounces julienned prosciutto and chill.

 Tomato Raita

Toss 2 chopped and seeded tomatoes with ¼ thinly sliced red onion, the juice of ½ lemon, ¼ cup chopped mint leaves, 1 teaspoon sugar, 2 teaspoons chili powder, and 1 tablespoon plain yogurt.

Tomato and Fried Spinach Salad

Place 2 large diced tomatoes and ½ thinly sliced red onion in a salad bowl. Toss with dressing made from ½ cup wine vinegar, 1 clove minced garlic, ½ teaspoon crushed red pepper flakes, and salt. In a large heavy pot, heat several inches of oil, at least 1 cup of which is olive oil, to 375°F. Add 1 pound dry, stemmed spinach leaves to the hot oil in three batches, frying each batch for 30 seconds and allowing the oil to return to frying temperature after each batch. (Be careful; the oil may splatter when

adding the spinach.) Drain on paper towels. Toss crisp spinach with other ingredients. Serve over toast.

 Roasted Tomato and Rice Salad

Roast 2 tomatoes directly over a high flame of a gas range or under a broiler, turning every 20 seconds to blister skins evenly. Run under cold water and rub with your fingers to peel. Coarsely chop tomatoes and toss with 3 cups warm cooked brown and/or wild rice, along with a dressing made from ⅓ cup olive oil, ¼ cup wine vinegar, the juice of 1 lemon, ¼ cup chopped fresh parsley, salt, and pepper.

 Marinated Tomato and White Bean Salad

In a salad bowl, mix 1 minced onion, 2 cloves minced garlic, ⅓ cup olive oil, ¼ cup wine vinegar, 2 tablespoons lemon juice, 2 tablespoons minced fresh parsley, 2 tablespoons chopped basil leaves, 2 sliced scallions, and 1 teaspoon chili pepper. Toss in 3 diced tomatoes and the drained contents of a 19-ounce can of white kidney beans and chill.

 Tomato Tonnato

In a salad bowl, mix 3 thinly sliced scallions, 1 clove minced garlic, ⅓ cup olive oil, ¼ cup lemon juice, 2 tablespoons minced fresh dill, salt, and pepper. Toss in 3 diced tomatoes and 6 ounces drained water-packed tuna. Chill.

 Spinach Salad with Tomato Vinaigrette

In a salad bowl, mix ½ minced onion, 1 clove minced garlic, 1 finely chopped tomato, ⅓ cup olive oil, ¼ cup wine vinegar, 1 tablespoon balsamic vinegar, 2 tablespoons minced fresh parsley, a pinch of crushed red pepper flakes, salt, and pepper. Toss in 1 pound cleaned spinach leaves and top with 2 cups garlic croutons and 2 tablespoons grated Parmesan.

Cherry Tomato and Grilled Onion Salad

Brown 1 thinly sliced large onion in 1 tablespoon vegetable oil. Toss in a salad bowl with 1 pint red cherry tomatoes and 1 pint yellow cherry tomatoes, all stemmed and halved, along with a dressing made from 1 clove minced garlic, ⅓ cup olive oil, ¼ cup wine vinegar, 1 tablespoon balsamic vinegar, 2 tablespoons chopped fresh flat-leaf parsley, salt, and pepper.

Tomato Walnut Salad

In a salad bowl, mix 1 thinly sliced red onion, 1½ cloves minced garlic, ⅓ cup walnut oil, 3 tablespoons cider vinegar, 2 tablespoons minced fresh parsley, a pinch of crushed red pepper flakes, ½ teaspoon sugar, salt, and pepper. Toss in 3 tomatoes cut into wedges and ½ cup coarsely chopped walnuts and chill.

Red and Yellow Tomato Salad

In a salad bowl, mix ½ minced onion, 1 clove minced garlic, ⅓ cup olive oil, ¼ cup wine vinegar, 1 tablespoon lemon juice, 2 tablespoons minced fresh parsley, 2 tablespoons coarsely chopped fresh herbs, salt, and pepper. Into this dressing, toss 1 cup stemmed red and 1 cup stemmed yellow cherry tomatoes that have been halved. Chill.

Chili Salad

In a salad bowl, toss 3 tomatoes cut into thin wedges, ¼ minced onion, the juice of 1 lime, 2 teaspoons chili powder, 1 teaspoon ground cumin, ¼ cup chopped fresh cilantro, ¼ cup corn oil, salt, pepper and 1 cup cooked and drained kidney beans.

Tomatoes with Green Peppercorn Tarragon Vinaigrette

In a salad bowl, mix 1 minced shallot, ½ clove minced garlic, ⅓ cup olive oil, ¼ cup tarragon vinegar, 2 tablespoons green peppercorns, 2 tablespoons chopped fresh tarragon leaves, salt, and pepper. Toss in 3 tomatoes cut into wedges and chill.

Curried Tomato and Onion Salad

In a nonstick skillet, cook 1 minced onion, 1 clove minced garlic, and 2 tablespoons grated fresh gingerroot until softened. Add 1 tablespoon peanut oil, 1 tablespoon curry powder, 2 teaspoons ground coriander, and 1 teaspoon sugar and continue cooking until mixture browns lightly. Remove from heat and transfer to a salad bowl. Add to the bowl ⅓ cup more peanut oil, ¼ cup orange juice, 1 tablespoon cider vinegar, 2 tablespoons minced fresh cilantro, and 2 tablespoons chopped mint leaves. Add hot chili powder, salt, and pepper to taste. Toss 3 tomatoes cut into wedges in this dressing and chill.

Tomato Slaw

Sprinkle ½ teaspoon kosher salt on a large platter. Place 2 sliced tomatoes in a single layer on the salt and sprinkle 1 teaspoon more over the top. Set aside for 15 minutes. Wrap tomatoes in a towel and squeeze to remove most of the moisture. Cut tomato slices into thin strips and toss with 4 thinly sliced scallions, 2 ribs diced celery, and a dressing made from 3 tablespoons mayonnaise, 1 table-spoon lemon juice, 1 teaspoon cider vinegar, 2 teaspoons orange marmalade, salt, and pepper.

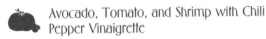

Orange, Tomato, and Tarragon Salad

Arrange 4 peeled navel orange sections, 4 thin to-mato wedges, and 4 thin red-onion rings on a plate. Spoon 2 tablespoons standard oil-and-vinegar dressing seasoned with 2 teaspoons chopped fresh tarragon over top. Serves 1.

Avocado, Tomato, and Shrimp with Chili Pepper Vinaigrette

Arrange ½ peeled and sliced avocado, 4 thin to-mato wedges, and 6 cooked and peeled shrimp on a plate. Spoon 2 tablespoons oil-and-vinegar dress-ing seasoned with a pinch crushed red pepper flakes, and ⅛ teaspoon chili powder. Serves 1.

Tomatoes Marinated in Olive Oil, Garlic, and Crushed Pepper

In a salad bowl, mix together ½ minced onion, 2 cloves minced garlic, ½ cup extra-virgin olive oil, the juice of ½ lemon, 3 tablespoons chopped fresh flat-leaf parsley, ¼ teaspoon crushed red pepper flakes, salt, and pepper. Toss in 3 tomatoes cut in wedges and chill. Serve with grated Parmesan.

Fresh Tomatoes and Pasta

Follow preceding recipe, but omit lemon and dice the tomato. Toss with 12 ounces hot cooked pasta and ⅓ cup grated Parmesan. Serve with additional Parmesan.

Fresh Tomato Sauce

In 2 tablespoons olive oil, sauté 1 cup chopped onion, 2 cloves minced garlic, and 1 dried chili pepper until the onion is just soft, about 2 minutes. Add 6 coarsely chopped skinned and seeded large tomatoes. Cook until tomatoes begin to lose their liquid and add 1 tablespoon tomato paste, salt, and pepper. Stir in ⅓ cup chopped fresh herbs and heat 1 minute more. Remove chili pepper. Serve with 12 ounces hot cooked pasta.

Tomato, Basil, and Feta over Pasta

In a skillet, warm 1 tablespoon olive oil, add 1 clove split garlic, and sauté 1 minute. Add 3 chopped tomatoes and ⅓ cup dry vermouth and cook over high heat until alcohol evaporates. Sea-son with a pinch of cayenne, salt, and black pep-per. Toss in 2 tablespoons chopped fresh basil and cook 20 seconds more. Remove garlic and toss with 12 ounces hot pasta and 6 ounces crumbled feta.

Fresh Tomato and Cream Sauce

In 2 tablespoons olive oil in a large skillet, cook 2 tablespoons minced onion, a pinch of crushed red pepper flakes, and 1 clove minced garlic over mod-erate heat just until softened. Add 4 chopped to-matoes and cook until they begin to release their liquid. Add 1 tablespoon minced fresh flat-leaf parsley and ½ cup heavy cream, and simmer until sauce thickens lightly, about 1 minute. Season with salt and pepper. Toss with 12 ounces hot cooked pasta.

Tomato Sauce with Fennel and Orange

In a large skillet over moderate heat, cook ½ chopped onion and 1 clove minced garlic in 2 tablespoons olive oil until soft. Add ½ teaspoon ground fennel seed, 1 tablespoon finely grated orange zest, and ½ teaspoon ground turmeric and cook another 30 seconds. Add the juice of 1 large orange, 3 chopped tomatoes, and a dash of hot pepper sauce. Simmer for 3 minutes until tomatoes begin to release their liquid. Season with salt and pepper. Serve over fish, chicken, veal, rice or hot cooked shell-shaped pasta.

Tomato Sandwich

Slice 1 French bread in half horizontally and spread with a thin layer of unsalted butter. Slice 1 tomato and cut slices in half. Lay slices overlapping down the length of one side of the bread, sprinkle liberally with salt and pepper, and top with the other half of the bread. Cut into 4 sections. Serves 2 to 4.

Grilled Cheese with Tomato and Mustard

Spread 8 slices bread with butter on one side, turn slices over, and spread with mustard on the other side. Place 3 slices Swiss cheese overlapping on the mustard side of each of 4 slices of the bread and place 2 tomato slices on top of each of the cheese-lined slices. Place remaining slices, mustard-side down, on top of the tomatoes and press each sandwich lightly to hold in place. Grill sandwiches on a dry griddle or skillet at moderate heat until bread is toasted and cheese has melted.

Tomato and Gorgonzola Grinder

Split 4 hoagie rolls horizontally and remove a trough of bread from each piece. Spoon 1 tablespoon oil-and-vinegar dressing along each trough and place total of ½ pound sliced tomato in the troughs, along with ¼ pound crumbled Gorgonzola. Top each grinder with 1 tablespoon ad-

ditional dressing, wrap each roll in foil, and bake at 400° F. for 15 minutes until cheese melts and bread is warmed through. Shred 4 lettuce leaves, and sprinkle the length of each grinder.

Mild Red Salsa

In a food processor, coarsely chop 1 small onion and 3 tomatoes. Add 2 tablespoons olive oil, 2 tablespoons chopped fresh cilantro, and enough water to make a saucelike consistency. Use as a dip or a sauce for plain meats.

Mild Green Salsa

In a food processor, coarsely chop 1 small onion, 1 clove garlic, and 8 peeled and stemmed tomatillos. Add 2 tablespoons olive oil, 2 tablespoons chopped fresh cilantro, and enough water to make a saucelike consistency. Use as a dip or a sauce for plain meats.

Cucumber Salad with Tomato Salsa

Thinly slice 2 cucumbers, toss with 1 tablespoon salt, and set aside. Rinse well and squeeze out excess moisture. Toss with ½ recipe Mild Green or Red Salsa (above).

Tomato Salsa with Garbanzos

Follow recipe for Mild Green or Mild Red Tomato Salsa (above), adding 1 small minced jalapeño pepper and ½ cup cooked, drained garbanzo beans.

Tomato and Olive Salsa

In a food processor, coarsely chop 1 small onion and 3 tomatoes. Add 2 tablespoons olive oil, ¼ cup chopped pitted green olives, 2 tablespoons brine from the olives, and enough water to make a sauce-like consistency. Use as a dip or a sauce for plain meats.

 Tomato Shallot Salsa

In a food processor, coarsely chop 3 shallots and 3 tomatoes. Add 2 tablespoons olive oil, 2 tablespoons chopped fresh cilantro, and enough water to make a saucelike consistency. Use as a dip or a sauce for plain meats.

 Avocado and Tomato Salsa

Toss 1 large diced avocado with 1 minced jalapeño pepper, 1 tablespoon chopped fresh cilantro, and Mild Red Tomato Salsa (opposite).

 Tomato and Corn Salsa

In a blender or food processor, coarsely chop 1 small onion, 3 chopped tomatoes, 1 canned jalapeño pepper, ½ cup cooked corn kernels, 1 tablespoon corn oil, and 1 teaspoon chili powder.

 Parmesan-Crusted Baked Tomato

Rub a sheet pan with 1 teaspoon olive oil. Place 4 thick tomato slices on the pan and drizzle 1 teaspoon additional olive oil over the slices. Make mixture of 2 tablespoons *each* bread crumbs and grated Parmesan and ¼ teaspoon *each* onion powder and garlic powder. Add salt and pepper. Place a thick layer of this mixture on top of each tomato and drizzle another 1 teaspoon olive oil over top. Bake at 425° F. for 20 minutes until golden brown.

 Rosemary-Grilled Tomato

Warm ¼ cup olive oil with 1 tablespoon dried crumbled rosemary for 2 minutes. Dip 4 thick tomato slices into the oil and grill 4 inches from a hot fire for 2 minutes, seasoning tops with salt and pepper and basting with more oil halfway through the grilling. Flip tomato slices and grill another 2 minutes, basting and seasoning in the same way. Transfer to serving plate and top with a few rosemary leaves.

 Grilled Tomato with Ranch Dressing

Warm ¼ cup olive oil with 1 clove minced garlic for 2 minutes. Dip 4 thick tomato slices into the oil and grill 4 inches from a hot fire for 2 minutes, seasoning tops with salt and pepper and basting with more oil halfway through the grilling. Flip tomato slices and grill another 2 minutes. Sauce each grilled tomato with 2 tablespoons buttermilk ranch dressing. Transfer to a serving plate and top with a bit of chopped fresh parsley.

 Grilled Tomato and Pesto

In a blender or food processor, finely chop 1 clove garlic and 2 tablespoons pine nuts. Add ⅔ cup firmly packed basil leaves and chop finely. Add ⅓ cup extra-virgin olive oil in a slow steady stream. Mix in 2 to 3 tablespoons grated Parmesan, salt, and pepper. Grill tomatoes as in the preceding recipes, but top with the pesto instead of ranch dressing.

 Gazpacho Cocktail

In a processor, finely chop 2 diced tomatoes, ¼ small diced onion, ½ clove garlic, ½ chunked cucumber, and 1 rib peeled and chopped celery. Add 2 teaspoons wine vinegar, 2 tablespoons olive oil, 2 cups spicy tomato juice, salt, and pepper. Chill and serve in chilled cups with spoons.

 Green Tomato Gazpacho

In a processor, roughly chop 6 ice cubes, 2 diced large green tomatoes, 1 small diced onion, ½ chopped seeded cucumber, and 1 clove garlic. Add 1 tablespoon white wine vinegar, 3 tablespoons olive oil, 1 teaspoon hot pepper sauce, salt, and pepper and process until finely chopped. Chill.

31

Fifty Ways to Eat Your Spinach—and Other Greens

Spinach is a culinary litmus test, distinguishing Popeye from Brutus and an inspired cook from a kitchen hack every time it's served. Its name alone can make a contented youngster cringe and send otherwise mature adults running for cover. Yet its natural affinity to everything from garlic to ham hocks has made it and other green leafy vegetables among the most widely eaten, if underappreciated, side dishes on the American table.

The challenge presented by spinach and practically all other dark green leaves is how to deal with their bitterness. From the acrid aroma of simmering kale to the overtly bitter bite of broccoli rabe and chicory, one's reaction to bitterness largely determines whether one loves or loathes these vegetables.

Nature doesn't help. Our palates are built to reject bitter foods. Bitterness is often an indication of harmful alkaloids in food. We have come to accept low concentrations of some bitter flavors, like qui-

nine and caffeine, only by modifying them with an addition of sugar, fat, fruit, or dairy products, or by balancing the bitterness with other strong flavors, such as lime juice, cinnamon, or chocolate.

The same approach can make greens more palatable to diners who would otherwise reject them as overly bitter. Collard, mustard, beet, and broccoli greens are typically counterbalanced by the subtle aroma of smoked meats, fruity olive oil, or a pungent jolt of garlic. We serve sweet and sour cabbage, creamed spinach, and Brussels sprouts with cheese sauce. We toss radicchio and escarole with creamy dressings and pungent vinaigrettes, or we shadow the sharpness of braised endive with shades of lemon juice, white wine, shallots, and chicken broth.

The bitterest of all greens are those in the chicory and endive families. Maturity, deeper green color, and exposure to sunlight all increase bitterness. Many growers try to limit exposure to sunlight, sometimes exposing only the outer leaves to keep all but the outside of the endive from coloring, thereby cutting down on off-flavors.

In addition to buying paler specimens, you can control bitterness during preparation. Soaking endive or chicory will increase bitterness, so rinse these vegetables quickly and dry them well.

Soon after they start cooking, the bitter components in the vegetable will be released and become more overt. Eventually this bitterness will dissipate, but in the interim it will become more pronounced. This means the most palatable ways of serving bitter greens are raw in salads, barely wilted in a flavorful mixture of herbs, acids, and oil, or braised until fully softened. Don't try serving these greens *al dente* unless a puckered palate is your idea of a good time.

ABOUT THESE RECIPES

About half of the following 50 recipes are for spinach; the rest are for less common greens. We assume you will add salt and pepper to your taste. They are written for 4 to 6 portions unless otherwise noted. Salads are intended as entrées.

The cooked spinach recipes are written for frozen spinach, although you can substitute fresh, remembering that 1 pound fresh spinach equals about 10 ounces frozen. Since spinach freezes well and these products are processed when the leaves are quite fresh, frozen spinach is frequently of higher quality than the fresh spinach available in the produce area of the market. Unless the spinach is being served raw and/or the fresh spinach is particularly good, the frozen product might be the better choice.

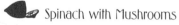 Spinach with Mushrooms

Brown 2 tablespoons minced onion and ¼ pound sliced mushrooms in 3 tablespoons butter. Add 20 ounces defrosted frozen chopped spinach and cook until most of its liquid evaporates. Finish with ½ teaspoon lemon juice.

 Garlic Spinach

Cook 2 tablespoons minced onion and 1 clove minced garlic in 2 tablespoons butter until soft. Add 20 ounces defrosted frozen chopped spinach and cook until most of its liquid evaporates. Finish with ½ teaspoon lemon juice.

 Spinach with Lemon and Parsley

Follow preceding recipe, substituting 2 teaspoons finely grated lemon zest and 1 tablespoon finely chopped fresh parsley for the lemon juice.

 Spinach with Capers

Follow recipe for Garlic Spinach (above), adding 1 tablespoon drained small capers along with the onion.

 Ricotta Creamed Spinach

Follow recipe for Garlic Spinach (above), adding ¼ cup drained ricotta cheese along with the lemon juice.

 Creamed Spinach with Herb Cheese

Follow recipe for Garlic Spinach (above), adding ¼ cup herbed cream cheese and 1 teaspoon sour cream in place of the lemon juice.

 Spinach with Warm Bacon Dressing

Follow recipe for Garlic Spinach (above) adding ¼ cup Warm Bacon Dressing (page 298) in place of the lemon juice.

Spinach with Roasted Peppers and Green Peppercorns

Follow recipe for Garlic Spinach (above), adding 1 diced roasted red bell pepper (page 442) and 1 teaspoon green peppercorns along with the onion.

 Spinach with Feta and Olives

Cook 2 tablespoons minced onion and 1 clove minced garlic in 2 tablespoons olive oil until soft. Add 2 tablespoons chopped oil-cured black olives and 20 ounces defrosted frozen chopped spinach and cook until most of the liquid evaporates. Stir in ⅓ cup crumbled feta cheese.

 Prosciutto and Fennel Spinach

Cook 2 tablespoons minced onion, 1 clove minced garlic, and ½ teaspoon ground fennel seed in 2 tablespoons olive oil until soft. Add 2 tablespoons minced prosciutto and 20 ounces defrosted frozen chopped spinach and cook until most of its liquid evaporates.

 Spiced Spinach

Cook 1 teaspoon *each* ground coriander and curry powder and a pinch *each* of black pepper, cayenne pepper, and grated nutmeg in 2 tablespoons butter for 1 minute. Add 20 ounces defrosted frozen chopped spinach and salt. Cook until most of the moisture evaporates. Remove from heat and mix in ⅓ cup plain yogurt.

Spinach, Corn, and Tomatoes

Cook 2 tablespoons finely chopped onion, 1 minced and seeded jalapeño pepper, and 1 cup corn niblets in 2 tablespoons butter until vegetables soften. Add 10 ounces defrosted frozen chopped spinach and cook until most of its liquid evaporates. Add 1 seeded chopped tomato and heat through.

 Creamed Spinach with Wild Mushrooms

Soak ½ ounce dried wild mushrooms (any variety) in ½ cup boiling water for 20 minutes. Squeeze out excess liquid, trim off hard ends, and chop mushrooms coarsely. Sauté mushrooms with 2 tablespoons finely chopped onion in 2 tablespoons butter until lightly browned. Strain soaking liquid and add to pan along with 20 ounces defrosted frozen chopped spinach. Cook until most of the liquid evaporates. Add ¼ cup heavy cream mixed with 1 egg yolk and cook gently for 1 to 2 minutes.

 Stir-Fried Spinach with Pine Nuts

Heat 1 tablespoon peanut oil in a hot wok. Add ¼ cup pine nuts, toss until browned, about 1 minute, and remove with a slotted spoon. Add ½ chopped onion and stir-fry 30 seconds. Add 1½ pounds fresh spinach leaves, trimmed of their stems, and stir-fry until wilted. Toss with pine nuts, ½ clove minced garlic, salt, and pepper.

 Spinach Strudel with Tomato Vinaigrette

Prepare preceding recipe. Place 1 sheet phyllo dough on a clean work surface and brush with melted butter. Layer 3 more sheets, brushing each with more butter. Spread half the spinach over the phyllo. Roll, jelly-roll style, and place seam-side down on a buttered sheet pan. Brush with more butter. Make another strudel the same way. Bake in a preheated 400° F. oven until golden brown, 30 to 35 minutes. Rest for 10 minutes. Slice each strudel in 2 portions, and serve each in a pool of Warm Tomato Vinaigrette (page 298).

Fifty Ways to Cook Most Everything

 ### Stir-Fried Shrimp with Spinach

Stir-fry ½ cup chopped scallion, a pinch of crushed red pepper flakes, and 1 tablespoon minced fresh gingerroot for 10 seconds in 2 tablespoons peanut oil. Add 1 cup shelled and deveined small shrimp, stir-fry 30 seconds more, remove, and set aside. Add 1½ pounds fresh spinach leaves, trimmed of their stems, and stir-fry until wilted. Add a mixture of 1 teaspoon cornstarch, a pinch of sugar, 2 teaspoons Chinese oyster sauce, and 1 teaspoon soy sauce and heat through. Finish with 1 teaspoon Oriental sesame oil and 1 tablespoon dry sherry.

 ### Stir-Fried Spinach with Hoisin Walnuts

Toast 1 cup walnut pieces in 1 tablespoon peanut oil heated in a wok until smoking, remove and set aside. Add 1 tablespoon hoisin sauce, 1 tablespoon sugar, and 1 clove minced garlic to the wok and cook until sugar caramelizes. Pour over nuts and toss to coat. Add 2 tablespoons oil to the wok along with 1 teaspoon grated fresh gingerroot. Add 1½ pounds fresh spinach leaves, trimmed of their stems, and stir-fry until wilted. Toss in the nuts and 2 sliced scallions.

 ### Spinach Timbales

Cook ¼ cup finely chopped onion and ½ clove minced garlic in 2 tablespoons butter until soft. Add 10 ounces defrosted frozen chopped spinach and cook until dry. Season with salt, pepper, and a dash of ground nutmeg. Mix ½ cup light cream, ½ cup milk, 2 eggs, and 1 egg yolk. Add to spinach and mix. Pour into four 5-ounce buttered ramekins, place in a shallow pan of warm water, cover ramekins with a sheet of parchment or wax paper, and bake at 350° F. for 40 minutes. Run a knife around the timbales to loosen and invert onto a

plate. Serve with Beurre Blanc (page 24), Red Pepper Coulis (page 25), or Warm Tomato Vinaigrette (page 298).

 ### Spinach and Blue Cheese Custard

Follow preceding recipe, adding 2 ounces crumbled blue cheese to the egg-milk mixture. Use 5 ramekins.

 ### Spinach Parmesan Soufflé

Cook ¼ cup flour in 4 tablespoons butter for 2 minutes in a heavy saucepan. Add 1½ cups milk, whisking constantly, and simmer several minutes until thick. Remove from heat and beat in 6 egg yolks, 1 at a time. Season liberally with salt and pepper. Add ½ recipe Garlic Spinach (page 272) and ½ cup grated Parmesan. Beat 8 egg whites with ⅛ teaspoon cream of tartar until firm peaks form. Fold into spinach mixture in 3 additions. Transfer into a greased 2-quart soufflé dish that has been dusted with Parmesan. Bake in 400° F. oven for 20 minutes, reduce heat to 350° F., and bake 20 to 25 minutes, until puffed and brown. Serve immediately.

 ### Broccoli Rabe Soufflé

Follow preceding recipe, substituting Broccoli Rabe with Garlic and Olive Oil (page 278) for the Garlic Spinach.

 ### Spinach Orzo Soup

Season 1½ quarts rich chicken broth with salt and pepper and bring to a boil. Add ¾ cup orzo and simmer for 12 minutes until orzo is tender. Meanwhile in a food processor or blender, puree 3 egg yolks with 10 ounces defrosted frozen chopped

spinach

spinach. Add a ladleful of the boiling soup to the egg yolk mixture, stirring constantly. Reduce heat so soup barely simmers and slowly pour egg mixture into the hot soup, stirring constantly. Cook over moderate heat, still stirring, until soup thickens lightly. Add 1 tablespoon lemon juice and serve.

Cream of Spinach Soup

Follow recipe for Garlic Spinach (page 272). Add 1 tablespoon flour in place of the lemon juice and cook 1 minute more. Add 3 cups chicken broth and simmer 10 minutes. Finely chop in a food processor or blender. Finish with 1 cup heavy cream and reheat.

Spinach and Wild Mushroom Soup

Soak ½ ounce dried wild mushrooms (any variety) in 1 cup boiling water for 20 minutes. Squeeze out excess liquid, trim off hard ends, and chop mushrooms coarsely. Sauté ½ pound sliced fresh mushrooms and the wild mushrooms with ¼ cup chopped onion in 2 tablespoons olive oil until lightly browned. Add 2 tablespoons flour, ¼ teaspoon dried thyme, and ¼ teaspoon crumbled dried rosemary and cook for 3 minutes. Strain mushroom soaking liquid, add to pan with 20 ounces defrosted frozen chopped spinach and 3 cups chicken stock, and simmer for 15 minutes. Add ½ cup heavy cream mixed with 1 egg yolk and cook gently for 1 to 2 minutes.

Spinach Pasta

Squeeze as much water as possible from 5 ounces defrosted frozen chopped spinach. In a food processor, blend spinach with 3 eggs and ½ teaspoon salt until smooth. Add 2 cups all-purpose flour and process until a ball of dough forms in the work

bowl of the processor. Knead on a floured board until very smooth and elastic. Cover and let rest for 10 minutes. Roll to desired thickness with a pasta machine or on a floured board with a floured pin, adding flour as necessary to keep the dough from sticking. Cut into noodles, cook in rapidly boiling salted water until *al dente*, 1 to 5 minutes, depending on thickness, and serve tossed with 3 tablespoons extra-virgin olive oil, ⅓ cup grated Parmesan, and 1 clove minced garlic.

Spinach Pilaf

Prepare 1 recipe Simple Rice Pilaf (page 240). When you fluff the rice, toss with ½ recipe Garlic Spinach (page 272).

Spinach Waldorf Salad

Toss 1 diced large apple, 1 cup walnut pieces, 1 rib sliced celery, ¼ cup diced red onion, 10 ounces stemmed and deveined clean spinach leaves, and ½ pound diced baked ham. Heat 3 tablespoons cider vinegar and 1 tablespoon sugar until sugar dissolves. Whisk into 1 tablespoon sour cream and ¼ cup mayonnaise and toss with salad.

Warm Spinach Salad with Chicken Livers

In a salad bowl, toss 1½ pounds stemmed and cleaned spinach leaves, 8 sliced large mushrooms, and ½ thinly sliced red onion. Cook 3 strips bacon until crisp, drain on paper towels, and crumble bacon into salad. Brown 1½ pounds cleaned chicken livers in the hot bacon fat. Mix ½ cup olive oil, the juice of ½ lemon, 5 tablespoons wine vinegar, 2 tablespoons sugar, salt, and pepper, add to pan, and simmer for 2 to 3 minutes. Remove from heat and stir in ½ cup plain yogurt. Adjust seasoning and pour over the spinach. Toss well.

 Watercress and Spinach Caesar Salad

In a salad bowl, mash 1 clove garlic and 4 anchovies with the back of a fork. Mix in 2 teaspoons brown mustard and 3 tablespoons wine vinegar. Slowly beat in 6 tablespoons olive oil. Toss stemmed leaves from 10 ounces spinach and 2 bunches watercress with this dressing. Garnish with 2 tablespoons grated Parmesan and 1 cup garlic croutons.

 Ruby Salad

Rinse, dry, and tear into bite-size pieces leaves from 1 head Romaine, 1 head radicchio, and 5 ounces fresh spinach. Toss with 8 sliced red radishes and 1 thinly sliced small red onion. Whisk 1 small clove minced garlic, ¼ cup red wine vinegar, ½ cup virgin olive oil, ½ teaspoon salt, and pepper. Toss with the vegetables and toss in ½ cup shelled pistachios.

Braised Belgian Endive

Trim wilted leaves and hard white bases from 4 fat heads of Belgian endive. Halve lengthwise and sear on both sides in 3 tablespoons olive oil. Add ½ cup white wine and boil off the alcohol. Add ½ cup chicken broth, salt, and pepper, cover, and simmer for 20 minutes. Add 1 tablespoon lemon juice and 2 tablespoons chopped fresh parsley and simmer for 5 to 6 more minutes until endive are fork-tender.

 Braised Endive with Ham

Follow preceding recipe, replacing olive oil with peanut oil and adding ¼ cup chopped ham with the endive.

 Wilted Chicory

Cook 3 strips bacon until crisp, remove bacon, and crumble. To the bacon fat in the pan, add 1 dried chili pepper, 1 chopped onion, and 2 cloves minced garlic and cook until onion is softened. Add ½ pound diced smoked turkey breast, 2 tablespoons dry sherry, ½ cup chicken stock, 1 tablespoon cider vinegar, 1 tablespoon mustard, and 1 tablespoon honey. Bring to a simmer, remove chili pepper, and season liberally with salt and pepper. Add 1 bunch stemmed, rinsed, and dried chicory, broken into large pieces, and cook just until wilted. Toss in the reserved bacon.

 Sweet Apple Sauerkraut

Drain and thoroughly rinse 1 pound sauerkraut. Set aside. Cook 1 chopped small onion in 2 teaspoons vegetable oil until soft. Add 2 large tart peeled and diced apples and cook another 2 minutes. Stir in 1 tablespoon brown sugar, 1 cup apple juice, and the sauerkraut. Simmer until all the liquid evaporates.

 Caraway Sauerkraut

Drain and thoroughly rinse 1 pound sauerkraut. Set aside. Cook 2 strips bacon until crisp, remove, and crumble bacon. To fat in pan, add sauerkraut, 2 teaspoons caraway seed, 1 teaspoon sugar, and 2 cups white wine. Simmer until all liquid evaporates, then stir in the crumbled bacon.

 Brussels Sprouts Simmered in Milk

Remove stem and any wilted leaves from 1 pint fresh Brussels sprouts. With a paring knife, cut a small X in the bottom of each sprout. Bring 2 cups water mixed with 2 cups milk to a gentle boil. Add sprouts and simmer for 10 minutes, until softened. Drain and toss with salt, pepper, and 2 tablespoons sour cream.

Brussels Sprouts Sautéed with Bacon and Apples

Cook Brussels sprouts as described in preceding recipe, but omit the sour cream. Cook 2 slices crisp bacon, remove, and crumble. Cook 2 tablespoons chopped onion and 1 peeled, diced tart apple in the hot fat. Add the cooked sprouts and heat through. Garnish with the bacon.

Stir-Fried Brussels Sprouts

Cook Brussels sprouts as described in Brussels Sprouts Simmered in Milk (opposite), but omit the sour cream. Halve the cooked sprouts and set aside. Dissolve 1 teaspoon cornstarch in juice of ½ lemon. Set aside. Mix 1 tablespoon light soy sauce, 2 teaspoons hoisin sauce, ¼ cup water, and 1 teaspoon ground ginger and set aside. Stir-fry ½ cup chopped onion in 1 tablespoon peanut oil for 30 seconds. Add sprouts and stir-fry 30 seconds more. Add soy mixture and bring to a boil. Stir the starch mixture, add, and simmer until thick. Add 1 tablespoon finely chopped lemon zest and 1 clove minced garlic and toss.

Sautéed Spring Greens

Rinse, dry, and stem 1 bunch Swiss chard and 2 bunches young dandelion greens. Boil in plenty of salted water for 5 minutes, drain, and season with salt and pepper. Cook 1 small finely chopped onion in 2 tablespoons olive oil until soft. Add greens and 1 clove minced garlic, toss in the hot fat for 1 minute, and place on a platter. Add 2 tablespoons drained capers and the juice of 1 lemon to deglaze pan and pour juices over the greens.

Sautéed Bitter Greens with Sweet Pepper Vinaigrette

Rinse, dry, and stem 1 head escarole and 1 head curly endive. Boil in plenty of salted water for 5 minutes, drain, and season with salt and pepper. Cook 1 small finely chopped onion, 1 diced roasted red bell pepper (page 442), and ⅓ cup diced smoked turkey breast or ham in 2 tablespoons olive oil until vegetables soften. Add greens and 1 clove minced garlic, toss in the hot fat for 1 minute, and place on a platter. Deglaze pan with 1 tablespoon sugar and 2 tablespoons red wine vinegar and pour juices over the greens.

Gratin of Chard

Trim stems from 2 pounds Swiss chard, rinse and dry leaves. Blanch for 45 seconds in boiling salted water, drain, and shake off excess water. Cook ½ pound cleaned, sliced mushrooms and 1 clove minced garlic in 3 tablespoons butter until softened. Add greens and remove from heat. Mix in ½ cup ricotta cheese, ¼ cup grated Parmesan, and 1 beaten egg. Mound in an 8-inch baking dish and sprinkle top with 2 tablespoons seasoned bread crumbs mixed with 2 tablespoons grated Parmesan. Bake at 375° F. for 35 minutes.

Gratin of Spinach

Follow preceding recipe, substituting 1½ pounds fresh spinach for the chard.

Chard with Chorizo

Rinse, dry, and stem 2 pounds Swiss chard and boil in plenty of salted water for 1 minute. Drain and season with salt and pepper. Cook 1 small finely chopped onion in 2 tablespoons olive oil until soft.

Add ½ cup chopped chorizo sausage, 1 clove minced garlic, and the greens. Toss in the hot fat for 2 minutes and mound on a platter.

Broccoli Rabe with Garlic and Olive Oil

Slice hard stem ends from 2 bunches broccoli rabe and cut the rest of the stalks in 1-inch sections. Rinse thoroughly and add the rabe, with any water still clinging to it, to 3 tablespoons olive oil, heated in a large skillet. Add a large pinch of crushed red pepper flakes and season liberally with salt and pepper. Cover and simmer over moderate heat for 10 minutes. Stir in 1 clove minced garlic and more olive oil, if desired.

Baked Broccoli Rabe with Cheese

Slice hard stem ends from 2 bunches broccoli rabe and cut the rest of the stalks in 1-inch sections. Rinse thoroughly. Boil in a large amount of rapidly boiling water for 10 minutes and drain. Mix in ½ cup ricotta cheese, ¼ cup grated Parmesan, and 1 beaten egg. Mound in an 8-inch baking dish, and sprinkle top with 2 tablespoons seasoned bread crumbs mixed with 2 tablespoons grated Parmesan. Bake at 375°F. for 35 minutes.

Kale with Sausage and Apple

In a large deep skillet or Dutch oven, brown ½ pound sliced Italian sausage with ¼ cup chopped onion in a thin film of oil. Add 1 cup apple juice and bring to a boil. Add 1 pound stemmed and rinsed kale leaves, cover, and simmer over moderate heat for 10 minutes, stirring occasionally. Meanwhile, cook 1 peeled diced large tart apple in 2 tablespoons butter until soft. Add 1 tablespoon brown sugar and cook until sugar melts. Combine with kale, salt, and pepper and serve.

Fried Kale

Stem 1 pound perfect kale leaves and leave whole. Rinse and dry thoroughly. Deep-fry at 375° F. a few at a time, until bright green, and crisp at the edge, 15 to 30 seconds. Blot off excess oil and toss with salt, pepper, and a dash of cider vinegar.

Kale Smothered with Bacon and Onions

In a large deep skillet or Dutch oven, cook 4 slices bacon until crisp, remove, and crumble. Add 2 sliced onions to the bacon fat and cook very slowly until golden brown. Stem and rinse 1 pound kale leaves and add to the onions along with any water still clinging to the kale. Cover and simmer over moderate heat for 10 minutes, stirring occasionally. Season with salt and pepper and serve.

Chilled Watercress Soup

Cook 1 finely chopped small onion in 3 tablespoons butter until soft. Add 1 tablespoon flour and cook 1 minute. Add 4 cups chicken broth and bring to a simmer. Add stemmed leaves from 3 bunches watercress, salt, pepper, and a grating of nutmeg and simmer for 10 minutes. Process in a blender until smooth and chill. Before serving, whisk in 1 cup sour cream or plain yogurt.

Watercress Cream Sauce

Wilt the stemmed leaves from 1 bunch watercress in 1 tablespoon butter with 1 finely chopped shallot. Add 1 cup heavy cream and simmer until lightly thickened, about 1 minute. Serve over poached fish, shellfish, eggs, or a grilled chicken breast.

32

Fifty Ways to Conquer Zucchini

The zucchini are coming! The zucchini are coming! Hiding under mulch and poking through the foliage, they are ready to take over your garden, your refrigerator, and half your life if you don't take immediate measures to stem their tide.

Every gardener/cook has faced the onslaught of zucchini, which descends each summer as the crops come in. But necessity is an inventive mother, offering unceasing quantities of zucchini breads, stews, soups, muffins, and sautés to help pull suffocating kitchen victims out from under the produce avalanche.

The trick to meeting such an invasion with the coolness of a cucumber is simple. You need only an oversized pot, a generous supply of freezer bags, and a recipe that can turn your kitchen into a processing plant. We have just such a formula, capable of spinning squash into culinary gold by the bushel.

We've christened it BZM, short for Basic Zucchini Mixture. The recipe yields an easy, all-purpose preparation that will last in your freezer well into the winter, ready to be whipped into everything from soup to cake in minutes.

The processing is simple, and once it's complete,

you're set to reap the harvest from your garden year round, baking zucchini breads for holiday gifts or preparing a summer-fresh soup in the middle of March.

BZM is a straightforward mix of zucchini, garlic, onion, and butter adaptable to many subsidiary preparations but flavorful enough to stand on its own. One of the drawbacks of zucchini to many diners is its watery blandness. Zucchini needs aromatics such as garlic or onion to give it a flavor base on which to build. Otherwise, the zucchini will behave like a flavor vacuum, absorbing any seasoning you add to it with no apparent benefit.

ABOUT THESE RECIPES

It is best to store this Basic Zucchini Mixture in 2- to 3-cup lots, which is a versatile, manageable quantity. Unless the amounts needed are unusual, we have not included salt and pepper in the following recipes, assuming that you will season each recipe to taste with both. All subsidiary recipes yield 4 servings unless otherwise noted.

Making and freezing a large quantity of the basic

mixture is your choice, of course. If you're interested only in making the occasional zucchini recipe, simply determine what fraction of the basic mix you need for the recipe you want and make enough for that recipe only.

We recognize that you may balk at the prospect of putting onion and garlic in the recipes for cakes, breads, and muffins. Rest assured that in such small quantities the flavors of these ingredients, as well as the zucchini, are imperceptible in baked goods. Like carrots in carrot cake, their function in these cases is to add and maintain moistness, not to contribute to the products' flavor. (Of course you *can* omit onion and garlic without affecting the results if you make BZM only for sweet recipes.)

Here's the recipe for the basic mix:

Basic Zucchini Mixture (BZM)

Cook 1 finely chopped onion and 1 clove minced garlic in 1 tablespoon butter and 1 tablespoon oil until soft. Add 5 pounds grated zucchini and stir over heat for 4 to 5 minutes. Let cool and drain. Squeeze in a clean kitchen towel to remove most moisture before using in any of the following recipes. Makes 8 cups.

 ## Zucchini Bread

Beat 3 eggs, 1 cup granulated sugar, and 1 cup light brown sugar until fluffy. Slowly add 2 cups peanut oil in a steady stream and 2 teaspoons vanilla extract, mixing constantly. Sift 3 cups flour, ½ teaspoon salt, 1 teaspoon ground cinnamon, 1 teaspoon baking soda, and ¼ teaspoon baking powder. Mix into the batter alternately with 2 cups BZM. Fold in 1¾ cups walnut pieces. Pour into 2 greased and floured 8-by-4-inch loaf pans and bake in preheated 325° F. oven for 1 hour 15 minutes or until a tester comes out with crumbs clinging to it. Unmold while warm. Serves 12.

 ## Zucchini Muffins

Follow preceding recipe, but bake in greased and floured 12-cup muffin tin, filling each cup about ⅔ full, for 30 minutes at 350° F.

 ## Lemon Zucchini Muffins

Add the finely grated zest and juice of 1 large lemon to recipe for Zucchini Bread (above) and replace baking powder with baking soda. Bake in 12-cup greased and floured muffin tin for 30 minutes at 350° F.

 ## Gingered Pecan Zucchini Bread

Follow recipe for Zucchini Bread (above), substituting 2 teaspoons ground ginger for half the cinnamon. Use pecans instead of walnuts and add ¼ cup minced candied ginger with the nuts.

 ## Zucchini Fruit Cake

Follow recipe for Zucchini Bread (above), replacing ½ cup BZM with 2 cups chopped dried fruit marinated overnight in 1 cup brandy, then drained.

 ## Tropical Zucchini Cake

Follow recipe for Zucchini Bread (above), replacing ½ cup of the BZM with ½ cup mix of chopped dried pineapple, papaya, and banana soaked in dark rum and drained and using shredded coconut instead of walnuts. Spread with icing made by beating together 8 ounces cream cheese, 4 tablespoons softened butter, 1 cup sifted confectioners' sugar, ½ teaspoon vanilla, and 1 tablespoon dark rum. Sprinkle ½ cup shredded coconut over the icing, if desired.

 ### Zucchini Cake

Beat 4 eggs with 1¾ cups sugar until fluffy. Slowly add 1½ cups peanut oil in a steady stream and 2 teaspoons vanilla extract, mixing constantly. Sift 2 cups flour, ½ teaspoon salt, 2 teaspoons ground cinnamon, and 2 teaspoons baking soda. Mix into batter alternately with 3 cups BZM. Fold in 1 cup walnut pieces. Pour into 2 greased and floured 9-inch layer pans and bake in preheated 350° F. oven for 50 minutes or until a tester comes out with a crumb clinging to it. Unmold, cool, and frost with icing made by beating together 1 pound cream cheese, ¼ pound softened butter, 2 cups confectioners' sugar, and 1 teaspoon vanilla extract. Serves 12.

 ### Zucchini Carrot Cake

Follow preceding recipe, substituting 2 cups grated carrots for half the BZM.

 ### Chocolate Zucchini Cake

With electric mixer, beat ½ pound butter, 2 teaspoons vanilla extract, and 2 cups sugar until light and fluffy. Beat in 5 eggs, 1 at a time. Add 2¾ cups sifted flour sifted with 1 teaspoon baking powder, 2 teaspoons baking soda, 2 teaspoons ground cinnamon, 1 teaspoon ground ginger, ½ teaspoon ground cloves, ½ teaspoon grated nutmeg, and 1 cup cocoa powder in several additions. Mix in 2 cups BZM and 1½ cups walnut pieces. Turn into greased and floured 10-inch tube pan and bake in preheated 325° F. oven for 1 hour 10 minutes, or until a tester comes out with only a crumb clinging to it. Cool for 10 minutes before removing from

pan. Dust with confectioners' sugar when completely cool. Serves 12.

 ### Two-Chocolate Zucchini Cake

Follow preceding recipe, substituting 1½ cups chopped white chocolate for the walnuts.

 ### Chocolate Gingered Zucchini Cake with Orange Glaze

Follow recipe for Chocolate Zucchini Cake (above), substituting 1 cup chopped candied orange peel and ¼ cup chopped candied ginger for the walnuts. Drizzle with icing made by beating together 8 ounces cream cheese, 4 tablespoons softened butter, 1 cup sifted confectioners' sugar, ½ teaspoon vanilla extract, 1 tablespoon dark rum, and 1 tablespoon orange liqueur.

 ### Zucchini Cornbread

Cook 3 tablespoons chopped onion in 2 tablespoons corn oil until soft. Add 1 cup BZM and heat through. Toss mixture with ¾ cup flour sifted with 1 tablespoon baking powder, ¼ cup sugar, ½ teaspoon salt, and 1¼ cups cornmeal. Add 1 beaten egg and 1 cup milk until mixture is uniformly moist. Brush hot ovenproof 9-inch skillet with another 1 tablespoon corn oil and spread batter evenly in skillet. Bake in preheated 425° F. oven for 25 minutes. Remove from pan and cool for 10 minutes.

 ### Multicolored Cornbread

Follow preceding recipe for Zucchini Cornbread, substituting 1 recipe Zucchini Sautéed with Roasted Peppers (page 442) for 1 cup BZM.

Fifty Ways to Cook Most Everything

 Zucchini Soup

Cook 1 finely chopped onion and 1 clove minced garlic in 2 tablespoons butter until soft. Add 3½ cups BZM, 1 teaspoon curry powder, ⅛ teaspoon cayenne pepper, and 3 cups chicken stock. Simmer for 10 minutes. Add 1 cup light cream and heat through. Serves 6.

 Chilled Curried Zucchini Soup

Cook 1 finely chopped onion and 1 clove minced garlic in 2 tablespoons butter until soft. Add 3½ cups BZM, 2 teaspoons curry powder, ¼ teaspoon cayenne pepper, 1 teaspoon ground coriander, and 3½ cups chicken stock. Simmer for 10 minutes. Add 1 cup plain yogurt and chill before serving. Garnish with chopped walnuts. Serves 6.

 Zucchini Apple Soup

Follow either of preceding two recipes, adding 1 peeled, cored, and diced apple to the soup with the BZM.

 Lemon Zucchini Soup

Follow recipe for Zucchini Soup (above), substituting 2 tablespoons lemon juice and ½ cup *crème fraîche* for the light cream.

 Zucchini Vichyssoise

Cook 2 thinly sliced leeks and 2 minced shallots in 2 tablespoons butter until soft. Add 1 cup diced and peeled potato, a pinch of nutmeg, and 4 cups chicken stock. Simmer until potatoes are tender. Puree through a food mill. Add 3½ cups BZM and simmer another 10 minutes. Finish with 1 cup light cream. Chill. Serves 6.

 Zucchini Minestrone

Cook 1 cup chopped onion, the chopped white of 1 leek, and 2 cloves minced garlic in 2 tablespoons olive oil until soft. Add 2 sliced carrots, 2 ribs sliced celery, 3 cups BZM, and ½ diced bell pepper. Cook 2 minutes. Add 1 teaspoon *each* dried thyme, savory, and basil and ½ teaspoon *each* dried rosemary, oregano, and sage. Cook 5 minutes more. Add 4 chopped canned tomatoes, 5 cups chicken broth, 1 tablespoon wine vinegar, and 1 tablespoon tomato paste. Bring to a boil and simmer for 10 minutes. Serve with grated Parmesan. Serves 8.

 Split Pea Zucchini Soup

Cook 1 diced onion and 2 cups diced smoked turkey in 2 tablespoons butter over moderate heat for 2 minutes, until onion softens. Add 5 cups chicken broth, 1 cup rinsed split peas, and a pinch of crushed red pepper flakes. Simmer until peas are tender, about 45 minutes. Stir in 2 cups BZM and simmer 5 minutes more. Adjust seasoning.

 Zucchini Lentil Soup

Follow preceding recipe, substituting lentils for the peas.

 Zucchini Chowder

Cook 1 cup chopped onion and 2 cloves minced garlic in rendered fat from 2 slices bacon until vegetables soften. Add 1 diced peeled potato, 1 teaspoon *each* dried thyme and basil leaves, ½ teaspoon dried marjoram or oregano, a pinch of crushed red pepper flakes, and ⅓ cup diced red pepper and sauté for 1 minute. Add 4 cups chicken stock and simmer until potato is tender. Add 2 cups BZM and 1 cup chopped peeled and seeded tomato and heat through.

 Zucchini Stuffing

Cook 1 finely chopped onion and 1 clove minced garlic in 2 tablespoons olive oil until soft, along with 2 teaspoons rubbed sage, 1 teaspoon dried thyme, and 1 teaspoon dried and crumbled rosemary. Combine with 2 cups BZM, 2 cups toasted bread cubes, 2 dashes grated nutmeg, and ½ cup chicken stock. Makes enough to stuff 2 frying chickens, 2 ducks, 4 large fish, or 1 roasting chicken, turkey, or capon.

 Zucchini Wild Mushroom Stuffing

Follow preceding recipe adding ¼ pound sliced fresh wild mushrooms to the onion mixture.

 Zucchini Rice Stuffing

Follow recipe for Zucchini Stuffing (above), substituting cooked rice for the bread.

 Zucchini Fruit Stuffing

Follow recipe for Zucchini Stuffing (above), substituting 1 cup cooked brown rice for the bread and adding 2 cups diced mixed dried fruit along with the BZM.

 Walnut Zucchini Stuffing

Cook 1 finely chopped onion and 1 clove minced garlic in 1 tablespoon *each* walnut and olive oils until soft, with 2 teaspoons dried basil, 1 teaspoon dried thyme, and 1 teaspoon dried and crumbled rosemary. Combine with 2 cups BZM, 1 cup toasted bread cubes, 2 cups chopped walnuts, a dash of grated nutmeg, and ½ cup chicken stock. Use as you would Zucchini Stuffing (above).

 Zucchini Sautéed with Roasted Peppers

In a nonstick skillet, cook 1 halved and thinly sliced onion and 1 clove minced garlic in 2 to 3 tablespoons olive oil until soft. Add 2 stemmed, seeded, and julienned roasted red peppers (page 442) and cook 1 minute. Add 3 cups BZM and 1 tablespoon finely chopped basil leaves and cook 2 minutes more.

 Red, White, and Green Zucchini

Follow preceding recipe, adding 6 ounces cleaned and sliced white mushrooms with the onion mixture.

 Zucchini Tabouleh

Soak 1½ cups bulgur in 2 cups boiling water about 20 minutes, until wheat is swollen and softened. Toss with Zucchini Sautéed with Roasted Peppers (above), the juice of 1 lemon, 2 tablespoons virgin olive oil, and ⅓ cup chopped fresh parsley. Season liberally with salt and pepper.

 Zucchini Sautéed with Tomatoes and Parmesan

Follow recipe for Zucchini Sautéed with Roasted Peppers (above), substituting ½ cup chopped tomatoes for the peppers and adding 2 tablespoons grated Parmesan at the end.

Fifty Ways to Cook Most Everything

 Pasta Primavera

Toss either of two preceding recipes with 12 ounces hot cooked pasta. Garnish with grated Parmesan.

 Zucchini Stuffed with Zucchini

Stuff 1 zucchini, split lengthwise and hollowed out, with Zucchini Sautéed with Tomatoes and Parmesan (page 283). Top each with 1 tablespoon additional Parmesan and bake at 350° F. for 20 minutes.

 Zucchini Sautéed with Thyme

In nonstick skillet, cook ½ cup chopped onion, 1 clove minced garlic, and 1 teaspoon dried thyme in 2 tablespoons olive oil until soft. Add 3 cups BZM and cook another 2 minutes.

 Garlic and Ginger Zucchini

Follow preceding recipe, doubling amount of garlic and adding 1 tablespoon grated fresh gingerroot with it. Substitute ½ teaspoon Oriental sesame oil for ½ teaspoon olive oil.

 Zucchini Timbales

Follow recipe for Zucchini Sautéed with Thyme (above), adding 1 cup milk and 2 beaten eggs after it is done cooking. Divide among 6 greased 5-ounce ramekins, cover with plastic wrap, and steam in flat-bottomed steamer until springy, about 10 minutes. Run a knife around the edge of each timbale and invert to unmold.

 Zucchini Quiche

In nonstick skillet, cook ½ cup chopped onion with 1 clove minced garlic and 1 teaspoon dried thyme in 2 tablespoons olive oil until soft. Add 3 cups BZM and cook another 2 minutes. Remove from heat, add 1 cup milk, 2 beaten eggs, and 1 cup grated Swiss cheese and pour into prebaked 8-inch pastry shell. Bake in a preheated 375° F. oven for 45 minutes.

 Zucchini with Walnuts

In nonstick skillet, cook ½ cup chopped onion, 1 clove minced garlic, and 1 teaspoon dried thyme in 2 tablespoons walnut oil until soft. Add 3 cups BZM and cook another 2 minutes. Add ¼ cup chopped toasted walnuts.

 Zucchini with Pine Nuts

In nonstick skillet, cook ½ cup chopped onion, 1 clove minced garlic, and 1 teaspoon dried basil in 2 tablespoons olive oil until soft. Add 3 cups BZM and cook another 2 minutes. Add 2 tablespoons toasted pine nuts.

 Zucchini Provençale

In nonstick skillet, cook ½ cup chopped onion, 2 cloves minced garlic, and 1 teaspoon *herbes de Provence* in 2 tablespoons olive oil. Add 3 cups BZM and ¼ cup chopped fresh tomato and cook another 2 minutes.

 Stir-Fried Zucchini with Caramelized Cashews

In a wok or skillet, toast 1 cup cashew pieces in 1 tablespoon hot peanut oil, remove and set aside.

Add 1 tablespoon hoisin sauce, 1 tablespoon sugar, and 1 clove minced garlic and cook until sugar bubbles. Add to nuts and toss to coat. Add 2 tablespoons oil and 1 teaspoon grated fresh gingerroot. Add 2 cups BZM and toss. Add nuts and 2 sliced scallions.

 Zucchini Pasta

In a food processor, blend 1 cup BZM, 1 large egg, 1 clove garlic, ¼ teaspoon salt, and ½ teaspoon olive oil. Add 2 cups flour and process until dough forms a ball in center of work bowl. Knead with additional flour until smooth and elastic. Roll out with floured pin or pasta machine to desired thickness and cut into desired shapes. Cook until *al dente* for 1 to 2 minutes in rapidly boiling salted water. Drain well and serve with pasta sauce of your choice.

 Zucchini Latkes

Mix 3 cups BZM, 3 lightly beaten eggs, and 2 tablespoons flour. Season well with salt and pepper. Fry heaping spoonfuls in hot vegetable oil until browned on both sides. Drain on paper towels and serve with tomato sauce or sour cream.

 Zucchini Potato Pancakes

Follow preceding recipe, substituting 1 cup rinsed, dried, peeled, and grated russet potatoes for 1½ cups of the BZM. Serve with sour cream.

 Garden Latkes

Mix ½ cup *each* peeled and grated carrot, potato, and apple with 1½ cups BZM, 3 lightly beaten eggs,

and 2 tablespoons flour. Cook as described in Zucchini Latkes (above). Serve with sour cream.

 Cottage Cheese Zucchini Pancakes

Follow recipe for Zucchini Latkes (above), substituting 1 cup drained cottage cheese for 1 cup BZM.

 Zucchini Burgers

Cook 1 minced onion, 2 cloves minced garlic, 1 finely diced carrot, and 1 diced roasted red pepper (page 442) in 2 tablespoons corn oil until soft. Mix with 2 cups BZM, 2 beaten extra-large eggs, 6 tablespoons seasoned bread crumbs, and a pinch of cayenne pepper. Refrigerate for 1 hour. Dredge ¼-cup portions in a mixture of 6 tablespoons *each* flour and seasoned bread crumbs and form into patties. Brown well in a thin film of oil. Drain.

 Turkey Zucchini Burgers

Follow preceding recipe, substituting ¾ pound ground turkey for bread crumbs and flour. You need not refrigerate before forming patties.

 Crab Zucchini Burgers

Follow recipe for Zucchini Burgers (above), using 1 pound lump crabmeat in place of the carrot and 1 cup of the BZM, and adding ½ teaspoon hot pepper sauce and 3 tablespoons mayonnaise to the mixture.

 Zucchini Meatloaf

With your hands, mix 2 pounds meatloaf blend (50 percent ground beef, 25 percent ground veal, 25

percent ground pork) with 1 minced medium onion, 2 eggs, ½ cup ketchup, 1 tablespoon Worcestershire sauce, 2 teaspoons mustard, and 2 cups BZM. Soak 2 slices bread with crusts removed in ½ cup milk and crumble soaked bread into meat mixture. Form mixture into a rough loaf and bake on a sheet pan or in a 6-cup casserole or 9-by-5-inch loaf pan in a 375° F. preheated oven for 1 hour. Makes about 6 servings.

Fifty Serious Salads

Salads have gotten a raw deal. Thrown together without thought, bathed in bottled dressing, and written off as "roughage" by the meat-and-potato mainstream, salads too often fail to get serious culinary attention. Even as salads have expanded from side dish to full entrée, they still haven't escaped the powerful lettuce-and-tomato stereotype.

We have to wonder why. A salad is olives, roasted peppers, and anchovies saturated with olive oil and garlic. It's a grilled chicken breast on a mound of winter greens peppered with bacon bits. It's poached scallops tossed in a tangle of pasta and a pesto vinaigrette, or grapefruit sections nestled into the crooks of shrimp and cloaked with guacamole.

Salads are hot, cold, tepid, and frozen, made from meat, poultry, seafood, vegetables, pasta, grains, beans, and fruit. They are raw as well as poached, roasted, grilled, and barbecued. There are marinated salads, tossed salads, composed salads, and molded salads. Salads start a lunch, finish a dinner, or provide a respite between courses.

About the only thing common among salads is flavor. Regardless of the type of salad, the flavor is always strong, bright, and sparkling. True to its name (from the Latin root *sal*, meaning "salt"), sal-ads have always been dishes that excite the palate. With a jolt of spice and a tart spark of acid, a salad perks the appetite and enlivens all other flavors in a meal. Whether salads are seasoned with lemon, vinegar, wine, garlic, or chili peppers, the reward is always the same—a bounty of flavor with a minimum of calories and fat.

These 50 recipes deliver salad ideas far in excess of their number, for within their ranks are recipes to spark a myriad of salad possibilities in your own culinary imagination.

ABOUT THESE RECIPES

All recipes are written for 4 portions unless otherwise noted. It is assumed that you will clean and dry all greens and season each salad with salt and pepper to your taste.

 Basic Green Salad

Break into bite-size pieces leaves from ½ head Boston lettuce and ½ head green- or red-leaf lettuce, and 6 leaves Romaine. Toss with ¼ cup any salad dressing and ¼ cup croutons.

Orange and Celery Salad

Cut 2 peeled and sectioned navel oranges in small pieces and toss with 4 ribs peeled, sliced celery. Toss with Orange Walnut Dressing (page 296) and ⅓ cup broken walnut pieces.

 Classic Caesar Salad

Toss Ceasar Dressing (page 297) with 1 head Romaine leaves, broken into bite-size pieces. Add ¼ cup grated Parmesan and 2 cups homemade Croutons (page 431) and toss.

 Mushroom Caesar Salad

Follow preceding recipe and add 8 cleaned, sliced mushrooms with the Romaine.

 Creamy Cucumber Salad

Peel, halve, seed, and thinly slice 1 large cucumber. Toss with 1 teaspoon kosher salt and set aside for 15 minutes. Rinse thoroughly and drain. Mix with Minted Yogurt Dressing (page 300).

 Iceberg with Three Tomatoes

Core and quarter 1 head iceberg lettuce. Place each quarter on a salad plate in a pool of Warm Tomato Vinaigrette (page 298). Arrange 3 wedges tomato to one side of the lettuce. Top with ½ recipe Real Russian Dressing (page 298).

 Gingered Carrot Salad

Blanch 2 pounds peeled, spiral-cut carrots in 2 quarts boiling water until barely tender, about 5 minutes. Toss with 1 recipe Spicy Ginger Vinaigrette (page 299) and chill thoroughly. Add 1 tablespoon chopped fresh chives. Serves 4 to 6.

 Creole Beet Salad

Simmer 1½ pounds small, rinsed beets in 2 quarts boiling water until tender, about 30 minutes. Add 1 pound peeled, diced carrots 4 minutes before beets are done. Drain well. Peel and dice beets and toss with carrots, 1 peeled, diced Granny Smith apple, ¼ cup minced scallion and Sweet and Sour Creole Vinaigrette (page 299).

 Creole Cole Slaw

In large bowl, mix Sour Cream Cole Slaw Dressing (page 298) with 2 tablespoons ketchup and 3 tablespoons hot pepper sauce. To dressing add 2 cored and coarsely grated large Granny Smith apples, 2 pounds cored and shredded cabbage, and 1 bunch thinly sliced scallions. Refrigerate several hours or overnight before serving.

 Endive, Beet, and Potato Salad

Break stemmed leaves from 1 head chicory, 1 head radicchio, and 1 head Belgian endive into bite-size pieces and toss with ½ pound cooked, peeled, and diced beets, ½ pound boiled, sliced red-skin potatoes, 4 ounces crumbled feta or goat cheese, and 1 cup walnut pieces. Toss with Garlic Herb Dressing (page 296).

 Russian Herring Potato Salad

Boil 3 pounds red-skin potatoes in 3 quarts salted water until tender, about 30 minutes. Drain and dice. While still warm, toss potatoes with drained and cubed contents of 1-pound jar of pickled herring, 1 finely chopped small red onion, and Real Russian Dressing (page 298).

 Tricolored Peppers with Herbs

Roast, peel, and stem 2 *each* large red, green, and yellow bell peppers and slice into strips (page 442). Toss with ½ recipe Garlic Herb Dressing (page 296).

 Peppers with Basil and Walnuts

Follow preceding recipe, but use only red or yellow peppers and add ¼ cup chopped fresh basil to dressing. Garnish with ⅓ cup chopped walnuts.

 Roasted Peppers with Black Olives and Anchovies

Roast, peel, stem, and seed 4 large bell peppers of any color and slice into strips (page 442). Toss with 24 pitted, oil-cured black olives, ½ finely chopped red onion, 1 clove minced garlic, 6 julienned anchovy fillets, ¼ cup olive oil, and 3 tablespoons wine vinegar. Serves 4 to 6.

 Spinach Salad with Roasted Peppers and Feta

Roast, peel, stem, and seed 4 large bell peppers of any color and slice in strips (page 442). Toss with 8 ounces crumbled feta cheese, ½ finely chopped red onion, 1 clove minced garlic, 2 ounces julienned Genoa salami, ¼ cup olive oil, and 3 tablespoons wine vinegar. Toss mixture with 10 ounces cleaned, stemmed spinach leaves. Serves 4 to 6.

 Asparagus-Orange Salmon Salad

Rub four ½-inch-thick salmon steaks with Oriental sesame oil. Grill 4 inches from a hot fire for 2 minutes per side, cool slightly, and remove skin and bones. Place each steak on a warm plate with 6 warm poached asparagus spears. Cloak with Sesame Tofu Vinaigrette (page 298) and garnish each plate with 3 orange rings and 1 teaspoon toasted sesame seeds.

 Sweet and Sour Smoked Turkey Potato Salad

In a small saucepan, heat 5 tablespoons cider vinegar and 3 tablespoons sugar until sugar dissolves. Transfer to large salad bowl and add 1 small finely chopped onion, 1 teaspoon salt, 1 tablespoon ketchup, and 3 tablespoons mayonnaise. Add 1½ pounds cooked, peeled, and diced warm red-skin potatoes, 2 ribs peeled and diced celery, and ¾ pound diced smoked turkey breast and toss well.

 Waldorf Potato Salad

Follow preceding recipe, but substitute sour cream or plain yogurt for the ketchup and ½ pound diced ham for the smoked turkey. Add 2 cored, diced Granny Smith apples.

 German-Style Potato Salad

Prepare Warm Bacon Dressing (page 298) with mayonnaise instead of ketchup. Toss with 1½ pounds cooked red-skin potatoes that have been peeled, cut into large dice and kept warm and 2 ribs sliced celery. Garnish with crumbled bacon left from making the dressing.

Fifty Serious Salads   289

Fifty Ways to Cook Most Everything

 Potato Vinaigrette with Mussels and Olives

Bring 1 clove minced garlic, ½ cup white wine, and ¼ teaspoon crushed red pepper flakes to a boil. Add 2 dozen scrubbed, debearded mussels and simmer until they open, about 3 minutes. Remove mussels with their shells and strain liquid in the pot through several layers of cheesecloth or toweling. Reserve strained liquid. Remove mussels from their shells, discarding shells and any mussels that do not open. In a bowl, combine 3 tablespoons mussel liquid, the mussels, another clove minced garlic, ¼ cup olive oil, 3 tablespoons wine vinegar, 2 tablespoons chopped fresh dill, and 20 pitted, halved oil-cured black olives. Toss well. Chop 1½ pounds red-skin potatoes that have been peeled, boiled, and kept warm into bite-size pieces and toss well with the other ingredients.

 Sour Cream and Caviar Potato Salad

In a bowl, blend 6 tablespoons sour cream, 2 tablespoons red wine vinegar, and ¼ cup peanut oil. Mix in 2 ounces salmon caviar, and 2 tablespoons thinly sliced fresh chives. Toss with 1½ pounds cooked red-skin potatoes, cut into bite-size pieces. Chill.

 Seafood Potato Salad

In a bowl, blend 6 tablespoons sour cream, 1 tablespoon red wine vinegar, 2 tablespoons lemon juice, and ¼ cup peanut oil. Mix in 2 ounces salmon caviar, 2 tablespoons thinly sliced fresh chives, and 1 tablespoon chopped fresh dill. Toss with 1½ pounds cooked red-skin potatoes cut into bite-size pieces and ½ pound *each* cooked and cleaned small shrimp and cleaned lump crabmeat. Chill.

 Marinated Tuna and White Bean Salad

Toss 1½ cups flaked freshly cooked or canned tuna, 1½ cups freshly cooked or canned drained white beans. ½ cup thinly sliced scallions, 1 small finely chopped red onion, and 1 clove minced garlic. In separate bowl, whisk 2 tablespoons olive oil, ¼ cup wine vinegar, and ½ teaspoon crushed red pepper flakes. Pour over salad and toss well. Garnish with 12 pitted, chopped oil-cured black olives. Chill well and serve on Romaine leaves.

 Crab, Orange, and Black Bean Salad

Toss together 1½ cups lump crabmeat, 1½ cups freshly cooked or canned drained black beans, ½ cup thinly sliced scallions, 1 small finely chopped red onion, and 1 clove minced garlic. In separate bowl, whisk 2 tablespoons olive oil, 2 tablespoons orange juice, 2 tablespoons wine vinegar, and ½ teaspoon crushed red pepper flakes. Add 2 tablespoons finely grated orange zest. Pour over salad and toss well. Garnish with 12 pitted, chopped oil-cured black olives. Chill well and serve on Romaine leaves.

 Southwest Garbanzo Turkey Salad

Combine 1 pound cooked and drained garbanzo beans, ⅓ cup thinly sliced scallions, 1 sliced roasted red pepper (page 442), and ½ pound diced smoked turkey breast. Toss with mixture of 3 tablespoons mayonnaise, 2 tablespoons chili powder, 1 tablespoon ground cumin, ⅓ cup corn or peanut oil, and 2 tablespoons hot pepper sauce. Just before serving, toss in 1 peeled, pitted and diced avocado and 2 tablespoons chopped fresh cilantro. Serves 6.

Tabouleh

Soak 2 cups bulgur in 2½ cups hot tap water for 30 minutes. Pour off any remaining water. Combine ⅓ cup olive oil, the juice of 1 lemon, 1 clove minced garlic, 1 small seeded and minced hot pepper, and 3 tablespoons *each* chopped fresh parsley, mint, and cilantro. Toss with the bulgur 2 cored, seeded, and chopped large tomatoes, 1 large peeled, seeded, and diced cucumber, and 3 tablespoons thinly sliced scallions. Chill.

 Grilled Lamb and Tabouleh Salad

Follow recipe for Tabouleh (above), but double quantity of dressing. Mix half the dressing with the soaked bulgur and combine the other half with 1 cup plain yogurt. Rub half the yogurt dressing into 2 pounds of 1-inch-thick boneless lamb steak and set aside for 30 minutes. Grill marinated lamb to desired degree of doneness. Slice steak and arrange on a bed of the tabouleh. Pour remaining yogurt dressing over top.

 Grilled Scallops and Shrimp Tabouleh

Follow recipe for Tabouleh (above), but double quantity of dressing. Mix half the dressing with the soaked bulgur and combine the other half with 1 cup plain yogurt. Marinate ½ pound *each* large scallops and large shelled shrimp in half the yogurt dressing for 30 minutes. Grill marinated shrimp 1 to 2 minutes per side, the scallops 1 minute longer. Arrange on a bed of the tabouleh, and pour remaining yogurt dressing over top.

 Bulgur Tortellini Salad

Soak 2 cups bulgur as described in Tabouleh recipe (above). Toss 1 pound hot cooked tortellini with bulgur. In a separate bowl, mix 2 tablespoons olive oil, 1½ cups plain yogurt, the juice of 1 lemon, 1 clove minced garlic, ¼ cup chopped fresh basil, and ¼ cup grated Parmesan. Toss with the bulgur and tortellini, cover, and refrigerate until ready to serve. Serves 6 to 8.

 Middle Eastern Bulgur Orzo Salad

Soak 2 cups bulgur as described in Tabouleh recipe (above). Toss ½ pound hot cooked orzo and bulgur. In a separate bowl, mix 2 tablespoons olive oil, 1½ cups plain yogurt, the juice of 1 lemon, 1 clove minced garlic, ¼ cup chopped fresh mint, and ¼ cup chopped fresh parsley. Toss with the bulgur and orzo. Add 1 peeled, seeded, and diced cucumber and 2 seeded, diced tomatoes, cover, and refrigerate until ready to serve. Serves 6 to 8.

 Summer Salmon Salad

Poach 1½ pounds boned salmon fillet in ½ recipe simmering Court Bouillon (page 430) until salmon flakes to gentle pressure. Cool to room temperature. Trim fillet of skin and excess fat and flake into a bowl. Toss with ⅓ cup Lemon and Olive Oil Dressing (page 296), 2 tablespoons chopped fresh dill, ¼ cup toasted pine nuts, and cayenne pepper.

 Pungent Tomato Salmon Salad

Poach 1½ pounds boned salmon fillet in ½ recipe simmering Court Bouillon (page 430) until salmon flakes to gentle pressure as in preceding recipe. Cool to room temperature. Trim fillet of skin and excess fat and flake into a bowl. Toss with ⅓ cup Sun-Dried Tomato Vinaigrette (page 297) and 2 tablespoons chopped fresh basil. Add 6 finely chopped oil-cured sun-dried tomatoes and cayenne pepper.

Smoked Fish Salad with Belgian Endive

Remove skin and bones from 1 pound of any smoked fish. Toss in bowl with ⅓ cup chopped celery, 2 tablespoons chopped chives, and Creamy Mayonnaise Dressing (page 300). Serve in center of a large platter surrounded by 3 heads Belgian endive, cored and broken into leaves, 1 peeled, sliced cucumber, and 1 seeded red bell pepper cut into strips. Garnish with 4 lemon slices.

 ## Grilled Fish Salad with Garden Greens

Rub four 4-ounce fish steaks or 4 small whole fish with 2 tablespoons olive oil, 1 tablespoon lemon juice, salt, and pepper. Grill or broil 4 inches from a hot fire for 8 minutes per inch of thickness, turning halfway through cooking time. Tear 1 head leaf lettuce and 1 head radicchio or arugula into small pieces. Combine with 6 finely sliced scallions and ¼ cup chopped fresh parsley. Toss with ½ recipe Balsamic Olive Oil Vinaigrette (page 297) and arrange to one side of each of 4 dinner plates. Place fish on the other side, overlapping salad by an inch or two. Moisten fish with some of remaining dressing. Garnish each plate with 2 sprigs watercress, 2 lemon wedges, and 1 lime wedge.

 ## Grilled Chicken Breast with Bitter Greens and Pine Nuts

Follow preceding recipe, substituting 2 split chicken breasts for the fish and grilling about 3 to 4 minutes per side. Use a combination of escarole, endive, radicchio, or arugula for the lettuces and garnish each salad with 1 tablespoon toasted pine nuts.

 ## Grilled Summer Squash Salad

Slice lengthwise 2 small zucchini and 2 small yellow summer squash. Marinate in Balsamic Olive Oil Vinaigrette (page 297) for 1 hour. Grill 2 minutes per side 4 inches from a charcoal fire and toss with enough dressing to moisten.

 ## Grilled Salmon Salad with Rosemary Vinaigrette

Slice 2 large russet potatoes into 1-inch-thick slices. Rub with some vegetable oil and grill over a hot fire for 4 to 5 minutes per side. Rub four 5-ounce salmon steaks with oil, salt, and pepper. After potatoes have cooked for 2 minutes, grill salmon 3 to 4 minutes per side. Rub 2 sliced ripe tomatoes with oil and grill 2 minutes per side. Skin salmon steaks, remove meat from center bones in 2 pieces, and arrange on a platter. Bank salmon with 1 pound snapped and blanched green beans, the grilled potato slices, and grilled tomatoes. Pour Creamy Rosemary Dressing (page 297) on top and garnish with rosemary sprigs.

 ## Composed Salad of Grilled Vegetables

Coat with olive oil 1 sweet potato cut into ½-inch-thick slices, 1 large zucchini cut into 1-inch-thick slices, 12 large mushrooms with stems trimmed, 1 medium eggplant, peeled and cut into 3-inch batons, 3 ears corn, husked and cut into thirds, 2 large beefsteak tomatoes, cored and thickly sliced, and the white part of 4 leeks, cleaned and split lengthwise. Grill vegetables over a hot fire; the whole process will take about 10 minutes. Start with leeks and sweet potatoes. After 2 minutes, add mushrooms, eggplant, and corn. After 3 minutes more, add zucchini and tomatoes. Turn all vegetables two or three times during cooking. Arrange on large platter and pour Mustard Vinaigrette (page 297) over all. Serve warm.

Grilled Chicken Salad with Asian Vegetables

Halve 2 carrots crosswise and slice each piece lengthwise in 3 strips. Brush carrot strips and 2 split, skinned, and boned chicken breasts with ¼ cup Soy Ginger Dressing (page 298) and grill 4 to 5 minutes per side until surfaces are seared and chicken is firm to the touch. Place 2 leaves Chinese cabbage on a large serving platter. Fan slices of chicken across cabbage. Pile 1 cup bean sprouts next to chicken. Fill remaining space on plate with grilled carrots. Toss ½ pound peeled, julienned jicama with 2 tablespoons dressing and pile atop carrot strips. Fan 16 pea pods across the bed of sprouts, place the peeled sections from 1 large navel orange on the cabbage to one side of the chicken, and garnish with 4 thinly sliced red radishes. Pour on remaining dressing and serve.

Red Cabbage Slaw

Core and shred 1 small head red cabbage. Toss in a large bowl with 2 coarsely grated carrots, 2 ribs peeled and diced celery, and 1 peeled, cored, and diced Granny Smith apple. Toss with Clear Cole Slaw Dressing (page 298). Serves 8.

White Cabbage Slaw

Core and shred 1 small head white cabbage. Toss in a large bowl with 2 coarsely grated carrots and 2 ribs peeled and diced celery. Toss with Sour Cream Cole Slaw Dressing (page 298). Serves 8.

Sweet and Sour Cole Slaw

Cook ½ pound bacon over moderate heat until crisp. Drain, and set aside bacon and fat to cool.

Trim 1 small head Savoy cabbage of tough outer leaves, remove stem, halve cabbage through its stem axis, and cut each half into paper-thin slices starting from rounded side and moving toward stem end. In a large bowl, toss cabbage, 1 grated carrot, 1 diced roasted red bell pepper (page 442), and 1 large rib peeled, diced celery. Crumble bacon slices and add to mixture. In deep skillet, cook 1 minced large red onion and 1 large clove minced garlic in the reserved fat until soft. Add ½ cup apple cider vinegar, 2 tablespoons sugar, and 2 tablespoons sour cream. Toss salad with dressing.

Bacon and Fruit Slaw

Follow preceding recipe, substituting 2 peeled, cored, and diced Granny Smith apples and 1 cup crushed pineapple for the carrot and roasted peppers.

Crab and Corn Slaw

Remove kernels from 4 ears of cooked white corn and toss in a large bowl with 1 pound cleaned lump crabmeat, 1 diced roasted red bell pepper (page 442), 2 ribs peeled, diced celery, ½ peeled, seeded, and diced cucumber, ¼ cup chopped fresh chives, and 1 small peeled, pitted, and diced avocado. Toss with Creamy Creole Dressing (page 299). Serves 6.

Smoked Turkey and Bitter Greens with Sweet Pepper Vinaigrette

Break 1 head escarole, 1 head curly endive, and ½ pound spinach leaves into larger-than-bite-size pieces, discarding stems and wilted leaves. Rinse thoroughly, dry, and toss in a large salad bowl with ⅔ cup finely chopped red onion and 12 sliced mushrooms. Grill 1 pound smoked turkey breast, cut in 12 thin slices and brushed lightly with vegetable oil, over a very hot fire just until surface sears. Bring Sweet Pepper Vinaigrette (page 299) to a boil over high heat. Immediately pour over greens and toss quickly. Greens will soften slightly from heat of the dressing. Divide greens among 4 plates and place 3 slices grilled turkey breast atop each. Serve immediately.

Warm Jerusalem Artichoke Salad with Lemon and Fennel

In large saucepan, bring to a boil 1 quart water, the juice of 1 lemon, and ½ teaspoon salt. Meanwhile, scrub 2 pounds Jerusalem artichokes with a mushroom brush under cold running water, cutting off hard ends or dark tips, and break into equal-size pieces. Add artichokes to boiling water and simmer until barely tender, about 5 minutes; they should still be crisp near their centers. Refresh under cold water and slice into bite-size pieces. Toss with the juice of another lemon. In a large skillet, heat 2 cloves minced garlic in 3 tablespoons olive oil and sauté for 30 seconds over moderate heat. Add 2 cups peeled and julienned celery root, 1 cup diced fennel, Jerusalem artichokes, and the lemon juice in which they are soaking. Cook 2 to 3 minutes or until vegetables are heated through. Remove from heat, stir in 2 tablespoons sour cream, and adjust seasoning.

Spinach Salad with Blue Cheese Dressing

In large salad bowl, combine 1½ pounds cleaned spinach leaves, 1 diced red onion, Blue Cheese Dressing (page 299), and ¾ cup chopped walnuts.

Steamed Vegetable Salad with Lemon Dill Dressing

Add 2 teaspoons chopped fresh dill to Lemon and Olive Oil Dressing (page 296). Set aside. Select a platter that will hold vegetables in a single layer. Arrange attractively on the plate 8 peeled baby carrots, ½ head broccoli florets, ¼ head cauliflower florets, 6 cherry tomatoes, and 8 small mushrooms. Place carrots and broccoli closer to the rim, tomatoes and mushrooms more toward the center. Cover platter with plastic wrap and microwave for 10 minutes at full power, or until carrots are just tender. Uncover and pour any juices on the plate into the dressing. Whisk dressing to make it smooth and thick and pour over vegetables. Serve hot.

Poached Winter Fruit Salad with Raspberry Vinaigrette

In a saucepan, combine 1½ cups white wine, ½ cup water, ½ cup sugar, 1 stick cinnamon, 1 clove, 1 slice fresh gingerroot, and a pinch salt. Heat until liquid simmers. Add 1 cored unpeeled sliced underripe pear to poaching liquid, simmer for 3 minutes, and remove pear slices to a warm platter. Add 1 cored unpeeled sliced Golden Delicious apple to the liquid, poach for 2 minutes, and transfer to the platter. Add 1 cup seedless red grapes to the liquid, simmer for 1 minute, and transfer to the platter. Add 2 peeled and sectioned tangerines to the poaching liquid, poach for 30 seconds, and transfer to the platter. Whisk 2 tablespoons poaching liquid into Raspberry Vinaigrette (page 297) until smooth. Pour dressing over poached fruit and serve warm.

Tossed Winter Greens with Warm Bacon Dressing

Break leaves from the stems of 2 heads escarole, curly endive, or chicory. Discard stems. Rinse and dry leaves, and toss with 2 finely chopped hard-cooked eggs, ¼ pound sliced cleaned mushrooms, and 1 thinly sliced red onion. Refrigerate. Toss with Warm Bacon Dressing (page 298) and garnish with crumbled bacon left from making the dressing. Serve immediately.

34

Fifty Bottle-Free Dressings

Salad dressing is as easy as one, two, three—one part vinegar, two pinches flavoring, and three parts oil. The measurements need not be exact and the technique requires nothing more than a flick of the whisk.

Why, then, is bottled dressing one of the most popular convenience foods in our culture? Why do we continue to pay so extravagantly for something that can be made at home in minutes for pennies?

For most of us, it's simply lack of practice. Most of us don't know that many homemade salad dressings keep for ages in the refrigerator and can be replenished quickly when supplies run low. Nor have most of us ever taken the time to see that hundreds of dressings stem from just three basic formulas and that to know these formulas is to have the entire cuisine of salads at one's fingertips.

All salad dressings are a mixture of fat and acid, usually oil and vinegar and usually mixed in a three-to-one proportion. Many salad dressings are simple vinaigrettes—Italian dressing, white and red wine vinaigrettes, lemon-and-oil dressings, warm bacon dressings, and sweet and sour salad dressings.

The only problem is that acids and fats do not readily blend together. If you mix them rapidly, they'll appear to blend, but that's just an illusion. After sitting for a few minutes the fat comes out of suspension and rises to the surface. That's why simple vinaigrettes must be shaken or whisked every time they're used.

To combat that separation anxiety, cooks have learned to rely on culinary emulsifiers to stabilize the fragile suspension of oil and vinegar. Emulsified salad dressings are held together by beating a simple vinaigrette into an egg yolk, commercial mayonnaise, or a fermented dairy product, all of which contain natural emulsifiers, to help the shaky oil-and-vinegar suspension remain thick and creamy for up to a week.

Emulsified salad dressings include creamy Italian vinaigrette, mayonnaise dressings, Russian dressings, buttermilk dressings, and most blue cheese dressings.

The third type of salad dressing holds the oil and vinegar together with a puree. This can be anything from the tomato in a tomato vinaigrette to the tofu in a creamy Japanese dressing. It might be the peanut butter in an Indonesian saté or a puree of basil and pine nuts in a pesto dressing.

Understand these three methods and any salad dressing is within your culinary grasp. These 50 recipes include examples of each type. Use them as starting points for your own creations if you wish, substituting an herb for the garlic in one or walnut oil for olive oil in another. Once you know the easy basic techniques that are the root of all dressings, bottled products will be nothing more than a part of your past.

ABOUT THESE RECIPES

Don't be confined by your lifelong habit of using dressings only with greens. Many of the following dressings pair splendidly with grilled meats and fish or work well as marinades. We've included a suggestion or two with some of the more unusual dressings. All make enough dressing for 4 servings, unless otherwise noted. The dressings made without eggs or dairy products have a longer refrigerated shelf life than those made with them.

Many cooks, responding to the danger of salmonella contamination in uncooked eggs, have stopped using salad dressings that call for raw or slightly cooked egg yolks. We've included a few such recipes because we consider them classics of salad making that belong in a chapter like this. You may want to skip them.

Oil and Vinegar Dressing

Whisk together ⅓ cup olive oil, 2 tablespoons wine vinegar, salt, and pepper.

Hot Pepper Vinaigrette

Follow preceding recipe, adding 2 teaspoons crushed red pepper flakes.

Lemon and Olive Oil Dressing

Whisk together ⅓ cup virgin olive oil, the juice of 2 lemons, 1 clove minced garlic, salt, and pepper.

Orange Walnut Dressing

Whisk together ⅓ cup walnut oil, the juice of 1 large orange, the juice of ½ lemon, and a pinch of grated nutmeg.

Lime Vinaigrette

Whisk together ⅓ cup olive oil, ¼ cup red wine vinegar, the finely grated zest and juice of 1 large lime, salt, and pepper.

Creamy Avocado Dressing

Follow preceding recipe, whisking into it 1 pureed, pitted, and peeled ripe avocado and a dash of hot pepper sauce.

Basic Wine Vinaigrette

Whisk together the minced whites of 4 scallions, ¼ cup white wine vinegar, ¼ cup white wine, ⅓ cup peanut oil, ⅓ cup virgin olive oil, ½ teaspoon salt, and pepper. Makes enough for 8 portions of salad.

Niçoise Vinaigrette

Follow preceding recipe, adding 2 cloves minced garlic and ¼ cup finely chopped oil-cured black olives.

Garlic Herb Dressing

Whisk together 2 large cloves minced garlic, ¼ cup red wine vinegar, ¾ cup olive oil, ½ teaspoon salt, pepper, 1 tablespoon minced fresh parsley, and 2 teaspoons dried herbs (basil, dill, oregano, chervil, tarragon, etc.). Makes enough for 8 portions of salad.

 Creamy Italian Dressing

Make preceding recipe and whisk in 2 tablespoons mayonnaise. Makes enough for 8 portions of salad.

 Balsamic Olive Oil Vinaigrette

Whisk together ½ cup olive oil, ¼ cup balsamic vinegar, 3 tablespoons lemon juice, 1 clove minced garlic, a dash of cayenne, salt, and pepper.

 Sun-Dried Tomato Vinaigrette

Follow preceding recipe, using the oil from oil-cured sun-dried tomatoes instead of olive oil. Add 6 minced sun-dried tomatoes.

 Mustard Vinaigrette

In a bowl, combine 1 clove minced garlic, 2 tablespoons Dijon mustard, 3 tablespoons wine vinegar, salt, and pepper. In slow, steady stream, whisk in ⅓ cup *each* peanut and olive oils.

 Tarragon Mustard Vinaigrette

Follow preceding recipe and add 2 teaspoons dried or 2 tablespoons fresh tarragon leaves.

 Creamy Rosemary Dressing

In small bowl, bruise 2 teaspoons fresh rosemary leaves with back of a wooden spoon. Add 1 small clove minced garlic, 1 teaspoon Dijon mustard,

and 1 large egg yolk. Whisk until lightly thickened. Add 2 tablespoons wine vinegar and 6 tablespoons peanut oil in a slow, steady stream, whisking continuously. When oil has been incorporated, season with salt and pepper.

 Creamy Orange Fennel Dressing

Follow preceding recipe, but use ¼ cup minced fresh fennel instead of the rosemary and 3 tablespoons orange juice in place of half the vinegar.

 Raspberry Vinaigrette

In small bowl, whisk together ¼ cup raspberry vinegar, ½ cup almond or walnut oil, a pinch of cayenne, and salt. Toss with ¼ cup fresh or unsweetened frozen raspberries. Use with delicate greens, chicken, or fruit salad.

 Sherry Vinaigrette

In small bowl, whisk together ¼ cup sherry vinegar, ½ cup almond or walnut oil, a pinch of cayenne, and salt. Toss with 2 tablespoons minced raisins soaked in dry sherry and drained. Use with delicate greens, chicken, or fruit salad.

 Caesar Dressing

Whisk together yolk of 1 soft-cooked egg, 1 clove crushed garlic, 2 minced anchovies, and 1 teaspoon Dijon mustard until lightly thickened. Blend in 1 tablespoon wine vinegar, the juice of ½ lemon, and 2 teaspoons Worcestershire. In a slow, steady stream, whisk in 6 tablespoons olive oil blended with 6 tablespoons vegetable oil. Season with salt and pepper.

Fifty Ways to Cook Most Everything

 ### Tonnato Caesar

Follow preceding recipe, adding 2 ounces canned oil-packed tuna, mashed, with the Worcestershire.

 ### Warm Bacon Dressing

In deep skillet, cook 1 minced large red onion and 1 large clove minced garlic in rendered fat of 3 bacon slices until soft. (Save bacon for another use.) Add ½ cup apple cider vinegar, 2 tablespoons sugar, 1 tablespoon ketchup, salt, and pepper. Use hot, tossed with strong-flavored greens such as escarole, chicory, endive, or spinach.

 ### Real Russian Dressing

Whisk together ¼ cup mayonnaise, ¼ cup sour cream, 2 tablespoons ketchup, and 3 tablespoons lemon juice. Fold in 2 tablespoons red or black caviar. Makes enough for 6 portions.

 ### Clear Cole Slaw Dressing

Mix 6 tablespoons vegetable oil, 6 tablespoons cider vinegar, ½ teaspoon sugar, and 2 teaspoons caraway seed. Season liberally with salt and pepper.

Sour Cream Cole Slaw Dressing

Blend 2 tablespoons orange marmalade with 1 tablespoon honey. Whisk in 3 tablespoons mayonnaise, ¼ cup sour cream, 3 tablespoons red wine vinegar, ¾ teaspoon salt, and ¼ teaspoon pepper.

 ### Poppy Seed Dressing

Use 2 tablespoons poppy seeds instead of the caraway seeds in Clear Cole Slaw Dressing (above), or add them to preceding recipe.

 ### Sesame Tofu Vinaigrette

In a food processor or blender, puree ¼ cup cubed tofu, 1 small clove minced garlic, 2 tablespoons Oriental sesame oil, 6 tablespoons peanut oil, 3 tablespoons rice wine vinegar, and 1 teaspoon soy sauce. Thin with a few drops of water, if necessary. Fold in ¼ cup toasted sesame seeds. Serve with poached vegetable salads, Chinese cabbage cole slaw, or fish and seafood salads.

 ### Soy Ginger Dressing

In small bowl, mash 2 tablespoons grated fresh gingerroot and 1 large clove minced garlic with the back of a spoon. Mix in 2 tablespoons low-sodium soy sauce, a pinch of cayenne pepper, a pinch of sugar, ¾ cup Oriental sesame oil, and 5 tablespoons rice vinegar. Adjust seasoning.

 ### Szechuan Ginger Dressing

Follow preceding recipe, but add 2 teaspoons crushed Szechuan peppercorns with the ginger and garlic.

 ### Warm Tomato Vinaigrette

Blend 1 cup tomato puree, ¼ cup virgin olive oil, 2 tablespoons white wine herb vinegar, 2 tablespoons chopped fresh parsley, salt, and pepper. Warm the dressing and serve on salad of chicken, seafood, spinach, pasta, or potatoes. Serves 4 to 6.

Sweet and Sour Creole Vinaigrette

Whisk together ⅓ cup ketchup, 2 tablespoons spicy mustard, 2 tablespoons sugar, 1 tablespoon prepared horseradish, 1 clove minced garlic, and 2 tablespoons apple cider vinegar. Whisk in 2 cups peanut oil in a slow, steady stream until oil has been incorporated and the dressing is thick. Season to taste with hot pepper sauce, black pepper, and salt. Use with hearty greens (though it would also be good with hamburgers, ribs, or broiled pork chops).

 Creamy Creole Dressing

Mix ½ cup mayonnaise, 2 tablespoons wine vinegar, the juice of 1 lemon, 1 teaspoon sugar, 1 teaspoon hot pepper sauce, salt, and pepper.

 Sweet Pepper Vinaigrette

In heavy saucepan, combine 2 finely diced roasted red bell peppers (page 442), 2 cloves minced garlic, ¼ cup sugar, ¾ cup wine vinegar, ¼ cup walnut oil, salt, and pepper.

 Blue Cheese Dressing

Blend 2 cloves minced garlic, ½ cup olive oil, 3 tablespoons red wine vinegar, ½ cup sour cream, 2 tablespoons milk, 4 ounces crumbled blue cheese, salt, and pepper.

 Warm Blue Cheese Dressing

Cook 2 cloves minced garlic in ¼ cup olive oil until soft. Add 3 tablespoons red wine vinegar and ⅔ cup heavy cream and bring to a boil. When mixture separates, remove from heat and stir in 4 ounces crumbled blue cheese until it melts. Season with salt and pepper. Serve over spinach salad.

 Roquefort Dressing

Follow either of two preceding recipes, but substitute 2 tablespoons lemon juice for 1 tablespoon of the vinegar and use Roquefort cheese instead of blue.

 Spicy Ginger Vinaigrette

Combine ¼ cup peanut oil, ¼ cup Oriental sesame oil, 2 tablespoons rice wine vinegar, the juice of 1 lemon, 1 clove minced garlic, ½ teaspoon crushed red pepper flakes, 1 tablespoon finely shredded fresh gingerroot, salt, and pepper.

 Garlic Ranch Dressing

Blend together ¼ cup mayonnaise, 1 teaspoon cider vinegar, 3 tablespoons buttermilk, 1 teaspoon seasoning salt (or salt-free seasoning blend), ½ teaspoon onion powder, 2 cloves minced garlic, and pepper.

 Yogurt Ranch Dressing

Follow preceding recipe, but use ¼ teaspoon garlic powder instead of fresh garlic and use plain yogurt instead of buttermilk.

 Basil Ranch Dressing

Follow recipe for Garlic Ranch Dressing (above), adding ¼ cup finely chopped fresh basil.

 Green Goddess Ranch

Blend ¼ cup mayonnaise, 1 teaspoon cider vinegar, 3 tablespoons buttermilk, 1 teaspoon seasoning salt (or salt-free seasoning blend), ½ teaspoon onion powder, 1 clove minced garlic, 1 minced anchovy fillet, 1 tablespoon minced fresh parsley, 1 tablespoon other fresh herb (basil, tarragon, or chervil), and pepper.

 ### Creamy Mayonnaise Dressing

Blend until smooth 3 ounces cream cheese, ⅓ cup mayonnaise, the juice of ½ lemon, salt, pepper, and a generous dash of cayenne.

 ### Pesto Mayonnaise Dressing

Follow preceding recipe, but replace cream cheese with ½ clove minced garlic, ⅓ cup finely chopped basil leaves, 2 tablespoons olive oil, and 2 tablespoons grated Parmesan.

 ### Minted Yogurt Dressing

Combine 1 cup plain yogurt, the juice of ½ lemon, 1 tablespoon olive oil, 1 tablespoon chopped mint leaves, salt, and pepper.

 ### Yogurt Cilantro Dressing

Follow preceding recipe, but substitute ¼ cup chopped fresh cilantro for the mint.

 ### Sweet Mustard Dressing

Whisk 2 egg yolks with 2 teaspoons mustard until yolks are pale. Mix in ¼ cup cider vinegar, 1 tablespoon apple juice, and 1 tablespoon honey. Whisk in 1½ cups vegetable oil in a slow, steady stream. Season with salt and pepper.

 ### Apple Cider Dressing

Combine ¼ cup cider vinegar, 2 tablespoons minced onion, 2 tablespoons apple juice, and 2 tablespoons honey. Whisk in ¼ cup safflower oil in a slow, steady stream. Season with salt and pepper.

 ### Sweet Balsamic Dressing

Combine 2 tablespoons balsamic vinegar, 2 tablespoons red wine vinegar, 2 tablespoons apple juice, and 2 tablespoons honey. Whisk in ½ cup olive oil in a slow, steady stream. Add 1 clove minced garlic, salt, and pepper.

 ### Guacamole Vinaigrette

In a blender, puree 2 peeled and pitted avocados, 2 cloves minced garlic, 3 tablespoons white wine vinegar, a dash of cayenne, salt, and pepper. Use as an alternative to Russian dressing.

 ### Salsa Vinaigrette

In a food processor or blender, finely chop 1 clove garlic, 4 or 5 seeded and stemmed pickled jalapeño peppers, 2 stemmed tomatoes, ¼ cup olive oil, and 1 tablespoon cider vinegar. Serves 6.

 ### Pesto Vinaigrette

In a food processor, puree 1 cup cleaned basil leaves, 1 clove garlic, and ¼ cup pine nuts. Add 2 tablespoons wine vinegar and ⅓ cup virgin olive oil and process. Season with salt, pepper, and 1 tablespoon grated Parmesan.

Fifty Easy Stews: Long Cooking Makes Short Work

By measuring culinary ease with a stopwatch, we have forgotten that there are ways to cook as old as fire itself that require some time—but little labor and even less attention. More time doesn't have to mean more work. Soups, casseroles, pot roasts, and stews infuse food with goodness that only time can give, and all we have to do to reap their benefits is slow down the cooking.

Speeding from one activity to the next, we risk thinking about eating the way we do fueling up the car—one more necessity, rather than one of life's greatest pleasures. And once that happens the quality of what we eat is bound to take a back seat to the speed of its preparation. A hand-built home-made hamburger has to be pretty good to warrant the time and energy required to produce it, while its 2-minute microwaved counterpart, trapped in a form-fitted disposable oven-to-table warming coffin, need only fill the belly to meet quality standards.

By slowing down, we can actually make meal-times easier. Stew simmers and spits lazily on the back burner while we play, it rests in a low oven while we rest in the next room, it steams gently in a fragrant broth while we run errands, finish up work, or just relax.

And the best part is that while we're occupied elsewhere, ingredients are being transformed in ways that faster food can't match. Flavors are blending, blossoming, and balancing and all we have to do is slow down, sit back, and serve up the rewards.

ABOUT THESE RECIPES

The following 50 stew recipes all take time but very little work. Except for the fish stews, they all can be made ahead and reheated. Frequently they are better after a day in the refrigerator. When a recipe calls for stew meat, the amount indicated refers to meat that is partially on the bone, unless otherwise noted. All recipes, unless otherwise noted, should be prepared in an 8-quart pot and make 6 to 8 servings.

There are lots of stews scattered elsewhere in this book, especially in the chapters on chilis (Chapter 13) and chicken legs (Chapter 22).

Beef Stew

Dredge 3 pounds beef stew meat in flour and brown in 2 tablespoons vegetable oil. Halfway through browning, add 2 cups chopped onions and 1 clove minced garlic. When browned, add 1 cup white wine, and boil for 3 minutes. Add 3 cups beef stock, 2 tablespoons Worcestershire sauce, 1 tablespoon tomato paste, and 2 chopped, skinned tomatoes. Cover and simmer for 30 minutes. Add 3 peeled and chunked potatoes, and 4 peeled carrots and 3 celery ribs cut in 2-inch lengths. Simmer 1 hour more.

Beef Stew with Roasted Garlic

Follow preceding recipe using olive oil instead of vegetable oil. While the stew cooks, roast 2 large heads garlic at 375° F. for 45 minutes or until soft to the touch. Cool slightly. Cut pointed end off each head and slip cloves from their peels. Mash the roasted garlic, 5 tablespoons white prepared horseradish, and 1 teaspoon Dijon mustard until smooth. Season with salt. When stew is done, remove solids with a slotted spoon to a serving platter. Bring liquid to a boil, whisk the puree into the boiling liquid, and pour over the meat and vegetables.

Beef and Vegetable Stew

Follow recipe for Beef Stew (above). Add 1 teaspoon crumbled dried rosemary, ¼ teaspoon ground allspice, and ½ teaspoon dried thyme with the onions. Replace potatoes with 2 peeled, diced turnips and 2 peeled, chunked sweet potatoes.

Sweet and Sour Beef Stew

Follow recipe for Beef Stew (above), replacing the white wine with ¼ cup cider vinegar and 3 tablespoons brown sugar.

Beef and Wild Mushroom Stew

Soak ½ ounce dried wild mushrooms (any variety) in warm water to cover for 30 minutes. Squeeze liquid from the mushrooms and rinse well. Set aside and strain soaking liquid through a coffee filter. Follow recipe for Beef Stew (above) using the soaking liquid in place of ½ cup of the beef stock. Use the soaked wild mushrooms in place of the potatoes.

Beef Stew with Rosemary and Ham

Dredge 3 pounds beef stew meat in flour and brown in 2 tablespoons vegetable oil. Halfway through the browning, add 2 cups chopped onions, 1 clove minced garlic, ⅓ cup chopped baked ham, and ½ teaspoon *each* crumbled dried rosemary, dried thyme, and finely grated lemon zest. When browned, add 1 cup white wine and boil for 3 minutes. Add 3 cups beef stock, 2 tablespoons Worcestershire sauce, and 1 tablespoon tomato paste, cover, and simmer for 30 minutes. Add 3 peeled and chunked potatoes, 4 peeled carrots and 3 celery ribs cut in 2-inch lengths, and 2 teaspoons dried mint. Simmer, covered, 1 hour more.

Boeuf Bourguignonne

Brown ¼ pound diced rindless slab bacon, remove, blot excess fat from bacon, and reserve.

Dredge 3 pounds beef stew meat in flour and brown in the hot fat. Halfway through browning, add 2 cups chopped onions, ¼ cup *each* diced carrots and celery, and 1 clove minced garlic. Add 2 cups hearty red wine and boil, uncovered, for 5 minutes. Add 3 cups beef stock, 1 bay leaf, ½ teaspoon dried thyme, 1 tablespoon chopped fresh parsley, and 1 tablespoon Worcestershire sauce. Cover, and simmer for 1 hour. Add 4 peeled carrots and 3 celery ribs cut in 2-inch lengths. Simmer 30 minutes more. Add ½ pound small mushrooms sautéed in butter and the reserved bacon and heat through. Remove bay leaf. Serve over noodles.

 Veal Bourguignonne

Follow preceding recipe but use veal stew meat instead of beef, chicken stock instead of beef stock, and dry white wine instead of red.

 Coq au Vin

Follow recipe for Boeuf Bourguignonne (opposite), using 4 pounds stewing chicken pieces instead of beef and chicken stock instead of beef stock.

 Beef Stew Provençale

Dredge 3 pounds beef stew meat in flour and brown in 3 tablespoons olive oil. Add 1 cup chopped onions, ½ cup *each* chopped carrots and celery, and 1 head peeled garlic cloves and brown lightly. Add 2 teaspoons *herbes de Provence*, the zest of ½ orange, 1 cup red wine, 3 cups beef stock, and 1 cup crushed plum tomatoes and bring to a simmer. Cook, covered, for 1½ hours. Quarter the artichoke hearts from 1 drained 8-ounce can and add to stew with ½ cup pitted oil-cured black olives.

 Chicken Stew Provençale

Follow preceding recipe, using 4 pounds sectioned chicken instead of beef, white wine in place of red, and chicken stock instead of beef stock.

 Lamb Stewed with Anise and Orange

Dredge 3 pounds lamb stew meat in flour and brown in 3 tablespoons olive oil. Add 1 cup chopped onions, ½ cup chopped carrots, 1 cup chopped fennel, and 1 head peeled garlic cloves and brown lightly. Add 2 teaspoons *herbes de Provence*, 1 teaspoon ground aniseed, the zest of ½ orange, ½ cup orange juice, ½ cup red wine, 3 cups beef stock, and 1 cup crushed plum tomatoes and bring to a simmer. Cook, covered, for 1½ hours. Add ½ cup pitted oil-cured black olives.

 Mussel Stew Provençale

Cook 1 cup chopped onions, ½ cup *each* chopped carrots and celery, and 1 head peeled garlic cloves in 3 tablespoons olive oil until vegetables soften. Add 2 teaspoons *herbes de Provence*, the zest of ½ orange, ½ cup white wine, 1 cup clam juice, and 1 cup crushed plum tomatoes and bring to a simmer. Cook, covered, for 10 minutes, add 4 dozen cleaned and debearded mussels, and simmer until mussels open, discarding any that don't. Serve over pasta.

 Shrimp Stew Provençale

Follow preceding recipe, using 1 pound cleaned large shrimp instead of mussels. After adding shrimp, return to a boil and remove from heat.

Fifty Ways to Cook Most Everything

Barbecued Beef Stew

Dredge 3 pounds beef stew meat in flour and brown in batches in ¼ cup corn oil. Add 1½ cups chopped onions, ⅓ cup chopped celery, and 1 clove minced garlic and cook in the fat in the pan until vegetables soften. Add ⅔ cup ketchup, 1 cup chopped tomato, 1 cup beef stock, 1 cup beer, 1 tablespoon molasses, 1 tablespoon hot pepper sauce, 1 tablespoon Worcestershire sauce, 1 teaspoon brown mustard, salt, pepper, and the browned meat. Cover and simmer for 1½ hours. Skim off fat and serve with beans or rice.

Barbecued Pork Stewed with Sausage

Follow preceding recipe, using chunks of pork shoulder instead of beef. Use chicken stock in place of beef. Add 1 pound sliced smoked sausage during last 30 minutes of cooking. Serves 6.

Barbecued Chicken Stew

Follow recipe for Barbecued Beef Stew (above), using chicken pieces instead of beef and chicken stock instead of beef stock. Reduce cooking time to 1 hour.

Veal Stew in the Style of Osso Bucco

Dredge 3 pounds veal stew meat in flour and brown in 2 tablespoons butter melted with 2 tablespoons olive oil. Halfway through the browning, add ⅔ cup finely chopped onions, ⅓ cup finely chopped carrots, ⅓ cup finely chopped celery, 1 clove minced garlic, and the zest of ½ lemon, cut in strips. When browned, add ½ cup white wine, 1½ cups beef stock, 1 cup chopped skinned plum tomatoes, ½ teaspoon dried thyme, 1 tea-

spoon dried basil, 1 bay leaf, salt, and pepper. Bring to a boil, cover, and place in a 350°F. oven for 2 hours, until tender. Skim off fat, remove bay leaf, and stir in ½ clove minced garlic, 1 tablespoon finely grated lemon zest, and 1 tablespoon finely chopped fresh parsley.

Turkey Stew Milano

Follow preceding recipe, using 4 pounds sectioned turkey legs instead of the veal.

Mediterranean Chicken Stew

Follow recipe for Veal Stew in the Style of Osso Bucco (above), but use 4 pounds stewing chicken pieces instead of the veal.

Lamb Stewed with Peppers

Dredge 3 pounds lamb stew meat in flour and brown in ¼ cup olive oil. Add ¾ cup chopped onions, ⅓ cup chopped celery, ⅓ cup chopped carrots, and 1 clove minced garlic and brown lightly. Add 3 cored, seeded, and chunked bell peppers of different colors, 1 teaspoon ground cumin, 1 teaspoon dried thyme, ¼ teaspoon dried oregano, ¼ teaspoon ground ginger, and 1 tablespoon sweet paprika. Cook another 3 minutes. Add 2 cups beef stock. Bring to a boil, stir in 1 tablespoon tomato paste, salt, and pepper, and simmer slowly, covered, for 1½ hours. Skim off fat.

Veal Stewed with Peppers

Follow preceding recipe, substituting veal stew meat for the lamb, dried basil for the cumin, and ½ teaspoon crumbled dried rosemary for the oregano and ginger.

Lamb Stewed with Red Curry

Dredge 3 pounds lamb stew meat in flour and brown in 3 tablespoons vegetable oil. Add 1 peeled and diced large carrot, 1 rib diced celery, and 1 finely chopped onion and cook until lightly browned. Add 1 teaspoon ground coriander, ¾ teaspoon ground cumin seed, ¼ teaspoon crushed red pepper flakes, 2 tablespoons flour and 1½ tablespoons curry powder and cook for 1 minute more. Add 5 chopped tomatoes, 2 cups beef stock, salt, and pepper and simmer, covered, for 45 minutes. Add 2 tablespoons dried mint and simmer, covered, for 30 minutes more.

 Brown Curry Duck Stew

Remove all visible fat from two 4-pound ducks and brown in 1 tablespoon olive oil. Follow preceding recipe from the point after the meat is browned. For the last 30 minutes, add 1 tablespoon ground aniseed instead of mint.

 Veal Stewed with Artichoke Hearts

Dredge 3 pounds veal stew meat in flour and brown in ¼ cup olive oil. Add 1 cup chopped onions, ⅓ cup chopped celery, and 3 cloves minced garlic and cook until softened. Add 1 bay leaf, 1 teaspoon crumbled dried rosemary, 1 teaspoon dried thyme, 1 teaspoon grated lemon zest, ¼ teaspoon ground ginger, and ½ cup white wine. Cook until alcohol evaporates. Add 2 cups chicken stock, salt, and pepper and simmer slowly, covered, for 1 hour. Add 2 tablespoons chopped fresh parsley, two 9-ounce packages defrosted frozen artichoke hearts, and 2 chopped, skinned, and seeded tomatoes. Simmer 10 minutes more. Skim off fat and remove bay leaf.

 Veal and Asparagus Stew

Follow preceding recipe, substituting chervil for the rosemary and using 1 pound medium-thick fresh asparagus, cut in 1-inch sections, instead of the artichoke hearts.

 Veal Stewed with Chick-Peas and Avocado

Follow recipe for Veal Stewed with Artichoke Hearts (above), replacing ginger with 1 tablespoon chili powder. Add 1 pound cooked chick-peas in place of the artichoke hearts. Garnish with 1 diced large avocado.

 Veal Shanks with Apples and Cream

Tie string around the equators of 4 pieces veal shank, each 2 inches thick, and dredge in flour. Brown in 2 tablespoons vegetable oil and remove. Reduce heat and add 2 tablespoons butter. Stir in sliced whites of 2 cleaned leeks, 2 ribs peeled and diced celery, and 2 cloves minced garlic. When softened, add ¼ cup applejack brandy and flame. Add 1 teaspoon dried thyme leaves, 2 teaspoons crumbled dried rosemary, ½ cup apple cider, 1 cup chicken stock, the finely grated zest of ½ orange, and 1 bay leaf. Cover and simmer 1½ hours. Add 2 peeled, cored, and chunked Granny Smith apples and cook, covered, another 30 minutes. Skim fat and stir in ½ cup heavy cream. Untie shanks and remove bay leaf before serving. Serves 4.

 Veal Stew Normandy

Follow preceding recipe, but use 3 pounds veal stew meat instead of tied veal shanks, omit the orange zest, and reduce initial cooking time to 1 hour. If desired, substitute *crème fraîche* for the heavy cream.

Pork Stewed with Apples and Prunes

Soak 12 pitted prunes in 1 cup boiling water until plump. Drain. Dredge 3 pounds pork stew meat in flour, brown in 2 tablespoons vegetable oil, and remove. Reduce heat and add 2 tablespoons butter. Stir in the sliced whites of 2 cleaned leeks, 2 ribs peeled and diced celery, and 2 cloves minced garlic. When softened, add ¼ cup applejack brandy and ignite carefully with a match. Add 1 teaspoon dried thyme, 2 teaspoons crumbled dried rosemary, ½ cup apple cider, 1 cup chicken stock, the prunes, the juice and finely grated zest of ½ lemon, and 1 bay leaf. Cover and simmer 1½ hours. Add 2 peeled, cored, and chunked Granny Smith apples and cook, covered, another 30 minutes. Skim fat. Remove bay leaf.

 Fresh Ham Hocks with Leeks and White Beans

Tie 8 ham hocks, each 2 inches thick, around their perimeters, and dredge in flour. Brown ¼ pound rindless slab bacon, cut in large dice. Remove and drain bacon pieces and brown ham hocks in the hot fat. Add the sliced whites of 6 cleaned leeks, ½ cup finely chopped carrots, 1 cup diced celery, 1 teaspoon dried thyme, and ½ teaspoon rubbed sage and cook until vegetables soften. Add 1 cup white wine and boil 2 minutes. Add 1 cup chicken stock, salt, and pepper and bring to a boil. Scatter reserved bacon over top, cover, and bake at 350° F. for 1 hour. Add 1 pound cooked, drained white kidney beans and bake, covered, 1 hour more. Skim fat. Untie hocks before serving.

Smoky Lamb Stew

Follow preceding recipe, substituting 3 pounds lamb stew meat for the tied hocks, using 2 cups chopped onion instead of leeks, and adding 2

diced roasted red peppers (page 442) with the cooked bacon.

 Sausage and Bean Stew

Follow recipe for Fresh Ham Hocks with Leeks and White Beans (above), substituting 1 pound sweet and 1 pound spicy Italian sausage, cut in 2-inch lengths, for the tied hocks. Do not dredge sausage. Bake only 30 minutes after adding the beans.

 Spring Lamb Stew

Dredge 3 pounds lamb stew meat in flour and brown in 3 tablespoons *each* butter and olive oil. When halfway browned, add 1 chopped large onion, 2 cloves minced garlic, 2 ribs chopped celery, and 2 chopped carrots. Add 1 cup white wine, boil 2 minutes, and add 2 cups beef stock, 1½ cups skinned chopped tomatoes, 2 bay leaves, ½ teaspoon *each* dried thyme and dried basil, 2 tablespoons chopped fresh parsley, 2 tablespoons finely grated orange zest, salt, and pepper. Simmer, covered, for 1 hour. Add ½ pound halved new potatoes and simmer, covered, 30 minutes more. Meanwhile, cook ¼ pound small mushrooms and ½ clove minced garlic in 1 tablespoon olive oil until softened. Add 2 sliced small zucchini and cook 2 minutes more. Blanch 1 bunch trimmed and peeled baby carrots for 3 minutes, drain, and add to stew. Remove bay leaves.

 Lamb Stewed with Asparagus

Cut 1 pound medium asparagus in 2-inch lengths. Cook in 1 tablespoon olive oil with 1 clove minced garlic until bright green. Add ¼ cup chicken stock, cover, and simmer for 2 minutes. Follow preceding recipe, but use this mixture in place of the mushrooms, zucchini, and carrots.

Moroccan Turkey Stew

Cook 3 chopped large onions and 1 head peeled garlic cloves in 4 tablespoons butter until soft. Add 2 small sectioned turkey legs, 1 teaspoon ground turmeric, 1 tablespoon ground coriander, 2 teaspoons ground cumin, 1 dried chili pepper, and 4 cups chicken stock. Bring to a simmer and cook, covered, for 1 hour. Add ½ pound coarsely chopped skinned plum tomatoes, 2 peeled carrots, 2 ribs peeled celery, ½ stemmed, peeled, and seeded acorn squash, 2 small zucchini, and ⅓ pound sweet potato, all cut in chunks. Simmer, covered, 30 minutes more. Serve over couscous, orzo, or other small pasta.

Spiced Veal and Squash Stew

Follow preceding recipe, but replace the turkey with 3 pounds boneless veal shoulder, cut in chunks and dredged in flour.

Pork Stewed with Red Cabbage

Brown ¼ pound diced rindless slab bacon, remove, blot off excess fat, and reserve. Dredge 3 pounds pork stew meat in flour and brown in half the hot fat. Add ½ cup chopped onions, ¼ cup chopped celery, and ¼ cup chopped carrots. Add 1 sliced small red cabbage and 1 tablespoon caraway seed and cook until cabbage is barely softening. Add 3 tablespoons red wine vinegar, 3 tablespoons brown sugar, and 3 cups brown stock, cover, and simmer for 1 hour. Serve with buttered boiled potatoes.

Duck Stewed with Red Cabbage

Remove all visible fat from two 4-pound ducks and cut each into 8 pieces. Follow preceding recipe, using the duck pieces instead of the pork. Do not dredge duck. Add 2 tablespoons flour when adding the cabbage.

Civet of Chicken

Dredge 4 pounds chicken pieces in flour and brown in 2 tablespoons butter melted with 2 tablespoons walnut oil. Remove chicken. Add 1 cup chopped onion and ¼ cup each chopped celery and carrots and cook until softened. Add 2 tablespoons flour and cook until browned. Add 1 clove minced garlic, 1 cup hearty red wine, 4 crushed juniper berries, 1 bay leaf, ½ teaspoon dried thyme, 1 tablespoon chopped fresh parsley, and a pinch of cloves. Boil for 2 minutes. Add 2 cups beef stock, 1 teaspoon tomato paste, salt, and pepper. Return chicken, cover, and simmer for 45 minutes. Meanwhile, sauté 12 mushrooms in butter until golden brown and add, with ½ ounce finely chopped bitter chocolate, when chicken is tender.

Civet of Beef (or Venison)

Follow preceding recipe, substituting 2 pounds boneless beef stew meat (or boneless venison cubes). Double amount of wine and increase simmering time to 1½ hours. (If using venison, marinate overnight in a mixture of the onion, celery, carrots, garlic, juniper, bay leaf, and red wine.)

Lamb Stew with Lots of Garlic

Dredge 3 pounds lamb stew meat in flour and brown in ¼ cup olive oil. Add 1 coarsely chopped onion and 40 cloves peeled garlic and brown lightly. Add 1 cup finely chopped peeled eggplant and cook for 1 minute. Add 2 cups white wine and boil for 3 minutes. Add 2 cups beef stock, 2 tablespoons tomato paste, 1 tablespoon *herbes de Provence*,

2 bay leaves, ¼ teaspoon ground allspice, salt, and pepper. Cover and simmer for 1 hour. Remove bay leaves.

 ### Veal and Garlic Sausage Stew

Follow preceding recipe, but use 2 pounds veal stew meat instead of lamb. Add 1 pound sliced garlic sausage with the onion and garlic.

 ### Catfish Corn Stew

Brown ¼ pound diced rindless slab bacon, remove bacon bits, blot, and reserve. Season 3 pounds catfish fillets with 1 tablespoon hot paprika, salt, and pepper and brown in the hot bacon fat. Remove. Add 1 cup diced onions, 2 ribs diced fennel, 2 cloves minced garlic, 1 diced red bell pepper, and ⅛ teaspoon crushed red pepper flakes and cook until softened. Add 3 cups uncooked corn kernels and cook for 5 minutes. Add 4 cups Quick Fish Stock (page 430), 2 tablespoons chopped fresh dill, and 1 tablespoon chopped fresh parsley and simmer, covered, 30 to 40 minutes, until corn is tender. Cut fish into large strips and add to simmering broth. Cook 8 minutes more and finish with ½ cup light cream.

 ### Piquant Monkfish Stew

Toss 3 pounds monkfish fillets, cut in bite-size chunks, in ¼ cup lemon juice, salt, and pepper. In a food processor, finely chop 1 onion, 2 cloves garlic, 1 stemmed and seeded jalapeño pepper, and 1 stemmed and seeded red bell pepper. Cook in 2 tablespoons olive oil until softened. Add 1 cup crushed tomato and 3 cups Quick Fish Stock (page 430) and bring to a boil. Meanwhile, finely process 6 tomatillos with 1 stemmed and seeded jalapeño pepper. Mix in ¼ cup chopped fresh cilantro and

1 diced avocado. Add the fish to the broth and simmer, covered, for 6 minutes. Stir in the jalapeño mixture.

 ### Mexican Bouillabaisse

Follow preceding recipe, replacing monkfish with ¾ pound large cleaned shrimp. Before adding shrimp to the broth, add 12 littleneck clams, and simmer, covered, for 3 minutes. Add shrimp, ½ pound cleaned sea scallops, and 16 cleaned and debearded mussels. Simmer for 3 minutes more. Discard any shellfish that does not open.

 ### Jamaican Jerk Pork Stew

In a heavy skillet over high heat, toast for 2 to 3 minutes 1½ teaspoons *each* coriander seed and cumin seed, ½ teaspoon black peppercorns, ¼ teaspoon crushed red pepper flakes, 1 clove and 2 teaspoons chopped fresh gingerroot. Grind finely in a spice mill. Strain and mix in 1½ teaspoons ground allspice and ½ teaspoon salt. Rub mixture into 3 pounds pork stew meat and refrigerate for 1 hour. Mix 2 tablespoons rum, 3 tablespoons ketchup, 1 teaspoon hot pepper sauce, and 2 tablespoons low-sodium soy sauce and set aside. Brown pork in 2 tablespoons vegetable oil and remove. Add 1 chopped onion and 2 tablespoons flour and brown lightly. Add 1 tablespoon brown sugar and cook until melted. Add 3 cups chicken stock, salt, and pepper, bring to a boil, return pork to broth, cover, and simmer for 1½ hours. Degrease, add the juice of ½ lemon, and serve over rice.

 ### Jerk Short Ribs

Follow preceding recipe, but use 4 pounds beef short ribs instead of the pork.

Blanquette of Veal

Cook ½ cup chopped onion, ¼ cup diced celery, and ¼ cup diced parsnip in 4 tablespoons butter until softened. Add ¼ cup flour and cook for 1 minute. Add 4 cups hot chicken stock and bring to a simmer. Add 2½ pounds boneless veal cubes, cover, and simmer for 1 hour. Add 12 small peeled boiling onions and 12 chunks peeled carrots and simmer, covered, 15 minutes. Add 12 trimmed mushrooms tossed in 1 tablespoon lemon juice and 1 cup frozen peas. Simmer 5 minutes more. Season with salt and white pepper. Finish with ½ cup cream.

 Turkey Blanquette

Follow preceding recipe, substituting boneless turkey breast for the veal. Reduce initial simmering to 30 minutes.

36

Fifty Useful Microwave Recipes

Occasionally, a piece of kitchen equipment redefines our very notions about cooking. Such was the case when affordable refrigeration turned every home kitchen into its own food distribution center and later when food processors debunked the pretensions of classic French cuisine for American cooks. Now it is the microwave oven that has infiltrated our daily meal preparations, causing us to mark cooking times in seconds rather than hours and to rethink exactly what labor-saving means.

As usual, new technology has brought with it new confusions. As we learn to master microwave techniques, there is a tendency to find more and better ways to flex our newfound microwave muscle. But our enthusiasm should not take the place of common sense. Many techniques—such as deep-fat frying, roasting, toasting, and most baking—are still better and more conveniently done by conventional cooking.

This is not a microwave cookbook, and this chapter is not intended to be comprehensive. Instead, the recipes we've chosen are those that use the microwave in ways that we have found make sense and complement the rest of this book.

ABOUT THESE RECIPES

One of the most exasperating things about microwaves and microwave recipes is their inconsistencies. Two ovens with different wattages cook the same food in different times, but frequently so do two ovens of the same wattage, or even the same oven on different occasions. You can put four apples in a microwave to bake and have one melt into oblivion minutes before the others are ready. For that reason, we have found it most accurate to give you a timing range whenever our testing has produced varying results. Test for doneness at the lower end of the timing range, then proceed in two steps to the upper end of the range, until the desired doneness is achieved.

All recipes in this chapter were tested in a 650-watt oven and again in a 700-watt model—with a carousel and without. If you have a low-power microwave, you'll need to increase the cooking times in these and most other microwave recipes, and if you have one of the newer 800-watt models, you will need to decrease it. You've probably already figured out a formula for adjusting cooking times to your unit. Use that formula, or try a 15-percent increase or decrease.

For our testing, all these recipes were microwaved at full power, either uncovered or covered tightly with microwave-safe plastic wrap. When you microwave under a tight cover, steam will build up. Be careful when releasing this steam, which is done by pricking the plastic before unwrapping. If your oven has no carousel, you'll get more even heating by rotating the dish a half turn halfway through cooking.

The recipes all make 4 servings unless otherwise noted.

 ### Baked Apple

Cut off the bottoms and peel the tops of 4 large Granny Smith, McIntosh, or Rome apples. Core and rub all cut surfaces with lemon juice. Place in a circle on a plate. Drizzle 1 teaspoon honey over each, cover with plastic wrap, and microwave 6 to 8 minutes at full power.

 ### Steamed Artichokes

Trim stems from 4 large globe artichokes and cut off the tops. Rub the surfaces with lemon. Place in a circle on a deep plate. Pour ¼ cup water over the artichokes, cover with plastic wrap, and microwave 18 minutes at full power. For artichoke hearts, follow the same procedure, but remove the leaves and scrape out the choke with a spoon after cooking.

 ### Blanched Asparagus

Place 1 pound trimmed thin asparagus stalks, layered up to 3 deep, in a rectangular dish, cover with plastic, and microwave 3 to 4 minutes at full power. Add another 1 minute for medium-thick asparagus.

 ### Crisp Bacon Strips

Place 8 slices bacon, side by side, in a rectangular dish lined with 4 sheets of paper towel, top with 2 more sheets, and microwave 7 minutes at full power.

 ### Finely Chopped Bacon with Rendered Bacon Fat

Place 4 strips chopped bacon on a plate, top with a sheet of wax paper, microwave for 2 minutes at full power, stir, and microwave 1 to 2 minutes more. Use in recipes calling for chopped bacon and/or rendered bacon fat.

 ### Baked Beets

Place 1 pound trimmed and scrubbed small beets in a shallow dish, cover with plastic wrap, and microwave at full power for 14 minutes. For 1 pound large beets (¼ pound or more each), wrap individually in plastic and microwave 15 to 18 minutes at full power.

 ### Berry Preserves

In a 3-quart bowl, toss 4 cups cleaned and trimmed berries with 1½ cups sugar and the finely grated zest of 1 lemon. Let rest 10 minutes. Cover with a double thickness of plastic wrap and microwave 9 minutes at full power. Uncover and stir, being sure to stir up any sugar from the bottom of the bowl. Return to the microwave uncovered and cook for 15 minutes more. Beat in 2 teaspoons lemon juice and 3 ounces liquid pectin and cook 1 minute more. Chill. Makes 1 pint.

Fifty Ways to Cook Most Everything

Blanched Broccoli

Separate 1 bunch broccoli into stalks and peel the stems. Place spoke-fashion on a 10-inch circular plate with the heads pointing toward the center. Put 1 or 2 tablespoons water on the plate, cover with plastic wrap, and microwave 5 minutes at full power.

Melted Butter

Cut chilled butter in small pats and place in a bowl at least 4 times the volume of the butter. Cover with wax paper and microwave ¼ pound for 1 minute, or ½ pound for 2 minutes, at full power. If frozen, add 30 seconds to either amount.

Brown Butter

Follow preceding recipe, but double the cooking times. Use on vegetables or sautéed meats.

Blanched Cabbage Leaves

Remove torn and wilted leaves from 1 head cabbage. Core out the stem completely. Place cabbage on a plate, base down, and microwave at full power for 3 minutes. Remove outer layers of leaves. If more blanched leaves are desired, return cabbage for 1-minute sessions until you have the number of leaves you want.

Blanched Cauliflower

Break 1 small head cauliflower into florets. Place in a single layer in a deep plate, add 1 tablespoon water, cover with plastic wrap, and microwave 4 to 5 minutes at full power, tossing once halfway through.

Melted Chocolate

Break 2 to 4 ounces chocolate into ½-ounce pieces. Place in a small bowl, cover with plastic wrap, and microwave 2 minutes at full power. Stir to finish. One ounce will melt in 1 minute; 8 ounces in 3 minutes 15 seconds.

Clams in Liquid

Place 24 clams in ½ inch poaching liquid or a sauce in a large enough pan so they sit uncrowded in 1 layer. Cover with plastic wrap and microwave 6 to 9 minutes, depending on size, at full power, until opened. Discard any that do not open.

Mussels in Liquid

Place 2 pounds large cleaned mussels in ½ inch poaching liquid or a sauce in a large enough pan so they sit uncrowded in 1 layer. Cover with plastic wrap and microwave 5 to 6 minutes at full power, until opened. Discard any that do not open.

Unsweetened Coconut Milk

Combine 2 cups shredded coconut (unsweetened) with 2 cups water in a 2-quart bowl. Microwave 5 to 6 minutes at full power, and strain, forcing as much liquid from the coconut as possible. For desserts, replace water with milk.

Toasted Coconut

Spread 1 cup grated unsweetened coconut over bottom of a 10-inch plate and microwave 3 to 4 minutes at full power, stirring twice.

Eggplant Puree

Poke 1 medium-size eggplant all over with a fork. Place on 2 sheets of paper towel on a plate and microwave at full power for 7 to 8 minutes, turning twice. Cut off stem, split lengthwise, and scoop out flesh.

Braised Fennel or Celery

Microwave 2 teaspoons olive oil in a 10-inch baking dish for 2 minutes. Toss 1 trimmed and julienned bulb fennel, ¼ cup finely chopped onions, 1 clove minced garlic, and ½ teaspoon crumbled dried rosemary with the oil and microwave 4 minutes at full power. Add 2 skinned, seeded, and finely chopped plum tomatoes and ¼ cup white wine, cover with plastic wrap, and microwave at full power for 8 minutes. Season with salt and pepper.

Individual Fish Fillets

Season 1 skinless, boneless fish fillet, about 4 ounces, as desired or according to your recipe. Wrap in plastic and microwave 1 to 1½ minutes at full power. Rest 1 minute before unwrapping. Serves 1.

Individual Fish Steaks

Season 1 bone-in fish steak, about 8 ounces and ¾ inch thick, as desired or according to your recipe. Wrap in plastic and microwave at full power for 2 to 2½ minutes. Rest 1 minute before unwrapping. Serves 1.

Whole Fish

Slash the sides of a 2-pound fish and rub with seasonings as desired or according to your recipe.

Wrap in plastic wrap and microwave 6 to 8 minutes at full power, flipping once halfway through. Let rest 1 minute, snip plastic, and remove fish.

Poached Fish

Place 1 pound fish fillets in a 1-inch-deep dish large enough to hold them in a single layer. Pour 2 cups desired liquid (stock, sauce, broth, wine, juice, etc.) over top, and cover with plastic. Microwave 2 minutes at full power. Let rest 1 minute.

Fruit Sauce

Toss 1 pint berries or 1 pint chopped pitted cherries, peaches, plums, or apricots with 2 tablespoons sugar in a 1-quart bowl. Cover and microwave 3 minutes. Puree with 3 tablespoons orange juice and 1 teaspoon lemon juice in a food processor.

Rhubarb Sauce

Toss 2 cups sliced rhubarb and ½ cup sugar in a 1-quart bowl. Cover and microwave 5 minutes. Puree in a food processor with 3 tablespoons orange juice and 1 teaspoon lemon juice.

"Roasted" Garlic

Rub 2 bulbs garlic with 1 teaspoon olive oil and season lightly with salt. Place on a plate, cover with plastic wrap, and microwave 5 minutes at full power. Let rest 5 minutes. Slice off the tapered end and push flesh out of the skins. Serve as an appetizer with olive oil and crisp toast or as a sauce thickener.

Fifty Ways to Cook Most Everything

 Cooked Greens

Trim and rinse 1 pound kale, collards, beet greens, turnip greens, or broccoli rabe. Toss with 2 tablespoons olive oil, a pinch of crushed red pepper flakes, and salt in a large rectangular baking dish. Cover with plastic wrap and microwave 6 minutes at full power. Uncover, stir, and microwave 2 minutes more. Mix in 1 clove minced garlic.

 Braised Leeks

Trim 1 pound leeks of dark green leaves and roots. Split lengthwise and rinse away all dirt. Place in a single layer in a rectangular baking dish, pour ¾ cup chicken broth over top, season with salt and pepper, and dot with 1 teaspoon butter. Cover with plastic wrap and microwave 9 to 11 minutes at full power.

 Scalded Milk

Pour 1 to 2 cups milk in a 1-quart bowl, cover with plastic wrap, and microwave 2 minutes at full power for 1 cup, 3 minutes for 2 cups. Use in any recipe calling for scalded milk.

 Baked Custard

Beat 2 eggs, ¼ cup sugar, and a pinch of nutmeg. Scald 2 cups milk and beat slowly into the egg mixture. Add 1 teaspoon vanilla extract and beat vigorously for 1 minute. Pour into four 8-ounce dessert dishes and place in a circle on a large plate. Sprinkle ½ teaspoon grated nutmeg over top of each. Place on a carousel (if you don't have one, you'll have to turn the plate several times during cooking), and microwave 3 to 5 minutes at full power, until custards are set at their edges. Re-

move to a cooling rack and cool to room temperature. Chill.

 Caramel Custard

Mix 2 tablespoons sugar and 2 teaspoons water in each of four 8-ounce ramekins or flat-bottomed dessert dishes. Place in a circle on a large plate, cover with wax paper, and microwave 3 minutes at full power. Remove paper and microwave at full power for 3 minutes more on a carousel (turn plate every minute if you don't have a carousel). Check each minute until sugar has caramelized. Cool until caramel becomes solid, about 5 minutes. Use the caramel-lined dishes for cooking custard, as directed in preceding recipe. When chilled, invert onto 4 dessert plates for serving.

 Custard Sauce

Beat 4 egg yolks and ¼ cup sugar. Scald 1⅓ cups milk as described in recipe for Scalded Milk (above) for 2 minutes and beat into yolk mixture with 1 teaspoon vanilla extract. Microwave 2 minutes at full power. Whisk and microwave for 1 to 1½ minutes more. Whisk in 1 tablespoon brandy or fruit liqueur and let cool.

 Toasted Nuts

Place 1 cup whole nuts in a 10-inch shallow glass pan, and microwave at full power for 5 minutes, stirring twice.

 Sweet Spiced Nuts

Microwave 2 teaspoons peanut oil in a 10-inch pie plate at full power for 2 minutes. Add 2 cups nuts of any type and microwave for 5 minutes. Add 3

tablespoons sugar, ½ teaspoon salt, ¼ teaspoon ground cinnamon, and ½ teaspoon cayenne pepper. Toss and microwave 3 minutes more at full power. Toss and cool.

Poached Pears

Peel and core 4 underripe, perfectly shaped pears. Mix 2 tablespoons honey with 1 teaspoon lemon juice, add 1 teaspoon vanilla extract and 2 tablespoons white wine, and brush pears with mixture. Wrap each pear in plastic wrap and place upright on a plate. Microwave 6 minutes at full power, either on a carousel or by rotating the plate 3 times during cooking.

Praline

Place 1 cup sugar in a bowl and microwave at full power for 8 minutes. Stir. Microwave 2 minutes more and stir. Microwave 1 minute more until a clear golden liquid results. Add 1 cup toasted nuts (opposite). Toss thoroughly, and spread out on an oiled sheet pan to cool. Serve as a confection or break into pieces and grind to a powder to use as a flavoring agent when baking mousses or making frozen desserts.

Irish Oatmeal

In a 1½-quart bowl, combine ½ cup coarse-cut Irish oatmeal and 2 cups water. Cover with plastic wrap and microwave at full power for 5 minutes. Uncover, stir, and microwave at full power for 8 minutes more. Let rest 1 minute and stir well. Sprinkle with 1 to 2 tablespoons brown sugar and serve with ½ to 1 cup cold buttermilk. Serves 2.

Opening Oysters

Place 6 oysters, convex-side down, in a single layer on a large platter. Cover with plastic wrap and mi-

crowave at full power for 1½ to 3 minutes. It is likely that some of the oysters will open before others. Remove them as that happens. It is not necessary to re-cover the plate once the oysters begin to open.

Steamed New Potatoes

Wash 1 pound small new potatoes well. With water still clinging to them, place in a single layer in a deep dish. Dot with 1 tablespoon butter and season with salt. Cover with plastic wrap and microwave 4 minutes at full power. Shake and microwave 4 minutes more. Let rest 1 minute and uncover.

Cooked Pumpkin

Stem and seed 1 pound pumpkin. Cut into 4-inch square pieces, and place skin-side down in a dish large enough to hold the pieces in a single layer. Cover with plastic and microwave 6 to 8 minutes.

Stewed Prunes

Combine 1 pound pitted prunes with the juice and julienned zest of 1 lemon, ⅓ cup orange juice, ¼ cup honey, and ½ cup water in a bowl. Cover with plastic wrap and microwave 3 minutes at full power. Uncover and stir in a pinch of ground cloves and ¼ teaspoon ground cinnamon.

Broccoli Rabe

Trim off the hard ends from 1 pound broccoli rabe. Cut into 1-inch lengths and toss with ¼ cup virgin olive oil, salt, and a pinch of crushed red pepper flakes in a large rectangular baking pan. Microwave 8 minutes at full power, tossing once halfway through.

Wild Rice

Mix 1 cup wild rice, 1 cup water, and 1 cup beef or chicken broth in 1-quart bowl. Cover with plastic wrap and microwave 15 minutes at full power. Pierce plastic with point of a small knife and microwave 12 minutes more. Let rest 10 minutes. Season with salt and pepper and fluff with a fork.

 Microwave Risotto

Microwave 3 tablespoons virgin olive oil 3 minutes at full power in a 10-inch deep-sided baking dish. Add 1 chopped onion and 2 cloves minced garlic, toss, and microwave 4 minutes at full power. Add 1 cup Arborio rice and toss. Microwave 2 minutes more. Add 1¾ cups chicken broth and microwave 8 minutes at full power. Stir in 1¾ more cups chicken broth and microwave 8 minutes more at full power. Let rest 3 minutes. Stir in ¼ cup grated Parmesan and 2 tablespoons butter.

 Winter Squash

Halve a 1-pound squash and scrape out seeds and fibers. Season each half as desired or according to your recipe, wrap in plastic, and microwave 7 minutes at full power for 1 squash, 12 minutes for 2.

 Caramelized Sugar

Place 1 cup sugar in a bowl and microwave 6 to 8 minutes at full power. Stir. Microwave 2 to 3 minutes more, stirring every minute, until a clear golden liquid results.

 Sugar Syrup

Combine 1 cup sugar with ⅓ cup water in a 4-cup bowl and stir to dissolve. Cover with plastic wrap and microwave 5 minutes at full power for soft-ball syrup (240° F.), 5½ minutes for firm-ball (245° F.), 6 minutes for hard-ball (250° F.), 7 minutes for soft-crack (270° F.), and 7½ minutes for hard-crack (300° F.) syrup. After 8 minutes, the syrup will begin to caramelize (320° F.). Prick plastic immediately. Use in recipes for making candy and icing.

 Sweet Potatoes

Rinse and prick skin of 2 large sweet potatoes. Place on a plate and microwave 12 to 13 minutes at full power, turning once halfway through.

 Blanched Hard Vegetables

Place 1 pound trimmed green beans or julienned carrots in 2 tablespoons water and microwave in a deep dish, covered with plastic wrap, for 7 minutes at full power.

 Soaked Wild Mushrooms

Mix 1 ounce dried wild mushrooms with ½ cup warm water in a bowl. Cover with plastic wrap and microwave 3 minutes at full power. Let rest 1 minute.

Fifty Ways to Have Your Health and Eat It Too

Like fast food, snack food, and diet food, health food is uniquely an American concept. Unlike the people of most other countries, who eat as best they can for as long as they can so that they may gain as much happiness as they can while they're at it, we Americans often seem compelled to compartmentalize our diets. We eat one way when we're in a rush, another when we want to impress, and still another when we're eating for health.

The term *health food* has been used since the last quarter of the 1800s, when utopian communities practicing their own ideas of dietary perfection began springing up throughout the Midwest and Plains states. They espoused eating less processed food, more whole grains, and less meat. In the 1920s, the focus became more scientific, emphasizing vitamins and other nutrients. But it wasn't until the late 1960s and early 1970s that a complete retail industry was built around health food, incorporating traditional American health-food values with a drugstore-like inventory and Asian and African ingredients.

Health food became ginseng and tofu, but it did not stop there. The industry continues to grow and now includes organic produce, hormone-free meats, low-fat and chemical-free alternatives to processed foods, hyper-allergenic foods, herbs, healthful snacks, natural cosmetics, and new-age book stalls.

ABOUT THESE RECIPES

The following 50 recipes take a broad overview of the health-food field. All are designed with a reduction of fat, sugar, calories, and cholesterol in mind. Many call for typical health-food ingredients, but most can be made without a special trip to the health-food store.

They include snacks, appetizers, entrées, and desserts. All are written for 4 portions.

 Apple Turnip Soup

Cook ½ cup finely chopped onion in 2 tablespoons butter over moderate heat until soft. Add 2 finely chopped peeled and cored large apples, 6

small to medium peeled and diced white turnips, and 4 cups chicken broth. Simmer for 15 minutes until turnips are soft. Season with salt and white pepper. Purée in a food processor or blender. Reheat, mixing in ½ cup cream.

Puree of Root Vegetable Soup

Cook the chopped whites of 3 cleaned leeks, ½ teaspoon dried thyme, 1 teaspoon dried dill, and 1 clove minced garlic in 1 tablespoon vegetable oil until vegetables soften. Peel and chop ½ pound celery root, ½ pound parsnips, ¾ pound red-skin potatoes, and 1 large carrot, and add with ½ pound scrubbed and chopped Jerusalem artichokes, 1 bay leaf, salt, and pepper. Cook gently for 5 minutes. Add 4 cups hot chicken broth and simmer until vegetables are tender, about 30 minutes. Remove bay leaf. Process finely in a food processor or blender, but do not make completely smooth. Reheat and add 2 cups milk and 1 tablespoon chopped fresh parsley. Serves 6.

Ginger Pumpkin Bisque

Cook the finely chopped whites of 3 cleaned leeks and 1 tablespoon finely chopped fresh gingerroot in 2 tablespoons vegetable oil until vegetables soften. Add 2½ cups pumpkin puree, 1 quart chicken stock, a dash of cayenne pepper, a dash of grated nutmeg, and 2 teaspoons light-brown sugar. Simmer 5 minutes. Season with salt and white pepper. Bring to a boil and stir in ½ cup room-temperature sour cream and 1 cup room-temperature buttermilk.

Jerusalem Artichoke Soup

Toss 1½ pounds scrubbed and sliced Jerusalem artichokes with the juice of ½ lemon. Cook in 4

tablespoons butter with 1 chopped onion, 1 peeled and chopped parsnip, salt, and pepper in a covered pot until soft, about 20 minutes, stirring occasionally. Add 3 cups chicken stock and simmer 20 minutes more. Puree soup in a blender or food processor and reheat. Finish with ¾ cup buttermilk. Do not reboil.

Smoky Lentil Soup

Cook ½ cup each diced onion, carrot, and celery in 2 tablespoons corn oil until softened. Add 1 cup diced skinless smoked turkey breast, 6 cups chicken or vegetable broth, ½ pound lentils, ½ teaspoon crumbled dried rosemary, ¼ teaspoon dried thyme, and 1 bay leaf. Simmer for 45 minutes until lentils are tender. Add 1 diced roasted red bell pepper (page 442) and 1 tablespoon tomato paste. Adjust seasoning. Remove bay leaf.

White Bean and Brown Rice Soup

Cook the chopped whites of 2 leeks, 1 teaspoon ground coriander, 1 teaspoon dried thyme, 1 cinnamon stick, and 2 diced carrots in 2 tablespoons peanut oil over moderate heat until vegetables soften. Add 1 cup brown rice and toss. Add 2 quarts chicken broth, 1 small chili pepper, salt, and pepper and simmer 45 minutes. Add 2 cups drained cooked white beans and heat another 15 minutes. Just before serving, remove chili pepper and cinnamon stick and stir in ½ cup chopped fresh cilantro and the juice of 1 large lemon.

Miso Soup with Dried Mushrooms

Combine 1 ounce any variety dried mushroom and 2 cups boiling water. Remove mushrooms, trim, and chop coarsely. Strain liquid through a coffee filter and dissolve 2 tablespoons soy miso in it. Set aside. Cook ¼ pound cleaned and sliced white mushrooms in ½ teaspoon vegetable oil until vegetables soften. Add 2 thin slices fresh gingerroot, the miso liquid, 3 cups chicken stock, and the chopped dried mushrooms and bring to a boil. Add 6 ounces cubed soft bean curd and simmer 2 minutes. Stir in 3 thinly sliced scallions.

 Miso Noodle Soup

Break 2 ounces buckwheat or whole-wheat noodles in 2-inch lengths and boil until soft in plenty of salted water. Drain and rinse with cold water. Dissolve 3 tablespoons red miso in 1 cup water. Mix with 3 cups vegetable broth, 1 strip kombu seaweed, and 1 teaspoon finely diced fresh gingerroot and bring to a boil. Add 6 ounces cubed soft bean curd and the noodles and simmer 2 minutes. Garnish with 3 thinly sliced scallions.

 Miso Soup with Brown Rice

Follow preceding recipe substituting 1 cup cooked brown rice for the cooked noodles.

 Corn and Cheese Potato Soup

In a heavy soup pot, cook the chopped whites of 3 leeks and 1 finely chopped onion in 1 tablespoon *each* oil and butter until softened. Add 1 pound peeled and diced red-skin potatoes, 2 cups corn niblets, a pinch of dried thyme, and 4 cups chicken or vegetable broth. Simmer 15 minutes, until potatoes are tender. Add 1½ cups milk, ½ cup light cream, salt, and white pepper. Heat slowly to a simmer. Carefully whisk in ¼ pound shredded sharp Cheddar tossed with 1 tablespoon cornstarch. Cook just long enough to melt the cheese. Serves 6.

 Avocado Grapefruit Salad

Cut the peel and white membrane from 2 large pink grapefruit. Carefully remove grapefruit sections by cutting on either side of the membranes that divide the sections. Place in a serving bowl and squeeze any remaining juice over top. Toss with 2 thinly sliced avocados, 1 tablespoon small fresh tarragon leaves, and salt.

 Spicy Black Beans

In a large saucepan, combine ½ pound soaked and drained black beans, 1 small chopped onion, 1 small carrot, ½ rib celery, 2 ounces chopped smoked turkey breast, 2 diced stemmed jalapeños, 1 whole clove garlic, 1 bay leaf, ½ teaspoon dried thyme, and 4 cups water. Simmer until beans are tender, about 1 hour. Remove carrot, celery, bay leaf, and garlic clove and drain off remaining cooking liquid. Toss beans with 2 cloves minced garlic, 1 teaspoon olive oil, and the juice of 1 lemon.

 Black Beans and Basmati Pilaf

Follow preceding recipe. When beans are almost finished, rinse 1 cup Basmati rice in several changes of cold water until water is clear. Cook ¼ cup finely chopped onion, ¼ cup diced carrots, and 2 tablespoons diced celery in 1 tablespoon olive oil until vegetables soften. Add rice and stir. Add 1¾ cups chicken broth, salt, and pepper, bring to a boil, reduce heat, cover, and simmer 15 minutes, until all the liquid has been absorbed. Remove from heat, rest for 5 minutes, and toss with the black beans.

 Spiced Sesame Chick-Peas

Heat 3 tablespoons olive oil with 2 tablespoons chili powder, 2 teaspoons ground coriander, and 1

clove minced garlic for 30 seconds. Add 2 cups cooked or canned drained chick-peas, ¼ cup toasted sesame seeds, and salt. Cook until chick-peas absorb the oil. Serve as a snack.

 ## Brown Beans and Rice

Cook 1 cup chopped onion, 2 finely chopped canned or fresh chili peppers, and 1 clove minced garlic in 1 tablespoon corn oil until softened. Add 3 tablespoons chili powder, 1 tablespoon ground cumin, 1 teaspoon dried oregano, and 2 teaspoons ground coriander and cook 1 minute more. Add 2 cups brown rice and stir. Add 5 cups vegetable, chicken, or beef broth, cover, and simmer until liquid has been absorbed and rice is tender. Add 2 cups drained, cooked kidney beans and heat through. Stir in 1 tablespoon chopped fresh cilantro.

 ## Healthy Hoppin' John

Cook 1 cup *each* diced celery and onion in 1 table-spoon corn oil until softened. Add ½ cup diced skinless smoked turkey breast, 7 cups chicken broth, ½ pound black-eyed peas, soaked, ¼ tea-spoon cayenne pepper, and 1 bay leaf. Simmer 45 minutes, until peas are tender. Add 1 cup brown rice, cover, and simmer until liquid has been ab-sorbed, about 45 minutes. Season with salt and pepper.

 ## Chick-Pea and Red Onion Salad

Toss together 2 cups drained, cooked chick-peas, ⅓ cup chopped red onion, 1 chopped ripe to-mato, 3 tablespoons lemon juice, 3 tablespoons extra-virgin olive oil, ⅛ teaspoon crushed red pep-per flakes, 2 tablespoons finely chopped fresh pars-ley, salt, and pepper. Chill.

 ## Protein-Packed Cornbread

Place a 9-inch iron skillet in a preheated 425° F. oven while you prepare batter. Mix ½ cup un-bleached flour, ¼ cup whole-wheat pastry flour, 1 tablespoon baking powder, ¼ cup light brown sugar, ½ teaspoon salt, 1¼ cups stone-ground cornmeal, and ¾ cup finely grated sharp Cheddar cheese. Cook 3 tablespoons finely chopped on-ions in 3 tablespoons corn oil until soft. Add 1 peeled, cored and diced large Granny Smith apple and cook 1 minute. Toss with dry ingredients. Beat in 1 egg and 1 cup milk. Brush hot skillet with 2 tablespoons oil and pour in the batter. Bake 20 to 25 minutes.

 ## Flan Provençale

Cook 1 finely chopped onion and 2 cloves minced garlic in 2 tablespoons olive oil. Add ¼ teaspoon crushed chili pepper, 1 peeled and diced small egg-plant, ½ finely diced red pepper, 4 chopped and seeded plum tomatoes, 6 chopped basil leaves, a pinch of dried oregano, salt, and pepper and cook until eggplant is soft, about 15 minutes. Stir in ¼ cup chopped pitted black olives. Spoon into pre-baked 9-inch Flaky Pastry Shell (page 435) and top with a mixture of 1 cup milk, 2 eggs, and ¼ cup grated Parmesan. Bake at 350° F. for 35 minutes.

 ## Stir-Fried Quinoa

Rinse 1 cup quinoa in several changes cold water. Combine with 2 cups water and ¼ teaspoon salt and bring to a boil. Simmer, covered, for 10 to 12 minutes until all the water has been absorbed and the quinoa is tender. Set aside. Stir-fry ¼ cup finely chopped onion, 1 rib diced celery, and ½ diced red bell pepper in 1 tablespoon peanut oil, then push mixture up the sides of the wok. Add another

1 tablespoon oil in the center, then the quinoa, and stir-fry 1 minute. Add 1 beaten egg, 1 teaspoon soy sauce, 1 cup bean sprouts, ½ cup shredded spinach, ¼ cup roasted peanuts, and 2 chopped scallions. Heat through.

Quinoa with Tofu and Mushrooms

Prepare quinoa as in preceding recipe. Stir-fry ½ pound trimmed small white mushrooms and 2 cloves minced garlic in 2 tablespoons peanut oil for 1 minute. Add 1 tablespoon soy sauce, 1 cup vegetable or chicken broth, and 12 ounces large-diced tofu and simmer 2 minutes. Add 3 sliced scallions, then 1 teaspoon cornstarch dissolved in 1 tablespoon water. Stir until lightly thickened and pour over quinoa.

Tofu and Soba

Boil 8 ounces buckwheat noodles (soba) in plenty of salted water until *al dente*. Drain and rinse with cold water. Cook ½ cup finely chopped onion and 3 cloves minced garlic in 2 tablespoons peanut oil until soft. Add ½ cup finely diced carrots, ½ cup finely diced red bell pepper, ¼ teaspoon crushed red pepper flakes, and 1 tablespoon finely chopped fresh gingerroot and sauté 2 minutes more. Add the noodles and cook until heated through. Add 2 tablespoons soy sauce, 1 cup vegetable or chicken broth, and 1 pound tofu cut in large dice. Simmer 2 minutes. Add 3 sliced scallions, then 1 teaspoon cornstarch dissolved in 1 tablespoon water. Stir until lightly thickened and finish with 1 teaspoon Oriental sesame oil and a pinch of sugar.

Stir-Fried Shrimp and Tofu in Yogurt

Cut 1 pound firm tofu into cubes and pat dry. Fry in 2 batches in 1 inch hot soy oil until lightly brown, about 3 minutes. Drain and remove all but 1 tablespoon of the oil. Add 1 pound cleaned large shrimp and 2 cloves minced garlic. Stir-fry just until shrimp colors. Add 1 cup white wine, salt, pepper, and ½ teaspoon ground Szechuan peppercorns and simmer 1 minute. Remove shrimp with slotted spoon. Reduce liquid to ⅓ cup. Add 2 tablespoons chopped fresh dill and ½ cup plain yogurt. Toss with shrimp and tofu. Serve over rice or pasta.

Grilled Teriyaki Tofu

Split 2 tofu cakes in half horizontally and marinate 30 minutes in Ginger Soy Marinade (page 17). Remove and brush each with 1 teaspoon Oriental sesame oil. Broil or grill slowly until lightly browned, basting with marinade every minute.

Grilled Tofu Steak with Pickled Ginger

Split 2 tofu cakes in half horizontally and brush with ½ cup steak sauce. Marinate 30 minutes. Drizzle each with 1 teaspoon Oriental sesame oil. Broil or grill slowly until lightly browned. Serve with ¼ cup Japanese pickled ginger (*gari*).

Sizzling Tofu

Mix ¼ cup cornstarch with 2 egg whites until smooth. Toss 1 pound cubed firm tofu in ¼ cup cornstarch, then in the egg-white mixture, and deep-fry at 375° F. until crisp and light brown on its surface. Remove with slotted spoon and drain on rack for 20 seconds. Serve with Ginger Soy Marinade (page 17) spooned over top. Garnish with 2 sliced scallions.

Fifty Ways to Cook Most Everything

 Tofu Rice Pudding

Process 10½ ounces soft silken tofu until smooth with ¾ cup milk, 1 tablespoon honey, 3 tablespoons light brown sugar, 2 teaspoons vanilla extract, a pinch of salt, 1 teaspoon ground cinnamon, a grating of nutmeg, and 2 egg whites. Stir in 1 tablespoon melted margarine, ¼ cup raisins, and 1 cup cooked brown rice and cook over low heat, stirring frequently for 10 minutes, until lightly thickened. Transfer to a bowl and chill.

 Souffléd Sweet Potatoes

Beat 1½ cups mashed cooked sweet potatoes, ¾ cup plain yogurt, 1 tablespoon light brown sugar, a grating of nutmeg, a pinch of ground cloves, the juice and finely grated zest of 1 orange, 2 egg yolks, salt, and pepper. Beat 4 egg whites to firm peak with ⅛ teaspoon cream of tartar and fold into the sweet potatoes. Turn into a 1½-quart soufflé dish, and bake at 400° F. for 35 minutes, until puffed and brown.

 Broccoli and Peppers Baked in a Bread

Slice the hard stem ends from 2 bunches broccoli rabe and cut the rest of the stalks in 1-inch sections. Rinse thoroughly. Add rabe, with any water still clinging to it, to 2 tablespoons olive oil, heated in a large nonstick skillet. Add a large pinch of crushed red pepper flakes and season liberally with salt and pepper. Cover and simmer over moderate heat 10 to 15 minutes, adding a bit more water if needed to keep broccoli from boiling dry. Stir in 1 clove minced garlic and 1 diced roasted red pepper (page 442). Cut top off a 1-pound round loaf of crusty whole-grain bread. Hollow out interior of the loaf and fill with the rabe and peppers, layered with ¼ pound shredded smoked cheese. Replace

top of bread and bake at 350° F. for 40 minutes. Serve in wedges.

 Spanakopita Bread

Cook ½ cup onion in 1 tablespoon olive oil until soft. Add 20 ounces defrosted frozen chopped spinach, a pinch of crushed red pepper flakes, salt, and pepper and cook until dry. Add 1 clove minced garlic and 2 tablespoons grated Parmesan. Bake in a bread as described in preceding recipe, using crumbled feta instead of smoked cheese.

 Garden Vegetable Tempura

With a pair of chopsticks or the wrong end of a wooden spoon, mix 2 egg yolks, 2 cups ice water, and 2 cups sifted flour just until a loose batter forms. There should still be some lumps. Toss ½ pound *each* small broccoli florets, cauliflower florets, and julienned carrots in ¼ cup cornstarch, shake off excess, and dip in batter. With tongs, pick up small bundles of vegetables and deep-fry a few at a time at 375° F. in vegetable oil until lightly browned. Drain on paper towels and serve with a mixture of ¼ cup soy sauce, 1 teaspoon honey, and 1 clove minced garlic for dipping.

 Three-Bean Tempura

Follow preceding recipe substituting 1 pound diced firm tofu, 1 cup bean sprouts, and ½ cup chopped peanuts for the vegetables. To fry, drop small handfuls of the batter-coated bean mix into the hot oil.

 Vitamin-A Tempura

Follow recipe for Garden Vegetable Tempura (above) using peeled and diced yellow sweet potatoes instead of cauliflower. Before frying the vegetables, rinse and dry 12 large perfect stemmed kale leaves. Deep-fry for 30 seconds until bright green and crisp at the edge. Serve the tempura on a bed of the fried kale.

 ### Broccoli Pasta

Blot away excess water from ½ pound cooked broccoli. In a food processor, blend with ½ teaspoon salt, 1 clove garlic, 2 large eggs, and 1 teaspoon olive oil. Add 3 cups flour and process until mixture forms ball of dough in center of workbowl. Knead several minutes on floured board, using additional flour as needed to keep dough from sticking. Let rest 10 minutes. Roll out to desired thickness with a pasta machine or rolling pin. Cut into desired shape noodles. Cook until *al dente* in rapidly boiling water and serve with tomato pasta sauce or with olive oil, grated cheese, and garlic.

 ### Whole-Wheat Wild Mushroom Pasta

In a food processor, grind to a powder 2 ounces dried wild mushrooms. Add ¾ cup whole-wheat pastry flour, ½ cup unbleached white flour, and ¼ cup semolina or bread flour and mix well. Add ½ teaspoon salt, 2 eggs, and 1 teaspoon olive oil and process until mixture forms a ball of dough in center of workbowl. Knead, rest, roll, cut, and cook dough as described in preceding recipe. Serve tossed with desired sauce.

 ### Broccoli-Stem Crudités with Warm Tofu Vinaigrette

Cut ½ pound peeled broccoli stems into 4-inch-long strips and soak in ice water. Meanwhile in a food processor, blend ½ clove garlic, 3 tablespoons Oriental sesame oil, ¼ cup safflower oil, 2 tablespoons rice vinegar, 1 teaspoon soy sauce, ¼ pound diced tofu, salt, and pepper until smooth. Heat gently in a heavy saucepan. Drain broccoli stems and serve with sauce.

 ### Eggless Tofu "Mayonnaise"

In a food processor, blend until smooth 8 ounces soft silken tofu, 2 tablespoons lemon juice, ½ teaspoon sugar, ½ teaspoon Dijon mustard, salt, and pepper. With the processor on, slowly add ½ cup unsaturated vegetable oil in a slow stream until incorporated. Adjust seasoning. Makes about ¾ cup.

 ### Asian Tofu Dressing

In a food processor, blend ½ clove garlic, 3 tablespoons Oriental sesame oil, ¼ cup safflower oil, 2 tablespoons rice vinegar, 1 teaspoon soy sauce, ¼ pound diced tofu, salt, and pepper until smooth.

 ### Tofu Tuna

Prepare either of 2 preceding recipes. Toss with 12 ounces drained and crumbled canned water-packed tuna, 1 shredded carrot, and 1 rib diced celery.

 ### Stir-Fried Broccoli with Apples

Dissolve 1 teaspoon cornstarch in the juice of ½ lemon and 2 tablespoons soy sauce. Mix in 1 tablespoon hoisin sauce and 1 teaspoon ground ginger. Set aside. Stir-fry ½ chopped onion in 1 tablespoon peanut oil for 30 seconds. Add 1 head broccoli, trimmed into bite-size florets, and 1 cored and diced Granny Smith apple. Stir-fry another 30 seconds. Add ½ cup water, cover, and steam 2 minutes. Stir starch mixture, add, and cook until lightly thickened. Toss with 1 tablespoon finely chopped lemon zest, 2 tablespoons toasted cashews or almonds, and 1 clove minced garlic.

Poached Salmon with Arugula

Bring 1 cup white wine, 2 cups water, the juice of ½ lemon, and 2 finely chopped shallots to boil. Reduce heat, simmer, and add 4 pieces of skinless salmon fillet, each 5 ounces. Cover and poach 6 to 8 minutes. Remove to a warm platter and reduce poaching liquid to ⅓ cup. Add 1 diced roasted red bell pepper (page 442) and any liquid from the fish plate and return to a boil. Remove from heat and mix in ½ cup chopped arugula leaves and ½ cup nonfat yogurt. Pour over fish.

Eggplant Chili

Cook 4 cups peeled and diced eggplant, 1 cup chopped onions, 1 diced bell pepper, 2 finely chopped canned or fresh chili peppers, and 2 cloves minced garlic in 1 tablespoon corn oil until vegetables soften. Add 2 tablespoons tomato paste, ¼ cup chili powder, 1 tablespoon ground cumin, and 2 teaspoons dried oregano and cook 5 minutes more. Add 2 tablespoons flour and cook 1 minute more. Add 3 cups beef broth, 1 teaspoon black pepper, and 1 teaspoon cider vinegar. Simmer, covered, for 30 minutes. Season with salt and 1 teaspoon to 1 tablespoon hot pepper sauce. Add 2 cups drained, canned white kidney beans and heat through.

Ratatouille e Fagioli

Cook 1 large chopped onion, 4 cloves minced garlic, and 2 stalks diced fennel in 2 tablespoons virgin olive oil until vegetables soften. Add 1 peeled and diced large eggplant, 1 diced bell pepper, ¼ cup wine vinegar, 1 cup chicken or vegetable stock, salt, pepper, and 1 tablespoon grated lemon zest. Simmer until stock evaporates. Add 1 teaspoon hot pepper sauce, 6 chopped, skinned, and seeded plum tomatoes, 2 sliced small zucchini, 2 cups drained canned cannellini beans, and 12 minced basil leaves. Simmer 5 minutes more. Serve warm with grated Parmesan.

Whole-Wheat Vanilla Yogurt French Toast

Beat 4 eggs, 1 cup buttermilk, ½ pint vanilla yogurt, and a pinch of salt. Add 8 thick slices slightly stale whole-wheat bread and let soak until liquid is absorbed. Lightly grease a nonstick skillet with butter. Add as many slices of the bread as will fit in a single layer and brown on each side over moderate heat, 3 to 4 minutes per side. Remove to a warm platter. Brown remaining slices in the same way. Serve with 2 cups fresh fruit.

Buttermilk Bran Hotcakes

Mix 1 cup 100-percent bran cereal, 1 cup wholewheat flour, 2 teaspoons baking powder, 1 teaspoon baking soda, and 2 tablespoons brown sugar. Mix 2 egg yolks, 2 cups buttermilk, 2 teaspoons vanilla extract, and 2 tablespoons melted butter. Stir into dry ingredients. In a clean bowl, whip the egg whites until soft peaks form. Fold the beaten whites into the batter. Heat a griddle until water dropped on its surface forms beads and bounces. Grease well and pour ¼ cup batter onto the hot griddle for each cake. Turn after 2 minutes, when top looks pocked and bottom is brown. Serve with 2 cups warm applesauce.

Whole-Wheat Brown Rice Pancakes with Caviar

Mix 1 cup whole-wheat flour and 1 cup unbleached white flour. Sift with 2 teaspoons baking powder, 1 teaspoon baking soda, 1 tablespoon sugar, and ½ teaspoon salt. Mix 2 egg yolks, ½ cup melted butter, and 2 cups buttermilk and stir into dry ingredients until smooth. Stir in 2 cups cooked brown rice. In a clean bowl, whip the whites until soft peaks form. Fold beaten whites into batter. Heat a griddle until water dropped on its surface forms beads and bounces. Grease well and pour ¼ cup batter onto the hot griddle for each cake. Turn after 2 minutes, when top looks pocked and bottom is brown. Top with 1 cup sour cream and ½ cup caviar. Serves 6.

 Wild Rice Pancakes with Corn and Roasted Pepper Salsa

Prepare batter as in preceding recipe, but use wild rice instead of brown rice. Serve pancakes with this salsa: Heat 2 cups corn niblets and a pinch of crushed red pepper flakes in 1 tablespoon corn oil for 1 minute. Add 1 tablespoon Hungarian paprika, the finely chopped whites of 3 scallions, 1 diced roasted red pepper (page 442), salt, and pepper.

 Stir-Fried Asparagus with Tofu and Almonds

Dissolve 2 teaspoons cornstarch in 2 tablespoons low-sodium soy sauce, ⅓ cup Chinese oyster sauce, and the juice of ½ lemon. Set aside. Stir-fry 1 pound trimmed asparagus, cut into 2-inch sections, in 2 tablespoons safflower oil until bright green. Add ½ pound diced tofu, a pinch of crushed red pepper flakes, and 1 cup chicken stock. Cover wok and steam 3 minutes. Add cornstarch mixture and toss until sauce thickens. Remove from heat and toss in 1 clove minced garlic, 2 thinly sliced scallions, and 1 cup toasted almonds.

 Sesame Brown Rice Pilaf

Cook ½ cup chopped onion and 1 clove minced garlic in 1 teaspoon peanut oil until soft. Add 1 teaspoon Oriental sesame oil and 1 cup long-grain brown rice, and toss. Add 2½ cups boiling water, a pinch of crushed red pepper flakes, salt, and pepper. Cover and simmer until all the liquid has been absorbed, about 35 minutes. Toss with ½ cup toasted sesame seeds and 2 teaspoons soy sauce.

 Dried Fruit Mush

Finely chop or grind 2½ cups coarsely chopped assorted dried fruits (raisins, dates, apricots, apples, pineapple) in a food processor or meat grinder, with a pinch of ground allspice, 1 teaspoon ground cinnamon, and ¼ teaspoon ground ginger. Mix in ½ cup walnut or pecan pieces. Wet your hands and form mixture into a rough log. Wrap in plastic and refrigerate. Serve in slices as a condiment.

Fifty Alternatives to Meat

Time was when a balanced meal was meat, potatoes, and a vegetable, in that order. But times have changed. Since many people want to cut down on their consumption of animal fat, meat is no longer the automatic main course. One of the best ways to find alternatives to meat is to look into cuisines that traditionally lack access to it as a main protein source. Because meats are luxury items in all but a handful of cultures, we need only leave the Western world to find a full array of inspired vegetarian dishes from which to choose.

From the chili-spiked beans and tortillas of Mexico to the fragrant vegetable curries of India, vegetarian cooking is ripe with rich flavors that can let you erase meat from your diet without regret—whether you choose to do so for a single dinner or an entire lifetime. Grill marinated vegetables and serve them with high-protein Middle Eastern sauces made from eggplant, chick-peas, and beans. Stuff cabbage with brown rice and vegetables or serve a spaghetti (or spaghetti squash) primavera, in a sauce overrun with garden produce.

Make stir-fries of vegetables, bean curd, and nuts. Or assemble antipasto salads speckled with cheese, roasted peppers, and fresh herbs. Make blini or latkes inundated with chopped vegetables to serve with yogurt and chives or make hearty soups thick with peanuts, chili peppers, and grains from East Africa. Try vegetable tempura from Japan or South American vegetable stews laden with hearty winter vegetables and the perfume of cilantro.

These foods are all based on the process of protein complementation—balancing the amino-acid deficiencies of one incomplete vegetable protein with the amino-acid strengths of another. For instance, most beans are low in the essential sulfur-containing amino acids and the amino acid tryptophan. These deficiencies limit the amount of protein that can be built from a diet of beans alone. But combine them with a grain, such as rice or corn, and the missing amino acids are right there. Hence, beans and grains eaten together provide much more usable protein than either one could provide alone—and in ways that eliminate cholesterol and saturated fats from the diet.

The argument that beans and grains are high-calorie starches has long been used against them by weight-conscious as well as health-conscious diners. But look at the facts. A 1-pound beef steak has more than three times the calories as a pound of cooked kidney beans. A pound of fat packs more than twice as many calories as a pound of starch. Considering that a typical serving of meat weighs 6 to 8 ounces and an average portion of beans or rice is closer to 5 ounces, the old starch-is-fattening argument has lost most of its weight.

ABOUT THESE RECIPES

The following recipes are hearty, highly nutritious entrées that rely on flavorful oils and a combination of spices and vegetables to supply filling alternatives to meat with far fewer calories and less cholesterol and saturated fat.

All recipes serve 4 unless otherwise noted.

Black Bean Tacos

Fill 8 warm taco shells with Refried Black Beans (page 429), 2 cups shredded lettuce, 1 diced avocado, and a salsa made by processing the chopped whites of 4 scallions, 3 large tomatoes, 2 seeded and stemmed jalapeño peppers, 2 tablespoons olive oil, 2 tablespoons finely chopped fresh parsley, 1 tablespoon chopped orange zest, and the juice of 1 orange.

Black Bean Falafel

In a food processor, puree ½ pound cooked or canned drained black beans, 3 tablespoons lemon juice, 3 tablespoons olive oil, 1 clove minced garlic, ⅓ cup tahini, ½ teaspoon ground coriander, ½ teaspoon ground cumin, and a pinch of dried oregano. Form into 2-teaspoon-size balls, dip in 1 beaten egg, and dredge in a mixture of ⅓ cup whole-wheat flour, ⅓ cup sesame seeds, salt, and pepper. Deep-fry at 375° F. in batches until golden brown and blot dry. Mix ⅔ cup tahini, 3 tablespoons lemon juice, 1 clove minced garlic, 1 tablespoon olive oil, and ½ cup plain yogurt. Spread interiors of 4 pita pocket breads with this mixture and fill with the black-bean balls. Top with more sauce, 2 chopped tomatoes, 1 cup shredded let-tuce, ½ cup diced cucumbers, and 2 tablespoons chopped fresh parsley.

Avocado Falafel

Follow preceding recipe, substituting cooked chick-peas for the black beans, 1 diced avocado for the lettuce, and fresh mint for the parsley.

Eggplant Falafel

Sauté 1 peeled and diced eggplant in ¼ cup olive oil with ¼ cup chopped onion, 2 cloves minced garlic, 2 chopped and skinned tomatoes, salt, pepper, and 2 teaspoons dried mint until eggplant is tender. Follow recipe for Black Bean Falafel (above), using chick-peas instead of the black beans and using the eggplant mixture in place of the tomatoes, lettuce, and cucumbers.

Pita Filled with Toasted Chick-peas, Avocado, and Eggplant "Caviar"

Roast 1 small eggplant for 45 minutes at 400° F. Let cool, split lengthwise, and puree the flesh in a food processor with ½ clove minced garlic, 2 tablespoons mayonnaise, 1 tablespoon olive oil, 1 tablespoon lemon juice, salt, and pepper. Spread interiors of 4 pita pocket breads with half this mixture. Fill pockets with Spiced Sesame Chick-Peas (page 319). Divide the remaining eggplant mixture, 1 diced avocado, and 1 diced tomato among pitas.

Chilied Corn Enchiladas

Cook 1 cup chopped onion and 1 clove minced garlic in 1 tablespoon corn oil until soft. Add 1 teaspoon chili powder, ½ teaspoon ground cumin, a pinch of crushed red pepper flakes, salt, black pepper, 1 large diced roasted red pepper (page 442), and 1 cup corn niblets and cook for 5 minutes. Spread 4 large wheat tortillas each with 3 tablespoons Refried Beans (page 429). Top each with 3 tablespoons of the chilied corn, spread in a line, and roll up tortillas. Place seam-side down in a baking dish. Top with 2 cups Quick Fresh Tomato Sauce (page 46) and sprinkle 4 ounces crumbled farmer cheese over top. Bake at 375° F. for 20 minutes.

 ## High-Protein Vegetarian Tostadas

Toss 1 diced large avocado, 1 tablespoon lemon juice, 2 cored and chopped tomatoes, salt, and hot pepper sauce. Toast 8 corn tortillas in thin film of corn oil. Place 2 tortillas on a plate. Top each with ⅓ cup Refried Beans (page 429), a dollop of the avocado mixture, ¼ cup alfalfa sprouts, and ½ ounce shredded Monterey Jack cheese. Garnish with 1 tablespoon julienned red radish.

 ## Mixed Grilled Vegetables with Black Bean Sauce

Trim 1 large red pepper and 1 large yellow pepper and cut into 6 spears. Cut 1 zucchini and 1 yellow squash in large chunks. Cut 1 large sweet onion in wedges. Slice 1 large tomato. Stem 12 large mushrooms. Toss vegetables in 1 cup Oil and Vinegar Dressing (page 296) and marinate for 1 hour. Meanwhile, process 2 cups drained, cooked black beans, 1 large clove garlic, 1 tablespoon minced onion, ¼ cup olive oil, 1 teaspoon hot pepper sauce, and salt in a food processor until smooth. Thin with ¼ to ⅓ cup orange juice to desired consistency. Grill or broil the vegetables until browned and tender. (Onion needs about 12 minutes; peppers, squash, and mushrooms, 6 to 8 minutes; tomatoes, 4 minutes.) Serve topped with the sauce

and garnished with 1 tablespoon toasted sesame seeds.

 ## Mixed Grilled Vegetables with Chilied Peanut Sauce

Prepare the grilled vegetables as in the preceding recipe and serve with a double recipe of Chilied Peanut Sauce (page 26) instead of with the black bean sauce.

 ## Mixed Grilled Vegetable Tostada

Follow recipe for Mixed Grilled Vegetables with Black Bean Sauce (above). Brown 4 tortillas in thin film of corn oil, spread with ¼ of the black bean sauce, and mound with the vegetables. Top with more black bean sauce, ¼ pound shredded Cheddar cheese, 1 diced avocado, and ¼ cup sour cream.

 ## Pumpkin Bisque

Cook ½ cup finely chopped onion in 2 tablespoons butter until soft. Add 2 tablespoons finely chopped fresh gingerroot, 1 cinnamon stick, and 1 dried hot chili pepper. Cook for another minute. Add 2 cups canned pumpkin, 4 cups vegetable stock, 2 tablespoons honey, 1 teaspoon apple cider vinegar, ¼ teaspoon grated nutmeg, salt, and pepper. Bring to a boil and adjust seasoning. Serve hot or cold garnished with ⅓ cup sour cream.

 ## Red Pepper Chowder Swirled with Chili Cream

Cook ½ cup finely chopped onion, 1 large clove minced garlic, and 1 rib diced celery in 2 tablespoons olive oil until vegetables soften. Add 4

roasted and diced red or yellow bell peppers (page 442), 2 cups corn niblets, 1 teaspoon curry powder, and ⅛ teaspoon cayenne pepper and cook for 30 seconds more. Add 5 cups vegetable stock, 1½ teaspoons paprika, salt, and pepper. Simmer for 20 minutes. Add ¼ cup finely chopped fresh parsley and 2 tablespoons lime juice. While soup is cooking, reduce 1 cup heavy cream by half, then puree in a food processor with 2 to 3 tablespoons canned chopped chili peppers. Serve chowder swirled with the chili cream.

Chili and Corn Chowder

Follow preceding recipe, replacing 3 of the roasted peppers with 2 cups drained, cooked kidney beans, and replacing the curry powder with 1 tablespoon chili powder. Add ¼ cup tomato paste with the stock.

Middle Eastern Chick-Pea Soup

Cook 1 finely chopped onion and 4 cloves minced garlic in 2 teaspoons Oriental sesame oil and 1 teaspoon peanut oil until softened. Add 1 teaspoon ground coriander and cook another 30 seconds. Add 1 quart vegetable stock and bring to a boil. Add 1 cup small macaroni and simmer 10 minutes. Add 1½ cups cooked or canned chick-peas and simmer 5 minutes more. Mix 1 extra-large egg yolk with ¼ cup lemon juice. Slowly whisk into the soup and simmer until soup thickens lightly. Do not boil. Add ¼ cup finely chopped fresh parsley.

Spicy Chick-Pea Soup

Cook 1 finely chopped onion and 4 cloves minced garlic in 1 tablespoon olive oil until soft. Add 1 diced bell pepper, 1 tablespoon finely chopped jalapeño pepper, 1 finely chopped peeled tomato,

¼ teaspoon dried oregano, 1 teaspoon ground cumin, salt, and pepper. Cook another minute. Add 1 quart vegetable broth and bring to a boil. Add ½ cup rice and simmer 10 minutes. Add 1½ cups cooked or canned chick-peas and simmer 5 minutes more. Mix 1 extra-large egg yolk with ¼ cup lime juice. Slowly whisk into the soup and simmer until soup thickens lightly. Do not boil. Add ¼ cup finely chopped fresh parsley.

Marinated Antipasto

Serve the following vegetable dishes, either at room temperature or warmed, with 1 loaf crusty bread and 1 cup brine- or oil-cured black olives: Sicilian Artichokes (page 248), Grilled Mediterranean Finger Eggplant (page 251), Mushrooms Boiled with Lots of Garlic (page 252), and Melange of Roasted Peppers (page 253).

Summer Antipasto

Serve the following vegetable dishes on a bed of Romaine lettuce, either chilled or at room temperature, with 1 loaf crusty bread: Asparagus with Lemon Oil (page 248), Marinated Tomato with Chèvre and Onion (page 264), Roasted Peppers with Black Olives and Anchovies (page 289), Grilled Summer Squash Salad (page 292), and Tabouleh (page 291).

Frito Misto (Fried Antipasto)

Serve Sweet Potato Chips (page 112), Fried Kale (page 278), and Winter Tempura (page 330) with Anchovy Mayonnaise (page 28).

Brown Rice and Roasted Pepper Salad

Rinse 2 cups brown-and-wild rice blend in several changes of cold water. Bring 5 cups water to a boil with 1 tablespoon soy sauce. Add the rice, cover, and simmer for 45 minutes until rice is tender and water has been absorbed. Toss with 4 diced roasted bell peppers (page 442) of assorted colors, ½ clove minced garlic, ⅓ cup olive oil, ¼ cup red wine vinegar, the juice of 1 lime, ¼ cup chopped fresh parsley, salt, and pepper. Serve warm or refrigerate. Serves 6 to 8.

Rice and Lentil Salad

Follow preceding recipe substituting 1 cup soaked lentils for half the rice. Add ¼ cup chopped red onion and 1 tablespoon dried mint with the peppers.

Risotto e Fagioli

Cook ¼ cup finely chopped onion in 2 tablespoons olive oil until soft. Add 1 cup Arborio rice and toss with oil. Add ½ cup white wine and, stirring frequently with a wooden spoon, cook over moderate heat until wine has been absorbed. Add 4¼ cups chicken broth to the rice, ½ cup at a time. Wait for each addition to be absorbed before stirring in the next, until the rice is *al dente* and a creamy sauce develops throughout the rice. Stir in 1 cup cooked drained, small white beans, ½ cup roasted pumpkin seeds, 1 tablespoon Oriental sesame oil, and ¼ cup grated Parmesan.

Squash Stuffed with Risotto

Cut a thin slice from the pointed ends of 4 acorn squash so that they can stand upright. Slice off stem ends and save as lids. Hollow out interior cavity, discarding seeds. Sprinkle inside of each squash with 1 teaspoon lemon juice and 1 teaspoon soy sauce. Set aside while preparing ½ the preceding recipe. Stuff squash with the risotto and replace

lids. Place in a baking pan with ¼ inch water, and bake at 400°F. for 45 minutes, until squash are soft.

Winter Tempura

Julienne 1 large peeled red beet, 2 peeled carrots, 2 ribs fennel, and 1 peeled sweet potato. Thinly slice the white parts of 2 leeks. Beat 2 cups ice water into 2 beaten egg yolks. Stir in 2 cups sifted flour, but not too thoroughly, leaving some clumps of flour. Toss each type of vegetable in this batter and deep-fry at 375° F. small handfuls in batches. Do the beets last. Hold the fried vegetables in a warm oven while the rest are being cooked. When all are cooked, deep-fry 8 sprigs of parsley for 10 seconds. Garnish vegetables with the fried parsley and serve with Dipping Sauce for Potstickers (page 205).

Carrot and Beet Latkes

Shred ½ pound *each* peeled carrots and beets and mix with 3 beaten eggs, 1 teaspoon lemon juice, 2 tablespoons flour, 1 teaspoon salt, pepper, and 3 tablespoons finely chopped onion. Fry heaping soupspoonfuls of this batter in ¼ inch hot oil in a deep skillet, flattening mounds to form pancakes about 3 inches in diameter. Brown well, 4 to 5 minutes per side. Drain on paper towels, and serve hot with sour cream.

Celery Parsnip Latkes

Follow preceding recipe, but use celery root instead of beets, parsnip instead of carrots, and the white parts of leek for the onion.

Sweet Potato, Carrot, and Apple Pancakes

Shred ¾ pound sweet potatoes, ¼ pound carrot, and ½ tart apple and mix with 3 beaten eggs, 1 teaspoon lemon juice, 2 tablespoons flour, 1 teaspoon salt, pepper, and 3 tablespoons finely chopped onion. Fry heaping soupspoonfuls of this batter in ¼ inch hot oil in a deep skillet, flattening mounds to form pancakes about 3 inches in diameter. Brown well, 4 to 5 minutes per side. Drain on paper towels, and serve hot with sour cream.

 ### Jerusalem Artichoke and Mushroom au Gratin

Sauté ½ pound sliced mushrooms in 2 tablespoons olive oil. Make an even layer of ½ pound scrubbed and sliced Jerusalem artichokes mixed with the sliced white part of 1 leek in an 8-inch shallow baking dish. Season liberally with salt and pepper and top with these layers: half the mushrooms, ¼ cup grated Swiss cheese, 1 tablespoon grated Parmesan, and ½ cup milk mixed with half and half in any proportion. Repeat layering of the same ingredients in the same proportion and same order, and bake in a preheated 375° F. oven for 1 hour, until the Jerusalem artichokes are tender and the top is bubbly and brown.

 ### Stir-Fried Sesame Asparagus

Stir-fry 1 small chopped onion and 1 clove minced garlic in 1 tablespoon peanut oil for 10 seconds. Add ½ pound carrot strips, ½ pound sliced mushrooms, 2 teaspoons finely chopped fresh gingerroot, and a pinch of crushed red pepper flakes. Stir-fry 30 seconds more. Add ⅔ cup water and 2 tablespoons light soy sauce and bring to a boil. Add 1 pound asparagus, trimmed and cut in 2-inch lengths, cover, and cook for 3 minutes. Add 2 thinly sliced scallions, 1 cup bean sprouts, and 1 teaspoon cornstarch dissolved in 1 tablespoon lime juice. Stir until liquid thickens. Finish with 1 tablespoon dry sherry, 1 teaspoon Oriental sesame oil, and ¼ cup toasted sesame seeds.

 ### Fried Rice with Vegetables

Follow preceding recipe, but add 3 cups cooked rice after mixture boils. Replace cornstarch and lime juice with 2 beaten eggs.

 ### Spaghetti Squash with Stir-Fried Vegetables

Boil 1 medium (about 10 inches long) spaghetti squash in a large pot of water for about 20 minutes. Cut off stem, halve lengthwise, clean out seeds, and scrape out flesh with a fork. Sauté squash in ¼ cup peanut oil with 1 clove minced garlic, salt, and pepper. Top with Stir-Fried Sesame Asparagus (above).

 ### Spaghetti Squash with Artichoke and Mushrooms

Boil 1 medium (about 10 inches long) spaghetti squash in a large pot of water for about 20 minutes. Cut off stem, halve lengthwise, clean out seeds, and scrape out flesh with a fork. Sauté squash in ¼ cup peanut oil with 1 clove minced garlic, salt, and pepper. Toss with ⅓ cup grated Parmesan and Artichoke and Mushroom Sauce (page 47).

 ### Marinated Mozzarella Salad in Tomatoes

Mix 3 tablespoons olive oil, 1 clove minced garlic, ¼ teaspoon crushed red pepper flakes, 2 minced oil-cured sun-dried tomatoes, and ¼ cup finely chopped basil leaves. Slice stem ends from 4 large tomatoes and hollow the tomato shells with a citrus knife. Remove seeds. Chop flesh and add it to the prepared sauce. Toss ¾ pound shredded mozzarella with the sauce and mound the mixture into the hollowed-out tomato shells. Garnish with 4 basil sprigs.

Fifty Ways to Cook Most Everything

 Chilied Corn Salad Stuffed in Roasted Peppers

Toss together 3 cups corn niblets, 1 pound cooked, drained kidney beans, the sliced whites of 1 bunch scallions, and 1 clove minced garlic. Separately, mix 3 tablespoons mayonnaise, 2 tablespoons chili powder, 1 tablespoon ground cumin, 3 table-spoons corn oil, 1 tablespoon hot pepper sauce, salt, and pepper. Combine with corn mixture and 2 tablespoons chopped fresh cilantro. Fill 6 large roasted, stemmed, and seeded bell peppers (page 442) with the corn mixture. Serves 6.

 Greek Marinated Mushrooms in Artichokes

Boil 4 artichokes, trimmed of stems and leaf spines in several quarts salted water until tender, about 30 to 40 minutes. Cool. Sauté 1 pound sliced mush-rooms in ¼ cup olive oil with 1 clove minced gar-lic until tender. Toss with juice of 1 large lemon, salt, pepper, and the sliced white parts of 3 scal-lions. Scoop the choke from the center of each artichoke and fill the cavity with a portion of the mushroom mixture. Moisten artichoke leaves with some of the liquid from the mushrooms.

 Caponata

Brown 1 pound peeled and diced eggplant in ¼ cup olive oil. Add 1 cup diced celery, 1 cup chopped onion, and 1 diced green pepper, cook-ing until vegetables soften. Add 1½ cups peeled, seeded, and chopped plum tomatoes, 1 teaspoon dried basil, ¼ teaspoon dried oregano, and 1 ta-blespoon minced anchovy. Cook until lightly thickened. Remove from heat and stir in ¼ cup chopped green olives, 1 tablespoon drained ca-pers, 2 tablespoons chopped fresh flat-leaf parsley, 2 tablespoons wine vinegar, 2 tablespoons virgin

olive oil, salt, and pepper. Serve with crusty bread and ½ pound sliced provolone.

 Ratatouille

Follow preceding recipe, but use oil-cured black olives instead of green olives, and use chopped fresh basil instead of parsley. Add 1 sliced zucchini and 1 sliced yellow squash with the tomatoes.

 Marinated Lentil Salad

Cook 1 chopped large onion in 2 tablespoons olive oil until soft. Add 1 clove minced garlic, 2 bay leaves, ¼ teaspoon crushed red pepper flakes, and 3 cups soaked lentils. Add 2 quarts salted water and simmer until lentils are tender, about 1 hour. Drain, mix in 2 tablespoons virgin olive oil and 3 tablespoons lemon juice, and let cool. Toss with ½ cup Mustard Vinaigrette (page 297), salt, pepper, and ¼ cup chopped fresh flat-leaf parsley. Chill. Serve garnished with 1 tomato, cut in wedges, and 12 oil-cured black olives.

 White and Black Bean Salad

Toss 2 cups each cooked or canned drained black beans and white beans, ¼ cup chopped fresh flat-leaf parsley, 1 diced roasted red pepper (page 442), ¼ cup chopped red onion, and ½ cup Garlic Herb Dressing (page 296). Garnish with 4 lemon wedges and 8 tomato wedges.

 Minted Curried Potatoes

Peel and brown 16 small red-skin potatoes in ¼ cup vegetable oil. Add 2 teaspoons black mustard seeds and cook 10 seconds. Add 2 finely chopped small onions and cook until soft. Add 1 clove minced garlic, 1 tablespoon finely diced fresh gingerroot, and ½ cup yellow split peas and cook 1 minute more. Add 2 teaspoons ground coriander seed, 2 teaspoons curry powder, 1 teaspoon ground aniseed, and ½ teaspoon crushed red pepper flakes. Stir and cook another minute. Add 3 cups water, salt, and pepper, cooking for 30 minutes until peas are soft and potatoes are tender. Add 2 tablespoons dried mint leaves and simmer another 10 minutes. Finish with ½ cup plain yogurt.

 Potatoes and Eggplant

Follow preceding recipe, substituting 1 pound peeled and diced eggplant for the split peas. Replace the mint with fresh cilantro.

 Cheese Gnocchi with Fresh Tomato Sauce

Scald 4 cups milk. Whisk in 1¼ cups semolina flour and cook gently, stirring constantly, until mixture becomes thick enough to pull away from the sides of the pan. Remove from heat and beat in ⅔ cup grated Parmesan, 2 extra-large egg yolks, and 4 tablespoons butter. Moisten bottom of a sheet pan and press gnocchi mixture into ½-inch-thick layer on the pan. Refrigerate until firm. Stamp out small circles of the dough and place in a buttered baking dish with the dough scraps. Pour 2 tablespoons melted butter over top, and sprinkle with ⅓ cup grated Parmesan. Bake at 450° F. for 15 minutes. Top with Quick Fresh Tomato Sauce (page 46).

 Herb Gnocchi with Parmesan and Butter

Follow preceding recipe, adding 1 tablespoon *each* finely chopped fresh basil and parsley and 1 teaspoon chopped fresh oregano to the dough with the Parmesan. Omit the tomato sauce.

 Pizza Rustica

Chop ½ pound fresh spinach in large pieces. Cook in covered pan with 2 tablespoons olive oil until tender. Uncover, raise heat, and cook until dry. Season with salt, pepper, and 1 clove minced garlic. Let cool. Mix with ¾ pound drained ricotta cheese, 3 eggs, 2 tablespoons chopped onion, 1 tablespoon chopped fresh parsley, ½ cup Parmesan, salt, and pepper. Line a 9-inch pie pan with Flaky Pastry (page 434). Fill with half the ricotta mixture. Make a layer of ¼ pound sliced mozzarella and ½ julienned roasted pepper (page 442). Top with remaining ricotta, ¼ pound sliced mozzarella, and the other roasted pepper half. Top with another round of pastry and crimp the edges. Slit the top crust and bake at 400° F. for 40 minutes until browned. Let cool 30 minutes before serving. Serves 6.

 Peasant Pie

Boil 3 peeled red-skin potatoes until tender in salted water, slice, and set aside. Sauté 4 cups shredded red cabbage, 1 chopped onion, 1 tablespoon chopped fresh parsley, 1 teaspoon dried basil, 1 teaspoon lemon juice, and ½ teaspoon ground fennel in 2 tablespoons butter until wilted. Season with salt and pepper. Sauté ½ pound sliced mushrooms in 1 tablespoon butter until tender. Line a 9-inch pie pan with Cream Cheese Pastry (page 434), spread with 4 ounces cream cheese, and top with potatoes, followed by 2 tablespoons chopped fresh dill, the cabbage, and the mushrooms. Top with another round of pastry and crimp the edges. Slit the top crust and bake at 400° F. for 40 minutes until browned. Let cool 30 minutes before serving. Serves 6.

Fontina Fondue with Garlic Roasted Potatoes

Toss 2 pounds chunked russet potatoes with 2 tablespoons olive oil and 1 teaspoon garlic salt and roast at 400°F. for 45 minutes, until browned and crisp. Meanwhile, rub the interior of a heavy pot with 1 cut garlic clove, add 2 cups white wine, and bring to a simmer. Add 3 tablespoons cornstarch dissolved in 6 tablespoons water and 2 teaspoons hot pepper sauce. Bring to a boil and stir until smooth. Remove from heat, then stir in ½ pound *each* grated Gruyère and Fontina cheese by the handful until melted. Season with salt and a pinch of cayenne pepper. Transfer to a fondue pot or keep warm in the pot and serve with potatoes and long forks for dipping.

 Cheddar Fondue with Apples, Pickles, and Toast

Follow preceding recipe, but omit the potatoes, substitute beer for wine, and substitute 1 pound shredded sharp Cheddar cheese for the Gruyère and Fontina. Serve with 2 large tart apples, 1 dill pickle, and 1 French bread, all cut in chunks.

 Leek and Chard Soufflé

Cook ¼ cup flour in 4 tablespoons butter for 2 minutes in a heavy saucepan. Add 1¼ cups milk, whisking constantly, and simmer until thick. Remove from heat and beat in 6 egg yolks, 1 at a time. Season liberally with salt and pepper. Set aside. Cook ½ cup finely chopped white part of leeks in 2 tablespoons olive oil until soft, add 1 pound blanched chard leaves and 1 clove minced garlic, and cook until dry. Chop finely and add to sauce with ½ cup grated Parmesan. Beat 8 egg whites with ⅛ teaspoon cream of tartar until firm peaks form. Fold into chard mixture in 3 additions. Transfer to a greased 2-quart soufflé dish dusted with Parmesan. Bake in a 400° F. oven for 20 minutes. Reduce heat to 350° F. and bake 25 more minutes, until puffed and brown. Serve immediately.

 Eggplant and Olive Soufflé

Cook ¼ cup flour in 4 tablespoons butter for 2 minutes in a heavy saucepan. Add 1¼ cups milk, whisking constantly, and simmer several minutes until thick. Remove from heat and beat in 6 egg yolks, 1 at a time. Season liberally with salt and pepper. Beat in Eggplant Puree (page 313), ¼ cup finely chopped olives, and ¼ cup grated Parmesan. Beat 8 egg whites with ⅛ teaspoon cream of tartar until firm peaks form. Fold into eggplant mixture in 3 additions. Transfer into a greased 2-quart soufflé dish dusted with Parmesan. Bake in a 400° F. oven for 20 minutes. Reduce oven to 350° F. and bake another 25 minutes, until puffed and brown. Serve immediately.

 Tarte Niçoise

Sprinkle a Flaky Pastry Shell (page 435), blind-baked in a 9-inch tart pan, with 1 tablespoon grated Parmesan. Scatter ½ cup shredded Gruyère cheese over bottom. Top with 1½ cups Ratatouille (page 332). Pour ½ cup milk beaten with 2 egg yolks, ¼ cup grated Parmesan, salt, and cayenne pepper over all. Bake at 350° F. for 40 minutes, until custard is set.

Tarte Lyonnaise

Prepare tart shell as in preceding recipe. Brown 2 large sliced onions in 2 tablespoons olive oil and top shredded cheese with the onions. Pour ½ cup milk beaten with 2 egg yolks, ¼ cup grated Parmesan, salt, and cayenne pepper over all. Bake as in preceding recipe.

Fifty Ways to Survive a Turkey

Sometimes it seems that we track our years one turkey at a time.

There was the first year we made Thanksgiving dinner, when emotions ran as raw as the turkey we nearly forgot to roast. Or the Thanksgiving we feasted like kings on a great browned gobbler, stuffed with peaches in brandy we had put up that July.

Each year, we assemble to appreciate a feast so large that no appetite can survive it. Try as we might, the meal always wins, leaving a week's worth of food in its wake. Thanksgiving dinner lingers in turkey parts, turkey soups, and hot turkey sandwiches. It comes to haunt as a meatloaf, a stir-fry, a casserole. It returns weeks later in a turkey pot pie, turkey sage croquettes or a turkey mushroom ragout.

The Thanksgiving feast is the meal of memories that won't let you forget. So to help you build those memories and survive the inevitable déjà vu of leftovers, we offer 10 memorable roast turkeys, each followed by 4 leftovers also worth remembering.

ABOUT THESE RECIPES

A whole roasted turkey should be cooked to an internal temperature of 170°F. To get an accurate reading, insert a meat thermometer into the thickest part of the breast or thigh meat.

Each of the roast turkey recipes makes 8 to 10 servings, plus leftovers. The leftover recipes serve 4 to 6.

You'll notice that we stuff our roast turkeys late in the roasting process. This is done to reduce overall cooking time.

By the way, don't ignore the Traditional Roast Turkey recipe. Even if you make one of the other roasts, a number of subsequent recipes use this one—and its stuffing—as a starting point.

 Traditional Roast Turkey—I

Season a cleaned 15-pound turkey inside and out with salt and pepper and place on a rack in a roasting pan. Roast in a preheated 450° F. oven for 30 minutes, reduce heat to 350° F., and roast for 3

Fifty Ways to Cook Most Everything

hours more, basting frequently with melted butter. Prepare stuffing by sautéing 1 cup minced onion and 2 ribs diced celery in 4 tablespoons butter until soft. Add 1 diced Granny Smith apple, 1 teaspoon *each* rubbed sage and dried chervil, ½ teaspoon dried thyme, and a pinch of nutmeg. Sauté 1 minute more, add 4 cups toasted bread cubes, the chopped and cooked turkey giblets, and 1 cup chicken stock, and mix to moisten. Season liberally with salt and pepper. Place the hot stuffing in the turkey cavity and roast 1 hour more, continuing to baste with pan drippings and butter.

 ### Turkey Noodle Soup

Cook 2 cups chopped onion and 1 cup *each* chopped celery and carrots in 1 tablespoon turkey fat or oil until softened. Add 3 tablespoons chopped fresh parsley, 2 tablespoons chopped fresh dill, 1 teaspoon dried thyme, 2 cloves, 2 teaspoons ground turmeric, salt, pepper, and 3 cups bite-size pieces boneless, skinless roasted turkey meat. Cook 3 minutes. Add 3 quarts chicken or turkey broth and simmer 15 minutes. Add 1 cup broad egg noodles and simmer another 15 minutes.

 ### Turkey Vinaigrette

In a bowl, combine ¼ cup cider vinegar, ¼ cup hazelnut or almond or walnut oil, ⅓ cup vegetable oil, 2 tablespoons orange juice, 2 finely chopped scallions, 1 clove minced garlic, ¼ cup chopped fresh parsley, a dash of cayenne, salt, and pepper. Toss with 4 cups diced roasted turkey meat, 2 ribs diced celery, ½ cup finely diced red onion, ½ cup sliced mushrooms, and 1 cup cooked rice or potatoes. Adjust seasoning.

 ### Hot Turkey Sandwiches

Slowly beat ½ cup cooled drippings from the roast turkey into 3 tablespoons flour until a smooth paste forms. In a large saucepan, bring another 2 cups drippings to a boil. Whisk in the paste a bit at a time and simmer for 20 minutes. Finish with 1 cup light cream, salt, and pepper. Warm a dozen or so slices roasted turkey breast in the gravy and serve over toast or fresh biscuits.

 ### Southern-Fried Turkey

Dip room-temperature leftover roast turkey parts in 1 egg beaten with 1 tablespoon honey, then dredge in bread crumbs. Allow to rest for 10 minutes and deep-fry at 375° F. until golden brown.

 ### Maple-Glazed Turkey Stuffed with Smoked Turkey Stuffing—II

Follow recipe for Traditional Roast Turkey (page 335). After first 2 hours of roasting, brush turkey every 20 minutes with glaze of ½ cup maple syrup, 1 tablespoon Worcestershire sauce, and 1 tablespoon peanut oil. For the smoked-turkey stuffing, cook the turkey giblets, chop and set aside. Sauté 1 cup minced onion and 2 ribs diced celery in the rendered fat from 6 slices bacon until soft. Add 1 diced Granny Smith apple, 1 teaspoon *each* rubbed sage and dried chervil, ½ teaspoon dried thyme and a pinch of nutmeg. Sauté 1 minute more, add 4 cups toasted bread cubes, 2 cups diced smoked turkey breast, 1 cup chopped walnuts, the giblets, and 1 cup chicken stock. Mix to moisten. Season liberally with salt and pepper. Place hot stuffing in the turkey cavity, and roast 1 hour more, continuing to baste with pan drippings and butter.

 ### Smoked Turkey Meatloaf

In a bowl, combine with your hands 2 pounds ground meat (50 percent beef, 25 percent veal and 25 percent pork), 2 cups leftover Smoked Turkey

Stuffing, 2 beaten eggs, ¼ cup ketchup, 2 table-spoons Worcestershire sauce, 2 teaspoons mustard, ¼ cup finely chopped onion, salt, and pepper. Form into a large loaf, layering ⅓ pound thinly sliced leftover turkey meat in 2 layers in the meatloaf. Bake in a preheated 375°F. oven for 1 hour.

 ### Sweet and Sour Turkey Salad

In a large bowl, combine ½ cup mayonnaise, 3 tablespoons maple syrup, 1 tablespoon hot pepper sauce, 2 tablespoons sweet orange marmalade, 2 tablespoons cider vinegar, salt, and pepper. Toss with 4 cups diced roasted turkey meat, ⅓ cup finely diced red onion, 1 cup halved orange sections, and 2 ribs diced celery.

 ### Sliced Turkey Breast with Chutney

Serve slices of turkey breast at room temperature with ½ cup mango chutney or other fruit chutney.

 ### Stir-Fried Turkey and Cranberries

Boil ½ cup cranberries, 2 tablespoons sugar, ¼ cup orange juice, and ½ teaspoon ground ginger for 1 minute. Let cool. Dissolve 1 tablespoon cornstarch in 1 tablespoon soy sauce and add to cooled cranberry mixture. Stir-fry 3 cups roasted turkey meat, cut in bite-size chunks, until lightly browned. Add ½ cup diced onion and 1 clove minced garlic. Cook 30 seconds. Add the reserved sauce and cook until thickened. Toss in ¼ cup sliced scallion.

 ### Orange-Glazed Turkey Breast with Brown Rice–Dried Fruit Stuffing—III

Follow recipe for Traditional Roast Turkey (page 335). Heat ¼ cup orange marmalade, 1 tablespoon Dijon mustard, ¼ cup orange juice, 1 teaspoon apple cider vinegar, salt, and pepper until smooth and liquid. After first 2 hours of roasting, brush turkey every 20 minutes with this glaze. Use the following stuffing: Cook 1 cup diced onion and 1 clove minced garlic in 2 tablespoons butter until soft. Add 1½ cups brown rice. Toss well. Add 3 cups boiling chicken stock, stir once, cover, and simmer gently for 40 minutes until all stock has been absorbed. Season with salt and pepper, and combine with 8 ounces mixed dried fruit that has been chopped, rehydrated in boiling water, and drained.

 ### Turkey Fried Rice

Stir-fry 1 cup chopped onion in 1 teaspoon peanut oil until lightly browned. Add ⅛ teaspoon crushed red pepper flakes, ½ cup diced celery, ½ cup diced red bell pepper, 2 cloves minced garlic, 1 teaspoon minced fresh gingerroot, and 2 cups bite-size pieces leftover turkey meat. Stir-fry 1 minute more. Add 2 cups Brown Rice–Dried Fruit Stuffing (preceding recipe) and 1 tablespoon soy sauce and stir-fry 2 minutes more. Finish with 2 teaspoons Oriental sesame oil and 4 sliced scallions.

 ### Cranberry Turkey Casserole

Brown ½ cup chopped onion in 1 tablespoon peanut oil. Add 1 clove minced garlic, 1 cup cranberries, and 2 tablespoons sugar and cook until cranberries pop. Add 1 cup chicken or turkey broth and toss with 3 cups bite-size pieces leftover turkey meat and 3 cups leftover Brown Rice–Dried Fruit Stuffing (above). Bake in a 2-quart casserole at 350° F. for 45 minutes.

Creole Turkey Salad

In large bowl, combine ½ cup mayonnaise, 3 tablespoons ketchup, 1 tablespoon hot pepper sauce, ¼ cup applesauce, 1 tablespoon sugar, 1 tablespoon vinegar, salt, and pepper. Toss with 4 cups diced boneless roasted turkey meat, ⅓ cup finely diced red onion, and 2 ribs diced celery.

Turkey Cranberry Turnovers

In small saucepan, cook ⅔ cup cranberries, 2 tablespoons sugar, and the juice and grated zest of ½ orange until berries pop. Mash lightly with a fork. In a skillet, sauté 3 tablespoons chopped onion in 1 teaspoon butter until soft. Add 1 cup finely chopped roasted turkey meat and the cranberry mixture to the onions and season well with salt and pepper. Using 2 frozen puff-pastry sheets, form 8 turnovers (page 445), using the turkey mixture as your filling. Bake 20 to 25 minutes, in preheated 400° F. oven.

Herbed Brandy Turkey with Wild Mushroom Stuffing—IV

Season a cleaned 15-pound turkey inside and out with salt and pepper. Place on rack in a roasting pan. Carefully lift breast and leg skin by slipping your fingers under it and disengaging it from the meat. Place ¼ cup fresh herb leaves and spoon several tablespoons brandy under the skin. Roast in preheated 450° F. oven for 30 minutes. Reduce heat to 350° F., and roast for 3 hours more, basting with more brandy every 20 minutes. To make stuffing, sauté 2 cups chopped onion in 4 tablespoons butter until soft. Add 1 pound each quartered fresh white and fresh wild mushrooms, and 1 teaspoon *each* dried thyme, crumbled rosemary, rubbed sage, and savory and cook until mushrooms lose their raw look. Add 1 cup fresh bread crumbs and cook 1 minute. Add 1½ cups hot chicken stock and ¼ cup tomato paste. Simmer until thick. Season with salt and pepper. Stir in ¼ cup chopped fresh parsley. Fill turkey cavity with this mixture 1 hour before it is done roasting.

Turkey Kiev with Herbed Cheese

Lay out 3 thin slices roasted turkey breast, overlapping slightly in a cloverleaf pattern. Place 1 tablespoon herbed cream cheese in the center and wrap turkey slices around the cheese. Secure loose ends with toothpicks. Repeat until you have 8 bundles. Beat 3 large eggs in a bowl with 2 tablespoons milk. Dip each bundle into the egg. Dredge heavily with seasoned bread crumbs. Dip into the egg again, then cover with more bread crumbs. Freeze the bundles. When ready to cook, dip the frozen bundles in egg again, then in another coat of bread crumbs. Deep-fry at 375° F. until golden brown, remove toothpicks, and serve immediately.

Turkey Mushroom Ragout

Sauté ⅓ cup chopped onion and 1 clove minced garlic in 2 tablespoons oil until lightly colored. Add 1 cup quartered mushrooms and 3 cups leftover roast turkey meat cut in large chunks. Sauté 1 minute. Add 2 cups leftover Wild Mushroom Stuffing (above) and ½ cup turkey drippings. Simmer for 5 minutes. Stir in 1 teaspoon fresh thyme leaves, salt, pepper, and 1 tablespoon chopped fresh parsley.

Leftover Turkey Chowder

In a large heavy soup pot over moderate heat, cook, in 2 tablespoons rendered bacon fat, the finely chopped white of 2 large leeks, 2 diced carrots, 2 ribs diced celery, 2 diced and peeled boiling potatoes, ½ diced red pepper, and 2 cups diced leftover turkey until vegetables soften. Add 2 cups sliced mushrooms, 1 teaspoon dried thyme, ½ teaspoon *each* ground sage and crumbled rosemary, and 1 bay leaf. Stir until mushrooms start to release their liquid. Add 1 quart chicken or turkey broth, season with salt and pepper, and simmer 20 minutes. Dissolve 1 tablespoon cornstarch in 1 cup cold milk and stir into the soup. Bring to a boil.

 ### Green Peppercorn Turkey Salad

In large bowl, mix ½ cup mayonnaise, 3 tablespoons drained, canned green peppercorns, ¼ cup herb wine vinegar, 1 clove minced garlic, salt, and pepper. Toss with 4 cups diced boneless roasted turkey meat, ¼ cup finely chopped shallot, 1 cup diced red bell pepper, and 2 ribs diced celery.

 ### Slow-Roasted Turkey—V

Season a cleaned 15-pound turkey inside and out with salt and pepper and place on rack in a roasting pan. Roast in preheated 450° F. oven for 45 minutes. Reduce heat to 170° F. and roast for at least 12 hours more to internal temperature of 170° F. It will not overcook; the bird will be amazingly juicy and tender.

 ### Turkey Nuggets

Dip 4 cups roasted turkey meat, cut into large chunks, into 2 eggs beaten with 1 tablespoon milk. Dredge in bread crumbs seasoned with salt and pepper and deep-fry at 375° F. until golden brown.

 ### Classic Turkey Salad

Toss 3 cups diced roasted turkey meat with ⅔ cup mayonnaise, 1 tablespoon cider vinegar, 2 ribs diced celery, ½ diced seeded cucumber, 1 shredded carrot, 1 tablespoon minced fresh parsley, salt, and pepper. Chill.

 ### Turkey Tabouleh

Soak 1 cup bulgur in 1½ cups cold water and 6 tablespoons olive oil until all liquid is absorbed. Toss in 3 cups diced roasted turkey meat, 1 diced apple, 3 sliced scallions, 1 clove minced garlic, ½ cup finely chopped fresh parsley, ¼ cup finely chopped red onion, 1 rib diced celery, ½ cup chopped almonds, 1 cup plain yogurt, salt, and pepper.

 ### Turkey Sloppy Joes

In a large skillet, sauté ½ cup chopped onion, ½ cup diced celery, and ½ cup diced green pepper in 2 tablespoons butter until lightly browned. Add 3 cups finely chopped leftover turkey meat and brown lightly. Add ¼ cup pan drippings from the turkey or ¼ cup gravy, 3 tablespoons ketchup, and 1 teaspoon hot pepper sauce. Simmer 1 minute more. Spoon onto 4 toasted hamburger buns.

Lemon-Honey Turkey with Corn Bread and Crab Stuffing—VI

Follow recipe for Traditional Roast Turkey (page 335). After first 2 hours of roasting, brush turkey every 20 minutes with glaze made from a mixture of ½ cup honey, ¼ cup lemon juice, 2 tablespoons walnut oil, salt, and pepper. One hour before turkey is done, place the following stuffing in the cavity: Combine 6 chopped scallions, 2 cloves minced garlic, 1½ pounds cleaned backfin crabmeat, the finely chopped zest and juice of 1 large lemon, and 3 cups crumbled corn muffins. Season with salt and cayenne pepper to taste.

Fifty Ways to Cook Most Everything

 ## Turkey Sautéed with Capers

Sauté 4 slices roasted turkey breast in 1 tablespoon clarified butter. Remove to a warm platter. Add 4 tablespoons butter to pan and cook until foamy. Add ½ cup capers and their liquid and cook until butter browns. Pour over the turkey.

 ## Buffalo Turkey

Dust with flour 4 cups roasted turkey meat cut into large chunks. Deep-fry at 375° F. for 1 minute and toss in 4 tablespoons hot melted butter mixed with ¼ cup hot pepper sauce.

 ## Lemon-Walnut Turkey Salad

In a bowl, combine ¼ cup lemon juice, ¼ cup walnut oil, ⅓ cup peanut oil, 2 tablespoons white wine vinegar, 2 finely chopped scallions, 1 clove minced garlic, ¼ cup chopped fresh parsley, a dash of cayenne, salt, and pepper. Toss dressing with 4 cups diced roasted turkey meat, 2 ribs diced celery, 1 cup chopped walnuts, and 2 tablespoons diced candied ginger. Adjust seasoning.

 ## Sliced Turkey with Lemon-Mustard Vinaigrette

Whisk together 1 large egg yolk and 1 tablespoon mustard until creamy. Add ¼ cup lemon juice. Whisk well. Slowly whisk in ¼ cup olive oil and ¼ cup peanut oil a bit at a time. Season with salt and pepper. Serve with cold sliced roasted turkey breast.

 ## Mustard-Glazed Smoked Turkey Breast—VII

Crush 1 tablespoon fresh thyme leaves and mix into ¼ cup brown mustard. Set aside for 10 min-utes. Brush onto a 4-pound smoked turkey breast. Roast turkey in a 350° F. oven for 1 hour, basting with the mustard every 15 minutes. Serve in thin slices.

 ## Smoked Turkey Salad

In a small saucepan, bring 2 diced roasted peppers (page 442), 2 cloves minced garlic, ¼ cup sugar, ¾ cup cider vinegar, ½ cup water, salt, and pepper to a boil, simmer for 3 minutes, and stir in ½ cup walnut oil. Keep warm while grilling or broiling 12 slices roasted smoked turkey breast. Toss pepper sauce with salad made from 1 head curly endive and ½ pound spinach leaves, both torn in small pieces, ⅔ cup finely diced red onion, and 12 sliced mushrooms. Arrange on plates, place grilled tur-key slices on top, and serve immediately.

 ## Grilled Smoked Turkey Breast with Mustard Glaze

Brush 4 thick slices roasted smoked turkey breast with 2 tablespoons mustard. Grill over high fire for 2 minutes per side.

 ## Melon Wrapped with Smoked Turkey

Cut a peeled, seeded honeydew into thin wedges, and wrap each with a thin 2-by-6-inch slice of smoked turkey breast.

 ## Turkey Benedict

Boil 2 quarts water with ¼ cup vinegar in a large skillet. Reduce to a simmer and poach 8 eggs just until whites are set, about 4 minutes. Remove eggs with slotted spoon and place each on half a toasted English muffin topped with 1 slice of smoked turkey breast. Top each egg with 1 tablespoon mayonnaise mixed with ¼ teaspoon Dijon mustard.

 ## Roasted Turkey Breast Studded with Hazelnuts and Garlic—VIII

In a blender or food processor, process 3 cloves garlic, ⅔ cup toasted hazelnuts, ¼ cup chopped fresh parsley, ½ teaspoon rubbed sage, salt, and pepper into a paste. With a thin, sharp knife, make deep slits into the meat of a 6- to 7-pound fresh turkey breast and stuff 2 teaspoons of the mixture into each slit. Brush the skin of the breast with equal parts olive oil and lemon juice and roast on a rack at 400° F. for 2 hours 15 minutes.

 ## Sliced Turkey Breast with Horseradish Sauce

Combine ½ cup mayonnaise, 3 tablespoons white prepared horseradish, and 1 tablespoon lemon juice. Serve with leftover turkey slices from preceding recipe at room temperature or chilled.

 ## Grilled Turkey Steaks with Steak Sauce

Brush 4 thick slices roasted turkey breast with 6 tablespoons steak sauce and grill over high heat for 1 to 2 minutes per side.

 ## Turkey Hazelnut Salad

In a bowl, combine ¼ cup white wine vinegar, 2 tablespoons fresh lemon juice, ⅓ cup walnut oil, ⅓ cup peanut oil, 1 finely chopped shallot, 1 clove minced garlic, ¼ cup chopped fresh parsley, a dash of cayenne, salt, and pepper. Toss with 4 cups diced roasted turkey meat, 2 ribs diced fennel, ½ cup toasted hazelnuts, and 1 cup halved orange sections. Adjust seasoning.

 ## Hazelnut Turkey Aïoli

Brush both sides of 4 thick slices Roasted Turkey Breast Studded with Hazelnuts and Garlic (above) with 2 tablespoons mayonnaise mixed with 1 clove minced garlic. Bread with ½ cup ground hazelnuts mixed with ¼ cup seasoned bread crumbs. Brown in 2 tablespoons *each* butter and peanut oil in a nonstick skillet.

 ## Apple Butter-Glazed Turkey with Apple-Sage Stuffing—IX

Follow recipe for Traditional Roast Turkey (page 335). After first 2 hours of roasting, brush turkey every 20 minutes with glaze made from ⅓ cup apple butter, 2 tablespoons cider vinegar, 1 tablespoon molasses, and 1 teaspoon salt. For the stuffing, double the apple and sage.

 ## Turkey Carcass Soup

In 4-quart soup pot, combine a large turkey carcass and bones with 1 cup white wine. Bring to a boil and cook until wine loses its sharp smell of alcohol. Add 2½ quarts water, bring to a boil, skimming away scum that rises to the surface, and simmer for 20 minutes. Add 1 quart chopped vegetables, 3 tablespoons chopped fresh parsley, 2 tablespoons chopped dill weed, 1 teaspoon dried thyme, 2 cloves, 2 teaspoons ground turmeric, salt, pepper, 1 envelope (¼ ounce) unflavored gelatin, and ½ cup pearl barley. Simmer 1 hour more. Remove from heat. Remove bones to a separate bowl and let cool. When cool, pick any edible bits of meat from the bones and return to the soup. Add additional leftover meat, if desired, and adjust seasoning.

Apple Turkey Meatloaf

In a bowl, combine with your hands 1 pound ground beef, ½ pound *each* ground veal and pork, 2 cups leftover Apple-Sage Stuffing (page 341), 2 beaten eggs, ¼ cup ketchup, 2 tablespoons Worcestershire, 2 teaspoons mustard, ¼ cup finely chopped onion, salt, and pepper. Form into a large loaf and layer ⅓ pound thinly sliced leftover turkey meat in 2 layers in the meatloaf. Bake in a preheated 375° F. oven for 1 hour.

 ### Baked Apples Stuffed with Turkey

Remove stems and cores from 4 large Rome apples. Hollow interior of each apple slightly with a melon baller and stuff each with a mixture of 1 cup chopped roasted turkey meat and crumbled stuffing. Brush with melted butter and a bit of honey and bake at 400° F. for 1¼ hours.

 ### Turkey Waldorf Salad

Combine 3 cups diced roasted turkey meat, 1 large diced apple, 2 ribs diced celery, ½ cup walnut pieces, 5 tablespoons mayonnaise, 1 tablespoon apple butter, 1 teaspoon cider vinegar, salt, and pepper.

Spicy Soy-Ginger Roast Turkey—X

Follow recipe for Traditional Roast Turkey (page 335). After first 2 hours of roasting, brush turkey every 20 minutes with glaze mixed from 2 tablespoons Oriental sesame oil, 3 tablespoons soy sauce, 2 teaspoons sugar, 2 tablespoons grated fresh gingerroot, 1 clove minced garlic, and 1 teaspoon chili paste. Omit stuffing.

 ### Stir-Fried Turkey with Ginger and Cashews

Dissolve 2 tablespoons cornstarch in mixture of 2 tablespoons low-sodium soy, ⅓ cup Chinese oyster sauce, and juice of 1 lemon. Stir-fry 4 cups roasted turkey meat cut in bite-size pieces and 2 tablespoons minced fresh gingerroot in 2 tablespoons peanut oil for 1 minute. Add 1 cup chicken stock, bring to a boil, add cornstarch mixture, and cook until thickened. Toss in 1 clove minced garlic, 2 sliced scallions, and 1 cup whole cashews.

 ### Oriental Turkey Salad

In a salad bowl, whisk together ¼ cup peanut oil, 1 tablespoon Oriental sesame oil, 2 tablespoons rice vinegar, ¼ teaspoon ground ginger, 1 clove minced garlic, 1 tablespoon soy sauce, and ½ teaspoon hot pepper sauce. Toss with 3 cups diced roasted turkey meat, ⅓ cup blanched pea pods, ½ diced red pepper, and 2 sliced scallions. Garnish with ¼ cup toasted sesame seeds.

 ### Sesame Turkey

Brush 4 thick slices roasted turkey breast with Oriental sesame oil and dredge in 1 cup sesame seeds seasoned with salt, black pepper, and cayenne pepper. Sauté in peanut oil until brown on both sides. Remove to a platter and deglaze pan with 1 clove minced garlic, 1 teaspoon Oriental sesame oil, and 2 tablespoons light soy sauce. Pour over turkey.

 ### Sliced Turkey with Soy Vinaigrette

In a bowl, combine ¼ cup rice vinegar, ¼ cup Oriental sesame oil, ⅓ cup vegetable oil, 2 tablespoons orange juice, 2 finely chopped scallions, 1 clove minced garlic, a pinch of ground ginger, ¼ cup chopped fresh cilantro, a dash of cayenne pepper, and soy sauce to taste. Serve over slices of room-temperature roasted turkey.

40

Fifty More-Than-Just-Meatloaves

A good meatloaf is hard to find. Blinded by fears of fat and a reverence for beef, too many people ignore the simple truth that the sensual charm of any ground meat mixture is in the filler, not the meat.

Once meat is ground, any textural quality it might have had is nearly gone. Baking it manages only to dry up what's left and turn it into the equivalent of edible gravel. Mix in an egg and you can get the gravel to hold together, but the result is more masonry than dinner.

To make a meatloaf succulent, you must refurbish its structure and replenish its moisture from the inside out. Do this either by adding liquid, along with a starch to absorb the moisture and hold it in the loaf, or by adding fat. Usually, both are done, forming what's commonly called filler.

Unfortunately, filler carries a seamy reputation, sullied by nuances of adulteration and deception. But makers of sausage, pâté, and meatloaf have known since ancient times that such adulteration is exactly what ground meat needs. With it, you add flavor, moisture, and consistency. Without it, all you've got is grit.

Liquid ingredients in a filler add flavor as well as moisture. Often they are condiments, such as ketchup, chutney, mustard, or relish. But they can also be sauces (anything from béchamel to Worcestershire), cooked vegetables, or cheeses.

Starchy ingredients that hold the moisture must be wet themselves. If they aren't, rather than contributing moisture to the meat, they will soak up other surrounding moisture in an effort to rehydrate themselves. Typically, bread soaked in milk, beer, wine, or broth is used, but cooked potatoes, rice, cereal, or pasta are other alternatives.

Added fat is the most controversial supplement these days. Though the amount of fat in many meatloaf recipes is excessive, deleting fat completely causes textural problems that are hard to overcome. If you do wish to cut back on the fat in a meatloaf, make sure you increase the amount of liquid and starch to make up the difference.

The following 50 recipes should give you enough meatloaf variations to take you into the next millennium. An hour of untended oven time is needed for most of these loaves, but the preparation is so quick and easy that most cooks can be done with the work in 10 or 15 minutes.

Fifty Ways to Cook Most Everything

If you're a fan of ground meat, be sure to see Chapter 23 for an assortment of burgers, meatballs, dumplings, and the like.

ABOUT THESE RECIPES

Most of these 50 recipes are built from either of two base recipes—one we call Mom's Meatloaf, the other a low-fat version made with ground turkey or lean beef without any additional fat. And both, unadorned, are fine recipes in their own right. These are followed by other variations using turkey, fish, veal, and crab. All make 4 to 6 servings, unless otherwise noted.

Mom's Meatloaf

With your hands, mix 2 pounds ground meat blended for meatloaf (50 percent beef, 25 percent veal, 25 percent pork) with 1 minced medium onion, 2 eggs, ½ cup ketchup, 1 tablespoon Worcestershire sauce, 2 teaspoons mustard, salt, and pepper. Soak 2 slices rye bread with crusts removed in ½ cup milk and crumble soaked bread into meat mixture. Form into a rough loaf and bake on a sheet pan, in a 6-cup casserole, or in a 9-by-5-inch loaf pan in a 375° F. preheated oven for 1 hour. Slice and serve.

Low-Fat Meatloaf

With your hands, mix 2 pounds lean ground beef or ground turkey with 1 minced medium-size onion, 2 egg whites, ⅔ cup ketchup, 1 tablespoon low-sodium soy sauce, 2 teaspoons mustard, salt, and pepper. Soak 1 cup fresh whole-grain bread crumbs and 1 cup quick oatmeal in 1 cup hot skim milk and mix into the meat mixture. Form into a rough loaf and bake on a sheet pan, in a 6-cup casserole, or in a 9-by-5-inch loaf pan and bake in a 375° F. preheated oven for 1 hour. Slice and serve.

Chilied Meatloaf with Chorizo

Follow recipe for Mom's or Low-Fat Meatloaf, adding 2 teaspoons ground cumin and ¾ pound chopped chorizo to the meat mixture.

Apple Sage Meatloaf

Follow recipe for Mom's or Low-Fat Meatloaf, adding 1 teaspoon ground sage, ½ teaspoon dried thyme, and 1 peeled, cored, and diced tart apple to meat mixture.

Meatloaf Cupcakes

Follow recipe for Mom's or Low-Fat Meatloaf, but instead of forming the meat into a loaf, form it into 12 large meatballs and bake them in a 12-cup muffin tin in a preheated 375° F. oven for 40 minutes. Remove from oven, mound 2 teaspoons grated Swiss cheese on each "cupcake," and broil until cheese melts, about 2 minutes.

Surprise Meatloaf

Follow recipe for Mom's or Low-Fat Meatloaf, forming the loaf around 2 peeled hard-cooked eggs, with their ends removed and placed end to end down the center of the loaf.

Wild Mushroom Meatloaf

Soak 1 ounce of any variety of dried wild mushrooms in 1 cup hot water for 15 minutes. Remove mushrooms and chop finely, discarding the tough ends. Follow recipe for Mom's or Low-Fat Meatloaf, adding chopped mushrooms to the meat mixture and substituting mushroom soaking liquid for the milk.

Oatmeal Meatloaf

Follow recipe for Mom's Meatloaf, substituting ½ cup quick oatmeal for the bread.

Roasted Pepper and Basil Meatloaf

Follow recipe for Mom's or Low-Fat Meatloaf, adding 2 diced roasted peppers and ½ cup chopped fresh basil to meat mixture.

Chicken Liver and Onion Meatloaf

Sauté 1 large, thinly sliced onion in 2 tablespoons vegetable oil until barely brown. Add ½ pound trimmed chicken livers and sauté just until livers are browned. Follow recipe for Mom's or Low-Fat Meatloaf, placing onion-liver mixture down the center of the loaf when you form it.

Sausage Meatloaf

Grill ½ pound link breakfast sausage until browned and firm. Follow recipe for Mom's Meatloaf, placing sausages in 2 rows down the center of the meat when you form the loaf.

Meatloaf Dijonnaise

Follow recipe for Mom's or Low-Fat Meatloaf, adding 2 tablespoons Dijon mustard to meat mixture.

Mexican Meatloaf

Follow recipe for Mom's or Low-Fat Meatloaf, adding 1 tablespoon chili powder, ⅔ cup hot salsa, and ⅔ cup cooked kidney beans to meat mixture.

Meat and Potatoes Meatloaf I

Follow recipe for Mom's or Low-Fat Meatloaf, crumbling ¾ pound skinned and cooked baked potato into basic meat mixture.

Meat and Potatoes Meatloaf II

Follow recipe for Mom's or Low-Fat Meatloaf, placing 2 whole baked potatoes, in their skins with their ends removed, end to end down the center of the meat mixture when you form the loaf.

Roasted Garlic and Green Peppercorn Meatloaf

Roast 1 head garlic in preheated 375° F. oven for 45 minutes until soft. Let cool, cut off pointed end of the head, and squeeze out the soft garlic. Follow recipe for Mom's or Low-Fat Meatloaf, adding the garlic with 2 tablespoons drained green peppercorns.

Macaroni Meatloaf

Follow recipe for Mom's or Low-Fat Meatloaf, adding 2 cups cooked macaroni and ½ cup chopped canned tomato to the basic mixture.

Prosciutto and Cheese Meatloaf

Cut 2 ounces mozzarella into 2 long sticks and roll each in 1 slice prosciutto. Follow recipe for Mom's or Low-Fat Meatloaf, placing prosciutto rolls end to end down the center of the loaf.

Ham Meatloaf

Follow recipe for Mom's or Low-Fat Meatloaf, adding ¾ pound chopped ham to meat mixture.

Ham and Cheddar Meatloaf

Follow recipe for Mom's or Low-Fat Meatloaf, mixing ½ pound chopped ham and ¼ pound shredded Cheddar in with meat mixture.

 ### Sweet and Sour Meatloaf

Mix 1 teaspoon hoisin sauce, 1 tablespoon cider vinegar, and 1 tablespoon honey. Follow recipe for Mom's or Low-Fat Meatloaf, basting surface of the loaf with this mixture before baking.

 ### Meatloaf Baked in a Bread

Cut off one end and hollow out center of 1 large loaf (1½ pounds) French bread. Follow recipe for Mom's or Low-Fat Meatloaf, stuffing the meat mixture into the hollowed-out bread. Wrap it in foil and bake in preheated 375° F. oven for 1½ hours.

 ### Lots-of-Olives Meatloaf

Follow recipe for Mom's or Low-Fat Meatloaf, mixing about 30 chopped, pitted black olives, and 30 pitted Spanish olives in with the meat mixture.

 ### Meatloaf with Spinach and Ricotta

Follow recipe for Mom's or Low-Fat Meatloaf, adding 5 tablespoons drained ricotta cheese, 1 clove minced garlic, and 1 cup cooked, drained chopped spinach to meat mixture.

 ### Meatloaf with Easy Tomato Sauce

Follow recipe for Mom's or Low-Fat Meatloaf and serve with following sauce. Sauté 1 cup chopped onion and 2 cloves minced garlic in 1 tablespoon olive oil until onion is soft, about 2 minutes. Add ½ cup wine and reduce to a third its volume. Add 3 cups chopped canned tomatoes, cook until tomatoes begin to release their liquid, and add ¼ cup tomato paste. Season to taste with a pinch of crushed red pepper flakes, salt, and pepper and simmer for 15 minutes. Stir in 1 tablespoon chopped fresh parsley and heat 1 minute more.

 ### Turkey Meatloaf

Soak 2 slices crustless bread (any type) in ½ cup milk. Crumble it into 1½ pounds ground turkey, ¼ pound ground veal, ¼ pound sausage, 1 minced small onion, 2 beaten eggs, ¼ cup ketchup, 2 tablespoons apple butter, 2 tablespoons soy sauce, and 2 teaspoons mustard. Mix well with your hands. Form mixture into a rough loaf and bake on a sheet pan, in a 6-cup casserole, or in a 9-by-5-inch loaf pan in a 375° F. preheated oven for 1 hour. Slice and serve.

 ### Turkey Meatloaf with Cranberries

Follow preceding recipe or recipe for Low-Fat Meatloaf made with ground turkey, replacing ketchup and apple butter with 1 cup whole-berry cranberry sauce.

 ### Turkey Meatloaf with Mint and Ricotta

Follow recipe for Turkey Meatloaf (above) or for Low-Fat Meatloaf made with ground turkey, replacing the ketchup with ¼ cup tomato sauce and the apple butter with 5 tablespoons drained ricotta cheese and 2 tablespoons dried mint leaves.

 ### Spicy Turkey Meatloaf with Chick-Peas

Follow recipe for Turkey Meatloaf (above) or for Low-Fat Meatloaf made with ground turkey, adding 1 teaspoon hot red pepper sauce, 1 teaspoon chili powder, and ½ cup cooked, drained chickpeas.

Apple and Bacon Turkey Loaf

Follow recipe for Turkey Meatloaf (opposite) or for Low-Fat Meatloaf made with ground turkey, adding 1 peeled, seeded, and diced tart apple to the meat mixture and laying 4 strips bacon over top of the meatloaf before baking.

Curried Chutneyed Turkey Loaf

Follow recipe for Turkey Meatloaf (opposite), substituting 2 tablespoons mango chutney for the apple butter and adding 2 teaspoons curry powder.

Fragrant Turkey Loaf with Pineapple

Follow recipe for Turkey Meatloaf (opposite), adding 1 teaspoon ground coriander, ¼ teaspoon ground turmeric and 2 ounces chopped dried pineapple. Substitute mango chutney for the apple butter.

Turkey Corn Bread Meatloaf

Follow recipe for Turkey Meatloaf (opposite) or for Low-Fat Meatloaf made with ground turkey, substituting 4 ounces corn bread for the bread in the meat mixture.

Turkey Loaf with Ham, Lemon, and Pistachios

Follow recipe for Turkey Meatloaf (opposite) or for Low-Fat Meatloaf made with ground turkey, mixing 1 cup diced turkey ham, 2 tablespoons minced fresh parsley, ¼ cup chopped pistachios, and 1 teaspoon finely grated lemon zest into the meat mixture.

Turkey and Walnut Meatloaf

Follow recipe for Turkey Meatloaf (opposite) or for Low-Fat Meatloaf (page 344) made with ground turkey, adding 1 cup toasted walnut pieces to the meat mixture.

Turkey Meatloaf with Aged Ricotta and Spinach

Follow recipe for Turkey Meatloaf (opposite), but substitute sour cream for the apple butter and add 4 ounces crumbled aged ricotta (available in cheese shops) and 1 cup cooked chopped spinach to the meat mixture.

Fresh and Smoked Turkey Meatloaf

Follow recipe for Turkey Meatloaf (opposite) or for Low-Fat Meatloaf made with ground turkey, adding 1 cup diced smoked turkey breast to the meat mixture.

Turkey Meatloaf with Bread Stuffing

Follow recipe for Turkey Meatloaf (opposite) or for Low-Fat Meatloaf made with ground turkey, replacing bread and milk with 1 cup cooked bread stuffing.

Tuna Loaf

In a bowl, combine ¾ cup mayonnaise, 1 beaten extra-large egg, 2 tablespoons chopped fresh parsley, 2 ribs diced celery, 1 tablespoon low-sodium soy sauce, ½ teaspoon hot pepper sauce, 1½ tablespoons lemon juice, 2 teaspoons Dijon mustard, three 6-ounce cans drained tuna, and 1⅔ cups fresh bread crumbs. Pour into a greased 1-quart loaf pan and bake at 350° F. for 45 minutes.

Tuna Loaf with Capers and Olives

Follow preceding recipe, substituting 3 tablespoons drained capers and ⅓ cup chopped black olives for the celery.

Tuna Noodle Loaf

Follow the recipe for Tuna Loaf, adding 1 cup cooked macaroni to the basic mixture.

Pesto Tuna Loaf

In a food processor, finely chop 2 cups fresh basil leaves. Blend in 1 clove minced garlic, 3 tablespoons virgin olive oil, and 2 tablespoons grated Parmesan. Follow recipe for Tuna Loaf (page 347), using basil mixture in place of ¼ cup of the mayonnaise.

Salmon Dill Loaf

Follow recipe for Tuna Loaf (page 347), replacing tuna with canned salmon and the parsley with chopped fresh dill weed.

Tartared Fish Loaf

Follow recipe for Tuna Loaf (page 347), adding 2 tablespoons pickle relish and 1 teaspoon white horseradish to the mayonnaise. If desired, you can substitute 1 pound of any cooked fish for the tuna.

Salmon Loaf Studded with Shrimp and Herbs

In a bowl, combine ¾ cup mayonnaise, 1 beaten extra-large egg, 1 tablespoon chopped fresh parsley, 2 teaspoons chopped fresh tarragon, 2 teaspoons minced fresh dill, 2 ribs diced celery, 1 tablespoon low-sodium soy sauce, ½ teaspoon hot pepper sauce, 1½ tablespoons lemon juice, 2 teaspoons Dijon mustard, three 6-ounce cans drained salmon, ¼ pound cooked and shelled chopped shrimp, and 1⅔ cups fresh bread crumbs. Pour into a greased 1-quart loaf pan and bake at 350° F. for 45 minutes.

Lasagna Meatloaf

Combine 1 pound ground beef, ¼ pound ground pork, 1 cup chopped onions, 1 clove minced garlic, ½ teaspoon dried thyme, ¼ teaspoon dried oregano, 1 teaspoon dried basil, 2 beaten eggs, and ¼ cup tomato sauce. Soak 2 slices crustless white bread in ½ cup white wine, crumble bread into meat mixture, and blend. Cook ½ pound lasagna noodles *al dente*. Cool under cold water. Mix 8 ounces drained ricotta cheese, 1 beaten egg, and ¼ cup grated Parmesan. Shred 8 ounces mozzarella cheese. Grease 2-quart loaf or baking pan with olive oil and line pan with noodles. Top with layers of meat, ricotta, mozzarella, and noodles, repeating 3 times, finishing with noodles. Top with 2 ounces additional shredded mozzarella. Cover with foil and bake at 350° F. for 1¼ hours. Cool in pan for 10 minutes. Invert on a platter, slice, and serve with any tomato pasta sauce. Serves 6 to 8.

Veal Loaf with Artichokes

In a bowl, combine 1½ pounds ground veal, ½ pound ground pork, ½ cup finely chopped onion,

1 clove minced garlic, ½ teaspoon crumbled dried rosemary, ¼ teaspoon dried thyme, and 2 beaten eggs. Soak 2 slices white bread in liquid from 6-ounce jar of marinated artichoke hearts. Crumble bread into meat mixture. Mix well with your hands, then carefully fold in the artichoke hearts. Form mixture into rough loaf and bake on a sheet pan, in a 6-cup casserole, or in 9-by-5-inch loaf pan, in a 375° F. preheated oven for 1 hour. Slice and serve.

Herbed Veal Loaf

In a bowl, combine 1½ pounds ground veal, ½ pound veal sausage, ½ cup finely chopped onion, ½ teaspoon dried tarragon, ½ teaspoon crumbled dried rosemary, ¼ teaspoon dried thyme, and 2 beaten eggs. Soak 2 slices white bread in ½ cup white wine and 1 tablespoon olive oil and crumble into meat mixture. Mix well with your hands. Form mixture into a rough loaf and bake on a sheet pan, in a 6-cup casserole, or in a 9-by-5-inch loaf pan in a 375° F. preheated oven for 1 hour. Slice and serve.

Layered Veal, Turkey, and Ham Loaf

In a blender or processor, process until smooth 12 eggs, 1½ cups ricotta cheese, and 1 cup grated Parmesan. Cover bottom of greased 2-quart loaf pan with wax paper and dust lightly with more Parmesan. Use 1 pound leg of veal cut into 10 scallops, 8 slices smoked turkey breast, and ½ pound thinly sliced prosciutto. Dip meat in the egg mixture and cover bottom of pan with 1 veal scallop. Top with turkey breast, then prosciutto. Place meats in alternating layers, ending with veal. Pour any additional egg mixture over top. Cover with foil, and place loaf pan in a larger pan of water. Bake in preheated 350° F. oven for 2 hours. Cool for 10 minutes, unmold, and slice. Makes 8 to 10 servings.

Crabcake Loaf

Mix ½ cup mayonnaise, 1 beaten egg, 1 tablespoon chopped fresh parsley, 1 tablespoon fresh dill, 1 tablespoon lemon juice, 2 teaspoons Worcestershire sauce, 1 teaspoon hot pepper sauce, 1 teaspoon dry mustard, 1 diced bell pepper, 1 pound cleaned backfin crabmeat, 1⅓ cups fresh bread crumbs, and 2 teaspoons paprika. Form into a loaf and bake on a sheet pan or bake in a 1-quart loaf pan in a preheated 350° F. oven for 45 minutes.

Fifty Tunas In and Out of the Can

Sometimes a can can't. A canned peach is no more like a fresh peach than chipped beef is like steak.

But sometimes a can can, providing us with food so convenient that it wipes out all cultural memory of the fresh food, making the canned product more natural to us than the food itself. Such is the case with tuna.

Until the culinary revolution of the 1970s, most of us had never eaten fresh tuna. We ordered chunk white tuna instead of tuna steaks and probably thought the fish swam packed in oil.

But all that has changed. Tuna is bonito and albacore; it's grilled over mesquite, sushied with ginger, and broiled with mustard. We slap it with pesto, cloak it in marinara, and crown it with chutney.

Yet it is unlikely that fresh tuna will ever usurp the position that canned tuna has achieved in our culture, and it's not our intention to press that point. Rather, it seems time to reintroduce the two tunas to one another in order to free ourselves from our national tuna rut. We've enjoyed surprising results trying fresh tuna in places where canned is traditionally used, as well as dressing up canned tuna with a pesto or guacamole sauce, treatments typically reserved for more upscale presentations made with fresh fish.

You can pursue the same course by reinventing your tuna noodle casserole with fresh tuna, or by making tomorrow's tuna sandwich from the tuna steak left over from tonight's dinner. Try canned tuna salad tossed with a garlic vinaigrette and roasted peppers instead of with celery and mayonnaise, or try a tuna platter where a grilled tuna fillet takes center stage.

Fresh tuna is readily available and quite easy to prepare. Buy it in steaks no more than an inch thick. The color of the meat will vary from light pink to beef red. The darker meat tastes slightly stronger, but both are equally good.

Before cooking the tuna, wash it well and press it lightly to make sure that the thickness is uniform throughout the steak. If need be, trim the thicker portions to ensure even thickness. Cut away the dark brown section located to one side or in the center of the steak. This section will have a grainier texture than the rest of the flesh and will have an overcooked liverlike flavor after cooking.

ABOUT THESE RECIPES

The first two recipes below—Poached Tuna and Grilled Tuna—can stand on their own as meals, especially with the serving suggestions accompanying each. But those two preparations are the basis for many of the recipes that follow, as is canned tuna.

The 50 recipes concentrate on the three tuna standards that are probably already in your repertoire—tuna salad, tuna casserole, and tuna croquettes. All we've done is given them a twist with new flavors and the opportunity to use fresh tuna where the can used to be. All recipes are written for 4 portions unless otherwise noted.

One footnote: As this is being written, some food companies have changed the size of the standard tuna can from 6½ ounces to 6⅛, and we were finding both sizes on store shelves. For lack of a better solution, we make reference below and elsewhere in this book to 6-ounce cans; that's really shorthand for 6-and-some-fraction. Which size you use will not affect any of the recipes in this book.

 ### Poached Tuna

Bring 2 cups white wine, 2 cups water, 2 tablespoons minced carrot, 2 tablespoons minced celery, ¼ cup minced onion, 3 strips lemon zest, the juice of ½ lemon, 6 peppercorns, ½ teaspoon salt, 1 whole clove, and 1 bay leaf to a boil. Turn down to a simmer. Add 1 pound tuna, cut in ½-inch-thick steaks, and poach for 4 minutes. Remove tuna, pat dry, and serve with a salsa (pages 164–165), a vinaigrette, or herbed sauce (Chapter 2), or use in any of the following recipes calling for Poached Tuna. Makes 1 pound or 2 cups flaked.

 ### Grilled Tuna

Rub four ½-inch-thick tuna steaks, each about 4 ounces, with a little vegetable oil. Grill or broil for 2 minutes per side. Serve with salsa (pages 164–165) or any sauce in Chapter 2 recommended for fish, or use in any of the following recipes calling for Grilled Tuna. Makes 1 pound or 2 cups flaked.

 ### Fresh Tuna Salad

Prepare Grilled or Poached Tuna and cool. Crumble and mix with 3 tablespoons mayonnaise, ¼ teaspoon crushed celery seed, salt, pepper, and 2 teaspoons lemon juice. Use as a sandwich spread or salad.

 ### Traditional Tuna Salad

Drain 2 (6-ounce) cans tuna and crumble. Toss with 1 rib peeled and diced celery, ¼ cup mayonnaise, 1 teaspoon lemon juice, salt, and pepper. Use as sandwich spread or salad.

 ### Fresh Tuna Pesto Salad

In a food processor, finely chop ¼ cup walnuts with 1 small clove garlic. Add 1½ cups fresh basil leaves and process until coarsely chopped. With the processor on, add ⅓ cup olive oil in a slow stream. Add salt, pepper, and ⅓ cup grated Parmesan. Toss pesto sauce with 2 cups chunked Poached Tuna, 2 ribs peeled and sliced celery, 1 seeded chopped tomato, 1 peeled, seeded, and chopped cucumber, and the juice of ½ lemon. Use as sandwich spread or serve on lettuce leaves for salad.

 ### Tuna Pesto Pasta Salad

Prepare pesto sauce from previous recipe and toss with 1 drained (6-ounce) can tuna, 1 cup cooked macaroni, 1 seeded and chopped tomato, and the chopped whites of 2 scallions.

Fifty Ways to Cook Most Everything

Marinated Tuna and Black Bean Salad

Toss 1½ cups flaked fresh cooked or canned tuna, 1½ cups drained cooked or canned black beans, ½ cup thinly sliced scallion, 2 teaspoons finely grated orange zest, 1 small finely chopped red onion, and 1 clove minced garlic. Make dressing by whisking together 2 tablespoons olive oil, 2 tablespoons orange juice, 2 tablespoons wine vinegar, ½ teaspoon crushed red pepper flakes, salt, and pepper. Pour over salad and toss well with 1 diced red bell pepper. Chill and serve on leaves of Romaine lettuce.

Tuna Chili Salad

Toss 1¼ cups drained, cooked or canned kidney beans, 2 tablespoons thinly sliced scallion, 2 tablespoons finely chopped fresh cilantro, 1 minced chili pepper, and 1 recipe crumbled Grilled Tuna or Poached Tuna, or 2 drained (6-ounce) cans tuna, with the following dressing. Whisk 3 tablespoons mayonnaise, 2 tablespoons chili powder, 1 tablespoon ground cumin, ⅓ cup corn or peanut oil, 2 tablespoons hot pepper sauce, salt, and pepper. Just before serving, toss in 1 diced avocado. Serve on a bed of Romaine lettuce garnished with 1 sliced tomato.

Tuna Taco

Fill 8 warm taco shells with previous salad. Top each with 1 tablespoon *each* finely shredded lettuce, finely chopped tomato, and grated mild cheese.

Tuna with Tarragon Mustard Vinaigrette

Drain 2 (6-ounce) cans tuna, crumble and toss with 1 teaspoon dried tarragon and the following dressing. Combine ½ clove minced garlic, 1 tablespoon Dijon mustard, and 1 tablespoon wine vinegar. In a slow, steady stream, whisk in 2 tablespoons *each* peanut and olive oils. Season with salt and pepper. Use as a sandwich spread or serve as a salad on a bed of watercress or Romaine lettuce leaves.

Tuna and Spinach Salad

Toss preceding tuna salad and dressing with 10 ounces cleaned and stemmed fresh spinach, 2 tablespoons chopped red onion, and 8 cleaned, sliced mushrooms

Tuna Herb Cheese Melt

Split 4 kaiser rolls and spread the interior of each bottom section with 1 tablespoon herbed cream cheese. Prepare Tuna with Tarragon Mustard Vinaigrette (above) and top each cheese-spread roll with a quarter of the tuna salad. Top each with 2 slices dill havarti and top-brown or broil until cheese melts. Top with remaining half of the roll.

Tuna Vinaigrette

Whisk together 1 clove minced garlic, 2 tablespoons red wine vinegar, 3 tablespoons olive oil, salt, pepper, and 1 tablespoon minced fresh parsley. Toss 2 drained (6-ounce) cans tuna with 2 ribs peeled and diced celery, 1 peeled and chopped tomato, and the dressing. Use as a sandwich spread or serve as a salad on a bed of Romaine lettuce leaves.

Tuna Gorgozola Grinder

Split 2 submarine rolls horizontally. Fill with preceding tuna salad and dressing, sprinkle with 3 tablespoons crumbled Gorgonzola cheese, and add the top of the roll. Wrap each in foil and bake in a preheated 400° F. oven for 15 minutes. Halve each sandwich.

Tuna Salad with Capers and Pine Nuts

Follow recipe for Tuna Vinaigrette (above), using 1 tablespoon drained capers and 2 tablespoons toasted pine nuts in place of the tomato.

Tuna and Roasted Pepper Salad

Toss together 1 large sliced roasted red bell pepper (page 442), crumbled Grilled Tuna, 2 tablespoons chopped fresh parsley, 1 clove minced garlic, 2 tablespoons red wine vinegar, 3 tablespoons olive oil, salt, pepper, and 1 tablespoon minced fresh parsley.

Tuna Creole Salad

Crumble Grilled Tuna and toss with 1 shredded carrot, 2 tablespoons finely chopped onion, 1 diced seeded apple and the following dressing. Whisk together 1½ tablespoons ketchup, 2 teaspoons spicy mustard, 1 teaspoon sugar, 1 teaspoon prepared horseradish, ¼ clove minced garlic, and 1 tablespoon apple cider vinegar. Whisk in ¼ cup peanut oil in a slow, steady stream until all has been incorporated and dressing is thick. Season to taste with hot red pepper sauce, black pepper, and salt. Use as a sandwich spread or serve as a salad accompanied by Creole Cole Slaw (page 288).

Tuna Lime Salad

Drain 2 (6-ounce) cans tuna and toss with a mixture of the thinly sliced whites of 3 scallions, 2½ tablespoons olive oil, 1 tablespoon wine vinegar, 1

teaspoon finely grated lime zest, 1 tablespoon fresh lime juice, a pinch of cayenne pepper, a pinch of grated nutmeg, salt, and pepper. Use as a sandwich spread or serve as a salad on a bed of Romaine leaves.

Tuna Guacamole Salad

Drain 2 (6-ounce) cans tuna, crumble, and toss with 1 seeded and diced tomato, 1 diced avocado, and a dressing made by pureeing 1 avocado with 1 clove garlic, 1 tablespoon white wine vinegar, a dash of cayenne, salt, and pepper. Use as a sandwich spread or a dip for raw vegetables.

Tuna Salsa Salad

In a blender or food processor, chop 1 clove garlic, 2 seeded and stemmed pickled jalapeño peppers, 2 stemmed and seeded plum tomatoes, 2 tablespoons olive oil, and 2 teaspoons cider vinegar until finely chopped. Toss with crumbled Grilled Tuna or Poached Tuna or 2 drained (6-ounce) cans water-packed white tuna. Use as a sandwich spread, a filling for 4 taco shells, or a dip for tortilla chips.

Tuna Nachos

Top 2 dozen tortilla chips with the previous salad. Arrange on a platter. Scatter 1 minced jalapeño pepper and 1 cup Cheddar cheese over top. Bake or microwave until the cheese melts. Sprinkle with ½ diced avocado and ½ diced tomato. Serve with ½ cup sour cream, if desired.

Bacon, Leek, and Tuna Sandwich

Cook 8 slices bacon until crisp, drain on paper towels, pour off half the fat, and sauté 2 sliced leeks and 1 sliced onion in the hot fat until lightly browned. Prepare Tuna Salsa Salad (above). Scoop onto 4 slices white toast, each spread with 1 teaspoon mayonnaise, and top with the leeks, onions, and bacon. Top each with another slice white toast, spread with another 1 teaspoon mayonnaise.

 ## Tuna Niçoise Salad

Whisk together the minced white of 2 scallions, 1 clove minced garlic, 2 tablespoons white wine vinegar, 3 tablespoons peanut oil, 2 tablespoons extra-virgin olive oil, salt, and pepper. Toss with crumbled Grilled Tuna or Poached Tuna, or 2 drained (6-ounce) cans water-packed white tuna, ¼ cup finely chopped oil-cured black olives, and 2 chopped anchovy fillets.

 ## Mediterranean Tuna Salad

Whisk 1 clove minced garlic, 1 tablespoon wine vinegar, 2 tablespoons orange juice, ¼ cup olive oil, salt, and pepper. Toss with crumbled Grilled Tuna or Poached Tuna or 2 drained (6-ounce) cans water-packed white tuna, 2 ribs diced fennel, 2 seeded and diced tomatoes, and 1 teaspoon finely grated orange zest. Serve with French bread.

 ## Tuna Caviar Salad

Whisk together 2 tablespoons mayonnaise, 2 tablespoons sour cream, 1 tablespoon ketchup, and 1 tablespoon lemon juice. Drain 2 (6-ounce) cans water-packed white tuna, crumble, and toss with the dressing. Fold in 2 tablespoons red or black caviar. Use as sandwich spread or serve with unsalted crackers.

 ## Tuna Teriyaki Salad

Cook 1 tablespoon grated fresh gingerroot and 1 clove minced garlic in 1 tablespoon peanut oil un-til soft. Remove from heat and add 1 tablespoon low-sodium soy sauce, a pinch of cayenne pepper, a pinch of sugar, 3 tablespoons Oriental sesame oil, and 2 tablespoons rice vinegar. Adjust seasoning and toss with crumbled Grilled Tuna, 1 julienned carrot, and 2 julienned scallions. Serve on a bed of bean sprouts, garnished with 8 snow-pea pods and 1 thin lemon wedge per portion.

 ## Tuna Pineapple Salad

Follow preceding recipe, substituting ½ cup crushed pineapple for the carrot.

 ## Grilled Tuna Sandwich

Mix ⅓ cup mayonnaise, ¼ teaspoon ground celery seed, and 1 tablespoon lemon juice. Set aside. Rub 1 tablespoon oil on surface of four 4-ounce tuna steaks. Season with salt and pepper. Grill until firm, 2 to 3 minutes per side. While tuna is cooking, split 4 kaiser rolls and spread inner surfaces with some of the mayonnaise. Place 1 lettuce leaf on one side of each roll. Place a grilled steak, tomato slice, and more mayonnaise on each.

 ## Grilled Tuna Special

Whisk 2 tablespoons mayonnaise, 2 tablespoons sour cream, 1 tablespoon ketchup, and 1 tablespoon lemon juice. Follow preceding recipe, substituting this dressing for the mayonnaise. Omit the lettuce and tomato, and top each tuna steak with 2 tablespoons cole slaw (either deli-style or the Red or White Cabbage Slaw on page 293).

 ## Tuna Melt with Apple and Cheddar

Spread 8 slices rye bread with a thin film of mustard. Place 2 peeled and seeded apple slices on each piece of bread. Prepare Fresh or Traditional

Tuna Salad (above) and top each slice of bread with a portion of the tuna. Place 2 thin slices sharp Cheddar over each mound of tuna. Top-brown or broil until cheese melts.

Real Tuna Sub Sandwich

Over the interior of each of 4 split submarine rolls, brush 1 tablespoon vinaigrette dressing of your choice (Chapter 34). Top with ¼ cup thinly sliced lettuce, 4 slices roasted red bell pepper cut in strips (page 442), 2 grilled 2- to 3-ounce tuna steaks, halved lengthwise, 2 tablespoons julienned cucumber, and 1 thin slice red onion, if desired. Top with 1 tablespoon additional dressing.

Tuna Po' Boy

Split 1 round loaf Italian bread horizontally. Remove some bread from interior of each side and dampen with 2 to 3 tablespoons of liquid from an 8-ounce jar of salad olives. Sprinkle a pinch of minced fresh garlic on each side. Place 2 ounces sliced provolone on each half. Prepare Tuna Vinaigrette (above), mound on bottom half of bread, spoon over the salad olives, and top with other side of bread. Cut in 4 wedges and serve or wrap in foil and warm for 20 minutes at 350° F. before slicing.

Tuna Tabouleh

Follow recipe for Tabouleh (page 291) adding crumbled Grilled Tuna, Poached Tuna, or 2 drained (6-ounce) cans water-packed white tuna with the vegetables.

Cold Grilled Tuna Platter

Mix 1 cup fresh chopped herbs (parsley, tarragon, basil, dill, etc.), 1 small clove garlic, and ½ cup mayonnaise. Add 2 teaspoons mustard and 1 tablespoon lemon juice. Slowly add ¼ cup peanut oil, whisking constantly, until sauce is smooth and thick. Split 4 hard-cooked eggs lengthwise. Mix yolks with 3 tablespoons of the sauce and season with a dash of hot pepper sauce. Mound back into the hard-cooked white halves. Prepare 4 steaks of Grilled Tuna and cool. Arrange each on a plate with 1 Romaine leaf, 2 slices ripe tomato, 3 slices cucumber, 3 thin avocado wedges, and 1 lemon wedge. Dollop fish with remaining sauce.

Traditional Tuna Platter

Prepare Traditional Tuna Salad (page 351) or any tuna salad in this chapter. Place 1 scoop in the center of a lettuce-lined plate. Surround with 1 sliced hard-cooked egg, 4 wedges ripe tomato, 8 cucumber slices, 2 black olives, and 1 lemon wedge. Serve with a salad dressing of your choice. (Or try any of these from Chapter 34: Creamy Avocado Dressing, Garlic Herb Dressing, Caesar Dressing, Blue Cheese Dressing, Garlic Ranch Dressing, or Real Russian Dressing.)

Real Tuna Noodle Casserole

Cook 2 tablespoons *each* finely chopped carrots and celery, and ¼ cup finely chopped onion in 4 tablespoons butter until softened. Add ¼ cup flour and cook for 2 minutes. Add 3 cups milk, stirring constantly, then add 1 whole clove, 1 small bay leaf, 6 whole peppercorns, ½ teaspoon dill weed, salt, and a dash of cayenne pepper. Simmer for 10 minutes. Strain and stir in 1 cup coarsely grated sharp Cheddar cheese, 2 teaspoons brown mustard, and chopped Poached Tuna (page 351). Boil ½ pound macaroni (any shape) to *al dente*, drain, and toss in the sauce. Pack into a 2-quart casserole, smooth surface, and sprinkle with ¼ cup grated Parmesan mixed with 2 tablespoons bread crumbs. Dot with 1 tablespoon butter and bake in preheated 400° F. oven for 20 to 25 minutes, until brown and bubbly. Serves 4 to 6.

Tuna, Orzo, and Feta

Follow preceding recipe, but double amount of dill weed, replace Cheddar with crumbled feta cheese, and replace mustard with chopped black olives. Use orzo as your macaroni.

Traditional Tuna Noodle Casserole (from scratch)

Cook 2 tablespoons *each* finely chopped carrots and celery and ¼ cup finely chopped onion in 4 tablespoons butter until softened. Add ¼ cup flour and cook for 2 minutes. Add 3 cups milk, stirring constantly, then add 1 whole clove, 1 small bay leaf, 6 whole peppercorns, ½ teaspoon dill weed, salt, and a dash of cayenne pepper. Simmer for 10 minutes. Strain and stir in 1 cup coarsely grated sharp Cheddar cheese, 1 cup sautéed mushrooms, 2 teaspoons brown mustard, and 2 drained (6-ounce) cans tuna. Boil ¼ pound macaroni (any shape) to *al dente*, drain, and toss in the sauce. Pack into a 2-quart casserole, smooth surface, and sprinkle with ¼ cup grated Parmesan mixed with 2 tablespoons bread crumbs. Dot with 1 tablespoon butter and bake in preheated 400° F. oven for 20 to 25 minutes, until brown and bubbly. Serves 4 to 6.

Tuna Tortellini Casserole

Follow the recipe for Real or Traditional Tuna Noodle Casserole (above), substituting provolone for the Cheddar and 1 pound cheese tortellini for the macaroni. Substitute finely chopped anchovy for the mustard.

Tuna, Fontina, and Ham Casserole

Follow recipe for Real or Traditional Tuna Noodle Casserole (above), adding ½ cup diced ham with the tuna and substituting Fontina cheese for the Cheddar.

Tuna- and Cheese-Stuffed Shells

Cook 2 tablespoons *each* finely chopped carrots and celery and ¼ cup finely chopped onion in 2 tablespoons butter until soft. Add 1 tablespoon flour and cook for 2 minutes. Add 1 cup milk, stirring constantly, then add ½ teaspoon dill weed, salt, and a dash of cayenne pepper. Simmer for 10 minutes. Stir in 1 cup coarsely grated mozzarella and 3 tablespoons grated Parmesan along with 1 cup chopped Poached Tuna. Boil 12 jumbo-shell macaroni until *al dente*, drain, cool, and fill with the tuna mixture. Arrange in a single layer in a baking dish. Pour 2 cups tomato pasta sauce and 1 cup shredded mozzarella over top. Bake at 350° F. for 45 minutes.

Roasted Pepper and Brown Rice Tuna Casserole

Cook ¼ cup finely chopped onion and 2 tablespoons finely chopped celery in ¼ cup olive oil until softened. Add 2 diced red or yellow roasted bell peppers (page 442) and 1 clove minced garlic and toss to coat. Add 2 tablespoons flour and cook for 2 minutes. Add ½ cup milk and 1 cup clam juice. Simmer for 5 minutes. Add 2 cups grated Cheddar cheese. Season with salt, pepper, and a dash of cayenne pepper. Mix in 1 cup crumbled Grilled Tuna or Poached Tuna or 1 drained (6-ounce) can tuna. Add 3 cups cooked brown rice and mix well. Adjust seasoning and pack into a 2-quart casserole. Smooth surface and sprinkle with ¼ cup grated Parmesan. Dot with 1 tablespoon butter and bake in preheated 400° F. oven for 20 to 25 minutes, until brown and bubbly.

Tuna Shrimp Casserole with Herbed Cheese

Cook ¼ cup finely chopped onion in 2 table-spoons olive oil and 2 tablespoons butter until soft. Add 8 ounces small cleaned shrimp and toss to coat with butter. Add 2 tablespoons flour and cook for 30 seconds. Add ½ cup milk and simmer for 1 minute, until thick. Add ½ pound herbed cheese until melted. Season with salt, pepper, and a dash of cayenne pepper. Mix in 1 cup crumbled Grilled Tuna or Poached Tuna or 1 drained (6-ounce) can white tuna packed in water. Boil ½ pound maca-roni (any shape) to *al dente*, drain, and toss in the sauce. Pack into a 2-quart casserole, smooth sur-face, and sprinkle with ¼ cup grated Parmesan mixed with 2 tablespoons bread crumbs. Dot with 1 tablespoon butter and bake in preheated 400° F. oven for 20 to 25 minutes, until brown and bubbly.

 Tuna Cassoulet

Boil 1 pound soaked navy beans in 2 quarts water until tender, about 1 hour, with ½ pound sliced hot smoked sausage, 1 tablespoon ground corian-der, 2 teaspoons ground cumin, 1 teaspoon ground ginger, 1 teaspoon dried mustard, and 1 tablespoon *each* chopped fresh dill and parsley. Drain. Cook ½ cup chopped onion in ¼ cup olive oil until soft. Add 3 cloves chopped garlic and ½ cup white wine. Cook until wine evaporates. Stir into the beans. Prepare Grilled Tuna, place in a 2-quart casserole in 2 layers, alternating with 3 lay-ers of the beans. Cover and bake in a preheated 325° F. oven for 1 hour.

 Curried Tuna Braised with Lentils

Boil 1 pound lentils in 2 quarts water until tender, about 45 minutes, with 1 stick cinnamon, 1 dried chili pepper, 1 bay leaf, and 1 tablespoon chopped fresh cilantro. Drain. Cook ½ cup chopped onion in ¼ cup peanut oil until soft with 1 tablespoon curry powder, 1 teaspoon ground coriander, 2 tea-spoons ground cumin, 1 teaspoon ground ginger, and 1 teaspoon dried mustard. Add 3 cloves chopped garlic and ½ cup chopped, skinned, and seeded tomato. Cook 2 minutes. Remove from heat and stir in 1 cup plain yogurt. Stir into the lentils. Prepare Grilled Tuna and place in a 2-quart casserole in 2 layers, alternating with 3 layers of the beans. Cover and bake in preheated 325° F. oven for 30 minutes.

 Tuna Fettuccine Primavera

Sauté ⅓ cup chopped onion in 2 tablespoons olive oil. Add 1 clove minced garlic, ½ cup chopped skinned and seeded tomato, 1½ cups diced vege-tables (zucchini, yellow squash, mushrooms, bell pepper, carrot, celery), ¼ cup frozen peas, and ¼ cup broccoli florets and stir-fry for 1 minute. Add 2 cups crumbled Poached Tuna or canned tuna and 1 cup light cream. Toss with ¾ pound hot cooked fettuccine, ¼ cup grated Parmesan, salt, and pepper.

 Tuna Croquette Fingers

Prepare ½ cup thick Bechamel Sauce (page 429). Beat 2 large egg yolks, 2 cups crumbled Poached Tuna or canned tuna, 2 tablespoons finely chopped scallion, 2 tablespoons minced fresh parsley, ⅛ teaspoon hot pepper sauce, 2 teaspoons lemon juice, and 1 teaspoon Worcestershire. Cover and refrigerate for 1 hour. Form into 24 fin-gers, each 4 to 5 inches long, and roll in seasoned bread crumbs until well coated. Dry on a rack for 20 minutes. Deep-fry, 4 at a time, at 375° F. until golden brown, about 3 minutes per batch. Serve with Warm Tomato Vinaigrette (page 298) or sauce of your choice.

 Deviled Tuna

Follow preceding recipe, adding 2 teaspoons mustard and 1 teaspoon hot pepper sauce to the tuna mixture and a dash of cayenne pepper to the bread crumbs.

 Tuna Burgers

Follow recipe for Tuna Croquette Fingers (above), forming tuna mixture into 4 burgers instead of fingers. Brown in ¼ inch hot olive oil in a skillet.

Serve on 4 warm burger buns, brushed with mayonnaise, and topped with 1 lettuce leaf and 2 tomato slices.

 Tuna Croquette Loaf

Follow recipe for Tuna Croquette Fingers (above) through refrigeration. Use ¾ cup Béchamel Sauce (page 429). Add 1 cup seasoned bread crumbs and 2 tablespoons mayonnaise to the mixture and pack into a small loaf pan. Cover and bake at 350° F. for 40 minutes.

42

Fifty Ways to Start the Day

Remember breakfast? No, not some skimpy continental affair, nor those instant meals where all you do is add water, but a *real* breakfast. Breakfasts with sausages, hash browns, and eggs, muffins, biscuits, popovers, and corn bread, grilled ham, bacon, and steak—all served up diner-style with a bottle of ketchup or country-style with plenty of gravy.

Breakfasts like these have fueled Americans for generations, and though such hearty country cooking is too filling and time-consuming to be eaten regularly by most modern working people, it is just the thing to warm the body and soul on a frigid winter's morning.

Country breakfasts are nostalgic, connecting us to the roots of American food, to a time when the good life comprised little more than working hard and eating well. Food like ham steaks, an inch thick and crosshatched with the scars from a hot coal fire, were served with potatoes or grits and maybe a pile of apple fritters and a cruet of maple syrup to help the ham along. There were overblown popovers halfway rising out of their tins, trout fried in bacon fat, mush with warm cream, farm cheese, buckwheat cakes, and any style of egg you'd ever want, provided it was fried.

Preparing such robust fare is more complex than slipping an English muffin in the toaster oven, but it is not nearly as time-consuming as you might expect. Breakfast breads like muffins, biscuits, and popovers can be mixed up in minutes, especially if you sift the dry ingredients the night before, leaving the addition of the liquids and the baking for the morning.

You can make a hearty breakfast by using leftover meat from the previous night's dinner. Ham is a natural, but so is chicken meat mixed with a gravy and served over biscuits. Slice last night's steak, sauté it quickly in bacon fat, and serve it with eggs for a quick and economical steak-and-egg breakfast.

A sure way to countrify breakfast is to serve more than one course. Have a hot cereal before eggs or serve hash brown potatoes as a side dish and finish with a simple dessert such as baked apples or a fruit compote.

ABOUT THESE RECIPES

Most people don't like cooking first thing in the morning. A good many of these recipes can be partially prepared the night before and finished quickly in the morning. All recipes make 4 servings unless otherwise noted.

Fifty Ways to Cook Most Everything

 ### Scrambled Eggs with Cheese

Beat together 8 large eggs, ½ teaspoon hot pepper sauce, salt, pepper, and 2 tablespoons milk. Melt 2 tablespoons butter in a large nonstick skillet over high heat until foamy and add the eggs. When a film of egg sets up across the bottom of the pan, about 5 seconds, move it toward the center with a spatula. Continue in this way until all the egg is mostly set but still quite wet. Turn heat to low, sprinkle 4 ounces shredded Cheddar cheese over the eggs, cover the pan, and cook 30 seconds more. Fold the egg over itself.

 ### Grilled Tomatoes

Cut 2 large tomatoes in ⅜-inch slices. Brush with ¼ cup melted clarified butter and season liberally with salt and pepper. Broil or grill 4 inches from a high flame for 2 minutes per side. Serve with eggs and meat.

 ### Poached Salmon and Eggs with Lemon Butter Sauce

In a deep skillet, boil 2 cups white wine, 2 cups water, ¼ cup white wine vinegar, salt, and pepper for 5 minutes. Turn down to a simmer and add four 6-ounce skinned salmon fillets. Poach for 3 minutes, remove, and keep warm. Combine 1 cup of the poaching liquid, 2 tablespoons lemon juice, and 1 tablespoon minced shallot and cook until reduced to ¼ cup. Keep warm. Meanwhile, break 8 eggs into the remaining poaching liquid and poach until whites are set. Remove with a slotted spatula and place 2 eggs on each salmon fillet. Whisk ¼ pound softened butter, a piece at a time, into the hot reduction, and spoon over the eggs.

 ### Poached Egg Tostadas

Prepare Refried Black Beans (page 429). Mash together 1 large peeled and pitted avocado, 1 tablespoon lemon juice, salt, and hot pepper sauce. Toast 8 corn tortillas in a thin film of corn oil for about 30 seconds per side. Poach 8 large eggs in acidulated water until whites are firm, 3 to 5 minutes. Top each tortilla with a layer of the refried beans, a handful of shredded Romaine, 1 poached egg, a dollop of the avocado mixture, and a dollop of chopped tomato.

 ### Eggs Steamed in Tomato Sauce

Simmer 4 cups canned crushed plum tomatoes over low heat for 10 minutes. Strain. Add 2 tablespoons extra-virgin olive oil, 1 tablespoon red wine vinegar, salt, and pepper. Pour into a skillet, crack 8 eggs over top, season with salt and pepper, cover, and simmer until egg whites are firm, about 5 to 7 minutes.

 ### Stir-Fried Scrambled Eggs with Shrimp

In a wok, stir-fry 1 cup cleaned, shelled baby shrimp, 3 sliced scallions, and ¼ clove minced garlic in 2 tablespoons hot peanut oil until shrimp are opaque, about 30 seconds. Add 6 eggs beaten with 1 tablespoon water, salt, pepper, and 1 teaspoon hot pepper sauce. As eggs set on the floor of the wok, scrape up with a spatula until all the egg is set.

 ### Stir-Fried Scrambled Eggs with Smoked Turkey

Follow preceding recipe, substituting diced smoked turkey breast for the shrimp.

Potato Leek Frittata

Sauté 1 sliced russet potato in 1 tablespoon *each* butter and oil in a large nonstick skillet until tender. Add 1 thinly sliced leek, 2 cloves minced garlic, ½ teaspoon crumbled dried rosemary, and a pinch of nutmeg. Simmer until leek is soft, season with salt and pepper, add 1 tablespoon olive oil, and heat briefly. Pour in 5 or 6 eggs beaten with 2 tablespoons water. Swirl pan until egg is distributed over bottom of pan. Cook for 3 minutes over moderate heat. Set under a broiler until browned and puffed, 2 to 3 minutes. Serve in wedges.

 Bacon Hash Browns

Cook 4 strips bacon in a large heavy skillet until crisp, remove from pan, and crumble. Grate 2 to 3 scrubbed large Idaho potatoes and soak in cold water for 1 minute. Drain and wring dry in a clean towel. Heat the bacon fat and pack the potatoes into the hot fat. Cook undisturbed until bottom is brown and crisp, 2 to 4 minutes. Sprinkle with reserved bacon, season liberally with salt, pepper, and cayenne pepper, break into sections, and flip. When potatoes are well browned, remove to a platter and serve.

 Onion and Garlic Hash Browns

Prepare potatoes as in preceding recipe. Heat 2 to 3 tablespoons oil in a large heavy skillet and pack potatoes and 1 cup finely sliced onion into the hot fat. Cook undisturbed until bottom is brown and crisp, 2 to 4 minutes. Season liberally with salt, pepper, and cayenne pepper, break into sections, and flip. Add 2 cloves minced garlic for last minute of cooking. When potatoes are well browned, remove to a platter and serve.

 Ham Steak with Apple Fritters

Render fat from 1 slice bacon. Brown a 1-inch-thick slice smoked ham on both sides in the hot fat. Add ¼ cup bourbon, ¼ cup apple cider, and ⅛ teaspoon crumbled dried rosemary. Lower heat, cover pan, and simmer 20 minutes, turning occasionally. Remove cover and reduce any remaining liquid over moderately high heat until it glazes the ham. Serve with Savory Apple Fritters (page 389) dusted with a mixture of 2 tablespoons brown sugar and ¼ teaspoon ground cinnamon.

 British Bacon

Cook 4 thick slices bacon in a skillet until crisp. Drain on paper. Lower heat and cook 4 slices Canadian bacon in the fat until lightly browned on both sides.

 Homemade Breakfast Sausage

Mix ¼ pound finely chopped fatback, 1 pound ground pork, ¼ cup minced onion, 1 teaspoon salt, a pinch of ground cloves, ½ teaspoon pepper, ½ teaspoon dried thyme, and 1 teaspoon dried sage. Cover and refrigerate overnight. Form into 12 patties and cook over moderate heat until firm and browned on both sides.

 Grilled Chutney-Glazed Ham Steak

Grill 2 large ¼-inch-thick smoked ham steaks 4 to 6 inches from a high flame until seared on both sides. Brush with 2 tablespoons strained mango chutney mixed with ½ teaspoon mustard.

Basic Buttermilk Pancakes

Sift 2 cups sifted flour with 1 teaspoon baking soda, 2 teaspoons baking powder, 2 tablespoons sugar, and ½ teaspoon salt. Mix in 2 beaten eggs and 2 cups buttermilk, then mix in 2 tablespoons melted butter. Heat 2 teaspoons butter in a skillet or on a griddle until foamy. For each pancake, pour ¼ cup batter on the hot surface. Cook over moderately high heat until pancakes are covered with bubbles. Flip and cook 1 to 2 minutes more, until pancakes feel springy. Keep warm while you prepare the rest of the pancakes, greasing pan with more butter for every batch. Serve with syrup, Fruit and Honey Topping (page 365) or Orange Butter (page 365). Makes 18 pancakes.

 Ricotta Cheese Pancakes

Beat together 2 cups drained ricotta cheese, 6 egg yolks, ¼ cup sugar, 6 tablespoons flour, and ½ teaspoon vanilla extract. Beat 6 egg whites to a soft peak with a pinch of salt and fold into the batter. Make 2- to 3-inch pancakes on a hot greased griddle and brown on both sides over moderate to high heat, flipping after 2 to 3 minutes. Serve immediately with fruit.

 Yeasted Maple Walnut Pancakes

The night before serving, dissolve 1 envelope (¼ ounce) active dry yeast in 1 cup warm water. Add 1 cup warm milk, 3 cups flour, and ½ teaspoon salt. Mix into a smooth batter. Cover loosely with plastic wrap and rest at room temperature overnight. Just before cooking, mix in ¼ cup pure maple syrup, ½ teaspoon baking soda dissolved in ¼ cup hot water, and 2 tablespoons melted butter. Stir in 1¼ cups finely chopped walnuts. Heat 2 teaspoons butter in a skillet or on a griddle until it

foams. Scoop ¼ cup batter onto hot surface for each pancake. Cook over moderate heat until the pancake is covered with bubbles. Flip and cook another minute or two, until pancake feels springy. Keep warm while preparing the rest of the pancakes, greasing the pan with more butter for every batch. Serve with syrup, Fruit and Honey Topping (page 365), or Orange Butter (page 365). Makes 12 pancakes.

 Buckwheat Pancakes with Sour Cream and Caviar

Mix ½ cup buckwheat flour, ½ cup whole-wheat flour, and 1 cup unbleached all-purpose flour. Sift with 2 teaspoons baking powder, 1 teaspoon baking soda, 1 tablespoon sugar, and ½ teaspoon salt. Mix 2 egg yolks, 4 tablespoons melted butter, and 2 cups buttermilk and stir into the dry ingredients until smooth. In a clean bowl, whip 2 whites until soft peaks form. Fold beaten whites into batter. Heat a griddle until water drops form beads and bounce. Grease well and pour ¼ cup batter onto griddle for each cake. Turn when top looks pocked and bottom is brown, about 2 minutes. Top with 1 cup sour cream and 6 tablespoons caviar. Serves 4 to 6.

 Sour Cream Walnut Waffles

Sift together 1 cup sifted cake flour, 1¼ teaspoons baking powder, 1 teaspoon baking soda, and 2 tablespoons sugar. Stir in ½ cup finely ground walnuts. Separate 3 eggs and beat the yolks with 2 cups sour cream and 2 tablespoons walnut oil. Beat into dry ingredients just until moistened. Beat whites with ¼ teaspoon salt to soft peaks and fold into batter. Brush a hot waffle iron with clarified butter and ladle on enough batter to fill two thirds of the surface. Cover iron and cook until brown and crisp on both sides. Remove and repeat with remaining batter. Serve with sour cream and fruit, or syrup.

Apple, Bacon, and Cornmeal Waffles

Cook 6 slices bacon until crisp. Blot, crumble, and reserve ¼ cup of the fat. Sift together 1 cup sifted cake flour, 2 teaspoons baking powder, ½ teaspoon baking soda, and 1 tablespoon sugar. Mix in 1 cup yellow cornmeal. Separate 2 eggs and beat yolks with 1 cup milk, 1 large peeled, seeded, and grated apple, and the reserved bacon fat. Beat into dry ingredients just until moistened. Beat whites with ¼ teaspoon salt to soft peaks and fold into batter. Make waffles as in preceding recipe. Serve with syrup.

Real Good French Toast

Beat together ¼ cup maple syrup, 4 eggs, 1 cup milk, 1 teaspoon vanilla extract, and a pinch *each* of grated nutmeg and salt. Soak 8 thick slices bakery-quality white bread in the custard until all has been absorbed. Brown in batches over moderate heat, in 4 to 6 tablespoons unsalted butter. Serve with syrup, Warm Pear Puree (page 402), Pear Honey (page 365), or Sautéed Fruit Salad (page 402).

Whole-Wheat Buttermilk French Toast

Combine 4 eggs, 1 cup buttermilk, 2 tablespoons sugar, 1 teaspoon vanilla extract, and a pinch of salt. Soak 8 thick slices slightly stale whole-wheat bread in this mixture until they absorb all the liquid. Lightly grease a nonstick skillet with butter. Add as many slices of the bread as will fit in one layer and brown on each side over moderate heat, 3 to 4 minutes per side. Remove to a warm platter. Brown remaining slices in the same way. Serve with 2 cups fruit yogurt.

Souffléed Cottage Cheese Sandwiches

Make 12 mini-sandwiches using 24 thin slices French bread and 1 cup drained cottage cheese. Separate 4 eggs and beat yolks with 3 tablespoons sugar until thick. Add 1 teaspoon vanilla extract, a pinch of grated nutmeg, and ⅔ cup milk. Beat whites to soft peak with a pinch of salt and fold into yolk mixture. Dip sandwiches into batter and brown on both sides in 4 to 6 tablespoons unsalted butter.

Honey-Dipped Corn Toast

Beat together 2 eggs, 3 tablespoons honey, 1 cup milk, salt, and 6 drops hot pepper sauce. Pour batter into a flat dish and soak 6 corn toaster cakes in the batter, in batches if necessary. Allow to soak for 10 minutes. Carefully lift soaked corn cakes with a spatula and transfer to a skillet to brown slowly in 4 tablespoons butter for 4 to 5 minutes. Turn carefully and cook another 3 to 4 minutes. Serve with butter and honey.

Buttermilk Biscuits

Mix 3 cups flour, 1 teaspoon salt, 1 tablespoon sugar, 4 teaspoons baking powder, and 1 teaspoon baking soda. Cut 4 tablespoons *each* butter and cold vegetable shortening into dry ingredients until mixture resembles coarse meal. Beat 2 eggs into 1½ cups buttermilk and mix all but ¼ cup into dry ingredients just enough to moisten. On a floured board with floured hands, push into a ½-inch-thick layer. Cut with a biscuit cutter and place close together on a cookie sheet. Brush tops with remaining liquid and bake at 400° F. for 15 minutes. Makes 18 biscuits.

Herb Biscuits

Follow preceding recipe, adding 2 tablespoons chopped fresh herbs with the flour.

Fifty Ways to Cook Most Everything

Whole-Wheat Sour Cream Biscuits

Mix 1½ cups flour, 1½ cups whole-wheat flour, 1 teaspoon salt, 1 tablespoon sugar, 4 teaspoons baking powder, 1 teaspoon baking soda, and ½ cup raisins. Cut 4 tablespoons *each* butter and cold vegetable shortening into the dry ingredients until mixture resembles coarse meal. Beat 2 eggs, 1 cup sour cream, and ½ cup milk and mix all but ¼ cup into dry ingredients just enough to moisten. Prepare dough, cut biscuits, and bake as described in recipe for Buttermilk Biscuits (page 363).

Cheese-Filled Biscuits

Shred 6 ounces Cheddar cheese. Prepare any of the previous biscuit doughs. Mix cheese shreds into the dough, patting dough into ½-inch-thick sheet. Form and bake biscuits as directed in Buttermilk Biscuits (page 363).

Maple Sugar Biscuits

Follow recipe for Buttermilk Biscuits (page 363), replacing ¼ cup of the buttermilk with maple syrup.

Bacon Biscuits

Cook 6 slices bacon until crisp. Blot, crumble, and reserve ¼ cup of the rendered fat. Sift together 3 cups flour, 1 teaspoon salt, 2 tablespoons sugar, 1½ tablespoons baking powder, and 1 teaspoon baking soda. Mix in 2 tablespoons chopped fresh chives and the crumbled bacon. Blend in 6 tablespoons cold shortening and the bacon fat until mixture resembles coarse meal. Beat 2 small eggs with 1 cup plus 1 tablespoon buttermilk and mix 1¼ cups of this mixture into the dry ingredients just until moistened. Prepare dough, cut biscuits,

and bake as described in recipe for Buttermilk Biscuits (above).

Poppyseed Buttermilk Scones

Mix together 1¾ cups flour, ¼ teaspoon salt, 2 teaspoons baking powder, ½ teaspoon baking soda, and 1 tablespoon sugar. Blend in 5 tablespoons unsalted butter until mixture resembles coarse meal. Beat 2 eggs with ⅓ cup buttermilk and mix into dry ingredients just until moistened. Pat on a floured board with floured hands into a 6-by-8-inch sheet. Cut sheet in half lengthwise. Spread ⅓ cup poppyseed paste over one half and top with the other half. Cut into three 1-inch strips and cut each strip into 8 triangles. Bake on an ungreased sheet pan in a preheated 450° F. oven for 15 minutes. Cool on a rack for 5 minutes. Makes 2 dozen.

Irish Soda Bread

Sift together 4 cups flour, 1 teaspoon baking soda, 1 tablespoon sugar, and ½ teaspoon salt. Beat in 1½ to 2 cups buttermilk, using just enough liquid to make a dough that can be gathered into a soft ball. On a floured board with floured hands, pat into an 8-inch round disk. Place on a greased cookie sheet and cut a deep X in the center of the loaf. Brush with any remaining buttermilk. Bake in a preheated 425° F. oven until puffed and brown, about 30 minutes. Serves 8 to 10.

Basic Popovers

Place a 12-well nonstick muffin tin or a 6-well deep popover pan in a preheated 450° F. oven. Beat 1 cup milk with 1 tablespoon melted butter. Sift 1 cup flour with a pinch of salt. Beat liquid into dry ingredients just until blended. Beat in 2 eggs, 1 at a time. Grease the hot tin with melted butter and sprinkle wells with flour. Divide batter evenly among the wells. Bake 15 minutes, reduce oven to 375°, and bake 10 to 12 minutes more, until fully puffed, brown and crisp all over the surface.

 ### Three-Cheese Popovers

Follow preceding recipe, adding a pinch of cayenne pepper and a pinch of garlic powder to the flour. When filling the tin, pour a few tablespoons batter in the bottom of each well. Distribute 3 tablespoons grated Parmesan, 2 teaspoons Romano, and 3 tablespoons finely shredded sharp Cheddar among the wells and fill with remaining batter.

 ### Pecan Popovers

Follow recipe for Basic Popovers (opposite) adding ⅔ cup finely chopped pecans and 2 tablespoons sugar with the flour. Dust greased pan with additional sugar rather than flour.

 ### Maple Popovers

Follow recipe for Basic Popovers (opposite), adding 1 tablespoon sugar with the flour and 3 tablespoons maple syrup with liquid ingredients. Dust greased pan with additional sugar rather than flour. Serve with additional syrup and sweet butter.

 ### Corn Popovers

Place a 12-well nonstick muffin tin or 6-well deep popover pan in a preheated 450° F. oven. Beat together 1¼ cups milk, 1 tablespoon melted butter, 3 beaten eggs, and 1 tablespoon honey. Sift together ¾ cup flour, 6 tablespoons cornmeal, and ¼ teaspoon salt. Whisk into batter. Grease hot tin

with melted butter, sprinkle with additional cornmeal, and divide batter among the wells. Bake 15 minutes, reduce oven to 375°, and bake 10 to 12 minutes more, until fully puffed, browned, and crisp all over the surface. Remove and serve with honey and butter.

 ### Fruit and Honey Topping

In a small skillet, heat ½ pint cleaned, stemmed, and sliced strawberries, 2 peeled and sliced bananas, and 2 dozen seedless grapes in 1 tablespoon *each* butter and honey until heated through. Stir in ½ teaspoon vanilla extract. Serve with pancakes, French toast, or waffles.

 ### Orange Butter

Beat ¼ pound butter until light and fluffy. Beat in ¼ cup sweet orange marmalade, 2 teaspoons frozen orange juice concentrate, and 1 teaspoon lemon juice. Use as a spread or a topping for pancakes, French toast, or waffles.

 ### Pear Honey

Bring to a boil 1¼ pounds finely chopped peeled and seeded pears, ¾ cup sugar, the juice of 1 lemon, a grating of nutmeg, and a pinch of salt. Simmer 30 minutes. Add 2 teaspoons finely grated lemon zest and simmer 5 minutes more. Let cool. Makes about 1½ cups. Use as a spread or on French toast, waffles, and pancakes.

 ### Real Oatmeal

In a heavy saucepan, bring 4 cups water and ½ teaspoon salt to a boil. Slowly add 1 cup Irish steel-cut oatmeal, stirring constantly. Do not allow the water to stop boiling. Cook oatmeal briskly until water starts to cloud. Turn down to a bare simmer, partially cover the pan, and simmer 30 minutes more, stirring briefly every 10 minutes. Stir in 2 tablespoons brown sugar and 2 tablespoons butter, if desired. Serve with cold milk, cream, or buttermilk.

 ## Sweet and Spicy Cornmeal Mush

In a heavy saucepan, cook ¼ cup onion, ¼ cup diced red bell pepper, 1 tablespoon minced chili pepper, and 1 diced apple in 2 tablespoons butter until softened. Add 4 cups water and bring to a boil. Meanwhile, mix 1 cup cornmeal, 1 teaspoon salt, and ½ cup cold water into a smooth paste. Whisk into the boiling liquid until completely distributed, along with 1 teaspoon hot sauce. Reduce to a simmer, cover, and simmer 15 minutes, stirring frequently. Serve with chilled cream and maple syrup.

 ## Muesli Cereal

In a large deep iron skillet, mix 2 cups quick or old-fashioned oatmeal, 1 cup slivered almonds, ½ cup sesame seeds, ½ cup flaked coconut, and ½ cup wheat germ. Stir until small pieces begin to color lightly, remove from heat, and continue stirring until cereal is uniformly lightly toasted. Stir in 1 cup raisins and a pinch of salt. Cool completely and store in a tightly closed container. Eat as is or in a bowl with milk. Makes 5½ cups or about 8 servings.

 ## Five-Grain Cereal

In a large deep iron skillet, mix 1 cup quick or old-fashioned oatmeal, ½ cup rye flakes, 1 cup natural cornflakes, ½ cup wheat bran, ½ cup rice bran, ½ cup slivered almonds, ¼ cup sesame seeds, and ¼ cup sunflower seeds. Stir until small pieces begin to color lightly, remove from heat, and continue stirring until cereal is uniformly lightly toasted. Stir in 2 cups raisins, 2 tablespoons brown sugar, and a pinch of salt. Cool completely and store in a tightly closed container. Eat as is or in a bowl with milk. Makes about 10 servings.

 ## Mushrooms Braised in Steak Sauce

Lightly brown 12 thickly sliced, large mushrooms in 2 tablespoons butter. Add 2 tablespoons steak sauce and simmer 1 minute. Stir in 1 tablespoon finely minced fresh parsley and serve with grilled breakfast meats or eggs.

 ## Melon with Lime

On a large circular platter, arrange 1 thinly sliced seeded ripe honeydew melon in a spoke pattern. Place 1 thin slice lime across each melon slice.

 ## Easy Sour Cream Coffee Cake

Mix 1 cup sour cream with 1½ teaspoons baking soda and set aside. Sift 2 cups flour with 1 teaspoon baking powder and set aside. Beat ¼ pound butter with 1 cup sugar until light and fluffy. Beat in 2 eggs, 1 at a time. Add 1 teaspoon vanilla extract and 1 cup raisins. Add sifted dry ingredients in 3 additions alternately with sour cream in 2 additions, starting and ending with dry ingredients. Pour into greased and floured 10-inch round pan. Mix together ¼ cup sugar, ½ teaspoon ground cinnamon, and ¼ cup chopped walnuts and sprinkle over top. Bake in a preheated 375° F. oven for 45 minutes. Cool on a rack and unpan. Serves 10.

Buttermilk Coffee Cake

Sift 2 cups sifted flour, 2 teaspoons baking powder, and 1 teaspoon baking soda. Mix in ¾ cup sugar, ¼ cup brown sugar, 1 teaspoon ground cinnamon, and ¼ teaspoon grated nutmeg. Cut 5 tablespoons plus 1 teaspoon chilled butter into dry ingredients until texture resembles coarse meal. Remove ½ cup of the mixture, combine it with ¼ cup chopped pecans or walnuts, and set aside. Mix ⅔ cup buttermilk, 1 beaten extra-large egg, and 1 teaspoon vanilla extract. Blend into remaining dry ingredients. Mix in ¾ cup chopped pecans or walnuts and ½ cup chopped raisins. Pour into greased and floured 9-inch baking pan and top with the crumb mixture. Bake at 375° F. for 40 to 45 minutes, until a tester comes out with a crumb or two clinging to it. Cool in the pan on a rack. Serves 8.

Date Nut Coffee Cake

Follow preceding recipe, adding ¼ cup chopped dates to the crumb mixture with the nuts. Use chopped dates instead of raisins.

Sweet Almond Coffee Cake

Follow recipe for Buttermilk Coffee Cake (above) using almonds in place of walnuts or pecans. Add ¼ teaspoon almond extract along with the vanilla. Substitute 2 ounces marzipan, cut in small pieces, for the chopped raisins.

43

Fifty Homemade Thirst Quenchers

Thirst hurts. It's more severe than hunger and worse than a burn; thirst thickens the tongue and stabs at the throat. It makes us see double and imagine swimming holes where there are none. It is one of the few pains that no one can ignore, for next to air we need nothing more than we need drink.

Fortunately for most of us, thirst is easy to beat. We live in a culture where thirst-quenching is big business. Sodas, beers, juices, shakes, frappés, punches, coffees, and teas compete for our dollars, but you can match any of them, and for a fraction of the cost, in your own kitchen.

Most drinks are simply flavored water, made either by mixing flavorful juices or liqueurs with still or sparkling waters and sweeteners, or by infusing flavors into water through steeping. The first method is how most punches and mixed drinks are made, the latter how teas and coffees are prepared.

Juices can be mixed, sweetened, and then thinned with water to become a drink, or they can be added when the beverage is served to flavor the drink more subtly. One of the most artful ways of doing this is to freeze the juice into tasty ice cubes. Plop these into a glass of wine or iced tea, then sip and wait. As the beverage chills, it is infused with the flavor of the ice.

Steeping infuses a liquid with the flavors of aromatic leaves, beans, or spices. The process is not difficult at all. In fact, if you know how to make a cup of tea, you already are an expert at steeping. Exotic iced teas, coffees, and cocoa can be made by mixing herbs, spices, tea leaves, coffee beans, blossoms, or citrus zests with boiling water. Allow the solids to steep in the water for at least 5 minutes. Strain it, warm it, or ice it, and it's done. Always make iced, steeped drinks on the strong side at first, because their flavor will be diluted once you add ice cubes.

For a cozy winter evening, nothing beats warm drinks. Flavored coffees, warm egg nog, or hot chocolates are all warm nonalcoholic elixirs that instantly take the bite out of a winter night, but for a more potent brew, we've included spiked renditions of each and an aromatic warm spiced wine punch.

Though most of us have been forced to abandon the unlimited consumption of milkshakes as our waistlines have expanded, these high-calorie, highly nutritious drinks need not be dropped completely from our diets. We have included a few shakes, made lower in calories by substituting yogurt for ice cream and punched up in nutrition with the addition of skim milk powder. For those obnoxious few who never need to watch their weight, there are some super-rich ice cream shakes, as well.

ABOUT THESE RECIPES

All of the following recipes make 4 portions, unless otherwise noted.

 ## Lemon-Lime Soft Drink

Mix ¼ cup *each* lemon juice and lime juice with 6 ounces apple juice concentrate. Dilute with 1 liter cold seltzer.

 ## Gingered Ginger Ale

Boil ¼ cup grated fresh gingerroot, 2 tablespoons sugar, and ⅛ teaspoon cayenne pepper in ⅓ cup water until most of the water evaporates. Remove from the heat, add ½ cup water, and cool to room temperature. Strain, chill liquid, and discard solids. Place 2 tablespoons in each of four 12-ounce glasses filled with ice, pour in 8 ounces ginger ale, and stir.

 ## Gingered Apricot Ale

Boil ¼ cup grated fresh gingerroot, 2 tablespoons sugar, and ⅛ teaspoon cayenne pepper in ⅓ cup water until most of the water evaporates. Remove from the heat, add 1 cup apricot nectar, and cool

to room temperature. Strain, chill liquid, and discard solids. Place ¼ cup in each of four 12-ounce glasses filled with ice, pour 8 ounces of ginger ale in each glass and stir.

 ## Sparkling Peach Melba

Crush 1 cup frozen raspberries and strain out the seeds. Mix with 2 cups peach nectar. Chill. Divide among 4 glasses, each ⅓ filled with crushed ice, fill each glass with seltzer, and stir.

 ## Raspberry Mint Seltzer

Alternate 4 raspberries and 3 mint leaves on each of 4 toothpicks or wooden skewers. Lightly bruise berries and mint with the back of a spoon. Fill four 12-ounce glasses with ice, place 1 skewer in each glass, fill with seltzer, and squeeze 1 lime wedge in each glass.

 ## Citrus Seltzer

Rub rims of 4 tall glasses with the outside of a lemon or lime half. Cut the lemon or lime half in 4 wedges and place in the glasses. Place 3 or 4 ice cubes in each glass and fill with seltzer.

 ## Grapefruit or Tangerine Seltzer

Bruise the colored side of 8 strips of grapefruit or tangerine peel with the back of a spoon. Skewer on 4 toothpicks or wooden skewers. Fill four 12-ounce glasses with ice, place 1 skewer in each glass, fill with seltzer, and squeeze 1 lime wedge in each glass.

Grapefruitade

Heat ½ cup sugar in 3 cups water until dissolved. Chill. Mix with 1 cup freshly squeezed grapefruit juice, 1 tablespoon lemon juice, and a pinch of salt. Chill and serve over ice.

Lemon-Limeade

Heat ¾ cup sugar and 1 quart water until sugar dissolves. Chill. Mix with ¼ cup *each* freshly squeezed lemon and lime juices and a pinch of salt. Chill and serve over ice.

Spicy Lemonade

Heat ¾ cup sugar and 1 quart water until sugar dissolves. Chill. Mix with ½ cup lemon juice and a pinch of salt. Chill and serve over flavored ice cubes as described in Iced Tea with Spicy Lemon Ice Cubes (opposite).

Honey Cranberry Cocktail

Blend ¼ cup honey, 3 cups cranberry juice cocktail, 1 cup orange juice, and the juice of ½ lime.

Double Orange Juice

Freeze 2 cups orange juice until solid. Cut into small cubes, and finely chop in a blender or food processor. Mix with 2 cups freshly squeezed orange juice.

 Minted Apple Juice

Bring 4 cups apple juice to a boil. Add 3 tablespoons dried mint and cool to room temperature. Strain and chill.

Strawberry Lime Frappé

In a blender or food processor, process 2 pints washed and stemmed strawberries, the juice of 1 large lime, 3 tablespoons sugar, and 8 ice cubes until smooth.

Cherry Raspberry Frappé

In a blender or food processor, process 2 cups cherry juice, 2 cups raspberry sherbet, 1 tablespoon lemon juice, and 4 ice cubes.

Fruit Cooler

In a blender or food processor, process 2 cups chopped fruit (any kind), ¼ cup grape juice, and 6 ice cubes until smooth. Combine in a pitcher with 2 cups seltzer and serve in 4 tall glasses over ice. Squeeze 1 lemon or lime wedge into each glass.

True Brewed Iced Tea

Pour 4½ cups boiling water over 6 teabags or 2 tablespoons loose tea and 2 strips lemon zest. Steep for 5 minutes. Strain and stir in 2 tablespoons sugar and 1 tablespoon lemon juice. Chill and serve over ice.

Sun-Brewed Iced Tea

Place 6 teabags or 2 tablespoons loose tea and 2 strips lemon zest in a jar. Add 9 cups water and 2 tablespoons sugar. Cover jar and place in the sun for 4 hours. Strain and add 1 tablespoon lemon juice. Chill and serve over ice.

Minted Iced Tea

Follow either of the two preceding recipes using 2 herbal mint tea bags in place of the lemon zest and lime juice instead of lemon juice. Garnish with mint sprigs.

 Double Iced Tea

Pour 8 cups boiling water over 6 teabags and 2 1-inch strips lemon zest. Steep for 5 minutes. Strain. Stir in 2 tablespoons sugar and chill. Pour 2 cups of the tea into an ice-cube tray and freeze solid. Add 1 tablespoon lemon juice and 1 tablespoon honey to remaining tea. Keep chilled and serve in glasses over the ice.

Spiced Iced Tea

Stud ½ orange with 3 whole cloves. Place in a pitcher with ½ lemon, 6 thin slices fresh gingerroot, 8 crushed coriander seeds, 1 cinnamon stick, 2 orange-spice tea bags, and 2 regular tea bags. Pour in 4½ cups boiling water and steep for 5 minutes. Remove tea bags and steep for 5 minutes more. Stir in 1 tablespoon honey. Strain and chill. Serve over ice.

Mint Julep Iced Tea

Pour 4½ cups boiling water over 5 mint tea bags and 1 Chinese black tea teabag. Steep for 5 minutes. Remove the teabags and stir in 2 tablespoons sugar. Chill. Crush 2 mint sprigs in each of four 12-ounce glasses. Fill glasses with ice and add 2 tablespoons bourbon to each glass. Fill the rest of the way with tea.

 Lemonade Iced Tea

Pour 4½ cups boiling water over 4 lemon teabags and 2 regular teabags. Steep for 5 minutes and remove teabags. Chill. Dilute one 12-ounce can frozen lemonade concentrate with the tea plus 1 can water. Serve over ice garnished with lemon wedges.

 Fruited Iced Tea Punch

Pour 4 cups boiling water over 5 fruit-tea teabags (raspberry, lemon, apple, orange, etc.) and 1 ginseng teabag. Steep for 5 minutes. Remove teabags and chill liquid. Add 24 ounces grape juice and serve over ice.

 Zesty Iced Tea

Pour 4½ cups boiling water over finely grated zest of 2 lemons, 2 oranges, and 2 limes, 4 lemon or orange teabags, and 2 regular teabags. Steep for 5 minutes. Remove teabags and stir in 2 tablespoons sugar. Chill and add juice of ½ lemon. Serve over ice.

 Iced Tea with Spicy Lemon Ice Cubes

Pour 2 cups boiling water over 1 teaspoon crushed red pepper flakes and 3 Lemon Zinger teabags. Steep for 5 minutes and strain. Chill and pour into an ice-cube tray. Freeze until solid. Prepare any of the preceding iced teas and serve over these ice cubes.

 Iced Mocha

Mix 4 cups cold coffee, ½ cup chocolate syrup, 1 cup milk or half-and-half, and ¼ teaspoon ground cinnamon. Pour over ice.

Iced Espresso with Rum

Dissolve 3 tablespoons instant espresso coffee in 2 cups boiling water with 1 tablespoon sugar and the finely grated zest of 1 orange. Cool. Pour ¾ ounce rum over ice in each of 4 glasses and fill glasses the rest of the way with the coffee.

Iced Spiked Coca

Mix 6 tablespoons cocoa powder, 6 tablespoons sugar, 1-inch piece cinnamon stick, and 1½ tablespoons instant coffee in ¾ cup boiling water and set aside to cool. Remove cinnamon stick and chill liquid. Add 1½ cups cold milk, 1½ teaspoons vanilla extract, and ¾ cup brandy or cognac. Whip 1¼ cups heavy cream until soft peaks form and fold into the cocoa mixture. Serve garnished with a sprinkling of ground cinnamon.

Banana Berry Kefir

In a blender, process 2 cups banana, 1 tablespoon honey, 1 cup vanilla yogurt, and 1 cup raspberry yogurt. Thin with 1 cup apple-raspberry juice. Chill.

Super-Protein Health Shake

In a blender, puree 2 bananas, ¼ cup frozen orange juice concentrate, and ¼ cup powdered milk. Add 1 cup vanilla yogurt and 2 cups lowfat milk. Beat 2 egg whites to a soft peak. Add 1 tablespoon sugar and beat until firm. Fold into fruit mixture.

Warm White Chocolate Egg Nog

Scald 4 cups milk and mix slowly into 2 lightly beaten egg yolks. Return to low heat and cook for 3 minutes, stirring constantly. Whisk in 4 ounces finely chopped white chocolate and ⅛ teaspoon grated nutmeg. Serve warm.

Mulled Cider

Bring to a simmer 12 chopped pitted dates, 12 chopped dried apricots, ½ cup raisins, ¼ cup chopped dried apple, ½ gallon apple cider, the finely grated zest and juice of 1 lemon, 1 cinnamon stick, 1-inch piece fresh gingerroot, 2 whole cloves, and ⅛ teaspoon grated nutmeg. Steep for 15 minutes. Serve in mugs, garnishing each with 1 cinnamon stick. Serves 10.

Liquid Chocolate Bars

Scald 3½ cups milk. Stir in 12 ounces finely chopped semisweet chocolate and bring to a bare simmer, stirring frequently. Top each cup with 1 tablespoon whipped cream.

Cappuccino Cocoa

Scald 4 cups milk with 1 stick cinnamon. Whisk in ¼ cup Dutch process cocoa, 3 tablespoons instant espresso, and ¼ cup sugar. Hold over low heat for 10 minutes. Remove the cinnamon stick, pour into cups, and garnish with ground cinnamon.

Hot Buttered Rum

Dissolve ¼ cup brown sugar in 1 cup boiling water. Add 1 teaspoon vanilla extract, 1 cup dark rum, and 2 tablespoons butter cut into small pieces. Stir until the butter melts.

Flaming Warm Spiced Wine

Bring 1 bottle (750 ml.) dry red wine, 2 tablespoons sugar, 1 cinnamon stick, 2 cloves, 2 strips orange zest, and 2 strips lemon zest to a boil in a covered pot. Ignite carefully, let flames die out, and serve.

 ### Modern-Day Mead

Bring ¼ cup honey to a boil in ½ cup water. Boil for 2 minutes. Add 1 cup brandy and serve.

 ### Café Brulot Slush

Bring 1½ cups sugar to a boil in 3 cups water. Add ½ cup instant coffee, a pinch of ground cloves, 1 cinnamon stick, and the finely grated zest of 1 large orange. Steep for 30 minutes. Strain and freeze until solid. Cut into small cubes and process in a blender until slushy with ¼ cup brandy.

 ### Mint Julep Slush

Steep 2 tablespoons dried mint leaves in 1¾ cups boiling water. Cool, strain, and mix with 1 cup cooled Simple Syrup (page 436) and 1¼ cups bourbon. Freeze until slushy, stirring about every hour. Serve garnished with fresh mint sprigs.

 ### Kahlúa and Cream Shake

Soften 1 pint coffee ice cream and blend with ½ teaspoon vanilla extract, ½ cup Kahlúa, and 1 cup milk. Beat ½ cup heavy cream to soft peaks and fold into ice cream mixture. Turn into 4 chilled glasses and top with 2 tablespoons finely ground espresso beans, if desired.

 ### Orange Cream Frappé

Soften 1 pint vanilla ice cream and blend with ½ cup Triple Sec and ¾ cup orange juice. Whip ½ cup heavy cream to soft peaks and fold into ice cream mixture. Turn into 4 chilled glasses and top with 2 tablespoons finely grated orange zest, if desired.

 ### Sparkling Kir Punch

Blend ½ cup creme de cassis, ¼ cup cooled Simple Syrup (page 436), and the juice of 1 lime. Add 1 bottle (750 ml.) dry white wine and 2 cups seltzer. Serve chilled.

 ### Berry Wine Punch

Toss 1 cup cleaned raspberries and 1 cup halved strawberries with 5 tablespoons confectioners' sugar. Add ¼ cup Madeira and add 1 bottle (750 ml.) dry white wine.

 ### "Champagne" with Grapefruit Ice

Mix 1 cup fresh grapefruit juice with 1 cup Simple Syrup (page 436), the juice of ½ lemon, and a pinch of salt. Freeze until solid, stirring mixture about every hour. Scoop into balls and divide among 4 champagne glasses. Pour 1 bottle (750 ml.) chilled inexpensive sparkling wine over top. (Don't use the good stuff for this.)

 ### Spicy Spiked Tomato Juice

Make flavored ice cubes as described in Iced Tea with Spicy Lemon Ice Cubes (page 371) and pour 32 ounces chilled tomato juice or vegetable cocktail juice, mixed with 1 tablespoon Worcestershire sauce, over the ice cubes.

 ### Super Vegetable Cocktail Juice

Combine 32 ounces vegetable cocktail juice, 2 Lemon Zinger teabags, 6 peppercorns, 1 dried chili pepper, and 1 teaspoon Worcestershire in a glass pitcher, cover with plastic wrap, and microwave at full power for 4 minutes. Remove teabags and chili pepper. Chill thoroughly. Serves 6.

 ### Shrimp Bloody Marys

Boil 1½ cups clam juice, 10 peppercorns, and 1 teaspoon ground celery seed. Add 8 large shrimp and return to a boil. Remove shrimp, cool under cold water, peel, and add the peels to the pan. Simmer 5 minutes more and cool. Clean and reserve shrimp. Strain cooled clam juice and mix with 1 tablespoon finely chopped celery leaves, 2 teaspoons finely chopped dill weed, 5 cups tomato juice, 1 tablespoon soy sauce, 1 tablespoon prepared horseradish, and 2 teaspoons hot pepper sauce. Serve in tall chilled glasses over ice. Add 1 ounce vodka per glass, if desired. Set 2 of the reserved shrimps on the rim of each glass with its inner side hooked over the rim, their tails facing outward.

 ### Gazpacho Cooler

In a food processor, finely chop in batches ⅓ cup coarsely chopped onion, 1 small clove garlic, ½ peeled and chunked cucumber, 1 rib sliced celery, ¼ chunked red pepper, ⅓ small seeded hot pepper, 2 cored tomatoes in chunks, 3 ice cubes, and 2 tablespoons red wine vinegar. Mix with ⅔ cup water, salt and pepper.

 ### Spicy Tomato Slush

Combine 3 cups spicy tomato juice or vegetable cocktail juice with the juice of 1 lime and ½ cup cooled Simple Syrup (page 436). Freeze until solid and cut into small cubes. In a blender, process until slushy with another ½ cup spicy tomato juice.

Fifty Homemade Snacks

Quadequina was not a great warrior, nor a famed peacemaker like his brother Chief Massasoit, but he sure knew how to pack a snack. When the Pilgrims threw their big pot-luck bash in the fall of 1621, he didn't bring the sweet potato casserole or his mother's recipe for corn bread stuffing. Instead, he made American gastronomic history by bringing the popcorn.

Popcorn set the stage for the scores of great American snack foods to follow. Not only is it quick and easy to prepare, but it can be eaten almost anywhere by the handful. Like corn chips, pretzels, and pizza, it lends itself to endless embellishment and like raisins and celery sticks it is inherently healthful.

Snack food needn't be synonymous with junk. Though many of the recipes that follow would hardly qualify as health food, all are made with wholesome ingredients and have been formulated with an eye toward eliminating excess fat, sugar, and salt.

ABOUT THESE RECIPES

In the name of Quadequina, we offer you the following 50 recipes for divine snacks. Most are very fast and easy, and those that take a little time to prepare make up for it with elaborate results. As for servings, who's to say what constitutes a portion of a snack? We've given guidelines for things like popcorn, but you should let your appetite and common sense steer you.

Several of these recipes are designed to be made ahead and stored—just right to have on hand for munching your way through the climax of a movie or the final inning, when a snack is essential but cooking is out of the question.

 Vanilla Popcorn

In a large heavy pot, heat ¼ cup corn oil over high heat until the oil smokes. Add 1 kernel popping corn and heat until kernel pops. Add 1 split vanilla bean and ¾ cup popping corn, cover pot, and shake gently until corn starts to pop. Shake vigorously until popping subsides. Remove from heat. Remove vanilla bean and toss popcorn with 1 tablespoon superfine sugar, salt, and 2 tablespoons melted butter. Scrape seeds from vanilla bean and add to the popcorn. Serves 6.

 Lemon Popcorn

Follow preceding recipe, but omit the vanilla bean, add the zest of 1 lemon in place of the sugar, and mix melted butter with 2 teaspoons lemon juice before adding.

Saffron Buttered Popcorn

Follow recipe for Vanilla Popcorn (opposite), but heat 3 tablespoons melted butter with ¼ teaspoon finely chopped saffron threads for 1 minute and use in place of the plain melted butter.

 Garlic and Parmesan Popcorn

In a large heavy pot, heat 2 tablespoons corn oil and 2 tablespoons olive oil over high heat until oil smokes. Add 1 kernel popping corn and heat until kernel pops. Add 2 split cloves garlic and ¾ cup popping corn, cover, and shake gently until corn starts to pop. Shake vigorously until popping subsides. Remove from heat. Remove garlic and toss popcorn with ¼ cup grated Parmesan, 1 clove minced garlic, a dash of cayenne pepper, and salt. Serves 6.

 Three-Pepper Popcorn

Follow preceding recipe, replacing Parmesan with 2 teaspoons coarsely ground black pepper and ¼ cup hot pepper sauce mixed with 2 tablespoons melted butter.

 Popcorn with Basil and Sun-Dried Tomatoes

Follow recipe for Garlic and Parmesan Popcorn (above), but replace Parmesan with grated aged provolone, and replace minced garlic with 6 finely chopped oil-cured sun-dried tomatoes, 1 tablespoon oil from the tomatoes, and 12 finely chopped basil leaves.

 Walnut Popcorn

In a food processor, chop ⅔ cup walnut pieces until oily. Set aside. Over high heat, heat ¼ cup walnut oil in a large heavy pot until oil smokes. Add 1 kernel popping corn and heat until kernel pops. Add ¾ cup popping corn, cover, and shake gently until corn starts to pop. Shake vigorously until popping subsides. Remove from heat. Mix in walnuts and salt to taste. Serves 6.

 Roasted Pepper Popcorn

Cook 2 tablespoons minced onion, 1 clove minced garlic, and 1 diced roasted red pepper (page 442) in 2 tablespoons olive oil until softened. Set aside. In a large heavy pot, heat 3 tablespoons corn oil over high heat until oil smokes, add 1 kernel popping corn, and heat until kernel pops. Add ¾ cup popping corn, cover, and shake gently until corn starts to pop. Shake vigorously until popping subsides. Remove from heat, toss with salt, cayenne pepper, and the vegetables. Serves 6.

 Spicy Crab Popcorn

Follow preceding recipe, but substitute this mixture for the vegetables: Cook the sliced whites of 4 scallions and 1 clove minced garlic in 1 tablespoon peanut oil. Add 4 ounces cleaned backfin crabmeat, salt, pepper, and 1 teaspoon hot pepper sauce and toss to coat.

 Bacon and Onion Popcorn

Brown and crumble 6 slices bacon. Cook 1 finely chopped small onion in 1 tablespoon of the hot bacon fat until softened and reserve. Place 2 tablespoons of the fat and 1 tablespoon corn oil in a large heavy pot and heat until the fat smokes. Add 1 kernel popping corn and heat until the kernel pops. Add ¾ cup popping corn, cover, and shake gently until corn starts to pop. Shake vigorously until popping subsides. Remove from heat. Toss with salt, the crumbled bacon, and the onion. Serves 6.

Molasses Mustard and Pretzels

Mix 5 tablespoons brown mustard, 2 tablespoons light molasses, and 1 tablespoon honey. Use as a dip with pretzel rods.

Spicy Cheese and Pretzels

Mix 2 tablespoons cream cheese and 2 ounces finely chopped Cheddar cheese in a bowl. Microwave for 1 minute, until melted. Stir in 2 to 3 tablespoons hot sauce. Serve warm. Use as a dip with pretzel rods.

Microwave Chocolate Dip

In a 4-cup glass measure, combine 2 ounces chopped unsweetened chocolate, 6 tablespoons sugar, 1 tablespoon vanilla extract, and ¼ cup milk. Cover and microwave for 5 minutes at full power. Remove cover, whisk until smooth, and blend in 1 tablespoon dark rum. Use as a dip for banana, orange sections, and pretzels or as an ice cream sauce.

Peanut Toffee Dip

Dissolve 2 tablespoons honey and 2 teaspoons instant coffee in ¼ cup boiling water. Whisk in 2 tablespoons butter and 6 tablespoons peanut butter. Use as a dip for pretzels or a sauce for ice cream.

Mustard Chutney Dip

Mix ¼ cup chopped mango chutney with ¼ cup brown mustard. Use as a dip with pretzel rods or

raw vegetables. Or spread on ham slices, roll up, and secure with a toothpick.

Bagna Cauda

Heat ½ cup olive oil and 2 tablespoons butter until butter foams. Add 1½ cloves minced garlic and cook until softened. Add ¼ cup finely chopped anchovy fillets and cook until anchovies become very soft. Season with salt and pepper. Serve warm as a dip with raw vegetables.

Warm Basil and Tomato Dip

Follow preceding recipe using ¼ cup chopped basil leaves and ¼ cup chopped tomato in place of the anchovies.

Hot Pepper Pecans

Toast 2 cups pecan halves in 2 tablespoons peanut oil for 1 minute. Add ½ cup sugar and cook until sugar caramelizes. Quickly turn out onto a sheet pan and sprinkle with 1 to 2 teaspoons salt, ¼ teaspoon ground cinnamon, and 1 teaspoon cayenne pepper. Store in tightly closed tin for a day or two. Serves 8.

Chili Pumpkin Seeds

Follow preceding recipe, substituting toasted pumpkin seeds for the pecans and 1 teaspoon chili powder for the cinnamon.

Sweet Curried Peanuts

Follow recipe for Hot Pepper Pecans (above), but use peanuts instead of pecans and ½ teaspoon curry powder instead of cinnamon.

Fifty Ways to Cook Most Everything

 Shrimp Chips

Mix ½ cup cornstarch with 1 teaspoon cayenne pepper. Butterfly 20 large shelled and cleaned shrimp. Dredge well in the cornstarch mixture. Place each between 2 sheets of plastic or wax paper and pound gently with a mallet until shrimp are paper-thin. Lift carefully from paper and dredge again in the starch. Deep-fry at 375° F. until firm, but still pale, remove, and blot. Hold up to several hours. Just before serving, fry again for another few seconds. Season with salt.

 Sesame Scallop Chips

Follow preceding recipe, but substitute sea scallops for the shrimp and mix 2 tablespoons ground sesame seeds with the cornstarch.

 Plantain Chips

Peel 2 large plantains by slitting the skin down the ridges of the peel. Cut off stem end and remove peel in sections. Slice plantains in thin slices. Fry in 1 inch hot peanut oil until lightly brown, remove, and blot off excess fat. Season with salt.

 Garlic Potato Chips

Slice 1 pound peeled russet potatoes in ⅛-inch slices. Deep-fry potatoes in batches in several inches of oil heated to 325° F. until chips are lightly browned. Drain. Increase oil temperature to 375° F. and deep-fry again until crisp. Drain and sprinkle with garlic salt.

 Spicy Sweet Nuts

Toast 2 cups mixed nuts in 2 tablespoons hot peanut oil for 1 minute. Add ½ cup sugar and cook until sugar caramelizes. Turn out onto a sheet pan and sprinkle with 1 to 2 teaspoons salt, ¼ teaspoon curry powder, and 1 teaspoon cayenne pepper. Serves 8.

 Spiced Brown Rice

Toss 2 cups cooked brown rice in 3 tablespoons Oriental sesame oil and 1 tablespoon chili powder. In a dry skillet, toast ¼ cup sesame seeds with 1 teaspoon ground coriander until seeds color lightly. Add rice and cook until grains are dry and separate. Serves 8.

 Prosciutto and Pear

Peel and core 2 large pears and slice each into 8 wedges. Wrap each wedge with 1 thin slice prosciutto, preferably imported. Serve immediately.

 French Bread Pizza

Brush 2 large tomatoes cut in 4 slices each with ⅓ cup Italian dressing and set aside for 20 minutes. Split 2 small French breads lengthwise. Brush insides of the bread with some of the liquid from the tomatoes and place under broiler for 1 minute or less to toast lightly. Place tomato slices on the breads and broil another 3 minutes. Top each with 3 ounces grated mozzarella and ½ ounce grated Parmesan. Broil until cheese melts. Serves 2 to 4.

 Gorgonzola and Onion French Bread Pizza

Lightly brown 3 thinly sliced onions in 1 tablespoon butter and 1 tablespoon olive oil. Season with ¼ teaspoon crushed red pepper flakes and salt. Split 2 small French breads lengthwise. Brush insides of the bread with 1 tablespoon olive oil and place under broiler for 1 minute or less to toast lightly. Spread onions on top and broil 3 minutes. Top each with 6 chopped black olives and 1 ounce crumbled Gorgonzola. Broil until cheese melts. Serves 2 to 4.

 ## Marinated Salad French Bread Pizza

Toss 8 ounces sliced mozzarella with 8 julienned oil-cured sun-dried tomatoes, 2 cloves minced garlic, ¼ teaspoon crushed red pepper flakes, ½ cup coarsely chopped basil leaves, salt, pepper, and 2½ tablespoons extra-virgin olive oil. Marinate for at least 1 hour. Remove cheese. Split 2 small French breads lengthwise, brush insides of the bread with some liquid from the marinade, and place under broiler for 1 minute or less to toast lightly. Scatter solids from the marinade on the breads and broil for another 3 minutes. Top each with the mozzarella and broil until cheese melts. Serves 2 to 4.

 ## Mini-Pizzas Provençale

Heat 2 cups olive oil with 3 cloves minced garlic and 1 teaspoon *herbes de Provence* until garlic bubbles. Add 1 cup chopped fresh basil leaves. Brush on slices of French bread. Top each slice of bread with 1 slice mozzarella, 1 slice tomato, and a thin coating of additional Provençal oil. Bake for 10 minutes at 450° F. until cheese melts. Blot with paper towel to absorb moisture before serving.

 ## Eggplant Grilled with Basil, Fontina, and Tomato

Brush 1 to 1½ pounds eggplant, cut into 8 slices, with ⅓ cup Italian dressing and allow to sit for 15 minutes. Grill slices over a hot fire or broil for 4 minutes. Flip and top each slice with 1 basil leaf, 1

sun-dried tomato, and ½ ounce Fontina cheese. Grill until cheese melts. Serves 4.

 ## Walnut Garlic Baguette

In a food processor, grind to a paste 2 cloves garlic, 1 cup walnut pieces, and 2 tablespoons olive oil. Slice 1 French bread in diagonal slices, as you would for garlic bread, and spread some nut mixture on each slice. Wrap tightly in foil and bake in preheated 400° F. oven for 20 minutes. Serve warm. Serves 4.

 ## Hot Pepper Oil

Heat 2 cups olive oil with 12 crushed dried chili peppers until peppers begin to bubble at their tips. Rest overnight. Brush onto slices of crusty bread.

 ## Sun-Dried Tomato Oil

Steep 1 cup finely chopped sun-dried tomatoes in 2 cups warm olive oil. Steep overnight before using. Brush on crusty bread and sprinkle ½ teaspoon grated Parmesan over top.

 ## Pine Nut and Garlic Butter

Toast ¼ pound pine nuts in an iron skillet until nuts are golden. In a food processor, finely chop nuts and ½ clove garlic. Add 1 teaspoon extra-virgin olive oil and process until completely smooth. Season with salt and serve as a spread on warm French or Italian bread or on vegetables.

 ## Cashew Date Butter

Process in a pulsing action in a food processor until finely chopped 10 ounces unsalted roasted cashews, a pinch of salt, 2 teaspoons light brown sugar, and 1 tablespoon peanut oil. Process with motor running continuously until smooth, about 3 minutes, scraping sides of the bowl periodically. Mix with ½ cup chopped pitted dates. Use as spread on bread or fruit slices. Serves 6 to 8.

 ## Chocolate Peanut Butter

In a food processor, finely chop 10 ounces unsalted roasted peanuts with a pinch of salt and 1 teaspoon peanut oil. Process until smooth, about 3 minutes, scraping sides of the bowl occasionally. Add 2 ounces melted semisweet chocolate and process to blend. Use as a spread on bread or fruit slices. Serves 6 to 8.

 ## Hot Pepper Peanut Butter

Blend ½ cup peanut butter, 1 tablespoon hot pepper sauce, ½ teaspoon chili powder, ¼ teaspoon ground coriander, ½ clove minced garlic, 2 teaspoons Oriental sesame oil and 1 teaspoon hot pepper oil. Spread on crackers or use as a dip.

 ## Gorgonzola Mousse

Blend 4 ounces crumbled Gorgonzola cheese, 1 tablespoon softened cream cheese, 2 tablespoons light cream, salt, and pepper. Serve surrounded by cherry tomatoes, celery sticks, carrot sticks, spinach leaves, or a selection of fruit.

 ## Smoked Salmon Mousse

Blend 6 ounces softened cream cheese, 2 tablespoons light cream, 2 ounces finely chopped smoked salmon, salt, pepper, and 1 teaspoon chopped fresh dill. Serve surrounded by cherry tomatoes, celery and carrot sticks, and spinach leaves.

 ## Healthful Snack Mix

Mix ½ cup roasted peanuts, ¼ cup toasted sesame seeds, ¼ cup roasted sunflower seeds, ½ cup toasted wheat germ, 1 cup whole almonds, ½ cup golden raisins, and ½ cup dark raisins.

 ## Unhealthful Snack Mix

Mix 1 cup salted peanuts, 1 cup pretzel sticks, 1 cup raisins, and 1 cup semisweet chocolate morsels.

 ## All-Almond Snack Mix

Mix 1 cup *each* whole unsalted almonds, smokehouse almonds, and spiced almonds.

 ## Lemon and Pepper Olives

Heat ½ cup olive oil with 2 cloves minced garlic, 1 teaspoon salt, and 1 teaspoon cracked pepper until garlic bubbles. Pour mixture over 2 cups drained canned black olives mixed with 1 thinly sliced lemon.

 ## Garlic Green Olives and Peppers

Toss 2 cups green olives and their brine, 6 cloves minced garlic, ⅛ teaspoon cayenne pepper, 1 diced roasted red bell pepper (page 442), and 1 tablespoon wine vinegar. Serves 4 to 6.

 ## Curried Black Olives

Cook 2 tablespoons finely chopped onion in ¼ cup olive oil until softened. Add 1 tablespoon curry powder, 1 teaspoon ground coriander, and 1 teaspoon ground cumin and cook 1 minute more. Add 2 tablespoons orange juice and 1 teaspoon cider vinegar and toss with 2 cups black olives. Serves 4 to 6.

 Cherry Fennel Compote

Simmer 1 pound stemmed cherries, ¼ cup sugar, a pinch of salt, the juice of 2 limes, 1 small stick cinnamon, 1 whole clove, ¼ cup kirsch, and ¼ teaspoon ground fennel seed for 5 minutes. Remove from heat and toss in ¼ cup fresh fennel leaves and the finely chopped zest of ½ lemon. Cool and serve as is, with cookies, or over ice cream. Serves 6 to 8.

 Prunes in Brandy

Simmer 1 pound pitted prunes, the juice of 1 lemon and 1 orange, the julienned zest of ½ lemon and ½ orange, 1 stick cinnamon, 2 whole cloves, ½ vanilla bean, 5 tablespoons honey, and ⅓ cup water for 3 minutes. Remove from heat and add ½ cup brandy. Cool and serve as is, with cookies, or over ice cream. Serves 8.

 Spanish Cauliflower

Brown 3 cloves minced garlic in ¼ cup olive oil. Remove from heat and toss with 2 cups blanched small cauliflower florets, 2 tablespoons dry white wine, 1 teaspoon paprika, 1 tablespoon lemon juice, salt, and pepper. Chill in liquid. Serves 4 to 6.

45

Fifty Ways to Tempt with an Apple

There are apples that beg to be baked and others destined for sauce. Some make perfect cake, balancing moisture and crumb with a spark of tartness and a floral scent, while others will swell into a pie, so opulently plump that a naïve cook might be tempted to take the credit. But anyone who knows apples knows that the praise belongs to the fruit, not the baker.

No fruit comes in as many varieties as apples, and no variety tastes, smells, crunches, or cooks exactly like another.

At one time, there were several hundred types of apples sold in American markets, but now the selection is usually fewer than ten. Red Delicious, Golden Delicious, Granny Smith, McIntosh, and Winesap are the easiest to find, with Rome, Stayman, Lady, and Fuji apples occasionally thrown in to break the monotony. But venture out to farm stands or outlying orchards and you are likely to find a cornucopia of apple varieties, ranging from overlooked classics like Gravensteins and Macouns to one-of-a-kind cultivated specialties.

Though specific varieties go hand in hand with certain preparations, like McIntosh for applesauce or Romes for baking whole, the success of most apple preparations is not dependent on varietals. Although a pie recipe written for a Rhode Island Greening apple will not be at its best when made with a delicate floral variety like Golden Delicious, anything tart, such as Granny Smiths, Winesaps, Northern Spies, Pippins, or Gravensteins will give good results.

Unfortunately, the most popular and widely marketed American apple is also the only apple lacking in culinary application. Though its crisp texture and exceptional juiciness make the Red Delicious a satisfying eating apple, its lack of tartness and perfume results in bland watery applesauce, tasteless and shapeless baked apples, and apple pies that are little more than sugar water.

ABOUT THESE RECIPES

Most of the following 50 recipes do not call for specific apples. They were tested with the types commonly available in the local supermarket—

Granny Smiths for pies, cakes, stuffings, and sautés; Romes for baking; McIntosh for applesauce; and Winesaps for an all-purpose substitution.

Unless otherwise stated, all sliced and diced apples should first be peeled, cored, and seeded.

A word of advice before you start: When processing a large number of apples, it is most efficient to do one step at a time. In other words, peel all the fruit, then core it all, then slice it all. While the peeled or cut apples are waiting for the next step, store them in a bucket of cold water spiked with cider vinegar. This will keep the apples from discoloring without adversely affecting their flavor.

Though our recipes provide cross-references to various pastries and toppings, many commercial products are of high enough quality that they would not compromise the finished dish. Feel free to use them.

A reassuring word if you're a novice baker: Pie crusts crack and cake edges crumble. Do not expect picture-perfect results anywhere this side of a picture.

All pies and cakes serve 8 to 10, and all other recipes serve 4, unless otherwise noted.

Some recipes below call for a nut streusel. Use whichever nut the recipe specifies in this recipe:

Nut Streusel. Mix ¼ cup flour with ⅓ cup brown sugar. Cut in 4 tablespoons chilled butter until mixture is the texture of coarse meal. Add 1½ cups chopped nuts.

Apple Walnut Pie

Cook 3 pounds thinly sliced apples in 4 tablespoons butter until softened with 3 tablespoons lemon juice, ⅔ cup sugar, a pinch of ground cloves, a pinch of nutmeg, and 1 teaspoon ground cinnamon. Stir in 2 tablespoons cornstarch dissolved in 2 teaspoons vanilla extract and 2 tablespoons rum and simmer for a few minutes until thickened. Cool. Mound apples into a 9-inch Flaky Pastry Shell (page 435) and top with 1 recipe Nut

Streusel (above) made with walnuts. Bake at 375° F. for 50 minutes. Cool before slicing.

Apple Pear Pie

Follow preceding recipe using underripe pears in place of half the apples.

Ginger Apple Pie

Follow recipe for Apple Walnut Pie (above) using almonds instead of walnuts and ground ginger instead of cinnamon. Add 3 tablespoons chopped candied ginger to apples after they have cooled. Use almonds in the Nut Streusel.

Praline Apple Pie

Follow recipe for Apple Walnut Pie (above). Use light brown sugar instead of granulated and bourbon instead of lemon juice. Use pecans in the Nut Streusel.

Apple Sour Cream Custard Pie

Cook 3 pounds sliced apples in 2 tablespoons butter until soft with ½ cup sugar, 1 teaspoon ground cinnamon, and 1 tablespoon lemon juice. Cool. Drain most of the liquid and mix apples with these custard ingredients: 5 tablespoons flour, ½ cup sugar, ¾ cup sour cream, a pinch of grated nutmeg, 2 teaspoons vanilla extract, ¼ teaspoon salt, and 1 beaten egg. Heap into prebaked Sweet or Flaky Pastry shell (page 435) and top with Nut Streusel (above) made with walnuts. Bake in a preheated 375° F. oven until browned and custard is set, about 1 hour 10 minutes. Cool before slicing.

Apple Butterscotch Custard Pie

Follow preceding recipe, cooking the apples with light brown sugar instead of granulated. Make the custard without sugar and with sweetened condensed milk instead of sour cream.

 ## Old-Fashioned Deep-Dish Apple Pie

Cook 8 sliced apples in 4 tablespoons butter until softened with ¾ cup sugar, ¼ cup brown sugar, 1 tablespoon lemon juice, and 1 tablespoon ground cinnamon. Mix 3 tablespoons cornstarch, 2 teaspoons vanilla, and 2 tablespoons whiskey and stir into the apples. Boil for 1 minute and cool completely. Pour mixture into a 9-inch deep-pie pan lined with Flaky Pastry (page 434) that has been brushed with mixture of 1 egg yolk and 1 tablespoon water. Top with another disk of Flaky Pastry, assembling as you would a two-crust pie. Bake in preheated 400° F. oven for 50 minutes. Cool before slicing.

 ## Apple Raisin Pie

Follow preceding recipe adding 1 cup raisins with the apples.

 ## Old-Fashioned Apple Cheddar Pie

Follow recipe for Old-Fashioned Deep Dish Apple Pie (above), adding 5 ounces coarsely grated Cheddar cheese to the apples after they have cooled.

 ## Tarte Tatin

Lay ¼ pound thinly sliced butter in bottom of 10-inch nonstick overproof skillet. Sprinkle with 1½ cups sugar. Pack 6 sliced large tart apples over sugar and cook over moderate heat until sugar has caramelized and apples are tender. Cool for 10 minutes. Place a 12-inch round of defrosted puff pastry over apples. Bake in 425° F. oven for 10 minutes, then reduce heat to 350° and bake until crust is crisp and brown, about 20 more minutes. Cool for 10 minutes, unmold upside down onto a serving platter, and wait 20 minutes before cutting.

 ## Upside-Down Maple Apple Pie

Follow preceding recipe substituting ½ cup maple syrup and ¼ cup brown sugar for half the sugar. Wait 1 hour after unmolding before cutting.

 ## Dried Apple Pie

Toss together ½ pound dried apples, 2 teaspoons ground cinnamon, and a pinch of ground cloves. Add 2 cups simmering apple cider, 1 cup water, and 2 tablespoons bourbon and set aside until apple slices are soft and plump, about 20 minutes. Mix in ¼ cup cornstarch, 1 cup applesauce, 2 teaspoons lemon juice, 1 cup confectioners' sugar, and ½ teaspoon vanilla extract. Fill a 9-inch pie pan lined with Flaky Pastry (page 434) with the apples, top with more Flaky Pastry, and assemble as you would a two-crust pie. Bake in preheated 400° F. oven for 45 minutes. Cool before slicing.

 ## Smoked Turkey and Apple Tart

Lightly brown ¼ cup chopped onion in 1 tablespoon butter with 8 ounces smoked turkey breast cut in thin strips. Deglaze with 2 tablespoons apple cider and add salt and pepper. Cool. Cover bottom of 9-inch pie pan lined with Flaky Pastry (page 434) with 4 ounces grated Fontina cheese. Make a layer of turkey mixture and top with 2 large, thinly sliced Granny Smith apples arranged in overlapping concentric circles. Bake at 375° F. for 40 minutes. Melt 3 tablespoons honey with 2 tablespoons brown mustard, brush over surface of tart, and bake for 20 minutes more. Cool before serving.

Ham and Apple Tart

Follow preceding recipe substituting baked ham for turkey and adding ½ teaspoon crumbled dried rosemary with the onion.

Apple and Sausage Pot Pie

Brown ¾ pound sliced Italian sausage in 1 teaspoon corn oil with 1 finely chopped onion. Add 1 large diced, unpeeled Granny Smith apple, ½ teaspoon dried thyme, ½ teaspoon crumbled dried rosemary, and 2 teaspoons flour. Cook 2 minutes. Mix in ⅓ cup white wine and ⅓ cup apple cider and simmer until thickened. Toss with 1 cup drained, rinsed sauerkraut. Place in 8-inch casserole, top with disk of Flaky Pastry (page 434) as you would assemble a pot pie, and brush top with mixture of 1 egg yolk and 1 tablespoon water. Bake at 400° F. for 30 minutes.

Apple and Chicken Pot Pie

Follow preceding recipe substituting bite-size chunks of boneless chicken for the sausage and adding ½ teaspoon rubbed sage with the herbs.

Apple Turnovers

Cook 2 large diced apples with ¼ cup sugar until tender. Dissolve 2 teaspoons cornstarch in 1 tablespoon lemon juice and stir into apples, cooking

until mixture thickens. Add 1 teaspoon vanilla extract. Cool and wrap in ½ pound defrosted puff pastry sheet, quartered. Assemble turnovers (page 445) and brush with 1 egg yolk mixed with 1 tablespoon water. Place on a baking sheet and bake in a 400° F. preheated oven for 20 to 25 minutes, until fully puffed and brown. Cool for 10 minutes before serving.

Apple Fennel Turnovers

Follow preceding recipe adding 1 rib finely chopped fennel with apples and 2 tablespoons fennel leaves with the vanilla. Substitute 3 tablespoons orange juice for the lemon juice.

Apple Cheddar Turnovers

Follow the recipe for Apple Turnovers (above) adding 4 ounces shredded sharp Cheddar to the cooled apple mixture. Use ¾ pound pastry, and make 6 turnovers. Serves 6.

Jewish Apple Cake

Toss 6 large, unpeeled, sliced apples with 1 tablespoon ground cinnamon and ⅓ cup sugar. Beat 4 eggs with 1⅔ cups sugar until thick and pale. Slowly add 1 cup peanut oil. Add 2 tablespoons lemon juice, 2 tablespoons orange juice, ¼ cup apple cider, and 2 teaspoons vanilla extract. Beat in 3 cups flour sifted with 1 tablespoon baking powder and ½ teaspoon salt. Spread a third of the batter across bottom of 10-inch greased tube pan. Layer with one third of apples. Repeat layers twice. Bake in preheated 350° F. oven for 1 hour 50 minutes, until tester comes out barely moist. Cool in pan on a rack.

Fifty Ways to Cook Most Everything

 Lemon Apple Cake

Follow preceding recipe using all lemon juice in place of orange-lemon-cider mixture. Add grated zest of 1 lemon with the cinnamon and sugar.

 Apple Walnut Cake

Follow recipe for Jewish Apple Cake (page 385), but toss apples with Nut Streusel (page 383) made with walnuts instead of tossing with cinnamon and sugar.

 Apple Crumb Coffee Cake

Mix 2 cups sifted flour, 2 teaspoons baking powder, 1 teaspoon baking soda, ¾ cup sugar, ¼ cup brown sugar, 1 teaspoon ground cinnamon, and ¼ teaspoon grated nutmeg. Cut in ⅓ pound butter until mixture resembles coarse meal. Toss ½ cup of this mixture and ½ cup chopped walnuts with 2 large diced apples, and reserve. Mix remaining dry ingredients with ⅔ cup buttermilk, 1 beaten extra-large egg, and 1 teaspoon vanilla extract. Turn half this batter into greased, floured 9-inch baking pan, top with half the apple crumb mixture, the remaining batter, and then the remaining apple crumb mixture. Bake at 375° F. for 45 minutes, until tester comes out with a crumb clinging to it. Cool before slicing.

 Apple Swirl Coffee Cake

Follow preceding recipe adding 3 tablespoons cocoa powder and ½ cup chopped raisins with the apples. Bake in 9-inch baking pan, layering 2 additions of crumb mixture between 3 layers of batter.

 Apple Cheddar Corn Bread

Mix ¾ cup flour, 1 tablespoon baking powder, ¼ cup sugar, ½ teaspoon salt, 1¼ cups yellow cornmeal, and ¾ cup shredded sharp Cheddar cheese. Mix in 3 tablespoons finely chopped onions that have been cooked in 2 tablespoons corn oil until softened with 1 large diced apple. Beat in 1 egg and 1 cup milk. Pour into a hot iron skillet greased with 1 tablespoon corn oil and bake at 425° F. for 20 minutes.

 Lemon-Glazed Baked Apples

Simmer together ¼ cup lemon juice, ¼ cup honey, ½ teaspoon ground ginger, and 2 tablespoons sugar until sugar dissolves. Add 6 tablespoons raisins, 1 teaspoon vanilla extract, a pinch of salt, and 1 tablespoon butter, stirring until butter melts. Core 4 Rome apples and remove 1 inch of peel from the top. Fill with the raisins and spoon glaze over top. Bake until soft, about 45 minutes, in preheated 350° F. oven, basting with more glaze every 10 minutes. Cool for 10 minutes.

Bourbon Pecan-Stuffed Baked Apple

Simmer ¼ cup bourbon, 1 tablespoon lemon juice, ¼ cup brown sugar, and a pinch of ground cloves until blended. Add ½ cup toasted pecans, 1 teaspoon vanilla extract, a pinch of salt, and 1 tablespoon butter, stirring until butter melts. Fill 4 cored Rome apples with the pecans and spoon glaze over top. Bake until soft, about 1 hour, in a preheated 400° F. oven, basting with more glaze every 10 minutes. Cool for 10 minutes.

 Wet Walnut Baked Apples

Follow preceding recipe substituting walnuts for pecans and apple juice for bourbon.

Applesauce

Combine 3 pounds coarsely chopped McIntosh apples, ¼ cup sugar, 1 tablespoon lemon juice, and a pinch of salt in heavy saucepan and bring to a boil, stirring frequently. Simmer for 8 to 10 minutes, until apples are tender. Run through a coarse strainer or food mill. Add ½ teaspoon ground cinnamon and sugar to taste, depending on sweetness of the apples.

 Microwave Applesauce

Follow preceding recipe, cooking ingredients in 3-quart bowl covered with plastic wrap at full power for 6 minutes. Carefully pierce plastic and remove. Stir, re-cover, and cook another 3 minutes at full power. Pierce again and uncover.

 Raisin Applesauce

Follow either of preceding two recipes, substituting 1 cup raisins for half the sugar.

 Spiked Applesauce

Follow recipe for Applesauce (above), adding 2 tablespoons bourbon with the apples and 2 tablespoons bourbon after cooking.

 Pear Applesauce

Follow recipe for Applesauce (above), using pears in place of half the apples. Use vanilla extract instead of cinnamon.

 Apple Butter

Simmer 2½ pounds quartered apples in a large heavy covered saucepan with ½ cup cider vinegar and ½ cup apple cider until tender. Push pulp and liquid through a coarse strainer or food mill. Return to pan and add ½ cup sugar, ¾ cup brown sugar, 1½ teaspoons ground cinnamon, a pinch *each* of ground cloves, ground allspice, and ground pepper, ⅛ teaspoon salt, and 2½ tablespoons lemon juice and simmer until very thick, stirring frequently near the end, about 40 minutes. Pack in jars. Makes 1 quart.

 Apple Charlotte

Melt ½ pound butter. Trim crusts from about 15 slices white bread. Line bottom of 6-cup soufflé dish or charlotte mold with whole slices or cut pieces, as needed, and brush with butter. Circle the side of the mold with half-slices placed on end, brushed with butter, and overlapping slightly. Trim bread flush with top of dish. Cook 8 large sliced tart apples in 4 tablespoons butter until softened with 2 tablespoons lemon juice, ¼ cup sugar, and 1 tablespoon vanilla extract. Drain well and fill the lined mold with the drained apple slices. Top with remaining butter-dipped bread slices, cutting pieces as needed, and bake in 375° F. oven for 45 minutes. Cool 1 hour and invert to unmold. Serve warm with a dessert sauce (Chapter 47). Serves 8 to 10.

 Apple Ginger Charlotte

Follow preceding recipe, adding 1½ teaspoons ground ginger with the apples and tossing drained apples with 3 tablespoons chopped candied ginger. Serve with Old-Fashioned Custard Sauce (page 400).

 Ham and Apple Charlotte

Follow recipe for Apple Charlotte (above), substituting this filling: Cook ⅓ cup chopped onion, 2

cloves minced garlic, and 8 large sliced tart apples in 4 tablespoons butter until softened with 2 tablespoons apple cider, 1 teaspoon dried thyme, ½ teaspoon crumbled dried rosemary, ½ teaspoon dried sage, and 2 cups diced baked ham. Drain well and stir in 1 tablespoon mustard. Fill lined mold with drained apple slices. Top with butter-dipped bread as directed and bake in 375° F. oven for 45 minutes. Cool for 1 hour and invert to unmold. Serve warm with 1 cup sour cream or *crème fraîche* mixed with 2 tablespoons Dijon mustard.

 Veal and Apple Torte

In a skillet, brown 2 pounds paper-thin veal scallops in a thin film of oil. Season lightly with salt and pepper and set aside. Cook 1 chopped onion, 2 cloves minced garlic, ½ teaspoon *each* crumbled dried rosemary and oregano, and 4 thinly sliced and peeled apples in 3 tablespoons butter until softened. Butter an 8-inch pan with removable sides and place a layer of veal over bottom. Cover with ¼ pound thinly sliced Fontina cheese and a third of the apple mixture. Repeat the layers twice more, and finish with remaining veal. Top with 8 sprigs fresh herbs and cover with a sheet of buttered parchment and a sheet of foil. Bake on sheet pan at 350° F. for 45 minutes. Rest for 20 minutes, remove sides of pan, and slice with a serrated knife. Serves 8.

 Broccoli and Apple Sauté

Cook the sliced white and light green sections of 2 leeks with 2 cloves minced garlic in 2 tablespoons butter until softened. Add 1 diced tart apple and cook until tender. Blanch 1 bunch broccoli florets in boiling salted water, drain well, and toss with the apples.

 Apple Stuffing

Lightly brown 2 sliced leeks, 1 cup chopped onion, and 2 cloves minced garlic in 4 tablespoons butter. Add 2 ribs finely diced celery, 2 pounds diced apple, 2 teaspoons *each* cider vinegar and sugar, and 1 teaspoon *each* crumbled dried rosemary and thyme. Simmer until apples are tender. Mix in 2 cups dried bread cubes.

 Braised Chicken with Apples

Scatter 1 onion, 1 rib celery, 1 carrot, and 1 apple, all coarsely chopped, in the bottom of roasting pan. Add giblets from a 6-pound roasting chicken and place chicken on top, breast side down. Roast at 400° F. for 30 minutes. Turn breast side up, and roast for 30 minutes more. Meanwhile, bring 3 cups apple cider to a boil with 1 teaspoon *each* dried rosemary (crumbled), thyme, and sage, ¼ cup frozen concentrated apple juice, and 1 teaspoon cider vinegar. Pour over chicken, turn oven down to 350° and cook for another 1 hour 45 minutes, basting with pan juices every 15 minutes. Serve with degreased pan juices. Serves 8.

 Braised Duck with Apples

Follow preceding recipe, substituting two 4-pound ducks, trimmed of their fat, for the chicken. Cook at 450° F. for 20 minutes before adding cider, then at 350° for 45 more minutes. Add 4 cored and quartered apples to pan along with cider and serve them with the duck. Serves 6 to 8.

 Creole Veal Shanks

Brown tops and bottoms of 4 floured 12-ounce veal shanks, which have been secured with string, in 2 tablespoons oil. Remove shanks, add 2 tablespoons butter to pan, and cook 1 diced onion, 2 ribs sliced celery, 2 cloves minced garlic, and 1 large diced apple until softened. Deglaze with ¼ cup bourbon and add ½ cup apple cider, 1 cup beef broth, the minced zest of 1 orange, 1 bay leaf, and 1 teaspoon dried thyme. Return veal shanks to pan and simmer, covered, for 1¼ hours. Meanwhile, sauté 2 sliced cored apples in 1 tablespoon butter until lightly browned. Remove shanks to a platter. Strain and degrease cooking liquid, add ½ cup cream, and pour over meat. Top with the sautéed apples.

Pork Braised with Apples

Follow preceding recipe, substituting a 3- to 4-pound pork roast for the shanks. Increase cooking time by 30 minutes, and omit the cream.

Sautéed Apples in Applejack

Cook 2 tablespoons minced onion in 2 tablespoons butter with a pinch of nutmeg. Add 3 sliced apples and sauté until lightly browned. Deglaze pan with ¼ cup applejack brandy and cook until apples are glazed. Serve with pork roast or poultry.

Sautéed Apple with Bacon and Onions

Cook 3 strips bacon until crisp, crumble, and reserve. Sauté ½ sliced onion in the rendered bacon fat. Add 3 sliced apples, a pinch of sugar, and ½ teaspoon dried thyme. Cook until softened. Deglaze pan with 2 tablespoons bourbon and top

with reserved bacon. Serve with roasted meat and poultry.

Apple Crisp

Toss 3 pounds sliced tart apples with ½ cup light brown sugar, 1 teaspoon ground cinnamon, ¼ teaspoon grated nutmeg, 2 tablespoons brandy, and 3 tablespoons cornstarch and pack into a large shallow buttered baking dish. Top with Nut Streusel (page 383) made with walnuts or almonds. Bake in preheated 350° F. oven for 45 minutes.

Apple Hazelnut Crisp

Follow preceding recipe, but top with Nut Streusel (page 383) made with hazelnuts.

Savory Apple Fritters

Into ½ cup sifted flour, whisk ½ cup milk, a pinch of salt, a pinch of dried thyme, and 1 beaten egg until smooth. Cut 2 cored apples into ½-inch-thick rings. Dredge rings in flour, dip into batter, and fry a few at a time in several inches of 375° F. vegetable oil until golden brown. Drain and serve with baked ham, pork, or poultry.

Sweet Apple Fritters

Follow preceding recipe, substituting ½ teaspoon vanilla extract for the thyme and sprinkling ⅓ cup confectioners' sugar over drained, cooked fritters.

46

Fifty Berried Treasures

Among the crown jewels of fruit, berries are the most radiant. But the real attraction of berries is more than surface-deep. It's in their elusive perfume and sweet-tart flavor, in the interior of the fruit, as firm and soft as flesh, in the honeyed sap that lingers on your fingers, and in the fragrant glaze across your palate that just won't quit.

One of the nicest things about serving beautiful berries is that, often, a cook should do as little as possible. Who could improve on a mound of golden raspberries touched with a few drops of liqueur, or on a single egg-size strawberry cloaked in contrasting skins of white and dark chocolate?

Perfect berries need nothing more than a dip in whipped cream or a pastry shell and a lacquer of glaze to dazzle any diner, but berries lacking in aroma, flavor, or color may need additional assistance. Hide the imperfection of these fruits under a pie crust or deep within a mouthful of muffin. Embellish their lack of sweetness with a balm of honey or intensify their fruit flavor with a jolt of vinegar and a swirl of preserves.

The following 50 recipes include simple elegant sauces for pouring over berries, sauces made from berries, tarts, pies, muffins, pancakes, cobblers, shortcakes, ice creams, mousses, parfaits, soups, preserves, and savory entrées.

ABOUT THESE RECIPES

Recipes that call only for berries are intended for use with whatever kind of berry you wish. Unless otherwise stated, all of the following recipes make 4 portions, except for the pies and tarts, which serve 6 to 8. All call for berries that have been cleaned and stemmed. All of them assume that you will add salt and pepper to taste for savory recipes and a dash of salt in sweet recipes.

Serve these 10 sauces with or over 1½ pints of berries.

 Strawberries in Grand Marnier

Mix 1 teaspoon sugar with 3 tablespoons Grand Marnier.

 Raspberries in Peach Schnapps

Mix 2 teaspoons sugar, 3 tablespoons peach schnapps, and ¼ teaspoon lemon juice.

Berries in Sambuca

Mix 1 teaspoon honey, 1 tablespoon sambuca, and ¼ teaspoon finely grated orange zest.

Strawberries in Microwaved Chocolate Fondue

In a 4-cup glass measure, combine 2 ounces chopped unsweetened chocolate, 6 tablespoons sugar, ¼ cup strong coffee, and ¼ cup milk. Cover and microwave for 5 minutes at full power. Remove the cover, whisk until smooth, and blend in 1 tablespoon of any liqueur. Cool for 5 minutes before serving with berries for dipping.

Strawberries with Caramel Lemon Glaze

In a small, heavy saucepan, cook ½ cup sugar with 2 tablespoons water until mixture turns pale amber at its edges. Immediately whisk in 1½ tablespoons butter and 2 to 3 tablespoons lemon juice. Allow to cool for 10 minutes.

Strawberries with Warm Rhubarb Sauce

Cook 2 pounds trimmed, peeled and thinly sliced rhubarb with ½ cup sugar until softened, about 10 minutes. Stir in 1 cup strawberry preserves. Serve warm, garnished with sour cream, if desired.

Strawberries with Walnut Mascarpone

Process ½ cup walnuts with 1 teaspoon sugar in a food processor until mixture becomes a paste. Scrape the workbowl, add ½ cup mascarpone and 1 tablespoon coffee liqueur, and process until smooth.

Blueberries with Rum and Lemon

Heat 1 tablespoon sugar in ¼ cup rum until dissolved. Add the grated zest and juice of ½ lemon. Cool and spoon over berries or ice cream.

Berries with Lime Crème Anglaise

Whisk 3 tablespoons fresh lime juice into Creme Anglaise (page 433).

Berries in Orange Brandy Crème Anglaise

Whisk 3 tablespoons orange brandy into Crème Anglaise (page 433).

These two berry sauces are spectacular over fruit salad, pound cake, or pancakes.

Strawberry Sauce

Melt 2 tablespoons strawberry preserves over moderate heat. Add 2 tablespoons brandy, a pinch of salt, and 1 pint sliced strawberries and cook until the berries begin to weep. Cool.

Sautéed Berry Syrup

Warm 1½ pints cleaned berries, 2 tablespoons unsalted butter, and 2 tablespoons sugar until the fruit is plump and glossy. Remove from heat and deglaze the pan with 2 tablespoons brandy or dark rum.

Nothing compares to the taste of homemade pastry, so for best results with the pies and tarts in this section, follow the recipes for Flaky Pastry (page 434) or Sweet Pastry (page 434). But if you're in a hurry, store-bought pastry shells or graham-cracker crusts will yield fully satisfactory results.

Deep-Dish Blueberry and Raspberry Pot Pie

Toss together 2 pints blueberries, 1 pint raspberries, ¼ cup cornstarch, 1 cup confectioners' sugar, and 2 tablespoons lemon juice. Pour into a 9-inch deep-dish pie plate and dot with 2 tablespoons butter. Prepare Flaky Pastry (page 434) and assemble as you would a pot pie. Bake 10 minutes in a 400° F. preheated oven. Reduce heat to 375° and bake 40 minutes more, until the top is uniformly brown. Allow to cool for 1 hour and refrigerate for at least another hour. Serve with whipped cream or vanilla ice cream.

 ## Strawberry Meringue Pie

Beat 5 extra-large egg whites with 1 teaspoon Berry Vinegar (page 397) until they barely hold a shape. Add 5 tablespoons sugar, 1 tablespoon at a time, and continue beating, until meringue is stiff, smooth and glossy. Set aside. Pack 3 pints strawberries into a prebaked Flaky Pastry Shell (page 435) in a solid layer. Mound the meringue on top of the berries and smooth into a peak, making sure the meringue overlaps the edge of the pie crust. Bake in a preheated 400° F. oven 7 to 8 minutes to brown the meringue. Cool for 30 minutes before serving, but serve within 1 hour.

 ## Two-Crust Strawberry Pie

Prepare a double recipe of Flaky Pastry (page 434). Toss 4 pints strawberries with 1 tablespoon lemon juice, a pinch of salt, 1¾ cups confectioners' sugar, and ¼ cup cornstarch. Assemble as you would a two-crust pie. Bake in a preheated 425° F. oven for 40 to 45 minutes until pastry is lightly browned and filling is bubbling. Cool on a rack for 30 minutes.

 ## Strawberry Rhubarb Pie

Follow the preceding recipe, replacing half the strawberries with 4 cups rhubarb cut into 1-inch pieces.

 ## Raspberry Nectarine Pie

Follow recipe for Two-Crust Strawberry Pie (above), substituting 1 pint raspberries and 1 quart skinless nectarine slices (use about 6 ripe nectarines) for the strawberries.

 ## Strawberry Phyllo Tartlets

Prepare 8 Phyllo Tartlet Shells (page 445). Coat the bottom of each pastry with Chocolate Glaze (page 433). Dip 2 pints perfect strawberries, 1 at a time, in warm glaze made by melting 1 cup strawberry preserves, simmering it 3 minutes, straining, and mixing in 2 tablespoons orange liqueur. Arrange berries in each shell. Cool for 10 minutes.

 ## Black-Bottom Raspberry Tart

Coat bottom of prebaked Flaky or Sweet Pastry Shell (page 435) with ¼ cup sour cream beaten into 1 cup melted semisweet chocolate morsels. Spread in an even layer. Spread cooled Pastry Cream (page 433) over the chocolate and cover with 1½ pints raspberries in closely packed concentric circles. Brush each berry with a warm glaze made by melting and simmering ½ cup red currant jelly and mixing in 1 tablespoon brandy. Chill to set glaze.

 ## Strawberry Cannoli Tart

Mix 1 cup drained ricotta cheese, 2 tablespoons sugar, 1 teaspoon lemon juice, ¼ cup shelled and chopped pistachio nuts, ¼ cup chopped raisins, and ¼ cup chopped candied lemon peel and spread across the bottom of a Flaky Pastry Shell (page 435). Top with 2 pints halved strawberries, closely packed in concentric circles, cut sides down. Brush the berries with glaze from preceding recipe. Chill to set glaze.

 Blueberry Sour Cream Corn Muffins

Mix 1 cup white cornmeal, ¼ cup flour, 2 tablespoons sugar, 1 teaspoon baking powder, and 1 teaspoon baking soda. Mix into this 1 cup blueberries, 3 tablespoons melted butter, and 1 cup sour cream beaten with 1 extra-large egg yolk. Beat the egg white to a soft peak and fold into the batter. Spoon batter into a liberally greased nonstick muffin tin. Bake in a preheated 400° F. oven for 15 minutes until puffed and browned. Cool on a rack for 3 minutes before removing from pan. Makes 9 muffins.

 Raspberry Banana Muffins

Sift 2 cups flour, ½ teaspoon baking powder, ¾ teaspoon baking soda, and ¼ teaspoon salt. Cream ¼ pound butter with 1 cup sugar until fluffy. Beat in 2 eggs. Puree 3 overripe bananas, ¼ cup sour cream, and 1 teaspoon vanilla extract. Alternately add dry ingredients in 3 additions and banana mixture in 2 additions to the egg mixture. Beat enough to incorporate. Fold in 1 pint cleaned raspberries and ½ cup chopped toasted almonds. Spoon into greased muffin tins and bake in a preheated 350° F. oven for about 25 minutes, until puffed, browned, and springy. Makes about 15 muffins.

 Blueberry Buttermilk Pancakes

Sift 2 cups unbleached flour, 2 teaspoons baking powder, 1 teaspoon baking soda, 2 tablespoons sugar, and a pinch of salt. Combine and beat in 2 cups buttermilk, 2 egg yolks, and 2 tablespoons melted butter until homogeneous. Beat 2 egg whites to soft peaks and fold into the batter along with 1 pint cleaned, dried blueberries. Cook on a griddle.

 Orange Raspberry Pancakes

Follow preceding recipe, adding 2 tablespoons finely grated orange zest to the dry ingredients and substituting raspberries for blueberries.

 Chocolate Raspberry Cobbler

Gently toss 1½ pints raspberries with 2 teaspoons cornstarch and place in an 8-inch baking dish. Cover with Streusel Topping (page 436) mixed with 1 ounce finely chopped semisweet chocolate. Bake in a preheated 450° F. oven for 20 minutes, until top is brown and berries are bubbling. Scatter ½ pint fresh raspberries on each of 4 dessert plates and pour the hot cobbler over top.

 Strawberry Lime Cobbler

In an 8- to 9-inch baking pan, moisten 2 teaspoons cornstarch with the juice and finely grated zest of 1 large lime. Toss 2 pints halved strawberries in this mixture. Top with Streusel (page 436) mixed with ¾ cup small hazelnut pieces. Bake in a preheated 450° F. oven for 20 minutes, until top is brown and berries are bubbling. Serve warm.

 Blueberry Shortcake Cobbler

Toss 2 pints blueberries with 1 cup confectioners' sugar, a pinch of salt, 2 teaspoons lime zest, and 3 tablespoons cornstarch, in an 8-inch baking dish. Cover top with Shortcake Biscuits (page 435) and bake at 350° F. for 45 minutes until biscuits are puffed and brown and berries are bubbling. Serve warm over ice cream or with whipped cream or yogurt.

Fifty Ways to Cook Most Everything

 Gingered Berry Cobbler

Toss 3 pints assorted cleaned and stemmed berries with 1 tablespoon candied ginger in a large baking dish. Top with Streusel Topping (page 436) mixed with 1 tablespoon candied ginger and ¾ cup finely chopped pecans. Bake in preheated 450° F. oven for 20 minutes, until top is brown and berries are bubbling. Serve hot or warm with ice cream, whipped cream, or yogurt.

 Peach Blackberry Crunch

Slice 2 pounds peeled, pitted peaches each into 8 wedges. Toss in a large rectangular baking dish with 1 pint blackberries, ⅓ cup sugar, 1 tablespoon raspberry vinegar, and 1 teaspoon vanilla extract. Cover with Streusel Topping (page 436) mixed with ¾ cup finely chopped almonds, ½ teaspoon ground cinnamon, 1 teaspoon vanilla extract, and ½ teaspoon almond extract. Bake in a preheated 400° F. oven for 30 minutes.

 Easy Tangy Strawberry Ice Cream

Scald 1 cup light cream, 2 cups milk, and 1 cup sugar and stir in ¼ cup cornstarch dissolved in ¼ cup lemon or lime juice. Cook another few minutes, stirring constantly, until the cream thickens. Cool to room temperature. Blend in 2 pints pureed strawberries and 1 pint sour cream. Freeze in an ice cream freezer according to manufacturer's directions. Makes ½ gallon.

 Raspberry Lemon Laban

Pour 3 cups lemon yogurt mixed with 3 cups vanilla yogurt into a cheesecloth-lined strainer. Tie the ends of the cheesecloth together over the top of the yogurt. Weight with a small plate on top and rest over a large bowl. Refrigerate at least 6 hours to drain. Unwrap and fold in 1 pint fresh raspberries.

 Strawberry Shortcake with Whipped Crème Fraîche

Prepare Shortcake (page 435). Whip 10 ounces *crème fraîche* with 3 tablespoons confectioners' sugar to a soft peak. Fold in 1 cup heavy cream, whipped to a firm peak and spread half on the bottom half of the split shortcake. Top with 1 pint cleaned, stemmed, and sliced strawberries. Top with the top section of shortcake, cover with remaining whipped topping, and decorate with 1 pint stemmed, whole perfect strawberries. Serves 8.

 Raspberry Shortcake with Lemon Whipped Cream

Prepare Shortcake (page 435). Fold 2 cups whipped cream into 2 cups prepared lemon pudding or Lemon Curd (page 434) and gently spread half the mixture over the bottom half of the shortcake. Top with 1 pint cleaned fresh raspberries and top half of cake. Top with remaining lemon cream and decorate with another 1 pint raspberries. Makes 8 servings.

 Warm Rhubarb and Strawberry Shortcake

Prepare Shortcake (page 435), but do not split. In a large heavy saucepan, cook 2 pounds thinly sliced rhubarb over moderate heat for 3 minutes. Add 1¼ cups strawberry preserves and ½ cup fresh orange juice and cook 5 minutes more. Cut shortcake into 8 wedges, place 1 wedge on each of 8 plates, top each with ¼ cup sliced strawberries and ½ cup warm rhubarb mixture. Finish with whipped cream or a scoop of vanilla ice cream. Makes 8 servings.

Triple-Dipped Strawberries

Dip 8 large perfect strawberries in 2½ ounces warm melted white chocolate, covering all but a ring at the top of each berry. Let excess run off and place coated berry on a sheet pan lined with wax paper. Refrigerate until chocolate is firm, about 10 minutes. Grasp cooled berries by their stems, and dip into 3 ounces warm, melted semisweet chocolate, leaving a ring of white chocolate exposed near the top. Return berries to the paper and refrigerate to firm the chocolate. Stir 2 tablespoons heavy cream into remaining melted chocolate while chocolate is warm, adding another if the chocolate binds up. When berries have cooled, dip the tips into the milk chocolate. Return berries to the paper and refrigerate to firm chocolate.

 Peaches Stuffed with Minted Blueberries

Cook 1 pint blueberries, 1 tablespoon sugar, and 1 tablespoon chopped mint leaves for 1 minute. Chill. Slice off tops of 4 large freestone peaches and reserve for "lids." Hollow out peaches with a melon baller and cut a thin slice from the bottoms so they sit upright. Rub cut surfaces with lemon juice. Fill the hollowed-out peaches with berries, place the "lids" on top, put peaches on a plate, surround with remaining berries, and crown each with a mint sprig.

 Easy Peach Melba

Toss 4 peach halves in 1 tablespoon sugar, ½ teaspoon vanilla extract, and 2 teaspoons brandy and set aside for 10 minutes. Mash ½ pint raspberries, 1 teaspoon honey, and 1 tablespoon framboise until saucy. Serve the peach halves next to scoops of vanilla ice cream, glazed with some of the marinating liquid. Spoon the raspberry sauce in a wide band overlapping the peach half and the ice cream.

  Low-Fat Peach Melba

Follow preceding recipe, but substitute Raspberry Lemon Laban (opposite) for the ice cream.

 Peach and Blackberry Parfait

Mix 3 large skinned, pitted, and chopped peaches with 2 teaspoons brown sugar, 2 teaspoons maple syrup, and ¼ teaspoon vanilla extract. Reserve 4 perfect berries from 1 pint blackberries and toss those remaining with 1 tablespoon honey and 1 teaspoon lemon juice. Form alternating layers of peaches and blackberries in 4 parfait glasses and top with 1 cup yogurt or sour cream, mixed with 1 tablespoon honey and ½ teaspoon vanilla extract. Decorate with reserved berries.

Blackberry Raspberry Parfait

Mix 2 pints raspberries, 2 teaspoons sugar, 2 teaspoons maple syrup, and ¼ teaspoon orange extract. Reserve 4 perfect berries from 1 pint blackberries and toss those remaining with 1 tablespoon honey and 1 teaspoon lemon juice. Form alternating layers of raspberries and blackberries in 4 parfait glasses, and top with 1 cup yogurt or sour cream mixed with 1 tablespoon honey and ½ teaspoon vanilla extract. Decorate with reserved berries.

 Easy Blueberry Borscht

Boil 1 cup dry red wine for 1 minute. Add 1 pint blueberries, ¼ cup sugar, and a pinch of salt. Return to a boil, remove from heat, and add 2 tablespoons lemon juice, 1 cup ice water, and 1 cup orange juice. Chill. Serve dolloped with sour cream, if desired.

Cranberry Borscht

Boil 1 cup dry red wine for 1 minute. Add 1 pint cranberries, ½ cup sugar, and a pinch of salt. Return to a boil, remove from heat, and add 2 tablespoons lemon juice, 1 cup ice water, and 1 cup orange juice. Chill. Serve dolloped with sour cream, if desired, and garnish with finely grated orange zest.

 ### Raspberry Grand Marnier Soup

Boil ½ cup sugar and 1 cup water. In a blender, purée with 1 pound defrosted unsweetened frozen raspberries, ¼ cup Grand Marnier, and a pinch of salt. Chill. Just before serving, mix 1 pint fresh raspberries into the soup and serve in chilled bowls.

 ### Strawberry Wine Soup

In a food processor, finely chop 2 pints strawberries with ¼ cup confectioners' sugar. Add ½ cup white wine, 1 cup buttermilk, and a pinch of salt. Blend briefly and chill. Serve in chilled bowls, each garnished with 1 sliced strawberry.

 ### Poached Fish with Raspberry Beurre Blanc

Poach 4 skinned fillets of flat fish or salmon in 2 cups Court Bouillon (page 430). Keep warm and discard half the pan liquid. Reduce remaining liquid to ½ cup. Add 2 tablespoons raspberry vinegar and 1 tablespoon minced shallot. Reduce to ⅓ cup, remove from heat, and swirl in 4 tablespoons butter and ½ pint raspberries. Pour over fish.

 ### Game Hens Braised with Blueberries

Brown 2 split game hens with backbone removed in 2 tablespoons *each* walnut oil and butter. Add 1 finely diced small onion, cook until softened, and add ½ cup white wine, ¾ cup chicken stock, and 3 tablespoons blueberry vinegar. Bring to a simmer, scraping floor of the pan, and cook for 20 minutes, turning the hens once or twice. Remove to a warm platter. Reduce pan liquid by half, and add 1 tablespoon black currant jelly and 1 pint blueberries. Simmer for 1 minute more. Pour finished sauce over the hens.

 ### Hens Braised with Cranberries

Brown 2 split game hens with backbone removed in 2 tablespoons *each* walnut oil and butter. Add 1 finely diced small onion, 1 clove minced garlic, and 2 teaspoons dried tarragon and cook until onion softens. Add ½ cup white wine, ¾ cup chicken stock, and 3 tablespoons raspberry vinegar. Bring to a simmer, scraping floor of the pan, and cook for 20 minutes, turning the hens once or twice. Remove to a warm platter. Reduce pan liquid by half and add 1½ cups whole cranberry sauce. Simmer for 1 minute more. Pour finished sauce over the hens.

 ### Strawberry Lime Preserves

In a 3-quart microwave-safe bowl, toss together 4 cups strawberries, 1½ cups sugar, and the finely grated zest of 2 limes. Set aside for 10 minutes. Cover with double thickness of microwave-safe plastic wrap and microwave at full power for 9 minutes. Uncover and stir, being sure to stir up any sugar that has collected at the bottom of the bowl. Return to the microwave, uncovered, and cook for another 20 minutes. Stir in juice of 1 large lime. Makes 1 pint.

Strawberry Top Topping

Rinse 4 cups strawberry trimmings (tops, hulls, rejected berries) and drain thoroughly. Combine in a large saucepan with 1 cup sugar, ½ cup water, and the juice of 1 lemon. Bring to a boil and skim off any dark residue that rises to the surface. Simmer for 5 minutes, strain out the solids, and return liq-uid to the pot. Simmer another 5 minutes, skimming frequently. Chill. Serve over ice cream, plain cakes, fruit, cheesecake, custard, or pancakes. Yields 1½ cups.

Berry Vinegar

Heat 1 pint blueberries, raspberries, or blackberries in 1 cup wine vinegar. Bring to a boil, remove from the heat, and allow to steep for 1 hour. Strain and store in tightly closed jar.

Fifty Dessert Sauces for Better Mental Health

When we rule the world, every city and town will have a Mental Health Food Store. It will be packed with hot fudge instead of ginseng tea and soft ice cream where the wheat germ used to be. For it's our unalterable belief that if you can't occasionally indulge in a few empty calories then there's far too little happiness in staying fit.

With that in mind, we propose the following: One thing gooey, once a week, for everyone. And to get you through the first year of our regime, here are 50 dessert sauces. All are fast, easy, and just the thing to top a scoop of ice cream, gild a fruit salad, or crown a humble slice of cake as you eat your way to better mental health.

ABOUT THESE RECIPES

All of these recipes yield enough sauce to top 4 to 6 servings of dessert.

 ### Quick Dark Chocolate Sauce

Combine ¾ cup sifted cocoa, ⅔ cup sugar, and a pinch of salt in a heavy saucepan. Slowly whisk in 1 cup cold water until smooth. Simmer 2 minutes, stirring frequently. Stir in 1 tablespoon unsalted butter and simmer 2 minutes more. Cool.

 ### Hot Fudge Sauce

Heat ½ cup heavy cream with 2 tablespoons butter until butter melts. Add ⅓ cup granulated sugar and ⅓ cup dark brown sugar, stirring until dissolved. Whisk in a pinch of salt and ½ cup sifted Dutch-process cocoa. Stir until smooth. Serve warm or reheat.

 ### Milk Chocolate Sauce

Combine ⅔ cup sifted cocoa and ¾ cup sugar in heavy saucepan. Slowly whisk in 1 cup milk until smooth. Bring to a simmer, stirring frequently. Add ¼ cup heavy cream and simmer for 3 minutes. Add 2 tablespoons butter and simmer another 3 minutes. Add 1 teaspoon vanilla extract. Cool.

Peanut Butter Chocolate Sauce

Follow preceding recipe, substituting ¼ cup creamy peanut butter for the butter.

Mocha Sauce

Combine ⅔ cup sifted cocoa and ¾ cup sugar in a heavy saucepan. Slowly whisk in 1 cup milk until smooth. Bring to a simmer, stirring frequently. Add ¼ cup heavy cream and simmer for 3 minutes. Add 2 tablespoons butter and simmer for 3 minutes more. Add 1 tablespoon instant coffee powder and 1 teaspoon vanilla extract. Cool.

White Chocolate Sauce

In a heavy enamel saucepan, scald ¼ cup heavy cream with ¼ cup milk. Remove from heat and whisk in 5 ounces finely chopped white chocolate. Serve warm.

Milk Chocolate Sauce with Almonds

In the top of a double boiler over simmering water, melt 8 ounces milk chocolate candy bar with almonds until soft. Whisk in ¼ cup boiling water until smooth. Serve warm.

Bitter Chocolate Sauce

Combine ¾ cup sifted cocoa, ½ cup sugar, and a pinch of salt in a heavy saucepan. Slowly whisk in ¾ cup cold water until smooth. Simmer for 2 minutes, stirring frequently. Stir in 1 teaspoon instant coffee powder and 1 tablespoon unsalted butter. Simmer 2 minutes more. Cool.

Peppered Chocolate Sauce

In a heavy saucepan, combine ¾ cup sifted cocoa, ½ cup sugar, ¼ teaspoon black pepper, ½ teaspoon ground cinnamon, ¼ teaspoon ground ginger, a pinch of ground cloves, and a pinch of salt. Slowly whisk in ¾ cup cold water until smooth. Simmer for 2 minutes, stirring frequently. Stir in 1 tablespoon unsalted butter. Simmer 2 minutes more. Cool.

Chocolate Rum Sauce

Combine ¾ cup sifted cocoa, ¾ cup light brown sugar, and a pinch of salt in a heavy saucepan. Slowly whisk in ⅔ cup cold water until smooth. Simmer for 2 minutes, stirring frequently. Stir in 2 tablespoons dark rum and 1 tablespoon butter. Simmer 2 minutes more. Cool.

Orange Chocolate Sauce

In a heavy saucepan, combine ¾ cup sifted cocoa, ⅔ cup sugar, and a pinch of salt. Slowly whisk in ⅔ cup cold water until smooth. Simmer for 2 minutes, stirring frequently. Stir in 1 tablespoon orange marmalade, 1 tablespoon orange liqueur, and 1 tablespoon unsalted butter. Simmer 2 minutes more. Cool.

Black Forest Chocolate Sauce

Combine ¾ cup sifted cocoa, ⅔ cup sugar, and a pinch of salt in a heavy saucepan. Slowly whisk in ⅔ cup cold water until smooth. Simmer 2 minutes, stirring frequently. Stir in 2 tablespoons sour cherry preserves, 1 tablespoon kirsch, and 1 tablespoon unsalted butter. Simmer 2 minutes more. Cool.

Fifty Ways to Cook Most Everything

 Chocolate Raspberry Sauce

Combine ¾ cup sifted cocoa, ⅔ cup sugar, and a pinch of salt in a heavy saucepan. Slowly whisk in ⅔ cup cold water until smooth. Simmer for 2 minutes, stirring frequently. Stir in 2 tablespoons seedless raspberry fruit spread, 1 tablespoon crème de cassis or framboise, and 1 tablespoon unsalted butter. Simmer 2 minutes more. Cool.

 Chocolate Mint Sauce

Combine ⅔ cup sifted cocoa and ¾ cup sugar in a heavy saucepan. Slowly whisk in 1 cup milk until smooth. Bring to a simmer, stirring frequently. Add ¼ cup heavy cream and simmer for 3 minutes. Add 2 tablespoons butter and simmer for another 3 minutes. Add 1 teaspoon vanilla extract and a few drops peppermint extract. Cool.

 Chocolate Banana Sauce

Combine ⅔ cup sifted cocoa and ¾ cup sugar in a heavy saucepan. Slowly whisk in 1 cup milk until smooth. Bring to a simmer, stirring frequently. Add ¼ cup heavy cream and simmer for 3 minutes. Add 2 tablespoons butter and simmer for 3 minutes more. In a food processor, purée 2 ripe bananas and add to sauce with 1 teaspoon vanilla extract. Stir and let cool.

 Praline Chocolate Caramel Sauce

Combine ½ cup sifted cocoa, ¾ cup light brown sugar, and a pinch of salt in a heavy saucepan. Slowly whisk in ⅔ cup cold milk until smooth. Bring to a simmer, stirring frequently. Simmer for 2 minutes. Stir in ¼ cup finely chopped toasted almonds, ½ teaspoon almond extract, and 2 table-

spoons unsalted butter. Simmer for 2 minutes more. Cool.

 Raspberry White Chocolate Sauce

In a heavy enamel saucepan, scald ¼ cup heavy cream with ¼ cup milk. Remove from heat and whisk in 5 ounces finely chopped white chocolate. Stir in ½ cup fresh or frozen raspberries. Cool.

 Old-Fashioned Custard Sauce

In a heavy saucepan, scald 2 cups milk with ¼ cup sugar. Meanwhile, in the top of a double boiler, beat 5 egg yolks, ¼ cup sugar, and a pinch of salt until thick and pale. Slowly whisk the hot milk into the yolks and sugar. Place over simmering water and stir with a wooden spoon until the custard coats the spoon lightly. Immediately pour into a container and stir in 1 teaspoon vanilla extract. Serve cool or warm.

 Coffee Custard Sauce

Follow preceding recipe, stirring 1 tablespoon instant coffee powder into the sauce with the vanilla extract.

 Chocolate Custard Sauce

Follow recipe for Old-Fashioned Custard Sauce (above), whisking in 5 ounces finely chopped semisweet chocolate just before the vanilla extract.

 Maple Custard Sauce

In a heavy saucepan, scald 2 cups milk with ⅓ cup maple syrup. Meanwhile, in the top of a double boiler, beat 5 egg yolks, ¼ cup sugar, and a pinch of salt until thick and pale. Slowly whisk the hot milk into the yolks and sugar. Place over simmering water and stir with a wooden spoon until the custard coats the spoon lightly. Immediately pour into a container and stir in 1 teaspoon vanilla extract. Serve cool or warm.

 ### Praline Custard Sauce

In a heavy saucepan, scald 2 cups milk with ¼ cup brown sugar. Meanwhile, in the top of a double boiler, beat 5 egg yolks, ¼ cup sugar, and a pinch of salt until thick and pale. Slowly whisk the hot milk into the yolks and sugar. Place over simmering water, and stir with a wooden spoon until the custard coats the spoon lightly. Immediately pour into a container and stir in ½ teaspoon vanilla extract, ¼ teaspoon almond extract, and ½ cup chopped toasted almonds. Serve cool or warm.

 ### Super-Rich Custard Sauce

In a heavy saucepan, scald 1 cup light cream, 1 cup milk, and ¼ cup sugar. Meanwhile, in the top of a double boiler, beat 6 egg yolks, ¼ cup sugar, and a pinch of salt until thick and pale. Slowly whisk the hot milk into the yolks and sugar. Place over simmering water and stir with a wooden spoon until the custard coats the spoon lightly. Immediately pour into a container and stir in 1 teaspoon vanilla extract. Serve cool or warm.

 ### Orange Custard Sauce

Follow preceding recipe, adding 2 tablespoons finely grated orange zest and 2 tablespoons orange-flavored liqueur to the sauce as it cools.

 ### Creamy Caramel Sauce

In a heavy saucepan, mix 1 cup light cream and 1 cup firmly packed brown sugar. Bring to a boil and

simmer for 2 minutes. Add 2 tablespoons butter, mix, and simmer for 2 minutes more. Serve warm or cool.

 ### Sour Cherry Coulis

In a heavy saucepan, combine 1 pint pitted sour cherries with 2 cups sugar and cook until the sugar dissolves and cherries release their juices. Add a pinch of salt and strain.

 ### Fresh Strawberry Sauce

Slice 1 pint hulled strawberries. Toss with ¼ cup sugar until sugar dissolves. Stir in 2 to 3 tablespoons fruit liqueur. Refrigerate.

 ### Fresh Raspberry Sauce

Slice 1 pint hulled strawberries. Toss with 1 pint washed raspberries and ¼ cup sugar until sugar dissolves. Stir in 2 tablespoons framboise and 1 teaspoon lemon juice. Refrigerate.

 ### Ginger Peach Sauce

Toss 2 cups diced, peeled, and pitted peaches with 2 tablespoons finely minced candied ginger and ¼ cup sugar until sugar dissolves and peaches start to release their juices. Stir in ½ cup Madeira or sherry. Refrigerate.

 ### Brandied Peaches

Dice 4 pitted, peeled peaches and toss with ¼ cup brown sugar until sugar dissolves and the peaches start to release their juices. Stir in ½ cup brandy. Refrigerate.

Warm Stir-Fried Grapes

In a saucepan, warm 3 cups red and green seedless grapes, 1 tablespoon butter, and 2 teaspoons sugar until grapes become shiny. Remove grapes and deglaze pan with 3 tablespoons sweet white wine and 1 teaspoon lemon juice. Season with a pinch of salt. Serve grapes and liquid immediately.

 ### Raspberries and Cream

Place 1 pint fresh or frozen raspberries and 2 tablespoons sugar in a bowl and mash with a fork. Mix in ¼ cup fruit liqueur. Refrigerate. Immediately before serving, stir in ¼ cup heavy cream.

 ### Blueberry Orange Sauce

In a heavy saucepan, bring 3 tablespoons sweet orange marmalade, 1 tablespoon honey, and ⅓ cup orange juice to a boil. Add 1 pint cleaned blueberries and cook until berries lose their silvery appearance and turn dark blue. Serve cool or warm.

 ### Warm Pear Puree

In a saucepan, bring 1 cup white wine, 1 cup water, and 2 tablespoons sugar to a boil. Add 1½ pounds peeled, seeded, and quartered pears and poach for about 7 minutes, until the pears are tender. Remove pears and set aside. Reduce pan liquid to 2 tablespoons. Puree pears with the reduced liquid and 2 tablespoons butter. Serve warm.

 ### Sautéed Fruit Salad

In a pan, warm 3 cups chopped fruit (cherries, berries, peaches, plums, bananas), 1 tablespoon butter, and 2 teaspoons sugar until fruit becomes shiny and starts to release its liquid. Remove fruit from pan and deglaze pan with 2 tablespoons fruit liqueur and ½ teaspoon vanilla extract. Serve immediately.

 ### Mango Coulis with Lime

Puree flesh of 2 large mangoes with the juice of 1½ limes and 2 teaspoons honey. Chill.

 ### Berry Concassé

Mix 2 cups coarsely chopped berries of any variety with ¼ cup sugar, ½ teaspoon vanilla extract, and 1 tablespoon lemon juice.

 ### Figs Preserved in Port

Remove stems from 5 ounces dried figs. Cover with boiling water and soak for 20 minutes until plumped. Drain and pack in a jar large enough to fit the figs with just 1 inch headroom. Fill jar with Port wine, cover, and allow to rest for at least 1 week before serving. Keeps indefinitely.

 ### Melba Sauce

In a blender or food processor, puree 1 pint fresh or frozen raspberries. Strain. Melt ¼ cup currant jelly and stir into raspberry puree. Chill.

 ### Suzette Sauce

In a saucepan, simmer the finely julienned zest and juice of 1 orange, the juice of ½ lemon, and 3 tablespoons sugar for 10 minutes. Stir in 1 tablespoon butter and 2 tablespoons *each* kirsch, rum, brandy, and orange liqueur. Serve warm.

Maple Whipped Cream

Whip 1 cup chilled heavy cream in chilled bowl using chilled beaters just until cream holds a shape. Add 1 tablespoon confectioners' sugar and 3 tablespoons maple syrup. Beat to a soft peak. Serve chilled.

 ## Chocolate Chip Whipped Cream

Whip 1 cup chilled heavy cream in chilled bowl using chilled beaters just until cream holds a shape. Add 1 tablespoon confectioners' sugar and 1 teaspoon vanilla extract. Beat to a soft peak and fold in ½ cup semisweet chocolate morsels. Serve chilled.

 ## Peanut Butter Cream

Heat ½ cup light cream with ¼ cup brown sugar until sugar dissolves. Whisk ½ cup peanut butter into cream until smooth. Add ½ teaspoon vanilla extract. Serve warm or chilled.

 ## Candied Ginger Cream

In a chilled bowl, whip 1 cup chilled heavy cream with 2 tablespoons confectioners' sugar, ½ teaspoon vanilla extract, and 1 tablespoon orange liqueur until very firm. Fold in 3 tablespoons finely chopped candied ginger. Serve chilled.

 ## Honey Walnut Sauce

In heavy saucepan, melt 3 tablespoons butter. Add 2 teaspoons cornstarch and stir to dissolve. Add ⅔ cup honey and bring to a boil. Add 1 cup walnut pieces and simmer for 2 minutes. Serve warm or cold.

 ## Honey Bourbon Sauce

Mix together equal parts bourbon and honey. Serve over coffee ice cream.

 ## Margarita Sauce

In small bowl, whisk 2 teaspoons frozen orange-juice concentrate with ½ cup tequila until dissolved. Add the juice of 2 limes and 2 tablespoons sugar. Mix to dissolve sugar and add ½ teaspoon salt. Serve chilled.

 ## Butter Rum Raisin

In a heavy saucepan, combine ½ cup sugar with 1 tablespoon cornstarch. Add 1 cup hot water and stir to dissolve. Add ¾ cup raisins and heat until sauce clears and thickens. Remove from heat, and stir in 2 tablespoons softened butter, 2 tablespoons heavy cream, 1 teaspoon vanilla extract, and 2 tablespoons dark rum. Serve warm or chilled.

 ## Wet Bourbon Pecans

In a heavy saucepan, melt 3 tablespoons butter. Add 2 teaspoons cornstarch and stir to dissolve. Add ⅓ cup dark corn syrup and ⅓ cup bourbon and bring to a boil. Add 1 cup pecan pieces and simmer for 3 minutes. Serve warm or cold.

 ## Orange, Scotch, and Espresso Sauce

In a jar, combine the juice and finely grated zest of 1 large orange, 1 tablespoon sugar, 1 teaspoon instant espresso powder, and ¼ cup Scotch whiskey. Cover and shake well. Serve over ice cream.

Fifty Ways to Charm with Chocolate

To a true chocoholic, chocolate is a food set apart, a food to which the usual rules do not apply. An overabundance of sugar is cloying and an overabundance of cayenne is painful, but too much chocolate? That's an oxymoron.

With that in mind, we've devoted a chapter to 50 chocolate opulences, none of which is restrained or restricted by diet, budget, or rational thought. These recipes range from homey puddings to elaborate tortes, and though some are impressive enough to serve on the most elegant occasions, not one is complicated or time-consuming to prepare.

So, if you swoon for chocolate chocolate cakes or chocolate chocolate-chip anything, loosen your belt a notch and try some of these desserts.

ABOUT THESE RECIPES

Most of these recipes call for either semisweet or unsweetened chocolate. Substitutions of one for the other are not recommended. Not only will it throw off the balance of sugar in the recipe, but it can also destroy the product's texture. Bitter chocolate not only has less sugar, but more chocolate per ounce than sweeter varieties. Using it in place of sweeter chocolate can make a mousse implode or a cake come out like a chocolate flapjack.

Many cooks are a little scared of working with chocolate. Chocolate is an emulsion of water in fat, and like all emulsions it is easily broken. A slight amount of moisture in melted chocolate will ruin its smoothness, causing the mixture to bind up like so much concrete. Ironically, you can relax the mess by adding a bit more warm liquid (up to 1 tablespoon per ounce of chocolate) or a bit more fat.

Melted chocolate will also seize if it gets cold. This makes sense when you realize that chocolate has a high proportion of fat and fat becomes firmer the colder it gets. If this should happen, warm the chocolate slightly and it will immediately relax.

To melt chocolate, chop it finely and place it in the top of a double boiler over barely simmering water. Stir until half melted, then remove from heat and stir until it's melted completely.

Chocolate can also be melted in a microwave oven in a bowl. Heat up to a few ounces at full power for 1 to 2 minutes. Remove and stir until melted.

Do not melt chocolate directly over a flame unless it is protected by the addition of butter or a liquid. Alone it will scorch easily.

The following recipes are written for 4 portions unless otherwise noted. All use lightly salted butter unless otherwise noted. Skip the mousse recipes if you're concerned about the safety of raw egg yolks.

Best-Ever Chocolate Pudding

In a saucepan, combine 2 ounces *each* chopped unsweetened chocolate and semisweet chocolate, ¼ cup sugar, and 2 cups milk. Bring to a gentle boil. In a bowl, mix ⅓ cup sugar, a pinch of salt, 2 tablespoons cornstarch, and 2 tablespoons cocoa powder and beat in 4 egg yolks until smooth. Whisk in 1 cup of the hot milk, then beat back into the saucepan. Bring to a boil while stirring and scraping side of the pan. If lumps form before it boils, remove from heat, whisk briskly to remove the lumps, and return to the heat. Whisk in 2 tablespoons unsalted butter and 1 teaspoon vanilla extract. Pour into 4 dessert dishes. Cover with plastic and chill. Serve with whipped cream, if desired.

Chocolate Walnut Pudding

Follow preceding recipe. Before serving, top each serving with 2 tablespoons coarsely chopped walnuts.

Chocolate Chocolate-Chip Pudding

Freeze 1 cup semisweet chocolate chips on a sheet pan. Follow recipe for Best-Ever Chocolate Pudding (above). Let cool for 10 minutes, stir in frozen chocolate chips, and pour pudding into 6 dessert dishes. Serves 6.

White Chocolate Amaretto Pudding

In a saucepan bring ¼ cup sugar and 2 cups milk to a gentle boil. In a bowl, mix ¼ cup sugar, a pinch of salt, and 3 tablespoons cornstarch and beat in 4 egg yolks and ½ teaspoon almond extract until mixture is smooth. Whisk in 1 cup of the hot milk, then beat back into saucepan. Bring to a boil while stirring and scraping side of the pan. If lumps form before it boils, remove from heat, whisk briskly to smooth, and return to heat. Whisk in 6 ounces finely chopped white chocolate, 2 tablespoons Amaretto liqueur, and 1 teaspoon vanilla extract. Pour into 4 dessert dishes. Cover with plastic and chill.

Chocolate Mousse

Melt 3 ounces chopped semisweet chocolate. Remove from heat and beat in 3 egg yolks and 2 tablespoons dark rum. The chocolate will first bind up but will then become smooth again. Beat 2 egg whites to a soft peak and fold into the chocolate in 2 additions. Beat ¼ cup heavy cream to a soft peak and fold in. Pour into 4 wine glasses, cover with plastic wrap, and chill. Top with whipped cream, if desired.

Chocolate Mousse with Chocolate Dumplings

Melt 2 ounces sweet chocolate and heat in a double boiler with ½ cup heavy cream for 10 minutes. Pour into a bowl set over ice until firm, stirring frequently. Prepare preceding recipe. Make ½-teaspoon-size dumplings of the chocolate mixture and layer 5 or 6 of them with the mousse in each dessert dish. Cover and chill.

Spiked Chocolate Mousse

Separate 3 eggs and beat the yolks into 4 ounces melted semisweet chocolate. Thin with 1 to 2 tablespoons of any liquor. Beat whites to a soft peak and fold into the chocolate. Pour into 4 dessert dishes. Chill and top with whipped cream, if desired.

 Honey Brandy White Chocolate Mousse

In a small saucepan, heat 3 tablespoons honey and 1½ tablespoons brandy until honey melts and mixture is heated through. Remove from heat and whisk in 5 ounces finely chopped white chocolate. Cool and fold in 2 cups unsweetened whipped cream. Spoon into dessert dishes and chill.

 Fruit in Chocolate Cups

Heat 4 ounces semisweet chocolate chips until half melted. Stir until smooth. Cool for 5 minutes. Set 4 cupcake papers in a muffin tin. Spoon several tablespoons chocolate into each cup. Using the back of a spoon or a small spatula, spread chocolate up sides of each cup, making an even layer without holes or thin spots. Refrigerate at least 30 minutes until chocolate hardens. Peel paper from the backs of the chocolate cups and refrigerate until ready to serve. Fill each cup with ⅓ cup fresh berries or chopped fruit and top with 1 tablespoon whipped cream and 1 teaspoon grated chocolate.

 Peaches and White Chocolate Mousse in Chocolate Cups

Prepare Chocolate Cups and Honey Brandy White Chocolate Mousse as in two previous recipes. Fill cups with mousse and top with 1 cup diced peaches tossed with 2 teaspoons orange liqueur and ½ teaspoon confectioners' sugar.

 Unbelievably Amazing Brownies

Melt ½ pound *each* unsweetened chocolate and butter together and set aside. Beat 5 eggs with 1½ cups firmly packed light brown sugar, 2 cups granulated sugar, 1 tablespoon vanilla extract, and 2 tablespoons instant coffee powder until thick and fluffy. Add cooled chocolate mixture until blended and beat in 1½ cups flour just until mixed. Fold in 2 cups walnut pieces and turn into a greased and floured 9-by-13-inch baking pan. Smooth top and bake in preheated 425° F. oven for 35 minutes. It will test wet inside. Remove from oven, cool on a rack, unmold, and refrigerate until firm. Cut into 24 squares.

 Date Nut Brownies

Follow preceding recipe, replacing walnuts with 1 cup pecan pieces and 1 cup chopped pitted dates.

 Plain Wonderful Brownies

Melt 5 ounces unsweetened chocolate with 11 tablespoons butter. Set aside. Mix 3 cups walnut pieces with 1 cup flour. Set aside. Beat 4 eggs with 2 cups sugar until light and fluffy. Add 1 tablespoon instant coffee powder and 2 teaspoons vanilla extract. Beat in the chocolate followed by the nuts and flour. Pour onto a greased and floured jelly-roll pan. Smooth top and bake in preheated 425° F. oven for 18 minutes. Cool on a rack and cut into 24 squares.

 White Chocolate Brownies

Grease a jelly-roll pan and line it with wax paper. Grease and flour the paper. Melt 10 tablespoons unsalted butter with the finely grated zest of 1 orange. Remove from heat and whisk in 2 tablespoons orange liqueur and 8 ounces finely chopped white chocolate until chocolate melts. In separate bowl, beat 5 eggs, with 1 teaspoon vanilla extract, ¼ teaspoon salt, and 1½ cups sugar until light and fluffy. Beat in chocolate mixture and 1 cup sifted flour. Bake in preheated 400° F. oven for 15 to 18 minutes, until a tester comes out with just a crumb clinging to it. Invert onto a cookie sheet, remove pan and paper, and invert back into baking pan. Cool completely on a wire rack. Cut into 24 squares.

White Chocolate Brownies with Chocolate-Dipped Almonds

Melt ½ cup semisweet chocolate morsels. Pour over ½ pound coarsely chopped almonds, set in a pie pan, and mix until well coated. Chill until chocolate is set. Break into individual pieces and set aside. Follow preceding recipe and fold chocolate-covered almonds into batter after the flour.

Triple Chocolate Brownies

Beat ¼ pound butter with ¼ cup brown sugar until smooth. Beat in 1¼ cups flour sifted with 2 tablespoons cocoa powder to form a firm dough. Press into a 9-inch square baking pan, and bake at 375° F. for 10 minutes. Meanwhile, beat 2 large eggs with ¾ cup brown sugar until thick. Add ¼ teaspoon salt, ½ teaspoon vanilla extract, and 2 tablespoons cocoa powder and beat for 2 minutes more. Fold in 6 ounces finely ground walnuts. Spread 3 tablespoons strained raspberry preserves over the baked dough. Top with prepared batter and bake for 25 minutes. Cool on a rack. Melt 6 ounces semi-sweet chocolate chips with 2 tablespoons honey, 2 teaspoons dark rum, and 2 teaspoons strong coffee. Spread over cooled cake and cool to set. Cut into 24 bars.

Chocolate Orange Brownies

Follow preceding recipe, adding 2 tablespoons finely grated orange zest to the batter. Use 4 teaspoons orange liqueur in place of the rum and coffee.

Use this chocolate glaze with the next five recipes:

Chocolate Glaze.

In a double boiler, melt 3 ounces semisweet chocolate and 2 ounces unsweetened chocolate with 6 tablespoons butter and 1 tablespoon honey. Stir until smooth, place over ice water, and continue stirring until slightly thickened. To coat, brush away any crumbs from the cake and place on a rack over a drip pan. Using an icing spatula, spread glaze evenly over top of cake, letting some run down the sides. Smooth sides, covering all surfaces with glaze. Transfer cake to a platter. Makes enough for 2 tortes or 1 layer cake.

Chocolate Almond Torte

Beat ¼ pound butter with ⅔ cup sugar until light and fluffy. Add 3 eggs, 1 at a time, followed by 4 ounces melted semisweet chocolate. Fold in 7 ounces (1½ cups) finely ground almonds. Grease an 8-inch layer pan, line bottom with parchment or wax paper, grease paper, and flour the pan. Pour batter into prepared pan and bake in preheated 375° F. oven for 25 minutes. Cool in pan on a rack for 30 minutes. Unmold, cool completely, and top with Chocolate Glaze (above). Serves 12.

Gâteau Bordeaux

Finely chop ½ cup raisins and toss with 3 tablespoons cognac. Set aside until raisins have absorbed the rum. Follow preceding recipe, using the raisins in place of ⅓ of the almonds.

 Creole Chocolate Torte

Beat ¼ pound butter with ⅔ cup sugar until light and fluffy. Add 3 eggs, 1 at a time, followed by 4 ounces melted semisweet chocolate. Fold in 5 ounces finely ground pecans, ¼ cup fine bread crumbs, and the finely grated zest of 1 orange. Grease an 8-inch layer pan and line the bottom with parchment or wax paper. Grease the paper and flour the pan. Pour batter into prepared pan and bake in preheated 375° F. oven for 25 minutes. Cool in pan on a rack for 30 minutes. Unmold and cool completely. Top with Chocolate Glaze (page 407) made with 1 tablespoon Grand Marnier in place of the honey. Serves 12.

 Bitter Chocolate Torte

Follow preceding recipe, substituting 3 ounces unsweetened chocolate for the semisweet.

 Chocolate Apricot Torte

Finely chop 12 dried apricots and soak in 3 tablespoons orange liqueur. Follow recipe for Creole Chocolate Torte (above), replacing the bread crumbs with the apricots and the pecans with almonds.

 Chocolate Souffléed Cake

Melt 9 ounces semisweet chocolate and 18 tablespoons butter. Combine 6 egg yolks and 6 tablespoons cornstarch and mix into melted chocolate. Beat 6 egg whites until they just hold a shape, add ⅓ cup sugar, and beat until firm. Fold whites into chocolate until completely incorporated. Line a greased 9-inch springform pan with wax paper or parchment, grease the paper, and flour the pan. Pour batter in pan and bake in a preheated 350° F. oven for 30 minutes. Cool for 10 minutes on a rack. Run a knife around the edge and remove the sides. Invert onto a serving plate and remove bottom of pan. Cool completely and dust top with confectioners' sugar before serving. Serve with 1 cup cold heavy cream whipped to soft peaks with 2 tablespoons confectioners' sugar. Serves 12.

 Mocha Torte

Follow preceding recipe, adding 2 tablespoons instant coffee powder with the egg yolks. Add 1 teaspoon instant coffee powder to the cream before whipping.

 Devil's Food Layer Cake

Whisk 6 tablespoons cocoa powder with 6 tablespoons water and bring to a boil. Whisk in 4 ounces chopped semisweet chocolate until melted. Set aside. Beat ½ pound butter with ½ cup dark brown sugar until light and fluffy. Add 6 egg yolks, followed by the chocolate. When combined, beat in ¼ cup sour cream. Add ¾ cup flour. Dissolve 2 teaspoons baking soda in 2 teaspoons hot water. Add to batter followed by another ¾ cup flour. Beat just until smooth. Beat 6 egg whites to a soft peak, add 3 tablespoons sugar, and beat until peaks are firm. Fold into batter and turn into 3 greased and floured 8-inch layer pans. Bake in preheated 350° F. oven for 25 minutes. Cool on racks and unmold. When completely cool, layer and ice with a frosting made by melting 8 ounces milk chocolate with 24 ounces semisweet chocolate chips. Beat in 1 teaspoon vanilla extract and 2 cups cream.

Chocolate Black Pepper Pound Cake

Sift 3 cups flour with 1 tablespoon baking powder, 1 cup cocoa powder, ½ teaspoon salt, ½ teaspoon allspice, and 1 teaspoon ground black pepper. Beat ½ pound unsalted butter with 3 cups sugar until fluffy. Add 1 teaspoon vanilla extract and 3 extra-large eggs, 1 at a time, beating until incorporated. Add 1¾ cups milk in 2 additions alternating with dry ingredients in 3 additions. Pour into greased and floured 10-inch Bundt pan and bake in a 350° F. preheated oven for 1 hour 10 minutes. Cool on a rack for 15 minutes. Unmold and cool another 30 minutes. Whisk together ⅓ cup melted semisweet chocolate chips with 6 tablespoons sour cream and spoon atop cake. Serves 12.

Chocolate Pâté

Sift 2 cups flour, ½ teaspoon salt, 1 teaspoon baking soda, 1 teaspoon ground cinnamon, and ¼ cup cocoa powder. Cream ¼ pound butter with 1 cup sugar. Beat in 1 teaspoon vanilla extract, 2 teaspoons rum extract, and 2 eggs, 1 at a time. Add half the sifted dry ingredients, ½ cup milk, and the remaining dry ingredients, beating just until incorporated. Beat in 2 cups raisins, 2 cups semisweet chocolate morsels, and ⅓ cup chopped candied ginger. Turn into a greased and floured loaf pan and bake at 350° F. for 1 hour 40 minutes. Cool in the pan for 15 minutes, unpan, and cool on a rack. Slice thinly with a serrated knife. Serves 16.

Chocolate Brandy Pudding Cake

Sift 1 cup flour, 2 teaspoons baking powder, ½ teaspoon baking soda, ¼ teaspoon salt, ¾ cup sugar, a pinch of ground cinnamon, and ⅓ cup cocoa powder. Add ½ cup milk, ¼ cup light cream, 1 teaspoon vanilla extract, and 4 tablespoons cooled melted butter. Spread in a 9-inch baking pan. Sprinkle a mixture of ¾ cup dark brown sugar, ¼ cup sugar, and ¼ cup cocoa powder over top. Combine ½ cup brandy with 1 cup boiling water and pour over all. Bake in preheated 350° F. oven for 50 minutes. Cool on a rack for at least 1 hour. Spoon onto plates and serve with whipped cream if desired. Serves 8.

Black Forest Pudding Cake

Sift 1 cup flour, 2 teaspoons baking powder, 2 tablespoons Dutch process cocoa powder, and ⅔ cup sugar. Beat in ¾ cup milk, 1 teaspoon vanilla extract, ½ teaspoon almond extract, and 2 tablespoons melted unsalted butter. Pour into a buttered 8-inch square baking pan. Bring to a boil ⅓ cup sugar, ½ cup firmly packed dark brown sugar, ⅓ cup cocoa powder, and 1 can (16½ ounces) pitted dark sweet cherries in syrup. Ladle over batter and bake in preheated 350° F. oven for 45 minutes. Cool on a rack for 30 minutes. Invert onto a deep-rimmed platter. Sauce in bottom of the pan will run over top of inverted cake. Cool and serve with whipped cream. Serves 8.

Chocolate Gingerbread

Pour 1 cup strong hot coffee over ½ pound butter and stir until melted. Whisk in 1 cup firmly packed dark brown sugar, 1 cup dark corn syrup, and 4 extra-large eggs until blended. In another bowl, sift together 2¼ cups flour, 1½ teaspoons baking soda, 2 teaspoons powdered ginger, 1 teaspoon ground cinnamon, and ⅛ teaspoon ground cloves. Beat into wet ingredients, followed by 2 ounces melted unsweetened chocolate, until batter is smooth. Pour into greased and floured 9-by-13-inch baking pan and bake in a preheated 350° F. oven for 45 minutes. Cool on a rack, cut into 16 squares, and serve with 1 cup chilled heavy cream beaten to a peak with 2 tablespoons honey and 1 teaspoon vanilla extract. Garnish with 2 tablespoons finely chopped candied ginger. Serves 12.

 ## Triple Chocolate Drops

Melt 7 ounces semisweet chocolate, 1 ounce unsweetened chocolate, and 6 tablespoons unsalted butter. Cool. Beat 2 extra-large eggs, 1 tablespoon instant espresso powder, 2 teaspoons vanilla extract, and ¾ cup sugar until thick and fluffy. Beat in the chocolate and ⅓ cup flour sifted with 1 teaspoon baking powder and ¼ teaspoon salt just until blended. Stir in 1½ cups semisweet chocolate morsels. Drop in 1½-tablespoon mounds, 2 inches apart, on greased cookie sheets, and bake in a preheated 325° F. oven for 17 minutes. Cool on the pan for 1 minute and remove with a slotted spatula to cool on a rack the rest of the way. Makes 16 to 18 large cookies.

 ## Peanut Chocolate Drops

Follow preceding recipe, replacing the chocolate morsels with 1 cup chunked milk chocolate and 1 cup unsalted roasted peanuts.

 ## Chocolate Chocolate-Chunk Cookies

Cream ½ pound softened butter, ¾ cup granulated sugar, and ¾ cup firmly packed brown sugar. Add 2 eggs and beat well. Mix in 1¼ cups flour sifted with ½ cup Dutch process cocoa powder, followed by 1 teaspoon baking soda dissolved in 1 teaspoon *each* hot water and vanilla extract. Beat in 1 cup additional flour, 1 cup walnut pieces, and ½ pound chunked semisweet chocolate. Place

1-tablespoon scoops on cookie sheets and bake at 375° F. for 12 minutes per batch. Cool pans for 1 minute and transfer cookies to cooling racks. Makes about 3 dozen cookies.

 ## Chocolate Peanut Pie

Melt 2 ounces unsalted butter. Stir in 2 ounces finely chopped semisweet chocolate until melted. Pour into a blind-baked deep-dish Flaky Pastry Shell (page 435) and chill to set. Beat 3 large eggs with ¾ cup light brown sugar, 1½ tablespoons flour, ¾ cup dark corn syrup, 1 teaspoon vanilla extract, and 2 tablespoons peanut butter until blended. Stir in 2 cups roasted unsalted peanuts. Pour into shell and bake in a preheated 350° F. oven for 1 hour. Cool for 2 to 3 hours. Serves 8.

 ## Chocolate Pecan Pie

Follow preceding recipe, replacing the peanut butter with melted butter and the peanuts with pecan halves. Add 1 tablespoon bourbon to the filling.

 ## Chocolate Chocolate Chocolate Parfait

Bring 3 tablespoons light corn syrup and 1½ tablespoons brandy to a boil. Remove from heat and beat in 5 ounces finely chopped white chocolate until melted. Whip 1½ cups heavy cream to a firm peak, fold into the chocolate, and chill. Crumble 2 dozen chocolate wafer cookies. Make a ½-inch layer of cookies in the bottom of 6 parfait glasses. Top each with 1 tablespoon semisweet chocolate morsels and 1½ inches of the mousse. Continue layering until you have 3 layers of each element. Cover with plastic and refrigerate several hours until firm. Garnish each with 1 large strawberry. Serves 6.

MeMe's Chocolate Roll

Separate 8 eggs. Beat yolks until light in color. Beat in ½ cup sugar, ½ cup cocoa powder, and 1 teaspoon vanilla extract. Beat whites and a pinch of salt to soft peak. Fold thoroughly into chocolate mixture. Generously grease and flour a 10-by-15-inch jelly-roll pan. Pour batter into pan, spread evenly, and bake in a preheated 375° F. oven for 10 minutes, until a tester comes out slightly moist. Cover with a damp flat-weave kitchen towel. Invert onto the towel, remove pan, and roll up in the towel. Soften an 8-ounce jar of marshmallow creme in a bowl of hot water. Unroll cake and spread marshmallow over its surface. Using the towel to help lift the cake, roll it up jelly-roll style, starting from a short side. Wrap finished roll in the towel and refrigerate for several hours or overnight. Unwrap and place on a long platter. Ice with 3 cups sweetened whipped cream, and decorate with 1 ounce shaved chocolate if desired. Serves 8.

Real Hot Chocolate Spiked with Scotch

Melt 12 ounces chopped semisweet chocolate and whisk in 3 cups scalded milk. Heat to serving temperature and stir in 2 tablespoons Scotch and 1 tablespoon instant coffee powder. Serve in mugs and top each with 1 tablespoon whipped cream, if desired.

White Chocolate Ice Cream

Heat 5 ounces finely chopped white chocolate and 2 cups heavy cream until chocolate melts. Set aside. Scald 2 cups milk with 1 clove and the finely grated zest of 1 orange. Beat 4 egg yolks with ½ cup sugar and slowly pour scalded milk into the yolks. Over low heat, stirring constantly, cook until lightly thickened, about 10 minutes. Remove from heat, stir in 1½ tablespoons vanilla extract and the cooled chocolate mixture. Refrigerate until completely chilled. Remove clove and freeze in an ice-cream freezer according to manufacturer's directions. Store in a tightly closed container in a freezer. Serves 6.

Chocolate Ice Cream with Raspberry Swirl

Follow preceding recipe, substituting semisweet chocolate for the white chocolate and using an additional 2 tablespoons sugar. Crush 10 ounces sweetened frozen raspberries with 2 tablespoons framboise or an orange-flavored liqueur. When the ice cream is almost frozen, swirl in the raspberries. Store in a freezer in tightly closed container.

Use this dipping chocolate for the remaining recipes:

Dipping Chocolate:

Melt 12 ounces semisweet chocolate. Add 4 more ounces, 1 ounce at a time, stirring until each addition is completely melted before adding the next. Set over warm water. Put the prepared centers into the dipping chocolate, one at a time. Coat completely and lift with a small fork. Shake off excess chocolate by lightly tapping the fork on the edge of the bowl. Remove any drips by running a fork across the edge of the bowl. Slide onto a cookie sheet lined with parchment or wax paper. Allow to cool until solid. Makes 1 pound dipping chocolate.

Chocolate-Covered Prunes with Marzipan "Pits"

Makes 18 small balls from 1½ ounces almond paste. Stuff each into 1 extra-large pitted prune through a small slit made in the prune's side. Prepare ¾ pound Dipping Chocolate (above) and dip the prunes. Refrigerate briefly to firm chocolate. Makes about 1½ pounds.

Chocolate-Covered Almond Apricots

Make 18 small balls from 1½ ounces almond paste. Stuff each into 1 extra-large dried apricot through a small slit made in the apricot's side. Prepare ¾ pound Dipping Chocolate (page 411), and dip the apricots. Cool for 30 minutes to set chocolate. Roll in 1½ cups finely ground almonds and refrigerate until chocolate is completely firm. Makes about 1½ pounds.

 Chocolate Fruit Squares

Finely chop or grind 2½ cups assorted coarsely chopped dried fruits (raisins, dates, apricots, apples, pineapple) in a food processor or meat grinder, with a pinch of ground allspice, 1 teaspoon ground cinnamon, and ¼ teaspoon ground ginger. Mix in 2 ounces shelled and skinned pistachios. Wet your hands and form into a 4-inch square. Wrap in plastic and freeze for 1 hour. Unwrap. Cut into 1-inch squares with a serrated knife and dip into ½ pound Dipping Chocolate (page 411). Makes 16 squares.

 Chocolate-Covered Pretzel "Porcupines"

Cool 4 ounces melted semisweet chocolate until it no longer feels hot to the touch. Break 8 ounces pretzel sticks into bite-size pieces and stir into the chocolate to partially coat. Spoon onto a paper-lined cookie sheet in rounded tablespoonfuls. Refrigerate for several hours until very firm, before dipping. Dip in ¾ pound Dipping Chocolate (page 411). Makes about 30 candies.

 Chocolate Peanut Crunch Balls

Mix 1 cup chunky peanut butter, ½ cup dark corn syrup, and 1 cup crisped rice cereal (such as Rice Krispies) until well blended. Moisten your hands and form rounded teaspoonfuls of this mixture into balls by rolling between your palms. Freeze for 1 hour. Dip in ½ pound Dipping Chocolate (page 411). Makes about 3 dozen.

 Chocolate Peanut Grahams

Follow preceding recipe, substituting crumbled graham crackers for the cereal.

 Chocolate-Covered Potato Chips

Dip 2 to 3 dozen (depending on size) thick-sliced ridged potato chips in ¾ pound Dipping Chocolate (page 411).

 Chocolate-Covered Chocolate-Chip Cookies

Dip 1 dozen chocolate-chip cookies, homemade or storebought, in ½ pound Dipping Chocolate (page 411).

 S'mores

Dip 2 dozen regular-size marshmallows in ½ pound Dipping Chocolate (page 411). Allow to set until chocolate is tacky, about 20 minutes. Roll in 2 cups graham cracker crumbs. Place on a paper-lined tray and chill until chocolate sets.

 Chocolate-Dipped Strawberries

Rinse 1 pint large perfect strawberries. Dip each strawberry in ½ pound Dipping Chocolate (page 411) in the following manner, rather than as described in the Dipping Chocolate recipe: Hold each strawberry by the stem and dip in the chocolate up to, but without covering, the stems. Set on a sheet pan lined with parchment or wax paper and cool until firm. Makes about 1 dozen.

49

Fifty Ways to Fill the Cookie Jar

The allure of cookies never ends, from our first bite of zwieback to our last midnight nosh. What else can mend hurt feelings with less fuss or nourish a sweet-starved appetite with more aplomb?

Much to their detriment, cookies have increasingly become a prepackaged commodity. While no food thrives from commercial processing, the charm of most cookies all but disappears as their natural shelf life is unnaturally extended from several days to several months.

There's not a prepackaged chocolate chip that can hope to compete with a real Toll House warm from the oven, nor a commercial butter cookie that's more than a hard shard of sugar when compared with a lacy tuile just peeled from its baking sheet.

The quality of most cookies is fleeting. If we don't make cookies ourselves, we must learn to accept less than the best. But with a few well-tested recipes and a basic understanding of cookie types, anyone armed with a mixer and a preheated oven can create batch after batch of homemade perfection with negligible effort.

Note that the following 50 cookie recipes include basic formulas, each followed by several variations. We have found this arrangement expedient as a means of giving you maximum cookie recipes in minimum space, but it's also a way to help you understand the structure of various cookie types. Once you understand what makes one cookie chewy and another crisp, you'll be better able to judge which recipe best fits your image of cookie perfection—and be better able to adjust when problems arise.

Soft cookies are large, thick, and cakey. Like cakes, they have a high proportion of liquid to dry ingredients, considerable leavener, and a moderate amount of fat and sugar. Many molasses cookies, hermits, and some oatmeal cookies are of this type.

Chewy cookies are achieved by lowering the proportion of liquid and raising the amounts of egg and sugar in the recipe. Note that most of the drop cookies included in this chapter follow this ratio.

A crisp cookie comes from a dough practically devoid of liquid and leaveners but high in flour, butter, and sugar. These would include cookies with a pastry base and shortbreads.

Fifty Ways to Cook Most Everything

Textural changes also occur by altering the size of the cookie and the oven temperature. Large mounds of batter and moderate baking temperatures yield softer or chewier cookies, while flattening the batter or raising the temperature of the oven makes the same dough come out crisper.

ABOUT THESE RECIPES

All of the following cookies are baked on ungreased cookie sheets 2 inches from one another, unless otherwise noted. When rolling cookie doughs, do so on lightly floured boards with a floured rolling pin. Whenever you transfer the rolled dough, formed cookies, or baked cookies, do so with a wide spatula. All baking times and temperatures are for preheated ovens. Because of the high sugar content of most cookies, they burn easily. For this reason, an oven's normal hot spots can prove disastrous in cookie baking. To help minimize the potential damage, it is advisable to rotate cookie sheets front to back and top shelf to bottom midway through baking time.

 ### Peanut Butter Jumbles

Cream together ¼ pound softened butter, 1½ cups chunky peanut butter, 1 cup brown sugar, and 1 cup granulated sugar. Beat in 3 eggs. Dissolve 1 tablespoon baking soda in 2 teaspoons vanilla extract, and add. Pour this batter over 4½ cups quick-cooking oats, 1 cup unsalted dry-roasted peanuts, and 1½ cups raisins. Mix to moisten. Drop in ¼-cup mounds 2½ inches apart on cookie sheets and bake at 350° F. for 18 minutes per batch. Cool for 2 minutes on the pan and transfer to cooling racks. Makes 2 dozen.

 ### Candy Store Jumbles

Follow preceding recipe, but add 1 cup plain M&M's and 1 cup peanut M&M's instead of the raisins.

 ### Walnut Butter Jumbles

Follow recipe for Peanut Butter Jumbles (above), but use Walnut Butter (page 428) instead of peanut butter and ½ cup chopped walnuts and 1 cup chocolate chips instead of the raisins.

 ### Oatmeal Jumbles

Follow recipe for Peanut Butter Jumbles (above), substituting 1 cup wheat germ for 1 cup of the quick-cooking oats, and ½ cup toasted sunflower seeds for ½ cup of the raisins.

 ### Chocolate Peanut Jumbles

Follow the recipe for Peanut Butter Jumbles (above), but mix ½ cup cocoa powder with the quick-cooking oats and substitute 1 cup *each* semisweet chocolate chips and semisweet chocolate chunks for the raisins.

 ### Chewy Chocolate Chip Cookies

Cream together ½ pound softened butter, ¾ cup granulated sugar, and ¾ cup firmly packed brown sugar. Add 2 extra-large eggs and beat well. Mix in 1¼ cups unsifted flour, followed by 1 teaspoon baking soda dissolved in 1 teaspoon *each* hot water and vanilla extract. Beat in 1 cup additional flour, 1 cup walnut pieces, and 2 cups semisweet chocolate chips. Place tablespoon-size scoops of batter on cookie sheets and bake at 375° F. for 12 minutes per batch. Cool on pans for 1 minute and transfer to racks. Makes about 4 dozen cookies.

 ### White Chocolate Chunk Cookies

Follow preceding recipe, substituting ¾ cup granulated sugar for the brown sugar, slivered almonds for the walnuts, and 8 ounces chunked white chocolate for the chocolate morsels.

 ## Chocolate Chunk Cookies

Follow recipe for Chewy Chocolate Chip Cookies (opposite) substituting 8 ounces chunked semisweet chocolate for the chocolate morsels.

 ## Chocolate Chocolate Chips

Follow recipe for Chewy Chocolate Chip Cookies (opposite) replacing ¼ cup of the flour with ⅓ cup cocoa powder.

 ## Espresso Oatmeal Chocolate Chip Cookies

Follow recipe for Chewy Chocolate Chip Cookies (opposite), dissolving 1 tablespoon instant espresso powder with the baking soda and adding ½ cup quick-cooking oats with the walnuts.

Use this pastry with the seven recipes in this section:

Sweet Cream Cheese Pastry.

Mix ¼ pound butter and ¼ pound cream cheese into 1 cup flour and 2 tablespoons sugar until smooth. Dust with flour and pat into a flat disk. Wrap in plastic and refrigerate at least 1 hour. On a floured board with a floured pin, roll disk to ⅛- to ¼-inch thickness.

 ## Apricot Marzipan Drops

Prepare Sweet Cream Cheese Pastry (above). Break 1 ounce marzipan into 12 nuggets. Make a slit in 12 extra-large dried apricots and stuff each with 1 marzipan nugget. Cut dough into 12 circles, each 3½ inches in diameter. Wrap each stuffed apricot in a circle of dough, pinching seam to seal. Place seam side down on a cookie sheet. Chill for 20 minutes and bake at 400° F. for 30 minutes. Cool for 10 minutes, dust with ¼ cup confectioners' sugar, and let cool completely. Makes 12 cookies.

 ## Apricot Schnecken

Prepare Sweet Cream Cheese Pastry (above). Brush dough with 1 tablespoon melted butter and spread with ⅓ cup warm apricot preserves. Sprinkle with ½ cup finely chopped dried apricots and cut dough into 16 wedges. Roll each wedge up, rolling from the edge to the point. Place point side down on cookie sheets, brush with 1 egg yolk mixed with 1 tablespoon water, and bake at 350° F. for 30 minutes. Makes 16 cookies.

 ## Chocolate Rugelach

Follow preceding recipe, substituting ⅓ cup finely chopped semisweet chocolate and ⅓ cup chopped walnuts for the preserves and dried apricots.

 ## Tiny Eccles Cakes

Mix 3 tablespoons melted butter, 3 tablespoons sugar, 1 cup dried currants, 2 tablespoons candied orange or lemon peel, and a pinch *each* of ground allspice and nutmeg. Prepare a double recipe of Sweet Cream Cheese Pastry (above) and cut into 2 dozen 3½-inch circles. Place 1 tablespoon filling in center of each circle, bring edges up around filling, and twist to seal. Turn over and flatten lightly with a rolling pin. Cut a small X in the top of each pastry, brush with 1 egg yolk mixed with 1 tablespoon water, and bake at 400° F. for 13 to 14 minutes. Cool on racks and dust lightly with confectioners' sugar. Makes 2 dozen.

Fifty Ways to Cook Most Everything

 Grand Marnier Almond Bars

Prepare ½ recipe Sweet Cream Cheese Pastry (page 415). Press pastry into bottom of foil-lined 8-inch-square baking pan, prick with a fork, and bake at 350° F. for 15 minutes. Meanwhile, simmer ⅔ cup coarsely chopped almonds, ½ cup light cream, ⅔ cup sugar, a pinch of salt, 1 tablespoon Grand Marnier, and ⅛ teaspoon almond extract for 10 minutes. Stir in the finely grated zest of 1 orange and spread mixture over surface of pastry. Bake at 350° F. for 30 minutes until bubbly and lightly brown. Cool in pan for 30 minutes. Unpan onto a cookie sheet, remove foil, and invert onto a rack. Cut with serrated knife into 16 bars.

 Pecan Pie Bars

Prepare ½ recipe Sweet Cream Cheese Pastry (page 415), but replace granulated sugar with brown sugar. Press pastry into bottom of a foil-lined 8-inch-square baking pan, prick with a fork, and bake at 350° F. for 15 minutes. Mix 1 egg with ½ teaspoon vanilla extract, 1 tablespoon bourbon, 2 tablespoons dark brown sugar, 6 tablespoons dark corn syrup, 2 tablespoons flour, and 1 cup pecan pieces, and spread over surface of pastry. Bake at 350° F. for 30 minutes until topping is set. Cool in pan for 30 minutes. Unpan onto a cookie sheet, remove foil, and invert onto a rack. Freeze for 30 minutes. Cut with a serrated knife into 16 bars.

 Chewy Gooey Lemon Pecan Bars

Follow preceding recipe adding 1 tablespoon finely grated lemon zest to the Sweet Cream Cheese Pastry dough. Replace the bourbon in the topping with the juice of ½ lemon.

 Hazelnut Crescents

Cream ½ pound unsalted butter, 2 teaspoons vanilla extract, and ⅔ cup sugar. Add ½ cup finely ground toasted hazelnuts and 2½ cups flour, beating just enough to incorporate. Form scant tablespoons of dough into elongated ovals and place on sheet pans, bending in the ends of each cookie to form a crescent. Bake at 350° F. for 19 minutes. Cool on pans for 3 minutes, dust with confectioners' sugar, and cool on racks. Makes 3 dozen.

 Anise Almond Drops

Follow preceding recipe, substituting almonds for hazelnuts and 1 teaspoon anise extract for half the vanilla. Form into balls instead of crescents and bake 22 to 24 minutes.

 Coconut Snowballs

Follow recipe for Hazelnut Crescents (above), replacing the hazelnuts with shredded coconut and forming cookies into small balls instead of crescents.

 Spiced Gumdrop Drops

Follow recipe for Hazelnut Crescents (above) but sift flour with ¼ teaspoon ground cinnamon, ¼ teaspoon ground ginger, and a pinch of cloves. Wrap each portion of dough around a small gumdrop and form into a rough ball. Bake 3 to 5 minutes longer.

 Shortbread

Mix 2 cups flour, ⅓ cup cornstarch, and ½ cup sugar. With your fingers, work ½ pound butter cut in ½-inch pieces and ½ teaspoon vanilla extract into the dry ingredients until smooth. Pat into ⅓-inch-thick disk and cut into 2-inch circles. Re-form the scraps and cut more. Bake on sheet pans at 350° F. for 17 to 20 minutes. Cool on a rack. Makes about 2 dozen.

Almond Shortbread

Follow preceding recipe, but add ⅔ cup finely ground almonds to the flour and use ¼ teaspoon almond extract in place of half the vanilla.

Ginger Currant Shortbread

Follow recipe for Shortbread (opposite), adding 1 teaspoon powdered ginger, ¼ teaspoon ground cinnamon, and a pinch of allspice to the flour. Knead 1 cup dried currants into the dough before forming cookies.

Walnut Chocolate Chip Shortbread

Follow recipe for Shortbread (opposite), but add ⅔ cup finely ground walnuts with the flour, and knead 1 cup semisweet mini chocolate morsels into the dough before forming cookies.

Walnut Brown-Edge Wafers

In a large saucepan, combine 4 ounces (1 generous cup) walnuts, finely ground, ½ cup granulated sugar, ¼ pound softened butter, 1 tablespoon flour, and 2 tablespoons heavy cream until the butter melts and the ingredients are blended. Add 1 small beaten egg. Drop tablespoons of batter on greased sheet pans 4 inches apart. With the back of a spoon, spread into 3-inch circles. Bake at 350° F.

for 9 minutes. Remove immediately with a wide spatula. Cool on racks. Makes 2 dozen.

Walnut Oat Lace Cookies

Combine ¾ cup sugar, ½ cup quick-cooking oats, ½ cup finely chopped walnuts, and 2 tablespoons flour. Mix well with ¼ pound melted butter, 1 beaten egg, and ½ teaspoon almond extract. Drop tablespoons of batter on greased sheet pans 4 inches apart. With the back of a spoon, spread into 3-inch circles. Bake at 350° F. for 9 minutes. Remove immediately with a wide spatula. Cool on racks. Makes 2½ dozen cookies.

Ginger Lace Cookies

Combine ¾ cup brown sugar, 1 cup quick-cooking oats, ½ teaspoon ground ginger, and 2 tablespoons flour. Mix well with ¼ pound melted butter, 1 beaten egg, and ½ teaspoon vanilla extract. Prepare dough and bake as in preceding recipe.

Honey Almond Tuiles

Cream 4 tablespoons butter, ¼ cup sugar, and 3 tablespoons honey. Beat in 2 egg whites, 2 tablespoons heavy cream, ¾ cup ground almonds, and ¼ cup flour. Drop tablespoons of batter on greased sheet pans 4 inches apart and spread with the back of a spoon into 3-inch circles. Sprinkle each cookie with 4 or 5 sliced almonds. Bake on top rack of a 425° F. oven for 6 minutes. Remove immediately with a wide spatula and cool draped over a rolling pin. Makes 12 to 16 cookies.

Chocolate Pistachio Drops

Melt 8 ounces semisweet chocolate with 6 tablespoons unsalted butter. Let cool. Beat 2 extra-large eggs, 1 tablespoon instant coffee powder, 1 table-spoon cocoa powder, 2 teaspoons vanilla extract, and ¾ cup sugar until thick and fluffy. Beat in the chocolate, followed by ⅓ cup flour sifted with 1 teaspoon baking powder and ¼ teaspoon salt just until blended. Stir in 1 cup chopped pistachio nuts. Drop in 1½-tablespoon mounds on greased cookie sheets and bake in a preheated 325° F. oven for 17 minutes. Cool on the pan for 1 minute, remove with slotted spatula, and cool completely on a rack. Makes 16 to 18 large cookies.

 ### Wheat Germ Brownies

Mix together ¼ cup vegetable oil, 2 lightly beaten extra-large eggs, 1 cup dark brown sugar, ½ cup chopped walnuts, 2 teaspoons vanilla extract, 1 cup wheat germ, ½ cup raisins, and a pinch of salt. Sift ½ cup powdered milk with ½ teaspoon baking powder and stir into the batter. Bake in a greased and floured 8-inch square baking pan at 350° F. for 35 minutes. Cool completely, unpan, freeze for 30 minutes, and cut into 2-inch squares. Makes 16.

 ### Oaties

Melt ¼ pound butter with 1 cup firmly packed light brown sugar. Beat in 2 eggs. Sift in 1 teaspoon baking powder and mix. Add 1 teaspoon vanilla extract, 2 cups quick-cooking or old-fashioned oats, ½ cup chopped walnuts, and ¼ cup chopped raisins. Mix thoroughly. Turn into a greased, foil-lined 8-inch square baking pan, smooth the top, and bake at 350° F. for 45 minutes. Let cool for 30 minutes and freeze for 1 hour. Invert, remove foil, and cut into 16 squares.

 ### Butterscotch Oaties

Follow preceding recipe, but replace the raisins with ½ cup butterscotch morsels.

 ### Janis Traven's Dried Cherry Bars

Mix ½ pound butter, ½ cup sugar, and 2 cups unbleached flour into a smooth dough. Press into a greased 9-by-13-inch baking pan and bake at 350° F. for 30 minutes. Mix 1 cup brown sugar, 4 lightly beaten eggs, 2 tablespoons flour, 2 cups chopped hazelnuts, and 1½ cups dried pitted cherries. Pour over crust and bake another 20 minutes. Let cool and cut into 24 bars with a serrated knife. Makes 2 dozen.

 ### Date Nut Bars

Follow preceding recipe, using walnuts instead of the hazelnuts and chopped pitted dates instead of the dried cherries.

 ### Peanut Butter Sandwich Bars

Cream 6 tablespoons butter with ¼ cup brown sugar. Add 6 tablespoons honey, 1 small beaten egg, and 1½ cups flour sifted with ¾ cup whole-wheat flour, ¾ teaspoon baking powder, and ½ teaspoon baking soda. With floured hands, pat half the dough into a greased and floured 9-inch square baking pan. Freeze for 20 minutes and refrigerate remaining dough. Spread 1 cup chunky peanut butter across surface of frozen dough. Roll dough from refrigerator between 2 sheets of wax paper until it is about 9 inches square. Top peanut butter with this sheet of dough, and push down on edges. Bake at 350° F. for 25 minutes. Cool for 10 minutes, unpan onto a rack, cool, and cut into 16 squares.

 ### Chocolate Peanut Butter Bars

Follow preceding recipe, using smooth peanut butter and sprinkling 1 cup semisweet chocolate morsels over the peanut butter before topping with pastry.

Raisin Bars

Follow recipe for Peanut Butter Sandwich Bars (opposite), replacing the peanut butter with the following filling: Simmer 1 cup raisins, ¾ cup water, 1½ tablespoons lemon juice, and 2 tablespoons honey until liquid is absorbed and fruit is softened. (Watch carefully; raisins can scorch near the end of the cooking time.) Let cool.

Butter Cookies

Beat ¼ pound butter, 1 egg yolk, 6 tablespoons sugar, ½ teaspoon vanilla extract, and 1 cup flour. Form dough into 2 cylinders, each 1½ inches in diameter. Wrap in plastic and refrigerate several hours to firm. Slice into ¼-inch-thick rounds, and place on greased cookie sheets. Brush with 1 beaten egg white and top each cookie with 1 blanched almond. Bake at 375° F. for 13 minutes. Let cool on racks. Makes 3 dozen.

Sugar Cookies

Follow preceding recipe, sprinkling each cookie with about ¼ teaspoon sugar instead of topping with an almond.

Spiced Cookies

Follow recipe for Butter Cookies (above), sifting ½ teaspoon *each* ground cinnamon and ginger and ⅛ teaspoon *each* ground cloves and powdered mustard (yes, mustard) with the flour. In place of an almond, sprinkle each cookie with ¼ teaspoon sugar mixed with a pinch of ground cinnamon.

Cardamom Currant Cookies

Follow recipe for Butter Cookies (above), sifting 1 teaspoon ground cardamom with the flour and mixing 1 cup currants into the dough. Eliminate the almonds.

Sablés

Follow recipe for Butter Cookies (above), adding ¼ cup finely ground almonds with the butter. Replace half the vanilla with almond extract.

Chocolate Butter Cookies

Follow recipe for Butter Cookies (above) beating 2 tablespoons bittersweet chocolate into the dough after the flour. Top with hazelnuts instead of almonds.

Pinwheels

Prepare ½ recipe *each* Butter Cookies and Chocolate Butter Cookies (both above), but instead of forming cylinders, roll each dough into 7-by-9-inch rectangles between sheets of wax paper. Remove a sheet of wax paper from each dough, and flip one dough onto the other, lining up edges as perfectly as possible. Remove top sheet of wax paper and use the bottom sheet to help lift the doughs. Roll jelly-roll style, starting with a long side. Wrap the spiraled roll in plastic wrap. Chill, slice, and bake as described in recipe for Butter Cookies (above). Omit the nuts from both recipes.

Almond Macaroons

Finely grind ½ pound almonds in a food processor. Add 1¼ cups sugar, ¼ teaspoon almond extract, and enough egg white to make a paste that can be molded—about 2 large whites. Divide into 12 prune-size balls, place on a sheet pan, and place 1 whole blanched almond on top of each. Bake at 350° F. for 20 minutes. Let cool for 1 minute and transfer to a rack. When cool, sprinkle with confectioners' sugar. Makes 1 dozen.

Hazelnut Macaroons

Finely grind ½ pound hazelnuts in a food processor. Add 1 cup sugar, 2 tablespoons currant jelly, ¼ teaspoon vanilla extract, and enough egg white to make a paste that can be molded—about 2 large whites. Divide into 12 prune-size balls. Place on a sheet pan and place 1 skinned hazelnut on top of each. Bake and finish as in preceding recipe.

Pine Nut Macaroons

Follow recipe for Almond Macaroons (page 419), using ground pine nuts in place of ground almonds. Sprinkle 5 or 6 pine nuts over each cookie instead of 1 almond.

Chocolate Macaroons

Finely grind 6 ounces almonds in a food processor. Add 2 ounces chopped unsweetened chocolate, 1¼ cups sugar, ¼ teaspoon vanilla extract, and enough egg white to make a paste that can be molded—about 2 large whites. Divide into 12 prune-size balls. Place on a sheet pan and place 1 whole blanched almond on top of each. Bake at 350° F. for 20 minutes. Let cool for 1 minute and transfer to a rack. When cool, dip tops into 3 ounces melted semisweet chocolate. Let cool until chocolate is firm.

Coconut Macaroons

Mix 4 cups grated coconut with 1 cup sugar and ¼ cup finely grated orange zest. Beat 5 egg whites until foamy with a pinch of salt. Add ¾ cup sugar and beat to firm peaks. Combine with coconut. Drop by tablespoonfuls onto greased cookie sheets. Bake for 20 minutes at 350° F. and remove immediately with a wide spatula. Let cool on racks. Makes about 3 dozen.

Fifty Gifts from the Kitchen

There is no greater pleasure for one who loves to cook than to share food with another who loves to eat. Yet many cooks at holiday time overlook the treasure trove of gift ideas in their cooking repertoires. They run from store to store in search of the perfect gift when all they needed to do was leaf through some recipes and preheat the oven.

If a recipe makes something solid enough to travel and moist enough to resist going stale, it can easily be converted into a portion size and presentation perfect for gift giving.

And who doesn't love to eat pound cakes sodden with booze and a ton of nuts, brownies damp enough to leave their mark on anything they touch, and homemade marmalade packed with pulp and bright-colored whiskers of rind? Try your favorite brownie or bar cookie wrapped in cellophane and tied up with ribbons or bake cakes in easy-to-cut sheets, mini-loaf pans, or muffin tins to yield enough individual portions to instantly satisfy the better part of your gift list.

Recipes for homemade jellies, preserves, and pickles are alien to most modern cooks, but they are typically inexpensive and technically easy, and they yield enough to fill a home pantry with each batch. Since the high sugar and acid contents of most sweet preserves and sour relishes make the possibility of bacterial contamination negligible,

they don't require tricky canning procedures, and are perfect for first-time canners.

Flavored vinegars, oils, and mustards are unbelievably easy and inexpensive to make at home, often requiring little more than the ability to mix and heat a few ingredients for a few minutes. Flavor mustard with peppercorns, honey, brown sugar, or wine. Infuse vinegars with herbs or fruit. Or scent oil with chili, garlic, or nuts.

With the help of a food processor or blender, you can whip up homemade nut butters in a few minutes. Peanut butter is the most popular, but don't stop there. Make cashew butter spiked with ginger or pecan butter sweetened with brown sugar and a jolt of bourbon. Stud walnut butter with morsels of figs or turn peanut butter into a confection with a generous fistful of roasted peanuts, raisins, and chocolate chips.

ABOUT THESE RECIPES

The following 50 recipes will take care of your gift lists for years with flavorful, heartwarming, belly-filling goodies. The yield for each is given at the end of the recipe. The addition of salt and pepper in most of the recipes is not mentioned, unless their presence or the amount called for is unusual; otherwise, add to taste.

 Gingerbread Muffins

Sift ¾ cup flour, ¾ teaspoon baking soda, a pinch of salt, 2 teaspoons ground ginger, and a pinch of powdered mustard. Set aside. Beat 1 extra-large egg, ¼ cup dark brown sugar, and 2 tablespoons granulated sugar until thick. Add 6 tablespoons molasses and 3 tablespoons oil in a slow, steady stream. Add dry ingredients in 2 additions, alternating with 6 tablespoons strong boiling hot coffee. Pour into 12 large muffin cups lined with cupcake papers and sprinkle tops with ½ cup finely chopped walnuts. Bake in preheated 400° F. oven for 18 minutes. Let cool. Dust with ¼ cup confectioners' sugar and wrap individually. Makes 12.

 Hot Pepper Gingerbread Muffins

Follow preceding recipe, but sift ½ teaspoon ground cinnamon, ¼ teaspoon ground cloves, ¼ teaspoon ground black pepper, a pinch of white pepper, and a pinch of cayenne pepper with the dry ingredients. Mix in 2 tablespoons grated fresh gingerroot after sifting. Replace walnuts with hazelnuts. Makes 12.

 Gingerbread Men

Bring ⅔ cup light molasses, ⅔ cup sugar, 1 tablespoon ground ginger, 1 tablespoon ground cinnamon, and 2 tablespoons instant coffee powder to a boil in 2-quart saucepan. Immediately stir in 1 tablespoon baking soda and pour over 10 tablespoons butter, cut in small pieces, stirring until melted. Beat in 1 beaten egg and 5 cups flour, kneading in the last cup until a smooth dough forms. Roll a third of the dough on a floured board to ¼ inch thick. Cut with a man-shaped cookie cutter and transfer to paper-lined cookie sheets. Repeat with remaining dough, then brush cookies

with mixture of 1 egg yolk and 1 tablespoon water. Make "eyes," "noses," "mouths," and "buttons" with scraps of dough or dried and candied fruit and brush again with the egg wash. Bake in preheated 325° F. oven for 25 minutes. Cool and tie a ribbon around the "neck" of each cookie. Makes 12 large or 18 small gingerbread men.

 Gingerbread Wreaths

Follow preceding recipe, but cut each portion of rolled dough with 3-inch leaf-shaped cookie cutter into 20 "leaves." Brush with 1 egg yolk mixed with 1 tablespoon water and arrange each group of 20 on a paper-lined cookie sheet overlapping one another in a wreath shape. Form scraps into clusters of "berries" and "stems," attaching to wreaths for decoration. Brush all with more egg wash before baking. Tie ribbons around wreaths for hanging. Makes 3 wreaths, each 6 portions.

 Fruitcake Brownies

Toss 1 cup raisins, 1 cup coarsely chopped pitted dates, 1 cup chopped dried apricots, and 1 cup chopped candied fruit with ¼ cup brandy. Cover and set aside for at least 24 hours. Toss in 2 cups coarsely chopped walnuts. Beat 4 eggs, ¼ teaspoon salt, 1 cup firmly packed dark brown sugar, and 1 teaspoon vanilla extract just enough to mix. Stir in 1 cup flour mixed with 1 teaspoon ground cinnamon, 1 teaspoon ground ginger, a pinch of ground cloves, and the finely chopped zest of 2 lemons. Pour over fruits and nuts and mix until all are moistened with batter. Pour into a greased 10-by-15-by-1-inch rimmed sheet pan and smooth top. Bake in preheated 325° F. oven for 35 minutes. Let cool. Mix 1½ cups confectioners' sugar, 2 tablespoons melted butter, and ¼ cup dark rum. Drizzle over cooled cake. Allow to dry for 10 minutes. Cut into 32 brownies.

Walnut Fig Bars

Follow preceding recipe, substituting 3 cups finely chopped stemmed dried figs for the dried and candied fruit and adding another 1 cup walnuts. Use bourbon instead of rum for icing.

 Sugar Plums

Make 1½ ounces almond paste into 18 small balls. Stuff each into an extra-large pitted prune through a small slit made in the prune's side. Wrap each prune in a 3-inch circle of Cream Cheese Pastry (page 434) rolled to ⅛-inch thickness, sealing edges with mixture of 1 egg yolk and 1 tablespoon water. Place seam side down on greased cookie sheet and bake in preheated 350° F. oven 30 minutes. Let cool 10 minutes, and dust with ½ cup confectioners' sugar. Makes 18.

 Pecan Shortbread

In a food processor, coarsely chop 1 cup pecan pieces. Add 2 cups flour, ⅓ cup cornstarch, and ½ cup sugar, and process to a fine meal. Add ½ pound chilled chopped butter and ½ teaspoon vanilla extract and process until mixture climbs side of workbowl. Knead until smooth and homogeneous. Pat and roll to ⅓-inch thickness. Cut into 2-inch circles and place on ungreased cookie sheets. Bake in preheated 375° F. oven for 20 minutes. Let cool. Makes 36.

 Praline Shortbread

Follow preceding recipe, substituting brown sugar for granulated sugar.

 Orange Liqueur Brownies

Melt 5 ounces unsweetened chocolate with 11 tablespoons butter. Add 1 teaspoon orange extract.

Let cool. Beat 4 eggs with 2 cups sugar until thick. Add 2 tablespoons orange liqueur, the melted chocolate, 1 cup sifted flour, and the finely grated zest of 1 large orange. Beat until smooth. Pour into a rimmed 10-by-15-inch sheet pan that has been lined with paper, buttered, and floured, and bake in a preheated 400° F. oven for 21 minutes. Invert onto the back of a sheet pan and remove pan and paper. Invert back into the pan and let cool on a rack. Cut into 32 brownies.

 Kumquat Pound Cakes

Mince and reserve 3 dozen seeded and juiced kumquats. With an electric mixer, beat 1 pound butter until fluffy with 3 cups sugar, 1 tablespoon vanilla extract, ½ teaspoon ground ginger, and ¼ teaspoon grated nutmeg. Add 10 eggs, 2 at a time, scraping to keep batter smooth. Mix in 4 cups sifted flour and the kumquats. Pour into 10 greased and floured mini-loaf pans and bake in preheated 350° F. oven for 45 minutes, until a tester comes out with a moist crumb clinging to it. Unpan, let cool, and wrap individually. Makes 8 servings.

 Cardamom Apricot Pound Cake

Follow preceding recipe, substituting dried apricots for the kumquats and 1 teaspoon ground cardamom for the nutmeg.

 Whiskey Pound Cakes

With an electric mixer, beat ¾ pound butter until fluffy with 3 cups light brown sugar, 1 tablespoon vanilla extract, ½ teaspoon grated nutmeg, and a pinch of ground cloves. Add 6 eggs, 2 at a time, scraping to keep batter smooth. Sift 3¼ cups flour with 2 teaspoons baking powder and mix into batter alternately with ½ cup whiskey mixed with ½ cup buttermilk. Pour into 8 greased, floured mini-loaf pans, and bake in preheated 350° F. oven for 45 minutes, until a tester comes out with a crumb clinging to it. Let cool, unpan, and wrap individually. Makes 8.

 ### Pistachio Tea Cake

With an electric mixer, beat ½ pound butter, ½ cup almond paste, 2 teaspoons almond extract, and 1 cup sugar until fluffy. Add 4 eggs, 1 at a time, scraping to keep batter smooth. Sift 1⅓ cups flour with 1 teaspoon baking powder, and stir in with ¼ pound finely ground shelled pistachio nuts. Turn into a greased, floured 9-by-5-inch loaf pan, and cover top with ⅓ cup chopped shelled pistachios. Bake 1 hour 10 minutes in preheated 350° F. oven. Let cool. Serves 8.

 ### Walnut Cupcakes

Sift 2 cups flour, 1 teaspoon baking powder, and a pinch of salt. Mix in ¾ cup finely chopped walnuts. Beat 10 tablespoons butter, 1½ cups sugar, and ½ teaspoon *each* vanilla and almond extracts until fluffy. Add 3 extra-large eggs, 1 at a time, beating until smooth. Add dry ingredients in 3 additions, alternately with 1 cup milk. Pour in 24 muffin tins lined with cupcake papers and sprinkle with ½ cup chopped walnuts. Bake in a preheated 350° F. oven for 25 minutes. Let cool and dust with ½ cup confectioners' sugar. Makes 2 dozen.

Two-Ton Nut Cake

Sift 3½ cups flour, 1 tablespoon baking powder, and 1 teaspoon grated nutmeg. With an electric mixer, beat ¾ pound butter with 2¼ cups brown sugar until fluffy. Add 6 eggs, 1 at a time, scraping to keep batter smooth. Add dry ingredients in 3 additions alternately with mixture of 1 teaspoon vanilla extract, ½ cup milk, and ½ cup bourbon. In a large bowl, toss batter with 2 pounds pecan pieces until well coated. Pack into a 10-by-4-inch greased, floured tube pan. Arrange ⅔ pound pecan halves in concentric circles over top of cake and bake in preheated 350° F. oven for 1 hour 45 minutes, covering with foil for the last 45 minutes. Let cool for 20 minutes, unpan, and slowly pour 1 cup bourbon over cake until fully absorbed. Let cool completely. Slice with a serrated knife. Serves 30.

 ### Almond Amaretto Cake

Sift 3½ cups flour, 1 tablespoon baking powder, and 1 teaspoon grated nutmeg. With an electric mixer, beat ¾ pound butter with 2¼ cups sugar until fluffy. Add 6 eggs, 1 at a time, scraping to keep batter smooth. Add dry ingredients in 3 additions alternately with mixture of ½ teaspoon vanilla extract, ½ teaspoon almond extract, ½ cup milk, and ½ cup Amaretto. In a large bowl, toss batter with 2 pounds almond pieces until well coated. Pack into a 10-by-4-inch greased, floured tube pan. Arrange ⅔ pound almonds in concentric circles over top of cake. Bake as in preceding recipe. Cool for 20 minutes, unpan, and slowly pour 1 cup Amaretto over cake until fully absorbed. Let cool completely. Slice with a serrated knife. Serves 30.

 ### Honey Rum Raisin Tea Cake

Soak 1 cup raisins, ¾ cup dark rum, and the finely grated zest of 2 oranges. Sift 2 cups flour, ¾ teaspoon baking powder, ¾ teaspoon baking soda, ¼ teaspoon salt, 2 teaspoons ground cinnamon, and 1 teaspoon ground ginger. Beat 3 large eggs, ¾ cup dark brown sugar, 3 tablespoons melted butter, and ¾ cup honey until well mixed. Mix in dry ingredients alternately with the raisin mixture and turn into buttered, floured 9-by-5-inch loaf pan. Bake in preheated 350° F. degree oven for 1 hour 10 minutes. Let cool 10 minutes and unpan. Serves 8.

Pepper Cheddar Skillet Corn Bread

Brush a 9-inch iron skillet with oil and place in 425° F. oven. Cook 3 sliced scallions and 1 diced red bell pepper in ¼ cup corn oil until softened. Let cool. Mix 1 cup yellow cornmeal, 1 cup flour, ¼ cup sugar, 3 teaspoons baking powder, and ½ teaspoon salt. Mix in sautéed vegetables, 1 cup milk, and 1 cup grated Cheddar cheese. Pour into the hot iron skillet and bake 35 minutes. Let cool. Loosen bottom of bread from pan. Serves 4.

 ## Savarin

Dissolve 2 teaspoons dry yeast in ½ cup warm milk. Stir in ½ cup flour, cover, and set in a warm place for 30 minutes. Beat 3 tablespoons sugar, 2 tablespoons flour, and ¼ pound softened butter. Add 6 eggs and beat until smooth. Mix 2 cups flour into the yeast mixture along with egg mixture. Pour into well-greased 8-inch Bundt pan, cover, and let rise for 45 minutes. Bake in preheated 350° F. oven for 40 minutes. While cake is baking, boil 2⅓ cups sugar and 5 cups water until reduced to 3 cups. Stir in ½ cup dark rum. Pour over baked savarin slowly so all the syrup is absorbed. Let cool for 45 minutes before unpanning. Serve with whipped cream.

 ## Orange Savarin

Follow preceding recipe adding ¼ cup finely grated orange zest to egg mixture. Serve with candied orange peel or candied orange slices along with the whipped cream.

 ## Baba au Rhum

Follow recipe for Savarin (above), but divide finished dough among 12 well-greased muffin tins. Reduce cooking time to 23 minutes. After baking, unpan babas and place them in a pan that will hold them in 1 layer before pouring syrup over them. Spoon any syrup that drips down into the pan back over the babas until all of it has been absorbed.

 ## Meatless Mincemeat

Melt 4 tablespoons butter with 1 cup molasses, 1 cup apple cider, and ½ cup brandy. Toss mixture with 1 pound raisins, 1 pound currants, 4 ounces *each* chopped candied citron, candied orange peel, and dried apricots, 4 pounds peeled, cored, and finely chopped Granny Smith apples, 15 crumbled unsalted crackers, 3 tablespoons ground cinnamon, 1 tablespoon *each* ground ginger, ground cloves, and grated nutmeg, the juice and zest of 1 lemon, 1 teaspoon salt, ½ teaspoon freshly ground pepper, and 1 cup sugar. Cover and refrigerate at least 24 hours. Makes 3 quarts.

 ## Cider Syrup

In large, heavy saucepan, bring ⅓ cup sugar and 5⅓ cups apple cider to a boil. Skim any scum that rises to surface and boil until mixture reduces to 1 cup. Let cool in decorative jar. Keep refrigerated. Makes 1 cup.

 ## Spicy Garlic Oil

Heat 2 cups corn, Oriental sesame, or olive oil with 6 dried chili peppers and 1 bulb peeled garlic cloves until garlic and peppers start to bubble from their tips, about 4 minutes. Remove from heat and let cool. Pour all into a decorative bottle. Makes 2 cups.

 ## Citrus Oil

Heat 2 cups peanut oil with strips of zest from 2 oranges and 2 lemons until strips bubble at their ends. Remove from heat and let cool. Pour all into a decorative bottle. Makes 2 cups.

Fifty Ways to Cook Most Everything

 Ginger Sesame Oil

Heat 2 cups Oriental sesame oil with ⅓ cup julienned fresh gingerroot until strips bubble at their ends. Remove from heat and let cool. Pour all into a decorative bottle. Makes 2 cups.

 Provençal Oil

Heat 2 cups olive oil, 4 sliced cloves garlic, and 2 tablespoons *herbes de Provence* until bubbles form all around garlic. Do not allow garlic to brown. Remove from heat and let oil steep 1 hour. Strain and pour into a clean bottle. Makes 2 cups.

 Orange Fennel Walnut Oil

Heat 2 cups walnut oil, ¼ cup finely chopped orange zest, and 2 tablespoons fennel seed until bubbles form all around fennel seed. Remove from heat and let oil steep 1 hour. Strain and pour into a clean bottle. Makes 2 cups.

 Herb Vinegar

Heat 1 cup chopped fresh herb (basil, tarragon, chervil, oregano, cilantro) in 2 cups wine vinegar. Bring to a boil, remove from heat, and let steep 1 hour. Strain and store in tightly closed jar. Makes 1 pint.

 Fruit Vinegar

Heat 1 pint chopped citrus fruit, pears, peaches, plums, grapes, and/or berries in 1½ cups wine vinegar. Bring to a boil, remove from heat, and let steep 1 hour. Strain and store in tightly closed jar. Makes 1 pint.

 Pear Vinegar

Heat 3 finely chopped ripe pears in 2 cups white wine vinegar. Bring to a boil, remove from heat, and let steep 1 hour. Strain. Place 1 large perfect pear in a tightly closing wide-mouth jar and pour strained vinegar over top. Makes 1 quart.

 Lemon Garlic Vinegar

Heat 1 head garlic, separated into cloves, ¼ cup finely chopped lemon zest, and 1½ cups white wine vinegar. Bring to a boil, remove from the heat, and let steep 1 hour. Strain and add the juice of 2 lemons. Store in a tightly closed jar. Makes 1 pint.

 Spicy Corn Relish

Brown 1 cup chopped onion in 1 teaspoon corn oil. Add 1 tablespoon pickling spice, 1 dried chili pepper, 1 cup water, ¾ cup cider vinegar, 1 bay leaf, and 3 tablespoons sugar. Bring to a boil. Add ⅓ cup peeled, diced carrot and simmer for 5 minutes. Add 4 cups cooked corn and 2 diced roasted red bell peppers (page 442) and heat through. Makes 1 quart.

 Curried Eggplant Chutney

Cook 1 cup chopped onion and 1 clove minced garlic in 1 tablespoon olive oil until softened. Add 1 tablespoon curry powder, 1 teaspoon ground cumin, and 1 teaspoon chili powder and cook 2 minutes more. Add 1 large peeled and diced eggplant, 1 cup chopped canned tomatoes, 2 tablespoons sugar, salt, pepper, and ¼ teaspoon ground saffron dissolved in ¼ cup vinegar. Simmer 15 minutes. Add ½ cup roasted peanuts. Makes 3 cups.

Sweet Spiked Walnuts

Simmer 2¼ cups walnut pieces in 1 cup strong coffee for 3 minutes. Add ¼ cup Scotch whiskey, 1½ cups sugar, and ½ teaspoon salt. Bring to a boil, stirring constantly. Add 2 ounces liquid pectin and boil for 2 minutes. Makes 2 cups.

 ## Coffee Bourbon Pecans

Simmer 2¼ cups pecan pieces in 1 cup strong coffee for 3 minutes. Add ¼ cup bourbon, ¾ cup granulated sugar, ¾ cup brown sugar, and ½ teaspoon salt. Bring to a boil, stirring constantly. Add 2 ounces liquid pectin and boil for 2 minutes. Makes 2 cups.

 ## Bitter Grapefruit Marmalade

Boil the julienned zest of 3 large grapefruits in water for 5 minutes. Strain and combine the drained zest with the juice of 6 large grapefruits (about 6 cups) and slowly bring to a boil. Simmer for 5 minutes. Add 3½ cups sugar, a pinch of salt, and 1 tablespoon lemon juice and stir until returned to a boil. Boil for 5 minutes. Add 9 ounces liquid pectin and boil 1 minute more. Pour into jars, cool, and refrigerate. Makes 6 cups.

 ## Lemon Green-Peppercorn Marmalade

Boil the julienned zest of 9 lemons in water for 5 minutes. Strain and combine drained zest with 5 cups lemon juice and 1 cup water and slowly bring to a boil. Simmer for 5 minutes. Add 3½ cups sugar and a pinch of salt and stir until returned to a boil. Boil for 5 minutes. Add 9 ounces liquid pectin and boil 1 more minute. Crush ⅓ cup drained canned green peppercorns with the back of a spoon and stir into the finished marmalade. Pour into jars, cool, and refrigerate. Makes 6 cups.

 ## Jalapeño Jelly

In a food processor, finely chop 1 large seeded bell pepper, 1 large seeded apple, and 12 seeded jalapeño peppers. Bring to a boil with 1½ cups cider vinegar and simmer for 15 minutes. Allow liquid to drip through a strainer and discard any pulp that remains. Heat liquid with ¼ teaspoon salt and 4¼ cups sugar, stirring constantly, until mixture comes to a boil that can't be stirred down. Boil for 3 minutes. Stir in 6 ounces liquid pectin and 4 diced, seeded jalapeño peppers and boil 1 minute more. Pour into 4-ounce jars. Let cool and refrigerate. Makes 3½ cups.

 ## Gingered Carrot Marmalade

In a food processor, finely chop 1 pound peeled carrots and a 1-inch piece fresh gingerroot. Simmer with 1 cup orange juice and 1 cup apple cider or rice vinegar for 10 minutes, skimming any scum that rises to the surface. Stir in 1 teaspoon salt and 4 cups sugar, stirring until the marmalade reaches a boil that can't be stirred down. Boil for 1 minute. Add 6 ounces liquid pectin and simmer 1 minute more. Pour into jars. Let cool and refrigerate. Makes 4 to 5 cups.

 ## Caramel Pear Preserves

In a heavy pot, cook 5 large diced pears in 1 cup water, the juice of 1 lemon, and 2 tablespoons white wine vinegar until pears soften. Add ¼ teaspoon salt, 2 cups granulated sugar, and 2 cups brown sugar. Stir until preserve reaches a boil that can't be stirred down. Boil for 5 minutes and add 9 ounces liquid pectin. Boil 1 minute. Pour into jars. Let cool and refrigerate. Makes 6 cups.

Marinated Herbed Mushrooms

Bring 1 pound scrubbed, trimmed small mushrooms, 1½ tablespoons lemon juice, 1½ cups dry white wine, 1 bay leaf, 4 finely sliced scallions, ⅔ cup olive oil, ¼ teaspoon dried thyme, and ¼ teaspoon ground coriander to a boil, reduce heat, and simmer for 5 minutes. Remove mushrooms and reduce marinade by a third. Return mushrooms, along with ⅓ cup chopped fresh parsley, to the pan, return to a boil, and let cool. Makes 3 cups.

 Easy Honey Mustard

Whisk 2 cups brown mustard with 1 cup honey. Makes 3 cups.

 Green Peppercorn Mustard

Crush 3 tablespoons canned green peppercorns with 1 teaspoon vinegar and 1 teaspoon dried tarragon. Bring to a simmer and stir into 1 cup Dijon mustard. Makes about 1¼ cups.

 Red-Wine Whole-Grain Mustard

Soak overnight ¼ cup mustard seed in 1 teaspoon red wine vinegar and 2 tablespoons red wine. Bring to a boil and stir into 1 cup Dijon mustard. Makes about 1½ cups.

 Heavy-Duty Hazelnut Truffles

Over low heat, melt 1 tablespoon butter with ½ cup heavy cream. Add 8 ounces finely chopped semisweet chocolate and stir until melted. Transfer to a bowl and whisk in 3 tablespoons Frangelico (or other nut-flavored liqueur) and 2 tablespoons strong coffee. Cool completely. Scoop into rough tablespoon-size balls, and roll in ¼ cup toasted ground hazelnuts mixed with 2 tablespoons confectioners' sugar. Place in foil or paper candy cups, if desired. Makes 12.

 Raisin Chocolate Chip Peanut Butter

In a food processor, finely chop 1½ cups unsalted roasted peanuts with a pinch of salt. Process continuously until smooth, about 3 minutes, stopping to scrape bowl periodically. When fully processed, mix in a bowl with ⅓ cup chocolate chips and ⅓ cup raisins. Makes 2 cups.

 Pecan or Walnut Butter

In a food processor, using the pulsing action, finely chop 1 pound pecan or walnut pieces, a pinch of salt, and 2 teaspoons light brown sugar. Process continuously until smooth, about 3 minutes, stopping to scrape bowl periodically. Makes 2 cups.

 Ginger Tahini

Toast 2 cups sesame seeds by shaking them in a hot skillet for 3 to 4 minutes, until they pop and color lightly. Process with a pinch of salt, a pinch of grated nutmeg, and ¼ teaspoon ground ginger in a pulsing action until finely chopped. Turn on the processor and process until smooth, about 3 minutes, scraping the sides periodically. Mix in ¼ cup minced candied ginger. Makes 2 cups.

Appendix A

Fifty Basic Preparations

In most cases, you'll arrive at this appendix via a reference written into another recipe. Most of the 50 basic recipes in this appendix are not intended to be stand-alone recipes but elements of other recipes. Some of the entries below are basic preparations for simple batters, doughs, sauces, and condiments, compiled here for your convenience.

As the title of this section implies, the recipes that follow are simple and straightforward. They are neither unique nor creative, so if you have your own tried-and-true corn bread or pie crust, by all means use it instead of ours.

COOKING BASICS

Refried Beans (Black, White, or Kidney)

Heat 2 teaspoons olive oil in a nonstick skillet. Add ¼ cup finely chopped onion and cook 2 minutes. Add 1 clove minced garlic and 2½ cups cooked beans with 1 cup of their liquid. While beans are cooking, mash them into a coarse paste with the back of a fork or wooden spoon. Cook until mixture is fairly dry. Set aside and keep warm. Makes 6 to 8 portions.

Béchamel Sauce (White Sauce)

Heat 2 cups milk until steam rises from its surface. Add 2 tablespoons finely chopped carrot, 2 tablespoons finely chopped celery, and ¼ cup chopped onion. Remove from heat and set aside for 10 minutes. Strain. Separately, cook 1 tablespoon flour in 1 tablespoon melted butter for 1 to 2 minutes, until bubbly. Add the hot milk, whisking until all lumps are gone. Simmer 10 minutes, stirring frequently with a wooden spoon. Season with a dash of grated nutmeg, salt, and pepper. (For thick béchamel, use 2 tablespoons *each* flour and butter. For extra-thick béchamel, to use as a base for soufflés and croquettes, use 4 tablespoons *each* flour and butter.) Makes about 2 cups.

Mornay Sauce (Cheese Sauce)

Prepare preceding recipe. Bring to a boil, remove from heat, and stir in ⅔ cup finely grated cheese until melted. Use a sauce for vegetables, fish, or as a base for soufflés. Warning: Do not boil any mixture that contains cheese. The additional heat will cause it to congeal and separate.

Fifty Ways to Cook Most Everything

Court Bouillon

Bring to a boil 2 cups water, 2 cups white wine, ½ cup chopped onion, ¼ cup *each* chopped carrot and celery, 1 bay leaf, a pinch of thyme, 1 tablespoon chopped fresh parsley, 4 peppercorns, 1 clove, and 1 tablespoon lemon juice. Simmer 15 minutes and strain. Makes 1 quart.

Clarified Butter

Melt ¼ pound butter over moderate heat until it separates. There should be foam on top, clear golden liquid in the middle, and solids on the bottom. Skim off the foam and carefully pour off the clear liquid, which is your clarified butter. Discard solid particles left in the pot. Yields about 6 tablespoons.

Chicken Broth or Chicken Stock

Place 5 pounds raw chicken backs, necks, gizzards, hearts, and trimmings in a large soup pot. Add 10 quarts cold water, bring to a boil, and skim away scum that rises to the surface. Turn down to a simmer. Add ¼ pound chopped carrots, 2 ribs chopped celery, 1 large chopped onion, the juice of ½ lemon, 2 teaspoons salt, 1 tablespoon peppercorns, 2 teaspoons dried thyme, 2 teaspoons fresh dill, 1 whole clove, 1 bay leaf, and 5 sprigs parsley. Simmer 3 hours. Strain and let cool. Refrigerate up to 5 days or freeze up to 2 to 3 months. Remove fat. Use for soups, sauces, and stews. Makes about 2 gallons.

Beef Broth or Beef Stock

Rub 5 to 7 pounds beef bones with oil and place on a rimmed sheet pan so bones don't touch. Roast in 450° F. oven until uniformly browned, about 30 minutes, turning every 10 minutes. Place in a large soup pot, add 10 quarts cold water, bring to a boil, and skim away scum that rises to the surface. Turn down to a simmer and cook 1 hour. Meanwhile, brown ¼ pound chopped carrots, 2 ribs chopped celery, and 1 large chopped onion in the fat left in the browning pans. Add to the pot with 2 tablespoons tomato paste, 2 teaspoons salt, 1 tablespoon peppercorns, 2 teaspoons dried thyme, 1 whole clove, 1 bay leaf, and 5 sprigs parsley. Simmer 6 hours. Strain and let cool. Refrigerate up to 5 days or freeze as long as 2 to 3 months. Remove fat. Use for soups, sauces, and stews. Makes about 2 gallons.

Vegetable Broth or Vegetable Stock

In a covered pot over moderate heat, cook 2 large chopped unpeeled onions, 1 head unpeeled garlic cloves, the chopped whites of 4 washed leeks, 1 pound washed mushrooms, 1 pound chopped carrots, ½ pound chopped parsnips, 10 chopped tomatoes, and 1 bunch chopped celery in 2 tablespoons vegetable oil, stirring occasionally, until vegetables soften. Add 1 bay leaf, 12 peppercorns, 2 teaspoons dried thyme, 1 tablespoon salt, 1 teaspoon ground turmeric, 2 cloves, and ⅓ cup chopped fresh parsley. Add 2 gallons cold water, bring to a boil, and skim scum that rises to the surface. Simmer 2 hours. Strain and let cool. Refrigerate up to 3 days or freeze as long as several months. Makes about 1½ gallons.

Quick Fish Broth or Fish Stock

Cook 1 finely chopped onion, 3 ribs finely chopped celery, 1 chopped parsnip, and 2 chopped carrots in 1 tablespoon vegetable oil until vegetables soften. Add 3 cups white wine and boil 5 minutes. Add 4 cups clam juice, 3 cups water, the juice and coarsely chopped zest of 1 large lemon, salt, pepper, 2 branches dill, and 2 sprigs parsley. Bring to a boil, skim away scum that rises to surface, and simmer 15 minutes. Strain and refrigerate up to 2 days or freeze up to several months. Use in any recipe calling for fish stock. Makes about 2 quarts.

Garlic Butter

Cook 4 cloves minced garlic in 1 tablespoon olive oil until aromatic and soft. Let cool and beat into 4 tablespoons softened butter. Let cool. Makes about 5 tablespoons.

Herb Butter

Cook 2 teaspoons minced shallots in 1 teaspoon olive oil until softened. Add 1 tablespoon minced fresh parsley, 2 teaspoons *each* chopped fresh basil and dill, and 1 teaspoon chopped fresh tarragon and heat long enough to wilt the leaves. Beat into 5 tablespoons softened butter. Let cool. Makes about 5 tablespoons.

Tomato Butter

Cook 1 clove minced garlic in 1 teaspoon corn oil until softened. Add 2 tablespoons tomato paste and 1 minced basil leaf, bring to a simmer, and let cool to room temperature. Mix into ¼ pound softened butter. Let cool. Makes about 9 tablespoons.

Croutons

Cut any kind of stale bread into ½-inch cubes. For each cup of bread cubes, toss with 1 tablespoon olive oil, ½ clove minced garlic, 1 teaspoon paprika, 1 tablespoon finely grated Parmesan, salt, and pepper. Spread out on an oiled sheet pan and bake in a 375° F. oven for 20 minutes, stirring every 5 minutes. Makes 1 cup.

Soft- and Hard-Cooked Eggs

Poke a small hole in the rounder end of 1 egg with a thumbtack or pushpin. Place in a pot of simmering water, return to a simmer, and cook 3 to 5 minutes for soft-cooked, and 12 to 15 minutes for hard-cooked. Do not allow water to boil. It does not matter whether pot is covered, so long as eggs are entirely submerged. Cool eggs immediately by draining and running under cold tap water.

Roasted Eggplant

Poke 1 medium eggplant all over with a fork. Place in 400° F. oven for 45 minutes, remove, and let cool for 10 minutes. Cut off stem. Halve lengthwise and scrape out flesh with a spoon. Makes about 2 cups.

Rendered Fat

Sometimes bacon fat or chicken fat is used for sautéing. First, the fat must be rendered. To render, cut the fat into small pieces and cook over moderate heat until melted. Remove any crisped bits of meat or skin with a slotted spoon.

Chicken Gravy

Cook 1 tablespoon flour in 2 tablespoons chicken fat, skimmed from pan drippings, for about 3 minutes. Add 2 cups chicken broth and/or the juices from a roasted chicken, whisking until all lumps are gone. Simmer 10 minutes, stirring frequently with a wooden spoon. Season with salt and pepper. If you'd like cream gravy, finish with ¼ cup light cream. Makes about 2 cups.

Beef Gravy

Brown ¼ cup *each* finely chopped carrots and celery and ½ cup chopped onion in 3 tablespoons beef fat, skimmed from pan drippings. Add 4 chopped canned tomatoes and 1 tablespoon tomato paste, cooking 3 minutes more. Add 2 tablespoons flour and cook until flour browns, about 10 minutes. Add 4 cups beef broth and/or juices from a roast beef and stir until smooth. Add 1 bay leaf, ½ teaspoon dried thyme, and 2 sprigs parsley. Simmer at least 30 minutes. Season with salt and pepper. Strain. Makes about 3 cups.

Homemade Mayonnaise

In a bowl using a whisk, or in a food processor, beat 2 egg yolks with 2 teaspoons mustard until lightly thickened. Add 2 tablespoons lemon juice. In a slow stream, mix in 1½ cups mild vegetable oil (safflower, corn, canola, peanut, sunflower, etc.) Season with salt, white pepper, and a dash of cayenne pepper, all dissolved in 1 tablespoon boiling water. Makes about 2 cups. (Warning: As with any preparation using uncooked egg, this recipe poses a risk of salmonella. Buy eggs from reputable sources, keep refrigerated, and use as soon as possible.)

Aïoli

Follow preceding recipe, using 2 cloves finely chopped garlic instead of the mustard, and using a mixture of ½ cup olive oil plus 1 cup mild vegetable oil.

Egg Pasta

In workbowl of a food processor, blend 2 extra-large eggs, ¼ teaspoon salt, and 1⅓ cups unbleached flour until a smooth stiff dough forms in center of workbowl. Cover and let rest 10 minutes. Roll out to desired thickness using a pasta machine or a rolling pin and cut into desired shape. Makes about ¾ pound.

Doctored Jarred Pasta Sauce

Cook 1 cup chopped onion, 3 cloves minced garlic, ½ teaspoon crushed red pepper, 2 teaspoons dried basil and ¼ teaspoon dried oregano in 2 tablespoons olive oil until vegetables soften. Add 1 cup white wine and reduce by half. Add 32 ounces jarred tomato pasta sauce and simmer 15 minutes. Serves 6 to 8.

Roux

A roux is equal amounts of flour and butter cooked together to a homogenous paste, used for thickening sauces and as a base for savory mousses and soufflés. Start by melting the butter in a heavy saucepan over moderately low heat, add the flour, and stir until incorporated. Continue stirring until desired color is reached. The longer a roux cooks, the browner and more flavorful it becomes. A white roux, used for cream sauces, soufflés and croquettes, cooks less than 2 minutes. A blonde roux, used for chicken gravies and other light sauces, cooks 3 to 6 minutes. And a brown roux, used for beef gravy and many stews, cooks 10 minutes or more. Take care not to splash brown roux, which can get dangerously hot.

Slurry

Mix 1 tablespoon cornstarch with 2 tablespoons water until smooth. Stir again just before adding to 2 to 3 cups boiling liquid to thicken liquid into a sauce.

Homemade Yogurt

Heat 1 quart milk until bubbles form around perimeter. Let cool to about 100° F. (warm to the touch) and remove any skin from the surface. Stir in ½ cup powdered milk and ¼ cup plain yogurt, cover with plastic wrap, and set in a closed oven with a pilot light, near a warm radiator or hot-water heater, or any location with a constant temperature of about 100° F. for 4 to 6 hours. When done, yogurt will be thickened like custard. Refrigerate several hours and it will become thicker. Makes 1 quart.

BAKING BASICS

Basic Bread and Pizza Dough

Dissolve ⅛ ounce (½ package) dry yeast in ½ cup warm water. Stir in 1 cup bread flour, cover loosely with plastic wrap, and set in a warm place to rise for 20 minutes. Add another ½ cup warm water and 1 teaspoon salt. Place in the workbowl of a food processor, add 1½ cups all-purpose flour, and process until dough forms a ball in center of bowl. You may need to add up to ¼ cup additional flour to form dough of proper consistency. Remove dough and knead lightly on a floured board. Place in a bowl brushed with olive oil and turn over. Cover lightly and set in a warm place to rise, about 1 hour. Punch down, divide in half, and form into loaves or pizza disks. Makes 2 small loaves, 2 large pizzas, or 1 of each.

Basic Quick Buttercream

Beat together until fluffy 9 tablespoons butter or margarine, 3 cups confectioners' sugar, a pinch of salt, 1½ teaspoons vanilla extract, and ¼ cup milk, coffee, lemon juice, or liqueur. Makes enough to frost 1 cake.

Basic French Buttercream

Beat 6 egg yolks until fluffy. Bring ⅔ cup sugar and ⅓ cup water to a boil and cook about 4 minutes (250° F. on a candy thermometer or until thick enough to form a loose blob when a small amount is dropped in a glass of water). Slowly pour hot syrup into egg yolks while beating at high speed. Continue beating until mixture is cool. Add ¾ pound softened butter a tablespoon at a time. Beat until fluffy. Makes enough to frost 1 large cake.

Chocolate Sour Cream Frosting

Beat ½ cup sour cream into 1 cup warm melted semisweet chocolate chips. Makes enough to frost 1 small cake. Double for larger cakes.

Chocolate Glaze

In a double boiler, melt 3 ounces semisweet chocolate, 2 ounces unsweetened chocolate, 6 table-spoons butter, and 1 tablespoon honey. Stir until smooth, place over ice water and continue stirring until slightly thickened. Makes enough for 1 small cake.

Corn Bread

Place a 9-inch iron skillet in a preheated 400° F. oven. Mix 1 cup yellow cornmeal, 1 cup flour, ¼ cup sugar, 1 tablespoon baking powder, and ½ teaspoon salt. Cook ½ cup chopped onion in 1 teaspoon corn oil until soft. Mix into dry ingredients with ¼ cup corn oil, 1 beaten egg, and 1 cup milk. Grease the hot skillet with 2 teaspoons corn oil and bake at 400° F. for 25 minutes. Unpan immediately. Serves 6.

Pastry Cream

Heat 1 cup milk, 3 tablespoons sugar, and a pinch of salt until milk bubbles at the edge. Beat another 3 tablespoons sugar with 3 large egg yolks until lightly thickened. Mix in 2 tablespoons cornstarch and 1 tablespoon flour until smooth. Stir in hot milk in a slow, steady stream. Cook over moderate heat, stirring constantly with a wooden spoon until mixture comes to a boil. Beat lumps out with a whisk. Transfer to a bowl and stir in 1 teaspoon vanilla extract. Cover loosely with plastic wrap and chill. Makes about 1½ cups.

Crème Anglaise

In a heavy saucepan, scald 1 cup milk, 1 cup light cream, and ⅓ cup sugar. Meanwhile, in top of double boiler, beat 6 egg yolks, ⅓ cup sugar, and a pinch of salt until thick and pale. Slowly whisk hot milk mixture into yolks and sugar. Place over simmering water and stir with wooden spoon until custard lightly coats spoon (180° F.). Immediately pour into a container and stir in 1 teaspoon vanilla extract. Serve cool or warm. Makes about 2½ cups.

Fifty Ways to Cook Most Everything

Lemon Curd

Beat 2 egg yolks, ½ cup sugar, and ¼ cup lemon juice until sugar is moistened. In a heavy nonstick or enamel-lined saucepan, mix another ½ cup sugar, 1½ cups water, and 2 tablespoons cornstarch. Cook over moderate heat until very thick, stirring frequently. Beat yolk mixture into the hot sauce in a slow, steady stream, and cook over low heat for 3 minutes, stirring constantly. Remove from heat and stir in 1 teaspoon vanilla extract, 1 tablespoon finely grated lemon zest, and 4 tablespoons softened butter. Cool completely. Makes 2 cups.

Egg Wash

Whisk 2 tablespoons water or milk into 1 whole egg, 2 egg yolks, or 2 egg whites. Makes about ⅓ cup.

Sponge Cake (Basic Génoise)

Beat 6 egg yolks with 1 cup sugar until very light and fluffy. Add 1 teaspoon vanilla extract. Fold in ¾ cup twice-sifted flour just until combined. Beat 6 egg whites with ⅛ teaspoon salt to a firm peak. Fold into batter. Bake in a greased and floured 10-inch layer pan at 350° F. for 20 to 25 minutes or in a greased and parchment-lined jellyroll pan for 15 minutes, until edges pull away from sides and center is springy. Unmold and cool or roll up sheet cake in a damp towel to cool. Makes 1 large layer or 1 sheet.

Toasted Nuts

In conventional oven, bake 1 cup whole nuts in a pie pan for 15 minutes at 350° F. stirring twice. For sliced or slivered nuts, bake for 10 minutes. On stovetop, heat a heavy iron skillet over high flame for 4 minutes, turn off the heat, add 1 cup whole, sliced, or slivered nuts and stir constantly until the nuts color, 1 to 3 minutes. In a microwave, place 1 cup whole nuts in shallow 10-inch glass pan and microwave at full power for 5 minutes, stirring twice.

Cream Cheese Pastry

Mix ½ pound *each* butter and cream cheese into 2¼ cups flour, 1 teaspoon sugar, and 1 teaspoon salt until smooth. Halve the dough, dust with flour, and pat each half into a flat disk. Wrap in plastic and refrigerate at least 1 hour. On a floured board with a floured pin, roll disks to between ⅛- and ¼-inch thickness. Use for crusts for savory pies, tarts, tartlets, etc. Bake as directed. Makes 2 crusts.

Flaky Pastry

In a large bowl using a pastry cutter, or in the workbowl of a food processor, blend 1½ cups flour, ¼ teaspoon salt, 6 tablespoons chilled unsalted butter, and 2 tablespoons plus 1 teaspoon chilled shortening until mixture resembles coarse meal. Add 4 to 6 tablespoons water, a few tablespoons at a time, until all the flour is moistened but the dough is still rough and unformed. Turn dough onto a clean board and quickly form into a flat disk. Wrap in plastic wrap and refrigerate at least 30 minutes. Bake as directed. Makes 1 crust.

Sweet Pastry

In a large bowl using a pastry cutter, or in workbowl of a food processor, blend 1½ cups flour, ¼ cup sugar, a pinch of salt, and 6 tablespoons chopped butter until mixture resembles coarse meal. Beat in 1 extra-large egg and 1 teaspoon vanilla extract until mixture is fully moistened. Turn onto a clean board and knead small handfuls of the dough until smooth. Form into a flat disk, wrap in plastic wrap, and refrigerate at least 30 minutes. Bake as directed. Makes 1 crust.

Sweet or Flaky Pastry Shell

Prepare one of the two previous recipes. Remove from refrigerator and roll on lightly floured board with a floured rolling pin into a disk at least 12 inches in diameter. Roll pastry loosely around the pin and transfer to a 9- or 10-inch tart or pie pan. Line pan with the pastry, crimp edges, and poke holes in the bottom of the pastry with the tines of a fork. Freeze for 20 minutes. Line pastry with foil and weight with uncooked rice, uncooked beans, or pastry weights. Bake in preheated 400° F. oven for 10 minutes. Remove foil and weights, reduce oven heat to 375° F., and return crust to oven until fully browned, about 30 minutes. (This is also known as a blind-baked pastry shell.) Makes 1 shell. (For more detailed explanations of Forming a Pastry Shell, Forming a Two-Crust Pie, Forming a Tart Shell, Forming Tartlet Shells, and Blind-Baking or Prebaking pastry, see those entries in Appendix B.)

Crumb Crust

Mix 3 cups plain cookie crumbs (any type), 2 tablespoons confectioners' sugar, 1 teaspoon ground cinnamon, and 4 tablespoons melted butter. Line the interior of a 9- or 10-inch pie pan by pressing mixture in a firm even layer. Line with foil and bake at 400° F. for 10 minutes. Remove foil and bake for 5 to 10 minutes more, until lightly browned. Cool. Makes 1 crust.

Pâte à Choux (Cream Puff and Eclair Pastry)

Bring 1 cup water to a boil with ¼ pound butter, cut into chunks, and a pinch of salt. Immediately dump in 1 cup all-purpose flour and beat vigorously until the batter forms a ball in the center of the pan. Remove from heat and beat in 4 or 5 eggs, 1 at a time, until mixture is smooth and glossy. Pipe through a pastry bag or spoon onto a parchment-lined baking sheet pan and bake at 400° F. until browned and puffed. Reduce oven heat to 350° F.

and continue baking until sides are firm. Poke holes in pastry bottoms and return to a 250° F. oven for 30 minutes until dried and crisp. Makes 12 large eclairs or 24 cream puffs.

Basic Pound Cake

Beat 1 pound butter with 3 cups sugar until light and fluffy. Beat in 1 tablespoon vanilla extract and 10 extra-large eggs, 1 at a time. Beat in 4 cups sifted flour just until mixed. Stir in the finely grated zest of 1 lemon, if desired. Bake in a greased 10-inch tube or Bundt pan for 1 hour 45 minutes, until a tester comes out clean. If cake begins to brown too much, cover with foil. Let cool for 15 minutes. Unmold and cool to room temperature. Makes 1 large cake.

Shortcake

Sift 4 cups sifted flour, ½ cup sugar, 2 tablespoons baking powder, 2 teaspoons baking soda, and ½ teaspoon salt. Cut in ½ pound butter, chilled and cut in chunks, until mixture resembles coarse meal. Separately, mix 1 cup light cream, ¼ cup buttermilk, and 2 lightly beaten medium eggs. Mix enough of the liquid into the dry ingredients to form a soft cohesive dough. With floured hands, pat out into a greased 9-inch layer pan. Brush with remaining liquid and bake at 375° F. for 35 minutes. Cool on a rack for 10 minutes. Unmold and let cool to room temperature. Slice in half horizontally using a long serrated knife. This cake cracks easily, so handle carefully; if it breaks, push it back together. Makes 8 to 10 portions.

Shortcake Biscuits

Prepare the same dough as in preceding recipe, but use only half the quantity of each ingredient. Pat dough out onto a floured board and cut 8 to 10 3-inch circles with a biscuit cutter. Brush tops with reserved milk mixture and a sprinkling of sugar. Bake on a sheet pan at 450° F. for 20 minutes, or as directed in your recipe. Makes 8 to 10 portions.

Simple Syrup

Bring ⅔ cup sugar and ⅔ cup water to a boil without stirring. Boil 1 minute and let cool. Makes 1 cup.

Streusel Topping or Crumb Topping

In a bowl, combine ¾ cup flour and ⅓ cup brown sugar. Cut 4 tablespoons chilled butter into dry ingredients until mixture resembles coarse meal. Makes about 1¼ cups.

Nut Streusel Topping

In a bowl, combine 1½ cups chopped nuts (any variety), ¼ cup flour, and ⅓ cup brown sugar. Cut 4 tablespoons chilled butter into dry ingredients until mixture resembles coarse meal. Makes about 2¼ cups.

Fruit Glaze

Melt 1 cup apricot preserves, orange marmalade, or currant jelly with 2 tablespoons sugar, and 2 tablespoons liqueur. Simmer 3 minutes, strain, and use while warm. Makes enough to glaze 2 tarts.

Appendix B

Fifty Basic Techniques

This appendix contains descriptions of basic cooking procedures, many of which you may be familiar with, others of which may be new to you. Some recipes in the main part of the book will include techniques that refer to this listing. If you're familiar with the procedure, just continue with the recipe; if you need a refresher, it's here for you.

This appendix is divided into two categories—cooking techniques and baking techniques.

Soaking Beans

There are two easy ways to rehydrate dried legumes. The traditional way is to let the beans sit overnight in water, using four times as much water as beans. A quicker way, using the same ratio of water to beans, is to bring the beans and water to a boil for 1 to 2 minutes, remove from heat, and let rest for 1 hour.

Blanching

This technique usually precedes additional cooking. Tomatoes, peaches, and almonds are blanched to remove their skins. Green beans and broccoli are blanched to soften their tough fibers. Veal is blanched to rid it of color, and smoked pork is sometimes blanched to reduce its aroma and salt content. The process is almost always the same. Bring a large pot of water, salted or not, as you prefer, to a boil. Drop the ingredient in the boiling water in small enough batches so the water never loses its boil and cook until the desired effect is achieved. For skinning, 30 seconds is sufficient. Softening tough fibers usually takes several minutes. To stop the cooking, remove the ingredient and plunge it into ice water. Then dry it.

Braising

A two-step technique for tough or fibrous ingredients. After dredging, the food is first browned and then simmered in liquid in a covered pot until tender. There should be just enough liquid to come no more than half way up the side of the food.

Breading

Coating an ingredient with crumbs can improve the texture and color of a food. The simplest method of breading is to moisten the food and cover it with crumbs, which gives a very light coating. Better coverage is achieved by first dredging the food in flour or starch to absorb any surface moisture that might steam during cooking and cause the breading to flake off. Then the dredged ingredient is coated with egg wash and rolled in bread crumbs. A thicker crust can be achieved by redipping in the egg and bread crumbs. The breaded food should sit on a rack for at least 10 minutes to give the egg a chance to dry, thereby "gluing" the bread crumbs in place. To keep from breading your hands as well as the food, use one hand for handling the food only in dry ingredients, the other for handling it after it's wet.

Broiling, Grilling, and Barbecuing

Grilling and broiling accomplish the same things from different directions. In broiling, the heat comes from above, while in grilling it comes from below. In both cases, the food must be tender and ¼ inch to 2 inches thick. It helps for grilled or broiled food to have a moderately high fat content to keep it from drying out, but even lean foods can be grilled or broiled if they have marinated or are basted during cooking. The food should be placed 2 to 4 inches from a high fire. Because the heat is kept constant, cooking is regulated by moving the food farther from or closer to the flame. The thinner the ingredient or the rarer you want it, the closer to the heat source it should go so as to quickly brown the surface of the food, leaving the interior less done. By moving the food away from the heat, the surface browns more slowly and the food has a chance to cook through before the surface chars. Do not confuse grilling with barbecuing. Barbecuing is a method of braising tough meats over an open fire. Either the fire must be quite low or the food must be placed far from the flame and while the food cooks, it is basted with sauce. In this way, tough fibers are softened in simmering liquid as the meat is infused with the flavors of the sauce. The result is a pungent meat that literally falls from the bone. Barbecue should never be charred. If it is, the fire was too hot. Hot fires are for tender foods, such as fish fillets, high-quality steaks and chicken breasts. The meats to choose for barbecuing are tougher and more flavorful, such as ribs, stew meats, and chicken legs.

Browning

Unlike sautéing, browning colors a food but does not cook it through. To brown, heat a thin film of oil or clarified butter until smoking. Add the food and cook until browned. Proceed with the recipe. Browning can also be done under a broiler, over a grill, or in the oven.

Butterflying

When meat is too thick to cook the inside without scorching the outside, it needs to be butterflied. Slit the meat horizontally, leaving one side attached. Then open the two flaps as you would a book and pound the center lightly to even out the thickness.

Cutting a Chicken

To section: Using a sharp, thin-bladed boning knife, remove wings by cutting through inside joint where the wing joins the body. When the knife hits bone, bend the wing toward the neck until the wing joint pops out, then cut through the joint. To remove the legs, cut through the interior joint where the thigh meets the body. Push the leg toward the back of chicken until joint pops, then cut through the joint. To separate the breast from the back, cut through the carcass with a large knife, starting at leg cavity and cutting up along back, through the ribs, to the neck. When you get to the shoulder, bend the back away from the breast, exposing shoulder joints, then cut through them. *To bone breasts:* Place the breast skin-side down and press down with the heel of your hand, directly on the center of the breastbone until you hear a pop.

Lift out the center breastbone. Run your fingers between the meat and the ribs, lifting each side of the rib cage off in a section. Run a knife along the collarbone and wishbone and remove. Turn the breast over and pull off the skin. Trim and, if desired, halve. *To section legs:* Slit the meat inside the joint where the drumstick meets the thigh. Pull drumstick back, away from its natural angle, until joint pops. Cut through the joint and disengage.

Opening Clams and Oysters

Shells should be tightly closed and washed well in cold water with a scrub brush. Protect your hand with dish towel or pot holder. Place the hinged end of the clam or rounded end of the oyster in the towel nestled into the fleshy pad at the base of your thumb. *For clams:* Place the sharp edge of a clam knife in the crack between the shells. Use the first three fingers of the hand that holds the clam to direct the knife between the two shells while steadily pushing it in. Once the knife is inside clam, run it around and against the interior of the top shell to cut the two muscles that hold the clam closed. *For oysters:* Dig the pointed end of an oyster knife or beer-can opener into the hinge of the oyster and pry upward. The hinge will pop. Run a knife around and across the flatter of the two oyster shells, cutting the muscle that holds the shells together. Let the liquor drip through a strainer into a bowl. The strainer will catch stray bits of shell or debris.

Preparing Softshell Crabs

Softshell crabs must be cleaned and killed before they are cooked. Remove the apron from the underside. Lift up the flaps on either side of the top shell (carapace) and remove the gills underneath. Cut off the eyes with a scissors or small knife, and push out the bile sac, which lies behind the eyes, through the opening made by the cut. Pat dry.

Cutting Vegetables

Julienne: A julienne is an ⅛-by-⅛-by-2-inch strip. Square off the vegetable and cut it in 2-inch lengths. Cut the lengths into ⅛-inch-thick slices, stack up 3 slices, and cut into ⅛-inch-thick strips. *Dice:* These cubes are cut in much the same way as a julienne. Square off the vegetable and cut into slices as thick as you want the diced vegetable to be. Large dice are about ¾ inch, medium about ½ inch, small about ¼ inch, and fine dice about ⅛ inch. Stack up a few slices and cut strips of the same width. Line up several strips and cut into cubes by slicing across the strips in the same width. *Slices:* Hold the food perpendicular to the blade of the knife and cut thin pieces down the length of the food. *Diagonal Slices:* Hold the food at a 45-degree angle to the blade of the knife and cut thin pieces diagonally across the length of the food. *Spiral-cuts:* An Asian style usually associated with stir-fries. Cut the vegetable on a diagonal, then give vegetable a quarter turn so that the cut surface is now facing upward. Cut another diagonal slice across the cut face. Turn another quarter turn, and slice again. Pieces will be multi-faceted, like jewels.

Deglazing

To deglaze, pour liquid into a hot pan in which an ingredient has been browned, roasted, or sautéed. Stir briskly until any brown bits clinging to the bottom or sides of the pan have been incorporated into the liquid. Use the liquid for making sauces and broths.

Degreasing

This simple process is used whenever you serve the liquid in which meat was cooked. The most effective method is to chill the whole thing until the fat on the surface congeals. It can then easily be skimmed off. If there is no time for this, skim large amounts of liquid fat with a large spoon or ladle either by dipping it just under the fat and moving the spoon across the surface of the liquid, or by placing a ladle into the liquid so that its rim just breaks the surface of the fat. Then by keeping the ladle very still at that level, the fat will flow off the surface of the liquid into the ladle. You can remove small amounts of fat by blotting the surface quickly with a folded paper towel.

Dredging

When a recipe directs you to dredge in flour or starch, trim the food well and pat it dry. Toss in a bag with starch or flour, or roll in a deep plate of flour or starch. Once the food is completely coated, pat it until all but a thin powdering of the starch or flour falls off. Too heavy a dredging can cause sautéed meats to be mushy and the batter for deep-frying to roll off after dipping.

Finishing

This term refers to adding ingredients to a sauce of reduced liquid to make it smoother, richer, more flavorful, or thicker. Typically, after the liquid is reduced, it is removed from the heat. Then, butter, cream, mustard, yogurt, or any other finishing ingredient is swirled in.

Flambéing, or Flaming

This technique rids a dish of harsh hard-liquor flavors by burning off the alcohol. It is often seen equally as a way of adding drama to food presentation. To flambé, heat the liquor and carefully touch its fumes with a flame, which will instantly ignite and continue flaming until the alcohol has burned away. Use a lighter, match, or gas burner, being careful that nothing flammable is in the way of the flame, such as dish towels. Do not use more liquor than is called for in an attempt to make a large flame. To extinguish a flambé prematurely, suffocate it with the lid of the pan. To get the same flavor effects without a flame, simply boil the liquor until the smell of alcohol dissipates.

Killing a Lobster or Crab

Like most shellfish, lobsters and crabs must be alive close to the time that they're cooked. For that reason, they are always bought alive or precooked. The easiest way to cook and kill a lobster or crab is to plunge the animal into a large pot of boiling water and simmer for the time stated in the recipe. If you're preparing a recipe calling for a sectioned lobster, the lobster must be cut apart before cooking. Place the lobster on its belly on a clean surface. Plunge a knife into the lobster's back, right behind the head. Cut the lobster in half lengthwise. Clean out the body, reserving the dark green roe and lighter green tomalley. Crack the claws. The lobster is now ready for broiling. For stewing or making soup, continue sectioning it. Remove the claws and tail sections by twisting them from the body. Cook immediately.

Marination and Maceration

Marination infuses food with external elements, while maceration extracts something already in a food. Marinades infuse foods with aromatics and moisture, while softening tough fiber and modifying harsh flavors. All marinades are a balance of acid, salt, oil, and seasonings. Each element performs a specific function: Acid and salt break down fiber, oil adds moisture, and seasonings improve flavor. A balanced marinade will open up the food's fiber to allow moisture and flavor to enter. To use a marinade, rub the food with the marinade, cover, and refrigerate. Refrigeration time depends on the size and density of the food, the strength of the marinade, and the desired effect. A cloudy marinade means the food has started to dehydrate and the marination has gone on for too long. Remove the food immediately and use as soon as possible. Maceration is typically done with acid, as with seviche (in which scallops are "cooked" with citrus juice), or with salt, as when curing a salmon or ham in a mixture of salt, spices, and sugar. The food should be covered with the macerating agent and refrigerated until the desired degree of dehydration takes place.

Doneness of Meat

Roasts: The temperature of a meat indicates how firm, dry, and red it will be, so judging doneness with a meat thermometer is a snap—if we can agree what rare, medium, and well-done mean. For beef, the current fashion for doneness is as follows: 125° F. is rare, 140° F. is medium and anything above 155° F. is well done. The doneness for medium-rare lamb is 130° F. and the minimum doneness for pork is 155° F. Poultry breast is done through at 165° F., legs at 170° F. *Steaks and chops*: Because a meat thermometer needs 2 inches of thickness to get a proper reading, it is not effective for determining the doneness of steaks and chops. Your finger is the better tool. Raw meat is soft enough to take the impression of a poking finger without any resistance, while well-done meat will spring back and not show a dent. Between those extremes, the cook's experience and the diner's preference must determine doneness. Here are guidelines: Blood-rare meat has a firm crust but an interior as soft as pudding. Rare meat gives slight resistance at the surface. Medium-rare meat is soft only in the very center. Medium-done meat springs back. Medium-well meat is firm. And well-done meat is almost hard enough to be considered a blunt instrument.

Cleaning Mussels

Make sure that mussels are alive by checking to see that they are tightly closed. If one is open, tap its shell sharply. It should close. If it doesn't, discard it. Clean the mussels by scrubbing their shells with a stiff brush to remove debris and barnacles. Pull off the "beard," a collection of silky filaments with which the mussel clings to rocks, by tugging on it sharply. Cook the mussels immediately.

Heating Cooking Oil

Oil for softening vegetables should be heated over high heat for less than 30 seconds. Oil for browning should be heated over high heat for at least 1 minute. Oil for sautéing should be heated until it smokes, about 2 minutes. Oil for deep-frying should be about 375° F. This temperature can be judged by using a deep-fry or candy thermometer, or by dropping a small bit of the frying food in the fat. If the oil is up to temperature, but not too hot, the food will bubble immediately and brown in no less than 1 minute.

Wrapping in Parchment

Cut a large heart out of parchment paper, big enough so that the food you are wrapping can sit comfortably on one side of the heart with a 1½-inch border all around. Place the food, any seasoning, and a small amount of sauce in the widest part of one side of the parchment heart, and fold the other side over the top. Starting with the rounded end, begin to fold the parchment in small, crisp creases along its open edge, making sure each triangular fold overlaps the one before it, thereby locking it in place. When you get to the pointed end of the heart, lock the "chain" of folds in place by twisting the point tightly.

Paupiettes

A paupiette is a thin fillet of meat, fish, or vegetable, usually rolled with a stuffing, tied in place, and braised, poached, or steamed.

Poaching

This technique cooks tender foods in liquid heated just below the stage where bubbles form. Bring the liquid to a simmer, add the food to be poached, and regulate the heat to keep the liquid just below a simmer. Cook until the desired results are achieved, turning as necessary.

Place a dumpling wrapper on a work surface. Brush the wrapper with egg wash. Place 1 teaspoon of filling in the center of the wrapper and fold the wrapper in half over the filling. Carefully pinch the edges of the wrapper together so that no air is trapped in the center. Crimp the edges, if desired. Flatten the straight side of the dumpling, and set on a tray on its flat side.

Reducing

This is a saucemaking term for when liquid is boiled away, causing flavors to intensify and a natural thickening to take place. To reduce a liquid, boil it vigorously but watch it closely near the end to keep it from scorching, especially if you are reducing a liquid by more than half. Liquid reduced to a sixteenth its original volume is called a glaze.

Roasting Bell Peppers

Place any number of bell peppers directly over the high flame of a gas burner or under a broiler until they char on one side. Give the pepper a quarter turn and char again. Continue until the pepper has blackened all over. Place in a loosely closed paper bag and let cool for 10 minutes. Peel by rubbing the blackened skin with your fingers. Wash the skin off your fingers rather than washing the peppers to avoid washing away the pepper's flavorful oils. Good-quality roasted red peppers are available in jars.

Sautéing

To sauté, heat a thin film of oil or clarified butter in a sauté pan until it smokes. Add a thin slice of boneless meat, dredged in flour, and cook just long enough to brown well on both sides. The meat must be thin enough and tender enough to cook to doneness in that amount of time. If it is thicker, it should be grilled, broiled, or pan-fried.

Simmering liquid barely bubbles. Foods to be simmered should be more than half covered with liquid and cooked in a pot, covered or uncovered, until tender. Boiling is more vigorous. Fibrous or starchy foods are submerged in a large amount of rapidly bubbling water until tender and then drained.

Steaming

Food is trapped in an enclosed steam-infused environment until it is cooked through. This can be a covered perforated basket or a covered plate perched above a pot of boiling water, a parchment wrapper baking in an oven, a plastic-wrapped bowl in a microwave oven, or a tightly sealed pressure cooker. Although steam is hotter than boiling water by a few degrees, it will not cook as quickly unless it is under pressure, as is the case in a pressure cooker or microwave.

Stewing

Stewing is exactly the same as braising and simmering, except the food is always in bite-size or slightly larger pieces and the liquid should almost cover the ingredient.

Stir-Frying

This technique is explained in depth in the opening section of Chapter 6.

Roasting Tomatoes

Place any number of tomatoes directly over a high gas flame or under a broiler and cook until the skin blisters and chars slightly. This will take only a few seconds. Turn the tomato with tongs until the skin has blistered on all sides, then peel the skin by slipping it off with your fingers. The result is a subtle pleasant smokiness.

Water Bath

This is typically used when dissipated rather than direct heat is preferred, as when baking eggs or cooking dishes thickened with egg yolk. To make a water bath, simply place the cooked food in its container in a larger pan of hot water and heat in the oven or over a low flame. It might be necessary to replenish the water during cooking. Water baths filled with ice water can be used for cooling hot foods.

Zesting Citrus Fruits

To remove the colorful skin—the zest—from a lemon, lime, orange, or grapefruit, peel thin strips with a vegetable peeler or zester. Finely chop, mince, or julienne these strips. To grate zest, rub the citrus fruit against the smallest tooth of a grater. Your strips are too thick if the underside contains any of the white layer of pith underneath the zest.

Caramelizing Sugar

Sugar will dissolve in water when heated, but the higher the proportion of sugar to liquid, the hotter the mixture must get before the mixture boils. Eventually the proportion of sugar will near 100 percent, at which point the liquefied sugar will become golden brown and very complex in aroma and flavor. It caramelizes. You can caramelize sugar either by mixing it with half as much water and boiling until it turns brown or by heating the sugar in a heavy pot by itself until it caramelizes. The wet method will take longer but needs no attention until the end of cooking. With the dry method, caramelizing occurs more quickly, but the sugar can burn in the blink of an eye if it is not stirred frequently.

Melting Chocolate

Melted chocolate scorches easily and will seize (or split) without warning if it comes in contact with the least bit of moisture. Techniques for melting it center on avoiding these pitfalls. Do not store chocolate in the refrigerator or freezer. They will cause beads of moisture to settle on the surface of the chocolate, which will make it seize when melted. Have all utensils perfectly dry, chop or grate the chocolate into uniformly small pieces, place the chocolate over simmering water or in a microwave oven, and heat until half melted. Remove from heat and mix until completely smooth. By finishing the melting away from the heat, the chocolate will be cool enough to use immediately in a recipe. Seized chocolate will become smooth if you add 1 tablespoon fat for every 8 ounces of chocolate or 1 tablespoon liquid for each ounce, but it can no longer be used for candy making.

Collars on Soufflé Dishes

To get a soufflé to rise high and straight, or when making a chilled or frozen soufflé, it is necessary to tie a collar around the soufflé dish in order to build up the sides. To do so, prepare a sheet of kitchen parchment or foil 3 inches longer than the perimeter of the soufflé dish and 3 inches wider than the height of the dish. Wrap it around the outside of the dish so the width of the paper extends beyond the rim of the dish by about 3 inches. Secure with string or staples. If using foil, mold it into place. Grease and dust the interior of the collar as you did the dish.

Icing a Cake

Place the cake on a flat cake plate that has been lined with 4 strips of wax paper to protect the outer edges of the plate. Brush away any crumbs. *Frosting:* Prepare the frosting. Dip a long cake-icing spatula into the frosting. Lift up a large blob and spread it around the side of the cake, keeping the spatula parallel to the side. Continue until the entire side is covered and a small rim has built up at the top of the cake. Spread more frosting over the top in swirls, going all the way out to the perimeter. Wipe the spatula clean. Holding the spatula parallel to the side, turn the cake to smooth the side. Wipe the spatula clean after each stroke. Remove wax-paper strips by pulling each piece by its narrow end. *Glazing:* Prepare glaze and pour ⅔ of it over top of the cake. With an icing spatula, spread it evenly over the top, letting some run down the side. Smooth the side, being sure all surfaces are covered with a layer of glaze. Use the remaining glaze as needed. Remove wax-paper strips by pulling each piece by its narrow end.

Lining Baking Pans

To line a baking pan of any size, cut a piece of kitchen parchment or wax paper to size by placing the pan on a sheet of the paper. Trace the perimeter of the bottom of the pan on the paper and cut out with a scissors. Lightly grease the interior of the pan and place the paper, penciled side down, over the bottom, smoothing out any bubbles or wrinkles.

Unpanning Cakes

The first trick to unpanning cakes is to make sure that the cake pan was prepared properly in the first place (see Lining Baking Pans, above). Allow the cake to cool in the pan long enough so that the pan is cool enough to handle but still slightly hot to the touch. Run a small sharp knife around the edge of the cake to loosen the sides. Cover the cake with wax paper, top with a rack or large flat plate, and invert. The cake will fall from the pan. Remove the pan and, if necessary, the paper, place a cooling rack over the cake, and invert again. Remove the top rack or plate and paper. Cool to room temperature.

If a cake doesn't come out of the pan using this method, shake the inverted pan vigorously from side to side. This should release any vacuums that could be holding the cake in the pan. Vacuums frequently form around the edges of cake during cooling, especially if the cake is soft and moist. If it still won't come out, bang the pan and its covering plate sharply on the countertop. This should break any sticky spots across the bottom of the cake. If it still won't come out, turn it right side up and loosen the sides again with a knife, but this time push the sides of the cake away from the sides of the pan with the flat side of the knife. Invert again. If it still won't come out, get on with your life and slice the cake right in the pan, lifting out the pieces with a flexible spatula.

Unpanning Cheesecakes

If the cake is very soft, as is the case with a crustless cheesecake, follow the preceding procedure, but loosen the sides by holding the warm cake on its side and letting gravity pull cake away from upper side. Rotate pan a quarter turn and let it drop from that side. Keep turning until the side of the cake has been loosened all the way around.

Grinding Nuts

When a recipe calls for ground nuts, it means the nuts should be ground to a powder. This can be done easily and well in a food processor, but don't overdo it or the nuts' oils will be released and the powder will turn into nut butter. Grind no more than 2 cups at a time and use the processor in 3-second pulses to get even results. For very oily nuts, such as pecans or cashews, it's helpful to add a small amount of flour or bread crumbs to help absorb the oil. Chopped nuts, even when finely chopped, are still coarser than ground nuts.

Forming a Pastry Shell (Standard or Deep-Dish)

Roll out the chilled pastry on a lightly floured board with a floured rolling pin to a 3/16-inch-thick disk at least 4 inches wider than the pan it will line. Roll the pastry loosely onto the pin, using a spatula to help lift the pastry if it should stick, and transfer to a pie pan. Line the pan with the pastry, making sure the pastry comes all the way down into the corner of the pan, and trim so that the edge of the pastry barely extends 1 inch beyond the rim of the pan. Fold this excess pastry behind the pastry lining the pan. Crimp the edges to seal them.

Forming a Two-Crust Pie

Roll the pastry and line the pie pan as described in the preceding entry. Trim the edge of the pastry so that it barely extends over the edge of the pan. Fill with pie filling. Roll out another pastry disk in the same way. Roll pastry around the pin and unroll over the top of the filling. Trim so that the edge of the top pastry extends 1 inch beyond the rim of the pan. Fold this excess pastry under the pastry lining the pan. Crimp the edges to seal them.

Forming a Tart Shell

Roll the pastry and line a tart pan with a removable bottom, using the procedures described in Forming a Pastry Shell (above). To finish the edge, press the pastry into the ridges in the side of the tart pan and roll a rolling pin over the top of the pan to cut off the pastry flush to the edge of the pan. *Forming tartlet shells:* Roll the pastry between 2 sheets of wax paper to ⅛-inch thickness. Refrigerate 30 minutes. Remove from refrigerator and remove top sheet of wax paper from the pastry. Cut into eight circles, each four to five inches in diameter. Using a small spatula, remove each pastry circle from the back sheet of wax paper and place in a 2- to 3-inch tartlet pan, crimp the edges, cover, and freeze at least 30 minutes.

Forming Phyllo Tartlet Shells

Melt 10 tablespoons unsalted butter and skim white foam from its surface. Brush a sheet of phyllo dough lightly with the butter, fold in half, brush lightly with more butter, and fold in half again, this time in the opposite direction. Brush with more butter and fold in half a third time, so the finished shape is roughly a square. Butter 1 cup in an 8- to 12-cup muffin tin. Line the cup with the folded sheet of phyllo, buttered side up. Fold under any edges that hang over. Don't worry if the edge is uneven or ragged; it is part of the charm of these tartlets. Poke the bottom of the pastry a few times with the tines of a fork. Repeat until you have 8 shells. Bake in preheated 375° F. oven for 10 to 15 minutes, until golden brown. Let cool.

Blind Baking or Prebaking

Line the chilled pastry shell(s) with foil, and fill with pastry weights, uncooked rice, or beans. Bake in a preheated 400° F. oven for 12 minutes. Remove foil and weights and bake 10 to 25 minutes more, depending on how much more baking the pastry will get once it is filled. Sweet pastry should be baked for the minimum time. Cool on a rack.

Assembly for Pot Pie

Roll out pastry to ³⁄₁₆-inch thickness. Cut a circle from the pastry wide enough to overlap the edge of the baking dish by 1 inch all the way around, and cut a 1-inch-wide strip long enough to wrap around the baking dish (it need not be in 1 piece). Dampen edge of pie plate with water and place pastry strip along rim, making sure ends overlap. Press down to secure. Brush this pastry rim with egg wash and cover with the pastry circle. Press edge to seal well, crimp edge, and cut a decorative opening in center of pastry to allow steam to escape.

Assembly for Turnovers

To form turnover pastries, roll ½ pound puff pastry on a lightly floured board into a 12½-inch square. With a sharp knife, trim ¼ inch from each side, leaving a 12-inch square of dough. Cut into quarters to make four 6-inch squares. Brush with egg wash and make a small mound of filling in the center of each square. Fold each square by bringing one corner to the opposite corner, forming a triangle with filling in the center. Gently push edges together to seal. With the dull side of a small knife, make vertical indentations in sealed edges of the turnovers. Cut a few small slashes in the top to serve as steam vents. For mini-turnovers: Roll, shape, and trim dough as for regular turnover pastry, but cut the 12-inch square of dough into 16 3-inch squares. Prepare, fold, make indentations, and cut steam vents as described above.

Appendix   C

Fifty Menus

Here are 50 suggested menus, using recipes from this book. Each menu includes a selection of dishes that balances foods, tastes, colors, and preparation time. Only a small fraction of the recipes in this book are used in these 50 menus, leaving you with considerable leeway to use them as a guide. Do so, mixing and matching your own favorites and adding your choice of beverage.

For page numbers, see the Index.

SUMMER SPICE
Grilled Pork Chops with Jerk Citrus Marinade
Tomato and Fried Spinach Salad
Corn Chili Salad
Chocolate Black Pepper Pound Cake

SUMMER COOKOUT
Chilled Curried Zucchini Soup
Middle Eastern Grilled Softshell Crabs
Tomatoes Marinated in Olive Oil, Garlic, and
  Crushed Pepper
Grilled Summer Squash Salad
Chocolate Fondue on a Grill

WINTER PICNIC
Chili Inferno
Brown Rice and Roasted Pepper Salad
Tossed Winter Greens with Warm Bacon
  Dressing
Apple Pear Pie
Mulled Cider

MEDITERRANEAN PICNIC
Grilled Eggplant and Smoked Mozzarella Grinder
  with Sun-Dried Tomato Oil
Golden Turmeric Tomato Relish
Sicilian Artichokes, served cold
Melon with Lime
Sun-Brewed Iced Tea

CHINESE PICNIC
Anise Tea Eggs
Mahogany Chicken Wings
Artichoke with Tofu Dressing, served cold
Rice and Lentil Salad
Sautéed Fruit Salad

Fifty Ways to Cook Most Everything

DO-AHEAD MENU

Mediterranean Chicken Stew
Roasted Peppers with Black Olives and
    Anchovies
Multicolored Corn Bread
Kiwi and Honeydew in Margarita Glaze

IMPRESS YOUR BOSS

Shrimp Bisque
Chicken Wellington
Marsala Mushrooms with Pancetta
Gratin of Chard
Raspberry Nectarine Pie

TRICKING PICKY EATERS

Chicken Soup with Tortellini
Rolled-up Lasagna
Zucchini Bread

KIDS' BIRTHDAY DINNER

Honeydew Mint Soup
Make Your Own Pizza
Julienned Vegetables with Lemon Honey Dip
Chocolate Ice Cream Cupcakes

OLD FAVORITES

Manhattan Clam Chowder
Pasta with Quick Meat Sauce
Classic Caesar Salad
Praline Apple Pie

NEW FAVORITES

Lime Bisque
Stir-Fried Red Curry Chicken
Warm Buckwheat Pasta and Sesame Salad
Composed Salad of Grilled Vegetables
Cardamom Apricot Pound Cake served with
    Sautéed Fruit Salad

ROMANTIC DINNER

Cajun Oysters
Squab Roasted with Garlic and Molasses

Ragout of Wild Mushrooms
Warm Orange Walnut Spinach Salad
Sinful Chocolate Tartlets

ROMANTIC BRUNCH

Stir-Fried Scrambled Eggs with Shrimp
Spinach Artichoke Bread
Coeur à la Crème served with Warm Pink Pear
    Puree

LOW-CALORIE ROMANCE

Lime-Laced Gazpacho
Snapper Steamed with Green Peppercorns
Confetti Brown Rice
Honeydew Filled with Champagne

SPRING HOLIDAY DINNER

Mediterranean Minestrone
Salmon en Papillote with Shrimp and Asparagus
Lemon Cilantro Turkey Breast
Fragrant Basmati Rice
Spinach Parmesan Soufflé
White Chocolate Ice Cream served with Orange,
    Scotch, and Espresso Sauce

WINTER HOLIDAY DINNER

Potato Cheese Soup
Fennel-Cured Bluefish
with Roasted Garlic Horseradish Paste and black
    bread
Herbed Brandy Turkey with Wild Mushroom
    Stuffing
Polenta
Brussels Sprouts Sautéed with Bacon and Apples
Apple Charlotte served with Crème Anglaise

RED, WHITE, AND BLUE HOLIDAY DINNER

Mixed grill of chicken, steaks, and ribs marinated
    in All-American Barbecue Marinade
Southwest Garbanzo Turkey Salad
Creole Cole Slaw

Corned Beef and Potato Salad
Two-Crust Strawberry Pie
Old-Fashioned Deep-Dish Apple Pie
Spicy Tomato Slush

HARVEST FEAST

Pumpkin Leek Soup
Peasant Pie
Roasted Game Hens with Orange Cranberry
    Marinade
Broccoli with Walnuts
Acorn Squash with Spiced Honey
Chocolate Gingerbread served with Candied
    Ginger Cream

A VEGETARIAN FEAST

Marinated Antipasto
Pizza Rustica
High-Protein Vegetarian Tostadas
Buttermilk Spoonbread with Garlic
Brown Rice and Vegetable Pilaf
Indian Braised Vegetables
Stir-Fried Apple Shortcake

HORS D'OEUVRE BUFFET

Marinated Mozzarella, Olives, and Sun-Dried
    Tomatoes
Smoked Salmon and Gruyère Cheesecake
Cold Crab and Avocado Taco
Shrimp Marinated in Wine and Lemon
Smoked Trout and Horseradish Deviled
    Eggs
Buffalo "Fins"
Herbed Biscuits with a Secret
Anchovy Olive Pesto on Toasts
Crudités with Sesame Chick-Pea Spread
Chicken Fingers with Roasted Pepper Dip
Sweet Sesame Meatballs
Chicken Spinach Potstickers
Country Pâté served with Green Peppercorn
    Mustard

DESSERT BUFFET

Blueberry Shortcake Cobbler
Strawberries with Warm Rhubarb Sauce
Jewish Apple Cake
Two-Ton Nut Cake
Kumquat Pound Cakes
Zucchini Bread
Black Forest Pudding Cake
Pecan Pie Bars
Sablés
Walnut Chocolate Chip Shortbread
Spiced Gumdrop Drops
Grand Marnier White Chocolate Truffles

CHOCOLATE EXTRAVAGANCE

Chocolate Pâté
Chocolate Butter and a basket of brioche
Raspberry Chocolate-Chip Muffins
Peaches and White Chocolate Mousse in
    Chocolate Cups
Unbelievably Amazing Brownies
Chocolate Bread Pudding
Gâteau Bordeaux
Real Hot Chocolate Spiked with Scotch
Raspberry Chocolate Bombe
Chocolate Peanut Crunch Balls
Triple-Dipped Strawberries

ITALIAN BISTRO

Clams in Tomato Vinaigrette
Grilled Chicken with Sauce of Prosciutto, Peas
    and Rosemary
Pasta with Herbs, Tomato, and Cream Sauce
Sautéed Bitter Greens with Sweet Pepper
    Vinaigrette
Strawberries with Walnut Mascarpone

EUROMEX

Carpaccio Jalapeño with Tortilla Chips
Mexican Stewed Monkfish
Grilled Chicken Breast with Roasted Pepper Salsa
Avocado Ice Cream
Spiced Cookies

Fifty Ways to Cook Most Everything

ENTERTAINING ON A BUDGET

Fish Bisque
Tuscan Chicken Legs
Hominy Soufflé
Broccoli Rabe with Garlic and Olive Oil
Devil's Food Layer Cake

ENTERTAINING WITHOUT A BUDGET

Lobster Bouillabaisse
Veal Chops Stuffed with Fontina and Sun-Dried
     Tomato
Spinach Strudel with Tomato Vinaigrette
Risotto Milanese
Raspberry Grand Marnier Soup
Bitter Chocolate Torte

PACK A LUNCH (KIDS)

Peanut Butter and Apple Raisin Sandwiches
or Roast Beef Pita Pocket
Healthy Snack Mix
Chewy Chocolate Chip Cookies

PACK A LUNCH (WORK)

Meatloaf with Sauerkraut and Mustard on Rye
or French Shrimp Salad Sandwich
Hot Pepper Pecans
White Chocolate Brownies with
     Chocolate-Dipped Almonds

GREAT LUNCH AT HOME

Crabcake Sandwich with Creole Tartar Sauce
or Grilled Eggplant and Smoked Mozzarella
     Grinder
Parmesan Fries
Café Brûlot Slush

SOUP-AND-SALAD I

Black Bean Soup with Orange and Cilantro
Grilled Lamb and Tabouleh Salad

SOUP-AND-SALAD II

Chicken Barley Soup
Warm Spinach Salad with Chicken Livers

SOUP-AND-SALAD III

Mushroom Chowder
Sweet and Sour Hot Sausage Potato Salad

ELEGANT FOOD ANYONE CAN DO

Spaghetti with Turkey Bolognese Sauce
Mushrooms in Balsamic Glaze
Mediterranean Braised Leeks
Honey Brandy White Chocolate Mousse

LOW-CALORIE GOURMET

Seafood Pot au Feu
Veal Scallops with Asparagus and Capers
Black Pepper Pilaf
Carrot and Red Pepper
Grapefruit Cloud

COLD-WEATHER COMFORT MEAL

Mushroom Barley Soup
Crusty Macaroni and Cheese
Spinach with Warm Bacon Dressing
Wet Walnut Baked Apples

NONTRADITIONAL BARBECUE

Grilled Orange-Spice Clams and Mussels
Grilled Lamb Steak Provençale
Charcoal-Grilled Potato Chips
Grilled Ratatouille
Bananas Grilled with Vanilla and Candied Ginger

DINNER ON THE QUICK

Basic Green Salad
Sautéed Turkey Breast with Sage Glaze
Side of spaghetti with Oregano Walnut Pesto
Strawberries in Microwaved Chocolate Fondue

DINNER FOR ONE

Fish en Papillote with Julienne of Garden
  Vegetables
Dirty Rice
Lemon-Glazed Baked Apples

PIZZA PARTY

Tomato, Basil, and Chèvre Pizza
Artichoke and Mushroom Pizza
Tuna, White Beans, and Olive Pizza
Pepperoni with Meat Sauce Pizza
Bolognese and Mozzarella Pizza
Hot Peppers, Bacon, and Gorgonzola Pizza
Banana and Walnut Dessert Pizza
Brown Sugar Curds Dessert Pizza

DINNER ON A HOT PLATE

Chorizo Chicken Chili
Iceberg with Three Tomatoes
Easy Peach Melba

EAT WITH YOUR HANDS

Shrimp on a Stick with Spicy Avocado Sauce
Baked Brie with Croissant
Cold Roast Szechuan Chicken
Spicy Potato Chips
Asparagus with Lemon Oil
Chocolate Pistachio Drops
Tangerines and Grapes

COUNTRY BREAKFAST

Sour Cream Walnut Waffles
Cottage Cheese Pancakes
Sautéed Berry Syrup
Homemade Breakfast Sausage
Onion and Garlic Hash Browns
Applesauce Walnut Muffins

CHAMPAGNE BRUNCH

Cherries in Orange Honey Over Melon
Poached Salmon and Eggs with Lemon Butter
  Sauce

Grilled Farmer Cheese and Smoked Salmon on a
  Bagel
"Champagne" with Grapefruit Ice
Eight-Hour Brandy Cheesecake

QUICK HEALTHFUL BREAKFAST

Honey Bran Muffins
Muesli Cereal
Avocado Grapefruit Salad
Double Orange Juice

INSTANT BREAKFAST

Peanut Butter Raisin Bran Breakfast Cookie
Super-Protein Health Shake

LOW-CHOLESTEROL THANKSGIVING

Mushroom Chowder
Baked Trout Stuffed with Fennel and Apple
Herbed Turkey Breast Baked in Salt Crust
Sweet Potato, Carrot, and Apple Pancakes
Green Beans in Thyme
Cranberry Orange Corn Muffins

ALL-SEAFOOD FEST

Honey-Cured Gravlax
Cod and Avocado Salad
Brochettes of Shark, Sturgeon, and Salmon
Shrimp Étouffée
Tex-Mex Clams
Portuguese Mussel Stew
Hardshell Crabs in Beer Bread
Chocolate Raspberry Cobbler

ALL STIR-FRIED

Mussels in Red Clam Sauce
Sweet Anise Chicken
Stir-Fried Beef Barbecue
Stir-Fried Carrots with Mint and Red Pepper
Stir-Fried Broccoli with Hoisin Almonds
Stir-Fried Spicy Peanut Shrimp
Stir-Fried Banana Split

Fifty Ways to Cook Most Everything

CELEBRATING THE UNLOVED

Apple Broccoli Borscht
Grilled Mediterranean Finger Eggplant
Stir-Fried Spinach with Hoisin Walnuts
Liver, Onions, and Sherry Vinegar
Chocolate-Covered Prunes with Marzipan "Pits"

NOTHING EXCEEDS LIKE EXCESS

Wild Mushroom Bisque
Veal and Apple Torte
Braised Belgian Endive
Potatoes au Gratin with Three Cheeses
Chocolate Coronary
Soft Irish Ice Cream

Index

Fifty Ways to Cook Most Everything

Fifty Ways to Cook Most Everything

About the Authors

Andrew Schloss, forty-one, is known by his readers and students for his inventive recipes and his ability to explain technical aspects of cooking in entertaining, understandable terms. His popular articles first appeared in *The Philadelphia Inquirer* in 1982, and he has subsequently been published in *The Washington Post*, *The San Francisco Chronicle*, the *Chicago Tribune*, the *San Diego Union*, and *New York Newsday*. He currently divides his time among writing, teaching, and consulting. He also does organizational work for The American Institute of Wine and Food.

Schloss is the former director of the culinary curriculum for The Restaurant School in Philadelphia and helped launch Philadelphia's restaurant renaissance with his critically acclaimed restaurant, In Season. He lives near Philadelphia with his wife, Karen, their three children, and their dog.

Ken Bookman, forty-four, was the food editor of *The Philadelphia Inquirer* from 1982 to 1990. He has been an editor at the *Inquirer* since 1977. He and Ruth Adelman live near Philadelphia.